I LOVE MY HONI HUNS
(very much)

JOHN ♥'s
JODI

SUCCESSFUL
SMALL BUSINESS MANAGEMENT

SIXTH EDITION

SUCCESSFUL
SMALL BUSINESS MANAGEMENT

LEON C. MEGGINSON
Mobile College

CHARLES R. SCOTT
The University of Alabama

WILLIAM L. MEGGINSON
The University of Georgia

Homewood, IL 60430
Boston, MA 02116

© RICHARD D. IRWIN, INC., 1975, 1978, 1982, 1985, 1988, and 1991

Sponsoring editor: *Karen L. Johnson*
Project editor: *Karen Smith*
Production manager: *Bette K. Ittersagen*
Cover designer: *Sailer and Cook Creative Services*
Cover illustrator: *Steve Johnson*
Artist: *Mike Benoit*
Compositor: *Arcata Graphics/Kingsport*
Typeface: *10/12 Primer*
Printer: *R. R. Donnelley & Sons Company*

Library of Congress Cataloging-in-Publication Data

Megginson, Leon C.
    Successful small business management.—6th ed. / Leon C. Megginson, Charles R. Scott, William L. Megginson.
        p.   cm.
    Rev. ed. of: Successful small business management / Leon C. Megginson . . . [et al.]. 5th ed.   1988.
    ISBN 0-256-08635-4
    1. Small business—Management.   I. Scott, Charles R.
II. Megginson, William L.   III. Successful small business management.   IV. Title.
HD62.7.S9
658.02'2—dc20   90–4566
                                                                    CIP

Printed in the United States of America

2 3 4 5 6 7 8 9 0   DO   7 6 5 4 3 2 1

Dedicated to our wives—
Joclaire, Addie, and Peggy
and
to the pioneer members of the
Southern Case Writers Association
and members of the
North American Case Research Association

This sixth edition of *Successful Small Business Management* has been completely revised and updated. Many new features have been added to make it even more helpful to the student and the instructor. Yet it retains the basic structure, approach, and writing style of previous editions, which have been adopted in hundreds of schools in the United States, Canada, and other countries.

TO THE STUDENT

Most people seek a sense of meaning, identity, creativity, independence, and achievement in their work and in their lives. One of the best ways to achieve this goal is to become the owner or manager of a small business. Managing such a business, however, is a complex, challenging, rewarding, and sometimes frustrating occupation. Success requires knowledge, desire, and hard work on your part, plus a certain amount of luck.

Our goal in this edition, as in previous editions, is to explore what successful small business ownership/management entails and how you can achieve it. Thus, our specific objectives in this edition are to help you:

1. Relate personal talents and desires to the requirements for owning and managing a small business.
2. Examine the preparation you need to make in order to become successfully involved in such a venture.
3. Develop forward-looking systems and human qualities useful in conceiving, organizing, and operating a small firm with limited resources.

To help you achieve these objectives, we have tried to (1) communicate the material in a clear, concise, conversational, and reader-oriented style; and (2) provide the means to help you to mesh basic concepts and practices through the use of cases and company examples.

Text, Examples, and Cases

Since the first edition was published in 1975, we have tried to develop a comprehensive body of material that provides you with down-to-earth, reality-oriented, basic concepts of how to start and manage a small business. Therefore, this edition continues to provide a balance of theoretical and practical material.

The book's 24 chapters are divided into 7 parts, with concepts and applications continuously intermixed. For example, the text material in the chapters presents contemporary ideas and philosophies about owning and managing a small business. Many current examples of actual business applications are also given to help you relate the concepts to actual practice. Then, three to six cases are included at the end of each part to help you see how "real-world" businesses are actually operated. These cases are based on real business situations and will help you apply what you have read in the chapters to actual business problems. Analyzing these cases allows you to make difficult decisions as business managers while still in the safety of the classroom.

Organization of the Book

Part I, The Challenge of Owning and Managing a Small Business, explains the important role of small business, the characteristics of small business owners, why one should own a small business, and some current opportunities and challenges in small business—including owning a franchise.

Part II, Planning for and Organizing a Business, discusses how to do strategic and operational planning, prepare and present a winning business plan, obtain financing, and organize the business.

Part III, Selecting and Leading Employees, tells how to recruit, select, train, compensate, motivate, and maintain favorable relationships with employees—and their union, when one is involved.

Part IV, Operating the Business, deals with such operating factors as locating and laying out facilities, purchasing and maintaining inventory, and assuring operations and quality controls.

Part V, Marketing Goods and Services, discusses selecting marketing strategies for developing a product, pricing it, selling and distributing it, and doing international marketing and marketing research.

Part VI, Financial Planning and Control, explains how to plan for profit, how to budget and control operations, and how to use the computer and management information systems to do these more effectively.

Part VII, Providing Present and Future Security for the Business, tells how to use insurance and crime prevention for better risk management, how to deal with laws and social responsibility and business ethics, how to compute and pay taxes, and how to plan for the future—including estate planning.

Aids to Learning

Each chapter begins with two relevant, thought-provoking quotations and Learning Objectives—which are coordinated with the chapter summary—that define what should be learned from the chapter. An Opening Focus, which describes an actual business's or business owner's experience, is related to the subject of the chapter. The text—written for the TV generation—provides ample visuals such as photos, tables, figures, charts, checklists, and cartoons, along with real-life examples that illustrate the concepts being discussed. Most chapters include a Computer Update to show how computers can improve small business operations.

Key Terms—important words or phrases that are defined in the chapter—are bold-faced in the text for easy recognition and then listed at the end of the chapter, showing the page where the word is defined. Most of these terms are also included in the Glossary at the end of the book. Other end-of-chapter features are a summary—called "What You Should Have Learned"—which is coordinated by number with the Learning Objectives, to help you review the text material; Questions to test mastery of the chapter; and a list of Suggested Readings for further study of the topics presented.

We hope this edition will stimulate your interest in small business. We also hope you will identify with the individuals profiled in the text and cases and through them and their experiences learn to be a better owner or manager of a small firm.

TO THE INSTRUCTOR

This sixth edition of *Successful Small Business Management* takes a practical, down-to-earth approach to planning, organizing, and managing a small business. While based on current research, theory, and practice, the material is presented from a "how-to" perspective, with many examples and applications from the business world.

The material explores the role of small business and its growing importance. It also discusses the reasons for and against owning such firms and stresses up-to-date thinking in preparing, starting, organizing, and operating a small business. It explains how to achieve optimum benefits from the limited resources available to small firms and how to plan for growth and succession.

Cases have been selected for each part, and each case can be identified with one or more chapters—as is done in the *Instructor's Manual.* Since there are 32 cases, one or more cases can be used with each chapter.

Features of This Edition

The strengths of previous editions have been retained. These include simple, clear, and concise conversational writing style, numerous visuals, and the use of applications to reinforce the basic concepts presented.

Some chapters have been rearranged to give better progression and to change emphasis. For example, franchising is presented earlier, planning has been condensed and consolidated into one chapter, legal and administrative organizing aspects have been placed in one chapter, operating the business has been reduced from three to two chapters, and separate chapters have been added to cover business laws, social responsibility and business ethics, and taxes and their treatment.

We have continued the popular Learning Objectives, an Opening Focus, and a list of Key Terms in each chapter. Most chapters also include a Computer Update, which explains how small businesses are benefiting from new computerized technology. We have moved all appendixes to the end of the text for easy reference. These include help for women, minorities, and potential entrepreneurs; checklists for choosing the type of business to enter; a sample business plan; checklists for handling union organizing; and a management self-evaluation. The Glossary of Frequently Used Business Terms has been retained, and a Glossary of Frequently Used Computer Terms has been added to this edition. These follow the Appendixes.

Each chapter begins with philosophical, thought-provoking quotations summarizing the main thought of the chapter. These are followed by Learning Objectives that prepare readers for what they should learn from the chapter and that are coordinated with the chapter summary. Next comes an Opening Focus, which is the biography of some person who is or has been involved in small business, or a case involving actual business situations and events in small firms. This focuses the tone for the chapter and gives students a reference point as they read the material.

Each chapter contains many types of visuals, including photographs, figures, tables, and—where appropriate—a limited number of cartoons. Examples, illustrations, and real-life vignettes are set off from the body of the text to help students apply the material they are learning to actual small business situations. Key Terms, which are words or phrases defined in the text, are boldfaced for easy recognition and also listed at the end of the chapter, along with the page where they can be found in the text, and many are included in the Glossary. Footnotes are used to give authority to, and cite the sources of, the material used so that readers can get further information if desired. They are grouped at the end of the chapter, however, to prevent "clutter" on the text page.

This edition has a greater variety of types of cases than the fifth edition. Eight new cases have been added and nine others deleted to update and broaden the coverage. Two cases have been divided—one case into matching parts of the text and the other into four parts. These divisions help to provide continuity when moving from the study of one subject area to the next. Also, there is one case—CleanDrum, Inc.—with seven parts that describe how the owner decided to start a business, then follows its progress for the first three years of operation—up to January 1990.

Several end-of-chapter features aid learning. Chapter summaries, called "What You Should Have Learned," are coordinated with the Learning Objectives to provide a basis for better review of the material. Short-answer and discussion-type review questions can be used for student assignments, class discussion, or quizzes. Finally, a list of Suggested Readings guides students and instructors to current material for further exploration of key topics.

Important Current Issues Facing Small Business People

We have included topics about which small business owners and managers are currently concerned. These include a full chapter on taxes and their payment and another on business laws and ethics. Also, topics such as marketing, particularly international marketing; developing and presenting the business plan; and use of computers have been strengthened. Next, the discussions of location and purchasing have been oriented more toward retailing and services and less toward manufacturing. The expanding roles of small businesses, franchising, women, minorities, and sources of financing are discussed from a practical, applications-oriented point of view. Finally, the functional areas are covered from a small business perspective.

The retained features of previous editions, plus current changes and additions, make this an excellent, up-to-date teaching tool, relevant to today's changing environment.

ACKNOWLEDGMENTS

Our thanks go to those who contributed cases to this edition—as well as to previous editions. Our recognition is shown by the List of Case Authors. Thanks are also due for the many contributions made through the years by teachers, entrepreneurs, managers, professional people, and members of the North American Case Research Association. Our special thanks go to Lyle R. Trueblood for his carryover contributions to this edition. And we appreciate the contributions of Charles E. Scott, Loyola College in Maryland, in the management information systems and computer areas. We also appreciate the research and writing contributions of Jay Megginson.

Comments from our reviewers and colleagues around the country—named in the List of Reviewers and Other Contributors—were most helpful.

It pleases us greatly to say thank you to our wives, Joclaire L. Megginson, Addie M. Scott, and Margaret P. Megginson, whose support and patience have lightened our task. Also, thanks go to Barbara Barefield, Juli Byrd, and Karen Tomlin for the assistance they gave us in preparing the text materials and especially the *Instructor's Manual*.

We have no adequate way of expressing our sincere appreciation to Suzanne S. Barnhill. This edition would not have been possible without her help in editing, correcting, revising, typing, and proofreading. Her contributions have been of inestimable value in improving this edition.

Finally, we would like to thank Mobile College and the J. L. Bedsole Foundation for their continued support.

If we can be of assistance to you in developing your course, please contact any one of us.

Leon C. Megginson
Charles R. Scott
William L. Megginson

List of Case Authors

Steven J. Anderson, *Austin Peay State University*

Suzanne S. Barnhill, *Fairhope, Alabama*

James W. Cagley, *University of Tulsa*

James W. Carland, *Western Carolina University*

JoAnn C. Carland, *Western Carolina University*

Gary B. Frank, *University of Akron*

Robert Gatewood, *University of Georgia*

Walter E. Greene, *University of Texas–Pan American*

Bruce Gunn, *Florida State University*

Joe L. Hamilton, *Container Corporation of America*

Scott D. Julian, *Louisiana State University*

Bob Justis, *Louisiana State University*

Robert McGlashan, *University of Houston at Clear Lake City*

J. Barry Mason, *University of Alabama*

Lester A. Neidell, *University of Tulsa*

Christoph Nussbaumer, *Austin Peay State University*

John E. Oliver, *Valdosta State College*

Shirley Olson, *Millsaps College*

William V. Rice, *University of Houston at Clear Lake City*

Gayle M. Ross, *University of Mississippi Medical Center*

Burton F. Schaffer, *California State University at Sacramento*

Arthur D. Sharplin, *McNeese State University*

William M. Spain, *SCORE*

Curtis E. Tate, Jr., *University of Georgia*

Albert J. Taylor, *Austin Peay State University*

Patrick Taylor, *Millsaps College*

John C. Thompson, *University of Connecticut*

Lyle R. Trueblood, *University of Tulsa*

Jeanne Whitehead, *Austin Peay State University*

J. B. Wilkinson, *Youngstown State University*

Walter Wilson, *University of Georgia*

List of Reviewers and Other Contributors

Thomas B. Barley, *Syracuse University*

Mary Jane Byrd, *Mobile College*

Chloe I. Elmgren, *Mankato State University*

Russell C. Eustice, *Husson College*

Gordon Heath, *Rochester Community College*

Gerald Horton, *University of Georgia*

Jack Jankovich, *Kansas State University*

James F. Molloy, Jr., *Northeastern University*

Britt Shirley, *Columbus College*

Jude Valdez, *University of Texas at San Antonio*

Fred A. Ware, Jr., *Valdosta State College*

Mark Weaver, *University of Alabama*

PART I
THE CHALLENGE OF OWNING AND MANAGING A SMALL BUSINESS

CHAPTER 1   The Dynamic Role of Small Business   2

CHAPTER 2   Why Own or Manage a Small Business?   26

CHAPTER 3   Opportunities And Challenges in Small Business   56

CHAPTER 4   Growing Opportunities in Franchising   80

Cases For Part I   106

PART II
PLANNING FOR AND ORGANIZING A BUSINESS

CHAPTER 5   How to Become a Small Business Owner   126

CHAPTER 6   Strategic and Operational Planning   132

CHAPTER 7   Preparing and Presenting the Business Plan   176

CHAPTER 8   Obtaining the Right Financing for Your Business   192

CHAPTER 9   Organizing the Business   222

Cases for Part II   247

PART III
SELECTING AND LEADING EMPLOYEES

CHAPTER 10   Managing Human Resources in Small Firms   270

CHAPTER 11   Leading and Motivating Employees   300

CHAPTER 12   Maintaining Relationships with Employees   330

Cases For Part III   352

PART IV
OPERATING THE BUSINESS

CHAPTER 13   Locating and Laying Out Facilities   368

CHAPTER 14   Purchasing, Operations, and Quality Control   400

Cases for Part IV   432

PART V
MARKETING GOODS AND SERVICES

CHAPTER 15   Developing Marketing Strategies   446

CHAPTER 16   Selling and Distributing the Product   488

CHAPTER 17   International Marketing and Marketing Research   520

Cases for Part V   548

PART VI
FINANCIAL PLANNING AND CONTROL

CHAPTER 18   Planning for Profit   564

CHAPTER 19   Budgeting and Controlling Operations   590

CHAPTER 20   Using Computers and Management Information Systems   614

Cases For Part VI   643

PART VII

PROVIDING PRESENT AND FUTURE
SECURITY FOR THE BUSINESS

CHAPTER 21   Risk Management,
Insurance, and Crime
Prevention   668

CHAPTER 22   Business Laws and
Business Ethics   692

CHAPTER 23   Taxes and Their
Treatment   722

CHAPTER 24   Planning for the Future   750

Cases For Part VII   773

Appendixes   793

Glossary of Frequently
Used Business Terms   829

Glossary of Frequently
Used Computer Terms   839

Index   841

CONTENTS

PART I
THE CHALLENGE OF OWNING AND MANAGING A SMALL BUSINESS

CHAPTER 1
THE DYNAMIC ROLE OF SMALL BUSINESS   2

Opening Focus: Sam Walton: Work, Ambition—Success   3

It's an Interesting Time To Be Studying Small Business   4

The Number of Small Businesses Is Growing   5

Small Businesses Generate Most New Employment   5

The Public Favors Small Business   6

Interest Increasing at Colleges and Universities   8

Trend toward Self-Employment   8

Small Business Is Attractive to All Ages   9

Computer Update: The Whiz Kids Strike It Rich   10

Defining Small Business—No Easy Task   11

What Is Small?   11

Diversity of Small Businesses   12

Distinction between a Small Business and an Entrepreneurial Venture   12

Size, Sales, and Employment   15

Some Unique Contributions of Small Businesses   16

Encourage Innovation and Flexibility   17

Maintain Close Relationships with Customers and Community   19

Keep Larger Firms Competitive   19

Provide Employees with Comprehensive Learning Experiences   19

Develop Risk Takers   20

Generate Employment   20

Some Problems Facing Small Businesses   20

Inadequate Financing   22

Inadequate Management   22

Burdensome Government Regulations and Paperwork   22

What You Should Have Learned   23

CHAPTER 2
WHY OWN OR MANAGE A SMALL BUSINESS?   26

Opening Focus: Victor K. Kiam II: How to Succeed as an Entrepreneur   27

Why People Start Small Businesses   28

To Satisfy Personal Objectives   28

To Achieve Business Objectives   33

Need to Mesh Objectives   35

Characteristics of Successful Small Business Owners   36

Desire Independence   37

Have a Strong Sense of Enterprise   38

Are Motivated by Personal and Family Considerations   39

Expect Quick and Concrete Results   39

Are Able to React Quickly   40

Are Dedicated to Their Business   40

Enter Business as Much by Chance as by Design   41

What Leads to Success in Managing a Small Business?   41

Serving an Adequate and Well-Defined Market   41

Obtaining and Using Accurate and Useful Information   42

Using Human Resources Effectively   42

Acquiring Sufficient Capital   42

Computer Update: The Maine Line
Company: Obtaining and Using
Accurate Information   43

Coping with Government Regulations   44

Having Expertise in the Field   45

Managing Time Effectively   45

Doing an Introspective Personal
Analysis   47

Analyzing Your Values   47

Analyzing Your Mental Abilities   49

Analyzing Your Attitudes   49

What You Should Have Learned   51

CHAPTER 3
OPPORTUNITIES AND CHALLENGES IN
SMALL BUSINESS   56

Opening Focus: Sherri Hill:
The World's Most Beautiful Women
Wear Her Dresses   57

Where Are the Opportunities?   58

What Are the Fastest-Growing
Industries?   58

Which Industries Have the Highest
Success Rate?   60

Factors Affecting the Future of an
Industry and a Business   60

Computer Update: The Robot Center:
Would You Like to Buy a Robot?   61

Some Practical Ideas for Small
Businesses   62

Some Progressive Small Businesses   62

Some Innovative Suggestions for Future
Small Business Opportunities   64

Growing Opportunities for Women and
Minorities in Small Business   64

Women   64

Minorities   66

Some Areas of Concern for Small
Business Owners   72

Poorly Planned Growth   72

The Threat of Failure   74

What You Should Have Learned   75

CHAPTER 4
GROWING OPPORTUNITIES IN
FRANCHISING   80

Opening Focus: Ray Kroc:
Father of Franchising   81

Extent of Franchising   82

What Franchising Is   83

Definition   85

Types of Systems   86

Why Franchising Is Growing in
Importance   90

Recent Rapid Growth   90

Causes of Rapid Growth   90

How to Tell if a Franchise Is Right
for You   91

Look at the Opportunities   92

See What the Franchise Can Do
for You   92

Investigate the Franchise   94

Study the Franchise Offering Circular   96

Check with Existing Franchisees   96

Obtain Professional Advice   96

Know Your Legal Rights   97

The Future of Franchising   98

Expected Areas of Growth   98

International Franchising   99

Minority Ownership of Franchises   100

Computer Update: Careers USA, Inc.:
Taking the High-Tech Road   101

Turning Your Dream into a Reality   101

What You Should Have Learned   102

Cases for Part I

I–1   Sue Thinks of Going into
        Business—CleanDrum, Inc. (A)   106

I–2   Our Hero Restaurant (A)   107

I–3   Glammourrammer Beauty
        Salon   109

I–4   Cironi's Sewing Center Loses a
        Franchise   113

I–5   Shaffer's Drive Inns   118

I–6   Wilson's Used Cars   120

PART II
PLANNING FOR AND ORGANIZING A
BUSINESS

✳CHAPTER 5
HOW TO BECOME A SMALL BUSINESS
OWNER   126

Opening Focus: Jerry and Mona
Samuel: Combining Old-Fashioned
Newsstand and Modern Gift Shop   127
How to Go into Business for Yourself   128
  How to Start a Business   128
  Steps in Starting a Business   128
  Computer Update: Computerized
  Business Start-Ups   130
Searching For and Identifying a
Needed Product   130
  How to Decide Which Product to Sell   131
  Choosing the Business to Enter   133
Studying the Market for the Product   135
  Methods of Obtaining Information About
  the Market   136
  Method Used to Study the Market   136
  Computer Update: Using Electronic
  Scanners to Study the Market   137
Deciding Whether to Start a New
Business, Buy an Existing One, or Buy
a Franchise   138
✓To Start a New Business?   138
  To Buy an Existing Business?   140
  To Buy a Franchise?   145
What You Should Have Learned   148

CHAPTER 6
STRATEGIC AND OPERATIONAL
PLANNING   152

Opening Focus: Space Services, Inc.:
Ushering in the U.S. Commercial
Space Industry   153
✓The Role of Planning   154
  Why Small Businesses Need to Plan   154
  Why Small Businesses Neglect
  Planning   154
✓Types of Planning   156

✓The Role of Strategic Planning   157
  Mission and Objectives   157
  Strategies   160
  Computer Update: What's Your
  Competition Up To?   161
The Role of Operational Planning   161
✓Setting up Policies, Methods, Procedures,
  Budgets, and Standards   162
✓Planning to Operate the Business   162
The Role of Financial Planning   166
  Estimating Income and Expenses   167
  Estimating Initial Investment   168
  Locating Sources of Funds   171
What You Should Have Learned   172

CHAPTER 7
PREPARING AND PRESENTING THE
BUSINESS PLAN   176

Opening Focus: Jim Busby:
Preparing and Using a "Living
Business Plan"   177
Purpose of the Business Plan   178
Preparing the Plan   180
  Who Should Prepare the Plan?   180
  Developing Action Steps   180
Components of the Plan   181
  Cover Sheet   181
  Executive Summary   181
  Table of Contents   183
  History of the Proposed Business   183
  Definition of the Business   183
  Definition of the Market   184
  Description of Product(s)   184
  Management Structure   185
✓Objectives and Goals   185
  Financial Analysis   185
  Appendixes   185
Presenting the Plan   185
  Writing the Plan   186
  The Written/Oral Presentation   187
Implementing the Plan   187

Computer Update: 20/20 Hindsight ... 188

Sample Business Plan ... 188

What You Should Have Learned ... 188

CHAPTER 8
OBTAINING THE RIGHT FINANCING
FOR YOUR BUSINESS ... 192

Opening Focus: Roy Morgan:
Pioneer in Air Medical Services ... 193

Estimating Financial Needs ... 194

Principles to Follow ... 195

Using Cash Budgets ... 195

Reasons for Using Equity and Debt
Financing ... 196

Role of Equity Financing ... 196

Role of Debt Financing ... 197

Types of Debt and Equity Securities ... 198

Equity Securities ... 198

Debt Securities ... 199

Sources of Equity Financing ... 200

Self ... 200

Small Business Investment Companies
(SBICs) ... 201

Venture Capitalists ... 202

Angel Capitalists ... 206

Other Sources ... 206

Sources of Debt Financing ... 209

Trade Credit ... 209

Commercial and Industrial Financial
Institutions ... 209

Small Business Administration
(SBA) ... 211

Small Business Investment Companies
(SBICs)

Industrial Development Corporations
(IDCs)

Economic Development Administration
(EDA)

Agricultural Loans

What Lenders Look for

What You Should Have Learned

CHAPTER 9
ORGANIZING THE BUSINESS ... 222

Opening Focus: Henry E. Kloss:
Proprietor, Partner, and Corporate
Owner ... 223

Selecting the Right Legal Form ... 224

Factors to Consider ... 224

Relative Importance of Each Form ... 224

Why Form a Proprietorship? ... 227

Why Form a Partnership? ... 227

Types of Partnerships ... 230

Rights of Partners ... 230

Tests of a Partnership ... 230

Why Form a Corporation? ... 231

How to Form a Corporation ... 231

How a Corporation Is Governed ... 233

S Corporations ... 234

Other Forms of Business ... 234

Trusts ... 234

Cooperatives ... 236

Joint Ventures ... 236

Setting Up the Organizational
Structure ... 236

Some Basic Organizational Concepts ... 236

Some Organizational Problems in Small
Firms ... 238

Basic Ways of Organizing a Business ... 240

Organizing by Types of Authority ... 240

Organizing by Grouping Activities ... 241

Preparing an Organization Chart ... 242

What You Should Have Learned ... 243

Cases for Part II

II–1   Sue Forms and Starts a
Business—CleanDrum,
Inc. (B) ... 247

II–2   Our Hero Restaurant (B) ... 251

II–3   Simmons Mountainside Satellite
Sales ... 254

II–4   The Mother and Child Shop ... 258

II–5   Metal Fabricators, Inc. ... 262

PART III
SELECTING AND LEADING EMPLOYEES

CHAPTER 10
MANAGING HUMAN RESOURCES IN
SMALL FIRMS   270

Opening Focus: Supreme Plumbing and
Heating Company: Where Are the
Workers?   271
✓Planning for Personnel Needs   272
  Determining Types of Employees
  Needed   272
  Developing Sources of Personnel   273
✓Recruiting Employees   279
  By Advertising   279
  From Employment Agencies   280
  By Using Employee Referrals   280
  By Scouting   280
✓Selecting the Right Person for the Job   281
  Gathering Information about the
  Applicant   281
  Computer Update: Compu-Scan: An
  Effective Tool for Preemployment
  Screening   286
  Job Offer   288
  Orientation   288
Training and Developing Employees   288
  Need for Training and Development   289
  Ways of Training Nonmanagerial
  Employees   289
  Outside Help with Training   291
Selecting and Developing Managers   291
  Selecting Managers   292
  Developing Managers   292
Complying with Equal Employment
Opportunity Laws   293
  Laws Providing Equal Employment
  Opportunity (EEO)   293
  Some Practical Applications of EEO
  Laws   294
  Enforcing EEO Laws   295
  Terminating Employees   295
What You Should Have Learned   296

CHAPTER 11
LEADING AND MOTIVATING
EMPLOYEES   300

Opening Focus: Murry Evans:
Developing Winning Teams   301
Good Human Relations Is Needed in
Small Firms   302
  What Is "Good" Human Relations?   302
  How Managerial Assumptions Affect
  Management Approach   303
Exercising Leadership   303
  Leadership Styles   304
  Effective Managers Use Various
  Leadership Styles   304
Communicating with People   304
  What Happens When you
  Communicate?   305
  Barriers to Effective Communication   306
  How to Improve Communication   306
Motivating Employees   307
  What Is Motivation?   308
  Why Motivate Employees?   309
  How to Motivate Employees   310
  Some Practical Ways to Improve
  Motivation   311
  Does Money Motivate Employees?   312
  Motivation Is More than Mere
  Technique   313
Appraising Employees' Performance   313
Compensating Employees   314
  Legal Influences   314
  Setting Rates of Pay   315
  Using Money to Motivate   315
  Compensating Managerial and
  Professional Personnel   318
  Employee Benefits   319
  Computer Update: Computer
  Specialists, Inc.: Flexible Spending
  Accounts   322
Need for an Integrated Approach   322
What You Should Have Learned   324

CHAPTER 12
MAINTAINING RELATIONSHIPS WITH EMPLOYEES 330

Opening Focus: Mary H. Partridge and Michael Levy: "His and Hers" Businesses 331
Protecting Employees' Safety 332
  Factors Influencing Safety 332
  The Occupational Safety and Health Act 333
Environmental Protection 336
Counseling Disturbed Employees 336
  Benefits of Counseling 336
  What Counseling Involves 336
  Areas Needing Counseling 337
Dealing with Employee Complaints 341
Imposing Discipline 341
  Encouraging Self-Discipline 341
  How to Discipline Employees 342
Dealing with Unions 343
  Laws Governing Union-Management Relations 344
  What Happens When the Union Enters 344
  Negotiating the Agreement 347
  Living with the Agreement 348
What You Should Have Learned 348

Cases for Part III
III–1 CleanDrum, Inc. (C) 352
III–2 Our Hero Restaurant (C) 354
III–3 The Beary Best Cookies 356
III–4 The Case of Sam Sawyer 363
III–5 The Pepper Bush 364

PART IV
OPERATING THE BUSINESS

CHAPTER 13
LOCATING AND LAYING OUT FACILITIES 368

Opening Focus: Teague Brothers Rug and Carpet Cleaners: Cleaning Persian Carpets 369

Developing Operating Systems 370
  What Are Operating Systems? 370
  How Operating Systems Work 371
  Systems Must be Coordinated 373
  How to Begin Operations 373
Choosing the Right Location 374
  Why Choosing the Right Location Is So Important 374
  Collecting Information about Potential Locations 375
  Some Important Factors Affecting Location Choice 376
Locating Retail Stores 379
  Types of Stores 380
  Types of Locations 381
Locating Manufacturing Operations 383
  Nearness to Customers and Vendors 383
  Availability and Cost of Transportation 385
Planning Physical Facilities 385
  Determine Product to be Produced 385
  Identify Operations and Activities 385
  Computer Update: Autodesk, Inc.: Designers Get into Their Designs 386
  Determine Space Requirements 386
  Decide on the Best Layout 386
  Implementing Your Plans 392
How to Improve Operations 392
  State the Problem 392
  Collect and Record Information 393
  Develop and Analyze Alternatives 394
  Select, Install, and Follow Up on New Method 394
Setting and Using Performance Standards 394
What You Should Have Learned 395

CHAPTER 14
PURCHASING, OPERATIONS, AND QUALITY CONTROL 400

Operating Focus: Anders Book Stores: Dealing with Hundreds of Vendors 401

The Importance of Purchasing 403

What Purchasing Involves 403

Why Purchasing Is so Important 403

Making Someone Responsible for Purchasing 404

Selecting the Right Vendors 405

Computer Update: The Independent Insurance Agents Association 406

Types of Vendors 406

Use Few or Many Vendors? 406

Investigating Potential Suppliers 408

Evaluating Vendors' Performance 409

Maintaining Good Relations with Vendors 409

Establishing an Effective Purchasing Procedure 410

How Purchase Orders Originate 412

Placing the Purchase Order 413

Receiving the Items 413

Using Computers to Aid Purchasing and Inventory Control 414

Controlling Inventory 414

Why Carry Inventory? 414

Types of Inventory 415

Cost of Carrying Inventory 417

Determining When to Place an Order 417

Determining How Much to Order 418

Determining How to Order 419

Operations Planning and Control 420

Handling Variations in Demand 420

Scheduling Operations 421

Computer Update: Lucinda Gray, Travel Agent: Let Her Fingers Do Your Scheduling! 425

Controlling Operations 425

Quality and Its Control 426

Small Businesses Need Quality Output 426

What Is Quality? 426

Improving and Controlling Quality 427

What You Should Have Learned 428

Cases for Part IV

IV–1 CleanDrum, Inc. (D) 432

IV–2 Connie's Confections 436

IV–3 Plastic Suppliers, Inc. 439

PART V
MARKETING GOODS AND SERVICES

CHAPTER 15
DEVELOPING MARKETING STRATEGIES 446

Opening Focus: Judy Pugsley: Marketing a Service 447

The Marketing Concept 448

Understanding the Consumer Decision Process 449

Determining Customer Needs 450

Meeting Customers' Needs 451

Implementing the Marketing Concept 451

Seeking a Competitive Edge 452

Developing a Marketing Strategy 453

Setting Objectives 453

Choosing Target Market(s) 453

Developing an Effective Marketing Mix 458

Types of Products and Their Life Cycles 458

Types of Products 459

Product Life Cycle 459

Computer Update: Your Personal Robot 461

Packaging 462

How to Price Your Product 463

Establishing Pricing Policies 463

Computer Update: TeleData Guide, Inc. 465

Cost-Oriented Pricing 465

How Prices Are Set by Small Businesses 466

Other Aspects of Pricing 470

Physical Distribution 472

Storing 472

Order Processing 473

Transportation 473

Credit Management   473
 Methods of Payment   473
 Setting Credit Policies   474
 Carrying Out Credit Policies   475
Strategy for Marketing Services   476
 Nature of Service Businesses   476
 How Services Differ   477
 Developing Service Marketing
 Strategies   478
Implementing Your Marketing
Strategy   480
 The Introductory Stage   480
 The Growth Stage   481
What You Should Have Learned   482

CHAPTER 16
SELLING AND DISTRIBUTING THE
PRODUCT   488
Opening Focus: Mel Farr:
Sales Superstar   489
Promoting the Sale of Products   489
Choosing a Distribution Channel   490
 Distribution Channels for Consumer
 Goods   490
 Distribution Channels for Industrial
 Goods   491
 Factors to Consider in Choosing a
 Distribution Channel   492
Selling through Intermediaries   493
 Brokers   493
 Independent Agents   493
 Wholesalers   494
 Retailers   494
Using Your Own Sales Force   496
 Producers   496
 Computer Update: Interac Corporation:
 "Your Order, Please"   497
 Retailing   500
 Personal Selling   501
 Steps in the Creative Selling Process   501
 Attributes of a Creative Salesperson   505
✓Advertising   506

Types of Advertising   506
Developing the Program   507
Setting the Budget   508
Selecting the Media   508
Developing the Message   510
When and How to Use an Advertising
Agency   511
Measuring the Results of Advertising   511
Merchandising, Sales Promotion, and
Publicity   512
 Merchandising   512
 Sales Promotion   513
 Publicity   513
Considering Ethnic Differences   514
What You Should Have Learned   515

CHAPTER 17
INTERNATIONAL MARKETING AND
MARKETING RESEARCH   520
Opening Focus: Porterfield Wilson:
From Shining Shoes to Importing
Foreign Cars   521
Opportunities for Small Firms in
International Marketing   522
 Growing Interest in International
 Marketing   522
 Two Aspects of International Marketing   522
Importing by Small Firms   523
 Reasons for Importing   523
 Some Problems with Importing   524
Exporting by Small Firms   524
 Some Common Myths about Exporting   524
 Some Opportunities and Risks for Small
 Firms   525
 Levels of Involvement   528
 Does the Firm Have Export Potential?   528
 Need for Market Research   529
 Which Approach Should Be Taken?   532
 Overcoming Barriers to Exporting   533
 Help *Is* Available   537
 Computer Update: Census Bureau
 Provides New Electronic Service   538

Marketing Research   539

  Why Do Marketing Research?   539

  Where Marketing Research Fits into
  Marketing   540

  How to Do Marketing Research   540

  Using Computerized Data Bases   543

  Example of Marketing Research   543

What You Should Have Learned   544

Cases for Part V

V–1 CleanDrum, Inc. (E)   548
V–2 Medical Services, Inc.   551
V–3 Angelo's Supermarkets   556

PART VI
FINANCIAL PLANNING AND CONTROL

CHAPTER 18
PLANNING FOR PROFIT   564

Opening Focus: Avian Corporation:
Getting Off the Ground   565

Need for Profit Planning   566

How a Business's Financial Position
Changes   567

  How the Financial Position Changes   568

  Importance of Accounting   569

  Computer Update: Using Personal
  Finance Programs to Run Small Firms   569

Financial Structure of a Business   570

  Assets   570

  Liabilities   572

  Owners' Equity   573

Profit-Making Activities of a Business   574

  Revenue and Expenses   574

  Profit   575

✓ How to Plan for Profit   575

  Need for Profit Planning   576

  Steps in Profit Planning   576

  Need for Realism in Profit Planning   576

Profit Planning Applied in a Typical
Small Business   577

  Step 1: Establish the Profit Goal   577

Step 2: Determine the Planned Sales
Volume   578

Step 3: Estimate Expenses for Planned
Sales Volume   578

Step 4: Determine Profit from Steps 2
and 3   581

Step 5: Compare Estimated Profit with
Profit Goal   581

Step 6: List Possible Alternatives to
Improve Profits   581

Step 7: Determine How Costs Vary with
Changes in Sales Volume   582

Step 8: Determine How Profits Vary with
Changes in Sales Volume   584

Step 9: Analyze Alternatives from a Profit
Standpoint   584

Step 10: Select and Implement the
Plan   585

What You Should Have Learned   586

CHAPTER 19
BUDGETING AND CONTROLLING
OPERATIONS   590

Opening Focus: VideoStar Connections:
The Importance of Staying Power   591

What Is Involved in Control?   592

  The Role of Control   592

  Steps in Control   592

Characteristics of Effective Control
Systems   593

  Timely   593

  Cost Effective   593

  Accurate   594

  Quantifiable and Measurable   594

  Indicative of Causes—When
  Possible   594

  Assigned to One Individual   594

  Acceptable to Those Involved with
  Them   594

Setting Performance Standards   595

Using Budgets to Set Standards   595

  Benefits of Budgets   595

  Types of Budgets   596

  Preparing the Operating Budget   596

Preparing the Cash Flow Budget   598

Using Budgetary Control   600

Computer Update: The Check Is in the Computer   601

Controlling Credit, Collections, and Accounts Receivable   601

Other Types of Budgetary Control   602

Using Audits to Control the Budget   603

Obtaining and Using Information on Performance   603

Indirect Control by Means of Reports   604

Comparing Actual Performance with Standards   604

Determining Causes of Poor Performance   605

Evaluating the Firm's Financial Condition   605

Comparing with Firm's Past Performance   606

Comparing with Similar Companies   606

Some Important Ratios and Their Meanings   606

Are Profits Satisfactory?   607

Are Assets Productive?   608

Can the Firm Pay Its Debts?   608

How Good Are the Firm's Assets?   608

How Much Equity Should a Firm Have?   609

Ratios Are Interrelated   609

What You Should Have Learned   610

CHAPTER 20
USING COMPUTERS AND MANAGEMENT INFORMATION SYSTEMS   614

Opening Focus: Herman Valentine: A Study in Minority Entrepreneurship   615

Importance of Information   616

Elements of a Management Information System (MIS)   617

What Information Is Needed?   617

Timing of Information Flow   621

Choosing an MIS   622

The Role of Computers in Small Business   622

What a Computer System Includes   624

Strengths and Weaknesses of Computers for Small Firms   624

Manual versus Computer MIS   626

Computer Update: Micro Support Resource Corporation: Training People to Call Back   628

Choosing Software   628

Choosing Hardware   630

The Accounting System as an MIS   630

Sales   631

Computer Update: The Hawthorne Hotel: Nineteenth-Century Hotel . . . Twentieth-Century Technology   632

Cash Income and Outgo   634

Accounts Receivable   634

Accounts Payable   635

Inventory   635

Expenses   637

Financial Statements   639

What You Should Have Learned   639

Cases for Part VI

VI–1   CleanDrum, Inc. (F)   643

VI–2   Osborne Computer Company (A) and (B)   647

VI–3   Pools, Inc.   653

VI–4   Horne Box, Inc.   659

VI–5   What Is Profit?   664

PART VII
PROVIDING PRESENT AND FUTURE SECURITY FOR THE BUSINESS

CHAPTER 21
RISK MANAGEMENT, INSURANCE, AND CRIME PREVENTION   668

Opening Focus: Business Risks International Inc.: Corporate Protection   669

Risk and Its Management   670

Types of Risk   670

Ways of Coping with Risk   671

Using Insurance to Minimize Loss due to Risk 672

Determining Need for Insurance 672

Types of Insurance Coverage 673

Guides to Selecting an Insurer 675

Noninsurance Methods for Dealing with Risk 676

Crime Prevention 677

Armed Robbery 678

Theft 680

Computer Update: Kroy Sign Systems: Watch that Sign—It May Be Watching You! 683

White-Collar Crime 684

Document Security 686

Computer Update: Computerizing Accounts Receivable: A Two-Edged Sword 687

Safeguarding Employees with Preventive Measures 687

What You Should Have Learned 688

Government Help for Small Businesses 704

Small Business Administration (SBA) 704

U.S. Department of Commerce 705

Other Government Agencies 705

Computer Update: The Commerce Department Reports by Computer 706

Handling Government Regulations and Paperwork 706

Dealing with Regulatory Agencies 707

How Small Firms Can Cope with Regulations 710

Choosing and Using a Lawyer 711

Choosing the Lawyer 711

Maintaining Relationships with Attorneys 712

Being Your Own Counsel 713

Socially and Ethically Responsible Behavior 714

Social Responsibility 714

Business Ethics 716

What You Should Have Learned 716

CHAPTER 22

BUSINESS LAWS AND BUSINESS ETHICS 692

Opening Focus: Georgio Cherubini: Engineer-Turned-Restaurateur Cooks Up Three-Star Success 693

Understanding the Legal Environment 694

Some Basic Legal Principles 695

Different Types of Laws 695

Some Basic Business Laws 697

The Uniform Commercial Code 697

Contracts 697

Sales 699

Property 700

Patents, Copyrights, and Trademarks 701

Agency 702

Negotiable Instruments 702

Torts 702

Bankruptcy 703

CHAPTER 23

TAXES AND THEIR TREATMENT 722

Opening Focus: Jack Bares: Estate Planning to Minimize Taxes 723

How the U.S. Tax System Operates 724

Who Pays the Taxes? 724

How Taxes Affect Small Businesses 726

Get Professional Help! 726

Types of Taxes 727

Taxes Imposed on the Business Itself 727

Taxes Paid to Operate the Business 727

Excise and Intangible Property Taxes 729

State and Local Sales and Use Taxes 729

Federal, State, and Local Income Taxes 730

Treatment of Federal Corporate Income Taxes 733

Employment-Related Taxes 736

Income Tax Withholding 736

Social Security Taxes   737

Unemployment Compensation
Insurance   738

Computer Update: Magnetic Media
Reporting   739

Workers' Compensation   740

Personal Taxes Paid by Owners
Themselves   740

Taxes on Amounts Withdrawn from the
Business   740

Taxes on Amounts Received from Sale
of the Business   741

Estate Planning to Minimize Taxes   742

Estate Planning Issues   742

Estate Planning Techniques   742

Recordkeeping and Tax Reporting   744

Maintaining Tax Records   744

Reporting Your Taxes   745

What You Should Have Learned   745

CHAPTER 24
PLANNING FOR THE FUTURE   750

Opening Focus: To Continue or Not
to Continue?   751

Role of Family-Owned Businesses   752

The Family and the Business   753

Family Hierarchy   754

Family Interactions   755

Family Limitations   757

Family Resources   758

Preparing the Next Generation   758

Preparing for Management
Succession   760

Why Succession Is a Problem   760

An Overlooked Problem   762

Plan Ahead!   762

Sudden Departure   763

Planned Departure   763

Making the Transition Easier   766

The Moment of Truth   767

Taxes, Estate Planning, and the Future
of the Business   768

Tax Planning   768

Estate Planning   768

Buy/Sell Agreement   769

Doing a Management Self-Evaluation   769

What You Should Have Learned   769

Cases for Part VII
VII–1   CleanDrum, Inc. (G)   773
VII–2   Our Hero Restaurant (D)   775
VII–3   The Roxy Dinner Theatre   777
VII–4   See Coast Manufacturing
         Company, Inc.   784
VII–5   The Son-in-Law   791

APPENDIXES
A   Help for Women   795
B   Help for Minorities   795
C   Some Useful Publications for
     Potential Entrepreneurs   797
D   Deciding Whether to Buy an
     Existing Business, Start a New
     One, or Buy a Franchise   799
E   A Sample Business Plan   803
F   Things You Can Do When a Union
     Tries to Organize Your Company   821
G   Things You Cannot Do When a
     Union Tries to Organize Your
     Company   823
H   General Management Self-
     Evaluation   825

**GLOSSARY OF FREQUENTLY USED
BUSINESS TERMS**   829

**GLOSSARY OF FREQUENTLY USED
COMPUTER TERMS**   839

INDEX   841

THE CHALLENGE OF OWNING AND MANAGING A SMALL BUSINESS

Because small businesses are so important and so numerous, Part I is designed to show the unique challenges involved in owning and/or managing one of them. The material covered should help you decide if pursuing a career in small business is the right course of action for you. The dynamic and challenging role of small business is covered in Chapter 1. Then, Chapter 2 discusses reasons for entering small business, along with the characteristics and objectives of such firms. Chapter 3 explores some opportunities in small firms, especially for women and minorities. The role of franchising in small business is discussed in Chapter 4.

1

THE DYNAMIC ROLE OF SMALL BUSINESS

There is an entrepreneurial revolution sweeping this country, and it's a great time for all of small business.—June Nichols, Southeast administrator, Small Business Administration

Small businesses may still fail in prodigious numbers, but the small business-owner is clearly a winner—an American folk hero, a source of jobs and growth, a role model, a cultural icon. . . . The entrepreneur has been transformed during the 1980s into a courageous taker of risks.—Bernard Wysocki, Jr., small business editor, *The Wall Street Journal*

LEARNING OBJECTIVES

After studying the material in this chapter, you will be able to:

1. Explain why now is an interesting time to study small business.
2. Define the term *small business.*
3. List the unique contributions of small businesses.
4. Describe the limitations of small businesses.

SAM WALTON: WORK, AMBITION—SUCCESS

According to *Forbes* magazine, Sam Walton is the richest man in America. Whether this is true or not is irrelevant, for Walton is a classic example of a small businessman who has succeeded. For him, the key is people. It is a key that has unlocked countless doors and showered upon him, his customers, and his employees (his "associates," as he calls them) the fruits of nearly 30 years of labor in building his highly successful company, Wal-Mart Stores, Inc. He is founder, chairman of the board, and chief executive officer. He is also quite active in Students in Free Enterprise, Inc.

In a recent interview, he said:

The goal of our business has always been to be the very best; and along with that, we believe completely that in order to do that you've got to make a good situation and put the interest of your associates first. If we really do that consistently, they in turn will cause . . . our business to be successful, which is what we've talked about and espoused and practiced. We fail many times to do it as well as we should, but it's still the key to what success we've had.

It would be difficult to overstate the success the corporation has enjoyed in its nearly three decades of existence. Beginning with a single store in Rogers, Arkansas, that he opened in 1962, Walton has seen his company expand to include over 1,300 stores in 25 states. Along the way, the company has also become one of the top-rated stocks on Wall Street and racked up sales of $20 billion in 1988. According to Walton, the reason for Wal-Mart's success is

. . . our people and the way they're treated and the way they feel about their company. The attitude of our employees, our associates, is that things are different in our company, and they deserve the credit. . . . There is, of course, a price that must be paid. It takes an immense amount of solid dedication and determination to excel and to achieve, and a driving desire and an ambition.

Walton admits he paid the price. "I wouldn't change, because I've enjoyed what I do," he insisted. "But it's long hours and it's a singular dedication and you have to give up some things with your family that I would like to have had."

Sam Walton, chairman and chief executive officer, Wal-Mart Stores, Inc.

Source: Wal-Mart Stores, Inc., in cooperation with Students in Free Enterprise, Inc.

It began in Kingfisher, Oklahoma, on March 29, 1918, the day Walton was born to Thomas and Nancy Walton. Thomas Walton was a banker at the time and later entered the farm mortgage business and moved to Missouri. Sam Walton and his younger brother J. L. "Bud" Walton lived with their parents in several towns in Missouri while his father pursued his business, struggling to keep food on the table in the depths of the Great Depression. Growing up, the future founder of Wal-Mart discovered early that he "had a fair amount of ambition and enjoyed working." He had to work, he said, and found various jobs—delivering papers, milking cows, and delivering the milk so that the family would have money while his father was on the road. He became the youngest Eagle Scout at Shelbina Junior High School, an honor he still recalls.

After graduating from the University of Missouri in 1940 with a degree in economics, he was a trainee with J. C. Penney in Iowa for a year and a half, married Helen Robson, and served three years in the U.S. Army. Then, in 1945, he and his brother bought a Ben Franklin store in Arkansas and by 1962 had 15 of them operating under the name "Walton's 5 & 10." After failing to interest Ben Franklin executives in the discount store concept, he opened his own store in Rogers, Arkansas, in 1962.

His strategy was to operate a discount store in a small community; in that setting, he would offer name-brand merchandise at low prices and would add friendly service. It worked! In 1970, the family-owned company went public. In 1972,

with 41 stores, sales of $72 million, and fewer than 3,000 employees, the corporation's stock was listed on the New York Stock Exchange. The next move was into wholesaling, with 23 Sam's Wholesale Clubs. Wal-Mart has been a success story from the beginning, and the end is nowhere in sight.

In summary, Walton's success is based on his faith in his "associates," his belief in small-town America—where he got his start—and his down-to-earth approach to life. He's famous for applying the Golden Rule to his stores, hunting with his bird dog, and driving his old 1979 pickup wherever he goes. Although he now owns a 1988 Ford pickup, he still enjoys driving the older model.

Sources: Correspondence with Students in Free Enterprise, Inc., Springfield, Missouri, and with Wal-Mart Stores, Inc.; "Letters to Fortune," *Fortune,* February 27, 1989, p. 135; and Kenneth R. Sheats, "How Wal-Mart Hits Main St.," *U.S. News & World Report,* March 13, 1989, pp. 53–55.

Why start a small business book with a profile of Sam Walton? He is not a *small* businessman now, but that is how he started in 1945. Walton encountered difficulties at first, then hit his stride and took off. Wal-Mart hasn't slowed down since. This is true of many large firms: most were once small businesses!

IT'S AN INTERESTING TIME TO BE STUDYING SMALL BUSINESS

This is a challenging and rewarding time to be studying small business. Owning and operating such a firm is one of the best ways to fulfill the "Great American Dream." More than 4 out of 10 Americans believe that owning a small business is one of the best paths to riches in the United States.[1] Every year, around a million people in the United States turn this dream of owning a business into a reality, and many of these dreams become true success stories.

Some of the reasons for the increased interest in small business are that:

- The number of small businesses is growing rapidly.
- Small firms generate most new employment.
- The public favors small business.
- There is increasing interest in small business at colleges and universities.
- There is a trend toward self-employment.
- Small business is attractive to people of all ages.

The Number of Small Businesses Is Growing

The story of progress in small business in this country is truly an amazing one. As an economic power, American small business ranks fourth in the world, behind only the U.S. economy as a whole and the economies of Japan and the Soviet Union.[2] According to John Sloan, president of the National Federation of Independent Business (NFIB), there are over 14 million small firms in the United States.[3]

Other estimates of the number of small firms vary from a low of about 13 million[4] to the U.S. Treasury Department's estimate of 19.8 million, as shown in Figure 1–1. Notice that the Treasury's estimate includes "large businesses which make up a tiny percentage of the total."

More important than the total number of small businesses, though, is the fact that the number of new firms is growing by 700,000[5] to 1,000,000[6] per year. Moreover, nine new firms are organized for every one that fails, and these businesses generate nearly half of our gross national product (GNP) during a typical year.[7]

Small Businesses Generate Most New Employment

In addition to other benefits, small businesses contribute greatly to employment, especially in the creation of new jobs. According to a survey by the

Figure 1–1   The 1980s Smiled on Small Businesses

Small businesses boomed in the '80s. Forecast: The '90s won't be as explosive.

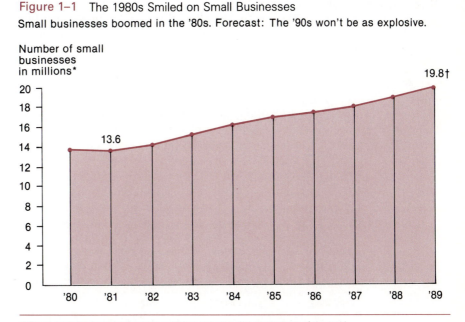

Number of small businesses in millions*

19.8†

13.6

* Figure includes large businesses, which make up a tiny percentage of the total.

† Estimate.

Source: USA Today, May 8, 1989, p. 1E. Copyright 1989, USA TODAY. Adapted with permission. (Original source: U.S. Treasury Department.)

U.S. Small Business Administration, businesses with fewer than 100 employees, representing slightly over half of all private employment, produce more than 60 percent of the total number of new jobs.[8] Robert B. Reich, a noted economist, stated in a recent book that "in recent years, the *Fortune* 500 have failed to generate a single new job."[9] However, "new and small-to-midsized firms have provided the bulk of the 20 million new jobs created in the past decade."[10]

This creation of jobs, however, varies according to the business cycle. It has been found that small businesses appear to produce relatively more jobs nearing the turning point of a business cycle and during the initial expansion phase of such a cycle. In turn, large businesses appear to perform best and create more jobs when nearing the turning point of an expansion. Thus, small businesses with fewer than 100 employees contributed around 89 percent of new jobs from 1978 to 1980, but only 38 percent of new jobs from 1980 to 1982.

As shown in Figure 1–2, the Small Business Administration confirms this tendency. While small firms created nearly 21 million jobs from 1978 to 1988, the number created varied from 5.8 million in 1978–80 to 1.5 million in 1980–82. The large increase from 1978 to 1980 was probably the result of the deregulation movement begun in 1978, which led to an expansion movement. During the second period, a recession wrung out most of the inflation resulting from the previous expansion.

The Public Favors Small Business

The owners and managers of these small firms generally believe in the free enterprise system, with its emphasis on individual freedom, risk taking, initiative, and hard work. For this reason, in a poll of 2,000 adults, the

Figure 1–2 Small Business, Big Employer

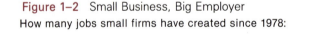

How many jobs small firms have created since 1978:

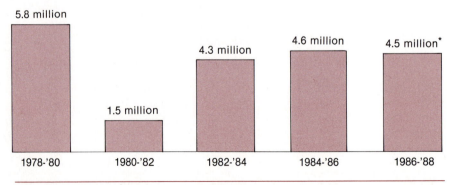

* Estimate.

Source: USA Today, May 9, 1988, p. 1E. Copyright 1988, USA TODAY. Adapted with permission. (Original source: Small Business Administration.)

Roper Organization found that people have a higher opinion of small firms than of large corporations (see Figure 1–3). In fact, according to a Wells Fargo study, the average small businessperson "is the unsung hero of the economy," leading the nation's economic growth during the 1980s.[11]

The public evidently favors keeping this segment of our economy healthy and flourishing. This conclusion was confirmed in a survey by Comprehensive Accounting Corporation, a nationwide accounting franchise specializing in small business. While 77 percent of those surveyed knew of the high failure rate of small firms, 53 percent of them would like to own a small business.[12]

As indicated by the opening quotation from June Nichols, the public's acceptance of small business has been reflected in government action. For

Figure 1–3   We Favor Small Business

We have a higher opinion of small companies than of large corporations

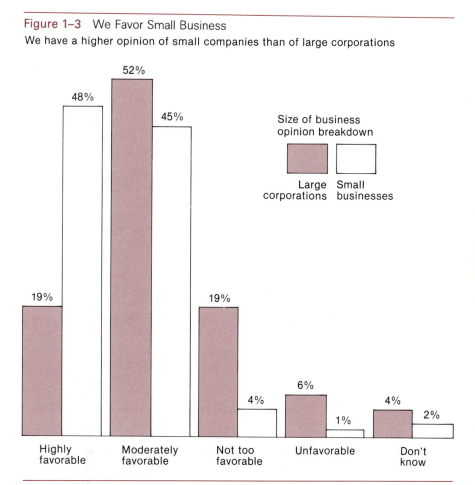

Source: USA Today, February 12, 1985, p. 18. Copyright 1985, USA TODAY. Adapted with permission.
(Original source: Roper Organization, Inc., poll of 2,000 adults.)

example, during fiscal year 1986, more than 98 percent of all government contracts were for $25,000 or less. Moreover, small business supplied over 18 percent of the total value of direct contract amounts bought by the federal government.[13]

Interest Increasing at Colleges and Universities

Another indication of the growing favor of small business is its acceptance as part of the mission of colleges and universities. For example, Foster McKay, a New York recruiting firm, found in a survey of recent M.B.A. graduates that 70 percent would prefer to own or work in a small firm, but most took jobs in large companies.[14] Also, a Roper poll of undergraduate students found 46 percent of them believing that *owning a business* is an excellent chance to get ahead.[15] Yet 35 percent of the students thought that *working for a large company* was an excellent way to get ahead, while only 20 percent thought that *working for a small business* would give them that opportunity. In other words, *owning* a small business is perceived as leading to success, while *working for* a large firm is seen as preferable to working for a small one.

Furthermore, small business management is becoming accepted as an academic discipline. Community colleges, especially, are now offering courses for small business owners. One study found that 90 percent of the community colleges offer such courses, while 75 percent of the public community colleges also provide training courses—often conducted on the company's own premises. This activity is "one of the fastest-growing areas in the community college field," according to a spokesman for the American Association of Community and Junior Colleges.[16] Many colleges and universities are now also offering specialized business courses, such as programs in family business, franchising, and international business, and many students are starting businesses to finance their education.

For example, Mark Frank went to Washington University at St. Louis to study accounting and finance. As a freshman, he noticed many students buying items such as computers, VCRs, and microwave ovens. But during summer break these items had to be carted home. He started renting the basement of his house on campus to store the items. With the profit from that, he bought 100 microwave ovens for about $90 each and rented them to students for $95 per year.

After two years, Mark, by then a senior, had earned an $18,000 profit.[17]

Trend toward Self-Employment

The growth rate for self-employment is greater than the growth rate of the general work force. For example, the Bureau of Labor Statistics found that the number of self-employed people in the United States increased 24 percent from 1974 to 1984, while the total work force grew only 21 percent during those years.

Small business experienced particularly dynamic growth in the mid-to-late 1980s as investors became more willing to assume the risk of starting or revitalizing small businesses. Many of these were middle-aged executives from large corporations who were eager to put their management skills to work in the "high-risk venture [of] reviving smaller companies in aging industries."[18]

Another evidence of this trend toward self-employment is the prediction that there would be 90 million U.S. households in 1990 and about 20 million businesses. And the number of businesses is growing three times as fast as the number of households.[19]

Small Business Is Attractive to All Ages

Entrepreneurship knows no age limits! From the very young to the very old, people are starting new businesses at an increasing rate. A particularly heartening trend is the entry of many teenagers and other young people into small business ownership.

For example, Howard Stubbs is known as "Mr. Hot Dog" in the South Bronx, an area known for its drug dealers, rubble-strewn lots, and burned-out buildings. As a 15-year-old student at Jane Addams Vocational High School, Stubbs borrowed $800 from friends and relatives to buy an umbrella-topped hot dog cart. Two years later, he grossed $10,000 from his stand. He buys hot dogs for 33 cents—with all the trimmings—and sells them for $1; soda costs 20 cents and sells for 75 cents.

Working at his stand on weekends and school holidays and during the summer, he also sells candy at school and gives haircuts to his friends—for $5.[20]

As indicated earlier, small businesses are being formed on college campuses at a rapid rate. For example, the Association of Collegiate Entrepreneurs (ACE), founded in 1983 at Wichita State University, now has hundreds of chapters throughout the world.[21] The Association found in one study that a third of all new companies are started by people under 30 (many still in their teens) and that these people possess certain characteristics that lead to success, as shown in Figure 1–4. Many of these small business owners made their fortune in computers or high-tech industries (see Computer Update).

A word of caution to young people is needed at this point. With all their self-confidence, energy, drive, and persistence, they must not forget their responsibility. If they start a business, they must learn that they can't just "turn it off and on" like a light switch. They can't take time off at will. If the business is to succeed, it must have longevity, and not shut down for holidays or vacations or when things aren't going well.

A recent study by the National Federation of Independent Business found that, while forming new businesses is attractive to young people, most owners of small firms are in their forties and fifties.[22] Also, 40 percent of

COMPUTER UPDATE

THE WHIZ KIDS STRIKE IT RICH

In 1972, at age 26, with a master's degree in aeronautical engineering from Stanford University, Sandra Kurtzig quit her job at General Electric to raise a family. In addition to caring for her two sons, she started developing computer programs in the bedroom of her apartment. She founded ASK Computer Systems to develop and market programs to help manufacturers keep track of inventory and work in progress. She and her company became so successful that she was referred to as the most successful woman entrepreneur in Silicon Valley.

She left ASK in 1985 to spend more time with her two sons. But when the company ran into trouble in 1989—slackening demand hurt earnings—the directors asked her to come back and help revive the firm, which she did.

William Gates was only 19 when he dropped his undergraduate work at Harvard to found Microsoft in 1975. After producing best-selling business software for companies such as IBM® and Apple®, as well as developing the popular computer game *Flight Simulator,* he was worth $313 million when he went public in 1986. He is now known as "one of the best people with the best ideas in the computer field." These talents have led him to extraordinary wealth and fame.

Sources: Kevin Anderson, "Whiz Kids Reap Riches from Offers," *USA Today,* February 5, 1986, p. 2B; Andrew Pollack, "ASK Computer Founder Severs Her Last Ties," *The New York Times,* February 22, 1989, p. C4; Stratford P. Sherman, "How to Beat the Japanese," *Fortune,* April 10, 1989, p. 145; and "Founder Acquires 490,000 ASK Shares," *USA Today,* November 20, 1989, p. 6B.

the nearly 1 million people who form new businesses each year already have some management experience, and one-fourth of them have managed or owned a business before.

Small business as a dynamic form of private ownership has become so popular that a whole new crop of journals and newsletters has sprung up to provide information and support. Many of these target specialized niches

---

Figure 1–4   Characteristics Needed by Young Entrepreneurs

Here's what the Association of College Entrepreneurs says it takes for teens to succeed in business:

- Self-confidence.
- A high level of drive and energy.
- Ability to deal with uncertainty, confusion.
- Persistence.

- Ability to set goals.
- An independent nature.
- Support and help from parents.

Source: Association of Collegiate Entrepreneurs, as reported in *USA Today,* February 20, 1986, p. 1B. Copyright 1986, USA TODAY. Reprinted with permission.

among small business people. Some of the more popular of these are: *Small Business Journal, Journal of Small Business Management, New Business Opportunities, Entrepreneurial Woman, Family Business Magazine,* and *Business Week Newsletter for Family-Owned Businesses.* There are also several new academic journals dealing with small business, including *Journal of Business and Entrepreneurship* and *Small Business Economics.*

Also many student organizations—such as the Association of Collegiate Entrepreneurs (ACE), the University Entrepreneurial Association (UEA), and Students in Free Enterprise (SIFE)—are being formed to encourage entrepreneurship and small business ownership.

For example, notice in the Opening Focus that Sam Walton is very active in SIFE. In fact, he founded the Wal-Mart Professorships for selected teachers in small business and entrepreneurship.

DEFINING SMALL BUSINESS—NO EASY TASK

Now that we've seen how much interest small businesses excite, what exactly constitutes a small business? There is no simple definition, but let's look at some qualified definitions.

What Is Small?

What is a small business? Superficially, this appears easy to answer. A number of firms that you patronize—such as the independent neighborhood grocery, the fast-food restaurant, the barbershop or beauty salon, the dry cleaners, the campus record shop, and the veterinarian—are examples of small businesses. However, when American Motors had 8,500 employees, it was considered a small business: the U.S. Small Business Administration deemed it eligible for a small business loan. Why? Because American Motors *was* small compared to its mammoth competitors—General Motors, Ford, and Chrysler, which bought it in 1987.

Qualitative characteristics are also important in describing small businesses. The Committee for Economic Development stated that a small business has at least two of the following four features:[23]

1. Management is independent, since the manager usually owns the firm.
2. Capital is supplied and ownership is held by an individual or a few individuals.
3. The area of operations is primarily local, although the market isn't necessarily local.

4.   The firm is small in comparison with the largest competitors in its industry.

Perhaps the best definition of small business is the one used by Congress in the Small Business Act of 1953, which states that a **small business** is one that is independently owned and operated and is not dominant in its field of operation.[24] We'll use that definition in this text.

Diversity of Small Businesses

Small firms come in many types and sizes, and defining and classifying them is difficult. The Small Business Administration (SBA), the federal agency that gives advice, financial assistance, and other services to small businesses, classifies them as follows.

Manufacturing firms use raw materials and semifinished parts to produce finished goods. Since the initial investment—the plant, machines, and equipment—is large, and operating costs and risks are high, relatively few such firms are truly small. A small manufacturing business is one where the "maximum number of employees may range from 500 to 1,500, depending on the industry in which [it] is primarily engaged."[25] These firms tend to provide parts and components to larger companies.

General construction firms build residences (both private and rental), commercial and industrial buildings, government offices and installations, and structures of other types. Small businesses are those whose average annual receipts for the past three years do not exceed $9.5 to $17 million, depending on the industry. They often do subcontracting for larger contractors, such as installing doors, windows, and cabinets in buildings.

Wholesalers buy finished products from manufacturers and other producers and resell them to retailers for sale to the ultimate consumer. A small firm has a maximum of 100 employees.

Retailers obtain goods from manufacturers, wholesalers, brokers, and agents and sell them to customers for use. Small retailers have annual sales not exceeding $3.5 million to $13.5 million, depending on the industry. Grocery stores, drugstores, and food service establishments are examples.

Service businesses perform essential, specialized, often technical services for customers, businesses, and institutions such as schools, governments, and hospitals. To be classified as small, they must have annual sales not exceeding $3.5 million to $14.5 million, depending on the industry. Their services are usually those the customers are unable or unwilling to provide, such as consulting, custodial and janitorial, accounting and tax, and automotive and appliance repair services.

Distinction between a Small Business and an Entrepreneurial Venture

We also need to distinguish between small businesses and entrepreneurial ventures. A small business (or Mom-and-Pop operation) is any business that is independently owned and operated, is not dominant in its field, and does not engage in many new or innovative practices. It may never grow large, and the owners may not want it to. These small businesspeople tend to enter business for reasons other than "making a lot of money." Thus, these owners usually prefer a more relaxed and less aggressive approach to running the business. In other words, they manage the business in a normal way, expecting normal sales, profits, and growth.

Case II–3, Simmons Mountainside Satellite Sales, at the end of Part II, is an excellent example of this "Mom-and-Pop" type of operation. Mr. Simmons' long-term goals are simply to continue doing what he is doing, and he "has no expansion or diversification plans."

On the other hand, an **entrepreneurial venture** is one in which the principal objective of the entrepreneur is profitability and growth. Thus, the business is characterized by innovative strategic practices and/or products. The entrepreneurs and their financial backers are usually seeking rapid growth, immediate—and high—profits, and a quick sellout with a large capital gain.

Look in dorm rooms across the nation and you will find the basic necessities of college life: books, clothes—clean and dirty, long distance phone bills, empty drink cans, and so forth. Tucked in a corner, or under a pile of clothes, you may find the greatest thing since Cliff Notes—a compact combination refrigerator, freezer and microwave oven.

In July 1989, a Sharon, Massachusetts, firm headed by Robert P. Bennett, introduced a new, technologically advanced multipliance called the MicroFridge®. It stands less than four feet tall and is billed as "the kitchen that fits in a file cabinet." The MicroFridge "multipliance" never exceeds 10 amps of electrical current and uses only one plug. Implementing an aggressive nationwide marketing strategy, Bennett is targeting the appliance to college students, office workers, and hotel guests.

Bennett, who holds two patents on the design, boasts that the unit "is a 500 watt microwave oven; a 2.9 cubic foot refrigerator; and a real zero degree, 0.7 cubic foot freezer that keeps frozen foods frozen." The high technology and performance, however, come with a $429 price tag.

Bennett's endeavor as president and cofounder of MicroFridge, Inc. is a classic example of an *entrepreneurial venture*. Using an innovative idea and an aggressive marketing plan, he hopes to dominate the field. His primary objective is high profit and rapid growth, with estimated 1989 revenues approaching $2 million. Bennett and his investor's venture has proven a success thus far.

MicroFridge is manufactured by Sanyo E&E Corporation with final assembly in San Diego, California. Financing has been provided by the founders and private investors.[26]

Source: Photo courtesy of MicroFridge, Inc.

It is not easy to distinguish between a small business owner and an entrepreneur; the distinction hinges on their intentions. In general, a **small business owner** establishes a business for the principal purpose of furthering personal goals, which include making a profit. The business is thus the primary source of income and will consume the majority of the owner's time and resources. The owner perceives the business as an extension of his or her personality, which is interwoven with family needs and desires.

On the other hand, the **entrepreneur** starts and manages a business for many reasons, including achievement, profit, and growth. Such a person is characterized principally by innovative behavior and will employ strategic management practices in the business.[27]

Notice in the Opening Focus that Sam Walton was an entrepreneur from the very beginning of Wal-Mart. He set out not only to make a profit but also to expand.

Of course, the owners' intentions sometimes change, and what started out as a small business becomes an entrepreneurial venture.

An example of this development is Texas Long Distance, a small Dallas firm. Bill Wiese, 65, a retired executive, his wife Chleo, his son Roger, and his nephew John started and operated the small business. The company began by using long-distance lines leased from discounters (such as Sprint) and secondhand switching equipment to find the cheapest route for each call. Customers could make up to 150 five-minute calls a month for only $75. Bill Wiese explained the objective of Texas Long Distance when he said, "Our goal is to have a good time and hopefully make some money at it."

But the business became an entrepreneurial venture in 1989 when it became a full-service long-distance company. The company's name was changed to Digital Network Inc., reflecting the changed nature of its activities. It had new switching equipment, more lines, and over 800 customers. With offices in Austin and Houston, as well as Dallas, the firm employed 25 to 26 people, including Scott Wiese, another of Bill's sons.[28]

Size, Sales, and Employment

As can be seen from Figure 1–5, the Internal Revenue Service classifies 96 percent of American businesses as small (with annual revenues of $1 million or less). Yet they generate only 13 percent of the total receipts each year, while the 4 percent of all firms that are classified as large generate 87 percent of all revenues.

Still, one of the greatest advantages of small businesses is their ability to create new jobs. Using the U.S. Bureau of the Census definition of small business (one having fewer than 500 employees), Figure 1–6 shows that, according to this definition, small businesses account for 80 percent of all employees in all business establishments in the United States. The small businesses with fewer than 100 employees provide over half (56 percent) of all business employment.

As can be seen from Figure 1–7, small firms with fewer than 500 employees are more prevalent in agriculture, contract construction, and wholesale and retail trade, where they provide over 90 percent of all employment. Yet they generate the most jobs in services (17,867,000 employees), retail trade (16,969,000), and manufacturing (11,845,000).

Figure 1–5 Percent Distribution of Business Establishments and Sales Receipts

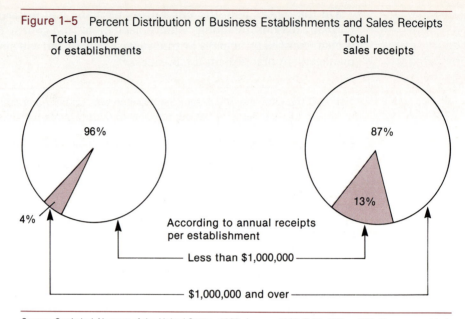

Source: Statistical Abstract of the United States, 1989, January 1989, Table 847, p. 516. Figures provided by the U.S. Internal Revenue Service.

As was discussed earlier in more detail, these figures show how important small firms are in generating employment opportunities.

There is now an apparent trend whereby the dominant position of small business in the retail sector is being eroded, according to an SBA economist, Edward Starr.[29] He believes the decline has been going on for at least 30 years. While retail sales have soared during that period, the number of retail outlets has remained almost constant. Chain-store outlets and bigger stores have absorbed the bulk of the added sales. Starr thinks other factors contributing to the decline are high-cost technology (such as point-of-sale scanners and computerized inventories, which reduce labor costs for larger stores), repeal of state "fair trade" laws (which opened the door to chain-store discounting), the rise of catalog shopping, and government regulations that disproportionately increased the paperwork burden of small business owners.

SOME UNIQUE CONTRIBUTIONS OF SMALL BUSINESSES

As indicated throughout this chapter, small firms differ from their larger competitors. Let's look at some of the major contributions made by small businesses that set them apart from larger firms.

Figure 1–6   Percent Distribution of Business Establishments and Employees by Size of Employer

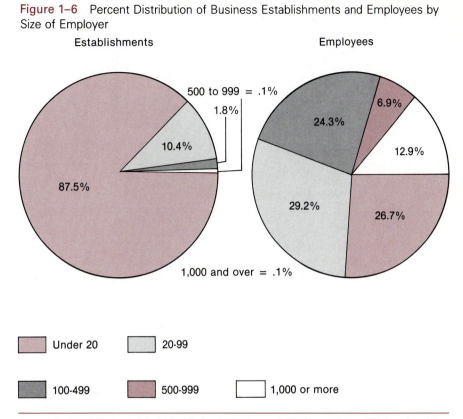

Establishments   Employees

500 to 999 = .1%
1.8%
10.4%
87.5%
6.9%
24.3%
12.9%
29.2%
26.7%
1,000 and over = .1%

Under 20   20-99

100-499   500-999   1,000 or more

Source: Statistical Abstract of the United States, 1989, January 1989, Figure 17.1, p. 512, based on data from Table 859, p. 523, provided by the U.S. Bureau of the Census.

Smaller firms tend to:

- Encourage innovation and flexibility.
- Maintain close relationships with customers and the community.
- Keep larger firms competitive.
- Provide employees with comprehensive learning experiences.
- Develop risk takers.
- Generate employment.

Encourage Innovation and Flexibility

Smaller enterprises are often sources of new ideas, materials, processes, and services that larger firms may be unable or reluctant to provide. Big companies are usually committed by their investment in tools, inventory, and personnel to producing the same product in large quantities over long

Figure 1–7 Percent Distribution of Employees in Large and Small Firms in Selected Industries

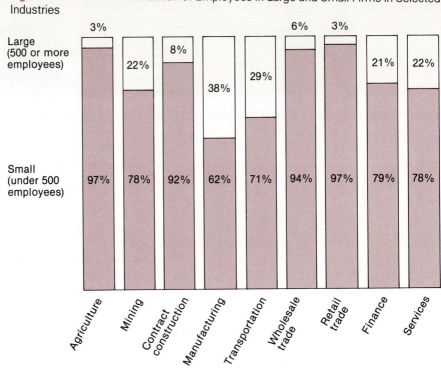

Source: Statistical Abstract of the United States, 1989, January 1989, Table 859, p. 523, based on data provided by the U.S. Bureau of the Census.

periods of time in order to benefit from economies of scale. This means that large firms may not be as flexible as smaller ones. If a small firm is to be successful, then, it must devote its efforts to developing and marketing innovative products and services.

These demands for innovation have forced smaller firms to be flexible. They tend to be able to switch their production readily in the face of changing market conditions and to adapt quickly to changing demands within their field and capacity. They can even change fields. In small businesses, experiments can be conducted, innovations may be initiated, and new ventures are started or expanded. As mentioned earlier, many of today's products originated in small businesses. This trend is especially true in the computer field, where initial developments have been carried on in small companies.

It is no coincidence that IBM didn't produce the first full-scale electronic computer, as IBM already owned 97 percent of the then popular punched-card equipment, which the computer would make obsolete. Instead, the Univac was conceived and produced by Univac Corporation, a small firm formed by Dr. John Mauchly and J. Presper Eckert. Although they were design experts, they lacked production and marketing skills; so they sold out to Remington Rand, which controlled the remaining 3 percent of the punched-card business. So the first giant computers at organizations such as the U.S. Census Bureau and General Electric's Appliance Park plant were Univacs. Nonetheless, IBM's marketing expertise overcame Remington's production expertise, and IBM soon dominated the mainframe computer industry.

Maintain Close Relationships with Customers and Community

Small, local businesses usually have a more intimate knowledge of their communities and therefore take closer interest in them. Also, a small business is usually in close touch with its customers, suppliers, and the community. It can do a more individualized job, thereby attracting customers on the basis of specialty products, quality, and personal services rather than solely on the impersonal factor of price resulting from mass production and mass marketing. While competitive prices and a reputation for honesty are important, an atmosphere of friendliness makes people glad to enter the store and to continue shopping there.

Notice in the Opening Focus that Walton started off his successful venture in small-town U.S.A., with a community setting and friendly, personalized service.

Keep Larger Firms Competitive

Smaller companies have become a controlling factor in the American economy by keeping the bigger concerns "on their toes." With the introduction of new products and services, small businesses help check the development of monopolies. Small businesses encourage competition—if not always in price, at least in design and efficiency. Good examples of this competition are the developments that have occurred in California's Silicon Valley, where the personal computer has been developed, perfected, and proliferated to the point where it affects almost everyone's daily life.

Provide Employees with Comprehensive Learning Experiences

Another unique characteristic of small business is that it enables employees, by handling different activities simultaneously, to have more varied experience than they could have in larger organizations. The small business provides employees with a greater variety of learning experiences in work activities not open to individuals holding more specialized jobs in larger organizations. Along with performing a greater variety of functions, people also have more freedom to make decisions. This freedom and the variety of activities and functions lend zest and interest to employees' work experience, so that small businesses train people to become better leaders and to develop their talents and energies most effectively.

Develop Risk Takers

It has been said that small businesses exemplify one of the basic American freedoms—risk taking, with its consequent rewards and punishments. The small business owner has relative freedom to enter or leave a business at will, to start small and grow big, to expand or contract, and to succeed or fail. This freedom is the basis of our economic system. Yet founding a business in an uncertain environment is risky. Much planning and study must be done before start-up. Even then, unforeseen changes can occur; so owners must see the need for change, make the right decisions, and make the changes. Certain legal and other requirements must also be met before one can start a new business (see Chapters 9 and 22). The same applies to closing a firm. The owner may have responsibilities to customers, employees, investors, and/or the community that prevent leaving at will.

Many large businesses appear to have lost their market appeal. These firms are cutting back, closing plants, and laying off people. This creates a quandary in the marketplace for the unemployed and the new entries into the work force. The risk taker with a small business provides a much-needed source of employment for these workers.

Generate Employment

As emphasized throughout this chapter, small businesses generate employment by creating jobs. The best estimate of new employment generated by small businesses came from David Birch, president of Cognetics, Inc., and a researcher at Massachusetts Institute of Technology. He found that, while the *Fortune* 500 companies "eliminated 3.5 million jobs" from 1980 to 1989, a net total of 17.5 million were added to the economy. And "about two-thirds of those new jobs have come from small businesses."[30]

In addition to providing employment for that many more people, these small firms serve as a training ground for employees, who then go on to larger businesses as experienced workers—at higher salaries. With their more comprehensive learning experience, their emphasis on risk taking, and their exposure to innovation and flexibility, these people become valued employees of the larger companies.

SOME PROBLEMS FACING SMALL BUSINESSES

Just as small companies make some unique contributions, there are some special problems that affect small businesses more than larger ones. These problems can result in limited profitability and growth, the decision to voluntarily close the business, or financial failure.

According to Bruce Phillips, chief economist for the U.S. Small Business Administration, startup firms don't fail as often as some people think. He found that "four out of 10 new businesses survive at least the first six years."[31] He also found that the vast majority of businesses that close do so for voluntary reasons, such as the desire to enter a more profitable business, the owner's death, legal changes, and disenchantment.

Figure 1–8   Why New Businesses Fail

Here's why new businesses fail, according
to a survey of small business owners:

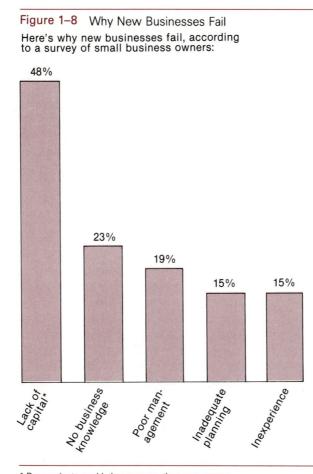

* Respondents could choose more than one answer.

Source: USA Today, March 13, 1987, p. 13. Copyright 1987, USA TODAY. Adapted with permission. (Original
source: Minota Corp., January 1987 survey of 703 businesses with lower than 500 employees.

A later survey of 2,994 new businesses commissioned by the National
Federation of Small Business and American Express also found that the
earlier, highly publicized studies were wrong when they found that fewer
than half of all new firms survived five years. It found that 77 percent of
the new businesses lived to celebrate their third birthday. Also, 75 percent
of new owners with no prior supervisory experience—and 77 percent with
extensive managerial experience—survived for three years.[32]

As you can see from Figure 1–8, a Minota Corporation survey of 703
businesses with fewer than 500 employees found that the main reasons
new firms fail are:

■ Lack of capital.

■ No business knowledge.

- Poor management.
- Inadequate planning.
- Inexperience.

Inadequate Financing

Notice that inadequate financing was first as a basic (primary/fundamental) cause of failure. *It cannot be stressed enough that the shortage of capital is the greatest problem facing small business owners.* Without adequate funds you are unable to acquire and maintain facilities, hire and reward capable employees, produce and market your product, or do the other things necessary to run a successful business. In fact, two small business consultants concluded that "most start-up businesses fail because of under-capitalization."[33] This problem will be emphasized throughout this text.

Inadequate Management

As shown in the previous discussion, inadequate management, in the forms of limited knowledge, poor planning, poor leadership, and no sense of direction, is the second problem facing small firms. Many owners tend to rely on one-person management and seem reluctant to vary from this managerial pattern. They tend to guard their position very jealously and therefore may not select qualified employees, or fail to give them enough authority and responsibility to manage adequately. Often problems are caused by **inbreeding,** whereby members of the family who are not capable are brought into the firm in positions of authority.

Managers of small firms must be generalists rather than specialists. Because they must make their own decisions and then live with those choices, managers are faced with a dilemma. Because the business's resources are limited, it can't afford to make costly mistakes; yet because the organization is so small, the owner can't afford to pay for managerial assistance to prevent bad decisions.

Burdensome Government Regulations and Paperwork

If you want to see small business managers become incensed, mention government regulations and paperwork. That is one of their least favorite subjects—and with good reason. At one time, smaller firms were exempt from many federal regulations and even some state and local ones. Now these firms are subject to the same regulations as their larger competitors. These regulations are unlimited, complex, and often contradictory, which explains why small business managers find it so difficult to comply with governmental requirements. While most businesspeople obey the law willingly, they find it difficult to do so because of conflicts over what the law really is and because of the time, effort, and cost involved.

But, as will be shown in Chapter 22, small businesses benefit from many of these regulations.

WHAT YOU SHOULD HAVE LEARNED

1. This is a challenging and rewarding time to be studying small business because the field is popular and is expected to continue growing in employment and productivity. The public attitude toward small business is favorable right now, too, and self-employment is so popular that around a million people per year—young and old—are starting their own small businesses.

2. Defining *small business* is difficult because the definition of smallness (in number of employees or annual sales revenues) varies widely depending on the industry. In general, a small business is independently owned and operated and not dominant in its field of operation. A clear distinction is difficult to draw between a small business and an entrepreneurial venture, as this depends on the intentions of the owners. If they start a small business and want it to stay small, it is a small business. If, on the other hand, they start small but plan to grow big, it is an entrepreneurial venture.

    Although 96 percent of American businesses can be classified as small, they generate only 13 percent of the total receipts each year. On the other hand, firms with fewer than 500 employees account for 80 percent of existing jobs in U.S. business and create 8 out of 10 new jobs year in and year out.

3. Small firms differ from larger ones in many ways, but their unique advantages include (*a*) flexibility and room for innovation, (*b*) the ability to maintain close relationships with customers and the community, (*c*) the competition they provide forces larger companies to remain competitive, (*d*) the opportunity they give employees to gain experience in many areas, (*e*) the challenge and freedom they offer to risk takers, and (*f*) the tremendous employment opportunities they generate.

4. Some of the problems that plague small companies more than larger ones—and place limitations on their development—are (*a*) inadequate financing, (*b*) inadequate management (especially as the firm grows), and (*c*) burdensome government regulation and paperwork.

KEY TERMS

small business, *12*

entrepreneurial venture, *13*

small business owner, *14*

entrepreneur, *15*

inbreeding, *22*

QUESTIONS

1. (*a*) Do you agree that this is an interesting time to be studying small business? (*b*) Why are you doing so?

2. All of us have personal experiences with small business—as an owner, employee, friend of the owner, or other relationship. Explain one or more such experience(s) you've had.

3. *(a)* What comes to your mind when you think of a small business? *(b)* How does your concept differ from the definition given in this chapter?

4. *(a)* Distinguish between a small business and an entrepreneurial venture. *(b)* If you were to start your own business, which would it be? *(c)* Why?

5. *(a)* How can you explain the growing interest young people have in small business? *(b)* Can you relate this to your personal small business experience?

6. *(a)* What are the unique contributions of small businesses? *(b)* Give examples of each from your own experience with small business or from small businesses that you patronize.

7. *(a)* What are some of the problems facing small businesses? *(b)* Again, give examples from your experience.

SUGGESTED READINGS

Cetron, Marvin J. "Think Big or Think Small: The Future of American Business Firms." *The Futurist* 22 (September–October 1988): 9–16.

Francese, Peter. "Small Companies Account for Most Job Opportunities." *Tulsa Daily World,* May 25, 1986, p. 10–B.

Gardner, Katie. "Student Entrepreneurs: Minding Their Own Businesses." *Washington Post Education Review,* April 9, 1989, pp. 5–7.

Hess, Karl. *Capitalism for Kids.* Wilmington, Del.: Enterprise Publishing, 1989.

"The Job Engine Is Going Great Guns." *Business Week,* March 30, 1987, p. 20.

"New Data on Job Growth Show Some Surprises." *The Wall Street Journal,* March 23, 1989, p. B1.

"The Rise and Rise of America's Small Firms." *The Economist,* January 21, 1989, pp. 67–68.

Skrzycki, Cindy, et al. "Risk Takers." *U.S. News & World Report,* January 26, 1987, pp. 60–67.

Szabo, Joan C. "The Job Machine Rolls On." *Nation's Business,* July 1988, p. 10.

Wysocki, Bernard, Jr. "The Wall Street Journal Reports: Small Business." *The Wall Street Journal,* February 24, 1989, pp. R1ff.

ENDNOTES

1. *USA Today,* October 25, 1985, p. 1A.

2. "Millions of New Jobs to Be Created in '86, Survey Shows," *Mobile* (Alabama) *Register,* March 31, 1986, p. 3–A.

3. George Melloan, "Small Firms Brace for Legislative Attack," *The Wall Street Journal,* May 5, 1987, p. 37.

4. "When You Start Your Own Business . . . ," *Parade Magazine,* August 21, 1988, p. 12.

5. "College Prof Says Entrepreneurship Coachable," *Mobile* (Alabama) *Press Register,* November 28, 1988, p. 3–B.

6. Mindy Fetterman, "Hot Line: Callers Eager to Be Own Boss," *USA Today,* May 9, 1989, p. 1A.

7. "Millions of New Jobs," p. 3–A.

8. "Is Job Creation a Small Feat?" *The Wall Street Journal,* November 21, 1988, p. A17.

9. Reich was quoted in Benjamin Barber, "Reinventing the Liberal Mission," *The Wall Street Journal,* November 16, 1989, p. A15.

10. Mortimer B. Zuckerman, "The Envy of Mr. Gorbachev," *U.S. News & World Report,* December 26, 1988, p. 124.

11. Nancy Rivera, "Small Businessmen Called Unsung Economic Heroes," *Tulsa Daily World,* October 27, 1985, p. G–3.

12. "The American Dream: Your Own Business," *Nation's Business,* November 1988, pp. 10–11.

13. Adline Clarke, "Climate Said Right for Small Businesses," *Mobile* (Alabama) *Press Register,* January 27, 1989, p. 12–D.

14. *The Wall Street Journal,* November 18, 1989, p. B2.

15. *The Wall Street Journal,* November 1, 1988, p. 1.

16. Roger Ricklefs, "Schools Increase Courses to Help Entrepreneurs," *The Wall Street Journal,* February 6, 1989, p. B1.

17. Suzanne Alexander, "Student Entrepreneurs Find Road to Riches on Campus," *The Wall Street Journal,* June 23, 1989, p. B1.

18. Steven P. Galante, "Corporate Executives Quitting to Buy Rust Belt Businesses," *The Wall Street Journal,* April 28, 1986, p. 27.

19. Tait Trussell, "The Untypical Typical Millionaire," *Nation's Business,* November 1988, p. 62.

20. Bethany Kanel, "South-Bronx Teen-Ager Relishes Being Known as 'Mr. Hot Dog,' " *USA Today,* May 9, 1988, p. 9E; and "ABC Evening News," November 14, 1989.

21. Katie Gardner, "Student Entrepreneurs: Minding Their Own Businesses," *Washington Post Education Review,* April 9, 1989, pp. 5–7.

22. Reported in Shelley Liles, "New-Business Owners Smart, Experienced," *USA Today,* May 8, 1989, p. 3E.

23. From *Meeting the Special Problems of Small Businesses* (New York: Committee for Economic Development, 1974), p. 14. Copyright 1974, Committee for Economic Development. Used with permission.

24. W. B. Barnes, *First Semi-Annual Report of the Small Business Administration* (Washington, D.C.: Small Business Administration, January 31, 1954), p. 7.

25. This and the following general size standards are based on *Business Loans from the SBA* (Washington, D.C.: Small Business Administration, June 1987), pp. 5–6.

26. Correspondence with Microfridge, Inc.

27. James W. Garland et al., "Differentiating Entrepreneurs from Small Business Owners: A Conceptualization," *Academy of Management Review* 9 (1984): 354–59.

28. *Fortune,* February 18, 1985, p. 91; and communication with Digital Network Inc.

29. Eugene Carlson, "Neighborhood Groceries Fading Away in Face of High Cost, Big Competition," *The Wall Street Journal,* December 7, 1988, p. 32.

30. Liles, "New-Business Owners Smart," p. 3E.

31. Reported in Shelley Liles, "More Small Businesses Succeeding," *USA Today,* May 8, 1989, p. 1E.

32. Roger Ricklefs, "Road to Success Becomes Less Littered with Failures," *The Wall Street Journal,* October 10, 1989, p. B2.

33. Stephen M. Pollan and Mark Levine, "Playing to Win: The Small Business Guide to Survival and Growth," Special Advertising Section, *U.S. News & World Report,* December 12, 1988, p. A20.

2

WHY OWN OR MANAGE A SMALL BUSINESS?

Entrepreneurship isn't an event, it's a career. True entrepreneurs do it over and over again whether they succeed or fail.—Charles W. Hofer, professor of management, University of Georgia

---

Guts, brains, and determination—key ingredients of the American entrepreneurial spirit—[have] sustained this nation through good times and bad, and launched it on an economic journey unlike any ever witnessed in history.—John Sloan, Jr., president and CEO, National Federation of Independent Business

LEARNING OBJECTIVES

After studying the material in this chapter, you will be able to:

1. Explain why people start small businesses.
2. Describe the characteristics of successful small business owners.
3. Explain the requirements for success in small business.
4. Assess how qualified you are to be a small business owner.

VICTOR K. KIAM II: HOW TO SUCCEED AS AN ENTREPRENEUR

In a famous TV commercial, Victor Kiam says, "I was a dedicated blade shaver until my wife bought me this Remington Microscreen shaver. . . . I was so impressed with it, I bought the company." Whether or not that was the reason for his purchase of Remington Products, Inc., Kiam did "pick up" the firm from Sperry Corporation in 1979 for a "mere" $25 million, most of which was provided by Sperry and various banks. Since then, sales have increased manyfold. Market share has more than doubled, and profits have skyrocketed. Since 1988, Kiam has been the majority owner of the New England Patriots.

Kiam's success has been based on the guiding principles he has followed since 1935, when he became an entrepreneur at the age of eight. That summer, when people stepped off the streetcar named *Desire* near where he lived in New Orleans, they looked as if they would drop if they didn't have something cold to drink. Victor's grandfather staked him to $5 to buy 100 bottles of Coca-Cola to sell to the suffering passengers. The young entrepreneur set his price at 10 cents, a 100 percent markup, expecting to make a substantial profit. Sales zoomed, and his supply of drinks was soon sold out. He and his grandfather were both shocked when Victor learned he had only $4 to show for his efforts. Since this new venture was launched during the Depression, most of the customers couldn't pay the 10 cents; being softhearted, Victor couldn't turn them away. While this business was a financial disaster, it did build much goodwill for him and taught him some valuable business lessons.

After acquiring an M.B.A. degree from Harvard in 1951, and after 18 years of selling foundation garments for Playtex and toothpaste for Lever Brothers, Kiam bought an interest in the Benrus Corporation, where he sold watches and jewelry for another 11 years. These 29 years of experience, not to mention his years as CEO at Remington, demonstrate that he fits the profile of a successful entrepreneur—a profile Kiam developed in his

Victor K. Kiam II, President, Remington Products, Inc.

Source: Remington Products, Inc.

best-selling book *Going for It! How to Succeed as an Entrepreneur.*

In the book, Kiam says a person has "the right stuff" if he or she can answer the following questions affirmatively:

- Am I willing to make sacrifices?
- Am I decisive?
- Do I have self-confidence?
- Can I recognize an opportunity when it presents itself and capitalize on it?
- Do I have confidence in my proposed venture?
- Am I willing to lead by example?

In his latest book, *Live to Win*, he explains how you can figure your "Personal Balance Sheet" and your "Intangible Balance Sheet."

Sources: Based on Victor Kiam, *Going for It! How to Succeed as an Entrepreneur* (New York: William Morrow, 1986) and *Live to Win* (New York: Harper & Row, 1989); Dave Nelson, "Patriots' Cleanup Man," *The New York Times*, November 14, 1988, p. 21; and correspondence with Remington Products.

The dynamic role of small business was examined in Chapter 1, using Sam Walton's founding of Wal-Mart as an example. This chapter presents some of the opportunities and challenges of owning and operating such a business, using Victor Kiam as an example. Although neither of these men is now a small business owner, they both were once, and you can learn much from their early successes.

The topics to be covered in this chapter are (1) why people start small businesses, (2) characteristics of successful small business owners, (3) what leads to success in managing a small business, and (4) doing an introspective personal analysis to determine whether you have the abilities to succeed in small business.

WHY PEOPLE START SMALL BUSINESSES

Owning and operating a small business provides an excellent opportunity to satisfy personal objectives while achieving the firm's business objectives. Probably in no other occupation or profession is this as true. But there are almost as many different reasons for starting small businesses as there are small business owners.

To Satisfy Personal Objectives

Small business owners have the potential to fulfill many personal goals by managing their own firms, for there are many opportunities, challenges, and new experiences. In fact, owning a small business tends to satisfy most of our work goals. (See Figure 2–1 for a survey of how important these goals are to us.) How these personal objectives are achieved depends on the knowledge, skills, and personal traits an owner brings to the business. A great deal depends on the type of person and the dedication he or she brings to the business.

The objectives of owners and managers of small businesses differ from those of managers of larger companies.[1] While the objectives of large corporations are many and varied, they can be summarized as: (1) the desire for security, (2) the desire for place, power, and prestige, and (3) the desire for high income and benefits. On the other hand, the primary objectives of small business owners and managers are: (1) to achieve independence, (2) to obtain income, (3) to help their families, and (4) to provide products not available elsewhere. In summary, small business owners tend to be achievement oriented, as opposed to managers of large firms, who tend to be power and prestige oriented.

To Achieve Independence

While all of the above objectives may lead someone to become the owner of a small business, the owner's primary motive can usually be summarized by the one word *independence* (see Figure 2–2). This word can best describe

Figure 2–1   What Are Our Work Goals?

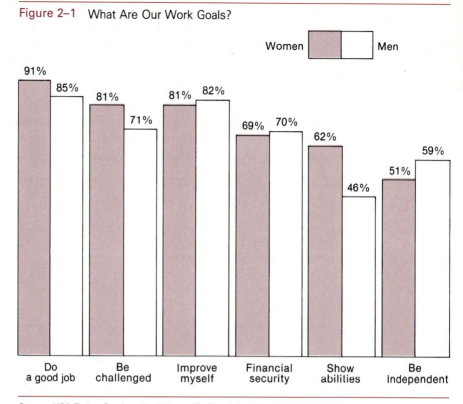

Source: *USA Today,* October 16, 1985, p. 1D. Copyright 1985, USA TODAY. Adapted with permission.
(Original source: *Working Woman* survey, October 1985.)

Figure 2–2   Which Road to Take?

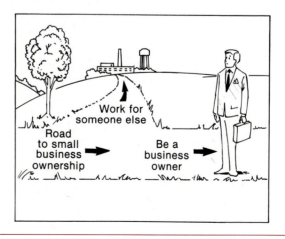

the goal of those who want to become the owners or managers of small firms; that is, freedom from interference or control by superiors. Small businesspeople tend to want autonomy to exercise their initiative and ambition. This autonomy often results in innovations and leads to great flexibility, which is one of the virtues of small businesses. The many people who eventually operate small firms know they are running a risk when they strike out on their own, but they hope to realize their goal of independence. In essence, owning your own business provides a feeling of satisfaction that is different from that resulting from managing a firm someone else has built, as the following example shows.

At age 59, after 30 years with a large New York firm, Robert Ritchie lost his job as a group financial executive. He then bought a little country inn and found that he was working longer hours and earning less money, but was enjoying himself more.[2]

To Obtain Income

Many people start a small business in order to obtain needed income or to supplement an otherwise inadequate source of funds. This need for funds varies with different people. For example, a retired person may want to earn just enough to supplement Social Security payments and possibly provide a few luxuries; that person will be content with a business that provides a small supplement to retirement income without jeopardizing that income.

Margaret Williamson began sewing when she was 10. She learned much from her mother, who was an excellent seamstress, and from home economics classes in high school. In the mid-1930s, she worked for the WPA, and later she sewed for her family, making all her daughter's school clothes.

In the 1960s, Mrs. Williamson began making and selling handicrafts to boost her Social Security income. The Alabama Cooperative Extension Service helped her with advice on marketing her crafts, including instructions on how to participate in craft shows and how to make effective displays. As a result of this training, she has had the opportunity to participate in many local craft shows and school bazaars, and has displayed items in local beauty shops and schools.

Many of the patterns Mrs. Williamson works with are of her own design, while some have been handed down to her from past generations of seamstresses in her family. Among the things she makes are clowns, afghans—both full-sized and crib-sized—sunbonnet brooms, crocheted scarves and collars, casserole carriers, sewing caddies, and dolls.

Source: Photo courtesy of Barbara Smith, Mobile College.

On the other hand, owning a business can provide the opportunity to make a great deal of money and to take advantage of certain tax benefits.[3] (Small business owners should consult their lawyers and tax accountants, though, to make sure they stay on the right side of tax laws, which have been modified to remove many of these benefits!) According to Thomas J. Stanley, a professor of marketing at Georgia State University, America's typical millionaire is a small-business entrepreneur.[4] And one is 10 times more likely to become a millionaire by owning one's own business. This affluent small business owner, on the average, is a 57-year-old man who works six days a week and "has mud on his shoes, drives a secondhand car, and has been married to the same woman for 32 years."

Yet not all small business owners and managers "make a lot of money." For example, small business chief executive officers made only $96,811 in 1988, as compared to the $1.08 million made by chief executive officers of the *Fortune* 100 firms.[5]

At times, a person may start a small business in order to survive, after being unable to find employment elsewhere or being discharged from a larger firm. Also, small businesses may be founded by athletes, whose bodies are a wasting asset and who must retire early. The athletes use their savings from their professional playing days to found a small business to provide them with later needed income, as shown in the following example.

Roger Staubach, former quarterback for the Dallas Cowboys (1969–1980), sold insurance and real estate in the off-season for Henry S. Miller Company. He and Robert Holloway, Jr., left Miller in 1977 and set up their own real estate business. In 1982, Staubach bought out his partner, and he is now the sole owner of a prosperous multimillion-dollar business.[6]

To Help Their Families

Small business owners are probably motivated as much by personal and family considerations as by the profit motive. For example, people often organize or operate a business out of a sense of obligation to the family.

For example, notice in Case III–3, The Beary Best Cookies, that Jeanne Parnell started her cookie business to "earn enough money to significantly contribute to the family income."

Students may return home to operate the family business so their parents can retire or "take life easier." They may form a firm to help their family financially. Or they may take over the business upon the death of a parent.

Burt Smukler and his wife, Janice, were going to graduate school after completing their undergraduate business program at State University (all names disguised). Janice had won a graduate scholarship, and Burt was going to be a graduate assistant. But his father died the week before graduation. At the request of his mother, they returned home to north Louisiana to operate the family automobile dealership.

To Provide Products Not Available Elsewhere

An elementary adage, "Necessity is the mother of invention," applies to the beginning of many small firms. In fact, most American economic development has resulted from innovations born in small firms. Relative to the number of people employed, they produce two-and-a-half times as many new ideas and products as large firms.[7] The first air conditioner, airplane, automobile, instant camera, jet engine, helicopter, office copier, aerosol can, heart pacemaker, foam fire extinguisher, quick-frozen foods, sliced and wrapped bread, vacuum tube, zipper, and safety razor, as well as many other breakthroughs, either emerged from the creativity found in small companies or led to the creation of a new business. The first full-scale commercial electronic computer, the Univac, was conceived and developed by a small firm—Univac Corporation—formed by Dr. John Mauchly and J. Presper Eckert.

Ann and Michael Moore were in the Peace Corps in West Africa when they noticed how peaceful the native children were. The mothers carried their children in pouches on their chest or back, held in place by straps over the shoulders and tied around the waist. The native mother could go about her work with her hands free, and the child was comforted by the closeness of its mother. The Moores started making the same kind of cloth pouch when they returned home. In 1981, they sold over $4.5 million worth of Snuglis worldwide. The home-sewn version sells for about $60, while the mass-produced ones can be had for around $30.[8]

Source: Courtesy of Snugli, Inc.

To Achieve Business Objectives

Since one distinction between small and big businesses is based on the needs, intentions, and objectives of the owner-manager, these factors deserve attention in deciding whether to own a small business. One of the most important functions the owner-manager must perform is setting **objectives,** which are the ends toward which all the activities of the organization will be aimed. Essentially, objectives determine the character of the firm, for they are the focal point of all its plans, policies, and programs; they give the business a direction and provide standards by which to measure individual performance.

Among the overall objectives important to a business are (1) service, (2) profit, (3) social, and (4) growth. These objectives tend to be interrelated, as shown in Figure 2–3. For example, the service objective must be achieved in order to attain the profit objective. Yet profits must be made if the business

Figure 2–3 How a Firm's Objectives Are Related

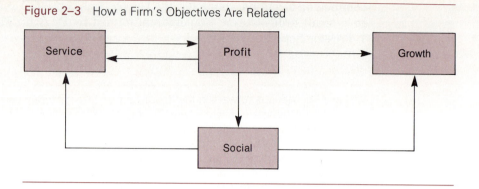

is to continue to reach the social and service objectives. Growth depends on attaining profit and social objectives, which are not necessarily inconsistent.

For example, the Music Box, a profitable portable radio from Koss Corporation of Milwaukee, monitors itself and turns on a warning light if its sound reaches levels that might damage hearing.

Service Objective

In general, the overall objective of a business is to perform a useful service for customers by producing and selling goods or services (or the satisfactions associated with them) at a cost that will ensure a fair price to the consumer and adequate profits for the owners. Thus, a person who aspires to operate a small business must set service as the primary objective—but with profit as a natural consequence. The pragmatic test for a small firm is: If the business ceases to give service, it will go out of business; if profits do not result, the owners will cease operating it.

When management makes decisions about the type of business to start or enter, the product(s) to offer, and the type(s) of customers to serve, it considers the service objective. Notice in the Opening Focus how Victor Kiam tried to help tired riders by providing them with cold drinks. The service objective—as well as the profit motive—prompted him to go into business.

Profit Objectives

We expect a private business to receive a profit from its operations because profit is acceptable in a free-enterprise economy and is considered to be in the public interest. The **profit motive,** simply stated, is entering a business to make a profit, which is the reward for taking risks—such as investing funds in an untried business and an uncertain market. Profits are needed to create new jobs, acquire new facilities, and develop new products or services. Profits are not self-generating, however; they result from satisfying the demand for a product. Goods or services must therefore be produced at a low enough cost to permit the firm to make a profit.

Profits, then, are the reward for accepting business risks and performing an economic service. They are needed to assure the continuity of a business.

For example, while Victor Kiam tried to help people by providing them with cold drinks, he also tried to make a profit. How long could he have continued in business at the rate he was losing money?

Social Objectives

As is discussed further in Chapter 22, a small business also has **social objectives.** It tries to help people in the community other than customers, such as employees, suppliers, the government, and the community itself. And it also must have a concern for protecting the environment. Even small firms have a social responsibility. Owners occupy a trusteeship position and should act to protect the social interests of all parties as well as to make a profit. The profit and social objectives are not necessarily incompatible.

Another important social contribution of the small organization is the opportunity to provide employees with a sense of belonging, identity, and esprit de corps. A small business is both an economic and a social system. It provides a sense of prestige that employees might lose in a larger company.

Growth Objective

A small firm should be concerned with growth and should select a growth objective early in its development. The objective will depend on the answers to several questions you, as a small business owner, must ask yourself:

- Will I be satisfied for my business to remain small?
- Do I want it to grow and challenge larger firms?
- Do I seek relative stability or mere survival?
- Do I seek a rate of profit that is only "satisfactory," considering my effort and investment, or do I seek to maximize profits?

Need to Mesh Objectives

Can personal and business objectives actually be integrated in small business establishments? Yes, if the emphasis is on optimizing objectives and minimizing company and personal conflicts. As will be shown in Chapter 11, communication plays an important part in the process. The close relationships between owners of small businesses and their employees, customers, and others speed up communication and make integration easier.

A survey of 97 small, owner-managed firms in the San Antonio area revealed a correlation between profitability, customer satisfaction, manager satisfaction, and psychic rewards. It also indicated greatly increased chances of success when the objectives of the business—service at a profit—are meshed with owner's personal objectives. The results of the study indicate that it is possible to integrate multiple objectives at different levels into a unified whole.[9]

People interested in a small business may be encouraged to observe how a business may have a simple beginning, yet provide a good income.

Addie Lindstrom had what she calls a ''cushy'' job as office manager for a giant forest products firm. While the working conditions, pay, and benefits were excellent, Addie wanted to do something different. So, after 22 years with the company, she borrowed $50,000, took a travel agent's training course, rented an office in the building where she worked, and opened her own travel agency. After working at the forest products firm from 6 A.M. to 10 A.M., she'd go down the hall to her agency and work till midnight.

After an auto crash that nearly killed her, Addie ran the agency from her hospital bed. She began specializing in services for disabled tourists. Two years later, having hired 10 new employees, Addie returned to her business—by then in the $2 million-plus range.[10]

CHARACTERISTICS OF SUCCESSFUL SMALL BUSINESS OWNERS

The abilities and personal characteristics of owners exert a more powerful influence on the fortunes of small companies than they do on those of larger firms. Whether a person has the characteristics needed to run a small business should be an important consideration in whether or not to own a small firm. Also, the methods and procedures adopted in such a firm should be designed not only to offset any personal deficiencies the owner may have but also to build on his or her strengths.

What characterizes owners of successful small companies? The Opening Focus on Victor Kiam presented one set of characteristics for small business entrepreneurs: willingness to make sacrifices, decisiveness, self-confidence, ability to recognize and capitalize on opportunities, and confidence in the venture.

A slightly different set of characteristics emerged from the 2,740 readers of *Venture* magazine who responded to the questions: "What type of person becomes an entrepreneur, and what psychological factors influence their future in business—and in life?"[11] The results showed that most of these entrepreneurs were firstborn children who had a positive relationship with their fathers. More than a third (36 percent) had held jobs before they were 15 years old, and 23 percent started their first business before they turned 20. Typically, these entrepreneurs were dedicated to their business, had a strong sense of enterprise, and were usually hard at work at the office by 7:30 A.M. Nearly all of the respondents (95 percent) had completed high school, 64 percent had graduated from college, and 30 percent held a postgraduate degree.

From these and many other sources, we conclude that the characteristics of those people who start and successfully manage small businesses are that they:

- Desire independence.
- Have a strong sense of enterprise.
- Are motivated by personal and family considerations.
- Expect quick and concrete results.
- Are able to react quickly.
- Are dedicated to their business.
- Enter business as much by chance as by design.

Desire Independence

As shown earlier in the chapter, those people who start small businesses seek independence and want to be free of outside control, whether this control is financial, governmental, or any other type of restraint on their initiative. They enjoy the feeling of freedom that comes from "doing their own thing" and making their own decisions—for better or for worse.

After spending 20 years working for others, Jean McMillen wanted to work for herself and do something new, different, and interesting. So, after three years of

Jean McMillen, owner of Mystery Bookshop

Source: T. R. Fletcher, "It's No Secret—Mystery Bookshop Offers 12,000 Volumes," *Bethesda* (Maryland) *Gazette,* March 16, 1989, p. A–45. (Photo by Rick Dugan.)

careful planning, much traveling, and looking at other shops, she and Ronald, her husband, opened Mystery Bookshop in Bethesda, Maryland, a boutique bookstore.

Devoted to a full range of services geared to mystery lovers, the shop caters to both young and old. It has 1,000 offerings for young readers, including "everything ever written about Nancy Drew." For older readers, there is a comfortable spot to rest and read. It has high-backed wing chairs, an antique chest, and lace antimacassars to recreate the atmosphere of an English country-house mystery.

According to Jean McMillen, they want to do more than just sell books. Instead, they provide a variety and depth of services (over 12,000 volumes, games, and murder mystery house parties) that other stores can't, and this gives McMillen the sense of achievement and independence she sought.[12]

Have a Strong Sense of Enterprise

The owners of small businesses have a strong sense of enterprise that gives them a desire to use their ideas, abilities, and aspirations to the greatest degree possible. They are able to conceive new ideas, plan them, carry them to a successful conclusion, and profit from the results of those plans. This is not always true in a larger organization, as the following example shows.

In 1985, at age 55, H. Ross Perot was the second richest man in America, worth $1.8 billion. But that wasn't always the case. In 1962, as an employee of IBM, he had twice gotten thumbs down on requests to do something "new and different." In a search for independence, he quit the company and founded Electronic Data Systems (EDS), a data processing firm, even though he also had to work for Blue Cross/Blue Shield to make ends meet. He sold the controlling interest in EDS to GM, which later removed him from GM's board because of his outspokenness. In 1988, he invested $20 million in Steven Jobs' endeavor to develop the Next® computer system.[13]

Another aspect of enterprise usually present in small business owners is their drive for achievement and their willingness to work long, hard hours to reach their goals. They are capable, ambitious, persevering individuals.

For example, after Victor Kiam took over Remington, sales increased eightfold, market share doubled, and profits skyrocketed.

This sense of enterprise has been emphasized in many different ways. For example, Irving Burstiner, author of *The Small Business Handbook*, found that among the most important "entrepreneurial personality traits" was "drive." He concluded that "something pushes these individuals."[14]

C. D. Peterson, a New York consultant who advises corporate managers who are interested in starting their own business, tells them that "the one thing they have to have is a strong, strong desire to start the business."[15] And Greenwich Group, an outplacement consulting firm, found that "starting their own business" appeals to 7 out of 10 displaced corporate executives. But when told how tough it really is, only one in three of the executives strikes out to become a small business owner.[16]

Joanne Marlowe began designing clothes for her friends when she was 14. In 1985, she opened her own fashion boutique in Evanston, Illinois. She projected her first-year sales to be $110,000 and planned to work 19 to 20 hours a day to earn that much. She said, "I work well under pressure."[17]

Are Motivated by Personal and Family Considerations

As shown earlier, small business managers are probably motivated as much by personal and family considerations as by the profit motive. They start and operate their businesses to help their parents, children, and other family members. As will be discussed in Chapter 24, there now seems to be a trend toward children helping their parents—financially and otherwise—to start small firms. This trend expands the past practice where the parent(s) helped the child, as the following classic example shows.

John H. Johnson, one of the nation's leading black entrepreneurs, heads Johnson Publishing Company, which owns *Ebony* and *Jet* magazines, radio stations, and a cosmetic firm. When asked what was the key to his success, Johnson answered, "My mother. . . . She made so many sacrifices. . . . She even let me mortgage her furniture [for $500] . . . to start my business. . . . I couldn't let her down." Now he's one of the nation's 400 richest individuals.[18]

Another exciting trend is the shift to more couples doing business together, as several of our previous examples have shown. Also, the SBA found that the number of joint proprietorship tax returns filed by wives and husbands jumped over 60 percent from 1980 to 1986, while the increase for all proprietorships was only 38 percent. As shown in Figure 2–4, the number of entrepreneurial couples in 1986 was 433,061.

Expect Quick and Concrete Results

Small business owners expect quick and concrete results from an investment of either time or capital. Instead of engaging in the long-range planning that is common in large businesses, they seek a quick turnover of a relatively small amount of capital invested in the firm. And they become impatient and discouraged when these results are slow in coming.

Figure 2–4 More Spouses Doing Business Together

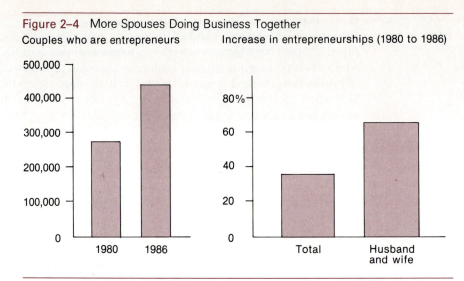

Couples who are entrepreneurs   Increase in entrepreneurships (1980 to 1986)

Source: Robert Lewis, "More Spouses Doing Business Together," *Mobile* (Alabama) *Register,* August 6, 1989, p. 2-D. Adapted with permission of Newhouse Graphics. (Original source: Small Business Administration.)

Are Able to React Quickly

Small businesses have an advantage over larger firms. Because they have fewer people making decisions, they can react faster to change. It is important for each owner to be sensitive to changes taking place both inside and outside the company and be ready to react quickly. For example, one characteristic of a small business enterprise is its vulnerability to technological and environmental changes. Because of its size, such changes have a great effect on its operations and profitability. A small business owner must therefore have the ability to react quickly.

Are Dedicated to Their Business

Small business owners tend to be fiercely dedicated to their firm. With so much of their time, energy, money, and emotions invested in the company, they want to ensure that nothing harms their "baby." Consequently, they have a zeal, devotion, and ardor often missing in owners and managers of big companies.

Most of the small businesspeople cited as examples in this text have this characteristic. Notice that Joanne Marlow was willing to work "19 to 20 hours a day" to attain her first-year sales goal of $110,000.

Enter Business as Much by Chance as by Design

It may not necessarily lead to success, but one interesting characteristic of many small business owners is that they get into business as much by chance as by design. These are the owner-managers who quite frequently ask for assistance in the form of management training and development. This type of individual differs sharply from those who attend college with the ambition to become professional managers and who gear their programs toward that end.

In 1981, Thurman Scheumack, while recovering from a broken neck, turned to the centuries-old craft of broom making as part of his therapy. He made such a good recovery and did such an admirable job of making the brooms that he was soon selling them to neighbors and others in Mountain View, Arkansas.

From their bustling workshop in the Ozark foothills, he, his wife, and their five employees now produce about 20,000 brooms each year. While most of their output is the standard kitchen models, the part Scheumack enjoys best is making brooms decorated with hand-carved faces on their handles. These are sold in galleries and gift shops throughout the country and at tourist attractions such as Colonial Williamsburg, Disneyland, and Disney World at prices ranging from $18 to $50.[19]

Another example of entering a business as much by chance as by design is Ralph Simmons in Case II–3, Simmons Mountainside Satellite Sales. Being in a small town with no prospects of getting cable, he bought a satellite dish so his elderly father could watch TV. After it was installed, Simmons received numerous requests from neighbors for help in buying and installing dishes. Before he knew it, he was in business.

WHAT LEADS TO SUCCESS IN MANAGING A SMALL BUSINESS?

Although it is difficult to determine precisely what leads to success in managing small businesses, the following are some important factors.

- Serving an adequate and well-defined market for the product(s).
- Obtaining and using accurate and useful operating and marketing information.
- Using human resources effectively.
- Acquiring sufficient capital.
- Coping with government regulations effectively.
- Both the owners and their teams having expertise in the field.
- Managing time effectively.

Serving an Adequate and Well-Defined Market

As is shown in Part V of this book, a demand for the business's product(s) must exist. One of the greatest assets small businesspeople can have is the ability to detect a market for a good or service before others do and then devise a way of satisfying the market. A company providing venture capital to small business entrepreneurs found that 90 percent of the 2 million U.S. millionaires owned their own firms. And the primary reason for this was that larger firms rejected the new—and often superior—ideas of employees, who then went out and started their own companies.[20]

For example, Ross Perot's sensitivity to the market enabled him to see the need for computer services and software before others at IBM and elsewhere did.

Obtaining and Using Accurate and Useful Information

Small business owners must stay regularly and frequently informed of the financial and market positions of the business. They must analyze and evaluate information and develop plans to maintain or improve their firm's position (see Computer Update). The "information explosion" of the 1980s has not been accompanied by an increased ability to interpret and use all the data available. Instead, information's increased complexity has overwhelmed the capacity of many small business owners. There are limits to what information owners can absorb and use in their operations.

Using Human Resources Effectively

Effective use of human resources is extremely important to small businesses because owner-managers have a closer and more personal association with their employees than managers in a larger business. These workers can be a good source of information and ideas. Their productivity can be greatly increased by allowing them to share ideas with the owner, especially if their contributions are recognized and rewarded. These issues will be expanded in Part III.

Acquiring Sufficient Capital

As shown in Chapter 1, a major problem for small business owners is obtaining sufficient investment capital—at a reasonable price—to acquire the resources needed to start and operate a business. Without adequate facilities, such as a building, furniture, fixtures, and tools and equipment, you can't operate effectively even if you hire capable people.

Owners who become successful have been able to obtain needed funds, either from their own resources or from others. They are willing to delay satisfying the desire for profit or dividends now, in the long-run interest of the business.

Case III–1, CleanDrum, Inc. (C), is an example of a new small business without enough money to hire a plant supervisor, which would allow the owner to go on the road to sell the service.

THE MAINE LINE COMPANY: OBTAINING AND USING ACCURATE INFORMATION

The Maine Line Company, based in Rockport, Maine, publishes greeting cards, note cards, and memo pads. Established in 1980 by Joyce Boaz and Perri Ardman and employing 18 people, the company operated for five years without computers. To obtain and use information more efficiently, thereby increasing employee creativity, the company decided to look into a computer system suitable for its needs and budget.

After a seven-month search, the Maine Line Company had an Altos system installed in May 1985. The system is used primarily for inventory control, billing, accounts receivable, and general ledger. The Altos allows the company to know exactly how much stock is on hand and precisely when

to restock. Because word processing slowed the primary functions of the system, Maine Line purchased two Sperry PCs to be used independently of the Altos system.

Aside from word processing, the personal computers distribute spreadsheet functions, and employees can analyze information on sales and account activity. With the Altos system and the two PCs, Maine Line can trace sales activity in each store selling its products, for a quick review of marketing efforts.

Maine Line was acquired by a large New Jersey corporation a few years ago. The store in Rockport, Maine, has scaled back operations but is still in business.

Joyce Boaz and Perri Ardman, Co-owners of Maine Line
Source: Photo courtesy of *Bangor Daily News.*

Source: "The Maine Line Company," *Venture,* November 1986, p. 80.

Figure 2–5   How to Deal with Cash Flow Problems

- Make finances your No. 1 priority. Monitor cash flow daily if possible.
- Consider replacing the person who handles your company's finances. Look for "a tough son-of-a-gun" who knows how to keep tighter control over costs.
- Speed up cash flow into the company. One way: Offer discounts to customers who pay their bills within 10 to 15 days versus 30 to 60 days.
- Turn as much inventory as possible into cash, even if it means selling inventory to your competitors.
- Put as many unpaid bills as possible on hold. But be sure to negotiate with your suppliers and your bank to stretch out payments. Don't leave lenders hanging.
- Cut employment. About 80 percent of potential cost savings will come from reducing your work force. As you cut back, though, try to keep your most productive workers.
- Cut your rental costs. Move to cheaper office space or cut back on the amount of space you use.
- Get rid of unproductive assets that cost money, such as outdated machinery that requires costly maintenance.

Source: Neil Churchill, as reported in David E. Gumpert, "Watch the Purse Strings," *USA Today,* May 8, 1989, p. 10E. Copyright 1989, USA TODAY. Excerpted with permission.

Not only is lack of investment capital a problem for small firms, so is the shortage of working capital. In fact, probably *the biggest crisis for small business is lack of cash.* And, according to Neil Churchill, professor of entrepreneurship at Babson College, dealing quickly with cash flow problems can mean the difference between success and failure. Churchill has provided several tips for successfully dealing with these problems, as shown in Figure 2–5.

Coping with Government Regulations

As discussed in Chapters 1 and 22, the day when small businesses were exempt from governmental regulation has passed. Equal employment opportunity, occupational safety and health, and environmental protection laws no longer exempt most small businesses; frequently, they add tremendously to the time and cost of operation. Government regulations and compliance directives are of major concern to small business owners, whose responses are varied and often rebellious. Not only must small business owners be able to handle red tape effectively, but it is especially important that they become involved in local governmental activities.

What can small business owners do about government regulation? Possible responses include:

- Learn as much as possible about the regulations, especially if they can be helpful to you. You will find throughout this text that there are many laws, regulations, and agencies—including the SBA—available to help smaller firms.
- Challenge detrimental or harmful laws, either alone—perhaps appearing before a legislative small business committee—or by joining organizations such as the National Federation of Independent Business.

- Become involved in the legal-political system, either to elect representatives who will help to change the laws or to run for office yourself.[21]
- Find a better legal environment, if possible, even if it means moving to a different city, county, or state.
- Learn to live with the laws and regulations.

Having Expertise in the Field

If you are to succeed in a business of your own, ambition, desire, drive, capital, judgment, and a competitive spirit are not enough. In addition, you'll still need technical and managerial know-how and expertise to perform the activities necessary to run the business. Some types of business, such as general retail establishments, may need only general skills. But the more technical and complex the business is, the greater the need for specialized skills, which can be acquired only through education, training, and experience, as the following example shows.

In 1989, Honeybee Robotics won a $1.5 million contract to operate a joint venture with Ford Aerospace to produce the "hands" for a robot that Martin Marietta would build for NASA. The robot, with two highly dexterous arms and twin video cameras, is to be used by astronauts to assemble the "Space Station Freedom," a permanently manned base to be put in low-earth orbit in the early 1990s.

While Honeybee was too small to get one of the major contracts with NASA on its own, it did have the highly specialized expertise to design and build sophisticated computer-driven robot systems, particularly robotic end effectors or "hands." Honeybee had made such camera-guided robot arms to pick up vials from conveyor belts and place them symmetrically in rows, accurate to within 1/1,000 of an inch. This technical expertise and experience was the reason Honeybee got the contract.[22]

Managing Time Effectively

The effective use of time is especially important to small business owners because of the many and varied duties that only they can perform. While managers of large corporations can delegate activities to others, freeing time for other uses, small business owners are limited in their ability to do so. The very characteristics that lead people to start small businesses tend to cause them to exercise a "hands-on" approach to managing their business. They therefore like to do things themselves rather than delegate authority to others. The final problem is the long hours worked per week by new business owners. As you can see from Figure 2–6, over half (53 percent) of such owners spend 60 hours or more working at their business. And over three-fourths of them spend 50 or more hours on the job.

Where do these long hours go? In a survey of people who've owned their businesses between three and four-and-a-half years, the most time is devoted to selling and production, as shown in Figure 2–7.

Figure 2–6   Hours per Week Worked by New Business Owners

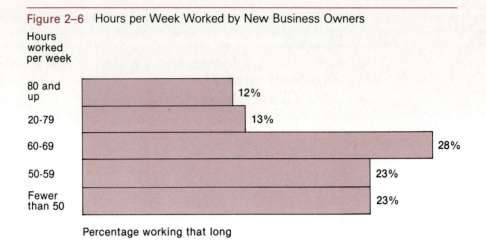

Hours
worked
per week

80 and up	12%
20-79	13%
60-69	28%
50-59	23%
Fewer than 50	23%

Percentage working that long

Source: National Federation of Independent Business, as reported in Mark Robichaux, "Business First, Family Second," *The Wall Street Journal,* May 12, 1989, p. B1. Adapted with permission of *The Wall Street Journal,* © Dow Jones & Company, Inc., 1989. ALL RIGHTS RESERVED.

Figure 2–7   Where the Time Goes

Surveyed entrepreneurs owning businesses between 3 years and 4.5 years old said they divide their work week as follows:

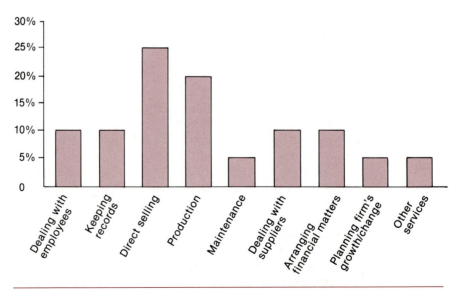

Source: National Federation of Independent Business, as reported in Carrie Dolan, "Entrepreneurs Often Fail as Managers," *The Wall Street Journal,* May 15, 1989, p. B1. Adapted with permission of *The Wall Street Journal,* © Dow Jones & Company, Inc., 1989. ALL RIGHTS RESERVED.

While there is no formula for effective time management, it is based on delegating activities that others can do, using a daily log to plan your activities, and limiting the time you spend on phone calls and meetings to what is necessary for the success of the business.[23] Some specific methods for saving your time include:

- Organizing the work, including delegating to subordinates as many duties as feasible.
- Selecting a competent assistant to sort out unimportant mail, screen incoming calls, and keep a schedule of appointments and activities.
- Using electronic equipment for letters and memos.
- Adhering to appointment and business conference times.
- Preparing an agenda for meetings, confining discussion to the items on the agenda, and making follow-up assignments to specific subordinates.

Plan your workday based on this analysis. You will probably find that it increases your effectiveness.

DOING AN INTROSPECTIVE PERSONAL ANALYSIS

Now that you have seen some of the characteristics of successful small business managers, as well as the requirements needed for success in a small firm, do you think you have enough of those characteristics to be successful? The following personal evaluation will help you decide this important question. No one of these items is more important than any other; rather, you need to determine whether the unique combination of qualities you have will help you succeed as a small business owner.

Analyzing Your Values

In order to manage a firm effectively, you need a value system and basic principles to use as guidelines for managerial decision making. The more important questions related to this value system include: What are your true motives? What real objectives do you seek? What relative weights do you give to service, profit, and social responsibilities? What type of interpersonal relations do you want to establish with employees?

Everyone has a philosophy, whether it is conscious or unconscious. Your philosophy will more than likely become your management philosophy, which in turn will determine your objectives. When these objectives are communicated, people will know what you stand for, in what direction you plan to go, what overall action you are most likely to take, and why you act as you do. In the business world, the greatest esteem seems to be granted to those people viewed as builders—that is, the ones who create a good or service and then go on to build companies based on their creations.

In summary, an analysis of your values helps you understand what you believe in and are willing to strive for. An infinite variety of philosophies is possible. However, we will limit discussion to two contrasts in philosophy: (1) individualism versus group-centered management and (2) activities-oriented versus results-oriented management.

Individualism versus Group-Centered Management

Characteristics associated with these philosophies vary, but the **individualist** generally tends to be highly self-reliant and a decision maker. Most of the strong-willed, powerful entrepreneurs of the 1890s and early 1900s (such as Henry Ford) were guided by this individualistic philosophy. On the other hand, many present-day corporate managers believe that their employees should be considered in all managerial decisions and actions. These **group-centered individuals** rely on planning and decision-making groups, use committees extensively, and consider the many mutual interests of management and employees.

Activities- versus Results-Oriented Managers

The **activities-oriented manager** stresses what must be done, tends to be a "one-person show," prescribes the organization structure, determines the tasks of subordinates, delegates decision-making authority, determines the best methods to perform the work, and exercises tight control over employee performance.

For an example of this type of small business owner, see Case I–5, Shaffer's Drive Inns. Mr. Shaffer had a "great man" image and was authoritarian, but his employees accepted his judgment as law because, in their opinion, "he was right 99 percent of the time."

The **results-oriented manager** prefers to use the full resources of employees, emphasizes goal setting, assists in achieving goals, wants both management and employees to develop self-commitment and self-direction for results, lets employees play a large part in determining the methods of work, and exercises control by result.

Steve and Barbara Chappell in Case III–2, Our Hero Restaurant (C), use this type of management. They both work alongside the workers and show their appreciation for the ability, honesty, and enthusiasm of those people.

Your philosophy depends on personal values—that is, what you consider right or wrong, desirable or undesirable. Your business objectives and resulting policies and procedures will be based on your value system and management philosophy, whether they are closer to individualism or group management, activities- or results-oriented management.

Analyzing Your Mental Abilities

If you still think you want to enter small business, make an analysis of your personal mental attributes in order to determine the type of business that will satisfy your personal objectives. Ask yourself questions such as these: Can I conceptualize my choice of a business; that is, can I visualize it in its entirety—physically and functionally? Can I see things logically, objectively, and in perspective? Can I generate ideas about new methods and new products? Am I technically oriented? Can I interpret and translate activities into a technical framework? Can I accurately interpret the feelings, wants, and needs of others?

Remember, *you don't have to have all these abilities to be a successful small business owner*. But an analysis of your abilities helps you understand what you can do if you try. It helps determine how you can move toward succeeding in business.

Analyzing Your Attitudes

Another way to determine whether you should become a small business owner is to analyze your attitudes. Consider such factors as your:

- Level of aspiration.
- Willingness to accept responsibility.
- Mental and emotional stability.
- Commitment to the idea of the small business.
- Willingness to take risks.
- Ability to tolerate irregular hours.
- Self-discipline.
- Self-confidence.

Try asking yourself questions about your attitudes in those areas. While you need not—and will not—have all the necessary attitudes, you should be able to develop them as much as possible.

What Is Your Level of Aspiration?

Aspiration is the motivational force that drives you. It is what you want to achieve in life. You may want to express this level in terms of education, marital or parental status, status in the community, physical or mental labor, service to others, or other achievements.

Are You Willing to Accept Responsibility?

The degree to which you are willing to accept responsibility determines the relationship you will have with the public and the customer. Are you willing to admit the mistakes you have made? Will you accept responsibility even though it may mean personal sacrifice? Are you willing to be responsible for the actions of others, even when you have delegated to them the authority to act?

Are You a Stable Person?

Are you impatient and unwilling to wait for success? Many people tend to reject opportunities that offer potential rewards in the distant future in order to accept opportunities that may promise current rewards but lack stability and security. The successful entrepreneur doesn't work that way. Would you?

Will You Be Committed?

The prospective small business owner needs to have the patience and the commitment to see an idea through to completion. Commitment is the trait that determines whether an individual will endure the trials, tribulations, and personal and family sacrifices necessary to move toward the achievment of objectives. How committed are you to the business you have dreamed of?

Are You Willing to Take Risks?

Are you willing to take the chance of "losing your shirt" to gain other benefits? Or do you "play it close to your vest" and seek the sure thing in life? The small business owner must be willing to take risks and must have the determination and perseverance to capitalize on those risks. It does make a difference! How do you rate?

Can You Live with an Irregular Schedule?

Small businesspeople don't operate on fixed schedules or timetables. How would you answer the following questions: Are you willing to forgo regular hours and be worried during your time off? Are you willing to give up your weekends if something goes wrong or it becomes necessary to prepare a proposal for that new contract? Or would you prefer regular hours, holidays, and vacations?

Are You Self-Disciplined?

The old cliché "Don't take too much out the front door" applied to early business owners. It still applies. It is important to leave sufficient resources in the business to supply working capital and provide for growth and contingencies. Are you willing to do this?

Are You Self-Confident?

Small business owners tend to have the independence and autonomy they seek, but with those benefits comes the responsibility of operating alone, without others to help. Therefore, you need to answer the following questions: Do you have confidence in yourself, and can you make decisions without help from others? Will you be secure enough in your own judgment to be willing to ask others for advice when needed?

If your answers to all the questions in this section were yes or if you feel that you can make them yes at some time in the near future, you may have the qualities that would make a small business venture a satisfying

Figure 2–8   Test Your Potential as an Entrepreneur

Do you have what it takes to be a success in your own business? Below is a list of 20 personality traits. Consider each carefully—and then score yourself on a scale of 0 to 4.* Tally your score and find out what kind of entrepreneur you would make.

Traits	Score
Ability to communicate	_____
Ability to motivate others	_____
Ability to organize	_____
Acceptance of responsibility	_____
Adaptability	_____
Decision-making capability	_____
Drive/energy	_____
Good health	_____
Good human relations	_____
Initiative	_____
Interest in people	_____
Judgment	_____
Open-mindedness	_____
Planning ability	_____
Persistence	_____
Resourcefulness	_____
Self-confidence	_____
Self-starting	_____
Willingness to listen	_____
Willingness to take chances	_____

* *Score Yourself:*

Choices	Points
Far below average	0
Just below average	1
Average	2
Just above average	3
Far above average	4

Key:
30 or lower: You're probably better off working for someone else.
31 to 50: Borderline, but you may make it in your own business.
51 to 65: You have qualities associated with an entrepreneur.
66 or higher: Shoo-in as a business owner, **if** you've answered honestly!

Source: USA Today, May 8, 1989, p. 3E. Copyright 1989, USA TODAY. Adapted with permission. (Original source: Adapted from Irving Burstiner, *Creativity/Leadership Self-Rating Chart.* © Irving Burstiner, 1974.)

and rewarding activity. The self-test in Figure 2–8 should help you decide whether you have these qualities.

While this test is designed for potential entrepreneurs, we feel the results also apply to all small business owners.

WHAT YOU SHOULD HAVE LEARNED

1. People start businesses for many personal and business reasons. The most important personal reason is to achieve independence. Their need to be able to exercise their own initiative and creativity leads entrepreneurs to take the risk involved in striking out on their own.

A second personal objective is to obtain income. But while income is an important consideration, many small business owners are satisfied to receive less than they could make by working for someone else, just to have their independence or to satisfy other needs.

Third, many small business owners are motivated by family considerations, such as taking over a family business to permit parents to retire or starting a family business to have more time with their families. It doesn't always work out this way!

Finally, some small businesspersons start businesses chiefly to provide a product or service not readily available elsewhere. As shown in the text, many of our most innovative products were either developed by small businesses or resulted in the formation of such businesses to produce and market them.

Entrepreneurs start businesses in order to achieve business objectives as well. These business objectives include providing services to their customers, making a profit, providing social benefits to society, and growing into large, profitable organizations.

These personal and business objectives must be effectively meshed for successful operations.

2. Although small business owners are as different as their businesses, some characteristics seem to be typical of the more successful business owners. Some of these characteristics are that they (*a*) desire independence, (*b*) have a strong sense of enterprise, (*c*) tend to be motivated by personal and family considerations, (*d*) expect quick and concrete results, (*e*) are able to react quickly to changing situations, (*f*) are dedicated to their business, and (*g*) enter business as much by chance as by design.

3. There are many factors that lead to success in small business, including the intangible factors of luck and timing. But the most prevalent factors leading to successfully managing a small business are (*a*) serving an adequate and well-defined market, (*b*) obtaining and using accurate and useful information, (*c*) using human resources effectively, (*d*) acquiring sufficient investment and working capital—at a reasonable cost, (*e*) coping with government regulations effectively, (*f*) having expertise in one's chosen field of business, and (*g*) managing one's time effectively.

    In essence, it is sticking to the basics that leads to success rather than using gimmicks or catering to fads.

4. If you are interested in becoming a small business owner, you should examine your values, mental abilities, and attitudes carefully in order to determine whether or not you have the characteristics required for success in small business. Your ability to think logically, generate new ideas, translate these ideas into technical specifications, make plans

for the business, and understand the feelings and needs of customers and employees are also important. And your success in any business depends on your level of aspiration, your willingness to accept responsibility, your ability to handle initial setbacks and disappointments, your commitment to the business, your willingness to take risks, your ability to live with an irregular schedule, your self-discipline, and your self-confidence.

KEY TERMS

objectives, *33*	group-centered individuals, *48*
profit motive, *34*	activities-oriented manager, *48*
social objectives, *35*	results-oriented manager, *48*
individualist, *48*	

QUESTIONS FOR DISCUSSION

1. Discuss the four personal objectives that people seek when starting a new business.
2. Explain the four business objectives they try to achieve.
3. Explain the interrelationship between the *service* and *profit* objectives.
4. *(a)* Are the social objectives really that important to small business owners? *(b)* Explain your answer.
5. *(a)* What are some of the characteristics found in successful small business owners? *(b)* Evaluate each of these as to their importance.
6. What factors lead to success in owning a small business?
7. Distinguish between *(a)* individualistic and group-centered management and *(b)* activities- and results-oriented management.
8. *(a)* How did you make out with the self-test in Figure 2–8? *(b)* Do you think the results accurately reflect your potential? *(c)* Explain.

SUGGESTED READINGS

Bacon, Donald C. "Entrepreneurial Bug Biting More Older Americans." *Nation's Business,* May 1989, p. 6.

Dolan, Carrie. "Entrepreneurs Often Fail as Managers." *The Wall Street Journal,* May 15, 1989, p. B1.

Donovan, Sharon. "Beginner's Luck Is Often Bad; Here's How to Improve It." *USA Today,* May 8, 1989, p. 3E.

"Hot Growth Companies." *Business Week,* May 22, 1989, pp. 90ff.

Johnson, Harriet C. "The Hard Part of Business—Staying Alive." *USA Today,* May 23, 1986, p. 4B.

Ricklefs, Roger. "Making the Transition to Small Business." *The Wall Street Journal,* February 28, 1989, p. B1.

Robichaux, Mark. "Business First, Family Second." *The Wall Street Journal,* May 12, 1989, p. B1.

Robinett, Stephen. "What Schools Can Teach Entrepreneurs." *Venture,* February 1985, pp. 50ff.

Tannenbaum, Jeffrey A. "Entrepreneurs and Second Acts." *The Wall Street Journal,* May 17, 1989, p. B1.

Wysocki, Bernard, Jr. "Digging for Dollars." *The Wall Street Journal,* February 24, 1989, p. R1.

ENDNOTES

1. "Labor Letter: They're Different!" *The Wall Street Journal,* May 2, 1989, p. 1.

2. Roger Ricklefs, "Making the Transition to Small Business," *The Wall Street Journal,* February 28, 1989, p. B1.

3. For more details, see Richard Greene, "Do You Really Want to Be Your Own Boss?" *Forbes,* October 21, 1985, p. 96.

4. Tait Trussell, "The Untypical Typical Millionaire," *Nation's Business,* November 1988, pp. 62ff.

5. *USA Today,* October 24, 1988, p. 1A.

6. Nelson A. Aldrich, Jr., "Private Lives: Staubach Co.," *Inc.,* December 1985, pp. 66–68.

7. *The State of Small Business: A Report to the President* (Washington, D.C.: U.S. Government Printing Office, March 1983), p. 54.

8. Eric Morganthaler, "Snuggling Business Booms as Babes in Pouches Proliferate," *The Wall Street Journal,* April 23, 1982, pp. 1, 29.

9. Hal B. Pickle and Brian S. Rungeling, "Empirical Investigation of Entrepreneurial Goals and Customer Satisfaction," *Journal of Business,* April 1973, pp. 268–73.

10. Joanne Davidson, "Broken in Body, Not Spirit," *U.S. News & World Report,* July 4, 1983, pp. 38–39.

11. Nancy Madlin, "The Venture Survey: Probing the Entrepreneurial Psyche," *Venture,* May 1985, p. 24.

12. T. R. Fletcher, "It's No Secret—Mystery Bookshop Offers 12,000 Volumes," *Bethesda* (Maryland) *Gazette,* March 16, 1989, p. A–45.

13. Katherine M. Hafner and Geoff Lewis, "Ross Perot Turns into an Angel for Steve Jobs," *Business Week,* February 9, 1987, p. 32; and Brian Reilly, "Steve Jobs Tries to Do It Again," *Fortune,* May 23, 1988, pp. 833ff.

14. Shelley Liles, "All It Takes Is That Overwhelming Drive," *USA Today,* May 9, 1989, p. 1E.

15. Roger Ricklefs, "Making the Transition to Small Business," *The Wall Street Journal,* February 28, 1989, p. B1.

16. *The Wall Street Journal,* May 30, 1989, p. 1.

17. Dennis Black, "Teens Make Big Bucks in Business," *USA Today,* February 20, 1986, p. 2C

18. Barbara Reynolds, "Pride and Inspiration Make *Ebony* No. 1," *USA Today,* April 16, 1986, p. 9A; and John H. Johnson with Lerone Bennett, Jr., *Succeeding against the Odds* (New York: Warner Books, 1989).

19. "Handmade Brooms Sweep up Sales," *USA Today,* February 10, 1989, p. 12B. Copyright 1989, USA TODAY. Adapted with permission.

20. Janice Castro, "Big vs. Small," *Time,* September 5, 1988, pp. 48–50.

21. See Ronald Brownstein, "So You Want to Go into Politics," *Inc.*, November 1985, pp. 98–100, 104, and 107, for an account of how some entrepreneurs are abandoning the freedom and privacy of business for the "perils of public office."

22. Mark Robichaux, "Fledgling Honeybee Learns to Fly with the Big Guys," *The Wall Street Journal,* May 12, 1989, p. D2.

23. Bill Symonds, "No, They Can't Stop Time, but They Can Help You Manage It," *Business Week,* May 22, 1989, pp. 178–79.

3

OPPORTUNITIES AND CHALLENGES IN SMALL BUSINESS

A wise man will make more opportunities than he finds.—Francis Bacon

The role of small and midsized firms . . . has never been more important to America's future.— Tom Peters, co-author of *In Search of Excellence*

LEARNING OBJECTIVES

After studying the material in this chapter, you will be able to:

1. Discuss some of the currently promising opportunities for small business.
2. Present some practical ideas for small business opportunities.
3. Explain some of the growing opportunities in small business for women and minorities.
4. Discuss some areas of concern for small business owners, especially the problem of poorly planned growth, and the prospect for failure.

SHERRI HILL: THE WORLD'S MOST BEAUTIFUL WOMEN WEAR HER DRESSES

Sherri Hill believes in taking advantage of opportunities when they knock! And opportunity knocked for her in 1985, when a contestant in the Miss Oklahoma pageant bought a dress from Sherri's small, family-run retail store in Norman, Oklahoma.

Wanting to "watch our dress," she and her partners—her sister and brother-in-law, and Vonda Vass, a marketing assistant—attended the pageant. During the show, they were distressed to see another contestant wearing the same design they had sold earlier. While their client was understanding about the duplication, it did upset Sherri and her partners.

Seeing the problem caused by more than one contestant wearing the same design, Mrs. Hill and her partners started doing their own designs.

Her name, "Temptations by Sherri Hill," is on all her dresses, which are sold on a registration basis. When one of her client stores sells a gown to a pageant contestant, it is registered to that person on a computer system so that no other contestant can buy the same design.

Soon after her designs were seen by the Miss Oklahoma and Miss USA pageant directors, she became the exclusive designer of gowns for the Miss Universe, Miss USA, and Miss Teen USA winners. At the 1988 Miss America contest, 48 women wore her gowns—and they were all different designs! At the 1989 Miss USA pageant, seven finalists were gowned by Mrs. Hill, as was Courtney Gibbs, the 1988 Miss USA, who was also present.

Most of the designs are made using several

Vonda Vass (left) and Sherri Hill show gowns worn by 1988 Miss USA contestants and a cocktail dress (held by Mrs. Hill) worn by 1989 contestants.

Source: Mobile (Alabama) Press Register. Photograph by Jay Ferchaud, © 1989. All rights reserved.

different kinds of beads, sequins, rhinestones, and pearls. The average gown costs from $1,500 to $1,600, while an all-rhinestone design, weighing 12 pounds, can cost as much as $5,600.

When a client comes into the store, she is first asked to sit down and talk, as Mrs. Hill and her partners try to emphasize the woman herself by focusing attention on her good points and best features. "If we accent those, we've got it made," she says.

Mrs. Hill doesn't restrict her clientele to pageant contestants. She also designs and sells gowns for brides and their mothers, proms and cocktail parties, debutante balls, and other special events.

Each of the partners contributes in his or her own way to the operation. Her sister, Kathy, contributes ideas for the dresses, while Vonda Vass does the marketing and works with the retailers.

What seemed like an embarrassing incident at the time proved to be the knock that opened a door to a successful new enterprise.

Source: Kathy Jumper, "Oklahoma Woman Designer of Gowns for Beauty Pageants," *Mobile* (Alabama) *Register,* February 28, 1989, pp. 1-B and 3-B.

In Chapter 1, we described the dynamic role of small business, and in Chapter 2, we explained why you might want to own and manage such a business. In this chapter, as the Opening Focus indicates, we discuss some of the opportunities available in small business, present some practical ideas for new businesses, explain some of the growing opportunities for women and minorities, and discuss some areas of concern for small business owners, especially the problem of poorly planned growth and the possibility of failure.

WHERE ARE THE OPPORTUNITIES?

There are many ways of exploring where opportunities exist for you to become a small business owner. First, you can study industry groupings or categories to see what types of small businesses are growing. Second, you can study the failure rates of industries dominated by small firms to see which ones are low risks. Third, you can see some innovative ideas that entrepreneurs are turning into successful businesses. From all these data, you can estimate where opportunities exist for a new business.

What Are the Fastest-Growing Industries?

What are the fastest-growing U.S. industries at the present time? According to the Bureau of Labor Statistics, nothing is growing faster than services—and this trend is expected to continue at least during this decade. This trend is evident in both the number of new jobs being created and the number of new firms being established. And most of these industries are dominated by small, private companies.

Figure 3–1 Where the New Jobs Will Be: These Industries Are Expected to Produce the Most New Jobs by the Year 2000.

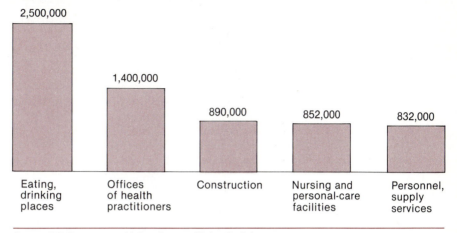

Source: U.S. Department of Labor, Bureau of Labor Statistics.

As you can see from Figure 3–1, the industries expected to produce the *most new jobs* by the year 2000 are:

- Eating and drinking places.
- Offices of health practitioners.
- Construction.
- Nursing and personal-care facilities.
- Personnel and supply services. (According to the Office of Advocacy of the U.S. Small Business Administration, except for construction and personnel/supply services, these are "small-business-dominated" industries.)

A similar picture emerges when we look at the number of *new firms expected to be established* during the 1990s. For example, as shown in Figure 3–2, services tend to dominate this group, also. Notice that 7 out of the 11 industries shown are in the service-performing areas.

American Business Information used a unique approach to determine the business categories that grew the most rapidly in 1988. It surveyed the Yellow Pages listings and found the following increases:

1. Facsimile communication equipment, 119.0 percent.
2. Money order services, 47.5 percent.
3. Exercise and physical fitness, 42.6 percent.
4. Bed and breakfast accommodations, 40.1 percent.
5. Collectibles, 37.3 percent.[1]

Figure 3–2   1990s Rage: Service

The hottest small businesses in the 1990s will be service firms such as accountants, lawyers, architects, and computer consultants. In this case, a small business is defined as having fewer than 100 employees.

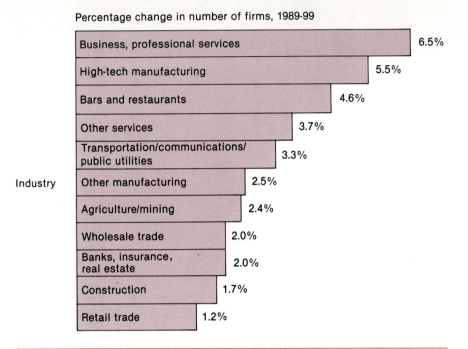

Percentage change in number of firms, 1989-99

Industry	Percentage
Business, professional services	6.5%
High-tech manufacturing	5.5%
Bars and restaurants	4.6%
Other services	3.7%
Transportation/communications/public utilities	3.3%
Other manufacturing	2.5%
Agriculture/mining	2.4%
Wholesale trade	2.0%
Banks, insurance, real estate	2.0%
Construction	1.7%
Retail trade	1.2%

Source: Cognetics, Inc., as reported in *USA Today,* May 8, 1989, p. 1E. Copyright 1989, USA TODAY. Adapted with permission.

Which Industries Have the Highest Success Rate?

We may have led you to believe up to this point that small businesses are being formed primarily by daring young entrepreneurs who use their college degrees to turn brilliant ideas into glamorous high-tech firms (see Computer Update). But these firms are only the most visible ones. Instead, most small firms are just that: small, limited in scope, and involving long hours of hard work to perform everyday activities needed by the general public.

Table 3–1 illustrates this point. As you can see, the SBA has found from its data that the 10 small-business-dominated industries with the lowest failure rates have tended to be businesses of this kind. Notice that these stable industries offer the public a service that is needed regularly by a large segment of the population.

Factors Affecting the Future of an Industry and a Business

Many changes are occurring in the environment that will affect the future of an industry and a business, and small business owners and managers

Table 3–1 Failure Rates for Selected Industries, 1983

In Washington, D.C., the Small Business Administration's idea of "small business" is any enterprise employing fewer than 500. That's a long way from family-run funeral homes and such, but there you are. The SBA does keep track of all sorts of businesses, though, and its data on success and failure are revealing. Here, according to the SBA, are the 10 fields dominated by small businesses where the failure rate was the lowest.

Industry	Failures per 100,000
Funeral services and crematoriums	10.9
Wholesale tobacco and tobacco products	22.6
Fuel and ice dealers	36.2
Laundry, cleaning, and garment repair	38.0
Drugstores	39.7
Hotels	40.4
Wood products	44.7
Personal services (secretarial, consulting, etc.)	45.2
Beer and wine wholesalers	45.7
Service stations	46.2

Source: Richard Greene, "Do You Really Want to Be Your Own Boss?" *Forbes,* October 21, 1985, p. 91. © Forbes Inc., 1985.

need to study them constantly in order to adjust to them. These factors can cause slow-growing industries to speed up or fast-growing ones to slow down. And an environmental change that provides an opportunity for one industry or business may pose a threat to others. For example, aging of the population may increase the need for retirement factilities but may reduce the need for industries supplying baby needs.

COMPUTER UPDATE

THE ROBOT CENTER: WOULD YOU LIKE TO BUY A ROBOT?

Timothy O. Knight, 19, was a student at the University of Santa Clara and author of 16 computer books when he and two partners decided that high-tech Silicon Valley would be the perfect place for a store devoted strictly to selling robots. In March 1985, they opened the Robot Center with a start-up cost of $22,250.

The store's most popular item is the 26-inch-high Omnibot 2000, which moves on command, plays tapes, and pours drinks (among other tasks). It sells for $500. The store's prices for other robots start at $40.

Knight says his next projects will include a series of books on the subject. He has already launched a robot magazine.

Source: "Retailing Robots," *Venture,* November 1985, p. 80.

Figure 3–3   Examples of Factors Affecting Industry and Business Trends

1. *Economics*—gross national product (GNP), interest rates, inflation (or deflation) rates, stage of the business cycle, employment levels, size and characteristics of business firms and not-for-profit organizations, and opportunities to serve foreign markets.
2. *Technology*—artificial intelligence, thinking machines, laser beams, new energy sources such as solar and thermal energy, amount of spending for research and development, and development of patents and their protection.
3. *Lifestyle*—career expectations, consumer activism, health concerns, desire to upgrade education and climb the organizational ladder, and need for psychological services.
4. *Political-legal*—antitrust regulations, environmental protection laws, foreign trade regulations, tax changes, immigration laws, child care legislation, and the attitude of governments and society toward the particular type of industry and business.
5. *Demographics*—population growth rate, age and regional shifts, ethnic moves and life expectancy, number and distribution of firms within the industry, and size and character of markets.

Figure 3–3 shows some selected examples of economic, technological, lifestyle, political-legal, and demographic factors that affect various industries and businesses. These factors will be discussed more fully in Chapters 5, 6, and 7.

SOME PRACTICAL IDEAS FOR SMALL BUSINESSES

As shown in Chapter 1, the more entrepreneurial small business owners tend to be innovative and to develop new ideas, and their businesses may later become big. What are some of the innovative ideas that are currently developing, which should lead to big businesses of tomorrow? These new types of business provide opportunities for those wanting to become small business owners.

Some Progressive Small Businesses

For its "Centennial Edition," reporters and editors of *The Wall Street Journal* selected a few of the companies that could "make our world different tomorrow." They looked for companies with innovative ideas and technologies that would lead into the next century, or ones that had found new ways to make and market products and services. Of the 66 companies chosen, 14 were small (with fewer than 500 employees). They are listed in Table 3–2. These companies have one thing in common: they're offering a new product, or a new application, or a modification of an old one.

For example, BSW Architects is revolutionizing architectural design by de-emphasizing the "art" aspect and emphasizing standardized designs to reduce construction costs and avoid problems in dealing with nit-picking code inspectors and regulators. It now operates in 30 states.

MIPS Computer Systems, Inc., is a pioneer in developing a new microprocessor that is the basis of the fast-growing computer work station market.

Steven Jobs' new company, Next, Inc., has combined the low-cost, easy-to-use qualities of PCs with the fancy graphics and increased horsepower of workstations. Since September 1989, when his sleek black computers hit the market, Next, Inc., has been battling with Apple®, IBM®, and Sun Microsystems® for the desktop market. IBM was so impressed with Next's new technology that it is using its distinctive software and three-dimensional look on its new high-powered workstation.[2]

Thinking Machines Corporation has gotten the jump on IBM, Digital Equipment Corporation, Intel, and many Japanese giants by linking together many computers to share the work simultaneously. Thinking Machines led the pack by connecting as many as 64,000 microprocessors in a single computer called the *Connection Machine.* The company is working toward machines approaching human capabilities in sight and reasoning.

Table 3–2   Small Businesses Expected to Be Leaders of the Future

Company (headquarters)	Founded	Chief executive	Employees	Main business
American Superconductor (Cambridge, Mass.)	1987	George McKinney	19	Superconductors
Biospherics (Beltsville, Md.)	1967	Gilbert Levin	480	Health and environment technologies
BSW Architects (Tulsa, Okla.)	1983	Robert P. Sober David E. Broach Robert C. Workman	100	Architecture
Codman Research Group (Lyme, N.H.)	1984	Philip Capter	12	Health data analysis
Compression Labs (San José, Calif.)	1976	John E. Tyson	160	Picture telephones
Echelon (Los Gatos, Calif.)	1988	M. Kenneth Oshman	45	Automated systems
HSST Corporation (Tokyo, Japan)	1985	Akira Hayashi	49	Magnetically levitated trains
Judicate (Philadelphia, Pa.)	1983	Jay D. Seid	26	Private court systems
Kurzweil Applied Intelligence (Waltham, Mass.)	1982	Raymond Kurzweil	89	Speech recognition devices
MIPS Computer Systems (Sunnyvale, Calif.)	1984	Robert C. Miller	370	Computer products
Nestor (Providence, R.I.)	1975	Michael G. Buffa	31	Neural-network computers
Next, Inc. (Palo Alto, Calif.)	1985	Steven P. Jobs	250	Computers
Northfield Laboratories (Evanston, Ill.)	1985	Richard DeWoskin	23	Medical research
Thinking Machines (Cambridge, Mass.)	1983	Sheryl Handler	280	Computers

Source: "At a Glance: Companies of the Future," *The Wall Street Journal,* Centennial Edition (1989), p. A3. Reprinted by permission of *The Wall Street Journal,* © Dow Jones & Company, Inc., 1989. ALL RIGHTS RESERVED.

Some Innovative Suggestions for Future Small Business Opportunities

Some other innovative ideas for small businesses are: specialized shopping, especially for dual-career families and shut-ins; desktop publishing; on-site auto tune-ups at the client's home; helping other small businesses computerize their activities; low-power TV stations for specially targeted audiences; presorting mail by ZIP codes for businesses sending out large mailings; at-home pet grooming; the use of fax machines for mass mailings and franchising fax vending machines; exotic family tours; utilization review firms to review hospital costs for employers, point out unnecessary treatments, and suggest cheaper alternatives; and specialized delivery services.

For example, Cuisine Express provides fast, effective delivery of meals from seven gourmet restaurants in Maryland to customers in the Bethesda, Chevy Chase, Glen Echo, and Somerset areas. Customers choose the restaurant and meal they desire and place an order with Cuisine Express's operator. The operator orders the meal from the restaurant, and a driver picks it up, delivers it to the customer, and collects. Upon delivery, the driver accepts Visa, MasterCard, or a personal check for the amount of the order.

GROWING OPPORTUNITIES FOR WOMEN AND MINORITIES IN SMALL BUSINESS

Small firms provide excellent opportunities for women and minorities to gain economic independence. The opportunities for women, blacks, Hispanics, and Asians are increasing in number and frequency, as will be shown by actual examples.

Women

One of the most impressive recent trends in small-business activity has been the escalating number of women starting their own business. This explosion of women-owned companies—up 84 percent from 2.5 million in 1980 to 4.6 million in 1989—has made the 1980s the "decade of women entrepreneurs."[3] Women now own about 28 percent of all small sole proprietorships, and they are starting twice as many new businesses as men. Women are expected to own half of the nation's small businesses by the year 2000.[4] As shown in Figure 3–4, the change in women-owned businesses is occurring faster in the nontraditional industries, such as transportation, construction, manufacturing, mining, and agriculture—as well as services, trade, and finance. However, 6 out of 10 women owners are still in:

- Public relations.
- Marketing.
- Data processing.
- Business service/personnel.
- Finance.
- Retailing.[5]

Figure 3–4 Increase in Women-Owned Businesses

Change in the number of women-owned and all nonfarm sole
proprietorships by industrial sector, 1980-85 (percent)

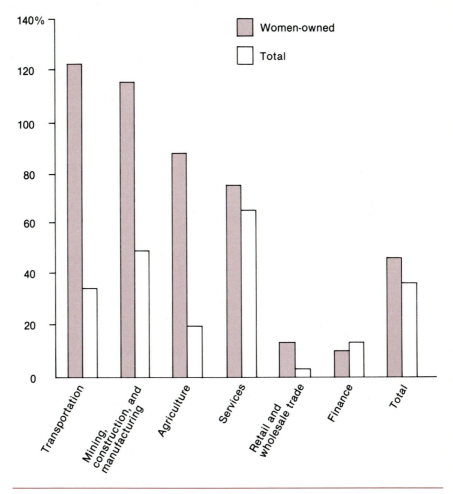

Source: U.S. Small Business Administration, Office of Advocacy.

A poll of National Association of Women Business Owners members
by *USA Today* found that these owners are not the mythical women who
inherited the family or their spouse's business. Instead, 90 percent of them
either (1) started the business for themselves (78 percent), (2) bought a
business (9 percent), or (3) bought a franchise (3 percent). They started
their businesses primarily to prove that they could succeed, to earn more
money, and to control their work schedule. As with all small business
owners (see Chapter 2), 57 percent of the women work more than 50

hours per week. The surveyed female entrepreneurs were highly educated, as only 5 percent of those responding had a high school education or less.

Opportunities for women entrepreneurs are growing all across the nation, as are the organizations to help women go into, and operate, their businesses. These include the Women's Economic Development Corporation in Minneapolis, Minnesota; the Women's Business Development Center in Chicago; the Midwest Women's Business Owners Development Joint Ventures in Detroit; and the American Women's Economic Development Corporation (AWED) in New York. AWED is a national organization dedicated to training women for business ownership. (*Note:* For counseling, call the toll-free hot line, 1-800-222-AWED. The nominal fee can be charged to major credit cards.) These centers received $1.6 million in matching grants under a new federal program providing technical assistance to women business owners.[6] Also, Young Women's Christian Association groups around the country have been helping for years.

Because of the difficulty of finding adequate markets at home, many businesses run by entrepreneurial women are now finding markets that were previously overlooked, namely, overseas markets. From all indications, these businesses are doing quite well.[7]

Yet there are many problems still facing women entrepreneurs, as shown in Figure 3–5. In order to overcome some of these problems, the Women's Business Ownership Act was passed in late 1988. It extended antidiscrimination laws to include commercial credit, as well as personal credit, for women. It also established a National Women's Business Council to submit to Congress a plan for women entrepreneurs.[8] Appendix A, at the end of this book, shows some sources of help for women entrepreneurs.

Minorities

Small business ownership also provides growing opportunities for minorities. Appendix B, at the end of this book, lists some sources of help for minorities either in or going into business. The Commerce Department's Minority Business Development Agency offers accounting, management, and marketing training and assistance at more than 100 minority business development centers across the United States. The SBA runs the 8(A) program, in which portions of federal government contracts are reserved for minority-owned firms. Although the details are covered in Chapter 8, in general the program helps economically disadvantaged business owners win federal contracts. SBA officials not only help owners write business plans but also provide technical and managerial advice and make annual performance reviews.[9]

The National Association of Investment Companies, which is the trade group for firms that invest in minority small businesses, periodically holds financial seminars at which investors present the standards they use for putting money into small, minority firms.[10]

Figure 3–5   Problems Faced by Women in Business

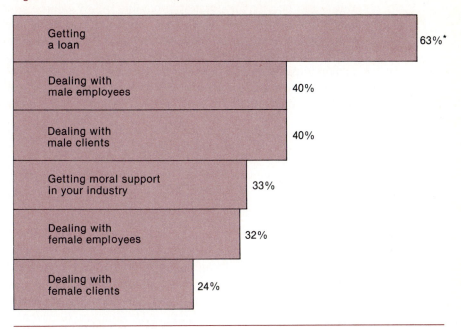

Getting a loan	63%*
Dealing with male employees	40%
Dealing with male clients	40%
Getting moral support in your industry	33%
Dealing with female employees	32%
Dealing with female clients	24%

* Percent responding. (Respondents could choose more than one answer.)

Source: USA Today poll, as reported in "She's the Boss," *USA Today,* June 21, 1989, p. 1A. Copyright 1989, USA TODAY. Adapted with permission.

Blacks

Today, small business offers many good opportunities for blacks. Small firms hire about 10-and-one-half times as many blacks as does big business, and about 6 percent of the self-employed are black. From 1977 to 1982, the number of black-owned businesses increased 47 percent—almost twice the growth rate for all nonfarm businesses.[11] Since then, the number of such businesses has increased around 63 percent. During the last 13 years, the total number of black businesses has grown from around 225,000 to about 375,000. Like other groups, not all black entrepreneurs succeed. But the larger ones do quite well, according to *Black Enterprise* magazine. Its 100 largest black-owned industrial and service companies grew 10.2 percent in revenues, as compared to 7.6 percent for the *Fortune* 500.[12]

Herman Valentine's Systems Management American Corporation, featured in our Chapter 20 Opening Focus, was included on this list.

While most black-owned businesses tend to be small, have small revenues, and be only moderately profitable, many efforts are being made to improve opportunities for blacks in business, and these efforts seem to be working. For example, in 1989 there were 255 black-owned Ford dealerships, 115 black-owned General Motors dealerships, and 71 black-owned Chrysler dealerships.[13] Also, in addition to the sources of help shown in Appendix B, the following is a good example of local efforts to improve opportunities for blacks in business.

"Buy Liberty," a $60,000 campaign to help blacks promote their businesses, was launched in Los Angeles in July 1986. Another thrust of the campaign, according to its chairman Anthony Essex, is "to promote black businesses to hire black youths."[14] A third goal is to add 200 new black businesses to the 4,000 already in the area.

The role of minority entrepreneurs is changing rapidly. Once concentrated primarily in Mom-and-Pop businesses such as barbershops, cleaners, and grocery stores, black businesspeople are now moving into such fields as electronics, advertising, real estate development, insurance, health care, computers (see the Opening Focus for Chapter 20, "Herman Valentine: A Study in Minority Entrepreneurship") and automobile dealerships (see the Opening Focus for Chapter 16, "Mel Farr: Sales Superstar").

Like his father, Ernest Bates, Jr., went into business. But while his father quit school after third grade to work, the son went to medical school. In 1978, Dr. Bates started a San Francisco company that supplies diagnostic imaging equipment to hospitals. The 50-year-old black neurosurgeon is chairman and chief executive officer of publicly held American Shared Hospital Services, which last year had sales of $7.5 million.[15]

Big companies are also helping blacks start small businesses. They do it through joint ventures, lending their personnel to help start—or advise—the business, providing low-cost facilities, and providing an assured market. All of these kinds of help are illustrated by the following example.

As part of its minority supplier program, McDonald's asked George Johnson and David Moore to start a business making croutons for its newly introduced line of salads. Johnson, 41, and Moore, 33, managers at a brewing company, had never run a business, knew nothing about baking, and had only one client—McDonald's. They invested $100,000 each and, with such an assured market, persuaded a Chicago bank to lend them $1.6 million. Also, a McDonald's bun and English muffin supplier bought a Chicago pork-processing plant and leased it back to their company, Quality Croutons, Inc.

The first croutons rolled off the line on May 4, 1987. Sales for 1988 exceeded $4 million, including sales to McDonald's, United Airlines, Kraft Foods, and Pizza Hut.[16]

Salad days: George Johnson, left, and David Moore raked in $4 million from crouton sales in 1988.

Source: Kevin Johnson, "McDonald's Recruits Duo to Make Its McCroutons," *USA Today,* January 27, 1989, p. 7B. Copyright 1989, USA TODAY. Used with permission. (Photo © 1989 by Richard Derk.)

Hispanics

As shown in Figure 3–6, the number of Hispanic businesses in the United States grew to about 200 percent during the 1970s, while the Hispanic population grew by only 64 percent. And there were around 611,000 such firms in 1987, doing about $35 billion worth of business. According to Salvador Gomez, the national director of U.S. Hispanic Chamber of Commerce, this progress has resulted from better education and developmental efforts by both private industry and government.[17] Private commitments to Hispanic companies are also rising rapidly.

One area in which Hispanic businesses are particularly booming is the food area. Previously this field was dominated by Mom-and-Pop Hispanic

Figure 3–6   Hispanic-Owned Businesses Are Growing Rapidly

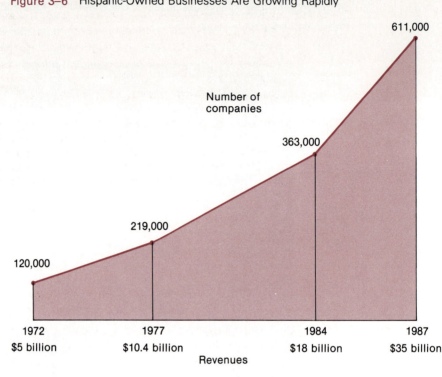

Number of companies

611,000

363,000

219,000

120,000

| 1972 | 1977 | 1984 | 1987 |
| $5 billion | $10.4 billion | $18 billion | $35 billion |

Revenues

* Projection.

Source: USA Today, November 2, 1984, p. 3B. Copyright 1984, USA TODAY. Adapted with permission. (Original source: U.S. Hispanic Chamber of Commerce.)

grocers. Now, though, supermarkets are beginning to invade the field because of the Hispanic view of shopping as an eagerly awaited social event.

The Hispanic market represents one of the fastest-growing groups of customers in the country, with about 22 million people. Since 1980, the Hispanic population has grown 34 percent, four times the overall U.S. growth rate. Now entrepreneurs are trying to cash in on this market.

For example, in 1987 Vons Companies, after two years—and $2.5 million— researching the market, started Tianguis, a three-store southern California supermarket chain. The store's shelves are stocked with Spanish items, including handmade tortillas, and mariachi singers stroll the aisles. Hispanics are driving from as far as 65 miles away to shop in the stores, as they like the products, the music, and the fact that "everyone speaks Spanish."[18]

Figure 3–7 Asians Benefit from Network

Recently arrived Asian immigrants establishing U.S. business enterprises gain support from cultural networks.

Readily available financial backing | Business contacts | Role models | Advice and training

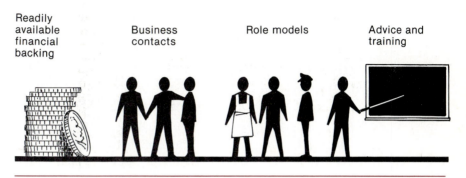

Source: Robert Lewis, "Asian Immigrants Find Large Profits in Small Stores," *Mobile* (Alabama) *Press Register,* March 5, 1989, p. G1. Adapted with permission of Newhouse Graphics. (Original source: U.S. Department of Commerce.)

Asians

The flood of Asian refugees into the United States in recent decades has resulted in a wave of Mom-and-Pop entrepreneurships. This seems to be the occupational choice of growing numbers of newly arrived families. Among other reasons, they tend to be motivated to open their own businesses because language and cultural barriers prevent them from obtaining wage or salary jobs. Being blocked from ordinary employment, Asians—especially Koreans—tend to go into business for themselves, even if it means setting up a street stand or opening a store in a poor, run-down neighborhood. As shown in Figure 3–7, Asian immigrants receive considerable support from cultural networks when they try to set up a small business.

For example, Dae Song, 36, arrived in Baltimore from Korea with $400. After losing the money, unable to speak or understand English, and not knowing what to do, he moved in with an aunt and started working in the family's dry cleaning business in a Washington suburb. After learning the business, he opened his own shop with help from a Korean support group. Each of the 30 members of the group contributed $1,000 as a loan to Dae Song. Eventually, each of these 30 will have access to the full $30,000 to finance a business of his own.[19]

But cultural factors alone do not explain the outstanding success of Asian entrepreneurs in this country. Instead, a study of 300 small businesses in California—the state with the highest concentration of Asian businesses—found several pragmatic differences between these entrepreneurs and businesses owned by non-Asians. Less than half as many of them had problems with general business knowledge, as compared to non-Asians. And while only 69 percent of non-Asian entrepreneurs had a business plan when they started their company, 84 percent of Asian entrepreneurs said they did. Finally, the Asians were more prone to use outside attorneys and accountants to assist them, along with the use of a personal computer. According to a spokesman for Pacific Bell Directory, which sponsored the study, Asian businesspeople are prospering not because they are Asians but because they understand key ingredients of running a successful business.[20]

SOME AREAS OF CONCERN FOR SMALL BUSINESS OWNERS

So far, the message of this discussion has been that opportunities abound for anyone with a good idea, the courage to take a chance and try something new, and some money to invest—or borrow. That's what small business is all about, But, as shown in Chapter 1, some areas of concern might limit these opportunities. For example, the success of smaller firms tends to be limited by factors such as inadequate management, shortages of working capital, government regulation and paperwork, and lack of proper record-keeping. But the two biggest concerns are (1) poorly planned growth that is too slow or too fast and (2) the danger of failure.

Poorly Planned Growth

Poorly planned growth appears to be a built-in obstacle facing many small businesses. For example, if the owners are incapable, inefficient, or lacking in initiative, their businesses flounder and may eventually fail. If the owners are only mediocre, their businesses continue to be small businesses. However, if the owners and/or managers are efficient and capable and their organizations succeed and grow, with poorly planned growth, they run the risk of losing the very things they seek from their small businesses.

Loss of Independence

The very act of growing means that owners may lose the independence they earlier sought. If nothing else, they must now please more people, including employees, customers, and the public. Owners also have many new problems, including hiring and rewarding managers. Thus, they now have the problem of managing other people—exercising the very power they may resent in others.

The South Texas Life Insurance Company began with Juan Ortiz selling ordinary-life policies and his wife, Rhonda, doing the paperwork (names disguised). Ortiz explained their growth into a major company this way:

Our company's success and growth was like a chain reaction. As business increased, we both started selling during the day, and then we'd prepare the policies and do the paperwork at night. We rapidly added sales reps and office personnel. I hired, trained, and supervised the reps, and my wife did the same with the officeworkers.

Next we hired specialized management people as we expanded into other types of insurance. We then expanded into other areas of Texas and surrounding states, which required more and different types of personnel and managers.

Somewhere along the line, we stopped being the owner-managers of a small company with its unique problems and rewards and became managers of a large company with all its problems. I do miss the early and exciting days, though, when I was personally involved in all aspects of the business.

Loss of Control

Many otherwise creative entrepreneurs are poor managers. They're able to generate ideas and organize the business but are unable to manage it on a day-to-day basis. If the firm becomes large enough to require outside capital for future success and growth, the owner-manager may lose autonomy over the company, as the following example shows.

Steven Jobs, 21, and Steve Wozniak, 19, two design and production geniuses, founded Apple Computer® in 1976 by selling Jobs' Volkswagen microbus and Wozniak's Hewlett-Packard scientific calculator. They managed its growth until 1980, when they sold stock in it to the public. Although they were worth $165 million and $88 million, respectively, they could not manage the day-to-day operations, and so John Sculley was hired away from PepsiCo in 1983 to manage the floundering firm.

In 1985, Wozniak sold his Apple stock and founded Cloud 9, an electronics firm producing infrared remote control devices to use with all electronic equipment. Jobs was ousted as chairman of Apple, sold all but one share of his stock, and—as shown in Table 3–2—founded Next, Inc.

Typical Growth Pattern

Historically, the ownership and management of small businesses have tended to follow a growth pattern similar to that shown in Figure 3–8.

Figure 3–8   Stages in the Development of a Small Business

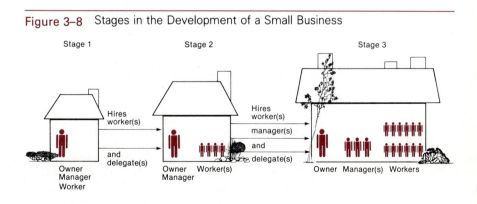

During stage 1, the owner manages the business and does all the work. As it enters stage 2, the owner still manages it but hires employees to help with the routine and/or management activities. Later, in stage 3, the owner hires a manager(s) to run the business. Thus the business takes on the form, characteristics, and many of the problems of a big business.

The length of service of professional managers (as opposed to owner-managers) in small businesses tends to be relatively short; they move from one company to another as they progress upward in rank and earnings. Often, owners must give managers a financial interest in the business in order to hold them.

The Threat of Failure

As shown in Chapter 1, the threat of failure is ever present for many small businesses, but this does not appear to discourage people from starting new ones. The number of new business incorporations each year increased from 319,000 in 1974 to around 1,000,000 in 1989.[21] But there have also been discontinuances and failures. **Discontinuances** are voluntary decisions to quit. They result from many factors, including health, changes in family situation, and the apparent advantages of working for someone else. Other businesses are **failures** as a result of inability to make a go of the business; things just don't work out as planned.

There are two types of failure: (1) **formal failures,** which end up in court with some kind of loss to the creditors, and (2) **personal (informal) failures,** where the owner cannot make it financially and so voluntarily calls it quits.

While there are relatively few formal failures, there are many personal ones. This kind of failure is more important numerically and probably emotionally as well. People put savings—or income—into a business only to see losses wipe out the investment. Creditors usually do not suffer; the owners tend to absorb the losses, putting up the funds to pay off their debts. The owner is the one who packs up, closes the door, and says, "That's it!" The following is a good example.

Sonny Brewer had edited the *Mobile Bay Monthly* in Mobile, Alabama, for two years when he decided to start a new magazine to serve Mobile Bay's Eastern Shore. Many people were enthusiastic; writers contributed stories and advertisers bought large ads. Using $5,000 of his own savings and $10,000 borrowed from his mother, Brewer published the first issue of the *Eastern Shore Quarterly* and mailed free copies to 10,000 carefully selected addresses.

Thi issue was well received, and subsequent issues were praised, but no one was buying the magazine. Despite subscription cards in each issue, only a few subscriptions trickled in.

The main problem was that the magazine was essentially a one-man band: Brewer alone, in addition to being editor and publisher, had to sell all the advertising. And collecting for the ads was as hard as selling them. To make matters worse, between issues Brewer was having to work odd jobs to make ends meet. Many of his expenses were being paid for with free advertising in the magazine.

After four issues, the *Quarterly* folded. Despite a very generous subscription offer in the last issue, only about 100 subscriptions had been received (at least 5,000 were needed to break even). Subscribers were reimbursed or compensated, the printer paid, and all other creditors satisfied, but Brewer had to borrow from friends to pay his utility bills. Ultimately, he sold his car to pay off his remaining debts. Now working at several other jobs, he still considers himself honor bound to repay his mother and so far has paid off $2,500 of that debt.

WHAT YOU SHOULD HAVE LEARNED

1. There are many opportunities for prospective small business owners. Some of the fastest-growing companies either are, or once were, small in their industry. Opportunities for starting new businesses seem to be especially good in business and professional services, high-tech manufacturing, bars and restaurants, and other services.

   Some of the industries with the highest success rates cater to basic human needs, such as funeral services, fuel and ice, and laundry and cleaning. Industries showing growth in employment include not only high-tech industries but also building trades and transportation. In summary, the opportunities seem to be in small firms, limited in scope, that involve long, hard hours working to satisfy basic human needs.

   Some of the factors affecting the future of an industry or business are *(a)* economics, *(b)* technology, *(c)* lifestyles, *(d)* political-legal, and *(e)* demographics.

2. Some practical suggestions for future small firms are specialized shopping, desktop publishing, helping business firms computerize their activities, applications of fax machines, utilization review firms to help employers reduce their health care costs, and specialized delivery services.

3. There are many opportunities in small business for women and minorities. Women, particularly, are starting new businesses at a rapid rate—twice that of men—so that they are expected to own half of all small firms by the year 2000. Women owning small firms tend to be well educated, capable, and committed owners.

   Blacks are also progressing in small business, but their firms tend to be small and less profitable than others. Still, blacks in entrepreneurial ventures are doing quite well.

   Opportunities for Hispanics are growing, especially in Mom-and-Pop food stores. The Hispanic market is growing fast and expects to provide many opportunities in the future.

Cultural networks, along with canny business practices—such as having a business plan and using computers—are aiding Asians as they flood into small business ownership.

4. Poorly planned growth can be a real problem for small business owners. The entrepreneur who is primarily interested in producing innovative products may be uninterested in management tasks, yet reluctant to surrender control to a professional manager. If the company needs to sell stock to capitalize rapid growth, the founders may lose another measure of control. Yet failure to grow can mean the death of an entrepreneurial venture; indeed, for all small businesses, there are problems associated with remaining small.

Another problem is failure. Many small businesses go out of business every year. Some discontinue for health, family, or other personal reasons, while others fail. Although relatively few of these are formal failures, or bankruptcies, personal failures resulting from unprofitability or general discouragement can be just as devastating for the small business owner.

KEY TERMS

discontinuances, 74	formal failures, 74
failures, 74	personal (informal) failures, 74

QUESTIONS FOR DISCUSSION

1. (*a*) Name the fastest-growing small businesses as indicated by the number of jobs. (*b*) Explain their growth.
2. Name the fastest-growing businesses as indicated by the number of new firms.
3. Explain the low failure rates of the firms listed in Table 3–1.
4. (*a*) What future do you see for the companies listed in Table 3–2? (*b*) Explain.
5. Evaluate the opportunities in small business for (*a*) women, (*b*) blacks, (*c*) Hispanics, and (*d*) Asians.
6. (*a*) How does success cause problems for some small businesses? (*b*) Can you give examples from your experience or suggest ways to avoid the problems of growth?
7. (*a*) Do you agree with the authors' practical suggestions for future small businesses? (*b*) Which of them do you think will not provide opportunities? (*c*) What other practical ideas would you suggest?
8. (*a*) Discuss the factors affecting the future of an industry or business. (*b*) What others would you suggest?

SUGGESTED READINGS

"Black-Owned Businesses." *Black Enterprise,* August 1987, p. 39.

Cetron, Marvin J., Wanda Rocha, and Rebecca Lucken. "Think Big or Think Small: The Future of American Business Firms." *The Futurist,* September–October 1988, pp. 9–16.

Farnham, Alan. "The Asians." *Fortune,* September 12, 1988, pp. 66–67.

Fitch, Ed, and Jennifer Pendleton. "WPP Hispanic Shops May Compete." *Advertising Age,* December 21, 1987, p. 34.

Hisrich, Robert D., and Candida G. Brush. *The Woman Entrepreneur: Starting, Financing, and Managing a Successful Business.* Lexington, Mass.: Lexington Books, 1985.

Howe, Marvine. "Asians in New York: High Ambition." *The New York Times,* April 17, 1989, p. A11.

"In Pursuit of Profits." *Black Enterprise,* November 1988, pp. 56–59.

"Looking to Immigrants for Entrepreneurship." *The Wall Street Journal,* November 14, 1988, p. B1.

Morrall, Patricia. *Directory of Women Entrepreneurs.* 2d ed. Atlanta: Wind River Publications, 1989.

Nelton, Sharon. "The Age of the Woman Entrepreneur." *Nation's Business,* May 1989, pp. 22–26.

Thompson, Roger. "Minority Entrepreneurs." *Nation's Business,* February 1987, p. 10.

ENDNOTES

1. Marcia Staimer, "Hottest Business Areas," *USA Today,* May 10, 1989, p. 1B.
2. Brenton R. Schlender, "How Steve Jobs Linked up with IBM," *Fortune,* October 9, 1989, p. 48.
3. Rusty Brown, "Women Entrepreneurs Dominate '80s," *Mobile* (Alabama) *Press Register,* January 18, 1986, p. 4–A; and "Women Entrepreneurs: Who Are They?" *USA Today,* June 21, 1989, p. 4B.
4. Adline Clarke, "Climate Said Right for Small Business," *Mobile* (Alabama) *Register,* January 27, 1989, p. 12–D.
5. "Women Entrepreneurs: Who Are They?" p. 4B.
6. Reported by Shelley Liles-Morris, "Federal Grants for Women in Business," *USA Today,* November 10, 1989, p. 4B.
7. Steven Golob, "Overcome Hurdles at Home: Export," *Nation's Business,* June 1988, pp. 47–49.
8. Shelley Liles, "Women Get Due Credit under Law," *USA Today,* May 8, 1989, p. 1E.
9. Jeanne Sadler, "New Rules for SBA Minority Program Make It Tougher to Gain Admission," *The Wall Street Journal,* August 17, 1989, p. B4.
10. "Any Programs for Minority Businesses?" *USA Today,* May 9, 1988, p. 1E.
11. Virginia Inman, "Black-Owned Businesses," *Inc.,* February 1986, p. 18.
12. "The Top 100," *Black Enterprise,* June 1989, pp. 57 ff.
13. Walter Scott, "Personality Parade," *Parade Magazine,* March 19, 1989, p. 2.
14. Pat Guy, "L.A. Blacks Push Black Business," *USA Today,* July 25, 1986, p. 2B.
15. Mark McNamara, "Entrepreneurial Surgeon," *Ebony,* April 1986, p. 84; and Linda M. Watkins, "Minority Entrepreneurs Venturing into Broader Range of Businesses," *The Wall Street Journal,* March 25, 1987, p. 33.
16. Kevin Johnson, "McDonald's Recruits Duo to Make Its McCroutons," *USA Today,* January 27, 1989, p. 7. Copyright 1989, USA TODAY. Adapted with permission.
17. Susan Antilla, "Hispanic Businesses Flourish," *USA Today,* November 2, 1984, p. 3B.
18. Alfredo Corchado, "Hispanic Supermarkets Are Blossoming," *The Wall Street Journal,* January 23, 1989, p. B1.

19. Robert Lewis, "Asian Immigrants Find Large Profits in Small Stores," *Mobile* (Alabama) *Press Register,* March 5, 1989, p. G–1.

20. "Asian Entrepreneurs: Success Isn't Cultural," *The Wall Street Journal,* April 3, 1989, p. B1.

21. Mindy Fetterman, "Hot Line: Callers Eager to Be Own Boss, *USA Today,* May 9, 1989, p. 1A.

4

GROWING OPPORTUNITIES IN FRANCHISING

Buying a franchise is probably the quickest, easiest, and most successful way of becoming an entrepreneur.—Colonel Harlan Sanders, founder of Kentucky Fried Chicken

Franchising . . . is changing not only our marketing system, but also our way of life.—Peng S. Chan, California State University, Fullerton; and Robert T. Justis, Louisiana State University.

LEARNING OBJECTIVES

After studying the material in this chapter, you will be able to:

1. Discuss the extent of franchising.
2. Define *franchising.*
3. Describe the two most popular types of franchises.
4. Tell why franchising is so rapidly growing in importance.
5. Explain how to evaluate opportunities in franchising.
6. Discuss the future of franchising, especially in international operations.
7. Turn your dream into reality.

RAY KROC: FATHER OF FRANCHISING

Ray Kroc, himself a billionaire, probably made more people millionaires in less time than anyone else in history. And he did it after he was 52 years old, in poor health, and working for a business that was at a standstill. Now his "brainchild"—McDonald's—has over 11,000 stores in 52 countries, and has over $16 billion in systemwide sales.

Kroc, a high school dropout, sold everything from paper cups in Chicago to real estate in Florida before he wound up selling electric milkshake mixers around the country. At that time—the early 1950s—"a hamburger and a shake" took anywhere from 15 to 30 minutes to prepare at the thousands of small, independent drive-ins haphazardly located around the country.

In 1954, Kroc received an order from a drive-in in San Bernardino, California, for eight machines that could make six milkshakes at a time. His curiosity led him to visit Richard and Maurice McDonald to see why they needed to make 48 shakes at a time. He found people lining up at a window, ordering, and leaving in about 30 seconds with bags of hamburgers, fries, and shakes—all for under a dollar. He thought the assembly-line operation, based on clean, instant service with a family atmosphere, was the most amazing merchandising operation he'd ever seen. He persuaded the brothers to let him be responsible for a complete franchising operation, including finding operators and locations, building drive-ins, and ensuring that they maintained the McDonalds' high standards. He left with a contract to franchise McDonald's worldwide and pay the brothers 0.5 percent of gross profit.

Kroc opened his first drive-in in Des Plaines,

McDonald's founder Ray Kroc.
Source: Photo courtesy of McDonald's Corporation.

Illinois, in 1955. By 1961, there were 200 of the golden-arches stores, and the McDonalds wanted to retire. Kroc bought their rights for $14 million. At the time, Kroc was earning millions of dollars a year from the franchises.

When he died in 1984, at age 84, Kroc was a billionaire. But his franchisees were also doing quite well, as each of them could expect annual sales of over $1 million per store and before-tax profit margins of 15 to 20 percent. By 1988, each of them could expect sales of about $1.6 million and a return of about 20 percent on their investment.

Kroc did for the fast-food industry what Henry Ford had done for the automobile industry. He was truly the "Father of Franchising."

Sources: Based on correspondence with McDonald's Corporation, Oak Brook, Illinois; as well as various other sources, including "The Top 1000," *Business Week*, Special 1989 Bonus Issue, p. 256; Eugene Carlson, "American Entrepreneurs: McDonald's Kroc Bloomed Late But Brilliantly," *The Wall Street Journal*, May 23, 1989, p. B2; and Barbara Marsh, "Going for the Golden Arches," *The Wall Street Journal*, May 1, 1989, p. B1.

This Opening Focus on Ray Kroc and McDonald's illustrates the exciting opportunities in one of the fastest-growing and most important segments of American business: franchising. This creative form of business has helped tens of thousands of entrepreneurs achieve their dream of owning a business of their own. As will be shown in this chapter, it is an appealing alternative to starting your own business. In Chapter 5, we will discuss the reasons to buy—and not to buy—a franchise. In this chapter, however, we present a more detailed look at franchising's role in small business.

EXTENT OF FRANCHISING

The U.S. Department of Commerce estimated that there were 516,000 franchised outlets in the United States in 1989 and that their sales totaled $661 billion.[1] As you can see from Figure 4–1, franchise sales nearly doubled in the last decade. Notice that since 1985 both sales and number of establishments have skyrocketed.

Figure 4–1   Franchising Takes Off

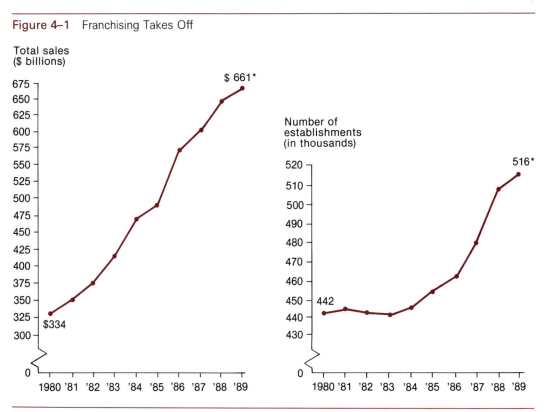

*Estimated.

Sources: Based on data from *Franchising in the Economy* (Washington, D.C.: U.S. Department of Commerce, various years); and Carol Steinberg, "Franchise Boom Still in High Gear," *USA Today,* May 8, 1989, p. 8E.

Figure 4–2   Franchising Encompassed 34 Percent of Retail Sales in 1988

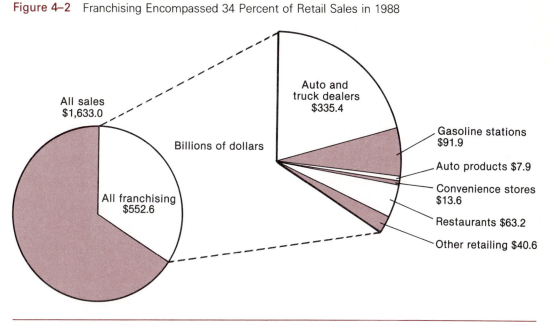

Source: U.S. Department of Commerce, *Franchising in the Economy, 1986–88* (Washington, D.C.: U.S. Department of Commerce); Chart 3, p. 15.

Franchising is particularly strong in retailing. Figure 4–2 shows that franchisors accounted for 34 percent of retail sales in 1988. Of all franchising receipts, 87 percent come from retailing.[2]

Franchising also provides direct employment for some 8 million people, including many younger and older workers who otherwise would be unable to find jobs. As popular and prevalent as franchisors are, however, they are not very well understood or recognized. So many new activities are now being franchised that you probably pass a dozen franchises each day without realizing it. For example, most automobile dealerships and many service stations are franchised arrangements.

Table 4–1 shows some typical franchises in various industries. You will notice after the name of each industry a number in parentheses. This is the number of franchises listed in that category in *Franchising in the Economy, 1986–1988*.

WHAT FRANCHISING IS

There are many different franchise arrangements. We will explain franchising by describing the process and parties involved. Then we will discuss the two most popular types.

Table 4–1   Franchise Areas and Examples of Franchisees

Automotive products/service (113)
  AAMCO Automatic Transmissions
  Express Lube
  Firestone Tire & Rubber
  Goodyear Tire & Rubber
  Jiffy Lube International
  Jiffiwash
  Midas International
  Precision Tune
  Tidy Car
Auto/trailer rentals (20)
  Avis Rent-A-Car System
  Budget Car and Truck Rental
  Hertz
  Thrifty Rent-A-Car Systems
Beauty salons/supplies (25)
  Command Performance
  Fantastic Sam's, The Original Family Haircutters
Business aids/services (122)
  H&R Block
  Business Consultants of America
  Comprehensive Accounting
  Francorp, Inc.
  Kelly's Liquidators
  Muzak
Campgrounds (3)
  Kampgrounds of America
  Yogi Bear's Jellystone Park Camp-Resorts
Children's stores/furniture/products (5)
  Lewis of London
Clothing/shoes (28)
  Athlete's Foot Marketing Associates
  Formal Wear Service
  T-Shirts Plus
Construction/remodeling materials and services (55)
  College Pro Painters (U.S.)
  Perma-Jack
Cosmetics/toiletries (7)
  Derma Culture
  Natural Cosmetics
Dental centers (6)
  Dental Power International
  Dwight Systems, Inc.
Drugstores (7)
  Health Mart
  Medicap Pharmacies
Educational products/services (29)
  Child Enrichment Centers
  Gymboree, Inc.
  Sylvan Learning Centers
Employment services (51)
  Career Employment Services
  Manpower, Inc.

Temporaries, Inc.
Equipment rentals (18)
  PCR Personal Computer Rentals
  Remco Franchises Enterprises
Foods (168)
  Baskin-Robbins Ice Cream
  The Bread Basket
  The California Yogurt Company
  Dunkin' Donuts
  Great Earth Vitamin Stores
  Hickory Farms of Ohio
  The Peanut Shack of America
  TCBY Enterprises
Foods—restaurants/drive-ins/carryouts (270)
  Arby's
  Burger King
  Captain D's
  Church's Fried Chicken
  Domino's Pizza
  El Chico
  Hardee's
  Kentucky Fried Chicken
  Mazzio's Pizza
  McDonald's
  Subway Sandwiches & Salads
  Wendy's Old Fashioned Hamburgers
General merchandising stores (2)
  Ben Franklin
  Coast to Coast Stores
Health aids/services (44)
  Health Clubs of America
  Pearle Vision Centers
  Physicians Weight Loss Centers
  United Surgical Centers
  Jazzercise
Home furnishings (42)
  Carpet Town
  Duraclean International
  Slumberland
Insurance (4)
  Pridemark
Laundry/dry-cleaning services (12)
  Dryclean—U.S.A.
  Martin Franchises, Inc.
Lawn and garden supplies/services (11)
  Liqui-Green Lawn Care
Maid services/home cleaning/party serving (16)
  Merry Maids
  Mini Maid Services
Maintenance—cleaning/sanitation services/supplies (26)
  All-Bright Industries Corporation of America
  Chem-Mark International

Table 4–1 *(continued)*

Roto-Rooter	Curtis Mathes
ServiceMaster	Entré Computer Centers
Motels/hotels (26)	MicroAge Computer Stores
Days Inns of America	National Video
Holiday Inns	Retailing other than computers/TV (150)
Quality Inns International	Art Management Services
Ramada Inns International	Frame World
Paint and decorating supplies (4)	Heritage Clock
Davis Paint	Radio Shack
Pet shops (5)	Sport Shack, Inc.
Docktor Pet Centers	Security systems (5)
Petland	Dictograph Security Systems
Printing (19)	Swimming pools (2)
Insty-Prints	California Pools
Postal Instant Press	Tools, hardware (5)
Real estate (28)	Ace Hardware
Century 21 Real Estate	Mac Tools, Inc.
Gallery of Homes	True Value
Realty World	Vending (5)
Recreation/entertainment/travel services and	Ford Gum & Machine Co.
supplies (28)	Water conditioning (3)
Batting Range Pro	Culligan International
International Tours	Miscellaneous wholesale/service business (41)
Putt-Putt Golf Courses of America	Oxygen Therapy Institute
Retail—computers/TV (13)	Together Dating Service
Compuadd	Your Attic
Computerland	

Note: Number in parentheses indicates the number of franchises listed in *Franchising in the Economy, 1986–1988.*

Source: Compiled from various sources, including franchisors' promotional materials, magazines, newspapers, and *Franchising in the Economy, 1986–88* (Washington, D.C.: U.S. Department of Commerce).

Definition

Franchising is a marketing system based on a legal arrangement that permits one party—the franchisee—to conduct business as an individual owner while abiding by the terms and conditions set by the second party—the franchisor. The **franchise** is the contract granting the right to do business and specifying the terms and conditions under which the business will be conducted. The **franchisee** is usually an independent local businessperson who agrees with the franchise owner to operate the business on a local or regional basis. The **franchisor** is the company that owns the franchise's name and distinctive elements (such as signs, symbols, and patents) and that provides operating systems, such as accounting, advertising, bookkeeping, marketing, and other services. While the franchisee is given the right to produce and market the franchisor's designated goods or services, that production and marketing must be done according to the terms of the licensing agreement. The contract specifies what the franchisee can and cannot do and prescribes certain penalties for noncompliance.

When Ray Kroc set up McDonald's as a franchisor, he controlled the trademark (or trade name), symbol (the golden arches), and operating systems. In turn, he permitted franchisees to use these under controlled conditions, for a fee. Kroc also controlled quality, including the family atmosphere and hygiene factors, that characterized the successful operations of the original drive-in.

Many franchising opportunities exist, as seen in block ads in the business section of daily papers and in various business publications, including the magazine *Franchising World.* The *1989 Franchise Annual* lists 4,185 franchisors, an increase of 754 over the previous year.[3] Yet a franchising opportunity does not automatically spell success. Caution is called for in dealing with franchisors who promise a guaranteed return on your investment, for contracts with these elusive or vanished companies often prove worthless.

Types of Systems

In general, based on the charter agreement between the franchisor and the franchisee, there are two types of franchising systems: product and trademark franchising and business format franchising (see Figure 4–3). **Product and trademark franchising** is an independent sales relationship between the franchisor and the franchisee in which the latter is given the right to use some of the franchisor's identity. Most franchisees concentrate on handling one franchisor's product line and identify their business with that firm. Familiar examples include automobile and truck dealerships, gasoline service stations, and soft-drink bottlers. The franchisor exercises very little control over the franchisee's operations; what control there is has to do with maintaining the integrity of the product, not with the franchisee's business operations. This arrangement is changing, however.

At one time, franchise agreements with auto manufacturers granted the dealer the exclusive right to sell the franchisor's cars in a given area, with the power to negotiate price and other terms and conditions of sale with customers. Now, many manufacturers are negotiating deals directly with their large purchasers, such as car rental agencies. The dealers merely deliver the cars for a small fee. Some dealers are complaining that this system makes their franchise practically worthless.[4]

Business format franchising is characterized by an ongoing business relationship between franchisor and franchisee that includes not only the product, service, and trademark (or trade name and logo), but also the other components of the operating system: marketing strategy and plan, operating manuals and standards, training programs for operating the system, quality control standards, accounting and financial control systems, and methods of communicating between franchisor and franchisee.

Figure 4–3   Types of Franchising Systems, Based on Charter Agreement

A. Product and trademark franchising

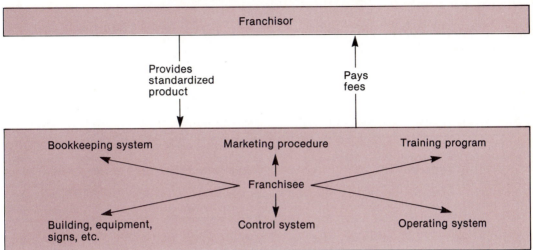

B. Business format franchising

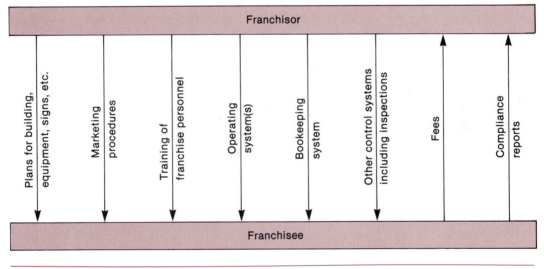

Best Western Motels is one of the largest—and best—examples of such a system. Its signs, logo, and operating system are standardized.[5]

In 1988, according to the U.S. Department of Commerce, more than 2,100 business format franchises operated in the United States—more than twice as many as the 900 in 1972. And they operated an estimated 368,000 units, up from 220,000 in 1975.[6]

Table 4–2   The Top 25 of the Franchise 100

Rank, (last year's rank), franchise, location	Parent company	Two-year average annual growth in franchised units	Type of business
1. (4) Subway, Milford, Conn.	Doctor's Associates Inc.	617	Fast-food restaurants
2. (1) Domino's Pizza, Ann Arbor, Mich.	Domino's Pizza Inc.	534	Fast-food restaurants
3. (2) Chem-Dry, Cameron Park, Calif.	Harris Research Inc.	482	Maintenance/cleaning
4. (11) Little Caesar's Pizza, Farmington Hills, Mich.	Little Caesar Enterprises Inc.	330	Fast-food restaurants
5. (10) Coverall, San Diego, Calif.	Coverall North America Inc.	321	Maintenace/cleaning
6. (8) Novus Windshield Repair, Minneapolis,Minn.	Novus Franchising Inc.	272	Auto maintenance
7. (16) "TCBY" The Country's Best Yogurt, Little Rock, Ark.	TCBY Enterprises Inc.*	263	Ice cream/yogurt
8. (7) Jani-King, Dallas, Tex.	Jani-King International Inc.	257	Maintenance/cleaning
9. (—) United Package Mailing Service, Richmond, Va.	Senpax Inc.	245	Packaging/shipping
10. (3) McDonald's, Oak Brook, Ill.	McDonald's Corp.*	224	Fast-food restaurants
11. (15) ServiceMaster, Downers Grove, Ill.	ServiceMaster LP*	220	Maintenance/cleaning
12. (17) Jiffy Lube, Baltimore, Md.	Jiffy Lube Int'l. Inc.*	202	Auto maintenance
13. (19) Decorating Den, Bethesda, Md.	Decorating Den Systems, Inc.	195	Home decorating
14. (14) RE/MAX, Englewood, Colo.	RE/MAX International Inc.	189	Real estate
15. (25) Better Homes & Gardens Real Estate Service, Des Moines, Iowa	Meredith Corp.*	182	Real estate
16. (12) Wendy's Old Fashioned Hamburgers, Dublin, Ohio	Wendy's International Inc.*	181	Fast-food restaurants
17. (6) Packy the Shipper, Racine, Wis.	PNS Inc.	171	Packaging/shipping
18. (18) Hardee's, Rocky Mount, N.C.	Imasco Ltd.*	167	Fast-food restaurants
19. (13) Fantastic Sam's, Memphis, Tenn.	Fantastic Sam's International Inc.	163	hair cutting
20. (22) Mail Boxes Etc. USA, San Diego, Calif.	Mail Boxes Etc.*	157	Business services
21. (5) Jazzercise, Carlsbad, Calif.	Jazzercise Inc.	147	Health/fitness
22. (26) Days Inns of America, Atlanta, Ga.	Sunrise Acquisition Corp.	134	Hotel/motel
23. (21) Arby's, Atlanta, Ga.	DWG Corp.*	126	Fast-food restaurants
24. (20) Rainbow Int'l. Carpet Dyeing & Cleaning Co., Waco, Tex.	Rainbow Int'l. Carpet Dyeing & Cleaning Co.	118	Maintenance/cleaning
25. (36) Nutri/System Weight Loss Centers, Willow Grove, Pa.	Diversified Services Group Inc.	105	Health/fitness

a. For 11 months.

b. Several franchise options available.

c. Varies with population of area served.

d. Amount determined by gross commission income.

e. Franchises are added only to an existing business.

f. Varies with number of guest rooms.

* Public company.

N.A. Not available.

Source: Venture, December 1988, pp. 36–37.

The fastest-growing industry groups, as far as business format franchising is concerned, are fast foods/restaurants, video, health/fitness, ice cream/yogurt, maintenance/cleaning, auto rental, and business services.

In 1988, *Venture* magazine compiled a list of the 100 fastest-growing U.S. business format franchises. The top 25 are shown in Table 4–2. *Venture* contacted 711 companies, but only 372 met its standards, which were that franchisors must:

Founded/ began franchising	Franchise fee ($)	Other start-up costs ($)	Real Estate†	Royalty fee	Advertising and other ongoing fees	Term of agreement (yrs.)	Total system company/ franchised units	Rank
1965/1974	$ 7,500	$ 27,900–70,900	L	8%	2.5%	20	10/1,823	1
1960/1967	6,500	78,200–128,000	L	5.5%	3%	10	1,103/3,206	2
1975/1977	1,500–7,600[b]	2,300–17,300	N	$50–$125/mo	None	5	0/2,867	3
1959/1962	15,000/20,000[b]	115,500–766,400	L.B.	5%	Up to 2%	10/20	441/1,352	4
1982/1982	3,800–14,000[b]	400–1,500	N	10%	None	10	9/973	5
1972/1985	2,900	5,600–6,900	N	6%	None	5	0/619	6
1981/1982	14,000/20,000[b]	78,000–259,500	L.B.C.	4%	3%	10	77/750	7
1969/1974	6,500–14,000[b]	1,800–11,000	N	10%	None	20	14/1,206	8
1979/1986	8,000–22,000[b]	14,900–28,300	N	5%	None	15	195/490	9
1955/1955	22,500	355,500–430,500	L	12%	None	20	2,399/7,512	10
1929/1948	13,600	13,400–18,400	N	10%	1%	5	0/3,737	11
1973/1973	35,000	90,800–141,200	L.C.	6%	3%	20	71/752	12
1969/1970	6,900–18,900[b]	6,300–28,700	N	Varies	2%	10	0/660	13
1973/1976	12,500–15,000	16,500–61,900	L.B.C	Varies	$50–$100/ agent/mo.	5	0/1,248	14
1978/1978	9,500–40,000[d]	0	C	0.5%–6%	1.25%–2.2%	3	3/1,337	15
1969/1972	30,000	254,500–860,000	L.B.C.	4%	2%	20	1,222/2,587	16
1978/1981	995/1,295[b]	0	N	25¢ or 50¢/pkg.	None	Indefinite	0/1,060	17
1960/1961	15,000	443,200–999,700	L.B.C.	4%	$245/mo.	20	963/1,985	18
1974/1976	25,000	33,700–95,500	L.B.C.	$140/wk.	$65/wk.	10	2/1,269	19
1980/1980	4,500–20,000	36,800–70,700	L.B.C.	5%	2%	10	4/568	20
1972/1983	500	1,200–1,900	L.B.C.	20%	None	5	0/3,784	21
1970/1972	29,000[f]	44,800–7,205,200	B.C.	6.5%	Varies	20	70/523	22
1964/1965	37,500	98,000–550,000	L.B.C.	4%	1.2%	20	197/1,654	23
1980/1981	15,000	5,660	N	7%	None	10	6/1,538	24
1971/1976	13,000–56,000	57,900–74,400	L.B.	7%	None	10	139/836	25

† L = Lease, B = Buy, C = Convert, N = None required.

- Offer a complete business format.
- Provide continuing support.
- Have begun franchising before 1987.
- Have at least 50 franchised units operating.
- Provide *Venture* with a disclosure document registered with the Federal Trade Commission.

The top 100 were then ranked by the average franchised unit growth in the United States in the past two years. Notice that Subway, Domino's Pizza, Chem-Dry, and Little Caesar's Pizza led the list.

WHY FRANCHISING IS GROWING IN IMPORTANCE

Before reading further, refresh your memory of how you've been involved with franchises during the past week. Have you or a friend worked at one? If so, which one? Have you shopped at any? Have you used any of their products at home, work, or school? Have any sponsored your favorite TV programs; if so, which ones?

Would your answers to any of these questions have been different a year ago? Five years ago? Ten years ago? How do the answers differ?

Recent Rapid Growth

During the past decade or so, franchising has been one of the fastest-growing areas of American business. From 1969 to 1989, the number of all franchised establishments grew from 384,000 to 516,000, and their sales ballooned from $116 billion to $661 billion (see Figure 4–1). The number of franchisors has also been rising steadily since 1972—as indicated earlier, from about 900 in 1972 to over 2,100 in 1988. This upward trend is expected to continue into the 1990s. Franchising "has become so diverse, it's no longer just a way of doing business, it's become a way of life," said Andrew Kostecka, franchising specialist for the U.S. Department of commerce's International Trade Association.[7]

Product and trademark franchising has tended to dominate the franchise field, but since 1972, while business format franchising has skyrocketed, the number of product and trademark franchises has declined rapidly. For example, over 100,000 service stations have gone out of business since that year. Conversely, business format franchising has accounted for much of the growth of franchising in the United States since 1950.

Causes of Rapid Growth

Essentially, there are four reasons why franchising has become so popular. First, a franchise operation has already identified a consumer need and created a product (either a good or a service) to meet that need—as well as a convenient and economical method of providing that product to customers. For example, in single-parent or dual-career homes, no one wants to spend precious time every night preparing meals. Instead, people head for a fast-food outlet, such as Hardee's. The reluctance to make dental or doctor's appointments weeks in advance—with a good chance of spending hours in the waiting room—has led to franchising of walk-in health care services. Increasing leisure time has resulted in franchising of recreational and exercise activities. In other words, franchises have emerged to cater to many consumer and business needs that were not being satisfied elsewhere.

Second, as Colonel Sanders said in the opening quotation, one of the best ways to succeed in small business is to buy a franchise from an established company, as the failure rate is much lower than for small independent businesses. While the Small Business Administration estimates that 25 to 33 percent of independent small firms fail in the first two years, the failure rate for first-year franchisees is only about 5 percent.[8]

A third reason for franchising's popularity is that, unlike independent owners of small firms who become ensnared in unfamiliar procedures and paperwork, franchisees have the support of established management, bookkeeping, marketing, operations, and control systems. And these systems give franchisees the benefit of that vast store of business experience without having to experience it for themselves. Yet, to a limited extent, you can still maintain your independence.

A final reason for franchising popularity is that many franchisors are establishing networks of subfranchisors to sell units within given territories—a state, a county, or a city. **Subfranchising** is sometimes referred to as **master franchising.** The subfranchisors do more than sell franchises. They can assist new franchisees in picking the site for a new unit, selecting the contractor to build it, designing the facility, training the employees, and finding an advertising agency to handle promotions. In addition to being a cheaper way to expand, subfranchising is considered by many fanchisors to be a more effective means of handling growth than delegating the task to their staff.

For the privilege of developing an exclusive region, subfranchisors pay substantial amounts—$150,000 to $1.5 million to one franchisor. In return, subfranchisors keep the lion's share—85 percent in the same example—of the franchise fee and royalties from units.[9]

A major drawback to franchising is the voluminous paperwork related to providing **disclosure documents** to potential franchisees. These statements, required by the Federal Trade Commission (FTC), provide background and financial position information about the franchisor and the franchise offering. Some opponents of subfranchising also believe that franchisors risk losing ultimate control over their systems. Furthermore, they believe that it can lead to quality problems at the unit level and to the collapse of the franchise's support network.

HOW TO TELL IF A FRANCHISE IS RIGHT FOR YOU

As you can see, opportunities abound in franchising today; it is an easy and relatively safe way of becoming an entrepreneur. However, there is still a need for intensive study and evaluation before entering into the franchise agreement. When you buy a franchise, you're relying not only on your own business expertise and experience but also on the franchisor's business ideas, skills, capital, and ethics.

Two highly publicized failures of the 1970s illustrate this point. Minnie Pearl Chicken failed because the franchisor lacked adequate capital to service the 1,840 franchisees, and Wild Bill Hamburgers was a "franchising fraud that fleeced millions of dollars from more than 100 investors."[10]

In buying a franchise, is there any way to protect yourself against such a disaster? While nothing is guaranteed to keep you from making a mistake, the risks are reduced if the actions discussed in this section are taken. See Figure 4–4 for further suggestions.[11]

Case I–2, Our Hero Restaurant (A), is an example of how one couple entered franchising. After writing to several franchisors, they saw an ad for new franchisees on napkins in an Our Hero restaurant. They answered the ad, found out a franchise was available in their area, and bought it.

Look at the Opportunities

In investigating whether a franchise is the way you want to go, first learn which ones are growing the fastest, in order to get in on growth possibilities. One way you can do this is to study *Entrepreneur* magazine's annual listing of the best performers, including various aspects of operations, such as sales, profits, and number of units.

Another excellent source of information on franchising possibilities is the U.S. Commerce Department's *Franchise Opportunities Handbook*, published annually.[12] Finally, the local Small Business Administration office or SCORE chapter, schools with small business development centers, chambers of commerce, and libraries can provide examples of franchising opportunities.

See What the Franchise Can Do for You

At this point, you should see what the franchise can do for you that you cannot do for yourself. We will go into greater detail about this in Chapter 5, but at this point you should decide whether you're willing to give up some of your independence by buying a franchise. It was emphasized in Chapter 2 that the desire for independence is one of the goals of small businesspeople. Whereas owners of regular small businesses may cherish their freedom to operate as they choose, many franchisees may be glad to receive the management training and assistance provided by the franchisor and be willing to abide by the provisions of the franchise contract regarding policies and operations.

For new small business owners with little business experience, the assistance they can get from the franchisor justifies some sacrifice of their independence, as shown in the Our Hero Restaurant case (Case I–2). When

Figure 4–4   How to Check Out a Franchise

The franchise
1. Does your lawyer approve of the franchise contract being considered?
2. Does the franchise call upon you to take any steps that your lawyer considers unwise or illegal?
3. Does the franchise agreement provide you an exclusive territory for the length of the franchise, or can the franchisor sell a second or third franchise in the territory?
4. Is the franchisor connected in any way with any other franchise handling similar merchandise or services?
5. If the answer to Question 4 is yes, what is your protection against the second franchisor?
6. Under what circumstances and at what cost can you terminate the franchise contract if you decide to cancel it?
7. If you sell your franchise, will you be compensated for goodwill?

The franchisor
8. How many years has the franchisor been operating?
9. Has it a reputation among local franchisees for honesty and fair dealing?
10. Has the franchisor shown you any certified figures indicating net profit of one or more franchisees that you have personally checked?
11. Will the franchisor assist with:
    a. A management training program?   d. Capital?
    b. An employee training program?   e. Credit?
    c. A public relations program?   f. Merchandising ideas?
12. Will the franchisor help find a good location for the new business?
13. Is the franchisor adequately financed to implement its stated plan of financial assistance and expansion?
14. Does the franchisor have an experienced management team trained in depth?
15. Exactly what can the franchisor do for you that you can't do for yourself?
16. Has the franchisor investigated you carefully enough to be sure of your qualifications?
17. Does your state have a law regulating the sales of franchises, and has the franchisor complied with that law?

The franchisee
18. How much equity capital will you need to purchase the franchise and operate it until it reaches the break-even point? Where are you going to obtain it?
19. Are you prepared to give up some independence in order to secure the advantages offered by the franchise?
20. Do you really believe you have the qualifications to succeed as a franchisee?
21. Are you ready to spend much or all of your remaining business life with this franchise company?

The market
22. Have you determined that an adequate market exists in your territory for the good or service at the prices you will have to charge for it?
23. Is the population in the territory expected to increase, remain the same, or decrease over the next five years?
24. Will the good or service be in greater, about the same, or less demand five years from now than it is today?
25. What is the competition in the territory for the good or service:
    a. From nonfranchised firms?
    b. From franchised firms?

Source: Franchising Opportunities Handbook (Washington, D.C.: U.S. Department of Commerce, January 1988), pp. xxxiii–xxxiv.

you buy a franchise, you'll pay up front to buy a building or rent space, renovate a store or office, lease or buy equipment and buy inventory, and provide other facilities. Then you'll pay the franchisor a one-time franchise fee and a monthly royalty fee (Table 4–2 shows the franchisee fee, other start-up costs, the royalty fee, and advertising or other ongoing fees for the leading franchises). For these fees and costs—ranging from around 3 to 7 percent—you can expect the kind of help shown in Figure 4–5. Those considering buying a franchise should ask themselves if they are willing to pay these fees, accept the franchisor's regulations, and give up a certain amount of their independence. Then, some franchisors even help potential franchisees make the self-evaluation as to whether they are willing to make the personal sacrifices, such as working long hours and putting in the hard work needed to succeed in the endeavor.

See the previously mentioned case, Our Hero Restaurant (A), for an example of the extensive assistance provided by a franchisor. According to Barbara and Steve Chappell, the franchisor provided a list of needed items "right down to Scotch tape." Also, the franchisor's ability to buy in bulk reduced the cost to the Chappells of some fixtures to 65 percent of retail and saved them thousands of dollars.

Investigate the Franchise

Investigating the franchisor and the franchise business as thoroughly as possible is very important. First, be sure to look at more than one franchise and investigate other, similar franchises in the same line of business. Review the brief descriptions of franchises in the *Franchise Opportunities Handbook*, published by the U.S. Department of Commerce and found in the government documents section of libraries. Call or write to several franchisors to see what benefits each offers that may not be available from other franchisors.

Dennis L. Foster, a California franchise consultant, is the author of *Rating Guide to Franchises*. This new reference helps evaluate franchises as to various aspects of performance. For example, it rates franchises on their training and management programs, advertising effectiveness, litigation record, franchise agreements, and satisfaction of current franchisees. Each of these elements is rated from one (the lowest) to four (the highest) stars. As it rates some of the most popular U.S. franchise businesses, from fast-food restaurants to hotels, it is an excellent source of information for potential franchisees.[13]

"I've always wanted to go into business by myself," said Susan McKay, currently the franchise owner of the first Handle With Care Packaging Store in Florida. She took the plunge into business ownership after doing a lot of research, planning, and "soul searching." She drew her list of possible franchises from ads in the

---

Figure 4–5   What a Franchise Can Do for You

The kind of help you can expect from a franchiser:

Site selection
  Varies by franchise, but the more help you get, the better. ''We do it all: find locations, demographic analysis, feasibility studies,'' says John Barry, vice president–franchise sales at the 700-unit West Coast Video based in Philadelphia.
In-store design plans
  This is a must to maintain uniform identity among franchisees. Look for companies that supply architectural drawings. (You'll pay renovation or construction costs.)
Lease negotiations
  A franchiser should help negotiate rent. Some, like Koenig Art Emporium of Milford, Conn., lease so much space in malls nationwide that ''we can cut a far better deal with the landlord,'' says President Robert Koenig.
Financial help
  Only 16 percent of franchisers will lend you money to buy their stores, the Commerce Department says, but many have contacts with lenders. Look for one that can help arrange financing.
Training
  You need more than an operations manual. You need training courses at company headquarters or regional training centers. Classes should cover store management, bookkeeping, employee training and product marketing. Get periodic updates.
Field support
  Don't let the franchiser take the money and run. Be sure company representatives will visit your store often. Some check stores monthly.
Advertising and marketing
  Mature chains typically collect a percentage of revenues, usually 2 percent, for a nationwide ad fund. Often new franchises design advertising materials but don't pay for national ad campaigns. In both cases, you usually have to pay for local ads.
Discounts on products and equipment
  If you require supplies, some franchisers operate distribution facilities. Be sure to ask whether the franchiser profits from what it sells you. You want group buying; it's less expensive. For instance, Koenig's 110 art supply stores have automatic inventory systems. Each week, franchisees receive merchandise free of freight charges from a central warehouse. Items are marked up to cover handling costs.
Research and development
  Expect constant upgrading of products and services. For instance, the 600-unit Ziebart Corp. of Troy, Mich., ($100 million in 1988 revenues) spends $500,000 a year on rustproofing research. Latest product: a super-rust protection.
Toll-free hot lines
  You need to be able to contact your parent company quickly. ''That's why they're buying into a franchise: for us to be there to answer questions,'' says Ellen K. Folks, president of Guarantee Girls, a housecleaning service based in Baton Rouge, La. Folks once owned a franchised store of a now-bankrupt firm. ''We only heard from them if we owed money,'' she says. ''I'm trying to give my franchisees what we never got.''

Source: Patrick J. Boroian, president of Francorp. Inc., as quoted in Carol Steinberg, ''What You'll Get for Franchise Fee,'' *USA Today,* May 8, 1989, p. 8E. Copyright 1989, USA TODAY. Excerpted with permission.

local paper. Also, as part of her research, she requested disclosure documents, then talked with current franchise owners. She warns, "If you have any questions at all, then have someone familiar with franchising look at it. Do all your research first!"[14]

Study the Franchise Offering Circular

A disclosure statement or prospectus of the franchise should be obtained and studied carefully. The Federal Trade Commission requires that franchisors give prospective franchisees a formal agreement and a franchise-offering circular at their first meeting. Circulars should contain at least the information listed in Figure 4–6. They provide background on the franchisor and its financial position, the financial requirements for a franchisee, and the restrictions, protections, and estimated earnings of the franchise.

Check with Existing Franchisees

Contact several of the franchise owners listed in the disclosure statement and ask them about their franchising experiences, as Susan McKay did. Seek those who have been in the business for at least one year and preferably for several years. They should be able to give the best advice about what to expect in the first year of operation—typically the period during which the success or failure of a new franchise is determined.

Obtain Professional Advice

A prospective franchise owner should obtain independent professional assistance in reviewing and evaluating any franchise being considered. The

---

Figure 4–6   Information Usually Included in a Franchise-Offering Circular

- The nature of the franchise.
- The business experience of the persons affiliated with the franchisor.
- Lawsuits involving the franchisor, its officers, directors, and management.
- Past or present bankruptcy filings involving the franchise or its officers.
- The franchise fee, initial payments, investment capital needed, and other fees.
- Any financial assistance available through the franchisor.
- Use of trademarks, trade names, logotypes, patents, copyrights, etc.
- Restrictions on goods and services that can be sold by the franchisee.
- Renewal, termination, repurchase, and modification agreements.
- Territorial protections granted to the franchisee.
- The extent to which a franchisee must participate in the franchise's operations.
- Conditions under which a franchise can be sold, repurchased or transferred to a third party.
- Names of past and present franchisees.
- Financial statements.
- Estimated or projected franchise earnings.

Source: Constance Mitchell, "Franchisees Shielded from Fraud," *USA Today,* September 13, 1985, p. 5B. Copyright 1985, USA TODAY. Reprinted with permission.

financial statements will reveal to a professional accountant, banker, or financial analyst whether the franchise company's financial condition is sound or there is a risk that it will not be able to meet its financial and other obligations. It is also important to check to see whether you will be required to stock items that you don't need or can't sell, or if the contract can be terminated for insufficient reason.

See Case I–4, Cironi's Sewing Center Loses a Franchise, for an example of a franchisor who canceled a contract because the franchisee refused to carry an unneeded item. The franchisor was also selling a major product to a competing dealer at a lower price.

Legal advice is unquestionably the most important professional assistance necessary before investing in a franchise. A lawyer can advise you fully about your legal rights and obligations in relation to the franchise agreement. Also, a lawyer may be able to suggest important changes in the contract that will provide improved protection for your interest. A lawyer will be aware of any requirements of state and local law that may affect the franchise and can assist with its taxation and personal liability aspects. According to one authority, finding a competent and compatible business attorney early in the game can save time, money, and—sometimes—sanity.[15]

Know Your Legal Rights

The International Franchise Association, the only U.S. international trade association serving franchisors in more than 50 countries, has a code of ethics that covers a franchisor's obligations to its franchisees. Each member company pledges that it will comply with all applicable laws and that its disclosure statements will be complete, accurate, and not misleading. Furthermore, it pledges that all matters material to its franchise will be contained in written agreements and it will accept only those franchisees who appear to possess the qualifications needed to conduct the franchise successfully. Fairness shall characterize all dealings between a member company and its franchisees, and it will not engage in a pyramid system of distribution, wherein a buyer's future compensation depends primarily on recruitment of new participants rather than on the sale of goods or services. This code is a fair one for both parties. If it is adhered to by franchisors, failures should be minimized and profits enhanced.

In considering the franchisee's rights, what happens if the franchisor attempts to buy back the franchise when it becomes very profitable? Should the franchisee be required to sell?

A distributor of Häagen-Dazs ice cream in San Diego said that he was forced to sell his franchise to the franchisor at a price he considered unfair. He was allegedly told that the distributor had the right to take over his major customers, whether he sold or not. Häagen-Dazs also terminated a long-term San Francisco area distributor who began distributing two competing local brands of superpremium ice cream.[16]

THE FUTURE OF FRANCHISING

The future of franchising is indeed bright. The number and variety of franchises in the United States is expected to continue to grow, probably at an increasing rate. As indicated earlier, franchises now account for over one-third of all retail trade, and the Commerce Department expects this figure to increase to one-half by the year 2000. Thus, we are now truly in a franchise revolution—or at least a franchise explosion.

Expected Areas of Growth

Some industries especially lend themselves to franchising and thus provide the best future opportunities. These are fast foods; motels; automotive parts, accessories, and servicing; convenience markets; and electronics. Not all franchises in these categories are of a quality worthy of selection, nor are they the only ones worthy of consideration; but they do appear to be the growth areas.

Fast Foods

The success of fast-food franchises is related to many factors. They include the demographic environment evidenced by the high percentage of young adults in the population; the large number of singles, both male and female; and the increasing percentages of homemakers working outside the home. Other factors that seem to have had a positive influence on success are product appeal to the palate of a significant segment of the market, fast service, a sanitary environment, and a building and sign that are easily recognizable.

At 26, Vince Millard, a seven-year, multi-unit Sonic Drive-In franchisee, expects to be a millionaire before he is 30 years old. He's come a long way since, as a 19-year-old, he was willing to make some sacrifices by investing in his first Sonic Drive-In in Lawrence, Kansas. However, he says, "It was a pretty proven deal. You did not have to make a big cash outlay, and the return on the money was great." As he had only a few dollars, he needed some partners to obtain the $500,000 needed to start the business. He also sold his interest in his family's hog farm to make his Sonic investment possible.

Millard checked into other industries and other fast-food franchises, and his research made him decide on the fast-food industry—for its greater return—and on Sonic, which was best for him personally. He liked Sonic's '50s-style drive-in. It is now ranked 12th among American fast-food restaurant chains. Vince's franchise has been phenomenally successful for him.[17]

Motels

During the past four decades, the motel industry has had phenomenal growth. The advent of the interstate highway system in 1956 and the affluence and mobility of the American public created a market for quality motels. Almost every interstate highway interchange became a potential motel site. We have seen the industry grow from Mom-and-Pop units (with an often questionable image) to an industry dominated by large corporate complexes. These corporations have company-owned motels and also a franchise division operating motels under the company trade name with cooperative participation by individual owners. Best Western is probably the largest—and also one of the best—such franchisors.

Automotive Parts, Accessories, and Servicing

Automotive franchises have been around for some time. The franchises have historically been retail outlets for parts and accessories. Some of the units have been affiliated with nationally known tire manufacturers. General Tire is a good example of these arrangements. A comparatively recent entry into the automotive franchise field is the specialty service shop. Some examples are those specializing in transmission repairs and parts, such as AAMCO Automatic Transmissions; those specializing in muffler and shock absorber repairs and parts, such as Midas International; shops providing technical assistance and specialized parts for "customizing" vans; and diagnostic centers with sophisticated computerized electronic equipment.

In recent years, there has been a significant growth in the wholesale-retail franchise auto parts outlets. Also, the number of automotive tune-up franchises, such as Precision Tune, has been growing as gasoline stations shift from full service to self-service. Many of the franchises use former service stations.

Convenience Markets

While the term *convenience market* is usually associated with food outlets, it may in fact cover other types of specialty shops. Some examples of convenience market franchises are Jitney-Jungle, the Bread Basket, T-Shirts Plus, and Health Mart.

Electronics

With the rapid growth in electronic fields such as music, video, TV, and computers, franchising has naturally followed. Radio Shack has long been a franchise, and its computers are standard equipment for school and business applications. Some other growing franchises are Computerland, Entré Computer Centers, and Software City. (See the Computer Update for one of the latest developments in the franchising of computer applications.)

International Franchising

A lucrative opportunity for franchising is developing outside the United States. The success achieved by some of the franchises in America has

Figure 4–7   International Franchising, 1986

Franchising companies: 354
Number of franchising outlets: 31,626

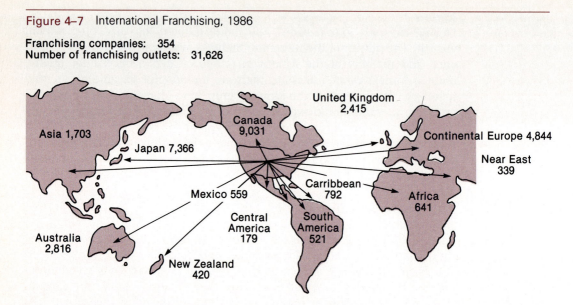

Source: U.S. Department of Commerce, Bureau of Industrial Economics, *Franchising in the Economy, 1986–88* (Washington, D.C.: U.S. Government Printing Office), p. 8.

resulted in international interest and opportunity. From 1971 to 1986, the number of U.S. franchisors operating internationally almost doubled, from 156 to 354, and the number of foreign outlets increased over ninefold, from 3,365 to 31,626. Of these franchisors, 30 provide business aids and services, and 27 have established restaurants.[18] Figure 4–7 shows the breakdown of the number of franchising outlets in various parts of the world. As seen in the table, Canada continues to be the most popular franchise market.

Fast-food franchises have been particularly successful abroad. Because the fast-food industry is not as well developed in other countries, U.S. franchises have the opportunity to be leaders in many markets.

Can you imagine capitalistic franchises flourishing in a country whose very name proclaims socialism? The Soviet Union has them, including McDonald's and Pizza Hut—as well as Pepsi bottlers.[19] Pepsi is advertising—in Russian—on Soviet TV.[20]

Minority Ownership of Franchises

Minority ownership of franchises has been increasing. The Commerce Department reported that, of 2,177 known U.S. franchisors, 572 reported 10,142 units owned by minority businesspersons. It was also estimated that minori-

---

CAREERS USA, INC.: TAKING THE HIGH-TECH ROAD

"We have to meet our clients' urgent needs if we expect to stay ahead in today's labor market," says Marylin J. Ounjian, president and CEO of Careers USA, Inc., a temporary and permanent placement franchise with 20 locations. "Employers keep work forces lean and add temporary employees when there is a sudden, unexpected surge in business. Our franchisees have to fill positions within hours of the need or risk losing the assignment to another company. The conventional method of manually thumbing through files was simply too slow for today's highly competitive business world."

To Ounjian, the logical solution was computerization. So Careers USA invested heavily in "SAM" (for Search, Administrative, and Management), an advanced computer system, to replace the old manual system. A typical example of the type of problem SAM can handle would be a request for a bilingual word processor who knows Word Perfect and medical terminology. SAM quickly seeks out and searches for people with those skills and then displays a listing of qualified temps with needed information for a customer. For its franchisees, SAM's search capabilities often spell the difference between business lost and business gained.

Source: "Taking the High-Tech Road," *Franchising World,* June 1989, p. 22.

---

ties owned 10,000 gasoline service stations and 236 automobile and truck dealerships.[21]

The primary agency that implements federal policies benefiting minority entrepreneurship is the Minority Business Development Agency (MBDA). Among its many other activities, it operates the **Minority Vendor Profile System,** a computerized data base listing some 30,000 minority firms. This system is designed to match minority entrepreneurs with available marketing opportunities.[22]

TURNING YOUR DREAM INTO A REALITY

You've been exposed to much information to help you decide whether or not you want to go into franchising. You've also been told how to investigate whether a franchise is right for you or not. Now, Figure 4–8 provides a step-by-step review of what is required to become a franchise owner. It also provides an estimate of the time required for each of the steps needed to become a franchisee. It should be pointed out that not all of these steps are required, nor are the time spans standard. This information is, however, a good generalization of the activities required by many franchisors and the time it takes to do each of them. It is the best model with which we are currently familiar.

Figure 4–8   What's Needed to Become a Franchise Owner

Step-by-step review of what needs to be done and how long it will take to turn the dream of owning your own business into the reality of opening day.

Phase	1 Decide to become a franchisee	2 Make decision and invest $_____	3 Real estate	4 Construction	5 Equipment and inventory
Action items	Investigate and select your franchise	Decide, buy, sign contract; pay $_____	Look for proper store site: a. Storefront type b. Build to specs, freestanding	Conform to franchise contract: a. Leasehold improvements b. Construct building per drawings	Order and install all equipment; order opening inventory—goods
Time span	3 months to 2 years	3 months	2 to 12 months	3 to 11 months	1 to 3 months

Phase	6 Hiring	7 Training	8 Pre-opening final check	9 Opening and operations	10 Contract term
Action items	Hire manager or assistant manager; hire crew; fill out state and federal forms	Get your training in franchisor's school; learn procedures and methods	Construction; punch list; permits; bank accounts; marketing plan; inventory	First soft opening; later grand opening ■ Employee daily work schedule ■ Daily sales reports ■ Cash register tapes, money ■ Deposit cash in bank nightly ■ Insure accuracy Pay royalty and advertising fees	Work and manage your own franchise
Time span	2 to 6 weeks	2 weeks to 2 months	1 day to 2 weeks	Select a Friday, Saturday, or Sunday	

Source: Franchising World, March/April 1989, p. 18.

WHAT YOU SHOULD HAVE LEARNED

1. Although you may not be aware that many familiar businesses are franchise outlets, franchising is increasingly popular and prevalent. Sales nearly doubled in the last decade, and the number of

establishments is also increasing. Almost any kind of business can be franchised, but franchising is strongest in retailing, accounting for 34 percent of retail sales in 1988 and 87 percent of all franchising receipts.

2. Franchising is a marketing system based on a legal arrangement that permits one party—the franchisee—to conduct business as an individual owner while abiding by the terms and conditions set by the second party—the franchisor. Under a franchise agreement, the franchisee contracts with the franchisor to pay a specified amount of money for the use of the franchisor's name, trademark, and/or other distinctive elements.

3. The two franchising systems in common use are (*a*) product and trademark franchising and (*b*) business format franchising. In product and trademark franchising, franchisees acquire the right to sell the franchisor's product and use its trademark, but are relatively free to design their own physical plant and operating methods. The franchised product may be the only product sold or only a part of the franchisee's business.

    In business format franchising, virtually every aspect of the franchisee's business is determined by the franchisor. For example, in fast-food restaurants, all food items and related goods are standardized and must be purchased from designated suppliers. Usually, management policies, accounting methods, reporting forms, designs, and furnishings are also prescribed by business format franchisors.

4. While product and trademark franchising is declining, business format franchising is growing rapidly in both numbers and importance. The variety of franchisors and the number of franchisees have risen steadily, so that franchises now account for over a third of all retail sales. This figure is expected to grow to 50 percent by the end of this decade.

5. Franchising is an ideal way for many people to enter business. They start with a known and proven product, tested operating methods, and much less chance of failure than in an independent business. If they have little business experience, they can rely on the experience and expertise of the franchisor to supply established management, bookkeeping, marketing, operating, control, and other systems. But prospective franchisees should carefully research the industry and the particular franchise in order to answer the question: "Is the assistance provided by the franchisor worth the required sacrifice of independence?"

    When the search has been narrowed to a particular franchisor, the prospective franchisee should study the franchise offering circular, check with existing franchisees, and obtain professional advice in order to understand his or her rights and obligations and the requirements of state or local laws. Franchisors who belong to the International Franchise Association subscribe to a code of ethics that provides protection to their franchisees.

6. The future of franchising looks good, especially for fast foods; motels; automotive parts, accessories, and servicing; convenience markets; and electronics. International franchising is one of the fastest-growing areas of new businesses. Minority ownership of franchises is also growing, and special efforts are being made to encourage minority franchising.

7. Information was presented to show the step-by-step process needed to turn your dream into a reality, along with the time span for each of the steps involved.

KEY TERMS

franchising, *85*

franchise, *85*

franchisee, *85*

franchisor, *85*

product and trademark
   franchising, *86*

business format franchising, *86*

subfranchising *or* master
   franchising, *91*

disclosure documents, *91*

Minority Vendor Profile
   System, *101*

QUESTIONS FOR DISCUSSION

1. What distingishes a franchise from an independent small business?

2. *(a)* What are the two most important forms of franchising? *(b)* Describe each.

3. Describe why franchising is growing so fast.

4. What makes franchising an attractive way to get into business?

5. How do you investigate the desirability of a franchise?

6. How can you decide whether a franchise is right for you? (Refer to Chapter 5 also.)

7. What are some expected areas of growth for franchising?

8. Why is franchising growing internationally?

9. What does Figure 4–8 tell you about the time required to start a franchise?

SUGGESTED READINGS

Brown, Buck. "Believing They Can Do Better, Franchisees Are Seizing the Reins of Their Companies." *The Wall Street Journal,* November 29, 1988, p. B1.

————. "Franchisers Now Offer Direct Financial Aid." *The Wall Street Journal,* February 6, 1989, p. B1.

Connelly, Mike. "U.S. Franchising Grows Attractive to Foreign Firms." *The Wall Street Journal*, December 22, 1988, p. B2.

"Franchise to the Rescue." *Franchising World*, February 1989, p. 12ff.

"Franchise Training Replaces School of Hard Knocks." *Franchising World*, April 1989, p. 30.

"Handicapped Sought as Firm's Franchisees." *The Wall Street Journal*, April 3, 1989, p. B1.

Kotite, Erika. "Building a Successful Franchise." *Entrepreneur*, February 1989, pp. 158ff.

Marsh, Barbara. "More Firms Target Women as Prospective Franchisees." *The Wall Street Journal*, April 19, 1989, p. B2.

Wells, Ken. "Fast-Food Industry Increases Tests of Sales on Credit." *The Wall Street Journal*, November 30, 1988, p. B1.

Whittemore, Meg. "Franchising Draw Minorities." *Nation's Business*, April 1989, p. 68.

Zinn, Laura, "Want to Buy a Franchise? Look Before You Leap." *Business Week*, May 23, 1988, pp. 186–88.

ENDNOTES

1. Carol Steinberg, "Franchise Boom Still in High Gear," *USA Today*, May 8, 1989, p. 8E.
2. U.S. Department of Commerce, *Franchising in the Economy, 1986–88* (Washington, D.C.: U.S. Government Printing Office), pp. 2 and 15.
3. *The 1989 Franchise Annual*, (Lewiston, N.Y.: Franchise News, Inc., 1989), p. H2.
4. Amal Nag, "Auto Dealers Say They're Bypassed in Sales to Fleet Buyers and Move to Halt Practice," *The Wall Street Journal*, June 21, 1983, p. 37.
5. Correspondence with Best Western Motels.
6. *Franchising in the Economy, 1986–88*, p. 2.
7. Constance Mitchell, "Franchising Fever Spreads," *USA Today*, September 13, 1985, p. 4B.
8. Barbara Marsh, "Franchisees Frolic but Focus on Deals at Annual Meeting," *The Wall Street Journal*, February 9, 1989, p. B2.
9. Ralph Raffio, "Double-Decker Franchising," *Venture*, November 1986, pp. 60–62, 64.
10. Constance Mitchell, "Franchisees Shielded from Fraud," *USA Today*, September 13, 1985, p. 5B.
11. See also Meg Whittemore, "Narrowing the Field," *Nation's Business*, October 1989, pp. 34–36; and "Finding the Right to Franchise," *Nation's Business*, February 1988, pp. 53–54, for further helpful advice.
12. The 1988 edition cost $16 and was stock number 003–009–00528–1, from the U.S. Government Printing Office, Washington, DC 20402–9325, (202) 783–3238.
13. Dennis L. Foster, *The Rating Guide to Franchises* (New York: Facts On File Publications, 1988).
14. "So You Want to Make It on Your Own," *Franchising World*, April 1989, pp. 10–15.
15. "You and Your Business Lawyer," *Franchising World*, April 1989, p. 20.
16. Sanford L. Jacobs, "Häagen-Dazs Distributors Find Big Profits, but Little Security," *The Wall Street Journal*, November 18, 1985, p. 33.
17. "So You Want to Make It on Your Own," pp. 10–11.
18. *Franchising in the Economy, 1986–88*, p. 8.
19. Monroe W. Karmin, "Earning a Fast Ruble," *U.S. News & World Report*, November 4, 1986, pp. 36–37.
20. Richard W. Stevenson, "Pepsi to Show Ad in Russian," *New York Times*, January 20, 1989, p. C5.
21. *Franchising in the Economy, 1986–88*, pp. 10–11.
22. Ibid., p. xxxv.

CASE I–1
SUE THINKS OF GOING INTO BUSINESS—CLEANDRUM, INC. (A)

CASE I–2
OUR HERO RESTAURANT (A)

CASE I–3
GLAMMOURRAMMER BEAUTY SALON

CASE I–4
CIRONI'S SEWING CENTER LOSES A FRANCHISE

CASE I–5
SHAFFER'S DRIVE INNS

CASE I–6
WILSON'S USED CARS

CASE I–1

SUE THINKS OF GOING INTO BUSINESS— CLEANDRUM, INC. (A)

Sue Ley had been a truck driver for a local oil company for about four years. During the previous nine years, she had served as a waitress and later worked as a forklift truck operator in the same company. In a recent interview, she said, "I was getting fed up with this type of work. I like working with people and thought I'd like to get into selling. One day a friend in personnel suggested that I get into marketing. When I indicated interest, she called my attention to the company's education program, which pays tuition for employees taking college courses. So I applied for it and was accepted."

Sue, whom the interviewers found to be a woman of above-average intelligence, personality, and drive, enrolled in the marketing program at the local university. She completed her marketing course work and graduated in three years with a business administration degree. She had continued driving the truck while working on her degree.

---

* The cases in this book are *actual situations* involving *real people* in *real organizations*, although the names of some of them have been disguised. The cases are designed to sharpen your analytical and reasoning ability, not to illustrate correct or incorrect handling of administrative problems. Some of these cases were written several years ago, but we have retained them because they remain excellent examples of what is involved in managing a contemporary small business.

When she approached her employer about the possibility of transferring to the marketing department, she was told that it would be "four or five years" before there would be an opening for her.

A short time after that, Sue's uncle suggested that she go into business for herself. He suggested that she start an oil drum cleaning business. The uncle, who had taken over Sue's grandfather's steel oil drum cleaning business about 200 miles away, advised her that she could make around $100,000 per year ($300,000 by the third year) if she started and ran a business of this sort. He offered to help her form a business and get it started.

Sue, who had been married and had two grown children, said, "I could not see any future with the oil company in marketing, and I did not want to drive trucks the rest of my life. I had saved $25,000 that I could put into the business. Why not?"

Questions for Discussion

1. What do you see as Sue's alternatives?
2. What are Sue's qualifications for going into business for herself?
3. What are Sue's deficiencies?
4. What do you think of the profit predictions of Sue's uncle?
5. What research do you recommend for Sue, and where can she find the needed material?
6. What do you recommend that Sue do?

Source: Prepared by William M. Spain, Service Corps of Retired Executives (SCORE), and Charles R. Scott, University of Alabama.

CASE I–2

OUR HERO RESTAURANT (A)

The last couple to leave the Christmas party held by Professor Brittain and his wife for the fall M.B.A. class in business policy were the Chappells. As they sat in the Brittains' living room, Steven Chappell said, "I don't know whether you ever eat hero sandwiches, but Barbara and I own the Our Hero Restaurant just off the campus."

An interesting conversation ensued during which both Barbara and Steve Chappell talked frankly about their joint effort to make a success of their fast-food venture. Although the general account of the start-up and operation of the Chappells' Our Hero franchise fascinated the Brittains, they were truly amazed to learn that Steve and Barbara were at that very time giving strong consideration to another location almost 700 miles away.

Steven Chappell was 25 years old when he and his wife Barbara opened the Our Hero Restaurant adjacent to the campus where they had been undergraduate students. He had been working as a research engineer on environmental projects for the state since graduating from college with an engineering degree over three years earlier. Barbara Chappell, a liberal arts graduate, was also employed by the state as a claims investigator in the welfare department. Married nearly four years, they had no children and still lived near the campus of New England University, the major public institution in the state. On a part-time basis, Steven Chappell had been pursuing an M.B.A. degree in the university's night courses and expected to receive his degree in the spring.

Prior to opening the restaurant, Steven Chappell had become increasingly dissatisfied with his state job. "Although the work was rewarding, advancement was sorely lacking with the state. Beyond the lack of room for growth, there didn't seem to be any difference in the rewards for doers and 'goof-offs.' Consequently, I had been keeping my eyes open for almost any kind of business opportunity that wouldn't require a large amount of capitalization."

Believing that the reward system was structured so that those who take a chance are repaid, the Chappells had sacrificed buying a house in order to develop a good financial position that would allow them to invest their savings in the right business. They hoped to start some part-time enterprise while they were still working.

With the idea in mind that they could find a small, shop-type business that would not require a 40-hour week—for example, a bookstore or smoke shop—they began writing to franchisors of such outlets. As luck would have it, on a visit to Steve Chappell's hometown (about 100 miles away upstate) they happened into what appeared to be a very successful Our Hero franchise. On the restaurant's napkins was an ad for the franchises, so Steve wrote to the company.

The franchisor, the Our Hero Company, was a New Jersey firm that had been in business for about 10 years, beginning with 12 company-owned stores that sold a unique sandwich unlike the hamburgers, filets of fish, and hot dogs sold by most fast-food chains at that time. In 10 years, the chain had grown to 120 outlets, all but 17 of them franchised.

The Chappells' correspondence with the Our Hero firm revealed that a franchise was available for the NEU area. Typical of the financial arrangement then current, a one-time franchise fee of $1,000 would be required. Upon examination, the feasibility of the venture seemed sound from all aspects to the Chappells, and in midyear they concluded an agreement to open a store of their own in Waretown, the site of NEU. With about $20,000 in savings accumulated from their four years of work, they hoped to have sufficient funds for all their initial needs.

Although still working full time at their state jobs, the Chappells spent as much time as possible on their Our Hero. "I drew up my own floor plans at work, began ordering equipment and materials during my lunch hours, and worked on constructing the store on weekends." It was in this planning stage that the franchisor was very helpful, furnishing a "list of all items necessary, right down to Scotch tape."

The Chappells received other benefits of their franchise too. They found that for refrigerators, microwave ovens, and other equipment, the Our Hero chain's ability to buy in bulk reduced their cost to 65 percent of retail and saved thousands of dollars. In addition, it was Steve Chappell's assessment that the Our Hero Company assisted significantly with marketing—first with its "instant advertising" and the familiarity the public had with its name, and second with the formulas it provided for amounts of meat on sandwiches, for markups, and for pricing.

With all of these types of support, Steve Chappell felt there was less risk to him because of the franchisor's experience and help. It meant that "very little trial and error was needed and gave me a better chance to break even; these were the main reasons I chose the Our Hero trademark over Steve Chappell's Grinders."

Questions for Discussion

1. What do you think of the Chappells' decision not to buy a house in order to save money to go into business for themselves?
2. (*a*) Evaluate the method(s) used by the franchisor to attract new franchisees. (*b*) What are some other methods that could be used?
3. (*a*) In view of the $1,000 one-time franchise fee and other start-up expenses, do you think $20,000 of savings is enough? (*b*) Explain.
4. (*a*) Evaluate the services offered by the Our Hero Company to new franchisees. (*b*) Are there other services they could offer? (*c*) Explain.
5. (*a*) Do you think the Chappells made the proper decision? (*b*) Explain.

Source: Adapted from a case prepared by John Clair Thompson, University of Connecticut.

CASE I–3

GLAMMOURRAMMER BEAUTY SALON

Mary Holifield was sitting in her office pondering her situation and the changes that she should make. "I'm very happy with my success so far," she told the casewriter, "but I feel that more could be done to improve the company's operations. I do feel, though, that I've had a lot of good advice from a SCORE member." She then reviewed what she had done since leaving school.

Mary is 1 of 13 children raised by parents with little money. After she left school, she got a job as an inspector in a local chicken processing plant, working on a rotating shift. She also registered at a local technical school, intending to study nursing. But the first demonstration of a baby being born turned her off nursing, and so she graduated with a cosmetology degree.

After working a second job as a lab assistant for two years, she decided to "get into hair" and obtained a job with a beauty salon. She dropped the lab job and continued the inspection job at the poultry plant.

After nine years, she had developed a clientele who asked for her when they came to have their hair done. Still, because the work at the beauty salon became "intolerable" for her, she started looking around for another opportunity.

During these years, Mary had married and had two children. She used the money from the inspection job to support the family and put her wages from the second job into savings. When she had accumulated about $8,000, she put the money into a CD. Mary had stated when she left school that she wanted to make sure her parents were taken care of financially. Her father had been a preacher and had not received a large salary. When he died, Mary used some of her savings to pay for the funeral. She later did the same for one of her sisters. Other members of the family could not afford to help.

Three years ago, after working two jobs for three years, she was driving down one of the main streets to visit her sister in the hospital when she saw a sign advertising a house for sale. She had looked at the house once before but had not realized it was for sale. "I called the number on the sign, and soon my real estate agent and I were meeting at the house with the daughter of the out-of-town owner. As soon as I walked in the door, I said, 'This is it. This is it.' The real estate man asked, 'Are you sure?' and I said, 'I love it! It's just what I want for my hair salon!' I just knew it."

The house, which was zoned for business, was located between an automotive business and a residence. "I had planned to be nearer my community, but now I think this is the best location—none better." Her husband was uncertain about her taking on this obligation, but she said to him: "You don't have to pay anything down on it." She used the CD as a down payment on the $45,500 house and used the rest of her savings for working capital. The bank agreed to a mortgage of $37,500 on the house.

"I started with one part-time and two full-time workers. I brought over enough customers from my former salon work to keep me busy. I work from 7:30 A.M. to 6 P.M. on Saturday and about three hours a day Tuesday through Friday." A full-time worker, an apprentice, works with her so that she has the highest production rate and sometimes even the highest production during the week even though she works fewer hours. Still, she does not want to give up her poultry inspection job because she has 19 years invested in it.

The full-time hairdresser works the regular shop hours of 10 A.M. to 6 P.M. Tuesday through Saturday. She came from out of town and so brought no customers with her, and it has been difficult to increase her client load. The part-time operator is still in training but already has some of her own clients.

About a year after opening, Mary contacted SCORE (Service Corps of Retired Executives) to obtain help. Dan, who had owned an advertising agency, was sent by SCORE to work with her. They spent many hours discussing methods of increasing the number of clients. Glammourrammer was—and is—listed in the telephone directory white pages and also advertises under "Beauty Salons" in the Yellow Pages. The Yellow Page ad is 1½ column-inches; it gives the salon's operating hours and lists its services: family styling, cuts, perms, coloring, manicures, facials, and scalp care operations. Mary and Dan's sessions resulted in the design and placement at the business of a large sign that can be seen from a nearby main street. Mary feels that the sign has helped to increase the business's clientele.

Another subject she and Dan discussed was the business practices she could use to improve her operations. She was particularly impressed with the importance of motivation and people-related practices.

While Mary has not had any formal training in business, she says, "At least I am ahead on my mortgage payments." Each month she sends her accounting papers to a relative in St. Louis for processing.

During the first year of operation, Mary had some incidents of trespassing and defacing of her property. She spent about $3,000 on a surveillance unit, and she had a fence put up to keep people from walking through the yard. "The little old lady next door was so sweet to me and kept an eye out for me. When she went into a nursing home, her son came in and tried to sell her house to me. My husband did not want it, and I had just moved into this business, so I did not buy it. If I had had enough drive, I would now own both these houses. The neighbors look out for me."

Mary discussed with Dan an idea she had for expanding her business: she thought she would like to add "toning," a method of working the muscles of the body to reduce weight, relax the muscles, and create a general sense of well-being. Mary had been reading some magazines and had seen pictures of the machines used in this activity. "The idea kept popping up," she said. Dan asked her if she thought she could make money on the machines, and she said she thought she could. They discussed the alternatives of renting—which included a percentage royalty—and of buying the machines. One company offered to waive the transportation cost if she used its name in her operation. She turned down this offer.

After determining the cost of the machines and other start-up costs, which included adding a large room to the back of the house, she and Dan estimated that she would need a $12,000 loan from the bank. She assembled her information, presented it to the bank, and obtained her loan. She eventually purchased five machines.

Neither Mary nor her workers knew how to conduct the toning operation. While thumbing through a magazine, she found an advertisement for a training program that would train her people. She arranged for the program and hired two women who would come on call to do part-time toning. The three operators and two toning specialists took the one-day program.

Mary and Dan discussed ways of attracting customers to come in for the toning. The two worked out a flier, with information on the location of the salon and the services to be offered, to be given to current and potential customers. Then they came up with a list of names, many of which were provided by Dan's daughter, who was a nurse in the nearby hospital. The fliers were mailed to the people on the list and given to employees and friends who would give them to others who might be interested in the toning or other services of the salon. Over 100 fliers were mailed, inviting people to an open house that was attended by quite a few. When they arrived, many asked to see the salon as well as the toning operation. Then they said, "I think I will get my hair done when I come for toning." Many signed up for toning on the spot, and others who just looked around and left have been coming back for toning. Dan taped the toning demonstration during training, and the tapes are available for potential and waiting customers to view. Also, two publicity releases were carried in the local newspaper.

The business has 300 to 400 customers who come in at various intervals—some as often as once a week, others less frequently, and some only once a year. The two toning specialists work full time at other jobs, but others in the shop can also do the toning when needed. The clients can be scheduled for their convenience and to fit the employees' schedules. Mary mentioned one unexpected scheduling limitation: "Many people do not know that I serve only Caucasians on Tuesdays and Thursdays, although at other times I will serve anyone. I need more publicity on this."

Questions for Discussion

1. (*a*) Was Mary ready to start a business? (*b*) Did she know enough about the running of a business? (*c*) Explain.
2. What personal assets did Mary bring to her business?
3. (*a*) Should Mary leave her inspection job to devote full time to the hairstyling business? (*b*) Explain.
4. (*a*) What are the good and bad points of the location analysis? (*b*) How important is the location to Mary?
5. Discuss the various decisions that Mary made during her three years in operation.
6. (*a*) What changes might be made to improve the company's performance? (*b*) Do you recommend any of them?

Source: Prepared by Charles R. Scott, University of Alabama.

CASE I–4
CIRONI'S SEWING CENTER LOSES A FRANCHISE

It started out as a beautiful spring day. Tony Cironi had spent the morning servicing sewing machines at East High School. He had deliberately timed his arrival to coincide with a visit to the school by Verna Robbins, educational supervisor of the Home Economics Division of Consolidated School District.

Over the previous four years, Tony had sold over 500 Elna sewing machines to the school district, and now the biggest contract yet was coming up. As part of a special state appropriation, the district had received funding for 150 replacement sewing machines. Tony felt he had an inside track because of his demonstrated ability to perform to contract specifications, and Verna would know when the winning bidder would be announced. Sure enough, as Tony was leaving the building, he saw Verna outside the administrative office. She motioned him over and said, "Tony, I just heard that yours was the winning bid! Congratulations! We think a lot of you here. I'm glad that you're going to get the business!"

After a start like that, what could spoil the day? Tony drove back to his store the long way—through the park. This was a big sale—over $80,000. Even though he had cut his price to rock bottom, he could anticipate a gross profit of $10,000, and ongoing service revenues from the school district would be at least $1,000 a year. But when he got back to the store and opened his mail, he got the shock of his life—White Sewing Machine Company was canceling his franchise!

Origins of the Conflict

A month earlier, Tony and Herb Hanson, the national sales manager for White Sewing Machine Company, had had a major altercation. Herb had just popped in, introduced himself, and initiated a conversation about how to increase sales of White sewing machines. Tony had responded, "How can I? You're distributing the best-selling White sewing machine model to Jo Ann Fabric Stores for $97 a machine while I pay $140." Herb said, "That's a different machine!" That was when Tony blew up. "The hell it's different! It's the same machine! You just slapped a different model number on it, sprayed it a different color, and let Jo Ann Fabrics label it. But customers aren't fooled—the Jo Ann Fabric salespeople make sure of that. And why should customers pay $200 at my store for a machine they can get at Jo Ann Fabrics for $149?" The conversation deteriorated at that point, and Herb left in a huff.

Two weeks later, Herb called and asked if he and the new district sales representative could stop by to discuss a new sales strategy for White sewing machines. That afternoon, Herb started off the discussion with a compliment: "Tony, you're doing a great job of selling the Elna sewing machine. No other dealer in the country does as good a job. But, as you know, we only distribute Elna in this area. Our primary concern is the White sewing machine. It is made in Cleveland, Ohio, and customers in this area are very brand loyal to us. We believe that you are not selling as many White sewing machines as you could. You really are not advertising and promoting our machine like you should. Also, you are not carrying our new knitting machine. All dealers are supposed to carry the full product line. So what we want to do today is work out an advertising campaign for the next six months and get a commitment from you to actively sell our products, including the new knitting machine."

Tony took a deep breath and said, "I do advertise White! And in terms of sales, I push the product as much as I can. I try to treat fairly all the brands I carry. But newspaper advertising in this town is expensive, and some brands are more profitable than others. Also, the advertising I do for Bernina is paid for 100 percent by Bernina, up to 3 percent of my gross sales for the brand. You pay only 50 percent of my advertising cost on the same basis. If you want me to increase my advertising for White sewing machines, you should change your policies. As far as the knitting machines go, forget it! I don't sell *any* knitting machines in the store!"

After this, the meeting broke up. Herb suddenly remembered that he and the new district sales rep had a late-afternoon appointment with a prospective new dealer back at the Cleveland office. He told Tony that he would be back within the week.

Decision Situation

As Tony read and reread the letter from White, several thoughts raced through his mind. Although the letter did not give any reason for terminating his franchise, events over the past month provided some clues. Clearly, White Sewing Machine Company felt that he was "shortchanging" the White brand of sewing machines. Yet Tony felt that he had been fair to White in allocating his advertising budget. After all, the gross profit margin on a White sewing machine was lower than on some of his other brands of machines (see Exhibits 1 and 2).

Exhibit 1   Cironi's Advertising Expenditures by Brand—1987

	Expenditures	Percentage of ad budget
Baby Loc	$ 3,150	15.0
Bernina	6,562	31.2
Elna	3,150	15.0
Necchi	1,400	6.7
Pfaff	5,552	26.4
Singer	420	2.0
White	788	3.7
Total	$21,022	100.0

Exhibit 2 Gross Profit Margin by Brand—1987

	Gross profit percentage
Baby Loc	45.0
Bernina	50.0
Elna	30.0
Necchi	40.0
Pfaff	45.0
Singer	12.0
White	30.0

On the other hand, Tony had to admit, even to himself, that he did not sell as many White machines as some of the other dealers in the area (see Exhibit 3). Part of the problem had to do with White's practice of supplying Jo Ann Fabrics with a popular machine model for distributor branding. Also, the other dealers that carried White machines often dis-

Exhibit 3 Local Area Sales and Market Share for Household Sewing Machines— 1987

Local area dealers	Sales	Area market share
Cironi's Sewing Center:	$300,500	37.6%
White	15,000	1.9
Elna	60,000	7.5
Pfaff*	70,500	8.8
Necchi*	20,000	2.5
Bernina*	75,000	9.4
Baby Loc*	40,000	5.0
Singer	20,000	2.5
Akron Sewing Machine:	$200,100	25.0
White	40,000	5.0
Elna	9,600	1.2
New Home*	10,500	1.3
Singer	140,000	17.5
Mollie's Sewing and Knitting Boutique:	$150,800	18.8
White	40,000	5.0
Elna	10,400	1.3
Riccar*	15,400	1.9
Singer	85,000	10.6
Jo Ann Fabrics (4 stores):	$148,600	18.6
Singer	81,400	10.2
Distributor brands†	67,200	8.4

* Exclusive dealership.

† Brands made exclusively for Jo Ann Fabrics by manufacturers (e.g., Sonata made by Singer).

counted their prices, using White machines as a price leader to generate store traffic. Most of the other sewing machine dealers carried other types of products, such as vacuum cleaners, to make up for what they lost on White. As a result, Tony had been hard pressed to realize a 30 percent gross margin on the White brand. Many customers shopped around and compared prices. Even those who chose White over other brands often went for the lowest price even if it was offered by a dealer who could not service or repair sewing machines.

Uppermost in his mind, though, was concern about his "winning" bid for the school district contract. Verna Robbins had specified a sewing machine with the following features: ability to fit into the existing cabinets, a free arm, and a drop-in bobbin. This last feature was an absolute "must" in her mind. Past experience with students losing a removable bobbin case or switching bobbin cases between machines had convinced her that a drop-in bobbin (with a stationary bobbin case) was a nonnegotiable requirement. A replacement bobbin case typically cost $8.95. Switching bobbin cases between machines usually causes expensive repairs because a bobbin case must be "balanced" for a particular machine. The only machine in his store that could meet these specifications was an Elna model. Consequently, he had put in a bid for 150 Elna machines. But Elna was distributed by White in his area! And, according to the letter from White, his franchise for Elna as well as White would be canceled within 30 days!

Tony was deeply disturbed. He began to question himself. How could he deliver on his bid if he was no longer a dealer for Elna? How would he get parts to repair the Elna machines that he had already sold to the school district? He wondered if White had the legal right to cancel his Elna franchise. If so, should he attempt to renegotiate his franchise agreement with White? Why would White do this to him? Was it a sound business decision for them? Was it an ethical decision on their part? Or were they just trying to pressure him? He considered his relative power in this situation—after all, he was the largest independent sewing machine dealer in the area. Most important, he wondered what he should do now.

As Tony pondered these questions, he reached for a copy of his Elna dealer agreement. The Elna and White dealer agreements were virtually identical. As he read his dealer agreement, several clauses seemed to leap out at him.

The Supplier hereby grants to Dealer the nonexclusive right to purchase from Supplier for resale to consumers Elna sewing machines and sewing machine parts, supplies, and accessories. Dealer agrees to maintain a stock of current Elna sewing machines and parts, supplies, and accessories, and an organization and facility as necessary, in Supplier's judgment, to provide adequate and proper sales, sales promotion, and services of Elna products at Dealer's location at: [store location]

The term of this agreement shall be of an indefinite duration. This agreement may be terminated by either party upon thirty (30) days' written notice to the other party.

Dealer shall provide prompt, competent, and efficient servicing on all Elna sewing machines sold by it or otherwise brought into its place of business for servicing. Dealer shall comply with warranty servicing policies as published by the Supplier and shall provide customer servicing in accordance with the Supplier's published procedures for premium sales, educator sales, courtesy sales, and school sales.

The Supplier reserves the right from time to time to sell and offer to sell Elna sewing machines and sewing machine parts and accessories directly in the same general marketing area served by Dealer. The Supplier also reserves the right to appoint such sewing machine dealers in the same general marketing area served by the Dealer as the Supplier, in its discretion, deems desirable.

The Dealer is not and shall not be deemed to be a joint venturer, partner, agent, servant, employee, fiduciary, or representative of the Supplier. The Dealer shall conduct its entire business under this Agreement at its own cost and expense.

This Agreement may be terminated by either party, with or without cause, subject to the applicable provisions of State law, if any, upon thirty (30) days' notice to the other party. The Supplier may terminate this Agreement if Dealer shall fail to comply with any of the terms hereof, or if a petition in bankruptcy shall be filed by or against Dealer, or if Dealer shall reorganize or shall make an assignment or conveyance of its property for the benefit of creditors, or if a receiver shall be appointed with authority to take possession of any of the property of Dealer, or if the Dealer fails to pay any amount due to the Supplier, or if the Dealer fails to conform to the business system or the standard of conformity and quality for the products and services promulgated by the Supplier in connection with the business system. The termination of this Agreement shall not release either party from the payment of any sum then owing to the other.

Questions for Discussion

1. (a) Does White Sewing Machine Company have the legal right to terminate Tony's franchise for the Elna brand? (b) Is White making a good business decision? (c) In your opinion, is White's decision ethical?
2. (a) What are the bases of power and authority of White Sewing Machine Company? (b) What are the bases of power and authority of Cironi's Sewing Machine Center? (c) Which party has the most power in this situation? (d) Why?
3. (a) What decision alternatives does Tony have in this situation? (b) Evaluate each of his alternatives. (c) How should Tony respond? (d) Why?

Source: Prepared by Gary B. Frank, University of Akron, and J. B. Wilkinson, Youngstown State University. The authors thank Bob Barnes, owner of Barnes Sewing Center in Akron, Ohio, for technical information regarding sewing centers.

SHAFFER'S DRIVE INNS

About 20 years ago the Shaffer family (mother, father, and son) decided to open a drive-in in a midwestern city of about 200,000 people. They observed that the general area was lacking a drive-in that provided such foods as malts and sandwiches with curb service and modern indoor eating facilities as well. They built a facility that filled these needs and named it Shaffer's Drive Inn.

The son, Albert Shaffer, put a lot of energy into managing the store and worked harder than most people realized. In fact, he was soon able to buy his mother and father out and gain exclusive control of the store for himself. It was 15 years before Albert Shaffer decided to build another store; 4 years later, he built a third one. He always issued stock for each store that he built but controlled at least 51 percent of the stock in each one.

Shaffer was respected and admired by his employees and had a "great man" image among them. He was an authoritarian leader, and his employees accepted his judgment as law because, in their opinion, he was right 99 percent of the time. When discussing restaurant business with his employees, Shaffer would never "tear into" them but would argue the point, listen to what they had to say, and then point out where they were either right or wrong. Once he had his mind made up, though, it usually stayed made up.

Some Organizational Problems

The organizational structure used by Shaffer's Drive Inns was complicated. There were two managers and an assistant for each store, and assistants were to be trained to become future managers. In addition to these managers in each store, there were kitchen help, curb boys, and so forth. Not only did this organizational structure have some serious flaws, but it led to some personality conflicts, as will be discussed later.

Shaffer's Drive Inns proved to be very popular. A lot of research went into the proper location for each of them, and each was located where it would make its appeal either to college students or to heavy automobile traffic. The Drive Inns became well known for their excellent service. These were Shaffer's specific objectives, and they were in tune with his business philosophy.

Shaffer's Drive Inns proved to be so popular that a decision was reached to build three more in a nearby city. These three stores opened during a month's period. It was at this point that Shaffer realized that his business was getting away from him. The people he chose for managers were well trained to go into the store, but they had very little contact with the main office and consequently were forced to make most of their own decisions. In addition, the two managers in each store were constantly bickering with each other. The tendency to pass the buck was a serious temptation. The employees were quick to realize they could play one manager against the other to achieve desired goals.

Choosing an Assistant

Shaffer believed in personal contact to get his views across. But as the stores were now becoming geographically separated, he was having a difficult time spending the proper amount of time at each. He decided he needed an assistant to be his "right-hand man" and carry on when and where he could not. He wanted someone from inside the organization who knew the ropes. Shaffer chose Marc Mason, known as a "self-made man," to be his unofficial assistant. Although Mason was entirely capable of handling the job, his selection caused serious complaints and criticisms from three of the store managers—Denney, Riley, and Nettles.

These three men had been with the organization for a combined time of over 30 years, and each one assumed for himself certain authority that he didn't actually possess. They were described as completely set in their ways and resisted any and every planned change. When Mason became Shaffer's unofficial assistant, they resisted every move he made in every conceivable way.

Denney had a high school education. He was known to argue just for the sake of arguing. He was not known as a go-getter and was content to work in the slowest store of the chain. He seemed to have an inferiority complex in that he thought he wasn't as good as everyone else. In the opinion of some of his associates, he was not even capable of managing his own money. His strongest feature was his length of service, for he had been with the organization so long that he assumed he had high status. Denney shared the managership of one store with Riley.

Riley was a quiet-spoken man; he seldom raised his voice to anyone. He was of average intelligence but was not able to communicate properly with his employees. As a result, he wasn't able to get as much out of his employees as he should have.

Nettles had once shared the management of a store with Mason. He was an ex-marine and was considerably older than Mason. Nettles was known "to be pretty sharp and to know quite a bit about the business." Nettles could never bring himself to believe that he had been bypassed by Mason and was frequently vocal about his feeling of dissatisfaction.

Mason, it was said, was treated very unfairly in the early days of his career. He was not brought into decisions or taken into the confidence of the man he worked with. However, he was a diligent worker and put in many hours of hard work. He was the type of man who really made a place for himself, and his long hours of hard work were eventually recognized by Shaffer.

Despite the growing communication problems, Shaffer went ahead with the plans for another Drive Inn (the eighth) in still another town. Now the lines of communication were really split. Shaffer, even with the assistance of Mason, was not able to devote as much time as he should to each of the stores. This left the store managers to their own discretion in many of their decisions. They started making more and more of their own decisions and relying less and less on Shaffer and Mason, much to Shaffer's displeasure. The problems that followed the opening of the eighth store caused Shaffer to seek outside help.

Questions for Discussion

1. What does this case show about the problems involved in organizing a small business?
2. What is shown about the problems resulting from growth of a small firm?
3. What were Shaffer's objectives in operating the business?

Source: Prepared by Joe L. Hamilton, Container Corporation of America.

CASE I–6
WILSON'S USED CARS

Toward the end of January 1979, Kevin Wilson, president of Wilson's Used Cars, thoroughly reviewed the past performance of the firm. Upon completion of this review he was quite pleased: sales in 1978 had increased by 59 percent and profit before taxes by 36 percent over the previous year. As far as Wilson was concerned, the future could not be brighter.

History

Wilson's Used Cars was founded by Kevin Wilson in January 1976 in a town in central California. When asked about his initial investment, Wilson stated:

I was able to open on a shoestring for two reasons. The lot belongs to my brother-in-law, and our first lease agreement was nothing short of a "sweet deal" for me. My payments for the first six months were only $50 per month. Today, of course, they are considerably higher since I no longer have a cash flow problem and can afford it.

Second, and perhaps more important, is the way I acquired my initial inventory. As a matter of fact, in looking back on it, the new-car dealers in our community literally set me up in the business. You see, most of the new-car dealers place only late model trade-ins on their used car lots and sell the older trade-ins at the auto auction or directly to used-car dealers like myself. Well, several of the new-car dealers are personal friends of mine and helped me during my first year by letting me have several cars on consignment.

On opening day, the initial inventory consisted of 12 automobiles with an average retail price of $800 each. During the months that followed, however, both sales and inventory grew at a rapid pace. Toward the end of 1977, over 30 cars were on the lot, with an average price of $1,200. By the end of 1978, the lot held over 40 cars with an average price approaching $1,350.

The Market

Several firms sold used automobiles in the market area of Wilson's Used Cars. According to Wilson, however, a large percentage of these firms were rather weak competitors: "Most of those idiots out there don't really understand the car game, and many go under. To be successful, you have got to be able to buy right, and you have got to be able to sell. In terms of buying, many rely too heavily on the wholesale book; and in terms of selling, I doubt very seriously whether some of those jokers could sell themselves out of a wet paper bag."

Wholesale Market

When a dealer buys cars either from a new-car dealer or through the auto auction, the wholesale book provides only a rough benchmark. If a particular model is "soft," or if considerable reconditioning is required, a figure of $300 or $400 "back of book" may be reasonable. On the other hand, fast-moving, "hot" items often sell above wholesale book. As Wilson said, "Knowing the market for these clunkers is essential if you're going to make it. If you pay too much for one, you'll take a loss when you sell it. If you don't offer enough, you won't get the cars to sell. It is as simple as that."

Retail Market

Wilson firmly believed that a thorough understanding of the retail market for used cars could only be acquired through experience:

I have been selling cars for years, and in terms of owning my own business, this experience has been invaluable as it taught me all of the tricks of the trade. A more important lesson, for example, is that understanding your customer and knowing what makes him tick is far more important than acquiring knowledge of the product you are selling.

Moreover, most of the people who come in here have two things in common. First, they don't know a hill of beans about automobiles. Of course, they often pretend to be knowledgeable by looking under the hood, or by sticking their fingers up the exhaust pipe, but let's face it, they are usually pretty stupid. Second, no one, and I mean no one, trusts used-car salesmen. As a result, the first order of business is to sell yourself, and there are numerous approaches that you may use to accomplish this feat.

Sales Techniques

In conjunction with the saying, "The first appearance is a lasting one," Wilson felt that a conservatively dressed salesperson would be far more successful than one who dressed "flashy." Typically, he approached customers in a beige shirt, brown slacks, a pair of brown brogues, and a light green sweater. He literally abhorred car salesmen dressed in something like a white silk shirt, plaid pants, white shoes, and a loud tie. "Whenever I see salesmen dressed like that," Wilson declared, "I keep waiting for them to do a cane dance or something, and I sure would never trust them."

Another technique that Wilson employed quite frequently to gain customers' trust was to advise against purchasing a particular automobile. Relative to this technique, Wilson stated, "You have to admit that for a car salesman to advise you *not* to buy an automobile is indeed a rare event. I believe, however, that this approach helps to establish a feeling of confidence towards me, and then when I do suggest that a particular automobile is a good buy and would satisfy the customer's needs, I stand a much better chance of closing the sale."

With respect to pricing, Wilson laughingly recalled his experiences when he first started out in the car business, "You know, . . ." he said:

I started selling cars part-time while I was a business administration major in college. At that time, I was being pumped full of flowery ideals by the college teachers and strongly believed that I could be totally honest with people and still be a success in the business world. Boy, was I in for a rude awakening!

My first job was with a small used-car lot here in town working evenings and weekends. Initially, for the first couple of weeks, I told the truth and nothing but the truth to all customers who came on the lot.

For example, my boss always gave me a list containing the asking price and minimum price of each car on the lot. Whenever someone would ask for the price of an automobile, I would actually take the list from my pocket and show it. I would explain that the minimum price was the rock bottom price we could sell the car for and that, as far as I was concerned, it was a fair price.

Using this approach, I didn't sell one car, not one lousy car. Oh, I got counter-offers, but I couldn't take them, for I had already quoted the lowest possible price. Needless to say, after a few weeks I was really hurting for money and finally began to play the game. It was then, and only then, that I began to sell cars.

Whenever a customer would ask for the price of an automobile, I would quote the asking price, which was usually substantially higher than the fair market value. After the customer recovered from the shock of hearing such a high price, I would follow up with, "I know the price is somewhat high, and I am sure that the owner would entertain a lower bid. Why don't you look the car over and present what you think is a fair price?"

More often than not, the customer would wind up paying a price that was higher than the minimum price acceptable to the owner. Believe me, at first I couldn't get over the irony of this situation. If the people out there would have let me be honest, they would have paid lower prices for their automobiles. But, as I stated before, I couldn't sell anything being *totally* honest.

The Future

The financial prospects for Wilson's Used Cars, according to Wilson, were bright. He knew how to play the game, and he was good at it. He did confess, however, that occasionally he wondered if there were some good way to incorporate into the car game more of those ideals that he had studied in college and still be a financial success. (See Exhibits 1 and 2.)

Exhibit 1

WILSON'S USED CARS
Income Statements
For the Years Ended December 31, 1977 and 1978

	1977	1978
Net sales	$228,000	$362,000
Cost of sales	172,000	275,000
Gross profit	56,000	87,000
Expenses*	42,000	68,000
Profit before taxes	$ 14,000	$ 19,000

* Includes Wilson's $1,500-a-month salary in 1977 and $1,800-a-month salary in 1978.

Exhibit 2

WILSON'S USED CARS
Comparative Balance Sheet
As of December 31

	1977	1978
Assets		
Current assets:		
Cash	$ 3,800	$ 6,300
Inventory	33,000	42,000
Other current assets	3,600	9,600
Total current assets	40,400	57,900
Fixed assets:		
Net fixed assets	8,300	9,800
Other noncurrent assets	2,300	3,300
Total assets	$51,000	$71,000
Liabilities and Net Worth		
Current liabilities:		
Short-term notes payable	$28,000	$37,000
Other current liabilities	4,000	5,300
Total current liabilities	32,000	42,300
Long-term debt	5,200	3,900
Other noncurrent liabilities	1,500	1,100
Net worth	12,300	23,700
Total liabilities and net worth	$51,000	$71,000

Questions for Discussion

1. Evaluate Wilson's entry into the used-car business, especially the low cost involved.
2. What does the case reveal about those who are willing to invest hard work in a business of their own?
3. Analyze the risks that confront Wilson.
4. How would you evaluate Wilson's pricing policy?
5. Discuss Wilson's comment on ideals he had studied.
6. What do you think of his philosophy of how to succeed?
7. (*a*) Is experience as important to success in small business as Wilson thinks? (*b*) Explain.

Source: Prepared by Burton F. Schaffer, California State University at Sacramento.

II

PLANNING FOR AND ORGANIZING A BUSINESS

Part I showed some opportunities in small business, as well as the characteristics of small businesses and their owners. It included some thoughts on studying the economic environment in order to increase the chances of success. These presentations involved general ideas rather than specific detail.

In this part, planning and organizing a small business are covered. The information presented is considerably more detailed, as it is a practical "how to do it" discussion of the activities involved in starting such a business. These include (1) having an idea for a new business, (2) obtaining the needed resources, including managerial talent, (3) doing production or operations, (4) marketing the product or service, and (5) profit planning. Notice the sequence of events from having the original idea to achieving the final result: making a profit (or suffering a loss).

Owners and managers of small firms must (1) get things done through others, (2) allocate scarce resources, and (3) make decisions so that objectives are reached. In doing these things, managers perform five functions: planning, organizing, staffing, leading, and controlling. Instead of organizing individual chapters around them, we discuss all these functions in various parts of the text.

The material in Chapter 5 explains how to become a small business owner; Chapter 6 shows how to do strategic and operational planning; Chapter 7 explains how to prepare and present a business plan; Chapter 8 discusses sources of operating and venture capital; and Chapter 9 discusses how to organize the business, from a legal and administrative point of view.

5

HOW TO BECOME A SMALL BUSINESS OWNER

To start and run a small business, you must know and be many things.—Small Business Administration

There is no such thing as growth industries. There are only companies organized and operated to create and capitalize on growth opportunities.—Theodore Levitt

LEARNING OBJECTIVES

After studying the material in this chapter, you will be able to:

1. Explain how to go into business for yourself.
2. Describe the steps involved in the procedure recommended for going into business.
3. Describe how to search for and identify a product.
4. Describe how to study the market you are entering, including sources of information.
5. Deciding whether to start a new business, buy an existing one, or buy a franchise.

JERRY AND MONA SAMUEL: COMBINING OLD-FASHIONED NEWSSTAND AND MODERN GIFT SHOP

Mona and Jerry Samuel started the News 2 U Store in the Muddy Branch Shopping Center in Darnestown, Maryland, in 1988. They went into business with the idea of "running a fun store" that would be different from others. The store is based on the old-fashioned idea of combining good service with a wide selection of goods for customers to choose from. This idea has led to economic success for the couple.

In keeping with the classic newsstand model, the Samuels stock over 1,500 titles of different newspapers and magazines. They carry 40 daily newspapers from around the country; between 70 and 80 computer magazines; and a variety of exercise, health, and running magazines. But it's hard to make a profit with just a magazine store, and so the owners added a gift shop with a wide range of candy and small gifts. In fact, they even sell "penny candy"—for a dime. According to the Samuels, they added the candy and gifts to make the business more interesting as well as to "provide financial security."

The old-fashioned idea has won acceptance even in a fast-paced, high-tech world, leading the Samuels to open two other stores in the fall of 1989. One store is located at the top of L'Enfant Plaza Metro in Washington, D.C., and the other in Rockville, Maryland.

The store is a family business. The parents, aged 42, divide the duties, with Mona selecting the gifts and novelty items and Jerry ordering the books, magazines, and newspapers. Their three children, aged 2½ to 13, assist by accompanying them to shows and testing out the toys and candy.

Source: Photo courtesy of Rick Dugan.

Source: Jenny Well, "Success of News 2 U Store Prompts Expansion," *Bethesda* (Maryland) *Gazette,* August 31, 1989, pp. 36–37.

As you can see from this case, many opportunities exist for enterprising people to go into business for themselves. As shown in Figure 5–1, the process begins when you have an idea for a new product or service, such as combining a newsstand and gift shop. Then you decide on the ownership and management of the business and obtain resources—in the form of people, buildings and equipment, materials and supplies, and the money to finance them. You then begin producing and selling the product or performing the service so that revenues come in to pay expenses and provide you with a profit—so that you can repeat the cycle.

While the concept is simple, the actual process is not as easy as it may appear from the figure or from the Samuels' experience. In fact, the actual process of choosing a business to enter is quite complex, as will be shown in this and the following chapters.

HOW TO GO INTO BUSINESS FOR YOURSELF

Chapter 2 cites many reasons for becoming the owner of a small business, and Chapters 3 and 4 describe some of the available opportunities. Those who do decide to take this important step must exercise care in planning for their business to ensure a reasonable chance of success. Now we would like to explain how to actually go into business—if that is what you would like to do.[1]

How to Start a Business

Once the decision is made to go into business, proper planning becomes essential. While there is no one tried and true procedure that will work for everyone who wants to become a small business owner, you should at least follow some logical, well-thought-out procedure. An excellent guide for starting a business is the Small Business Administration's *Checklist for Going into Business.*[2] Similar material is discussed in this chapter and Chapters 6 and 7. The next Computer Update suggests some shortcuts available if you have a computer.

Steps in Starting a Business

Assuming you've decided you *really* want to start a new business, how do you do it? We've tried to compress all the details into the following eight steps:

1. Search for and identify a needed product. (Technically, a product can be either a physical good or a service. To prevent repetition, we will use the term *product* to mean a physical good or a service.)
2. Study the market for the product, using as many possible sources of information as feasible.
3. Decide whether to start a new business, buy an existing one, or buy a franchise.

Figure 5–1   How a Business Is Formed and Operates

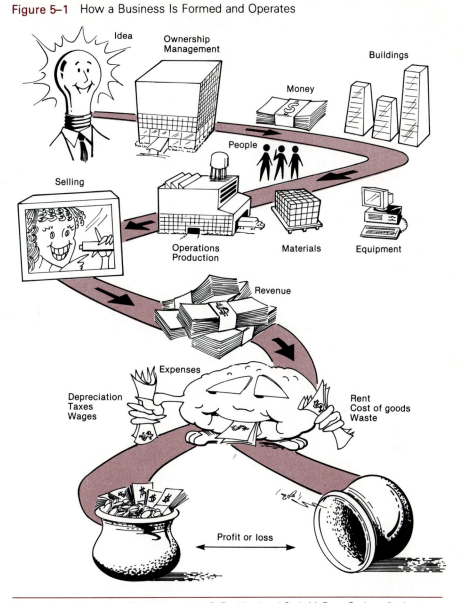

Idea

Ownership
Management

Buildings

Money

People

Selling

Operations
Production

Materials

Equipment

Revenue

Expenses

Depreciation
Taxes
Wages

Rent
Cost of goods
Waste

Profit or loss

Source: Adapted from Leon C. Megginson, Lyle R. Trueblood, and Gayle M. Ross, *Business* (Lexington, Mass.; D. C. Heath, 1985), p. 7.

4. Make strategic plans, including setting your mission, strategic objectives, and strategies.

5. Make operational plans, including setting policies, budgets, standards, procedures, and methods and planning the many aspects of producing and marketing the product.

COMPUTER UPDATE

COMPUTERIZED BUSINESS START-UPS

There is now a host of computer software to help people start a new business. One of the latest is *Venture,* developed by the University of Southern California and Star Software Systems. Used with IBM-compatible systems, it provides a business plan, word processor, file manager, general ledger, spreadsheet, and information on obtaining financing and corresponding with customers. (Note: For further information call 1-800-242-7827.)

How to Write a Business Plan, developed by the American Institute of Small Business, provides practical information on how to create a business plan. It offers tips on sales forecasting, marketing and competitive analyses, and projected balance sheets, cash flow data, and profit and loss statements. It can be used with Apple's Macintosh as well as IBM-compatibles. (Note: For further information on creating a business plan, call 1-800-328-2906.)

---

6. Make financial plans, including estimating income and expenses, estimating initial investment, and locating sources of funds.
7. Develop these plans into a detailed business plan.
8. Implement the plan.

The first three of these steps are covered in this chapter in considerable detail. Steps 4, 5, and 6 are covered in detail in Chapter 6. And in Chapter 7 you will learn how to prepare and present a sample business plan. Implementing the business plan is covered throughout the rest of the text.[3]

See Case II–4, The Mother and Child Shop, for an excellent example of how to plan and start a new business. Mick and Cathy McGregor went through all these steps in opening (and later managing) their maternity/children's store. They began with the desire to go into business and ended up expanding the store after its successful opening.

SEARCHING FOR AND IDENTIFYING A NEEDED PRODUCT

Many small business owners fail because they see the glamour of some businesses—and the apparent ease with which they are run—and think, "I just know I can make a lot of money if I start my own business." A few do succeed without adequate preparation, but the majority will fail. While proper planning does not ensure success, it improves the chances of succeeding.

Planning starts with searching for a product to sell or a service to perform. According to William A. Sahlman, who teaches entrepreneurial finance at

Harvard, "Being bright-eyed and bushy-tailed isn't necessarily a barometer of success. If people succeed, it's because they know an industry cold and perceive some need or service that no one else has seen."[4] So first find your product.

The list of possible products is almost unlimited, considering the variety of goods and services offered by the nearly 20 million U.S. businesses now in existence. What types of businesses are available? Not all the fields are open, but there is very likely a potential niche for a new business. You just have to find it. Some of the most successful small firms find a "niche within a niche" and never deviate from it.

For example, Tom Turrisi, who plays guitar with his left hand, started a left-hand guitar club. In 1980, the club evolved into a Springfield, Virginia, business—Shane Musical Instruments—which designs and sells guitars.[5]

How to Decide Which Product to Sell

How can the potential product be found? Magazines and newspapers recount stories of people who have started new businesses and have succeeded. Some new businesses were at one time uncommon or innovative, such as selling front pouches for parents to carry children in, selling or renting videotapes, and selling computer software. Talking to large companies may help you to identify opportunities that can be handled better by a small business. Newspapers are filled with advertisements for "business opportunities"—businesses for sale, new products for sale by their inventors, and other opportunities to become one's own boss. Bear in mind, though, that *these ideas are not always feasible, so proceed with caution.*

"I had secured sufficient financial backing, I'd set up fine inventory and cash management systems! I was ready for business, then it hit me . . . I had no product or service!"
Source: *Management Accounting,* May 1988, p. 77.

Don't forget to look to the past for a "new" product. Consumer tastes run in cycles, so it may be time to reintroduce an old product.

For example, a new magazine, *Victoria,* is devoted to Victorian-style decorating; and old-fashioned clothes for children—at thoroughly modern yuppie prices—are sold in trendy stores and catalogs.

The Windsor Court Hotel, a prestigious new hotel in New Orleans, serves old-fashioned English tea and scones each afternoon in its fashionable lobby.

In addition, the subject of needed products and services often comes up in social conversation. Hobbies, recreation, and work at home require study, training, and practice that can lead to products of new design or characteristics. Bankers, consultants, salespeople, and anyone else can be good sources of ideas. But it takes observation, study, vision, and luck to recognize the appropriate product for your business.

The idea for the Mother and Child Shop came to Mick McGregor when a friend mentioned in conversation at a party that some store space was available in a local shopping complex.

One suggestion for anyone remotely interested in going into business is to post a sheet of paper in a prominent place and write down every idea that comes up. Over the course of time, a long list of possibilities will accumulate. The longer the list, the greater the chance of finding the best product for you. See Figure 5–2 for an example.

The search for and identification of a product require innovative and original thinking, after putting the ideas together in an organized form. For example, if the chosen product is now being provided by competitors, what change is necessary for you to compete successfully—or avoid competition altogether? Can an original approach be used in serving the public? Not always, as the following example shows.

In December 1986, things looked good for Steven Freeman, aged 29. He was soon to marry and get his M.B.A. from the Wharton School, and he was going to use an old idea to revolutionize Manhattan's real estate market: he would use a computer data base to match buyers and sellers. But in September 1988, after investing about $30,000 of his family's money, he quit; not enough people were willing to pay for the service to make it profitable.[6]

Looking into the future requires widely diverse reading and contacts with a wide variety of people. Constant questioning of changes that are occurring and critical analysis of products and services being received pro-

Figure 5–2   Daily Idea List

IDEA LIST
Instruction manual for sewing.
Put on mystery parties.
Toothpaste holders.
Cleaner for bathtub.
Weighing scale on washing machines.
Make simple wood toy cars.
Do maintenance in homes of incapacitated.

vide ideas. Innovation is alive and well and will continue its surge ahead. Each new idea spawns other ideas for new businesses.

Choosing the Business to Enter

In choosing the business to enter, first eliminate the least attractive ideas from consideration and then concentrate on selecting the most desirable one. It is important to eliminate ideas that will not provide the challenges, opportunities, and rewards—financial and personal—that you are seeking. Be rather ruthless in asking, "What's in it for me?" Also ask yourself, "What can I do to be of service to others?" Questions like those in Figure 5–3 will also be helpful. Be sure not to eliminate "long shots" too soon. Also, concentrate on the thing(s) you would like to do, not on what someone else wants for you.

After eliminating the unattractive ideas, get down to the serious business of selecting the business to which you plan to devote your energy and resources. One way of doing this is to get a group of friends, a diversified group of small business managers, or a few **SCORE (Service Corps of Retired Executives)** members together and ask them what kinds of products are needed. Then ask them if those needs are being met adequately. If not, what would be necessary to satisfy the needs? Try to get them to identify not only existing types of businesses but also as many new kinds of businesses as possible. Then consider the kinds of products that are not now available but are needed and could find a market if available.

Figure 5–3 Questions to Ask to Help Eliminate Possible Businesses

1. How much capital is required to enter and compete successfully in this business?
2. How long will it take to recoup my investment?
3. How long will it take to reach an acceptable level of income?
4. How will I live until that time?
5. What degree of risk is involved? Am I willing to take that risk?
6. Can I make it on my own, or will I need the help of my family or others?
7. How much work is involved in getting the business going? In running it? Am I willing to put out that much effort?
8. Do I want to acquire a franchise from an established company, or do I want to start from scratch and go it on my own?
9. What is the potential of this type of business? What are my chances of achieving that potential?
10. Is sufficient information available to permit reaching a meaningful decision? If so, what are the sources of information?
11. Is it something I would enjoy?

There are several self-help groups of entrepreneurs in various parts of the country that can be called upon at this—and later—stages. These groups help potential entrepreneurs find their niche, and then assist them in surviving start-up, operating—and even personal—problems.

One such group—Master-Mind—operates in Palo Alto, California. It meets twice monthly to help small business owners develop new business ideas and cope with "their pressure-cooker world." Master-Mind tries to avoid concerns about direct competition among group members by including a wide variety of businesses. Also, those with new business ideas feel secure in the group because everyone agrees that the discussions are to be confidential.[7]

When obtaining advice from outsiders, though, remember that it is your resources that are at stake when the commitment is made, so the ultimate decision must be yours. Don't let someone talk you into something you are uncomfortable with.

After discussing the need for the product with other people, the next step is to select the business that seems best for you. To be more methodical and objective in your evaluation, you might prepare a checklist. Figure 5–4 shows a list used by a consultant with the MIT Enterprise Forum who helps people decide what business to enter. Are any of the collected choices very exciting to you? If not, make another list! If these lists are long enough, at least one idea will match your ability, training, experience, personality, and interests, which you should also consider when choosing a business to enter.

Initially you may want to make more than one choice and leave yourself

Figure 5–4   Business Selection Survey Checklist

Capital required	Degree of risk involved	Amount of work involved	Independent ownership or franchise	Potential of the business	Source of data

some options. Remember to consider your personal attributes and objectives in order to best utilize your capabilities. Let your mind—not your emotions—govern your decisions.

A psychology professor doing research in learning theory believed that the "right" space between lines and the "right" height of letters would simplify the early development of writing and learning skills of primary school children. He wanted to produce and sell products such as lined writing paper, with alphabetical letters of the "right" height, and alphabet cereal using these ideas.

The SBA counselor to whom he turned was impressed with the professor's commitment but told him there were existing products almost identical to his. The counselor contacted several authorities, who agreed that the ideas had no proprietary value.

The professor, too committed to his ideas to listen to reason, resigned his university position to devote full time to the project, even though he had a family and no other means of economic support. After his business failed, he went back to teaching at a different school.

STUDYING THE MARKET FOR THE PRODUCT

Once you have selected the product and business, the next step is to look at the market potential for them. If no market exists, or one cannot be developed, you would be foolish to pursue the project any further. On the other hand, there may be a market in a particular location or in a particular segment of the population that needs your product.

Small businesses usually select one segment of the population for their customers, or choose one product niche, since they do not have sufficient resources to cover the whole market. Also, small businesses cannot include as large a variety of products in their efforts as large businesses can. Hence, a small business must concentrate its efforts on a segment that it can serve effectively.

Harriette Rose and her husband, Dr. Martin Katz, uncovered a mini-niche in the giant U.S. food-service industry, which they've since turned into a profitable business. They found that the catering industry has some 3,300 firms competing for close to $1 billion a year of business. The Katzes figured that busy people giving a catered party wouldn't have the time or the know-how to choose the best vendors, so they set up New York's Gourmet Advisory Services Inc., to do it for them. The Katzes call themselves "party planners," and for a 15 percent commission they'll arrange the menu, the decor, even the mood for a catered affair.[8]

Methods of Obtaining Information about the Market

There are many ways to identify a market, and all can be generally classified as market research. **Market research** consists of gathering, recording, classifying, analyzing, and interpreting data related to the marketing of goods and services. (This is discussed in detail in Chapter 17.) Formal research programs can be very valuable in giving direction, but they can also be expensive. Computers are helping to increase the amount of information gathered, while reducing the cost (see the next Computer Update).

Some specific means of collecting data include a search of existing literature. The first places to look in a library are the "technical section" and the "government documents section." You should examine Bureau of the Census data on subjects such as population, business, housing, and agriculture. Computers are now used to gather and interpret many types of previously unavailable information, and many new indexes have been created to simplify the search for specialized information.

The SBA can be a helpful source of data, as can the research divisions of chambers of commerce, colleges, trade associations, and local business leaders, bankers, and congressional representatives. Talking with others—even potential competitors—can yield useful information.

The U.S. Department of Commerce is a particularly good source of information. Its district offices have well-stocked libraries of census data, and there is usually a staff member to help you find what you need. The Department of Commerce publishes an especially useful book, *Measuring Markets: A Guide to the Use of Federal and State Statistical Data.*[9] Appendix C at the end of this book lists some other publications that you can possibly use, along with their sources.

Method Used to Study the Market

In estimating your sales and market share, there are four things you need to do. First, you should determine the size of the industry you are about to enter and the size of the market segment you are targeting. Second, you should estimate your competition and figure out its market share. Third, you should determine how you stack up against the competition. Finally, you need to estimate your own sales volume.[10]

COMPUTER UPDATE

USING ELECTRONIC SCANNERS TO STUDY THE MARKET

More than half of the supermarkets in the United States now use electronic scanners, which essentially are computerized checkout machines that read the bar codes on merchandise labels. Originally used to speed the checkout process, these electronic scanners are now being connected to central computers to do market research as well. The computers gather, record, and analyze valuable information essential for speedy and effective managerial decisions. Analysts predict that profit margins, which average only about 0.5 to 1.5 percent, could very well double in the near future.

Hannaford Brothers, the Maine-based owner of Shop-n-Save stores, is an example of how well the new system works. Such data as shipping expenses, warehouse handling requirements, bulk displays, energy needs of various stores, and the amount of time canned corn stays on the shelf before being bought are sent to Shop-n-Save's headquarters. This information is processed into "Plan-a-Grams" that give managers a shelf-by-shelf, detailed description of where to put stock to increase profit.

Expected future developments include electronic shelves that give nutrition and cost information about products at the press of a button. This innovation could be operative by the time this book is published.

Sources: Correspondence with Hannaford Brothers; and S. Weinstein, "A Conversation with Hannaford's James Moody," *Progressive Grocer*, April 1988, pp. 119–20.

Estimating the Size of the Market

Before launching a business, you should find out if the market for it is large enough to accommodate a newcomer. An analysis of the answers to the following questions can give you an insight into how to solve the problem.

- How large is the industry?
- Where is the market for the company, and how large is it?
- Are sales to be made to a selected age-group, and how large is that group?
- What are the size and distribution of income within the population?
- Is the sales volume for this kind of business growing, stable, or declining?
- What are the number and size of competitors?
- What is the success rate for competing businesses?
- What are the technical aspects (state of the art) of the industry?

Estimating the Competition

In studying the market area, the number of similar businesses that have merged with a competitor or been liquidated should be determined. A high number of these activities usually signals market weakness. Analysis of competitors' activities may also indicate how effectively a new company can compete. Is the market large enough for another firm? What features—

such as lower price, better product, or more promotion—will attract business? Can these features be developed for the new firm?

Determine the kinds of technology being applied by other firms in the industry. For example, do other machine shops use hand tools, or do they employ state-of-the-art equipment, including robots? The level of technology is significant in determining operating costs.

Estimating Your Share of the Market

You should be able to arrive at a "ballpark" figure for your sales volume and your share of the market. In doing so, select reasonable and conservative figures. First, determine the geographic boundaries of the market area. Then, from your knowledge of the potential customers in the area, estimate how much of the product might be purchased. Finally, make an "educated guess" as to what part of this market you might attract as your share.

DECIDING WHETHER TO START A NEW BUSINESS, BUY AN EXISTING ONE, OR BUY A FRANCHISE

By now, you have probably decided what type of industry you want to enter and have done an economic feasibility study of that industry and the potential business. The next step is to decide whether to start a new business from scratch, buy an established business, or buy a franchise. As shown in Figure 5–5, many prospective business owners find themselves in a quandary over which direction to take. The material in this section may be helpful in making the choice more effectively. Also, Appendix D at the end of this book has a checklist to guide this evaluation.

To Start a New Business?

The characteristics of successful owners of small businesses indicate a tendency towards starting their own business from scratch. Their sense of individuality leads them to want the recognition that the success is all theirs. Often, the idea selected is new, and the businesses for sale at the time do not fit the desired mold. Also, the facilities needed should be new so that the latest ideas, processes, and procedures can be used. Size of company, fresh inventory, new personnel, and new location can be chosen to fit the new venture.

All this is exciting and—when successful—satisfying. But the venture is also challenging because everything is new, demands new ideas, and must overcome skepticism. Because everything is newer, a larger investment may be required.

Reasons for Starting a New Business

Some of the advantages of starting a new business lie in the owner's freedom to:

- Define the nature of the business.
- Create the preferred type of physical facilities.

Figure 5–5   Which Road to Take?

- Take advantage of the latest technology, equipment, materials, and tools.
- Obtain fresh inventory.
- Have a free hand in selecting, training, developing, and motivating personnel.
- Design a management information system.
- Select the competitive environment—to a certain extent.

Kathy Kolbe became angry when trying to find some stimulating educational materials for her two children. She raised such a fuss about the lack of materials in her children's schools that she was appointed to head a committee to develop a program for gifted children. Finding no materials for them in educational catalogs, she decided to write and produce her own, which she called "Think-ercises." She offered these materials to several publishers, but they rejected her offer, considering the market too small to be profitable. She took $500 from her savings and launched a firm called Resources for the Gifted. She wrote catalogs and sent them to around 3,500 schools and parents. While orders came in, her first few years were tough because of a fire, embezzlement, and personal problems. After six years, however, she was grossing $3.5 million a year.[11]

Reasons for Not Starting a New Business
Some of the disadvantages of starting a new business are:

- Problems in selecting the right business.
- Unproven performance in sales, reliability, service, and profits.
- Problems associated with assembling the resources—including the location, building, equipment, and materials.

- The need to select and train a new work force.
- The lack of an established product line.
- Production problems associated with starting up a new business.
- The lack of an established market and channels of distribution.
- Problems in establishing basic management systems and controls.

Also, the risk of failure is higher in small business start-ups than in acquiring a franchise or even buying an existing business.

To Buy an Existing Business?

Buying a business can mean different things to different people. It may mean acquiring the total ownership of an entire business, or it may mean acquiring only a firm's assets, its name, or certain parts of the business. Keep this point in mind as you study the following material. Also remember that many entrepreneurs find that taking over an existing business isn't always a "piece of cake," as the following example shows.

According to Elliott B. Ross, a former management consultant who is now chairman of Du-Wel Products Inc., a Bangor, Michigan, die-casting concern, the actual process of buying the company "was the most stressful business experience I ever had. Lawyers are always finding problems that nobody thought were there."[12]

Reasons for Buying an Existing Business

Some advantages of acquiring an established business are that:

- Capable personnel are already available and working.
- The facilities (building, equipment, and inventory) are already complete.
- A good or service is already being produced and distributed to an existing market.
- Revenues and profits are being generated.
- The location may be very desirable.
- Financial relationships have been established with banks and trade creditors.

Shortly before Christmas of 1985, the owner of the Speedy Bicycle Shop suddenly decided to sell the business because of a terminal illness. Don Albright, at that time the manager of a branch of the shop, arranged to buy the branch store. When the former owner decided to close the store without warning, Don alerted all the customers who had layaways to come and collect their purchases in order not to lose their deposits.

This gained Don a lot of goodwill when he reopened the branch shop as his own. Although he had to come up with a lot of capital to purchase new inventory, he had had the experience of managing the shop before he owned it. Don seems to have made a success of the business. It is now a teen hangout, sells skateboards as well as bicycles, and sponsors a BMX racing team.

Reasons for Not Buying an Existing Business

Some disadvantages of buying an ongoing business are:

- The physical facilities and product line may be old or obsolete.
- The employees may be stagnant and have a poor production record or attitude.
- Relations with unions may be poor.
- The inventory may contain an excessive amount of "dead stock."
- A high percentage of the assets may be in poor-quality accounts receivable.
- The location may be bad.
- The financial condition and relations with financial institutions may be deteriorating.

A group of investors was considering buying a coal mine in West Virginia. The market for coal was favorable, so the potential owners thought they had "a good deal." On examination, however, they found that the local coal was of such poor quality that the market would not accept the firm's product. The group wisely decided not to invest.

To Buy or Not to Buy

Even if there are several existing operations to choose from, the evaluation of alternatives finally must come down to one business to buy or not to buy. Then that business alone must be thoroughly evaluated before the final decision is made. This procedure can be compared to the steps involved in the first flight of an experimental plane or launching a space shuttle. As shown in Figure 5–6, the countdown involves several days, or even weeks, of intense preparation before the pilot climbs into the cockpit. Then comes the final countdown. Up until the last few seconds, the flight (mission) can be aborted, but from that point "All systems are go." The same tends to be true when buying an established business. Up to a given point, the buyer can change the decision to buy. Beyond that point, the decision is final. Money that has been put in escrow to assure the purchase will be lost if you decide against buying it.

A word of caution is needed here. Past success or failure is not sufficient foundation for a decision of whether or not to buy a given business. Instead, you must make a thorough analysis of the present condition of the business

Figure 5–6   To Go or Not to Go

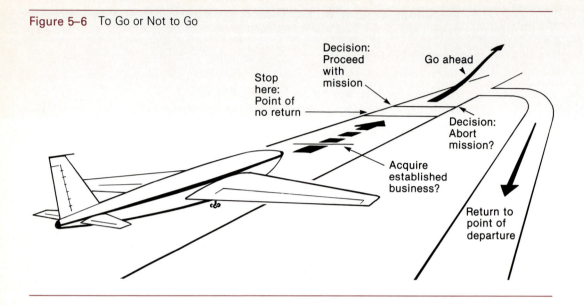

and an appraisal of what the business might do in the future, as shown in Figure 5–7.

Checklist B of Appendix D spells out some important questions to be asked when making the decision to buy an ongoing business. The number of each question here corresponds to its number in the checklist.

1. Why is the business available for purchase?   This question should help establish the validity of the owner's stated reason for selling the business. Some reasons provide a challenging opportunity, as this example shows.

Robert Sinclair had dropped out of college in his senior year for financial reasons. After working several years for a building supply firm, he went to work for a partnership engaged in diversified construction of commercial buildings. He was made manager of the metal door division. The partners were so busy with their other activities that they gave him little assistance or interest. Bob was left to run the division himself. Finally, he offered to buy the division from the partners, and they accepted. He is now the owner-manager of Sinclair Construction Company and two other small activities.

---

2. What are the intentions of the present owners?   After selling a business, former owners are free to do what they wish unless restricted by contract. What has been said before the sale and what happens afterward may not be the same. Some questions needing answers are: Will the present owner remain in competition? Does he or she want to retire or leave the area? What is the present owner's physical and financial health?

Figure 5–7   Buying an Existing Business—Tips for Making an Analysis and Appraisal

Although it may not appeal to true entrepreneurs, buying, rather than starting, a firm does have certain advantages: A quicker return on one's investment of time and money. To get those advantages, advises attorney Mitchell Kossoff, whose clients have taken both routes, "Make sure you are buying a business with a good location, an existing plant or facilities, competent employees, some market penetration, a solid base of paying customers, usable inventory and good relations with suppliers and creditors." But Kossoff warns, "This analysis is too complex for an individual to do alone. You'll need the services of lawyers, accountants, business brokers, business appraisers, consultants and bankers."

"They will examine balance sheets, income tax returns—both federal and local—and other financial statements prepared by a CPA for the seller," says accountant and attorney Stuart Rosenblum. "Have your accountant go over the financial statements and put your attorney to work performing a lien and judgement search on the owners and the hard assets of the business."

Find out why the seller wants to sell. Is the client base diminishing? Are there supply problems or employee problems? Maybe the plant and facilities are obsolete, there are disputes with the landlord, or creditors are after the seller. "Never take the seller's word for why he or she is selling," Rosenblum warns. "Try and dig deep and find the real reason."

Once you have determined the value of the tangibles in the business, you must place a value on the intangibles—often called "goodwill." This can include its relations with customers, banks and suppliers.

Next, decide how much the business is worth. "It has to be a better investment than other, more traditional investments," Kossoff says. "Consider the rate of return, analyze the assets, then subtract from them the liabilities."

The financial arrangements you make with the seller are limited only by law and your accountant's creativity.

Source: Stephen M. Pollan and Mark Levine, "Playing to Win: The Small Business Guide to Survival & Growth," *U.S. News & World Report,* December 12, 1988, Special Advertising Section, p. A12.

One Sunday, Ron Sikorsky was reviewing the classified ads in the newspaper and spotted an item of interest: "For reasons of health, owner willing to sacrifice successful, profitable sandwich shop, priced for immediate sale." Ron dashed over to the Submariner. The place was full, and business was great. (All the owner's friends just happened to need a sandwich that day.) Ron was able to engage the owner in negotiation. Following some haggling, the principals shook hands, and Ron wrote a check for $10,000 of his savings.

A month later, Ron was chagrined to learn that the business had been ready to fold when he took the bait. The former owner's friends were gone, and business was terrible. The $10,000 received by the former owner had proved to be a "miracle cure" for his ill health.

---

3. Are environmental factors changing?   The demand for a firm's product may rise or fall because of such factors as population characteristics, neighborhood, consumer habit, or changes in zoning, traffic pattern, environment, tax law, or technology.

The owners of a Florida company processing large cans of grapefruit juice decided to build a new, more efficient plant. As soon as the facility was completed, they found themselves competing with a new plant producing fresh-frozen juice concentrates.

4. Are physical facilities suitable for present and future operations? To be suitable, facilities must be properly planned and laid out, effectively maintained, and up-to-date.

Ramon Gutierrez and his wife had been running the Lone Star Drugstore for 40 years—largely without making changes and improvements. After the death of his wife, Gutierrez, who was approaching 70, decided to sell the business. He was unable to find a buyer. His equipment was so antiquated and in such poor condition that it was useless to others. He finally sold his stock and prescription file to another pharmacist.

5. Is the business operating efficiently? A prospective buyer should know whether a business will need to be "whipped into shape" after purchase. Are the personnel effective? Is waste excessive or under control? Is the quality of the product satisfactory, and is the inventory at the proper level and up to date? The following two actual situations are examples of waste and obsolescence.

a.   *An example of waste:* A potential buyer of a carpet mill noticed that the mill's employees were slicing off one to three inches on each side of the carpets as they were being produced. In the follow-up analysis, he found that if the machines were properly set, the mill could save $10,000 per day,

b.   *An example of inventory obsolescence:* In 1970, the owner of a hardware store decided to sell the business. A prospective buyer found 200 horse collars among the antiquated stock.

6. What is the financial condition of the firm? It is important to know whether the firm is a good financial risk. This can be determined by checking variables such as the validity of financial statements, the cash position, the cash flow through the business, various financial ratios, the amount and terms of debt, and the adequacy of cost data.

7. How much investment is needed? Remember that the investment includes not only the purchase price of the existing firm but also capital needed for renovations, improvements, and start-up activities, such as ordering new stock, advertising and promotion, and legal and license fees.

8. What is the estimated return on investment? This estimate should be realistic and not based on wishful thinking. It should include potential losses as well as potential gains.

Other factors to consider.   One important factor that should always be considered is the price asked for the firm. Sometimes, for some reason, a successful, ongoing business can be bought at a fraction of its dollar cost or replacement value. But while you may be lucky enough to get such a bargain, be very wary of pitfalls. For example, a retailer may offer to sell a business for "the current price of assets—less liabilities." But the accounts receivable may be a year or more in arrears, while the inventory consists of unsalable goods. Also, the extent of liability should be verified. Be sure to have a CPA audit the records and verify the inventory and its value.

A grocer who wanted to sell her store reduced her retail prices in order to attract a large number of customers. It mattered little to her that many items were reduced to cost or less. A potential buyer saw the crowd of customers, thought the store was a good buy, and bought it. About three weeks after assuming ownership and management, he had to replenish the stock. He had to raise his prices, but then his sales dropped off, and he was very unhappy over his situation. Soon, he was forced out of business.

Another element to consider is your managerial ability. Some people have a special talent for acquiring ongoing businesses that are in economic difficulty. They can come into the business and initiate changes that turn it around. If you have—or can develop—this special talent, the ability is valuable to society and profitable to you, the new entrepreneur.

An experienced small businessman recently sold one of his businesses. He searched for an existing business to get involved in. His interests included managerial challenge, economic growth, and profit. After looking at several possibilities, he acquired a small company that manufactured a top-quality airport service vehicle. The company needed additional capital and more effective management. The new owner was able to bring these two ingredients into the company and make it a success.

To Buy a Franchise?

According to the *Pacific Bell Directory,* "Franchising is now the most popular form of business available."[13] Even though franchising is expanding rapidly and appears to be very successful, some franchsors have failed, and some franchisees have had severe losses. The general subject of franchising has been covered in Chapter 4.

Reasons for Buying a Franchise

Franchise agreements normally spell out what both the franchisor and franchisee are responsible for and must do, as well as the goals of the parties. Each party usually desires the success of the other. The franchisor brings methods of operation and business images to aid the franchisee, as shown in Figure 5–8.

If you decide to start your own business, you can obtain guidance from experienced people by obtaining a franchise. Franchises are available in a wide range of endeavors. On the other hand, there may be no franchise to fit your original idea or your particular talents.

David and Tamara Kennedy, of Sausalito, California, once made their living skippering and being a Cordon Bleu chef aboard privately owned yachts around the world. But they were drawn to an ad by a nautical bookstore franchise—Armchair Sailor Bookstore—seeking to expand nationally. "Must have a love of the sea and know how to sail," it said. "While we won't become millionaires," they admit after buying a franchise, "we love what we're doing and are doing something we know about. It's been a learning experience for both of us."[14]

Another reason for buying a franchise is that it is already in operation and probably has many of the requirements for success. The market niche has been identified, and sales activities are in place. Also, the business may already be located, managed, and running. The questions to ask about

---

Figure 5–8 Services Provided by Competent Franchisors

1. Start-up assistance, such as market information, site location, building and equipment design and purchase, and financial help.
2. A proven and successful system for operating the business.
3. A standardized accounting and cost control system for business records. These records are audited periodically by the franchisor's staff. In many instances, standard monthly operating statements are required. The franchisor develops a set of standard performance figures based on composite figures of reporting franchisees and returns a comparative analysis to the franchisee as a managerial aid.
4. In some instances, financial assistance where minimum equity requirements are met by the potential franchisee. This financing covers land, building, equipment, inventory, and working capital needs.
5. Assistance with the purchase of the site and the construction of a standardized structure with a design identified with the franchise.
6. A training program to help train employees to operate and manage the unit. (The more successful franchisors have their own special training schools, such as McDonald's Hamburger University and the Holiday Inn University.)
7. A well-planned and well-implemented national or regional advertising program, establishing and maintaining a uniform image.
8. A set of customer service standards. These are created by the franchisor and its professional staff, who make regular inspection visits to assure compliance by the franchisee.
9. Sensitivity and responsiveness to changing market opportunities.
10. The advantage of discounts for buying in large quantities.

franchises are: How much help do I need? Can a franchise help me enough to more than cover the costs of the franchise?

Other reasons for buying a franchise are (1) to obtain a well-developed marketing program and (2) to have an operating training program for yourself and all your staff.

Most potential and new small business owners do not have all the competencies or resources to get started successfully. The franchisor can provide supplemental help through its experience and concentrated study of the field. These talents come from both successes and failures in the past. A study of the services listed in the contract in comparison with your needs shows the value to you.

Reasons Not to Buy a Franchise

A franchise is not a guarantee of success. It can cost more than the benefits from its purchase. Including expenses such as the initial investments and fees, as well as royalty payments, a franchise can be costly, as noted in Chapter 4. It may not fit the owner's desires or direction, or it may not give the franchisee enough independence.

However, a careful study of the contract, the operations, other franchises, and literature reduces the risk of a poor franchisor-franchisee relationship. Overpriced, poorly run, uninteresting, and white elephant franchises must be eliminated from consideration.

A man put up $2,000 as a guaranteed investment for gum and candy machines. The franchisors promised to find good locations for the machines. These failed to materialize, however, because all the desirable locations were already in use. The franchisor disappeared, and the man lost his $2,000.

Even in the best franchise situations, franchisors tend to hold an advantage, as shown in Figure 5–9. Usually, this relates to operating standards, supply and material purchase agreements, and agreements relating to the repurchase of the franchise. Also, there are constraints as to the size of

---

Figure 5–9   How Franchising Benefits Both Franchisee and Franchisor

Selected benefits to the franchisee	Selected benefits to the franchisor
1. Brand recognition	1. Faster expansion and penetration
2. Management training and/or assistance	2. Franchisee motivation
3. Economies of large-scale buying	3. Franchisee attention to detail
4. Financial assistance	4. Lower operating costs
5. Share in local or national promotion	

Source: Leon C. Megginson, Lyle R. Trueblood, and Gayle M. Ross, *Business* (Lexington, Mass.: D.C. Heath, 1985), p. 124.

the territory and the specific location. Moreover, you sometimes have no choice about the layout and decor.

However, careful study of franchisors' past records and contract offerings can lead to selection of a potentially successful franchise operation. Checklist C in Appendix D suggests how to analyze the desirability of buying a franchise.

WHAT YOU SHOULD HAVE LEARNED

1. The first thing to do in becoming a small business owner is to decide whether that is what you *really* want to do. Then, proper planning becomes essential to chart your new venture. The time of starting your new business is also important.

2. Although there is no set procedure for choosing and starting a business, there are certain well-defined steps that can be taken to help ensure success. They are: (*a*) search for and identify a needed product, (*b*) study the market for the product, including the size, competition, and your estimated share, (*c*) decide whether to start a new business, buy an existing one, or buy a franchise, (*d*) make strategic plans, including setting a mission, objectives, and strategies, (*e*) make operational plans, including setting up policies, budgets, procedures, and plans for actually operating the business, (*f*) make financial plans, including estimating income, expenses, and initial investment, and locating sources of funds, (*g*) prepare a business plan, and (*h*) implement the business plan.

3. The product to sell can be found by: (*a*) reading books, papers, and other information, (*b*) having social and business conversations with friends, support groups, businesspeople, and others, (*c*) listening to new ideas and innovative thinking, and (*d*) using checklists, questioning people, and doing research yourself.

4. Studying the market for the problem involves estimating: (*a*) the size of the market, (*b*) the competition and its share of the market, and (*c*) your own sales and share of the market.

5. Next, you should ask yourself whether you want to: (*a*) start a new business, (*b*) buy an existing one, or (*c*) buy a franchise. There are compelling arguments for and against each of these alternatives. Starting your own business means having no prior commitments and that the business is truly your own. But this process is time consuming and quite risky.

   When you buy an existing business, you acquire established markets, facilities, and employees. In spite of these advantages, you must make sure when you buy that all aspects of the business are in good shape and that you are not inheriting someone else's problem(s).

   Buying a franchise may help bring success in a hurry, as it provides successful management and operating procedures to guide the business. But you must be able to succeed on your own, for a franchise does not ensure success. Also, the cost may be high, or the franchisor may not perform satisfactorily.

KEY TERMS

Service Corps of Retired
   Executives (SCORE), *133*

market research, *136*

QUESTIONS FOR DISCUSSION

1. (*a*) Is planning really as important in starting a business as the authors say? (*b*) Defend your answer.
2. What are some important factors to consider in choosing the type of business to enter?
3. (*a*) How can you identify a business you would like to own? (*b*) What characteristics do you have that would help make that business successful?
4. (*a*) How do you go about determining the market for a product? (*b*) Your share of that market?
5. What kinds of answers to the questions in Figure 5–3 would lead you to eliminate a business from consideration?
6. What are some of the characteristics you should consider in studying the potential market for a proposed business?
7. What are some reasons for and against starting a new business?
8. What are some reasons for and against buying an existing business?
9. What are some reasons for and against buying a franchise?

SUGGESTED READINGS

Atkins, Norman D. "Putting Ideas into Action." *Venture,* February 1986, p. 107.

Eckert, Lee. "Owning the Store." *Entrepreneur,* February 1989, pp. 42–45.

Greene, Richard. "Do You Really Want to Be Your Own Boss?" *Forbes,* October 21, 1985, pp. 86–87.

Hisrich, Robert D., and Candida G. Brush. *The Woman Entrepreneur: Starting, Financing, and Managing a Successful Business.* Lexington, Mass.: Lexington Books, 1985.

Ricklefs, Roger. "Crisis Consultant." *The Wall Street Journal,* February 24, 1989, p. R31.

———. "Schools Increase Courses to Help Entrepreneurs." *The Wall Street Journal,* February 6, 1989, p. B1.

Stevenson, Howard H., and William A. Sahlman. "How Small Companies Should Handle Advisors." *Harvard Business Review* 26 (March–April 1988): 28–33.

Szabo, Joan C. "SCORE Advises Small Businesses." *Nation's Business,* March 1988, p. 12.

"What the SBA Can Do for You." *USA Today,* May 8, 1989, p. 1E.

ENDNOTES

1. This section is based on F. J. Roussel and Rose Epplin, *Thinking about Going into Business?*, U.S. Small Business Administration Management Aid No. 2.025. This and other publications are available for a small processing fee. Write SBA, Office of Business Development, Box 15434, Fort Worth, TX 76119, for free order forms 115A and 115B.

2. Management Aid No. 2.016. Order from the SBA at the address given in footnote 1.

3. See Stanley W. Angrist, "Entrepreneur in Short Pants," *Forbes*, May 7, 1988, pp. 84–85, for a different approach.

4. Keith H. Hammonds, "What B-School Doesn't Teach You about Start-Ups," *Business Week*, July 24, 1989, p. 40.

5. Jeanne Saddler, "Specialized Firms Stick to the Straight and Very Narrow," *The Wall Street Journal*, May 19, 1989, p. B2.

6. Hammonds, "What B-School Doesn't Teach You about Start-Ups," p. 41.

7. Jeanne Saddler, "Entrepreneurs' Support Group Eases Stress," *The Wall Street Journal*, April 27, 1989, p. B2.

8. Carter Henderson, *Winners* (New York: Holt, Rinehart & Winston, 1985), p. 34.

9. You can order this and other U.S. Census publications from the Bureau of the Census, U.S. Department of Commerce, Washington, DC 20233. Other documents can be bought from the U.S. Government Printing Office, Washington, D.C. 20402.

10. For further information on how to do this, see Stephen M. Pollan and Mark Levine, "Playing to Win: The Small Business Guide to Survival & Growth," *U.S. News & World Report*, December 12, 1988, Special Advertising Section, pp. A10, A12.

11. Otto Friedrich, "Seven Who Succeeded," *Time*, January 7, 1985, pp. 40–44.

12. Roger Ricklefs and Udayan Gupta, "Traumas of a New Entrepreneur," *The Wall Street Journal*, May 10, 1989, p. B1.

13. "Franchising: The Take-Out Recipe for Success," *Small Business Success* 11 (1989): 27. Copyright by Pacific Bell Directory.

14. Ibid., p. 28.

6

STRATEGIC AND OPERATIONAL PLANNING

The hardest—but best—part of being an entrepreneur is getting the business off the ground.— Phil Romans, founder of Stix Eating Spa

*If there's one thing certain about business today, it's change. . . . To meet change head-on, you must predict it, plan for it, and use it.—*J. Neal Thomas, head of Arthur Young's Entrepreneurial Services

LEARNING OBJECTIVES

After studying the material in this chapter, you will be able to:

1. Tell why planning is so important—yet is so neglected—in small businesses.
2. Distinguish between strategic and operational planning.
3. Explain the role of strategic planning, and give some examples.
4. Explain the role of operational planning, and give some examples of what is involved.
5. Explain the role of financial planning, and give some examples of it.

SPACE SERVICES INC.: USHERING IN THE U.S. COMMERCIAL SPACE INDUSTRY

"Long live free enterprise!" shouted some 300 observers as the 37-foot-long *Conestoga I* rocket lifted off from a makeshift launch pad on the Texas Gulf Coast on September 9, 1982. David Hannah, Jr., chairman of Space Services Inc. (SSI), said to his fellow investors: "I think we're going to make a lot of money with this."

The launch culminated years of effort—and some disappointments. The original *Conestoga*, aptly named for the covered wagons used by early American pioneers, blew up while being tested the week before launch. The firm hired an experienced California contractor and a former astronaut, "Deke" Slayton, as president and flight director. With the help of a $2.5 million investment, these two people, along with six other full-time employees, succeeded in developing the *Conestoga I*.

After spending $6 million just to achieve one successful launch, SSI then raised the $15 million needed to develop, supply, and manage low-cost launch vehicles, launch sites, launch activities, and related services. It plans to offer these commercial systems and services to a broad range of customers in the private sector and government agencies—especially as an alternative to the manned space shuttle. Since the 1986 *Challenger* explosion, there has been renewed interest in unmanned space programs.

By the early 1990s, this privately financed venture is expected to have a fleet of telecommunications and earth-scanning satellites. At least "a dozen" energy companies have expressed interest in doing business with SSI, especially to monitor oil flows at untended offshore wells and to conduct geological surveys from space.

These plans came closer to reality on March 29, 1989, when SSI launched the nation's first private spaceship into a 15-minute suborbital

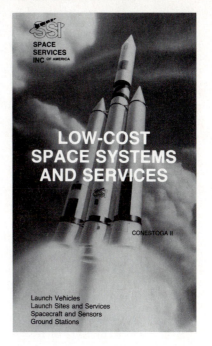

SPACE SERVICES INC OF AMERICA

LOW-COST SPACE SYSTEMS AND SERVICES

CONESTOGA II

Launch Vehicles
Launch Sites and Services
Spacecraft and Sensors
Ground Stations

flight that was expected to usher in the age of U.S. commercial space industry. *Consort I*—costing between $1 and $2 million, standing 52 feet tall, and weighing 6,000 pounds at lift-off—was launched from the White Sands Missile Range, New Mexico. It carried six experiments assembled by the University of Alabama–Huntsville's Consortium for Materials Development in Space, which is one of 16 commercial development consortiums sponsored by NASA.

SSI plans several similar launches in the next couple of years and is applying for a license to be the first private contractor to send a satellite into orbit. It believes there is a big future for this type of activity.

Source: Correspondence with Space Services Inc. of Houston, Texas, and others, including "Up, Up, Away," *USA Today,* March 30, 1989, p. 3A; and "Spaceship's Flight Lasts 15 Minutes," *Mobile* (Alabama) *Register,* March 30, 1989, p. 6–A.

The Opening Focus illustrates some of the problems involved in planning, organizing, and developing a new business. It also illustrates some of the eight steps required to start a new business. The first three of those steps were discussed in Chapter 5, and steps 7 and 8 will be covered in Chapter 7. Steps 4, 5, and 6 are explained in detail in this chapter, which covers:

- The role of planning.
- The role of strategic planning.
- The role of operational planning.
- The role of financial planning.

THE ROLE OF PLANNING

In order to become an effective small business owner-manager, you must look ahead. In selecting the business to enter, as discussed in the last chapter, you are doing just that—planning for the future.

As shown in Figure 6–1, planning should be the first step in performing a series of managerial functions, as it sets the future course of action both for the business as a whole and for each part of it. **Planning,** which is the process of setting objectives and devising courses of action to achieve those objectives,[1] answers such questions as: What business am I in? What finances do I need? What is my sales strategy? Where can I find needed personnel? How much profit can I expect?

Why Small Businesses Need to Plan

Planning is one of the most difficult activities small business owners have to do. Yet it is essential because, before taking action, managers must know where they are going and how to get there. Outsiders who invest or lend money need to know what are a firm's chances of success—and their chances of making money. Plans provide courses of action, information to others, bases for change, and a means of delegating work. In summary, well-developed plans can:

- Interest moneyed people in investing in your business.
- Guide the owner and managers in operating the business.
- Give direction to and motivate employees.
- Provide an environment to attract customers and prospective employees.

Why Small Businesses Neglect Planning

Although planning is so important, it is one of the most difficult managerial activities to perform. For this reason, small businesspeople, preoccupied with day-to-day operations, often neglect planning or must force themselves to do it. They should remember that, while predicting the future is risky, doing no planning can be disastrous.

We've suggested one reason why so many small business owners and

Figure 6–1   How Planning Relates to Other Managerial Functions

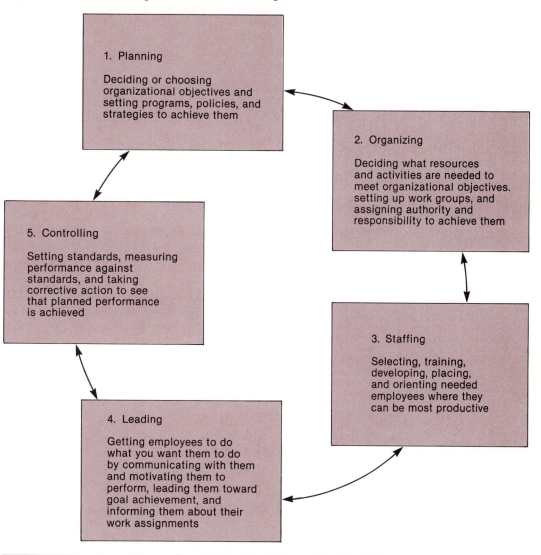

managers neglect planning, despite its importance: day-to-day activities leave them little or no time for planning. Some other reasons are:

- They fear the problems and weaknesses planning may reveal.
- They lack knowledge of how to plan.
- They feel that future changes cannot be planned for.

In summary, planning requires original thinking, takes time, and is difficult to do, but it does help one to see potential problems and prepare to cope with them.

Types of Planning

As shown in Figure 6–2, planning is usually divided into two types according to the nature of the planning and the distance into the future for which the planning is done. These criteria set the level in the organization where the planning is usually done and the amount of research required to do it.

The first type, which is long-range, high-level planning, is called **strategic planning.** It consists of (1) setting the company's mission and establishing the objectives that need to be attained in order to accomplish it and (2) determining strategies, which are the methods used to achieve those objectives.

Operational planning is needed to carry out the strategic plans and operate the business. It sets (1) policies, (2) methods, (3) procedures, (4) budgets, and (5) standards.

Figure 6–2 Some of the Most Important Types of Plans and Planning Functions

Types of plans and planning functions	Examples
Strategic planning:	
Mission: The long-term direction of the business.	To provide financial security at low cost.
Objectives: Shorter-term ends to meet mission.	
For total firm.	Earn a 20 percent return on investment by 1993.
For functional area.	Increase penetration of market by 25 percent by 1994.
Strategies: Means to achieve an end, or courses of action needed to achieve objectives.	
For total firm.	Establish control procedure to control costs by 1993.
For functional area.	Use 1 percent of sales to improve and expand service.
Operational planning:	
Policies: Guides to action that provide consistency in decision making, particularly in repetitive situations.	Personnel policy: Promote from within, giving preference for promotions to present employees.
Methods and procedures: Prescribed manner of accomplishing desired output.	Employee selection: complete application, test, interview, investigate, select.
Budgets and standards: Plans for future activities using measures for control.	Cash budget for planning use of money.

THE ROLE OF STRATEGIC PLANNING

Strategic planning is perhaps the most important type of planning that owners and managers of small business must do, for a strategic plan is the major, comprehensive, long-term plan that determines the nature of the business. Unfortunately, only about a third of small firms use long-range strategic planning.[2]

As shown in Figure 6–2, strategic planning consists of two parts: the firm's mission and objectives, and its strategies. Some examples of strategic planning are shown in Figure 6–3.

Mission and Objectives

Companies must plan ahead for varying lengths of time into the future. The **mission** is a long-range vision of what the business is trying to become. It is concerned with broad concepts such as the firm's image, with the basic services the firm plans to perform (e.g., "entertainment" instead of just "movies"), and with long-term financial success. Once set, missions are rarely revised.

A clear definition of your mission enables you to design results-oriented objectives and strategies. To deviate from your true mission can have adverse results, as the following example shows.

George Patterson and a partner founded City Gardens Inc. in Boston to sell and maintain plants for offices. Within a few years, however, the original mission had become blurred. The partners had opened a retail flower store in Boston, a garden center in Washington, D.C., and a branch office in Atlanta. "We lost a lot of money, and we were going nowhere," says Patterson.

What business were they in? "Plants" seemed the only way to describe it. What business should they be in? The answer, they decided, was "interior landscaping," since their competitive edge was their expert knowledge of the local market. So they got rid of their non–interior landscaping activities.[3]

Figure 6–3   Examples of Strategic Planning Activities

1. Selection of the type of business to enter.
2. Formulating the mission of the company.
3. Deciding whether to start a new business, buy an existing one, or buy a franchise.
4. Choosing the product or service to sell.
5. Decision on the market niche to exploit.
6. Selection of the location for the business.
7. Choosing the type of organization to use.
8. Determination of financial needs.

Figure 6–4   Firm's Objectives for 1991, 1992, and 1993

	1991	1992	1993
Total net profit (income) after taxes	$_____	$_____	$_____
Return on investment (ROI) (net income after taxes/total assets)	_____	_____	_____
Return on equity (ROE) (net income after taxes/equity)	_____	_____	_____
Total sales volume (units)	_____	_____	_____
Total sales volume ($)	_____	_____	_____
Return on sales (ROS) (net income after taxes/sales)	_____	_____	_____

To attain a _____ percent share of market by the end of 1992.

To have a _____ percent debt-to-equity ratio in the capital structure initially, declining to _____ percent debt-equity at the end of 1992.

To develop a new product by the end of 1993.

Objectives are the goals that give shorter-term direction to the business and serve as benchmarks for measuring performance. Meeting these objectives leads to the accomplishment of the mission. Examples of objectives might include "To increase total sales by 8 percent a year" and "To introduce within the next two years a new product aimed at the middle-class consumer." Objectives are more specific than missions and are revised more frequently. Figure 6–4 illustrates how objectives can be set for a small business.

Formulating the mission and objectives for a small business involves two important considerations: the firm's external environment and the internal resources that give it a competitive edge.

The External Environment

The external environment includes clients, competitors, the economy, technology, and many other influences. Changes caused by the introduction of videotapes, computer hardware and software, lasers, and population aging, for example, have been a blessing to some companies and a death warrant to others. The expanding communication and transportation systems have made management—even of the smallest companies—keep abreast of a constantly widening range of events. The needs and desires of clients, often following fads, may change so rapidly that changes go unnoticed.

Sally Von Werlhof started Salaminder Inc. in 1974 to design, produce, and sell only top-of-the-line American-made western apparel. Growth was steady and manageable until the 1980 movie *Urban Cowboy* caused the demand for western wear to skyrocket. Salaminder was swamped with orders and expanded to 60 employees. But sales plummeted in July 1981, when the fad died just as suddenly as it had begun.[4]

Even the international environment can favorably or adversely affect a small business's operations, as the following example shows.

In the early 1980s, when China began to emphasize private enterprise and enter joint ventures with Americans, Clark Copy International Corporation, a small, five-year-old company making plain-paper copiers in a cramped plant near Chicago, formed a joint venture with China. It signed a 20-year agreement to sell China 1,000 copiers, along with parts for another 5,000 machines. But in the late 1980s, China de-emphasized private enterprise, and this—along with the student protests of 1989, fueled by imported copiers and fax machines—could adversely affect Clark's position.[5]

Internal Resources and Competitive Edge

The internal resources found in every small business include those listed below. Also, to be competitive, the resources must include the characteristics listed.

1. **Human resources** include both management and nonmanagement people and include positions such as production supervisors, sales personnel, financial analysts, engineers, and key operating employees. To make the company competitive, these people must be motivated, imaginative, qualified, team members, dedicated, and discerning.
2. **Physical resources** include buildings, equipment, warehouses, inventories, and service and distribution facilities. To be competitive, these resources must be strategically located, be productive, be low in operating costs, be effective distributors, and make the proper product or service.
3. **Financial resources** include cash flow, debt capacity, and new equity availability. To make the company competitive, company finances must be adequate to maintain proper levels of current assets, to take advantage of opportunities, for sales promotion, and for proper management.

If a small firm has exceptionally good resources and they are effectively used, it can have a **competitive edge** over its competitors. Therefore, a proper evaluation of available resources may permit you to avoid activities that appear attractive but are really more costly than profitable, and to concentrate on more productive activities.

For example, in the case of Salaminder Inc., Sally Von Werlhof tried to diversify beyond the limits of her resources. She found, however, that the production process for a new line of $5 pot holders took as long as that for a $50 garment. A new line of children's clothes cost only $3 less to make than one for adults that sold for $40 more.

Since the production system was not designed for these changes, Von Werlhof had to retreat. She discontinued unprofitable products that did not conform to the company's basic process and concentrated on licensing Salaminder designs to other producers. Sales increased by 50 percent.[6]

As you can see from these examples, a small business must align its mission, objectives, and resources with its environment if it is to be most effective. The proper evaluation of its competitive edge can make a small firm's planning more realistic and lead to greater profitability.

Strategies

Strategies are the means by which the mission and objectives sought by a small business can be achieved. A basic question in setting strategies is: How should the business be managed in order to achieve its objectives and fulfill its mission? To be most effective, strategies should give a business a competitive advantage in the marketplace (see Computer Update). They should combine the various activities (such as marketing, production or operations, research and development, finance, and personnel) in order to use the firm's resources most effectively.

Figure 6–2 shows a strategy for achieving a 20 percent return on investment by 1993. The installation of a control system should help raise and maintain a more satisfactory profit performance. Figure 6–2 also shows how to set planned profit and compute what must be done to achieve it.

Figure 6–5 shows how a strategy can be set up to fulfill the mission of a small business. Notice that John Smith will provide certain services and policy coverage to clients so that they will have maximum personal financial security at the lowest possible cost.

Management by objectives (MBO) is an excellent method—strategy—for attaining goals. Many companies have found these programs most helpful in aligning the employees' goals with the firm's strategic objectives. MBO emphasizes goal orientation, with employees setting objectives for themselves. Their managers meet with them to discuss, change, and/or reach

---

Figure 6–5

Mission/Strategy of
John Smith, General Agent
Tulsa, Oklahoma

To provide the maximum amount of personal financial security at the lowest possible cost while maintaining the highest quality of personal individualized service.

To serve the financial needs of businesses, individuals, and their families in the Tulsa area through guaranteed income to meet loss from death or disability, through these services and policy coverages:

- Estate tax planning.
- Qualified pension and profit sharing.
- Group life and health.

- Ordinary life.
- Business interruption.

COMPUTER UPDATE

WHAT'S YOUR COMPETITION UP TO?

Miller Business Systems Inc. of Dallas plugs information obtained from customers into computer "profiles" of its competitors, which it then studies for ways of outmaneuvering these rivals. During a recent routine scan of those profiles, John W. Sample, Miller's vice president of sales and marketing, noticed that a competitor had hired nine furniture salesmen in a 10-day period. He believed that was a tip-off to a probable push by the competitor in the office furniture market. Sample had Miller's salesmen make extra calls on their accounts and was able to blunt the competitor's sales drive. His conclusion: "Your best customers can sometimes be your best sources of information."

Source: Steven P. Galante, "More Firms Quiz Customers for Clues about Competition," *The Wall Street Journal*, March 3, 1986, p. 21.

---

agreement on those objectives, how they can be accomplished, and how they relate to achieving the firm's overall objectives.

In a well-designed MBO program, each employee is provided with appropriate feedback on results compared with the objectives set. Employees are expected to overcome obstacles that stand in the way of their achieving those objectives. Near the end of a designated period, employees prepare reports for review and discussion with their supervisor.

THE ROLE OF OPERATIONAL PLANNING

Why do so many small businesses fail? Probably the underlying reason in most cases is *lack of proper operational planning.* Three types of planning will improve a small business owner's chances of success: (1) operational planning before starting the business, (2) a business plan to attract investors, financiers, and prospective employees, and (3) continuous planning after the business starts operating.

Operational planning is vital whether you decide to plan a new business from the beginning, take over an existing firm, or buy a franchise, as it helps potential entrepreneurs avoid costly blunders. It also should save time and result in a more polished final product.

As shown in the previous chapter (Figure 5–1), the business process involves putting the proper financial, physical, and human resources into an organization. These inputs are converted through some form of operations or production into the goods and services, the outputs of the business. Figure 6–6 shows how these outputs are then distributed to other processors, assemblers, wholesalers, retailers, or the final consumer. Businesses can be set up to perform any one or more of the parts of this total process.

Figure 6–6   The Business Process

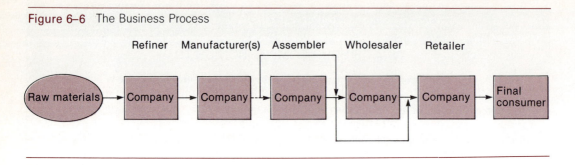

Setting up Policies, Methods, Procedures, Budgets, and Standards

As you can see from Figure 6–2 (page 156), operational planning starts with setting policies, methods and procedures, budgets, and standards. These form the basis for the other part of operational planning.

Policies guide action. They exist so that managers can delegate work and employees will make decisions based on the philosophy and thinking of the owner of the business.

Methods and **procedures** provide employees with instructions for performing their jobs. They comprise detailed explanations of how to do the work properly, and in what order it should be done.

Budgets set the requirements needed to follow the strategies and accomplish the objectives. For example, a cash budget shows the amount and times of cash income and outgo. It helps the manager determine when and how much to borrow. **Standards** establish the level of productivity expected of employees, facilities, and materials. Standards serve as incentives to motivate but also provide early warning of poor performance.

Planning to Operate the Business

The second part of operational planning—planning to operate the business—includes:

- Determining a location.
- Planning operations and physical facilities.
- Developing sources of supply from which to obtain materials and supplies.
- Planning personnel requirements.
- Setting up the legal and organizational structure.
- Determining an approach to the market.
- Establishing an efficient records system.
- Setting up a time schedule.

Determining a Location

The type of business to be operated influences most location decisions. It relates to access to customers, suppliers, employees, utilities, and transportation, as well as compliance with zoning regulations and other laws. The mission of the business is a basic consideration in seeking the right location.

Each type of firm has its own set of factors to consider and gives priority to those that most affect the business. Retailer location is based primarily on a marketing analysis. A manufacturing plant is concerned with costs and availability of labor, utilities, and transportation. Service organizations use different combinations of marketing cost factors in selecting their locations. These factors will be covered in detail in Chapter 13.

Planning Operations and Physical Facilities

You should decide early which part of the business process your firm will perform (see Figure 6–6). It is very difficult for a small firm to handle all the functions in the business process; therefore, you should choose the part you are best suited for. For example, an owner who is sales oriented may decide to be a retailer, while another person may choose to assemble a product. Some large companies foster and aid small businesses that will perform such services for them.

A firm's ability to sell its product is based on its ability to produce that product, as well as on its market potential. Good selection and efficient arrangement of physical facilities, then, is important. Too much capacity increases costs, which can reduce the competitive position of the company; too little capacity reduces the availability of goods and causes loss of sales. Therefore, you must try for proper balance of production and sales volume. Planning starts with the estimate of sales and the operations needed for the services and products. Using these estimates, the machines and skills needed for the demand can be determined.

Another decision you must make is whether to buy facilities outright or lease them. Any such choice between purchase and lease of plant and/ or machinery is based on differences in initial investment cost, operating performance and expense, and tax considerations. A photocopier is an example of an item that should probably be leased rather than purchased. Because of rapid improvements—and the need for prompt and proper maintenance— leased copiers will probably give more dependable service than purchased ones.[7] More details on locating and laying out facilities will be provided in Chapter 13.

Developing Sources of Supply for Goods and Materials

The largest expense for companies selling products usually is materials and/or goods; this cost is often more than 50 percent of the cost of goods sold. Therefore, the ability to purchase goods at favorable prices can lead to profitability—or vice versa. Lowest-cost materials do not necessarily mean inferior quality, and small firms should take every opportunity to reduce costs. But small businesses usually find it difficult to compete with large ones on a price basis only. Instead, they can more successfully compete on the basis of better quality, service, delivery, and so forth. The firm must be sure to have sources of supply that meet the company standards in all ways, including competitive prices. This topic is covered in greater detail in Chapter 14.

Planning Personnel Requirements

Personnel planning can be one of the most frustrating tasks that small business managers must face. Perhaps the primary reason for this is that the small business is not big enough to hire the specialized people needed. Prospective owners therefore need to estimate how much time they will spend in the business, for the less time the owner can devote to the business, the more important it will be to get capable employees. Not only will more employees be needed, but they must be able to work with less supervision than in larger firms.

Some important questions to ask yourself are: How many workers are needed? Where will they be obtained? How many managers will I need? How much to pay them? These and similar questions are discussed in Chapters 10, 11, and 12.

Setting Up the Legal and Organizational Structure

An organization structure must be developed, taking into consideration the legal and administrative aspects of the business. Both legal and administrative structures offer several options. Keeping in mind the basic premise that "My business is very personal," you must select the structure that is in your own best interest.

"I believe in keeping things simple and to the point."

Source: Reprinted from *The Wall Street Journal;* permission Cartoon Features Syndicate.

The legal form of a business may be a proprietorship, partnership, corporation (general or S Corporation), holding company, or cooperative. The administrative structure of the company should be based on factors such as (1) the strategic plan, including the main mission and objectives of the business, (2) the owner's personal and business objectives, (3) the plans, programs, policies, and practices that will achieve those objectives, and (4) the authority and responsibility relationships that will accomplish the mission or purpose of the firm. Organization is discussed in greater detail in Chapter 9.

Determining Approach to Market

The volume of sales and sales income of a small firm depend on its marketing strategies and activities.[8] If a study of the environment determines that there is a large enough market for its product(s), plans must be made to capture enough of the total market to be successful. Even if the company's service is the best, potential customers must be informed about it. Many methods of marketing are in use; the ones used must be chosen for the particular business.

Some years ago, a man living in New England conceived of a rubber, instead of metal, dustpan. He had a dozen samples of the new product custom-made in a variety of colors and headed to Boston to hawk his wares in Filene's and Jordan-Marsh. Neither seemed interested in the dustpan.

Still, he was sure that housewives would buy his product. As he was returning home, the idea of market testing the dustpan by calling on homemakers hit him. Pulling into a residential street, he parked his car and set out to ring doorbells. Just 45 minutes later, he returned to his car with only two pans left.

Convinced that his idea was good, Earl Tupper developed a company—Tupperware—to market the product directly to customers.

Once a target market is chosen, provision must be made for sales promotion and distribution to that group. The product to be offered should again be studied carefully to determine the special features to present to the potential customers. What qualities make it special to the customer? Are there features to emphasize, such as the ease of installation or low maintenance? Should the company use newspaper advertising or mailings to publicize the product? These and other questions are discussed in more detail in Chapters 15, 16, and 17.

Establishing an Efficient Records System

In starting a simple business, simple records and information systems can be used. But they must also be designed to help you control your business by keeping track of activities and obligations, and also to collect certain types of information demanded by outside organizations such as government agencies. For example, you must maintain records of such data as:

- The number of hours each employee works and the wages and benefits paid.
- Inventories, accounts receivable, and accounts payable.
- Taxes paid and owed.
- Units of each product sold.
- The date an employee is hired.

Records help to settle problems such as grievances, lawsuits, and returned merchandise; they also relieve people of carrying too much information around in their heads.

Accounting systems must be designed to keep track of company finances. Incoming revenues and outgoing expenses are processed into accounts that record changing values of assets, liabilities, and equity. The system for planning and controlling the finances can be based on a budget system that sets goals against which actual results can be compared. A member of SCORE can help you set up such a system.

For example, a SCORE counselor helped Sue Ley with her finances and set up a simple bookkeeping system for CleanDrum, Inc. (Case V–1).

The system of records for employees has expanded greatly during recent years as employee pay systems have become more complex and as government and legal controls have increased. Efforts to match skills to jobs and promote the proper person require records of factors such as experience, performance, education, and training. Records of accidents help identify unsafe practices.

Many other records are needed to help make the small business operate successfully. Management information systems should be selected and designed to aid management in decision making. Records and management information systems are discussed in Chapter 20. The SBA's Management Aids No. 1.017, *Keeping Records in Small Business*, would be quite helpful to you.[9]

Setting Up a Time Schedule

Once you decide to go ahead with the formation of your business, you should establish a time schedule to provide an orderly and coordinated program to follow. The schedule should probably include the prior planning steps as well as writing the business plan and implementing the steps leading to the running of the company. Many of these steps can be and often are performed simultaneously.

THE ROLE OF FINANCIAL PLANNING

Financial planning involves (1) estimating income and expenses, (2) estimating initial investment, and (3) locating sources of funds. These factors are covered in detail in Chapter 8.

Estimating Income and Expenses

The steps described so far set the stage for determining the profit (or loss) from operating your new business. Income from sales (also called *revenue*) can be estimated by studying the market; expenses (also called *costs*), such as purchases of material and supplies, utilities, physical facilities, personnel, and sales promotion, also can be estimated. Expense estimates can be obtained from past experience and other sources, such as knowledgeable people, a library, or a trade association. After all costs have been estimated, they can be totaled and subtracted from the estimated sales income to obtain the expected net profit (or loss), as shown in the worksheet for Dover Enterprises (name disguised) in Figure 6–7.

When making your estimates, remember two key points. First, these expense and income (or loss) estimates are usually for only one year of

Figure 6–7

DOVER ENTERPRISES
Worksheet for Estimated Annual Income,
Expenses, and Profit (Loss)*

	Units sold					
	10,000		20,000		30,000	
Income						
Sales income ($5/unit)		$50,000		$100,000		$150,000
Cost of goods sold:						
Production cost ($1.62/unit)	$16,200		$32,400		$48,600	
Shipping boxes and labels ($0.04/unit)	400		800		1,200	
Depreciation (mold)	2,500		2,500		2,500	
Total production expenses		19,100		35,700		52,300
Gross profit		30,900		64,300		97,700
Other operating expenses						
Salaries	30,000		30,000		30,000	
Telephone	3,000		3,500		4,000	
Rent	2,100		2,100		2,100	
Insurance	400		400		400	
Office expense	1,000		1,100		1,200	
Sales promotion	7,000		8,000		9,000	
Freight	1,000		2,000		3,000	
Travel	4,000		4,000		4,000	
Taxes and licenses	4,000		4,000		4,000	
Miscellaneous	1,000		2,000		3,000	
Total operating expenses		53,500		57,100		60,700
Net profit (loss)		($22,600)		$ 7,200		$ 37,000

* Projections for three levels of sales.

operations. However, if you also make an income analysis for an expected typical year in the future as well as for the first years, the exercise can provide valuable information for planning purposes.

Second, while total expenses do move up and down with sales volume, they do not vary as much. Some expenses, such as materials, rise in direct proportion to increases in sales volume and drop as sales volume drops. These fluctuating costs are called **variable expenses.** Other expenses, such as depreciation on buildings, do not vary in value as sales volume rises or falls. They are called **fixed expenses.** There are also expenses, such as supervision, that combine variable and fixed costs.

Changes in sales volume drastically affect the amount of net profit: as sales volume rises (say from 10,000 to 20,000 units), losses are reduced and profits may rise; as sales volume drops (say from 20,000 to 10,000), profits drop and losses may occur. An in-depth discussion of profit planning, including break-even analysis, may be found in Chapters 18 and 19.

Don't forget to also prepare a personal budget!   You—and your family—must have enough income to live on during the time when you are moving from being an employee to becoming an employer. If your standard of living drops too drastically, it will probably be devastating to your family. So, in addition to determining the expected income and expenses of the business, also estimate your continuing needs—and where you will get the resources to satisfy them.

Estimating Initial Investment

You will need money or credit to start your business. You must pay for items such as buildings, equipment, material, personnel, inventory, machines, business forms, and sales promotion at the outset—before income from sales starts providing the means to pay these expenses from internal sources. Credit may be extended to help sell the products, but this only adds to operating expenses.

The worksheet in Figure 6–8 provides a logical method of calculating the initial cash needs of a new business such as Dover's. The figures in column 1 are estimates that have already been calculated for the income statement for the first year. The amount of cash needed is some multiple of each of the values in column 1, as shown in column 3. The total of these multiple values is an estimate of the money needed to start the business and is shown in column 2.

Note that the cash needed to start the business—shown in column 2—represents the delay between paying money out for expenses and receiving it back as revenue. The item called *starting inventory* is an illustration of buying goods in one period and selling them in the next. But inventories of goods and supplies—in the form of purchases and recurring inventories—continue to exist for the life of the business. Therefore, funds obtained from investments in the business or from loans must continue for its life unless they are paid off.

Cash should not sit idle but should be used to earn income. The amount

Figure 6–8

DOVER ENTERPRISES
Estimated Monthly Expenses and Starting Costs
December 1, 1986

Estimated monthly expenses			
Item	(1) Estimate of monthly expenses based on sales of $100,000 per year	(2) Estimate of how much cash you need to start your business (see column 3)	(3) What to put in (2) (Multipliers are typical for one kind of business. You must decide how many months to allow for in your business.)
Salary of owner-manager	$ 2,500	$ 5,000	2 times column 1
All other salaries and wages	—	—	3 times column 1
Rent	175	525	3 times column 1
Travel		1,000	As required
Advertising	700	2,100	3 times column 1
Delivery expense	100	300	3 times column 1
Supplies	100	300	3 times column 1
Recurring inventory and purchases	—	—	Check with suppliers for estimate
Telephone and telegraph	300	900	3 times column 1
Other utilities	—	—	3 times column 1
Insurance		400	Payment required by insurance company
Taxes, including Social Security	325	1,300	4 times column 1
Interest	—	—	3 times column 1
Maintenance	—	—	3 times column 1
Legal and other professional fees	—	—	3 times column 1
Miscellaneous	200	600	3 times column 1

Figure 6–8 *(concluded)*

Starting costs you have to pay only once		
Fixtures and equipment: Telephone, $203; mold, $11,280; computer, $750	$12,233	Enter total from separate list
Decorating and remodeling	—	Talk it over with a contractor
Installation of fixtures and equipment	—	Talk to suppliers from whom you wish to buy these
Starting inventory	5,000	Suppliers will probably help you estimate this
Deposits with public utilities	—	Find out from utilities companies
Legal and other professional fees	—	Lawyer, accountant, and so on
Licenses and permits	(Part of taxes above)	Find out from city offices what you have to have
Advertising and promotion for opening	(Part of advertising above)	Estimate what you'll use
Accounts receivable	1,200	What you need to buy more stock until credit customers pay
Cash	1,000	For unexpected expenses or losses, special purchases, etc.
Other		Make a separate list and enter total
Total estimated cash you need to start with	$31,858	Add up all the numbers in column 2

Source: This basic worksheet is based on *Checklist for Going into Business,* Management Aids No. 2.016 (Washington, D.C.: Small Business Administration, 1983), p. 4.

of cash a business needs, and has, will vary during the year, since most businesses have busy and slack periods. To keep the investment and borrowing low, cash flow projections must be developed. The worksheet in Chapter 19 (Figure 19–2) illustrates a form that is used to make cash flow projections and then to compare the projection with what actually happens.

There are many sources from which you can get information to help estimate what these start-up costs are. The SBA has forms similar to the one in Figure 6–8, another entitled "Monthly Cash Flow Projection," and many others. Also, various financial firms and certified public accountants have computed some helpful standard figures.

For example, Baum & Krasnoff, a New York CPA firm, estimates that start-up costs for a manufacturing company with $100,000 of assets would be $108,300; a retail store with the same assets would need $123,800; a wholesale company with light warehousing would need $149,500, while with heavy warehousing it would need $282,000; and a service organization would need between $53,300 and $177,900.[10]

Locating Sources of Funds

Once the amount of funds needed for capital expenditures and for beginning operations is known, you must find sources for those funds. The ability to raise funds is one of the significant determinants of the size and type of business to enter, as is the method of financing the business. There is no one best method. While some have advantages over others, the attitudes and desires of investors or lenders determine the sources of financing available at a given time. The many sources from which to obtain funds to start and operate a business boil down to two: (1) the owner's funds and (2) funds from others. These two sources are discussed in detail in Chapter 8; so only the highlights are discussed here.

Before approaching a funding source, decide how much money you and others will put into the business and how much should come from loans. Every company has owners and investors who run the risk of losing their money but also stand to gain if the business is successful. Because of this risk, some security is usually given to those who lend money to the firm at a fixed rate of return. Thus, they do not stand to gain a great deal if the business succeeds; on the other hand, if it fails, their risk is low.

For example, Don Dover had invested in Dover Enterprises funds from his own reserves and from those of three relatives. All investors owned the company and made up its board of directors. Don, as president, also managed it on a day-to-day basis.

Using Your Own Funds

Some small business owners believe in investing only their personal funds and not borrowing to start or operate a business venture. Others believe that they should use little of their own money and, instead, obtain as much leverage as possible by using their interest in the business as a basis for obtaining funds from others. Normally, control of a company is exercised by owners, who take the risks of failure but also make the decisions. To maintain control, you must continue to invest more personal funds than all the other investors combined. Moreover, control can be maintained only so long as lenders do not become worried about the safety of their money.

Using Funds from Others

Several sources of outside funds are available. For example, it may be possible to find potential investors with excess funds who are interested in investing in a venture opportunity. Such people might be found among relatives, friends, or others through an attorney, certified public accountant (CPA), banker, or securities dealer.

Many individuals or groups are willing to lend money to a business but are not willing to assume the risks of ownership. They include private individuals, private financial institutions, merchandise and equipment vendors, and government agencies. There are many outright grants available from government agencies to start new businesses, especially for minorities and women.

Sources of funding for small firms will be covered in detail in Chapter 8.

WHAT YOU SHOULD HAVE LEARNED

1. Not only is planning one of the key managerial functions, but it is usually done first since everything else depends on it. Effective planning establishes directions and goals for the owners of a small firm. But planning is especially difficult in small firms, where management is often fully engaged in day-to-day operations and "can't see the forest for the trees." Still, investors and employees, as well as managers, need some idea of where the company is coming from and where it's going, and they can often provide useful input for the actual planning process.

   Some barriers to planning by managers of small firms are fear of learning things they would rather not know, the unpredictability of plans, their uncertainty, and especially the lack of adequate time to plan.

2. Strategic planning—the first phase of planning, from which other plans are derived—determines the very nature of the business. Next comes operational planning, which sets policies, methods and procedures, budgets and standards, and other operating plans.

3. Strategic planning includes the company's mission, which tells what type of business you are in. The mission is affected by the firm's external environment and its internal resources and competitive edge. Once

the mission is determined, a company can establish its objectives, which state the goals it hopes to reach and provide a way of keeping score on its performance. Strategies are formulated as the means to be used to reach the objectives.

4. Operational planning, which includes policies, budgets, standards, procedures, and methods, *forms the basis for preparing the business plan.* It involves planning the overall operations of the business, including (a) determining its location, (b) planning operations and physical facilities, (c) developing sources of supply for goods and materials, (d) planning personnel requirements, (e) setting up the legal and organizational structure, (6) determining the approach to the market, (f) establishing an efficient records system, and (g) setting up a time schedule.

5. Financial planning involves (a) estimating income and expenses, (b) estimating investment requirements, and (c) locating sources of funds. Income and expenses should be estimated to make sure that the proposed business will be profitable. Estimates should be based on the firm's first year of operation, as well as a typical "good" year, since investors may be willing to assume some risk of loss at the beginning to achieve greater gains when the company is established. Also, estimates should be made of personal needs during the transition period.

These projections permit the prospective new owner to estimate the initial investment needed. Revenues should more than provide operational income after the company is established, but a certain amount of capital will be needed for start-up costs, and that investment cannot be recovered immediately.

Finally, sources of funds must be determined. The two sources are (a) the business owner(s) and (b) others, either private individuals or lending institutions.

KEY TERMS

planning, *154*

strategic planning, *156*

operational planning, *156*

mission, *157*

objectives, *158*

human resources, *159*

physical resources, *159*

financial resources, *159*

competitive edge, *159*

strategies, *160*

management by objectives (MBO), *160*

policies, *162*

methods and procedures, *162*

budgets, *162*

standards, *162*

variable expenses, *168*

fixed expenses, *168*

QUESTIONS FOR DISCUSSION

1. *(a)* Explain why planning is so badly needed by small businesses. *(b)* Why is it so often neglected?

2. *(a)* What are the two overall categories of planning? *(b)* What is the essential difference between the two?

3. *(a)* What is strategic planning? *(b)* Explain the two components of strategic planning.

4. Discuss the factors that should be considered in formulating a business's mission.

5. What is operational planning?

6. Explain each of the following: *(a)* policies, *(b)* methods and procedures, *(c)* budgets, and *(d)* standards.

7. *(a)* In planning to operate the business, what are the eight factors that must be planned for? *(b)* Explain each.

8. What is involved in financial planning?

9. What are the two sources of funds for a small business?

SUGGESTED READINGS

Blanchard, Kay. "Management Training." *Business Credit,* October 1988, p. 12.

Checklist for Going into Business. Management Aids No. 2.016. Washington, D.C.: Small Business Administration, 1985.

"Finding Workers in a Tight Market." *Nation's Business,* February 1988, p. 21ff.

"Keeping the Life Blood Flowing." Excerpt from *Being the Boss: How to Make a Success of Your Small Business. Accountancy,* June 1988, p. 144.

Peters, Thomas J., and Robert H. Waterman, Jr. "A Bias for Action," Chapter 5 of *In Search of Excellence.* New York: Harper & Row, 1982.

Roussel, F. J., and Rose Epplin. *Thinking about Going into Business?* Management Aids No. 2.025. Washington, D.C.: Small Business Administration, 1986.

"Where to Start: The Best Way to Begin the Planning Process Is to Challenge Basic Assumptions." *Inc.,* November 1985, p. 132.

ENDNOTES

1. B. Bird and M. Jalinek, "The Operation of Entrepreneurial Intentions," *Entrepreneurship Theory and Practice,* Winter 1988, pp. 21–29.

2. *The Wall Street Journal,* October 31, 1986, p. 37.

3. "Where to Start: The Best Way to Begin the Planning Process Is to Challenge Basic Assumptions," *Inc.,* November 1985, p. 132.

4. Donna Fenn, "Growing by Design," *Inc.,* August 1985, p. 86.

5. See Chapter 17 for further details.

6. See Fenn, "Growing by Design," p. 86, for further details.

7. An excellent guide to leasing can be found in Robert S. Cunningham, "Ten Questions to Ask Before You Sign a Lease," *Inc. Magazine's Guide to Small Business Success,* pp. 20–22.

8. M. H. Morris, et al., "The Role of Entrepreneurship in Industrial Marketing Activities," *Industrial Marketing Management,* November 1988, pp. 337–46.

9. Can be obtained free from SBA, Box 15434, Fort Worth, TX 76119.

10. Stephen M. Pollan and Mark Levine, "Playing to Win: The Small Business Guide to Survival & Growth," *U.S. News & World Report,* Special Advertising Section, December 12, 1988, pp. A24–A25.

7

PREPARING AND PRESENTING THE BUSINESS PLAN

Businesses don't plan to fail, they just fail to plan.—Old business adage

---

A completed business plan is a guide that illustrates where you are, where you are going, and how to get there.—Charles J. Bodenstab

LEARNING OBJECTIVES

After studying the material in this chapter, you will be able to:

1. Tell why a business plan is needed and what purpose it should serve.
2. Explain how to approach the preparation of the business plan.
3. List the components of a business plan.
4. Suggest ways to write and present the plan.
5. Prepare a sample business plan.

JIM BUSBY: PREPARING AND USING A "LIVING BUSINESS PLAN"

At 39, James L. Busby had become a legendary figure on the financial scene in Mobile, Alabama. Busby is founder, major stockholder, and CEO of QMS Inc. (formerly Quality Micro Systems), a profitable company that makes and markets computer print systems to meet today's needs for state-of-the-art computer printing. QMS's newest system is KISS, the first intelligent laser printer that is both smart and simple. KISS produces crisp, near-typewriter-quality output at 400 characters per second and works with Lotus®, WordStar®, and any other software that will print to a Diablo 630®, Epson FX-80®, or QUME Sprint®.

After graduating with an electrical engineering degree from the University of Alabama—where he'd taken computer courses and designed and built his own computer—Busby served in the U.S. Army Signal Corps, working with computers. Upon returning to Mobile, he was employed for four-and-a-half years at International Paper Company and Scott Paper Company, working with computerized systems, while studying for an M.B.A. in the evenings.

He became intrigued by Scott's roll-wrapping system, which was controlled by a computer except for labeling. On the way home from class one night, he nearly wrecked his car when the solution to the labeling problem came to him. He stayed up all night working out the details. Now here was his big chance to found his own company, but he knew that he needed money.

He wrote up a business plan, which showed that he needed $10,000—and someone outside to furnish the money. Then he went to a stockbroker, who told him to see a banker, who then said: "If you can raise $5,000, the bank will match it with a $5,000 loan." Busby called everyone he knew but could not raise the funds. After a week, he called the banker to tell him that he could not get the $5,000. The next day, the banker called to say that he had studied Busby's business plan. If Busby and his wife would

both sign the note, the bank would lend them the $10,000. They agreed and received the loan to start the firm. Busby and his brother-in-law Mike Dow started the company while still working full time at other jobs.

QMS was ranked 70th in *Forbes* magazine's 1986 ranking of the 200 "Best Small Companies in America." According to *Forbes*, QMS had a 21.7 percent five-year average return on equity.

Like other high-tech growth companies, QMS had to reposition itself after the 1987 crash. Now, Busby and his staff are moving QMS into its next growth stage. They regard the company's overall business plan—as well as each department's plan—as the "backbone of the company." It is a "living business plan" that has resulted in over $215 million in sales in its fiscal year 1989 from its 1,200 employees worldwide.

Source: Correspondence with QMS and other sources, including Cammie East, "Meet a Mobilian: James L. Busby, A Technological Person, Built a Career with His Homemade Computer," *Mobile* (Alabama) *Press Register*, June 2, 1985, p. 2–G; and Adline Clarke, "QMS Breaks Ground on New Facility," *Mobile* (Alabama) *Register*, October 5, 1989, p. 8–A.

As Jim Busby discovered, a new business results from the prospective owner's having both a good idea for producing and selling a product and the personal abilities and drive to carry out the idea. For example, a survey of the 665 fastest-growing private companies found that 88 percent "succeeded by taking an ordinary idea and pulling it off exceptionally well."[1] Yet other things such as buildings and machines, personnel, materials and supplies, and finances are also needed. Where do these things come from? How? They result from the extensive strategic, operational, and financial planning described in Chapters 5 and 6. And all that planning is formalized in the **business plan,** which is a tool for attracting the other components of the business formation package, the people and the money. A well-developed and presented business plan can provide the prospective small business owner with a "road map to riches."[2]

The importance of the business plan was demonstrated in 1989, when Eastern Airlines' unsecured creditors said they would not "give credence to offers to buy the bankrupt firm until the bidder submitted a credible business plan."[3]

PURPOSE OF THE BUSINESS PLAN

The business plan could be the most useful and important document you, as an entrepreneur, ever put together. When you are up to your ears in the details of starting the business, the plan keeps your thinking on target, keeps your creativity on track, and concentrates your power on reaching your goal.

The plan can be used as a powerful money-raising tool to attract venture capital, for those relatively few small business entrepreneurs who are willing to dilute control of their company. Although few owners use a plan to attract venture funds, many more use a formal business plan to obtain loans from lending agencies.

For example, when Steven and Barbara Chappell were ready to start up their Our Hero franchise, their savings were not adequate to pay the rent and other expenses. So they drew up a 20-page plan—including blueprints, personal data, itemized lists of requirements for materials and supplies, and statistics from the Our Hero franchisor—and presented it to four banks. Since all of them offered to lend the required funds, the Chappells negotiated with the bank that offered the best terms. (See Case II–2 for details.)

But an effective plan does more than just help convince prospective owners and others that the new business is sound. It provides a detailed blueprint for the activities needed to finance the business, develop the product, market it, and otherwise manage the new business. Business plans are also used for the continuing operations of a firm.

For example, a *Venture* survey of 1,090 small business owner-managers found that 89 percent of them used the business plan to set employee goals, and 85 percent used it to establish records for management.[4] They also used it to help "run the business," and to serve as a yardstick to measure how the business was running.

An effective business plan investigates in detail the feasibility of an idea. It should therefore include a detailed analysis of:

- The proposed product.
- The expected market for it.
- The strengths and weaknesses of the industry.
- Planned marketing policies, such as price, promotion, and distribution.
- Operations or production methods and facilities.
- Financial aspects, including expected income, expenses, profits (or losses), investment needed, and expected cash flow.

In addition, a properly developed and well-written business plan should answer questions such as:

- Is the business formation package complete?
- Would it be attractive to venture capitalists?
- Does the proposed business have a reasonable chance for success at the start?
- Does it have any long-run competitive advantages to the owner? To the investor? To employees?
- Can the product be produced efficiently?
- Can it be marketed effectively?
- Can the production and marketing of the product be economically financed?
- Can the new company's business functions—operations, distribution, finance, and personnel—be properly managed? Are the needed people available?
- Can the prospective owner express the plans for the proposed business in writing in a clear, concise, and logical way so that it is easily understood and convincing to potential investors or lenders?

In summary, if the plan is properly developed and written, it provides more than mere numbers on paper. It performs three other important functions as (1) an effective communication tool to convey ideas, research findings, and proposed plans to others, especially financiers, (2) the basis, or blueprint, for managing the new venture, and (3) a measuring device, or yardstick, by which to gauge progress and evaluate needed changes. Developing and writing a business plan takes much time, effort, and money, but the results can make the difference between success and failure.

PREPARING THE PLAN

When developing a business plan, you should consider the firm's background, origins, philosophy, mission, and objectives (see Chapter 6), as well as the means of fulfilling that mission and attaining those objectives. A sound approach is to (1) determine where the business is at present; that is, recognize its current status, (2) decide where you would like it to be; that is, clarify your philosophy about doing business, developing the firm's mission, and setting objectives, and (3) determine how to get there; that is, identify the best strategies for accomplishing the business's objectives. Figure 7–1 shows one approach to preparing a business plan.

Who Should Prepare the Plan?

If the prospective owner is the only one involved in the business, he or she should prepare the plan with the advice and counsel of others. But, if the business is to be organized and run by more than one person, all of them should prepare it as a team. Raymond O. Leon, a consultant for new business start-ups, suggests letting each manager prepare a part of the plan.[5] We also recommend having other key employees help in the planning stage, as it will improve communication and motivation.

Developing Action Steps

The small business owner can collect needed information from the steps taken up to this point (as discussed in Chapters 5 and 6), as well as from business associates and legal, management, and accounting consultants. Conversations with people both inside and outside the firm are useful in gathering and evaluating this information.

The focus of the plan should be on future developments for the business, with specific steps set up to deal with specific aspects, such as product development, marketing, production or operations, finance, management, and accountability. Realistic, measurable objectives—that is, objectives that are attainable with some difficulty—should be set, and the plan's steps should be delegated, monitored, and reported regularly.

Questions such as the following are useful in developing action steps: Who will be responsible for each course of action? What is the time frame

---

Figure 7–1   How to Prepare a Business Plan

- Survey consumer demands for your product(s) and decide how to satisfy those demands.
- Ask questions that cover everything from the firm's target market to its competitive rank.
- Establish a long-range strategic plan for the entire business.
- Develop short-term, detailed business plans for every part of the business, involving all owners, managers, and employees.
- Plan for every facet of the corporate structure. That includes operations, sales development, general and administrative functions, and distribution.
- Prepare a business plan that uses staff time sparingly.

for each objective? What are the barriers to achieving the objectives? How can those barriers be overcome? Have the necessary controls been considered?

COMPONENTS OF THE PLAN

Because the business plan is such an important document, it should be arranged logically and presented clearly to save the reader time and effort and to prevent confusion. Although the information that should be included tends to be standardized, the format used is not. (Figure 7–2 presents one acceptable format.)[6]

Regardless of the specific format chosen, any plan should include at least the following:

- Cover sheet.
- Executive summary.
- Table of contents.
- History of the proposed business.
- Definition of the business.
- Definition of the market.
- Description of the product(s).
- Management structure.
- Objectives and goals.
- Financial analysis.
- Appendixes.

In the following sections, we discuss each of these items and what should be included in them.

Cover Sheet

The cover sheet presents the identifying information so that readers will immediately know the business name, address, and phone number. Also, they will know who the principals are.

Executive Summary

An **executive summary,** or statement of purpose, of the plan must be a real "grabber," as it must motivate the reader to go on to the other sections. Moreover, it must convey a sense of plausibility, credibility, and integrity. Your plan may be one of hundreds evaluated by representatives of lending institutions. They evaluate the initial worth of the plan on the basis of this executive summary; if it elicits sufficient interest, the remainder of the document may be assigned to other persons for review. Because the executive summary outlines the business plan, its major objectives, how these objectives will be accomplished, and the expected results, it is some-

Figure 7–2   Format of a Typical Business Plan

1. Cover sheet
   Business name, address, and phone
     number
   Principals
   Date
2. Executive summary
   Brief summary of plan
   Major objectives
   Product/service(s) description
   Marketing strategy
   Financial projections
3. Table of contents
   Each section listed, with subheads
4. History
   Background of principals, or company
     origins
   Product/service(s) background
   Corporate structure
   Brief outline of company successes or
     experiences, if any
5. Definition of the business
6. Definition of the market
   Target market
   Market penetration projections
   Analysis of competition
7. Description of products or services
   What is to be developed or sold
   Status of research and development
   Patents, trademarks, copyrights
   Append catalog sheets, photographs, or
     technical information

8. Management structure
   Who will enact plan
   Organization structure
   Employee policies
   Append additional detail such as
     résumés
9. Objectives and goals
   Revenue forecasts
   Marketing plans
   Manufacturing plans
   Quality assurance plans
   Financial plans
10. Financial data
    Projected income statements (three
      years)
    Projected cash flow analyses (first
      year, by months)
    Projected balance sheets (three years)
    Cost-volume-profit analyses where
      appropriate
    Projected statements of changes in
      financial position
11. Appendixes
    Narrative history of firm in detail
    Management structure (charts,
      résumés, etc.)
    Major assumptions
    Brochures describing products
    Letters of recommendation or
      endorsement
    Historical financial information (at least
      three years)
    Detail of objectives and goals
      Products and services
      Research and development
      Marketing
      Manufacturing
      Administration
      Finance

Source: Business Planning (New York: Peat, Marwick, Mitchell & Co., Private Business Advisory Services, 1984), appendix, pp. 22–23.

times first sent to potential investors to see if they have any interest in the venture.

Even though the summary is the initial component of the plan, it should be written after the plan has been developed. Remember, *the executive summary is just that—a summary—so keep it short!* It may be difficult to get so much information on one or two pages, but do so.

Figure 7–3 presents a sample outline of the executive summary required

Figure 7–3   Sample Outline of an Executive Summary

I. Summary
    A. Company
        1. Who and what it is
        2. Status of project/firm
        3. Key goals and objectives
    B. Product/service
        1. What it is
        2. How it works
        3. What it is for
        4. Proprietary advantages
    C. Market
        1. Prospective customers
        2. How many there are
        3. Market growth rate
        4. Competition (list three to six by
            name and describe)
        5. Industry trends
        6. How the firm will compete
        7. Estimated market share
           a. In one year
           b. In five years

II. Financial Projections
    D. Operations
        1. How product/service will be
            manufactured/provided
        2. Facilities/equipment
        3. Special processes
        4. Labor skills needed
    E. Channels of distribution:
        How product/service will get to end
        users
    F. Management team
        1. Who will do what
        2. Their qualifications
        3. Availability
    G. Sources and application of funds
        1. Present needs
        2. Future needs

One-page profit and loss statement showing annual totals for first three years, including detailed costs of goods sold and overhead (general and administrative) breakdowns.

Source: Entrepreneur Application Profile used by Venture Capital Exchange, Enterprise Development Center, The University of Tulsa, Tulsa, Oklahoma.

of all individuals and firms seeking equity capital from the Venture Capital Exchange of the University of Tulsa. We recommend that your summary also contain sections on the ownership and legal form of the business.

Table of Contents

This part of the plan gives readers an overview of what's in it. Consequently, it should be written concisely, in outline form, using alphabetical and numerical headings and subheads.

History of the Proposed Business

Pertinent background information on the person(s) organizing the business, as well as a description of their contributions, should be discussed at this point. Explanations of how the idea for the product or firm originated and what has been done to develop the idea should also be included. If the owner or owners have been in business before, that should be discussed, and any failures should be explained.

Definition of the Business

It is now time for you to define your business. More is needed than just a statement of what the firm does—or plans to do—and a listing of its functions, products, or services. This definition should tell what customer needs the business intends to meet. In writing this component, it might be helpful to search for relationships between how the owner perceives the business and what the customers think the business does. Think about questions such as these:

From the owner's perspective:
  What do you think you will sell?
  What is your largest line of inventory?
  Where is the greatest profit made?

From the customers' perspective:
  What do they think they need or want to buy?
  What is the best-selling item?
  On what product or service is most personnel time spent?

Are the answers to these questions closely aligned and compatible, or are they divergent? If they are compatible, there is a good chance of success; if divergent, then the business may be in trouble.

The sales manager of an FM radio station evaluated the results of efforts to sell advertising and found that advertising customers obtained 45 percent or more of their business volume from the black community. Yet members of this community made up a meager portion of the station's listening audience, and the station had never attracted the desired volume of advertising revenue. A shift to black disc jockeys and a program format attuned to this community produced a substantial increase in advertising revenues.

Definition of the Market

The market definition is one of the most important—and most difficult— components of the business plan to develop. The definition should indicate the target of your marketing efforts, as well as the trading area served. It must answer questions such as: Who buys what and why? What are your customers like? The competition also should be appraised carefully, showing any weaknesses you plan to exploit.

Description of Product(s)

This section should describe all of the firm's existing or planned products. The status of all research done and development under way should be described, along with discussions of any legal aspects, such as patents, copyrights, trademarks, pending lawsuits, and legal claims against the firm. Are any government approvals or clearances needed? Catalog sheets, photographs, and other visuals, if available, are helpful and should be included.

Notice that the Chappells (Case II–2) included blueprints in their plan when they submitted it to the four banks.

Management Structure

This is the place to describe your management structure, especially the expertise of your management team. Explain how they will carry out the plan. Employee policies and procedures could also be discussed. To repeat: It is important to demonstrate the ability and dedication of the owner and managers.

Objectives and Goals

This part outlines what your business plans to accomplish, as well as how and when it will be done and who will do it. Sales forecasts, manufacturing or service plans, quality assurance plans, and financial plans should be discussed. Other items of interest to potential investors include pricing and predicted profits, advertising and promotion strategies and budgets, a description of how the product(s) will be distributed and sold, and what categories of customers will be targeted for initial heavy sales effort and which customers for later sales efforts.

Financial Analysis

One important purpose of the business plan is to indicate the expected financial results of operations. The plan should show prospective investors or lenders why they should provide funds, when they can expect a return, and what the expected rate of return on their money is. At this point in the new business's development, assumptions—or educated guesses—are made concerning many issues. For example, assumptions must be made about expected revenues, competitors' actions, and future market conditions. Assumptions, while necessary, should be designated as such, and financial projections should be realistically based on how increased personnel, expanded facilities, or equipment needs will affect the projections. The budgetary process used—or to be used—is an important part of the business plan. And prices should reflect actual cost figures for the raw materials and operating costs.

A restaurant owner in a college town was not sensitive to the relationship between food cost and price. He was in financial difficulty and sought the aid of the Small Business Administration. A SCORE volunteer was assigned as a consultant. His first question was: "What's the most popular item on your menu?" The restaurant owner replied, "Our $5.25 steak dinner." The consultant asked for a scale and a raw steak. He showed the businessman that the raw steak cost $4.30. Obviously, the reason for the steak dinner's popularity was the markup of less than 22 percent on the steak alone. It was also the underlying cause of the business's financial troubles.

Appendixes

Other components needed in the plan are the firm's organizational structure—including organization charts. This part should include résumés of the officers and directors and also identify the key personnel and any outside board members. If the key personnel have any special expertise that increases the chances of success, this should be mentioned. Historical financial information, with relevant documents, should be included. Brochures, news items, letters of recommendation or endorsements, and similar items should be included as well.

The SBA has several free publications to help you draw up a business plan. For example, SBA Management Aids No. 2.007 is a *Business Plan for Small Manufacturers.*[7]

PRESENTING THE PLAN

A SCORE adviser says to clients, "In the first five minutes of perusing the executive summary, investors decide whether to reject or further consider a proposal." Therefore, *presenting* the business plan is almost as important as *preparing* it. All the work is in vain if interested persons—investors, lenders, and potential managers and key personnel—don't buy it. There are two aspects of presentation: (1) actually writing the plan and (2) presenting the plan to the targeted audience.

Writing the Plan

The usual rules of effective writing are quite important in writing the plan. John G. Burch, a writer on entrepreneurship, gives the following suggestions, among others:[8]

1. *Be honest,* not only by avoiding lies but also by revealing what you actually feel about the significant and relevant aspects of the plan.
2. Use the *third person,* not the first-person "I." This practice forces you to think clearly and logically.
3. Use *transitional words,* such as *but, still,* and *therefore,* and active, dynamic verbs as a means of leading the reader from one thought to another.
4. Avoid *redundancies,* such as "future plans." Such repetition adds nothing to the presentation.
5. Use *short, simple words,* where feasible, so the plan will be easy to understand.
6. Use *visuals* such as tables, charts, photos, and computer graphics to present your ideas effectively.

The plan should be prepared in an 8½ x 11-inch format, typewritten and photocopied, with copies for outsiders attractively bound. Most business plans can—and should—be presented effectively in 25 or 30 pages or less. Of course, the plan should be grammatically correct and should always be proofread before it is presented.

The plan should be reviewed by people outside the firm, such as accounting and business consultants, other businesspeople, and attorneys, before it is sent to potential investors or lenders. Other helpful reviewers might include a professional writer, editor, or English teacher.

When pertinent, the cover and title page should indicate that the information is proprietary and confidential. However, there is always the chance that this practice might offend a potential investor.

The Written/Oral Presentation

In an oral presentation, the entrepreneur or owner-manager presents the plan in person to investors or lenders. Presenting your plan involves creative skills on your part in order to give the impression that you have (or plan) a profitable and stable business, and that its chances of continuing that way are good. Your hearers will be looking very carefully at *you,* to see what kind of person *you* are, for you *are* the business—and vice versa. Both written and oral presentations should be very positive in nature and quite upbeat.

The plan should be delivered from the hearer's point of view, not the entrepreneur's. The oral presentation, as well as the written one, should demonstrate that the business is market driven, that there is a market for the product, and that the business has a feasible plan for aggressively selling it—at a profit. You should provide visual aids for key segments of the plan, and the presenter should be prepared for specific questions concerning:

- The adequacy of the research and development behind the product.
- The validity of the market research.
- The owner's understanding of the business.
- The financial projections and why they will work.
- The relative priority of the objectives.
- The owner's "ability to make it happen."[9]

The amount of detail in the market data and financial projections will vary according to the plan's purpose. If it is to raise equity or debt financing, more detail is needed; if it's to improve operations and motivate employees, less detail is needed.

Even the best-prepared plan, though, may not be accepted by potential investors. The Computer Update illustrates one of business history's classic rebuffs.

IMPLEMENTING THE PLAN

Now you are ready to take the plunge! It is time to get a charter, obtain facilities and supplies, hire and train people, and start operating. Using the capital structure plan and the sources of funds you have developed, obtain the funds and put them in a checking account for your business purchases. Obtain the services of an attorney to help acquire the charter

---

COMPUTER UPDATE

20/20 HINDSIGHT

Forty years ago, J. Presper Eckert, Jr., one of the inventors of ENIAC®, the first digital computer, fired off a business plan to IBM, hoping it would yield an investment to produce and distribute the UNIVAC®, the first giant electronic computer. IBM president Thomas J. Watson, Sr., after careful review, responded that it was the company's opinion that the world would eventually need only 12 computers and Eckert's machine was therefore of no interest to IBM.

Source: USA Today, September 26, 1989, p. 1E.

---

if the business is to be incorporated and to obtain occupational licenses and permits and take care of other legal requirements.

Once the funds, charter, and permits are in hand, refer to the timetable and start negotiating contracts; purchasing equipment, materials, and supplies; selecting; hiring, and training employees; establishing a marketing program; setting the legal structure in place; and developing an information system to maintain the records needed to run the business.

You are now a small business owner! You are operating your own business, you have all the risks, and you hope to receive the benefits and rewards of being on your own. Be ready for unforeseen problems, however, that may occur during the start-up period.

SAMPLE BUSINESS PLAN

A sample business plan is presented as Appendix E at the end of this text. It is a proposal for a new start-up pickup business. Notice that it closely follows the form presented in Figure 7–2.

WHAT YOU SHOULD HAVE LEARNED

1. Although a business plan is especially important for obtaining funds from potential investors and lenders, it can also be valuable as a blueprint for operating success. The research and analysis required to write an effective plan help the owner (or prospective owner) to focus on the company's goals, its markets, expected performance, and problems that might be encountered. The plan keeps the prospective owner from jumping into an enterprise without adequate thought and planning. After the business is started, the plan serves as a yardstick against which performance can be measured.

2. The best person to prepare the plan is the owner. If the business is to be run by more than one person, key executives should also help with the preparation. The people who have a personal and financial stake in the business can best define its mission, philosophy, and objectives and determine how it should be organized and operated. The preparers of the plan should consult with professionals and businesspeople for information and advice about specific aspects of the business. The owners must be clear about exactly how the business will be set up and managed and the schedule that will be followed in starting and developing it.

3. The plan should be logically organized and should include at least a letter of transmittal, a title page, a table of contents, the detailed components of the plan, appendixes, and a bibliography. The detailed components should begin with an executive summary, which is a short abstract or overview designed to encourage interested persons to read or hear the rest of the plan.

    The plan should include a history of the business, including background information on the people organizing it and the origin of the idea for the product or business; define the business; describe customer needs; show how the business objectives mesh with personal goals; define the prospective market for the business; appraise the competition; describe the product; show plans for product development, promotion, and distribution; explain the firm's organizational structure; summarize employee policies and benefits; review product research and development; and mention applicable patents, trademarks, and the like.

    If the plan's purpose is to raise funds, detailed financial projections of expected sales, profits, and rates of return should be emphasized.

4. A well-written business plan should be honest, logical, interesting, thorough, and easy to understand. It should probably be reviewed by outsiders qualified to judge its content and/or style before it is presented to interested persons.

    The plan should be presented by the owner in person, from the hearer's point of view, and using a marketing approach. The important point is to create an impression of a profitable and stable business run by capable and responsible people. The presenter should use visual aids and be prepared to answer a variety of questions.

5. From the discussions in this and the two previous chapters, you should be able to prepare an effective business plan.

KEY TERMS

business plan, *178*   executive summary, *181*

QUESTIONS

1. What is the purpose of a business plan?
2. How can a business plan be useful even to a prospective business owner who does not need outside capital?
3. (*a*) Do you think that the preparation of a business plan is as important as the authors claim? (*b*) Explain.
4. (*a*) Who should prepare the plan? (*b*) Why? (*c*) Why should the writer get help from outside professionals and businesspeople?
5. What should the business plan include?
6. How should a business plan be written and presented?

SUGGESTED READINGS

DeCordoba, Jose. "Wanted: Good Managers." *The Wall Street Journal,* February 24, 1989, pp. R16, R20.

Ferenbach, Carl. "The Birth of the Financial Entrepreneur." *The Wall Street Journal,* March 4, 1987, p. 30.

Gumpert, David E. "Don't Let Optimism Block Out Trouble Signposts." *USA Today,* May 8, 1989, p. 10E.

Hasmer, LaRue, and Roger Guiles. *Creating the Successful Business Plan for New Ventures.* New York: McGraw-Hill, 1985.

Hotch, Ripley, "Surviving a Start-up with Sleeves Rolled Up." *Nation's Business,* April 1988, p. 4.

Pollan, Stephen M., and Mark Levine. "Playing to Win: The Small Business Guide to Survival & Growth." *U.S. News & World Report,* December 12, 1988, Special Advertising Section, pp. A9–A19.

Postrel, Virginia I. "Capital: What Investors Look For." *Inc.,* November 1986, p. 18.

Stern, Jeffrey A. *How to Become Financially Independent Before You're 35.* Boston: Little, Brown, 1986.

Thompson, Roger. "Business Plans: Myth and Reality." *Nation's Business,* August 1988, pp. 16–22.

Weiner, Steve. "Business 101." *Forbes,* August 24, 1987, p. 52ff.

ENDNOTES

1. "Behind Success: Ordinary Ideas," *USA Today,* May 30, 1989, p. 7B.
2. Lee Eckert, J. D. Ryan, and Robert J. Ray, *Small Business: An Entrepreneur's Plan* (New York: Harcourt Brace Jovanovich, 1985), p. 272.
3. Christi Harlan, "Judge Clears Sale of Eastern Air Shuttle, Slates Monday Hearing on Rival Bids," *The Wall Street Journal,* May 17, 1989, p. A4.
4. Cynthia C. Ryans, *Managing the Small Business* (Englewood Cliffs, N.J.: Prentice-Hall, 1989), p. 73.
5. Raymond O. Leon, "Get Full Value from Your Plan," *Nation's Business,* August 1988, p. 21.
6. See "Raising Venture Capital: From Locating Investor to Cutting Deal," *Journal of Accountancy,* February 1988, pp. 105–9, for a different format.
7. Write SBA, Box 15434, Fort Worth, TX 76119, for your free copy.
8. John G. Burch, *Entrepreneurship* (New York: John Wiley & Sons, 1986), pp. 377–82.
9. *Business Planning* (New York: Peat, Marwick, Mitchell & Co. Private Business Advisory Services, 1984), pp. 17–18.

8

OBTAINING THE RIGHT FINANCING FOR YOUR BUSINESS

Money is the seed of money.—Jean-Jacques Rousseau

Many of the financial problems plaguing small businesses are avoidable, provided entrepreneurs analyze their own funding needs objectively and with sufficient lead time to act decisively.—Small Business Administration

LEARNING OBJECTIVES

After studying the material in this chapter, you will be able to:

1. Explain the importance of proper financing for a small business.
2. Tell how to estimate financial needs, and explain some principles to follow in obtaining financing.
3. Explain why equity and debt financing are used and describe the role each plays in the capital structure of a small firm.
4. Distinguish the types of equity and debt securities.
5. Describe some sources of equity financing.
6. Describe some sources of debt financing.
7. Explain what a lender looks for in a borrower.

ROY MORGAN: PIONEER IN AIR MEDICAL SERVICES

Roy Morgan, president of Air Methods Corporation of Englewood, Colorado, was a pioneer in providing rapid air medical services. After helping to develop the first hospital helipad in Salt Lake City, at Holy Cross Hospital, he brought in the first patient by helicopter, flying him in on the skids of a Bell 47 , which was the method used during the Korean War.

Morgan then flew a Bell 47 to do power line patrol and line maintenance work for the Public Service Corporation of Colorado. After seeing three fire fighters, seriously burned in a helicopter wreck, having to wait for primitive medical

attention, he saw the critical need to provide rapid medical response for people working in remote areas. He approached several Colorado hospitals during the late 1970s and interested St. Mary's Hospital in Grand Junction in the project. But first he had to have a helicopter.

Roy, his wife Dorothy, and friends Austin Clark and Ralph Mulford scraped together enough money to form a corporation and make the down payment on a helicopter. Roy and his wife took out a second mortgage on their house; sold a camper, a pickup truck, and their stock in Western Airlines; and emptied their savings account to get the funds. Their friends made similar sacrifices. The incorporators had a Texas company convert the copter to provide medical services and started the contract with St. Mary's Hospital Air Life in August 1980.

In 1982, Air Methods started an Air Life program for the North Colorado Medical Center in Greeley, Colorado. This time, three other friends, David Ritchie and Dennis and David

Source: Photos courtesy of Air Methods Corporation.

Source: Photo courtesy of Tom A. Ross III of Copiah-Lincoln Junior College.

Beggrow, helped make the down payment on a second helicopter and took Air Methods stock as their compensation.

Between 1983 and 1988, eight more programs were added in Denver (two programs); Texarkana, Arkansas; Minneapolis/St. Paul; Bend, Oregon; Salt Lake City; Des Moines; and Jackson, Mississippi (shown in the photo at right). By 1989, Air Methods had 19 helicopters and aircraft, all of which were medically dedicated and equipped to fly on instruments; the firm had more than 60 pilots on salary. All pilots must be college

graduates, as promotions are from within, and Morgan wants pilots to be able to become managers immediately as the need arises. Smokers are not hired because of the problems of impaired breathing and night vision and the danger of smoking around oil, gas, and oxygen.

According to Morgan, "obtaining financing is no longer a problem." He says they've done everything they said they would do, made all payments on time, and sacrificed in so many ways that money is now available for their type of operation.

Source: Information obtained by Gayle M. Ross, of the University of Mississippi Medical Center, Jackson, Mississippi; and from other sources, especially Barney Green, "Profile of an Operator," *Hospital Aviation,* January 1989, pp. 10–15.

This case shows the importance of obtaining the right financing for your business. As has been shown repeatedly in this text, *sufficient capital is essential not only for small business start-ups but also for their continued operation.* In fact, one of the main reasons for the high failure rate of small businesses is inadequate or improper financing. All too often, insufficient attention has been paid to planning for financial needs—thereby leaving the new business open to sudden but predictable financial crises. Or the owner has been unable to secure adequate funding to allow the firm to weather an unexpected business slump. Even firms that are sound financially can be destroyed by financial problems. Indeed, one of the difficulties most commonly experienced by rapidly growing firms is that they are unable to finance the investment needed to support sales growth.

ESTIMATING FINANCIAL NEEDS

The degree of uncertainty surrounding a small firm's long-term financial needs primarily depends on whether the business is already operating or is just starting up, as mentioned in the Opening Focus. If a business has an operating history, its future needs can be estimated with relative accuracy, even with substantial growth.

Even for an existing business, however, an in-depth analysis of its *permanent* financial requirements can be valuable. It may show the current method of financing the business to be unsound or unnecessarily risky. For example, an analysis of this nature may show that fixed assets, such as buildings, machine tools, and other equipment, are being financed with short-term bank loans that have an interest rate several points higher than the prime rate. As a general rule, small businesses' long-lived assets, such as buildings and other facilities, should be financed with long-term loans, while short-lived assets, such as inventory or accounts receivable, should be financed with short-term loans.

Principles to Follow

A new business, or a major expansion of an existing business, should be evaluated with great care, paying particular attention to the capital requirements. If the firm is soundly financed, then seasonal and short-term fluctuations in sales revenue should prove mere annoyances rather than mortal threats.

The assets of a business should be financed with equity funds, or with debt funds having a maturity approximately equal to the productive life of the asset. However, no business can be financed entirely with debt funding, nor would such a capitalization be desirable—even if creditors were willing to lend all the funds required. Such a capital structure would be extremely risky, both for the creditors and for the business.

Working capital includes the current assets, less current liabilities, that a firm uses to produce goods and services and to finance the extension of credit to customers. This grouping of assets includes items such as cash, accounts receivable, and inventories. Management of working capital, important for all business firms, is often a central concern for managers of small businesses because these firms are often undercapitalized and overdependent on uninterrupted cash receipts to pay for recurring expenses. Therefore, small business managers must accurately assess their working capital needs in advance and obtain sufficient financial resources to cover these needs, plus a "buffer" for unexpected emergencies.

Using Cash Budgets

An important tool that small business managers can use to project working capital needs is a **cash budget.** Such a budget estimates (1) the out-of-pocket costs that will be incurred during the next year to produce goods or services for sale, and (2) when revenues from these sales are to be collected. In most businesses, sales are not constant over the year, so revenues vary a great deal from one period to another, while the costs of producing the product tend to be relatively constant. For example, most retailers have their greatest sales period from Thanksgiving to Christmas. Yet, if they extend their own store credit, they do not receive payment for those sales until the following January or February—or even later. Also, the small producer may have produced the goods continuously the previous summer and consequently had to bear the out-of-pocket costs of production for up to six months before actually receiving cash payments.

In general, therefore, when sales are made on credit, the selling firm must *carry* the costs of production itself for an extended period of time. A cash budget can help the manager to predict when these financing needs are greatest and to plan the firm's funding operations accordingly. An accurate assessment of seasonal financing needs becomes especially important if commercial bank loans are used, since bankers usually require a borrower to be completely free of bank debt at least once a year.

REASONS FOR USING EQUITY AND DEBT FINANCING

Equity is an owner's share of the assets of a company. The exact nature of this ownership claim depends on the legal form of organization. For proprietorships and partnerships, the claim on the assets of the firm is that they are the same as the owner's personal assets.

Equity in a corporation is evidenced by shares of **stock,** either common or preferred stock. **Common stockholders** are the true owners of the firm, and their financial claim is to the profit left over after all other claims against the business have been met. Common stockholders almost always retain the right to vote for company directors and/or on other important issues; they thereby exercise effective control over the management of the firm. These voting rights are monetary votes (one vote per share) rather than people votes (one vote per shareholder); if one person owns 50 percent of the common shares, plus one share, that person can control the firm.

For example, Albert Shaffer (Case I–5) always issues stock for each new Shaffer's Drive Inn store he opens, but retains control of 51 percent of the stock in each one.

Preferred stockholders, on the other hand, have a claim to the firm's profits that must be satisfied before any can be distributed to the common stockholders as dividends; but they often pay for this superior claim by giving up their voting rights.

The assets of the firm that are financed by funds provided by the owner(s) and/or stockholders are called **equity capital.** The other kind of capital, or funding, that a firm uses is called **debt capital,** which comes from lenders, who will be repaid at a specified interest rate within an agreed-upon time span. The lenders' income does not vary with the success of the business, while the stockholders' does.

Role of Equity Financing

The role of equity financing is to serve as a buffer that protects creditors from loss in case of financial difficulty. In the event of default on a contractual obligation (such as an interest payment), creditors have a legally enforceable claim on the assets of the firm. It takes preference over claims of the common and preferred stockholders. Therefore, funding a business with debt is less expensive to the profitable firm than outside equity (stockholder) funding, particularly since interest payments are a tax-deductible expense for the firm, whereas dividend payments are not. The Tax Reform Act of 1986, by lowering corporate tax rates from 46 percent to 34 percent, reduced this "tax subsidy" for debt but did not eliminate it. From an investor's point of view, common stock investments should have a higher financial return than debt investments (since equity securities are riskier), and this has in fact been the case throughout modern U.S. history.

Role of Debt Financing

As stated above, debt financing consists of funds that the firm has borrowed and is contractually obligated to repay by a certain date. Principal and interest payments, as legally enforceable claims against the business, therefore entail substantial risk for the firm (or for the entrepreneur if the debt is guaranteed by personal wealth).

In spite of the risks involved, small businesses use debt financing for several reasons: (1) the cost of interest paid on debt capital is usually lower than the cost of outside equity, and interest payments are tax-deductible expenses; (2) by employing debt funding, an entrepreneur may be able to raise more total capital than from equity sources alone; and (3) since debt payments are fixed costs, any remaining profits belong solely to the common stockholders. This last strategy, employing a fixed charge to increase the residual return to common stockholders, is referred to as employing **financial leverage.** In recent years, many aggressive management teams have also employed debt financing to buy out public stockholders or other outside investors. This is called a **leveraged buyout (LBO).**

For example, Phillip J. Netznik, the company's outside accountant until the founder's death in 1984, bought the Norman Equipment Company of Bridgeview, Illinois, in an LBO in 1986. He refurbished it from top to bottom. He removed most of the senior executives, squeezed cash out of inventories and accounts receivable, and injected new enthusiasm into the firm's marketing and employee relations program.

Within a year of the purchase, sales had increased 7 percent and profits soared by 333 percent.[1]

One type of debt financing that is becoming more popular is leasing facilities and equipment from someone outside the business instead of buying them. A **lease** is a contract that permits you to use someone else's property, such as real estate, equipment, or other facilities, for a specified period of time. While a lease is not usually classified as debt, it is in many respects financially very similar.

Leases with a contract length essentially equal to the economic life of the asset, requiring the lessee to maintain the asset and make payments that fully recover the asset's cost, are called **capital leases.**

Shorter-lived leases, called **operating leases,** are most commonly used for vehicles and certain types of equipment. From the small business owner's point of view, the benefits of both types of lease are that the lease payments are tax deductible and that it may be possible for the business to lease equipment when it would be unable to secure debt financing to purchase such equipment.

For example, Goudreau Corporation, of Danvers, Massachusetts, used a lease agreement to solve a financing problem in 1986. To bid on construction jobs, Goudreau had to put up a surety bond, and the bonding company (which guaranteed that the company would finish the job satisfactorily) would approve only $10 in bonding for every dollar Goudreau had in the bank. This made cash a very important asset (since it effectively limited the firm's ability to bid on jobs), so Goudreau turned to an equipment leasing company for financing of the trucks, machinery, and other fixed assets needed to continue growing. By 1989, Goudreau Corporation had sales of $5 million and used over $200,000 worth of leased equipment.[2]

TYPES OF DEBT AND EQUITY SECURITIES

Various types of securities are used by small U.S. companies. Some of them are used only rarely by very small businesses, and many can be issued only by corporations (not by proprietorships or partnerships). A number of securities are described below. This listing is incomplete but sufficient to illustrate the richness and variety of financial sources that are a hallmark of the American financial system. Potential small business owners should always remember that if they have a viable project, financing can be obtained from some source!

Equity Securities

To start operating, all corporations must have some equity capital. **Common stock,** which represents the owners' interest, usually consists of many identical shares, each of which gives the holder one vote in all corporate elections. Common stockholders have no enforceable claim to dividends, and the liquidity of the investment will depend largely on whether or not there is a public market for the firm's stock.

In addition to the required common stock, a corporation may issue **preferred stock.** Such securities have a fixed par value (the value assigned in the corporation's charter, usually $100 per share) and entitle the holder to a fixed dividend payment. The amount of the dividend is usually expressed as a percentage of par value, such as 8 percent (equal to $8 per year). This dividend is not automatic; it must be declared by the firm's board of directors before it can be paid. Nor is it a legally enforceable claim against the business. However, no dividends can be paid to the common stockholders until preferred stock dividends have been paid. Moreover, preferred dividends that have been missed typically cumulate and must be paid in full before payments can be made to common stockholders. Preferred stock usually conveys no voting rights to its holder.

Debt Securities

Debt securities, including such items as bonds and loans, can be classified in many ways, the most important of which are by method of placement, maturity, denomination, security required, and method of interest payment.

Method of Placement

The method of placement refers to whether the debt securities are sold to the public or issued privately to a financial institution. In general, publicly issued debt (such as bonds or commercial paper) is more commonly used by larger firms, whereas small companies rely more on private loans from financial institutions such as commercial banks, insurance companies, or finance companies.

Maturity

The second factor, maturity, is perhaps the most commonly used method of classifying debt securities. The typical distinction is among **short-term securities** (those with maturities of one year or less), **intermediate-term securities** (those with maturities of one to five years), and **long-term securities** (those with maturities of more than five years). As we will discuss more thoroughly in the next section, commercial banks prefer to make short- and intermediate-term loans; other financial institutions, such as insurance companies, prefer to make long-term loans.

Denomination of the Loan

If a company negotiates a loan from a bank or other single lender, the denomination of the loan is simply the full amount borrowed. On the other hand, if securities are sold to the public or are privately placed with several lenders, most companies will issue the debt in the form of **bonds.** These debt securities have a standard denomination, method of interest payment, and method of principal repayment. The most common denomination for corporate bonds is $1,000.

Security Required

Large, well-established companies can often issue **debentures,** which are bonds backed only by the faith and credit of the issuing firm. These are unsecured: no explicit collateral is pledged as backing for them. Some of the better-established and more financially sound small businesses may also be able to have unsecured debt—especially short-term bank loans— but secured debt is more often the rule. Long-term debt secured by real property is a **mortgage loan,** whereas a **chattel mortgage loan** is debt backed by some physical asset such as machinery, transportation equipment, or inventory. Furthermore, many of the "unsecured" loans that banks extend to small businesses require personal guarantees by the manager or directors of the firm. Such loans are in fact collateralized by the personal assets of these individuals.

Method of Interest Payment

Interest on debt securities can be paid in many different ways. First, the stated interest percentage or dollar amount may be paid periodically, for example, monthly, quarterly, semiannually, or annually. Second, the interest may be deducted from the amount borrowed at the time the loan is made, thus paying the interest in advance (as with bonds that are sold at a discount to their face value). This procedure effectively increases the interest rate, for the lender has the use of your interest for a longer period of time. Or the total amount—principal and accumulated interest—may be paid at maturity or when the loan is terminated.

Finally, a loan can be repaid in several equal installments that cover both interest payments and repayment of principal. These self-amortizing loans have the advantage of a regular repayment schedule that can be easily budgeted for out of a firm's cash flow.

SOURCES OF EQUITY FINANCING

Obtaining sufficient equity funding is a constant challenge for most small businesses, particularly for proprietorships and partnerships. The only way to increase the equity of these two types of firms is either to retain earnings or to accept outsiders as co-owners. For corporations, the choices may be more varied. Some of the more frequently used sources of equity funding are discussed here.

Self

People who start a small business must invest a substantial amount of their own funds in it before seeking outside funding. Outside investors want to see some of the owner's own money committed to the business as some assurance that she or he will not simply give up operating the business and walk away from it. Many owners also prefer using their own funds because they feel uncomfortable risking other people's money or because they do not want to share control of the firm with anyone else.

From a practical point of view, just where do small business entrepreneurs get their initial start-up funds? The following examples from actual cases included in this book will show you.

Sue Ley used $25,000 of her savings to start CleanDrum, Inc. (Case I–1). She later gave up a 50 percent interest in CleanDrum to a partner who invested $32,000. Finally, she took out a $60,000 unsecured loan from the bank.

Barbara and Steve Chappell used all $20,000 of the savings that they had accumulated from working for four years to start Our Hero Restaurant (Case I–2).

Adam Osborne sold his computer publishing company to McGraw-Hill to obtain the capital to found Osborne Computer Company in 1981 (Case VI–2). Later he used outside equity and debt financing and was preparing to offer a $50,000 public stock offering in 1983 when the company went bankrupt.

Small Business Investment Companies (SBICs)

Small business investment companies (SBICs) are private firms licensed and regulated by the Small Business Administration to make "venture" or "risk" investments. SBICs supply equity capital and extend unsecured loans to small enterprises that meet their investment criteria. Being privately capitalized themselves (although backed by the SBA), the 500 or more SBICs are intended to be profit-making institutions. Therefore, they tend not to make very small investments.

SBICs finance small firms in two general ways: (1) by making straight loans and (2) by equity-type investments that give the SBIC actual or potential ownership of the small firm's equity securities. SBICs also provide management assistance to the businesses they help finance.

A specialized type of SBIC—a Section 301(d) SBIC (formerly called a minority small business investment corporation)—helps small firms owned and managed by socially or economically disadvantaged persons, including those with military service during the Vietnam War years.

SBICs prefer to make loans to small firms rather than equity investments,

"I run a small investment firm . . . Unfortunately it used to be a large investment firm!"
Copyright 1989 by Doug Blackwell.

so we will discuss them further under "Sources of Debt Financing" later in this chapter.

Venture Capitalists

Entrepreneurs often complain that it is "lonely at the top." If so, a venture capitalist can serve as a form of "security blanket" when needed. Traditionally, venture capital firms have been partnerships composed of wealthy individuals who make equity investments in small firms with opportunities for fast growth, such as Federal Express, Apple Computer, and Nike. In general, they have preferred to back fast-growth industries (usually high-tech ones), as the ultimate payoff from backing a successful new business with a new high-tech product can be astronomical.

These traditional venture capitalists have been joined in recent years by professionally created and managed venture capital funds set up by corporations, institutions, and even state and local governments. For example, 11 states had venture capital pools by 1988, with funding worth $39.8 million. Another 27 states had research and development grant programs. The goals of these programs are the same as for other types, namely (1) to fund promising local start-up businesses, (2) to provide low-cost debt financing for others, and (3) to provide a bridge to private funding for those firms that would otherwise not attract other forms of financing.[3]

Venture capital became much more important after the passage of the **Tax Reform Act of 1978,** which lowered the marginal income tax rate from 35 percent to 28 percent for long-term capital gains. The results were dramatic, as you can see from Figure 8–1. The annual commitment of new funds by venture capitalists grew from $68 million in 1977 to $4.9 billion in 1987, but dropped to $3 billion in 1988.[4] The October 1987 stock market crash and the growing uncertainty about the U.S. economy have made venture capitalists more cautious about investing in small firms.

As shown in Figure 8–2, consumer-related businesses, computer hardware and services, and medical and health care firms receive the greatest share of new venture capital investments.

Venture capitalists *are not* a good source of funding for new businesses—especially the Mom-and-Pop variety. At least that seems to be suggested by the fact that in 1988 more than half of all venture capital went to expand existing businesses rather than to start new ones.[5]

Foreign firms are now providing considerable venture capital for small American firms. For example, Japanese companies in recent years have drastically increased their investment in small U.S. firms with promising ideas and products, even projects that commercial banks won't touch. While Japanese firms have been financing small- and medium-sized U.S. firms for years, the pace escalated in 1989.[6] These foreign financiers tend to have a longer-term point of view concerning return on investment than American investment capitalists, so they have more patience with companies in which they invest than U.S. investors have.

Figure 8–1   The Venture Capital Pool

While the amount of venture capital under management rose 20% to $29 billion 1987, overall outlays to entrepreneurs rose 34% to $3.9 billion.

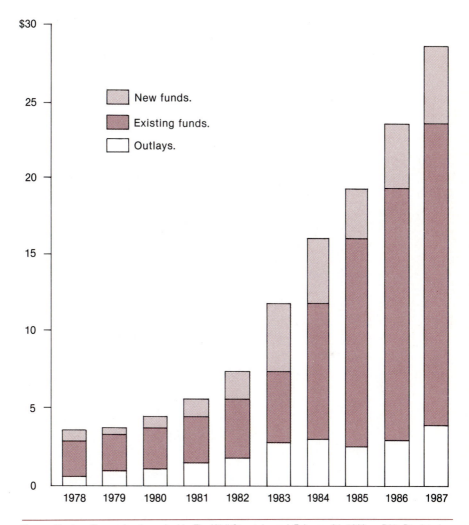

Source: Venture Economics, Inc., cited in *The Wall Street Journal,* February 24, 1989, p. R25. Reprinted by permission of The Wall Street Journal, © Dow Jones & Company, Inc., 1989. ALL RIGHTS RESERVED.

Tu Chen, chairman of Komag Inc., a Milpitas, California, maker of high-quality hard disks for computers, relies heavily on Japanese venture capitalists. Chen, an American citizen, started the company in 1983 with an initial boost from domestic capital, but since then he's relied increasingly on the Japanese—especially Asahi Glass Company, his principal backer in Japan.[7]

Figure 8–2 How Venture Capital Is Invested

Percentage of dollar amount invested in 1988, by type of company

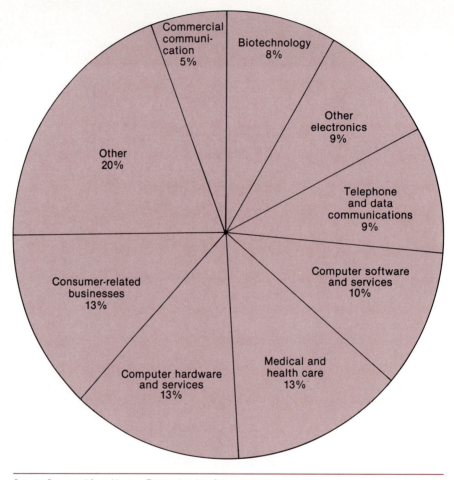

Source: Computed from Venture Economics, Inc. figures.

Foreign stock exchanges are other sources of venture capital. They tend to have easier regulations for listing, require less paper work, and have lower legal and administrative costs.

For these and other reasons, the Vancouver (Canada) Stock Exchange (VSE), is a popular source of venture capital for many small U.S. firms. VSE specializes in natural resource exploration companies, and small new technology firms, such as Neti Technologies Inc., an Ann Arbor, Michigan, software firm; and Sellectek (now operating as Global–Pacific Minerals, Inc.), a Menlo Park, California, software distributor. Sellectek used VSE to raise $1.5 million.

As of January 29, 1990, with its Vancouver Computerized Trading System (VCT), VSE became the first North American stock exchange to fully convert from the

Figure 8–3   Vancouver Computerized Trading System (VCT)

Source: Photo courtesy of Vancouver Stock Exchange.

traditional "outcry market" to a fully auomated trade execution system (Figure 8–3). Now, all trading takes place in the offices of member brokerage firms.

VSE has a "two-tier" system that recognizes the stages of development of companies as they grow and mature. Its rules and regulations are designed to (1) provide a niche for venture companies, and (2) maintain the integrity of the marketplace. Also, by using VSE—rather than making deals with private U.S. venture capitalists—entrepreneurs can keep greater control of their businesses. VSE has a proven record of performance, as shown by its third place (after the Toronto and New York exchanges) in trading volume.[8]

Many venture capitalists rely more heavily on the executive summary of a business plan (see Chapter 7) than on the plan itself in making investment decisions. So many long and complex plans are presented to them that they need a quick way to evaluate proposals in order to quickly discard those they do not want to consider further. The percentage of business plans accepted by venture capitalists for investment purposes is very low. For example, the top 20 venture capital firms invested in only 54 of the 33,100 plans they received in 1987.[9]

You should be aware when approaching either a venture capitalist or an SBIC for possible funding that they will not view your business the same way you do. While you may be content to remain relatively small in order to retain personal control, this is the last thing a professional investor will want. An SBIC or a venture capitalist will invest in a firm with the expectation of ultimately selling the company either to the investing public (through an initial public stock offering) or to another, larger company. This potential conflict of goals can be very damaging to the new business owner unless the differences are explicitly addressed before external financing is accepted.

Angel Capitalists

An often overlooked source of external equity funding is wealthy local businesspeople and other such investors. Known as **angel capitalists,** these investors will usually accept lower rates of return on the investments they make than will professional venture capitalists, and they will also accept smaller investments (the minimum investment for most professional venture capital firms is at least $100,000). While the true importance of these angel capitalists is hard to measure, it has been estimated that they provide up to four times as much total investment capital for small businesses as do the professional venture capital firms.[10]

The Massachusetts Bay Transportation Authority (MBTA) and the New York City Police Pension Fund are two examples of angel capitalists.

In 1989, the MBTA set aside $20 million from its retirement fund to lend to small businesses within its area of operations. Jack Gallahue, its executive director, set the interest rates on the loans as much as 2 percentage points lower than the rates small businesses were then paying for their loans.

The New York City Police Pension Fund set aside $50 million in 1989 to lend to small businesses. These loans were to be guaranteed by the SBA.[11]

Venture capital networks are a cross between venture capitalists and angel capitalists. They consist of individuals who made their wealth through entrepreneurial efforts and now want to invest in products or industries that are similar to the ones in which they made their fortune. The main objective is to help the local economy.

Other Sources

In some cases, the small business entrepreneur may be able to acquire equity financing from small investors: friends, relatives, wealthy acquaintances, or local businesspeople. This is particularly true for tax-sheltered investments such as real estate–related limited partnerships. The Tax Reform Act of 1986 reduced the incentive to use these tax-sheltered investments but did not eliminate it entirely.

Business Incubators

A big movement now encouraging the financing and development of small businesses is business incubators. **Business incubators** are usually old buildings, such as factories or warehouses, that have been renovated, subdivided, and rented to new companies by entrepreneurs, corporations, universities, governments, or groups such as chambers of commerce. Their purpose is to shelter young enterprises, offer moral support, and provide support services, including low overhead, until they are ready to go out on their own. The number of such incubators grew from a handful in 1980 to over 500 in 1988.[12]

Chicago's Fulton-Carroll Center, housed in a 100-year-old former factory, is one of the best-known U.S. business incubators. The Center, run by director June Lavelle, provides management assistance, low rent, shared services, and cooperation with other entrepreneurs. Three-fourths of the employees come from within a three-mile radius, and most are minorities. As of 1988, of the 142 businesses that had been housed, 42 had "graduated" and moved on, while 23 had failed.[13]

The Fulton-Carroll Center and its director, June Lavelle
Source: Photos courtesy of Fulton-Carroll Center.

Venture Capital Clubs

Another form of assistance is offered by individuals running venture capital networks, which use computers to provide a form of "dating" service to match people who need modest amounts of capital with those who have it. Some business groups, such as chambers of commerce, are setting up

venture capital clubs to bring together people with new business concepts and those interested in financing such ideas. For a fee, they will help you apply for funding from a venture capitalist. Some of these clubs are affiliated with local economic development agencies, while others are run by universities.[14]

The New York Venture Group holds regular monthly breakfasts to bring together would-be entrepreneurs and venture capitalists and other money sources. For a modest fee, people who think they have a salable idea can grab the mike and make a quick pitch to the assembled money men, who have also paid to get in. There are enough promising ideas to keep entrepreneurs and potential backers—including Japanese—coming back.[15]

Employee Stock Ownership Plans (ESOPs)

For existing small businesses, another source of financing is **employee stock ownership plans (ESOPs),**[16] to be discussed in Chapter 11. The company reaps tax advantages and cash flow advantages from passing shares to workers. The plan also makes employees think like owners and tend to be more productive.

Your Customers

Your customers are another source of financing. It happens often, and in many ways. For example, mail-order vendors—especially those who use TV commercials—require the customer to pay when ordering; they then have that money for operations—while the customer waits several weeks for delivery of the goods. Also it is customary for artisans and contractors to require a substantial down payment before beginning to produce the product.

For example, Diane Allen, a portrait artist, requires a down payment of one-third before she will begin a portrait. This money not only assures that the contract will be honored but also can be used to buy supplies and cover other expenses.

An innovative new source of start-up financing has become available for high-tech entrepreneurs in recent years. This involves obtaining capital from an established potential client.

An example is Conner Peripherals Inc., of San Jose, California, which entered into a partnership with COMPAQ Computer of Houston, Texas, whereby COMPAQ would make two $6 million investments in exchange for 49 percent of Conner's stock. The latter firm, which had only recently been launched by founder Finis Conner, had no revenues, and the partnership agreement with COMPAQ (which called for the development of advanced-technology disk drives) came only after Conner had approached several venture capitalists without success.[17]

SOURCES OF DEBT FINANCING

Although the more entrepreneurial small businesses may aggressively seek the kinds of equity funding we have been discussing, most small businesses are more likely to use debt financing. This is true at least in part because there are more sources for such financing, several of which are described here.

Trade Credit

Trade credit refers to purchases of inventory, equipment, and/or supplies on an open account in accordance with customary terms for retail and wholesale trade. In general, trade credit is one of the most important sources of debt financing for small business because it arises spontaneously in the normal course of operating the business.

Firms seeking new and expanded wholesale and retail markets for goods have the option of using **consignment selling.** Small auto, major appliance, and farm equipment dealers consider consignments a form of trade credit because payments to suppliers are made when the products are sold rather than when they are received in stock.

Commercial and Industrial Financial Institutions

These institutions may provide the small business owner with borrowed funds. The proportion of funds such institutions make available ranges from 25 to 60 percent of the value of the total assets. Usually, the cost of such financing is higher than that of other alternatives, but such funds may be the most accessible. These institutions may help the new business by (1) making loans on fixed assets, (2) arranging for lease-purchase arrangements, and (3) providing accounts receivable financing.

Commercial Banks

In the past, commercial banks have been a good source of credit for business borrowers who have funds of their own and proven successful experience. More recently, because of the higher rate of return, banks have shifted a greater portion of their funds into consumer financing. The large demand for funds in recent years has pushed interest rates and terms of bank loans to higher levels and less favorable terms. A well-prepared business plan, as described in Chapter 7, should help lower a firm's interest rate and possibly even extend the term of the loan. Even then, however, you may find it more advantageous to finance the business with a personal loan.

For example, Bob Mallard's major financial problem (Case VI–3) was finding adequate financing for Pools, Inc. Because banks required so much collateral for business loans, he chose to finance expansions of his business with personal loans.

If your business is successful, you may want to open up a **line of credit** with your bank. This is an arrangement whereby the bank permits an ongoing business to borrow up to a set amount—say $50,000—at any time during the year without further red tape. The business writes checks against its account, and the bank honors them up to the maximum amount.

Usually, except for businesses with an exceptionally high credit rating, the business is required to pay up all unsecured debts for a short period—say 10 to 15 days—each year to prove its creditworthiness. This is usually done when the firm's cash level is at its highest in order not to inconvenience the borrower too much.

In addition to borrowing funds, the small business owner should also consider the following services offered by commercial banks: general accounting, payroll accounting, income tax service, lockbox collections to expedite payments and cash flow, and various other personalized and computerized services.

Bruce W. Neurohr has made a point of courting several layers of management at Bank South ever since he switched banks in 1988. He learned the importance of a good personal relationship with one's banker the hard way when his former bank refused to renew a $550,000 line of credit unless some other responsible person guaranteed the loan. Yet Neurohr's Atlanta-based temporary help agency had been profitable since it began in 1982. Both Neurohr and Bank South executives are happy with the current working relationship, which includes a $1.5 million line of credit, and Neurohr even boasts that now his bankers take him out to lunch.[18]

Other Financial Institutions

Historically, **savings and loan associations (S&Ls)** have been a place to finance the mortgage on a house. But since Congress gave them the authority to make commercial loans, they have become another source of debt funding, especially for small firms. The advantages of S&Ls include (1) the smallness of their staffs and commercial loan operations, which means that the borrower will have access to higher-level officers rather than the lower-level employees in banks and larger institutions; (2) greater flexibility in loan terms, since they can amortize the loan over a longer period; and (3) quicker decisions. On the other hand, the recent crisis in the S&L industry, and Congressional legislation designed to deal with it, seem likely to severely restrict commercial lending by S&Ls for many years to come.

Commercial finance companies are another relatively new source of debt financing for small firms. As banks and S&Ls come under increased pressure to reduce their outstanding risks, these companies often give better—and longer-term—deals to small businesses, especially to buy equipment.

Pacific Envelope Company of Anaheim, California, was able to finance a total of $400,000 for used production equipment at a five-year fixed rate of 11 percent. C.I.T. Financial Corporation, which does equipment and commercial financing, provided the money without deducting it from the firm's line of credit, as the bank would have done. Also, the bank would lend only 80 percent of the $400,000.[19]

Major Nonfinancial Corporations

Major producing corporations often finance certain types of activities that are closely related to their operations. They may either provide the funding themselves through their financial subsidiaries or help the owner find it. This source of funding is used primarily by entrepreneurial ventures, not businesses of the Mom-and-Pop type.

General Electric, Westinghouse, and others have been active in helping finance mobile homes and apartments. The mobile home manufacturers install the appliances of a specific supplier, which then helps finance the manufacturer. In addition, the appliance-financing subsidiary often finances the sale of the home to the ultimate consumer.

Insurance Companies

Insurance companies may be a good source of funds for a small firm, especially real estate ventures. The business owner can go directly to the company or contact its agent or a mortgage banker. While insurance companies have traditionally engaged in debt financing, they have more recently demanded that they be permitted to buy an equity share in the business as part of the total package.

Small Business Administration (SBA)

One of the primary purposes of the SBA is to help small firms find financing, as is true of many other government agencies.[20] Though banks are limited by regulation or law as to the terms of their loans, the SBA tends to permit longer periods of repayment and make other concessions to small firms. The usual repayment period is five years or less. The longer maturities are primarily for disaster-type loans.

As far as credit risk is concerned, the SBA has requirements very similar to those of banks.[21] In other words, the borrower must be a good credit risk and must meet the eligibility requirements shown in Table 8–1. Eligibility for loans varies by industry and SBA program.

Table 8–1   Eligibility for SBA Business Loans [7(a) and 7(a)(11)], by Industry Type

Type of industry	Restrictions
Manufacturing	Maximum number of employees may range from 500 to 1,500, depending on the industry in which the applicant is primarily engaged.
Wholesaling	Maximum number of employees not to exceed 500.
Services	Annual receipts not exceeding $3.5 million to $14.5 million, depending on the industry in which the applicant is primarily engaged.
Retailing	Annual sales or receipts not exceeding $3.5 million to $13.5 million, depending on the industry.
Construction	General construction average annual receipts not exceeding $9.5 million to $17 million, depending on the industry.
Agriculture	Annual receipts not exceeding $0.5 million to $3.5 million, depending on the industry.

Source: Catalog of Federal Domestic Assistance (Washington, D.C.: USGPO, 1989), pp. 813, 817–18.

The SBA has been limited in its financial activities in recent years by Congressionally imposed restraints. For example, the total number of SBA loans and loan guarantees to small businesses declined from 31,700 in 1980 to 17,100 in 1987, and their total value declined from $3.86 billion to $3.23 billion.[22] The types of loans and guarantees the SBA can provide to small firms and the ways they can be used are discussed in the following sections.

Guaranteed Loans

Guaranteed loans have been the most popular in recent years. The SBA 7(a) loan program can provide small businesses with financing for real estate acquisition; building construction, renovation, or expansion; purchase of machinery and equipment; purchase of inventory; and working capital.

Ten years ago, John Horne started Horne Box, Inc. (Case VI–4), with $1,000 of equity and a $250,000 SBA loan, secured by his personal assets. Manufacturing equipment was obtained through a capital leasing agreement; office equipment was financed with a note payable; and materials were purchased with trade credit.

Repayment of debt is also permitted where existing short-term credit is not meeting the financial needs of the business (see Table 8–2 for details). The SBA guarantees the lender up to 90 percent of the loan to a maximum of $500,000. Maturity may be up to 25 years, but the typical loan has a five- to seven-year term. The borrower may contact the SBA directly or go through a bank with a policy of making SBA-guaranteed loans. Using the bank as an intermediary seems to produce more satisfactory results. As with other SBA-financing programs, demand for these loans has outstripped

Table 8–2 SBA-Guaranteed Bank Loans

Loan program	Purpose	Maturity limit	Maximum loan	Guarantee limit
Regular business loans	To provide guaranteed loans to small businesses unable to obtain funding in private credit market	Up to 25 years, though most are for shorter periods.	$750,000[a]	90%
Development company loans	Used by development companies to assist small businesses with plant acquisition, construction, or expansions (including acquisition)	10 or 20 years (504 programs) 25 years (502 program)	$1,875,000[b] in a package with other lenders $750,000[c]	40% of total loan ($750,000 SBA guarantee) 90%
Pollution control financing	Assistance for planning, design, and installation of pollution control facilities or equipment	Long-term (not specified)	$1,000,000	90%
International trade	For acquisition, construction, renovation, modernization, improvement, or expansion of productive facilities or equipment in the U.S. for production of goods and services involved in international trade	Not specified	$1,000,000	Not specified
Physical disaster loans	To provide loans to victims of designated physical disasters for uninsured losses	30 years for businesses unable to obtain credit elsewhere (3 years for those able to obtain credit)	$500,000[d]	Direct loans by SBA (not guaranteed)
Small general contractor loans	To assist small construction firms finance residential or commercial construction or rehabilitation of property for sale	Short-term	Not specified	Not specified
Seasonal line of credit	To provide financing for small firms having a seasonal loan requirement due to seasonal increase in business activity	Short-term	Not specified	Not specified
Export revolving line of credit	To provide financing for exporting firms for the purpose of developing or penetrating foreign markets	Short-term	Not specified	Not specified

[a] FY (fiscal year) 1989 obligations: $2,261,000,000
[b] FY 1989 obligations: $35,000,000 (guarantee)
[c] FY 1989 obligations: $330,000,000
[d] FY 1989 obligations: $280,000,000

Source: Your Business and the SBA (Washington, D.C.: SBA Office of Public Communications, 1989). Supplementary information also gathered from *Catalog of Federal Domestic Assistance* (Washington, D.C.: USGPO, 1989). Other loan programs not detailed here include veterans' loans, small business energy loans, and handicapped assistance loans.

Table 8–3   Who Are the Lenders?

The most active lenders in providing long-term credit to small businesses under the SBA loan guarantee program are ranked by the amount loaned in 1988.

Name of lender	Number of loans granted	Amount of loans (in millions)
The Money Store (operated nationwide)	493	$143.1
Truckee River Bank (California)	218	69.0
Southwestern Commercial Bank (Texas)	170	52.3
ITT Small Business Finance (operated nationwide)	168	42.1
Gulf American SBLC (Florida)	134	40.0
The Merchants Bank (Vermont)	198	34.9
Independence Mortgage (Texas)	92	30.5
Adobe S&L (California)	166	30.3
Government Funding, Calbidco (California)	128	28.1
Banco Popular (Puerto Rico)	97	24.8
Total SBA-guaranteed loans	14,988	$2,419.7

Source: Small Business Administration.

supply in recent years. Table 8–3 shows the lenders who were most active in granting these loans in 1988.

As mentioned in Chapter 3, the Women's Business Ownership Act, passed in 1988, provides SBA-guaranteed "miniloans" of under $50,000 for women.[23]

Direct Loans

Direct loans usually fit into one of the four categories:

1. *Minority-owned business loans.*   Significant interest has been shown in this type of loan, especially on the part of blacks, Native Americans, and Hispanics.
2. *Loans to women.*
3. *Catastrophe or disaster loans.*   These loans are made in an area where some form of physical or economic disaster has struck.
4. *Small loans.*   Business firms such as contractors rehabilitating property or providing energy conservation are eligible.

Direct loans have been restricted because of the limited supply of funds. But there are many other potential sources of funds for small companies.

Participating Loans

With participating loans, the SBA makes a portion of the total loan on a direct cash participation basis, and a bank or other lender provides the remainder. In this type of loan, the SBA assumes a subordinate position to the other lender in the event of liquidation. Due to limited funds, only a few of these loans are made.

Small Business Investment Companies (SBICs)

In addition to indirect equity financing, as previously discussed, SBICs also make qualified SBA loans. The SBA matches each dollar an SBIC puts into a loan. Loans are usually made for a period of 5 to 10 years. An SBIC may stipulate that it be given a certain portion of stock purchase warrants or stock options, or it may make a combination of a loan and a stock purchase. The latter combination has been preferred. From 1980 to 1988, SBICs made 22,074 disbursements, worth $3.8 billion, to small firms.[24]

Industrial Development Corporations (IDCs)

Industrial development corporations have freedom in the types of loans they are able to make. While they make many types of development loans, their most popular ones are **501 loans** and **503 loans.**

501 Loans

These loans are granted by state-chartered industrial development corporations, whose initial capital is provided by member commercial banks that are also members of the Federal Reserve System. These corporations make term loans, working capital loans, mortgage loans, and contract performance loans, and they can borrow up to half of the loan amount from the SBA.

503 Loans

These loans, called *the best loan program in town,*[25] are made under the Certified Development Company Program to facilitate inner-city development, neighborhood revitalization, and the like. The business owner puts up equity equal to 10 percent of the package; the bank supplies 50 percent, with a first mortgage at market rates; and the remaining 40 percent comes from the sale of SBA-guaranteed debentures at the U.S. Treasury rate.

Economic Development Administration (EDA)

The EDA makes a variety of direct loans to industries located in economically depressed communities or in communities that are declared regional economic growth centers. This financial assistance usually starts where the SBA authority ends, at $500,000.

The direct loans made by the EDA may be used for fixed assets or working capital. In addition, the EDA may extend guarantees on loans to private borrowers from private lending institutions, as well as guarantees of rental payments (from qualified lessors) on fixed assets.

The prospective small business owner should contact the local planning and development commission or chamber of commerce to determine qualification for EDA financial assistance.

Agricultural Loans

A number of sources of funds for agricultural loans are federally funded. The Cooperative Extension Service or one of its local agents may be checked for information concerning availability and procedures. Sources of such funds include the Federal Land Bank Association, the Production Credit Association, and the Farmers Home Administration.

These government loans and guarantees have drawbacks, of course. There's the usual paperwork and "red tape." These frequently result in delays in obtaining the funds. Also, the amount of the loan is often less than you need.

WHAT LENDERS LOOK FOR

What do lenders look for when considering a loan to a small business? In essence, the basics apply today as they did in the past. First, the lender wants to see if you can live within the income of the business, if the loan is for a new business. Given your expected revenues and expenses, will you be able to repay the loan? How much collateral can you put up to insure the lender against your inability to repay?

Second, if the money is for an existing business, the lender will look at its track record. If there are problems, you will be expected to explain what's going to happen to make a difference in the future. Do you have a new business plan? Are you going to buy new equipment or technology? Is there a new marketing plan?

To a large extent, your ability to attract money will depend on the lender's perception of your character as well as your ability to return the money. There are three things that help determine a lender's perception of you.

First, *income* is important. You will be asked questions such as: How well do you live within your means? Have you learned to manage your money effectively, so that the funds will be productive rather than wasted? The lenders will also look at your capacity for managing and using the money you have requested. It is a trite, but true, saying: If you can't manage your personal finances effectively, it will be difficult for you to manage the assets of a new or growing business.

Second, the lender will also look at your *stability*, to see how long you've lived in a given residence or neighborhood, as well as how long you've worked at a particular job or run a business. While none of these items alone will prevent your obtaining the loan, if they show an overall picture of instability, you may have to explain why you've changed so many times. Have you changed jobs for better opportunities? Have you moved up in socioeconomic level as you've moved from one residence to another?

Third, your *debt management* record is also important. Lenders will search for evidence that you have been able to pay off your debts. They'll ask questions such as: How good is your loan repayment history? Have you paid on time? Have you filed for bankruptcy? As with the other factors, you will need a satisfactory explanation of your debt management in order to obtain funds.

In summary, your request for financing will almost certainly be checked by some major credit company. The most frequently used ones are TRW and the U.S. Credit Bureau, and these use computerized reference services. Therefore, knowing that your credit record will be checked immediately by the computer, you should ask for a credit printout (which can be obtained for a few dollars) before you apply for funds. This will give you an opportunity to correct any errors or misunderstandings in your credit record.

Figure 8–4 provides you with some steps to use in developing a better relationship with investors, along with some questions that the investor should ask you.

Remember that, while lenders should have an interest in how financially sound your business is, *they should not have a voice in managing it.* If you permit them to, they in reality become partners and must share responsibility for any failures.

Figure 8–4   How to Improve the Entrepreneur-Investor Relationship

There are at least five steps you should take in order to assure a good working relationship with the investor. They are:

1. Establish the range of funds you will need.
2. Identify the investor's skills and abilities that could help enhance your venture.
3. Find an investor with interests and personality traits similar to yours.
4. Find a long-term investor, not one who wants to "make a quick buck" and get out.
5. Find an investor with more to offer you than just money, so that you may avoid having to hire outside consultants.

There are certain things the investor should find out about you.

1. Can you and the investor work together as a team?
2. Do you appear to be flexible and willing to accept new management if the project is highly successful?
3. Are you truly committed to this endeavor, and are you willing to expend the energy and resources to make it a success?
4. Can you accept constructive criticism, feedback, and assistance?
5. Do you have definite, fixed, realistic goals, and where do you plan to be in, say, one year? Five years? Ten years?

WHAT YOU SHOULD HAVE LEARNED

1. Providing for financial needs is crucial to the success of a small business, which may be undercapitalized and living hand to mouth. Sufficient short- and long-term financing are needed to provide for fluctuations in sales or an unexpected business slump.

2. For a start-up venture, the assets of a business should be financed with equity, or with debt funds having a maturity about equal to the productive life of the asset. Also, enough working capital to carry the company through periods when expenses are immediate and receipts are delayed is important. A useful tool for estimating financial needs is the cash budget, which projects not only the amounts of expense and revenue for the year, but also their timing, so that mismatches can be covered with adequate working capital.

3. The two major sources of funds for a small business are equity financing and debt financing. While equity financing never has to be repaid—as a debt does—it provides an interest in the business, including a share of the profits and a voice in decision making. Both kinds of financing are needed for a sound capital structure.

   Debt financing can be risky for a small business because debts must be repaid whether the company is profitable or not. However, it is less expensive than equity financing, as interest payments are tax deductible and the lender, regarding a debt investment as less risky than an equity investment, does not require as high a rate of return.

4. The most usual types of equity securities are common and preferred stock. Common stock conveys voting rights but has no enforceable claim to dividends. Preferred stock entitles the shareholder to a fixed rate of dividend whenever profits are sufficient. Although dividends are not guaranteed, any unpaid ones must be paid to preferred stockholders before any dividends are paid to common stockholders. Preferred stockholders usually have no voting rights.

   Debt securities include loans and bonds, which may be classified according to their maturities as short-, intermediate-, and long-term. Loans made by a lender in standard denominations are called *bonds*. Long-term debt secured by real property is a mortgage loan, whereas a chattel mortgage is backed by some other physical asset.

   A lease can be a form of debt financing. If it pays for the property over the term of its useful life, it is a capital lease. An operating lease, which is shorter lived, may still permit a company to use equipment it cannot secure debt financing to buy.

5. Sources of equity financing include funds from the owner, family and friends, small business investment companies (SBICs), venture capitalists, angel capitalists, business incubators, venture capital networks, venture capital clubs, employees, and customers.

6. Sources of debt financing include trade credit, commercial and financial

institutions, the SBA, SBICs, industrial development corporations (IDCs), the Economic Development Administration (EDA), and agricultural loans. Commercial and financial institutions include commercial banks, savings and loan associations, commercial finance companies, nonfinancial corporations, and insurance companies.

The SBA finances business ventures through guaranteed loans, direct loans, and participating loans. IDCs make 501 loans with funds borrowed partially from SBA and 503 loans with funds assembled from a combination of owner equity, conventional mortgage loans, and SBA-guaranteed debentures. The EDA can make larger loans than the SBA in areas of regional growth or economic depression.

7. When deciding whether or not to finance a small business, lenders look for factors such as (*a*) ability to repay the debt, (*b*) the owner's and the business's financial and business track record, and (*c*) the owner's income, stability, and debt management.

KEY TERMS

working capital, *195*

cash budget, *195*

equity, *196*

stock, *196*

common stockholders, *196*

preferred stockholders, *196*

equity capital, *196*

debt capital, *196*

financial leverage, *197*

leveraged buyout (LBO), *197*

lease, *197*

capital leases, *198*

operating leases, *198*

common stock, *198*

preferred stock, *198*

short-term securities, *199*

intermediate-term securities, *199*

long-term securities, *199*

bonds, *199*

debentures, *199*

mortgage loan, *199*

chattel mortgage loan, *199*

Tax Reform Act of 1978, *202*

angel capitalists, *206*

venture capital networks, *206*

business incubators, *206*

venture capital clubs, *208*

employee stock ownership plans (ESOP), *208*

trade credit, *209*

consignment selling, *209*

line of credit, *210*

savings and loan associations (S&Ls), *210*

501 loans, *215*

503 loans, *215*

QUESTIONS FOR DISCUSSION

1. Discuss the basic rules to follow in financing a business venture.
2. Why should small business managers assess working capital needs in advance?

3. What are some of the reasons small business entrepreneurs use *(a)* equity financing? *(b)* debt financing?

4. What are the factors that determine the classification of debt securities?

5. List and discuss the primary sources of equity financing.

6. List and discuss the primary sources of debt financing.

7. Compare equity financing to debt financing.

8. Evaluate the role of the SBA in providing operating and venture capital.

SUGGESTED READINGS

Angell, Robert J. "The Effect of the Tax Reform Act on Capital Investment Decisions." *Financial Management,* Winter 1988, pp. 82–86.

Anstaett, Kurt W., Dennis P. McCrary, and Stephen T. Monahan, Jr. "Practical Debt Policy Considerations for Growth Companies: A Case Study Approach." *Journal of Applied Corporate Finance,* Summer 1988, pp. 71–78.

Connell, R., and B. Phillips. "Finding Funds for Small Firms." *Management Today,* November 1988, p. 143ff.

Greenfield, W. M. *Developing New Ventures.* New York: Harper & Row, 1989.

"Growth through Strategic Sponsorship." *Accountancy* 102 (October 1988): 171–72.

"Informal Investment Booming for Small Business Start-ups." *Journal of Accountancy* 166 (December 1988): 17.

Ou, Charles. "Financing Patterns of Small Business." *Working Paper,* Office of Economic Research, U.S. Small Business Administration. Washington, D.C.: U.S. Government Printing Office, 1988.

Pratt, Stanley E., and Jane K. Morris. *Pratt's Guide to Venture Capital Sources.* 13th ed. Wellesley Hills, Mass.: Venture Economics, 1989.

Ricklefs, Roger. "Small Businesses Look Ever More Alluring to Big Banks," *The Wall Street Journal,* December 13, 1988, p. B2.

Sahlman, William A. "Aspects of Financial Contracting in Venture Capital." *Journal of Applied Corporate Finance,* Summer 1988, pp. 23–26.

Walker, Ernest W., and J. William Petty II. *Financial Management of the Small Firm.* 2d ed. Englewood Cliffs, N.J.: Prentice-Hall, 1986.

ENDNOTES

1. Edmund L. Andrews, "No Guts, No Glory," *Venture,* February 1988, pp. 31–40.

2. Don Nichols, "For Sale or Rent, No Money Down," *Venture,* April 1989, p. 54.

3. Abby Livingston, "State Capital," *Venture,* May 1989, p. 57.

4. James M. Poterba, "Venture Capital and Capital Gains Taxation," *Working Paper No. 2832,* National Bureau of Economic Research (Cambridge, Mass.: January 1989); and Shelley Liles, "Venture Capitalists' Investments Fall," *USA Today,* July 14, 1989, p. 6B.

5. "Venture Capital Disbursements Decline 21% to $3 Billion in 1988," *Venture Capital-Journal,* June 1989, pp. 10–12.

6. Eugene E. Carlson, "Japanese Bankroll U.S. Firms," *The Wall Street Journal,* November 2, 1989, p. B1.

7. Marj Charlier, "Patient Money," *The Wall Street Journal,* February 24, 1989, p. R21.

8. Correspondence with the Vancouver Stock Exchange.

9. Christina B. Schlank, "Them That Got, Gets," *Venture,* June 1988, p. 36.

10. Ellen L. James, "Desperate for Dollars," *Venture,* May 1988, p. 64.

11. "Pension-Fund Money Goes to Small Business," *The Wall Street Journal,* August 25, 1989, p. B1.

12. Andrew J. Sherman, "Washington Watch: New Director of Business Incubators Offered by IVCI," *Business Age,* May 1989, p. 64.

13. Correspondence with June Lavelle.

14. Call (203) 323-3143 for a copy of the *1989 Directory of Venture Capital Clubs* ($9.95), which has phone numbers for 115 clubs around the world.

15. Selwyn Feinstein, "The Breakfast Club," *The Wall Street Journal,* February 24, 1989, p. R8.

16. Jonathan B. Levine, "Louis Kelso's Baby Is Making Daddy Proud," *Business Week,* May 8, 1989, p. 130.

17. Joel Katkin, "Natural Partners," *Inc.,* June 1989, pp. 67–80.

18. Ellen E. Spragins, "Courting Your Banker," *Inc.,* May 1989, p. 129.

19. "Capital: The Commercial Finance Alternative," *Inc.,* August 1986, p. 84.

20. As Congress periodically passes new legislation that determines the kind of assistance the SBA provides, contact the nearest district office of the agency to determine what types of assistance are currently available to you.

21. "Small Business Statistics: Who the Lenders Are," *The Wall Street Journal,* February 24, 1989, p. R25.

22. U.S. Department of Commerce, *Statistical Abstract of the United States, 1989* (Washington, D.C.: U.S. Government Printing Office, 1989), p. 527.

23. Mindy Fetterman, "Callers Ignite the Hot Line," *USA Today,* May 10, 1989, p. 2B.

24. U.S. Department of Commerce, *The State of Small Business: A Report to the President* (Washington, D.C.: U.S. Government Printing Office, 1989), p. 142.

25. "Finance: The Best Loan Program in Town," *Inc.,* August 1986, p. 85.

9

ORGANIZING THE BUSINESS

Good order is the foundation of all good things.—Edmund Burke

To me, going public [incorporating] would be like selling my soul.—Carlton Cadwell, manufacturer

LEARNING OBJECTIVES

After studying the material in this chapter, you will be able to:

1. Name the legal forms a small business can have.
2. Explain the reasons for and against forming a proprietorship.
3. Explain the reasons for and against forming a partnership.
4. Explain the reasons for and against forming a corporation.
5. Discuss some other legal forms the business can take.
6. Describe how to select the best organizational form for the business.
7. Discuss some basic ways of organizing the business.

HENRY E. KLOSS: PROPRIETOR, PARTNER, AND CORPORATE OWNER

Henry E. Kloss is one of a very rare group in U.S. business—successful inventor-entrepreneurs. His first venture into business, as a young undergraduate at Massachusetts Institute of Technology, was designing, making, and selling cabinets for stereos to pay his way through school.

After military service, Kloss returned to Cambridge, where his skills as a cabinetmaker, combined with his interest in electronics and sound, led him to Edgar Villchur, who had an idea for an acoustic suspension system. They formed a partnership, Acoustic Research, in 1954 and pioneered in the production of acoustic suspension speakers, which made all other types of loudspeakers obsolete. Half the company went to the outsiders who put up the money, and equal shares went to Kloss, who brought in his cabinet proprietorship, and Villchur, who had the new idea. Eventually, a disagreement over day-to-day management put Kloss and two top managers, Malcolm Low and Anton Hoffman, on one side and Villchur on the other. Kloss, Low, and Hoffman were forced out and sold their interest for about $56,000.

They then formed KLH Corporation to produce a low-cost, full-range speaker. They expanded their product base by adding items such as the Dolby noise reduction system. In fact, their sales doubled from $2 to $4 million in the year after they were the first to use transistors in a consumer product—a portable stereo. Kloss sold his interest to Singer for $1.2 million of Singer stock in 1964, after Low and Hoffman left. (Unfortunately for him, Singer stock was the second biggest loser on the New York Stock Exchange the next year.) Kloss ran KLH for Singer until 1967; but when Singer refused to build a large-screen TV set he had designed, he sold his stock to Singer for $400,000.

Kloss then spent two years developing a working model of the large-screen set—called Videobeam—in his basement. But by then he was out of money; so he founded Advent Corporation to produce high-quality, low-priced speakers as well as the Videobeam. Advent had constant financial problems due to its low prices for the high-quality speakers and TV sets. Its bankers

forced Advent to raise new capital in 1975, resulting in Kloss's being demoted from president to chief scientist and then leaving the company.

Kloss spent the next two years perfecting a low-cost method for manufacturing the tubes for his large-screen TV. In 1979, he founded Kloss Video with $800,000 raised from friends and became its president and treasurer. Its two-piece, large-screen projection set, the Novabeam, which sold for about $3,300, had sharper and brighter images than its competitors. At the top price its stock reached, in 1983, Kloss's 60 percent share of Kloss Video was worth about $15 million at market.

After 1983, Kloss Video's operating earnings and stock price steadily declined. Operating losses were experienced in subsequent years, culminating in a massive loss of $4.5 million on sales of $12.9 million in 1987. Based on these results, Kloss Video's board of directors removed Kloss as president and replaced him with a manager of their choosing. Later that year, Kloss Video was acquired by Video Display Corporation.

Immediately after his removal, Kloss started a new corporation—Cambridge Sound—in nearby Newton. For $497, it will deliver to your door its Ensemble speaker system, consisting of four separate units: two woofers and two tweeters. His motto is "quality and affordability."

Source: Correspondence with Henry Kloss and Kloss Video; and other sources, such as Kloss Video 10–K filings and proxy statements for the years 1984–1987; and Hans Fantel, "Henry Kloss's Mail-Order Speakers," *The New York Times,* February 19, 1989, p. H32.

The Opening Focus illustrates an important decision facing new small businesses; namely, what legal form the business should use. In his first business, at MIT, Kloss operated alone as a proprietorship. As his needs changed, he took in partners. Then he incorporated when more funds were required.

Even in failure, the wisdom of his choice of organizational forms was evident. The net losses suffered by Kloss Video were not ruinous for Kloss personally, and the fact that the business was organized as a corporation meant that it could continue operations—and eventually be acquired by another company—even after Kloss himself had been removed as president. Also notice that he was able to walk away and start a new business, which was also a corporation.

SELECTING THE RIGHT LEGAL FORM

Going into business for yourself and being your own boss is a dream that can become either a pleasant reality or a nightmare. Though it may be satisfying to give the orders, run the show, and receive the income from the business, other factors must be considered when choosing the legal form for your organization. Income tax considerations, the amount of free time available, responsibility for others, and family wishes must also be considered in choosing a proprietorship, partnership, corporation, or other legal form for the new business.[1]

Factors to Consider

When choosing your business's legal form, ask several basic questions. For example, to what extent is your family able to endure the physical, psychological, and emotional strains associated with running the business? Second, how easy is it to start the business, operate it, and transfer your interest in it to your heirs or others? Third, to what extent are you and your family willing to accept the financial risks involved, including being responsible both for your own business losses and debts and for those of other people? Finally, how much information about yourself, your family, and your economic status are you willing to make public?

Of course, the choice of legal form does not have to be irrevocable. Instead, the usual progression—as with Kloss—is to start as a proprietorship or partnership and then move into a corporation.

Relative Importance of Each Form

As you can see from Figure 9–1, the proprietorship is by far the most popular form of business in the United States. Around 71 percent of all businesses are proprietorships, while only 19 percent are corporations and 10 percent are partnerships. Notice in Figure 9–2 that the proprietorship is more popular in services, retail trade, and manufacturing, while the corporation is more popular in wholesaling.

While the proprietorship is the most popular form, it accounts for only a small share of total revenues. As Figure 9–1 shows, proprietorships generate only around 6 percent of all revenues, while corporations account for 90 percent, and partnerships provide around 4 percent.

Figure 9–2 shows that corporations dominate the business receipts in all areas. However, proprietorships and partnerships account for significant revenues in services and retail trade.

Proprietorships also appear to be the most profitable form. As shown in Figure 9–1, they accounted for only 6 percent of revenues, yet received 25 percent of profits. Partnerships accounted for 4 percent of revenues but suffered $17.4 billion of *losses*. Corporations received 75 percent of the profits on 90 percent of the sales. These numbers should be interpreted with caution, however, since "proprietorship" profits include net financial return to owners. Much of that return would be included in wage and salary expense if the firm were organized as a corporation. That expense could have been deducted from profit.

Figure 9–1   Relative Position of U.S. Proprietorships, Partnerships, and Corporations

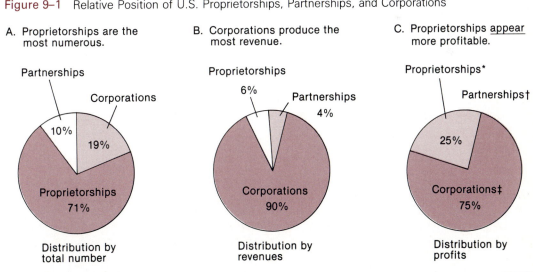

A. Proprietorships are the most numerous.

B. Corporations produce the most revenue.

C. Proprietorships <u>appear</u> more profitable.

Partnerships

Corporations

10%

19%

Proprietorships
71%

Distribution by total number

Proprietorships

6%

Partnerships
4%

Corporations
90%

Distribution by revenues

Proprietorships*

Partnerships†

25%

Corporations‡
75%

Distribution by profits

* Profits of $78.8 billion.
† Losses of $8.9 billion.
‡ Profits of $240.1 billion.
Source: U.S. Department of Commerce, *Statistical Abstract of the United States, 1989* (Washington, D.C.: U.S. Government Printing Office, 1989), Table 846, p. 516.

Figure 9–2 Comparison of Proprietorships, Partnerships, and Corporations in Selected Industries

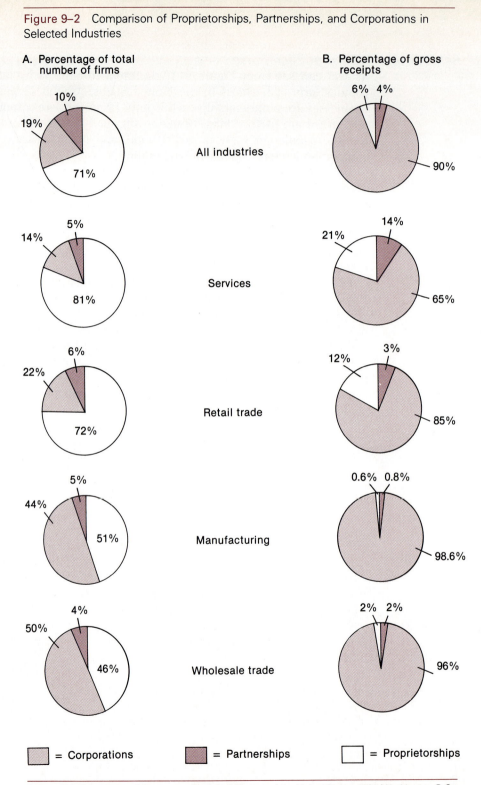

A. Percentage of total number of firms

B. Percentage of gross receipts

All industries

Services

Retail trade

Manufacturing

Wholesale trade

☐ = Corporations   ☐ = Partnerships   ☐ = Proprietorships

Source: U.S. Department of Commerce, *Statistical Abstract of the United States, 1989* (Washington, D.C.: U.S. Government Printing Office, 1989), Table 848, p. 517.

WHY FORM A PROPRIETORSHIP?

A **proprietorship** is a business that is owned and operated by one person. It is the oldest and most prevalent form of organization, as well as the least expensive to form. Most small companies prefer this type of operation because of its simplicity and the owners' desire for individual control over their businesses. In addition to being simple to enter, operate, and terminate, it provides for relative freedom of action and control. Finally, the proprietorship has a unique tax advantage. As will be shown in Chapter 23, it is taxed at the owner's personal income tax rate. In these respects, you may find it an attractive form to use; around 13 million proprietors now do.

Notice how easy it was for Henry Kloss to begin operating as a proprietor while a student at MIT. All he had to do was find a place to design, make, and sell his cabinets. He probably did not even have to pay taxes. Also, he was independent, with no co-owners to cause him problems.

At least two major negative factors, however, should be considered when choosing to become a proprietor. First, the business and its owner are one and the same, and they cannot be separated from a legal point of view. Consequently, the business legally ends with the proprietor's death, and some legal action must be taken to restart it. Second, if the business does not have enough funds to pay all of its obligations, the owner must use personal assets to pay them.

Figure 9–3 shows the advantages and disadvantages of owning a proprietorship.

WHY FORM A PARTNERSHIP?

According to Section 6 of the Uniform Partnership Act, adopted by most states, a **partnership** is "a voluntary association of two or more persons to carry on as co-owners a business for profit." The partnership is similar to the proprietorship but is more difficult to set up, operate, and end. Partnerships are generally more effective than proprietorships in raising financial resources and in obtaining better ideas, management, and credit. Also, as with the proprietorship, profits are taxed only once—on each partner's share of the income—not twice, as in the corporation. But if all profits are distributed to the partners rather than kept as retained earnings, there may not be sufficient equity capital for expansion.

As shown in Figure 9–4, however, the partnership has its own drawbacks. For example, the death of any one of the partners terminates the life of the partnership, and legal action is needed to revive it. This disadvantage may be overcome, however, by an agreement among the partners stating that the remaining partner(s) will purchase the interest of the deceased

Figure 9–3   Weighing the Advantages and Disadvantages of a Proprietorship

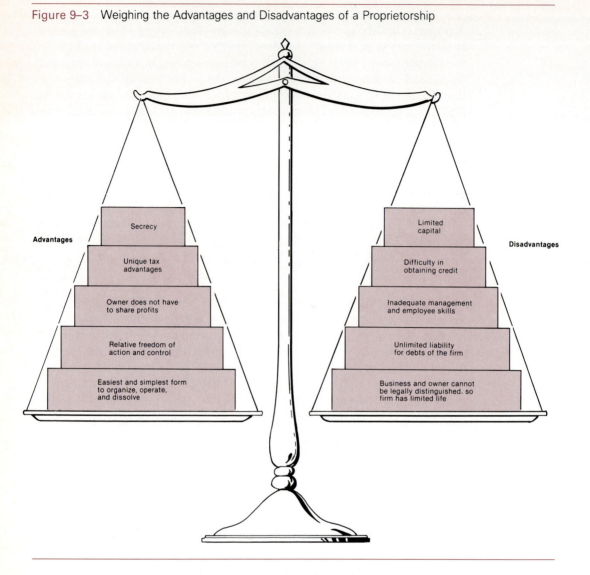

Advantages

Secrecy

Unique tax advantages

Owner does not have to share profits

Relative freedom of action and control

Easiest and simplest form to organize, operate, and dissolve

Disadvantages

Limited capital

Difficulty in obtaining credit

Inadequate management and employee skills

Unlimited liability for debts of the firm

Business and owner cannot be legally distinguished, so firm has limited life

partner from his or her estate. Further, the partnership itself usually carries insurance to cover this contingency.

Partners are responsible for the acts of each and every other partner. Thus, the members of a general partnership—or the general partners in a limited partnership (see next section)—have unlimited liability for the debts of the firm, so that even the personal property of each general partner can be used to satisfy the debts of the partnership. Also, a partner cannot obtain bonding protection against the acts of the other partner(s). Therefore, each partner is bound by the actions of the other partners, even if the action is detrimental to the interest of the partnership.

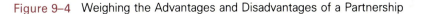

Figure 9–4   Weighing the Advantages and Disadvantages of a Partnership

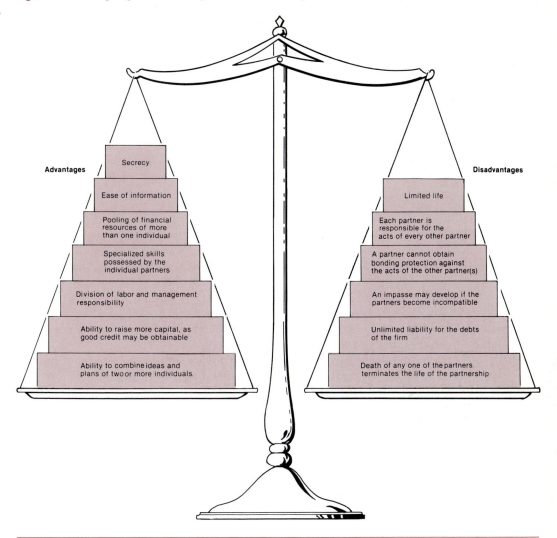

An impasse can easily develop if the partners disagree on basic issues. Thus, the business can become inoperative (or even dissolve) when a conflict can't be resolved.

This is what happened to Acoustic Research when there was a disagreement over day-to-day operations. Kloss and the others pulled out and sold their interests, but Villchur stayed in.

Types of Partnerships

Partnerships may be general or limited. In a **general partnership,** each participant is held liable for the acts of the other partners. In a **limited partnership,** there are one or more general partners and one or more limited partners. The firm is managed by the general partners, who have unlimited personal liability for the partnership's debts. The personal liability of the limited partners is limited to the amount of capital contributed by them.

Limited partners may be employees of the company but may not participate in its management. An attorney should be consulted for other limitations and requirements.

In some states, the law applied to limited partnerships permits a corporation to serve as a general partner. This arrangement, in recent years, has led to obtaining capital funds through the sale of limited partnership shares.

Rights of Partners

If there is no agreement to the contrary, each partner has an equal voice in the management of the business. Also, a majority of the partners has the legal right to make decisions pertaining to the daily operations of the business. The consent of all partners is required to make fundamental changes in the structure itself. Each partner's share of the profits is presumed to be his or her only compensation; in the absence of any agreement otherwise, profits and losses are distributed equally.

Ordinarily, the rights, duties, and responsibilities of the partners are detailed in the **articles of copartnership.** These should be drawn up during the preoperating period and revised as needed. They should spell out the authority, duties, and responsibilities of each partner.

Notice that Barbara and Steven Chappell were equal and fully responsible owners of Our Hero Restaurant (Case II–2). She handled personnel and payroll duties, while he was in charge of store operations, accounting, and long-term planning.

Tests of a Partnership

It is sometimes difficult to tell whether a business is a proprietorship, partnership, or corporation. The major determinants are: (1) the intent of the owners, (2) co-ownership of the business, and (3) carrying on the business for a profit. Also, no formalities are required to create a partnership. Thus, a proprietor may form one and not realize it. As a general rule, the sharing of profits and having a voice in the management of the business are sufficient evidence to imply the existence of a partnership.

A partnership is required to file Form 1065 with the IRS for information purposes. The IRS can—and sometimes does—challenge the status of a partnership and may attempt to tax it as a separate legal entity.

WHY FORM A CORPORATION?

In one of the earliest decisions of the U.S. Supreme Court, Chief Justice John Marshall defined a corporation as "an artificial being, invisible, intangible, and existing only in contemplation of the law." In other words, a **corporation** is a legal entity ("artificial being"), whose life exists at the pleasure of the courts of law.

The formation of a corporation is more formal and complex than is required for the other legal forms of business. The minimum number of persons required as stockholders varies with individual state laws. Commonly, the number varies from three to five. The procedure for formation usually is legally defined and requires the services of an attorney. Incorporation fees normally are based on the corporation's amount of capital.

The corporate form offers small business owners several primary advantages. For example, the corporation is separate and distinct from the owners as individuals, and so the death of one stockholder does not affect the life of the corporation. Also, each owner's liability for the firm's debts is limited to the amount invested; so personal property cannot be touched (with certain limited restrictions, such as loan guarantees, nonpayment of taxes, and malfeasance) to pay the debts of the business. Finally, since the owners are not required to become involved in the firm's operations, large amounts of capital can be raised relatively easily. Figure 9–5 illustrates these advantages.

Notice that Henry Kloss found it advantageous to incorporate when he needed more capital but wanted to restrict his liability and reduce the chances of disruption from partners. This made it easier for him to sell his interest to Singer, and to raise money from friends when he organized Kloss Video.

The corporate form's many offsetting disadvantages, also shown in Figure 9–5, might keep you from choosing it for a business. The main problem is double taxation, as the corporation pays taxes on its profit, and then individual owners pay taxes on their dividends. As will be shown later, this is one reason for using an S Corporation. Also, the area of operations is limited, and the process of incorporation is complex and costly.

How to Form a Corporation

As indicated, it is relatively difficult to form a corporation. **Articles of incorporation** must be prepared and filed with the state in exchange for a corporate **charter,** which states what the business can do and provides other information. Also, the procedure, reports, and statements required for operation of a corporation are cumbersome, and, because the owners' powers are limited to those stated in the charter, it may be difficult for the corporation to do business in another state. The legal requirements for incorporating vary from state to state; so it might be advantageous to find a state favorable to business in which to incorporate—such as Delaware.

Figure 9–5   Weighing the Advantages and Disadvantages of a Corporation

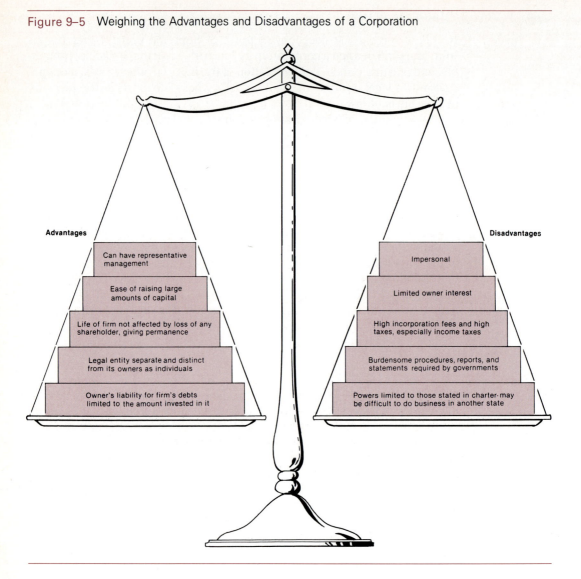

Advantages

- Can have representative management
- Ease of raising large amounts of capital
- Life of firm not affected by loss of any shareholder, giving permanence
- Legal entity separate and distinct from its owners as individuals
- Owner's liability for firm's debts limited to the amount invested in it

Disadvantages

- Impersonal
- Limited owner interest
- High incorporation fees and high taxes, especially income taxes
- Burdensome procedures, reports, and statements required by governments
- Powers limited to those stated in charter-may be difficult to do business in another state

Delaware's incorporation requirements are so lenient that, despite its small size, it charters more corporations than any other state. However, Texas has fewer filing requirements and simpler forms than any other state, though Tennessee is a close second.[2]

While forming a corporation, but before it is completed, a signed agreement should be made to protect against any member(s) of the group taking off on their own to start a competing business. This agreement at least makes it possible to recover damages that may be incurred.

In order to protect the incorporators, a buy-sell arrangement should be included in the articles of incorporation. This arrangement details the terms by which stockholders can buy out each other's interests. Also, if the success of the venture is dependent on key people, insurance should be carried on them. This type of insurance protects the resources of the firm in the event of the loss of these people (see Chapter 21).

Adequate bond and insurance coverage should be maintained against losses that result from the acts of employees and others. Also, liability coverage and workers' compensation insurance should be carried.

How a Corporation Is Governed

The initial incorporators tend to run the corporation after it is formed. But they are assisted by other stockholders, directors, officers, and executives.

Stockholders

The stockholders are the owners of the corporation. In a small corporation, one or a few people may own most of the stock and therefore be able to control it. In a large corporation, however, holders of as little as 10 percent may be able to control the company. Often, the founder and/or family have controlling interest and can pick the people to be on the board of directors.

Board of Directors

The board of directors represents the stockholders in managing the company. In a small business, the owners often consider the board not necessary, as the stockholders and top executives are the same. But a board can bring breadth to the planning in the corporation. The board helps set goals and plans marketing, production, and financing strategies and growth patterns. Despite these advantages, some owners prefer to run the company alone, without someone "looking over their shoulders."

There are many sources of effective directors. Among the possibilities are: (1) experienced businesspeople, (2) investors, (3) bankers, and (4) professionals, such as attorneys, CPAs, or business consultants. What you look for is the expertise or influence they have that can help you.

It is becoming more difficult to obtain competent outsiders to serve on corporate boards—especially of small companies—because liability suits may be filed against them by disgruntled stockholders, employees, customers, or suppliers.[3]

Corporate Officers

While their titles and duties vary, corporate officers usually include the chairman, president, secretary, and treasurer. Within limits set by stockholders and the board, these officers direct the day-to-day operations of the business.

S Corporations

In addition to limited liability, corporations with no corporate shareholders or incorporated subsidiaries and with 35 or fewer shareholders can reduce, under certain circumstances, the burden of taxes and their associated administrative expenses. An **S Corporation** (formerly called a *Subchapter S corporation*) is established primarily to eliminate multiple taxation of income and the attendant paperwork. Also, it does not process certain taxes. For example, regular corporations must deduct Social Security taxes on paid income to owners employed by the firm, and the firm must pay the employer's share of the taxes. But if an owner receives an outside salary above the maximum from which such taxes are deducted, the S Corporation neither deducts nor pays Social Security taxes on the owner's income.

If the income from corporate operations is distributed to the stockholders, they pay taxes on it at their individual rates. While the payment process is similar to that of a partnership, the corporation must file a special federal income tax return. The 1986 income tax revisions made the S Corporation much more attractive to small businesses. The maximum individual tax rate of 28 percent (33 percent with surcharge for higher incomes) is lower than the 34 percent maximum on corporations. For this reason, many small businesses may choose to swtich to this organizational form to reduce income taxes.

There are, however, significant costs to electing S Corporation status. For one thing, these corporations can issue only one class of stock—common. This may effectively limit capital financing in some cases, as other forms of stock are preferred by many venture capitalists—and they can't be issued by the S Corporation. Another disadvantage is that all shareholders must be individuals, estates, or some type of personal trust.[4] Therefore, no other corporation or partnership may make an equity investment in the company.

OTHER FORMS OF BUSINESS

Other legal forms can be used by a small business owner. The most popular of these are the trust, the cooperative, and the joint venture.

Trusts

For estate and other reasons identified under federal and state tax laws, the trust arrangement establishes a method of providing the owner of a business with certain tax advantages. A popular form in recent years has been the **real estate investment trust (REIT).**

A trust is designed to overcome some of the disadvantages of the general partnership, as it provides continuity of life as well as ease of transferring ownership. A **trust** differs from a corporation in that it is established for a specific period of time or until certain designated events have occurred. The trust receives specific assets from the person or persons establishing it and is administered by a trustee or a board of trustees. The trust covenant defines the purpose of the trust, names the beneficiary or beneficiaries, and establishes a formula for the distribution of income and trust assets.

Cooperatives

A **cooperative** is an organization owned by and operated for the benefit of patrons using its services. Usually, the net income of the cooperative is returned to the patrons at the end of each year, resulting in no profits and no taxes to the cooperative. To receive the advantages of a cooperative, an organization must meet the classification and operating requirements of federal and state governments. The cooperative form of business is usually

---

Delta Pride Catfish Inc. of Indianola, Mississippi, the United States' farm-raised catfish capital, is such a cooperative. Catfish farming—the nation's largest aquaculture industry—is done primarily by small farmers who don't have the expertise or resources to do their own advertising and marketing. So they join cooperatives that provide aggressive marketing and even financing. Delta Pride, the largest U.S. processor of fresh fish, is a farmer-owned cooperative numbering 180 members. Each member receives one share of stock for each acre of catfish in production. Delta Pride, whose members own 64,000 acres of catfish ponds, employs 1,890 people and had sales of $135 million in 1988.

John Folse, Delta Pride's executive chef and national spokesman, introduced catfish to Moscow when he was invited to coordinate America's first Soviet-American culinary exchange in 1988.[5]

Executive Chef John Folse, of Delta Pride Catfish Inc.
Source: Courtesy of Delta Pride Catfish Inc.

associated with farm products—processing and marketing farm products and purchasing, selling, and financing equipment and material.

Joint Ventures

Working relationships between small and big companies are quite popular these days and may become even more so in the future. The usual arrangement is a **joint venture,** which is a form of temporary partnership whereby two or more persons or firms join together in a single endeavor to make a profit. For example, two or more investors may combine their finances, buy a piece of land, develop it, and sell it. At that time, the joint venture is dissolved.

Now, many small businesses are using their research and development of innovative ideas to form joint ventures with larger companies that provide them with marketing and financial clout, as well as other expertise.

For example, SolarCare, Inc., a small Bethlehem, Pennsylvania, company, tried with only limited success to sell SunSense, a towelette moistened with sunscreen lotion and wrapped in foil. It was having financial difficulties and tried to attract a venture capitalist, but the 1987 stock market crash dashed hopes for the deal.

SolarCare put together a comprehensive tie-up with the Plough Inc. unit of Schering-Plough Corporation. SolarCare will focus on production and R&D work, and Schering will have first-refusal rights to new products. Schering, in turn, will play a huge role in marketing SolarCare's "SunSense by Coppertone." Thus, SolarCare keeps its name on its product and gains a potential distributor for new products while retaining its identity.[6]

Another example of a joint venture was given in Chapter 2, where we described the project in which Honeybee Robotics teamed up with Ford Aerospace to produce the "hands" for a robot to be built for NASA by Martin Marietta.

In summary, in an endeavor where neither party can achieve its purpose alone, a joint venture becomes a common and viable option. Usually, income derived from a joint venture is taxed as if the organization were a partnership.

SETTING UP THE ORGANIZATIONAL STRUCTURE

After deciding upon the legal form for the business, the operational, or administrative, structure must be organized. **Organizing** involves determining the activities necessary to achieve the firm's objectives, dividing them into small groups, and assigning each group of activities to a manager with the necessary authority and expertise to carry them out in the correct manner. A major problem for many small business owners is that they do not organize their activities properly. The following material should help you understand how best to organize a business.

Some Basic Organizational Concepts

An important concept of organization to follow is **unity of command,** whereby *each employee should be directly responsible to only one superior* *for carrying out a given duty.* (When employees report to two bosses concerning the same assignment, they may become frustrated if they receive conflicting instructions from the two.) *It is difficult to adhere to this principle in a small business, but it should be attempted.*

In assigning work to subordinates, try to arrange for their responsibility to equal their assigned authority, although this is not always feasible. Sometimes, in the short run, managers must assume responsibilities greater than their authority. Also, try to give subordinates sufficient authority to carry out their responsibilities. Otherwise, they lack the means of performing their duties.

Delegation means passing along to subordinates the responsibility for doing certain activities, giving them the authority to carry out the duties, and letting them take care of the details of how the job is done. Many owners and managers of small firms find it difficult to delegate authority. Some never do learn, while others give only lip service to the principle. You need to learn to delegate if you answer yes to most of the questions in Figure 9–6.

While these concepts should be applied to small businesses as they grow larger, they must often be adjusted when applied to Mom-and-Pop businesses, as the following example shows.

The Pepper Bush (Case III–5) had two cooks, five full-time and two part-time waitresses, and three dishwashers. There was no formal organization structure or job descriptions. All workers were expected to do whatever needed to be done: if the waitresses were too busy, a cook might serve some tables or work the cash register. The Pepper Bush was quite profitable.

A **job description** is a written statement of duties, responsibilities, authority, and relationships. Except in small Mom-and-Pop shops, such a statement should be provided to employees to inform them of the limits to what they can and cannot do. Remember, though, that if authority is to be delegated for certain duties, it must be relinquished to that employee; yet the manager cannot relinquish responsibility for seeing that those duties are performed.

Figure 9–6   How Well Do You Delegate?

1. Do you do work an employee could do just as well?
2. Do you think that you are the only one who actually knows how the job should be done?
3. Do you leave work each day loaded down with details to take care of at home?
4. Do you frequently stay after hours catching up?
5. Are you a perfectionist?
6. Do you tell your employees how to solve problems?
7. Do you seem never to be able to complete the work assigned to you?

Source: Claude S. George, *Supervision in Action: The Art of Managing Others,* 4th ed., © 1985, p. 283. Reprinted by permission of Prentice-Hall, Inc., Englewood Cliffs, New Jersey.

The owner of Cajun Products, a small seafood processing plant in Louisiana, established three departments and appointed a manager for each. He specified the following responsibilities:

1. The production manager was responsible for all processing and shipping. He was also designated assistant general manager and was delegated authority to make all operational decisions in the owner's absence.
2. The sales manager was responsible for advertising, customer solicitation, and customer service.
3. The administrative manager was responsible for personnel, purchasing, and accounting.

The owner gave each manager a detailed statement of the function of his department and the extent of his authority. Also designated were the actions that the managers could take on their own initiative, as well as the actions that required the approval of the owner-manager.[7]

Another important concept used in small businesses is that decisions are best made by the person closest to the point of action, as he or she usually knows more about what is going on. Also, authority should be exercised by a single person, usually the one responsible for performing the task. Time should not be wasted in unnecessary consultation and cross-checking before acting.

Watch carefully each supervisor's or manager's **span of control**—the number of employees reporting to a manager. Having responsibility for too many people or too many diversified types of work will reduce the supervisor's ability to handle the work. Those supervisors with more activities to control will successfully manage fewer people, and vice versa. Supervisors may have 10 or more employees reporting to them because of the similarity and repetitive nature of their work. On the other hand, middle managers may have fewer employees for whom they are responsible, because of the diversity of their work. Be especially careful of how many managers report directly to the owner-manager. If that number becomes too large, the operation of the business could be severely hampered.

Division of labor (specialization), whereby employees do the work they are best suited for, should be used whenever feasible. While it leads to increased expertise, it can also lead to problems such as boredom, fatigue, alienation, and lack of initiative. This concept is hard to apply in very small businesses.

Some Organizational Problems in Small Firms

One of the most common weaknesses in small business is that the owner or top manager does almost everything and delegates very little to others. This practice prevents the manager from devoting time to more pressing needs. It also prevents employees from developing into well-rounded workers.

The president of a small wholesale hardware company was also chairman of the board and treasurer. He handled all financial affairs, supervised accounting operations, and dealt with the firm's attorney. He made all decisions on prices, discounts, wages, salaries, and sales commissions, and controlled all sales territory assignments. He made recommendations to the board on the payment of dividends. Moreover, he was active in community organizations. Although he did all these things, the company's organization chart included an executive vice-president, vice-president, merchandise manager, sales manager, and operations manager.[8]

This example describes a manager who perhaps believes that no one else can make decisions and therefore does not delegate authority. It also illustrates another common organizational weakness of small firms: when the owner-manager is unavailable, the organization tends to become paralyzed. Another frequent problem is that the owner or top manager reverses decisions made by other managers. Perhaps the owner has not developed policies to cover the major repetitive situations and business functions. Sometimes the problem is that joint owners don't coordinate with each other.

For example, Joe Benson, as president, and Jerry Rogers, as general manager, of Metal Fabricators, Inc. (Case II–5), went their separate ways without informing each other. The resulting disagreements hampered the firm's performance. Nothing was done, however, because the majority stockholder devoted very little time to the business.

Problems, or weaknesses, also develop when the business operates loosely in its early years of operation and does not become more formalized as growth occurs. Imagine, for example, that the owner initially performs all managerial activities. With expansion, however, the business bogs down, and bottlenecks develop when the other cannot—or does not—delegate some of those duties to other people. Some other indications of trouble are:

- Sales or production can't keep up with its work load.
- The owner holds too many meetings attended by too many people, resulting in wasted hours and excessive costs.
- Administrative expenses grow more rapidly than sales.
- The owner directs too much attention to following proper procedures or resolving conflicts rather than to "getting production out."
- The attention of key people is not directed toward key activities of the firm and their performance.

The owner *must be careful*, however, *not to have rigid job classifications so that some employees are standing around idle while others are swamped with work.*

Finally, small business owners and managers need to be held accountable for their actions. Thus, as the business grows, so does the need for a meaningful board of directors or advisers.

BASIC WAYS OF ORGANIZING A BUSINESS

Small businesses can be organized in many ways, but the two most frequent ways of organizing small firms are by (1) types of authority granted and (2) how activities are grouped together.

Organizing by Types of Authority

You may already be familiar with the organizational forms based on types of authority. They are (1) the line organization and (2) the line-and-staff organization. Within these formal types of organization is found another type—the informal organization.

As shown in Chapter 3, a business may start with just a few people but with such a variety of duties that no one can specialize in any one task. Almost everyone is engaged in some of the activities of producing and selling the firm's product. The owner—or manager—has a direct line of command over employees doing such things as operations, finance, and selling the product. This is called a **line organization,** as shown in Figure 9–7.

As the firm grows and more employees are added, they tend to become specialized. Some specialists advise and perform services for those doing the operations, financing, and selling. Examples of these staff people are accountants (or controllers), personnel officers, and legal staff. This type of organization is called a **line-and-staff organization** (see Figure 9–8).

An **informal organization** always exists within the formal structure

Figure 9–7   A Simplified Line Organization

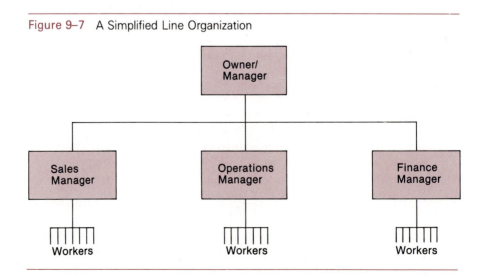

Figure 9–8   A Simplified Line-and-Staff Organization

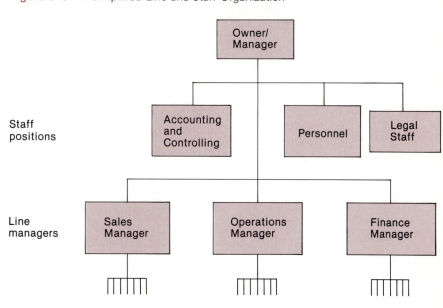

of a business. This organization consists of the many interpersonal relationships that arise as a result of friendships that develop on and off the job. Two examples are the **informal leader** and **grapevine communication** systems. The perceptive small business manager will determine who the informal leaders are, obtain their support for the company's progams, and encourage them to "sell" the programs to the rest of the employees.

What informal organizations do you belong to? A morning coffee group? A group get-together once a week?

Organizing by Grouping Activities

When a small company's formal organization structure is developed, the activities can be divided into small, workable groups in several ways. The most important bases for such organizations include:

1. *Function performed.*   Like skills are grouped together to form an organizational unit, such as production, marketing, or finance. The highest level of the organization should probably be structured on this basis (see Figure 9–7).

2. *Product sold.*   Activities may be grouped according to the product sold, such as menswear, ladies' wear, and so forth.

3. *Process used.*   Small manufacturing companies often base their organization on operating processes, such as welding or painting. Service-type firms can also use this basis. For example, a bank has windows for paying and receiving, desks for making loans, and offices for setting up trusts.

4. *Geographic area served.*   If a business requires a strong local marketing effort, organizing the sales force by areas or territories can be appropriate. This is frequently done by grocers and banks.

5. *Types of customers served.*   A firm's customers may, for example, be classified as industrial, commercial, institutional, or governmental.

6. *Project being managed.*   For example, a construction firm may be working on two projects—a store and an apartment complex. Each project needs separate managers and workers.

7. *Individual abilities of subordinates.*   Work may be assigned to people according to their particular talents. A limitation, however, is that the organization structure tends to change whenever a key employee is replaced.

Preparing an Organization Chart

There is no magical organizational structure that is best for all businesses—either large or small. Instead, you should use whatever structure seems to make sense in a given situation. The test is: Does it work at an acceptable cost? The people who own, manage, and operate the business are the important variations, not the legal form. Therefore, they should be concentrated on because they are the key factors. While there is truth in these observations, the following discussion is relevant to organizing most small firms.

Begin by setting up a series of authority and responsibility relationships expressed in a formal **organization chart.** Even if the business is small, a chart can be useful as a reminder of how people might operate more effectively. The most frequently used organization chart has the traditional formal organization structure, which may be described as a triangle or pyramid (see Figures 9–7 and 9–8).

A chart serves as a useful tool for establishing present relationships, for planning the development of the business, and in projecting personnel requirements. Therefore, a list of job titles and job specifications should accompany the chart (see Chapter 10 for details).

If the business is small and unincorporated, perhaps no one has the title of president or any other management title. A tight, formal organizational structure could stifle creativity and reduce initiative. Instead, the organization structure might be similar to that shown in Figure 9–9. It represents what actually occurs in Our Hero Restaurant (Case II–2).

As firms grow beyond a certain size, some specialized skills are usually required that the owners or top managers do not possess. They should first attempt to obtain outside, part-time assistance to aid, say, the sales

Figure 9–9 Organization of a Small Unincorporated Business

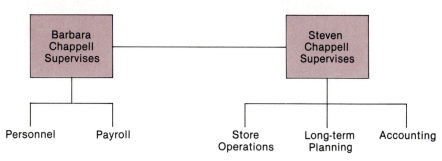

| Personnel | Payroll | | Store Operations | Long-term Planning | Accounting |

Source: Case II–2, Our Hero Restaurant (B).

manager, who may lack accounting training. Or an owner might bring in a manager because he or she no longer has time to manage operations.

WHAT YOU SHOULD HAVE LEARNED

1. Although the small business owner's choice of legal form—usually a proprietorship, partnership, or corporation—is important, it is not final, for many businesses progress from one form to another. While most small businesses are proprietorships, they generate only a small proportion of business revenues. Yet they seem to be quite profitable. Corporations and partnerships make up most of the other U.S. businesses, and corporations account for most of the revenues and profits.

2. A proprietorship is a business owned and operated by one person. It is simple to organize, operate, and dissolve, and it provides much freedom for the proprietor. The owner gets all the profits (if any), is not required to share trade secrets or details of operation with anyone else, and has some unique tax advantages. Since the business is legally inseparable from its owner, it ends when the owner dies. The owner is personally liable for all the debts and obligations of the business, may find it hard to raise money or get credit, and may find that management and employee skills are limited.

3. A partnership, which is jointly owned by two or more people, is automatically dissolved by the death of any partner. The partners share its profits, its management, and its liabilities (though limited partners may participate in profit without sharing liability or management responsibility). The partnership can combine the ideas, skills, and financial resources of several people. But it can also be difficult to dissolve, even when partners no longer see eye to eye. Moreover, except

for limited partners, all the partners bear responsibility for the actions of any one partner, and bonding protection against such actions is not available.

4. A corporation is a separate legal entity or "person" of its own. The fact that the owners are not personally responsible for its liabilities makes possible the raising of large amounts of capital, provides representative management, and assures the continuity of the business regardless of what happens to the individual owners.

    Its main disadvantages are: double taxation (the corporation pays a tax on its profits and shareholders pay taxes on dividends); the expense and paperwork of incorporation; and the limitations of its charter, which may make it difficult to operate in another state. Still, it may be the best form for a small business as it grows.

    Stockholders have the right to make any decision submitted to them for a vote, but are dominated by the owner. The board of directors, which is elected by the stockholders, should include a broad spectrum of businesspeople who should help make plans. But the day-to-day operations of the business are directed by company management.

    A form of corporation especially suitable for small business is the S Corporation. For simpler businesses (those with 35 or fewer shareholders and no corporate shareholders or incorporated subsidiaries), this form offers relief from multiple taxation and some of the burdensome paperwork.

5. Other forms of business include trusts; cooperatives, businesses owned and operated by patrons; and joint ventures, partnerships formed for specific, limited purposes.

6. Some important organizational concepts that apply to small firms as they grow are unity of command, authority equal to responsibility, making decisions where they are to be implemented, span of control, division of labor (specialization), and delegation. Following these principles helps the owner or manager to delegate, tends to eliminate tensions, and eases employee frustrations. Problems arise when managers are incompetent or the company is top-heavy, with more managers than needed for the number of employees.

7. Small firms are usually organized by type of authority structure or by the way activities are grouped. The simplest authority structure is the line organization, where orders are handed down a chain of command from the top level to the bottom. With growth, specialized staff people are needed to do activities not strictly related to operations, selling, or finance. They have the right to make suggestions to employees in their particular area of expertise. This is a line-and-staff structure. Informal organizations, which are found in any business, should not be ignored, since their leaders and grapevine communications can reinforce or counteract management activities.

An organization chart showing the chain of command and the way activities are grouped can be a useful tool for operations and planning.

KEY TERMS

proprietorship, *227*

partnership, *227*

general partnership, *230*

limited partnership, *230*

articles of copartnership, *230*

corporation, *231*

articles of incorporation, *231*

charter, *231*

S Corporation, *234*

real estate investment trust
(REIT), *234*

trust, *234*

cooperative, *235*

joint venture, *236*

organizing, *236*

unity of command, *236*

delegation, *237*

job description, *237*

span of control, *238*

division of labor
(specialization), *238*

line organization, *240*

line-and-staff organization, *240*

informal organization, *240*

informal leader, *241*

grapevine communication, *241*

organization chart, *242*

QUESTIONS FOR DISCUSSION

1. What are some of the basic questions to ask when deciding on the legal form to choose for a small business?
2. Define: (*a*) proprietorship, (*b*) partnership, (*c*) corporation, (*d*) trust, (*e*) cooperative, and (*f*) joint venture.
3. What are some (*a*) advantages and (*b*) disadvantages of a proprietorship?
4. What are some (*a*) advantages and (*b*) disadvantages of a partnership?
5. What are some (*a*) advantages and (*b*) disadvantages of a corporation?
6. Distinguish between (*a*) general partnership and (*b*) limited partnership.
7. Distinguish between (*a*) corporation and (*b*) S Corporation.
8. (*a*) Explain some of the basic organizational concepts used in organizing a small business. (*b*) How well do they apply to a small business?
9. Describe some of the organizational problems small firms have.
10. Distinguish between organizing the business by (*a*) type of authority and (*b*) grouping the activities.

SUGGESTED READINGS

Andrews, Edmund L. "I'll Take a Limited Partnership with a Twist, Please." *Venture,* May 1988, pp. 70–72.

Armitage, Jack. "Real Estate Tax Shelter—S Corporation or Limited Partnership." *CPA Journal,* May 1986, pp. 34–39.

Darrough, M. N., and N. M. Stoughton. "A Bargaining Approach to Profit Sharing in Joint Ventures." *Journal of Business* 62 (April 1989): 237–70.

"Latest Board Advice Is Keep It in the Family." *The Wall Street Journal,* January 5, 1989, p. B1.

Lazerson, Mark H. "Organizational Growth of Small Firms: An Outcome of Markets and Hierarchies." *American Sociological Review* 53 (June 1989): 330–42.

Magette, Kurt R., and Thomas P. Rohman. "Choice of Business Entity after the Tax Reform Act of 1986: The Brave New World." *Review of Taxation of Individuals,* Winter 1988, pp. 38–65.

"Market Watch: Directory of Acquisitions, Growth Companies, and Joint Ventures." *High Technology Business* 8 (October 1988): 65–68.

"Pros and Cons of S Corporations." *National Petroleum News,* November 1988, p. 2ff.

"Protecting Yourself against Your Partners." *Canadian Business,* November 1988, p. 11ff.

"Recent Rulings Support S Corporation as Joint Venturer." *Journal of Taxation* 70 (January 1989): 63–64.

Ridley, Michael P. "Preliminary Legal Considerations in Forming a New Enterprise." *Pratt's Venture Capital Journal,* 1987, pp. 62–65.

Schulman, Bruce D. "How to Choose a Business Partner." *Bottom Line,* February 28, 1989, pp. 5–6.

Wylie, Peter, and Mardy Grothe. "Breaking Up Is Hard to Do." *Nation's Business,* July 1988, pp. 24–25.

ENDNOTES

1. For further information on this subject without consulting a lawyer, see A. James Barnes, Terry M. Dworkin, and Eric L. Richards, *Law for Business,* 3d ed. (Homewood, Ill.: Richard D. Irwin, 1987), or any other good basic law book.

2. "New Businesses in Some States Have Less Red Tape to Fight," *The Wall Street Journal,* June 7, 1983, p. 33.

3. Laurie Baum and John A. Byrne, "The Job Nobody Wants," *Business Week,* September 8, 1986, pp. 55–61.

4. For more details, see Steven P. Galante, "Tax Package Would Enhance Attractions of S Corporations," *The Wall Street Journal,* September 15, 1986, p. 37.

5. Correspondence with Carolyn Ann Sledge, Assistant Director of Marketing for Delta Pride; and "Fish Tale: Mississippi to Moscow," *The New York Times,* May 21, 1988, p. 6.

6. Cecile Sorra, "SolarCare Resorts to a 'Big Brother' to Lighten Its Task," *The Wall Street Journal,* July 14, 1989, p. B2.

7. One of the authors of this text served as consultant to the firm.

8. Robert E. Schellenberger and Glenn Boseman, "The Mid-City Wholesale Hardware," in *Policy Formulation and Strategic Management: Text and Cases* (New York: John Wiley & Sons, 1982), pp. 262–72.

CASE II–1

SUE FORMS AND STARTS A BUSINESS—CLEANDRUM, INC. (B)

CASE II–2

OUR HERO RESTAURANT (B)

CASE II–3

SIMMONS MOUNTAINSIDE SATELLITE SALES

CASE II–4

THE MOTHER AND CHILD SHOP

CASE II–5

METAL FABRICATORS, INC.

CASE II–I

SUE FORMS AND STARTS A BUSINESS— CLEANDRUM, INC. (B)

Sue Ley decided to form an oil drum cleaning company. (See Case I–1 for earlier details). She approached the local Small Business Development Center to find out if there was a large enough market for such a company in her geographic location. The center surveyed 200 firms that could use the service and found that there was a sufficient market for such a quality service. It found that other firms were performing the service, but the quality was not high enough.

Using information furnished by her uncle, Sue had an accounting firm prepare projected balance sheets, income statements, and changes in cash for five years (see Exhibit 1). At the request of her banker, she approached potential customers and obtained letters indicating their willingness to do business with her "if high quality, good service, and competitive prices were offered." She then prepared a business plan. On the basis of the SBDC report, financial projections (as shown in Exhibit 1), the letters, a personal history, and interviews with the loan officer, the bank approved a $60,000 loan for Sue. With an additional $25,000 of her own money and incorporation arranged by a lawyer, Sue was ready to go into business.

Sue rented a building. Her uncle located and arranged for purchase of the necessary machinery (at the "special" price of $59,000). When it arrived, he failed to come, as promised, to supervise its installation. (She later learned that he had bankrupted her grandfather's business and that the quality of the equipment he had purchased was suspect.) Without experience\

Exhibit 1

Page 1

CleanDrum, Inc. (A Proposed Corporation)
1987 through 1991

Contents	Page
Accountants' Compilation Report	1
Projected Balance Sheets	2
Projected Income Statements	3
Projected Statements of Changes in Cash	4
Summary of Significant Projection Assumptions	5–6*

Accountants' Compilation Report

1. Development costs $100,000
    Working capital   50,000

    Total cash required $150,000
2. Estimates:

Year	Unit drum sales	Number of employees	Cost per drum
1987	31,000	4	$4.00
1988	38,000	4	4.00
1989	44,000	5	4.00
1990	50,000	5	4.50
1991	50,000	5	4.50

* Not included here.

or advice, it took Sue three months to hire mechanics, plumbers, and electricians to set up and connect the equipment. She also hired six laborers whom she trained during this time. All this delayed her start-up and drained much of her cash.

By visiting her uncle at his plant for two weeks, Sue tried to learn enough about the operation to enable her to run her own company—even though the equipment was not the same. However, sales of only 500 drums the first month of operation resulted in insufficient income to cover her direct labor costs. In the first four months, she drove a truck during the daytime hours four days a week and ran the drum-cleaning operations until 11 each night. The rest of the time, she was on the road selling CDI's drum-cleaning service. She centered her sales activities on the firms that had responded positively to the SBDC survey, especially those that had provided letters saying they were interested. She had expected her uncle to help her sell, but he did not. CDI's losses continued.

Her banker insisted that she quit her truck driving and concentrate her full energies on her business or close it. At the end of the year, CDI

Exhibit 1 *(continued)*

Page 2
CLEANDRUM, Inc. (A Proposed Corporation)
Projected Balance Sheets
1987 through 1991 (December 31)
(in $ thousands)*

	1987	1988	1989	1990	1991
Assets					
Current assets:					
Cash	$ 50	$ 97	$138	$196	$247
Fixed assets:					
Equipment	100	100	100	100	100
Less: accumulated					
depreciation	15	37	58	79	100
Net fixed assets	85	63	42	21	—
Unamortized organization costs	4	3	2	1	—
Total assets	$139	$163	$182	$218	$247
Liabilities and Stockholders' Equity					
Current liabilities	22	25	29	33	—
Long-term debt	88	63	33	—	—
Total liabilities	110	88	62	33	—
Stockholders' equity:					
Capital stock	1	1	1	1	1
Paid-in capital	19	19	19	19	19
Retained earnings	9	55	99	165	227
Total stockholders' equity	29	75	119	185	247
Total liabilities and stockholders' equity	$139	$163	$182	$218	$247

* Values have been converted into thousands of dollars.

had cleaned and sold about 18,000 drums, but Sue was still $30,000 in the hole.

Early the next year, Edie Jones became interested in investing in the company. Edie had a degree in environmental engineering, had no experience in business, and was married to the owner of a successful business. She invested $32,000 in DCI and became a 50 percent owner of the company.

Questions for Discussion

1. Evaluate the research Sue did before going into business.
2. How do you evaluate Sue's business plan, including the financial information?
3. If you were a banker, would you have loaned Sue the money? Explain.

Exhibit 1   (continued)

Page 3
CLEANDRUM, Inc. (A Proposed Corporation)
Projected Income Statements
For years ending December 31
(in $ thousands)*

Item	1987	1988	1989	1990	1991
Sales	$367	$441	$514	$588	$588
Cost of sales:					
Materials	143	172	222	254	254
Labor	45	45	60	65	70
Freight	15	15	15	15	15
Total cost of sales	$203	$232	$297	$334	$339
Gross profit	$164	$209	$217	$254	$249
Expenses:					
Depreciation	15	22	21	21	21
Payroll taxes	12	12	14	15	16
Repair and maintenance	7	7	7	7	7
Rent	12	12	12	12	12
Utilities	18	18	20	22	22
Salaries	45	45	46	50	53
Insurance	10	10	10	10	10
Office expense	3	3	3	3	3
General tax, legal, accounting	5	5	5	5	5
Travel and automobile	6	6	7	7	8
Telephone	5	5	5	5	5
Amortized organization expense	1	1	1	1	1
Interest	16	14	10	7	3
Total expenses	$155	$160	$161	$165	$166
Net income before taxes	$ 9	$ 49	$ 56	$ 89	$ 83
Income taxes	—	3	12	23	21
Net income	$ 9	$ 46	$ 44	$ 66	$ 62

* Values have been converted into thousands of dollars.

4. What do you think of the uncle and his activities—and nonactivities? Should Sue have gone back to him for help?

5. Was the banker wise in stopping Sue from driving the truck?

6. What do you recommend that Sue do now?

Source: Prepared by William M. Spain, SCORE, and Charles R. Scott, University of Alabama.

Exhibit 1   *(concluded)*

Page 4
CLEANDRUM, Inc. (A Proposed Corporation)
Projected Statements of Changes in Cash
For years ending 1987 through 1991
(in $ thousands)*

Items	1987	1988	1989	1990	1991
Net income	$ 8	$ 46	$ 44	$ 66	$ 62
Add: Amortization	1	1	1	1	1
Depreciation	15	22	21	21	21
Cash for operations	25	69	66	88	84
From long-term debt	130				
From sale of stock	20				
Total income	$175	$ 69	$ 66	$ 88	$ 84
Cash applied:					
For equipment	$100				
To pay long-term debt	20	22	26	29	33
Organization costs	5				
Total	$125	$ 22	$ 26	$ 29	$ 33
Increase (decrease)					
in cash	50	47	40	59	51
Cash balance, beginning	—	50	97	137	196
Cash balance, ending	50	97	137	196	247

* Values have been converted into thousands of dollars.

CASE II–2
OUR HERO RESTAURANT (B)

Having obtained a franchise from the Our Hero Company to open a restaurant in Waretown, Steven and Barbara Chappell began the arduous task of planning for its opening. They were immediately faced with several new problems.

Opening Problems

Having chosen Waretown because it was their home and because they foresaw a solid fast-food market in the campus area, the Chappells began looking for a site for their restaurant. The task of finding a location proved difficult. Waretown was a small community utterly dominated by New England University (NEU) and its 15,000 students. This domination extended to university ownership of much of the land surrounding the campus itself, as Steve Chappell found. Since the university was not interested in making its property available by either selling or leasing, Chappell became discouraged and began to have second thoughts. Soon, however, he determined to concentrate on the other alternatives.

I acquired from the town hall the names of all commercial property owners and began a letter-writing campaign to find a store location. To every owner who didn't respond, I sent a second letter. To every owner who still didn't respond, I made a phone call.

Finally, this effort paid off with the discovery of one private owner who might lease space to the Chappells. His property was a new building just being completed at the southeastern edge of the campus. Upon inquiry, Steve Chappell found that it was not yet leased but that much interest had already been shown in it. Thanks to his persistence in contacts with the owner by letter and by telephone, Steve finally was able to secure the space he needed.

The location was nearly ideal. Within two blocks were two very large dormitory complexes. Aside from the dormitories' cafeterias and the university snack bar a few blocks away, there were only four competitors in the immediate area. All others were a mile away across the campus on its northwestern edge or even more remote.

The store itself was to be located in approximately 800 square feet in the lower half of a two-story structure. Access was possible from two streets, one of which was Alderburg Road, the main thoroughfare through the south edge of the campus. A gas station and another building on Alderburg Road left only a wide driveway between them back to the Our Hero, and limited customer parking at the door to only eight cars.

But the Chappells' start-up problems weren't over. With the rent due in a few days, they discovered that their savings were not going to be adequate and that they needed additional financing. Steve Chappell therefore drew up a 20-page business plan—including blueprints, personal data, Our Hero statistics, and itemized requirements for materials and the like—and presented it to four banks. Fortunately all offered to lend the required funds, and he negotiated with the bank that tendered the best terms.

The restaurant layout plan was for a long counter, with no seating, separating the customers from the food preparation area. The menu was quite limited. It featured only 16 sandwiches, most of them variations on the meat ingredients in the basic hero sandwich, each in a choice of four sizes. About a dozen condiment and trimming items—pickles, olives, peppers, lettuce, tomatoes, cheese, oil, salt, pepper, and so on—could be added, and sandwiches could be warmed in a microwave oven, although most were not. A soft-drink dispenser and cigarette machine were the only other pieces of equipment.

Things must have fallen into place, because three years ago, in August, we opened the store after two months of work, one week after school had finished for the summer. On our tenth day open, we exceeded what I had calculated to be our break-even point, and we never went under it again. By the time the first week of school came around that fall, both my wife and I had quit our jobs to become full-time sandwich shop operators.

Looking back on the experience later, Steve Chappell added that the first six months are the make-or-break period in any new business: "It either breaks even or needs additional financing and sinks further into the hole, with liquidation also a possibility." It obviously pleased him that his Our Hero far exceeded expectations and soon became the largest-volume store in the Our Hero chain.

Subsequent Operations and New Problems

The Chappells soon found out that they could identify patterns in their expanding business volume: "The school had no meal plans on weekends; consequently, with about 85 percent of the store's business from students, about 50 percent of all our volume was on weekends." They also found that the systems provided by the Our Hero chain were not designed for the continuous high volumes they were experiencing. Therefore, they began experimenting and by trial and error devised means to deal with their problems.

Luckily the store had been built with doors at opposite ends of the long main counter. Since there was no provision for seating, it was fairly easy to develop a linear process: in one door, order and pay, pick up the freshly prepared sandwich, and out the other door.

Initially, with the original methods, the store had been able to prepare 30 to 40 sandwiches per hour; with such revisions as precutting and preportioning, it was able to achieve rates of over 100, a record of 128, and the confidence that "we can do even better."

As Steve Chappell put it, concerning the first year of operations:

After months of "catching up," we were able to get our staffing up to proper levels, develop a supervisor system, revamp some food preparation techniques, and rearrange our working areas. As a result, we had experienced a 45 percent increase in sales one year later.

A problem that persisted, however, was that of working with suppliers to obtain just the right qualities the Chappells wanted in their sandwiches. Bread was the number one problem because of the lack of bakeries able to furnish the preservative-free, high-quality product Steve Chappell demanded. Finally such a bakery was located 30 miles away, and luckily it was willing to make deliveries six days a week, meaning that only on Sunday was bread not delivered on the same day that it was to be used.

Freshness was the second part of the bread problem; since the restaurant did not toast its sandwiches to assure crispness, the bread had to be fresh that day (except for Sundays), and the Chappells stayed open only as long as the delivery held out, often ending service before the nominal 2 or 3 A.M. closing times because they had run out of bread. Steve Chappell recognized that the limit was to an extent self-imposed, since he kept close records of bread requirements so as to order precisely and not have to throw out unneeded bread.

Questions for Discussion

1. Evaluate the procedure the Chappells used in selecting a site for their business. Would you have done it differently? How? Why?
2. Evaluate their handling of additional financing.
3. Evaluate the Chappells' layout and operation system. How would you rate it? What are its weaknesses? Its strengths?
4. Evaluate the material ordering procedures. Would you recommend any changes in the procedures? What? Why?
5. Do you agree with Steve's policy of tying the closing time to the bread supply?

Source: Adapted from a case prepared by John Clair Thompson, University of Connecticut.

CASE II–3

SIMMONS MOUNTAINSIDE SATELLITE SALES

"Once a small businessman, always a small businessman!" So says Ralph Simmons, the owner and operator of an earth station satellite company in a small mountain town in north Georgia. When asked how he happened to get into this particular business, Mr. Simmons replied that his decision was helped by his elderly father's desire to watch television. Being in a small town with no cable and no prospects of getting it, because of living in a cove surrounded by mountains, Mr. Simmons bought his father a satellite dish. Mr. Simmons' son-in-law, who had just graduated from college with a technical degree, helped to install the system. After considerable effort, the dish was installed. Requests began to come in from neighbors who wanted help in installing dishes. Going into business seemed a natural!

Background

Mr. Simmons had been involved in several successful enterprises throughout his 60 years, including a fast-food franchise, a local eatery, and several converted apartment buildings. In anticipation of retirement, he had sold his businesses, carrying the mortgages on these businesses himself. Mr. Simmons intended to live on the monthly payments and spend his winters in Florida. But the challenge of something new and the promise of large profits were too great. Besides, his son-in-law had just finished college and had as yet not taken a job. So a new business was born!

Mr. Simmons began his new shop in April 1982 by initially capitalizing on the demand from friends and neighbors for earth station satellites. He acquired a dealership from a major manufacturer of satellite systems and set up shop in a used mobile home on the main highway between two small towns. No money had been wasted in beautification of the site. The unpaved parking area could handle three cars and did not puddle badly in the rain. There were no storage facilities for the inventory, which was stacked outside. One immediate neighbor was a business selling septic tanks and backhoe services. Overhead was at an absolute minimum and visibility at an absolute maximum.

After establishing and stocking the store, Mr. Simmons placed his son-in-law in charge and left for Florida. The advertising was done by word of mouth, with some ads in the local weekly newspaper. With a large satellite dish prominently displayed in front to attract passersby, little advertising was necessary. Potential customers would watch the large color TV inside and ask about the systems. Sales the first year were a phenomenal 100 dishes despite the short year. Most of the sales occurred in the spring and just before Christmas. This seasonality was obviously affected by climate because snow accumulates between January and March. Two additional full-time employees had to be hired to help with the installation of the systems. All four employees receive salaries. Additional help is sometimes hired on an hourly basis.

Sales Results

In the second year of operations, Mr. Simmons took a more direct interest in the business. He spent less time in Florida and more time in actual management of the operation. Over 200 units were sold, but at a decreased sales price. All sales were cash, since any financing requirements must be arranged by customers with their banks in advance. In the first year, a system sold for as much as $6,000 with the average sale being $4,000. In the second year, the $6,000 system sold for $3,000 and some systems were as low as $1,600. The average sales price was $2,000. Mr. Simmons declared that gross profit margins were about 30 percent for both years. When asked if he had considered other means of advertisement after the initial interest had worn off, Mr. Simmons contended that the effect of word-of-mouth advertising and his reputation in the community were adequate. Since he had no desire to grow too large, thereby losing control of the business, the potential market in his 25-mile dealership is more than adequate. The county population is 14,000, with another 35,000 people residing in contiguous communities. Mr. Simmons sees sales continuing to grow.

Purchasing and Inventory

Mr. Simmons has discovered that he can obtain a 10 percent discount on purchases if he buys 10 dishes at a time; so he has taken advantage of the excess cash inflows from the mortgage payments on other businesses to build up a fairly sizable inventory. Large purchases also save freight charges, since dishes must be delivered by truck. Since he carries only fiberglass dishes, outside storage does not seem to be a problem. Mr. Simmons believes that other types of dishes are not as effective and therefore does not carry them. At the time of the caseworker's visit, 6 satellite dishes of different sizes were installed for demonstration purposes, and 10 dishes were stacked beside the porch. Inventory of the electronic components for systems is kept low because these items can be obtained quickly and are subject to technological obsolescence.

Simmons' Family and the Business

Evidently Mr. Simmons intends to keep this a family business, eventually passing control to his son-in-law or selling the business outright as he has his previous ventures. Although he speaks highly of his son-in-law, who runs the place, Mr. Simmons is clearly the boss, keeps the books, and has control of the cash. The son-in-law provides the technical expertise required in installation and maintenance of the equipment. "Good service," declares Mr. Simmons, "is the most important aspect of the business, and delineates us from our competitors." Separate financial statements of financial data about the business are not available. Mr. Simmons is sure that the company is highly profitable, as indeed it should be with the low overhead, but he does not have the store set up as an independent corporation. The business is owned by the family corporation which receives income from the mortgage payments on businesses previously sold and income from an apartment building currently owned and operated. The operations of the satellite enterprise are commingled with the other operations of the corporation. Separate financial data are not available. Mr. Simmons does not need separate accounting to know that his business interests are profitable because he is closely involved with their day-to-day operations. Exhibit 1 contains Mr. Simmons' estimates for his operational expenses and investment in the company.

The Competition

Mr. Simmons considers his competition as primarily hobbyists: people who maintain full-time jobs in other fields but dabble on the weekends and at night installing dishes. And, indeed, in the immediate area there is only

---

Exhibit 1   Financial Data for Simmons' Mountainside Satellite Sales

Monthly expenses:		Assets:	
Officers' salaries	$4,000.00	Antenna inventory	$10,000.00
Other salaries	2,000.00	Office trailer	2,000.00
Lot rent	100.00	Truck	10,000.00
Utilities	100.00	Trailer-mounted satellite dish	8,000.00
Advertising	20.00	Demonstration antennae	12,000.00
Insurance	150.00	Office furniture and equipment	1,500.00
Vehicle expense	75.00	Tools and equipment	3,500.00
Miscellaneous	500.00		

one other business actually specializing in the home satellite systems, and that shop was started in mid-1983. Within the 25-mile radius of the dealership, which includes two small towns and two small communities, six businesses are engaged in satellite retailing. Mr. Simmons believes he has the largest firm and the best equipment. His dealership is with one of the largest manufacturers in the industry, but competitors also have dealerships with leading manufacturers. None of the firms does significant advertising, and all are locally owned and operated. Approximately 12 other businesses that deal in other products have satellite systems available for their customers, but none appears to have any significant influence on the market.

Mr. Simmons and the Future

When asked about past problems and future expectations, Mr. Simmons declared that once the initial technical problems of figuring out how to install the systems had been overcome, they were "off and running." The expertise required to locate and beam in on the satellites and understand the electronic components of the systems has now been established. Mr. Simmons sees no other problems of any significance. His long-term goals are simply to continue doing everything just the same, since he does not anticipate any changes that would affect his business. He has no expansion or diversification plans. When asked about the new technological advances such as the "K band" and private cable systems, he claims that different types of people than his customers would be interested in such things. Mr. Simmons does not foresee the possibility of market saturation at any time in the immediate future. If any such problems did develop, he would probably just get out of the business!

Questions for Discussion

1. Evaluate Mr. Simmons' approach to entrepreneurship.
2. Do you think Mr. Simmons' plan of selling for cash only was a good idea? Explain.
3. Evaluate Mr. Simmons' inventory policy.
4. Do you think he should have stocked and sold other types of antennas?
5. What are your thoughts concerning Mr. Simmons' relationship with his son-in-law?
6. Evaluate Mr. Simmons' legal form of organization. Do you think that he should form a partnership with the son-in-law or incorporate?
7. Do you think Mr. Simmons' attitude of "status quo" is best for the company, or might he profit by adding the "K band" units to his sales line? Explain.
8. Do you agree with Mr. Simmons that he doesn't need separate accounting to know that his business interests are profitable? Explain.

Source: Prepared by JoAnn C. Carland and James W. Carland, Western Carolina University.

CASE II–4
THE MOTHER AND CHILD SHOP

As Mick McGregor describes it, "I've never really been the type to devote myself to just one thing for very long. Trying something new has always been fascinating for me." Maybe that's why a married man, with a first child due shortly and a full-time job, who is working on a Ph.D., would decide to fill his free moments by starting his own business.

Deciding on the Type of Business

Mick had toyed with the idea of starting a business but had never really done much about it until a friend and neighbor of his, Jack Pollach, mentioned at a large Halloween party that there was some store space available in a shopping complex in town. Jack was developing plans for a candy store and discussed his ideas with Mick. He also mentioned that there were a few stores still to be leased.

Mick was intrigued by this idea of starting a store and encouraged by his friend's actions. He had some money set aside for investment and felt that putting this into a small business could be a profitable decision. The problem, however, was deciding what kind of store it should be. What products should be carried? The town Mick lived in was a community of about 65,000 located about 65 miles from one large city and about 150 miles from another. Mick's reasoning was that he needed to find some store or goods that his town didn't have yet but was ready to have. In other words, he needed something for which there was a market but for which people had to go to the larger cities at the present time.

Off and on during November, Mick pondered this problem. There really wasn't a specific thing he was interested in selling; he was just trying to maximize his chances of success by coming up with a "sure-thing" stock of merchandise. After all this effort, it was actually Mick's wife, Cathy, who wasn't very interested at all in going into business at that particular time, who gave him the idea. Cathy was due to have their first child late in November. During that last week, she commented to Mick that she would certainly be happy when her pregnancy was over if for no other reason than that she would be able to buy attractive clothes again.

Maternity clothes were sold only as a sideline by a few of the larger stores in town. Their selection was, at best, limited. The comment didn't register immediately with Mick, but later that evening the full impact hit him. It seemed like the very idea he had been looking for. He didn't have much time to act on the idea right away, however, for four days later their child was born.

Studying the Market

Once mother and child were home and as settled as possible, Mick began to pursue his idea vigorously. He first spent several evenings at the local library reading about manufacturers and suppliers of maternity clothing and specifically about their marketing. His main concern was deciding whether or not the town was large enough to support a maternity shop. He thought that the best way to do this was first to develop a list, from within his state and three adjacent states, of cities that were approximately the same size as his. Then he would determine how many of these had maternity clothing shops. This would give him an idea of how active the market was in similar, nearby cities and whether such a store in a city of this size was, in fact, feasible. To do this Mick first went to the latest census information and listed those cities within his four-state sample that had populations of 60,000 to 75,000. To get the names of merchants in these towns, he first went to the trade journals and noted the stores in the towns on his list and the lines they carried. He also was able to find telephone books for most of the cities and determine whether any maternity clothing shops were indexed. From this he found that nearly 80 percent of the cities on his list had at least one shop like the one he was considering, and about 25 percent had two or more shops. Mick concluded from these findings that his idea was at least generally sound.

He next wanted to find out some specific information about his own community in order to decide if the store was practical in his own city. He was able to find data on both the per-family income and the amount of money spent on mothers' and children's clothing each year for his area and other areas on his list. His area compared very favorably with the others on this basis. Finally, from the county planning commission, Mick obtained information on the estimated population increase over the next 5 and 10 years and the areas of projected growth within the county. These data told him that the county would grow by 10 to 15 percent for the next 5 years and by 15 to 25 percent over the next 10. In addition, areas near his tentative site were projected to increase in population. From all these data, Mick was greatly encouraged. He felt that he had a sound idea that was indeed supported by all the marketing information he could find.

It also occurred to him during this time that a better bet might be to have a combination maternity and baby store. Women who had become familiar with the store and its merchandise during their pregnancy might thus be influenced to come back afterward to buy clothing for their babies. The combination seemed natural and was quickly adopted.

Deciding on Management

By mid-December, then, Mick had the idea for a combination maternity-children's store which appeared to have very little competition nearby and which tentatively could be located in one of the largest and busiest shopping centers in town. That all seemed fine. The next question was, Who's going to run this thing? Mick wasn't confident enough in his idea to quit his job and his graduate education to go into it full time. The logical choice, at least to him, seemed to be Cathy. Cathy, having been a mother for all of two weeks, was less than wildly enthusiastic about the prospects of managing a store, too. But she agreed if two conditions were met: (1) that a full-time salesclerk would be hired, and (2) that a room in the back of the store could be designed for the baby.

Deciding on Operations

That problem solved, Cathy and Mick moved on to the next one—finding out something about how to run a business like this. In mid-December, while they were visiting Cathy's parents in one of the nearby large cities, they decided that the best way to find this information might be to talk with someone in the business. So they selected a maternity store that Cathy and her mother knew, and drove over to talk to the owner. In retrospect Mick describes that afternoon as perhaps the most important of that time period, both informationally and psychologically. The owner and his wife were extremely helpful and encouraging, discussed many financial and managerial details, and sent Mick and Cathy on their way feeling very confident of their decision to start this business. The effect of the visit was so positive that in early January Mick and Cathy signed a three-year rental lease with the owners of the shopping complex for a 1,500-square-foot store.

Among other things that they found out from the friendly store owner was that the next buying show for the region was to be held on January 28 and 29. This show was the main opportunity for comparing all the clothing lines' styles and prices for the coming spring and summer. The shortness of the time until the show was disconcerting. If they went to the show and bought merchandise, that meant they would have to open for business in a few months to sell the spring and summer clothing. If they didn't buy merchandise at this show, they most likely would have to wait several months for the fall-winter show. They decided to take the risk and try to open their store with the spring clothing.

To have a chance of meeting this deadline, Mick and Cathy decided to divide responsibilities. Cathy, because of her recent experience with maternity clothing, was in charge of selecting manufacturers' lines and styles and buying the inventory. Mick, calling on his undergraduate background of industrial engineering and his graduate training in business, took responsibility for designing and preparing the store layout and deciding on the financial and managerial aspects of the store.

Cathy suggested that the store stock high-quality, name-brand merchandise. She would pick styles and particular items at the show, depending mostly on her own tastes and advice gathered from product vendors.

Estimating Capital and Operating Expenses

Mick's immediate problem before the show was to decide how much inventory to carry initially. From his estimates of per-family income and amount of money spent on mothers' and children's clothing, and mainly from his discussion with the store owner, Mick estimated that first year sales would be about $50,000. He also decided he would be happy if the store broke even the first year. Knowing from his business courses that inventory should turn over about four times a year and cost of goods sold should be about 60 percent of sales, it was simple to estimate an initial inventory costing about $7,500.

Mick then estimated operating expenses, using actual figures when known and trade statistics for the others. The total was $18,000 for the first year, so he set the working capital requirements at $3,000 (two months of operating expenses).

Finally, Mick estimated the cost of fixtures and initial supplies by comparing prices in the catalogs of several fixture suppliers. The estimate was $4,500, bringing the total initial cash requirements for inventory, fixtures, supplies, and working capital to $15,000. Mick and Cathy had $10,000 in personal savings to invest and, by presenting the information they had collected to a local banker, had no difficulty borrowing the remaining $5,000.

Mick then categorized the various items the store would be carrying into the following groups: maternity casual wear, maternity dresses, lingerie, and children's wear. Again going back to his previous discussion with the same store owner, he decided to divide his inventory among the categories in the proportions 30 percent, 30 percent, 7 percent, and 33 percent, respectively. This information on total inventory and how it should be divided among product groups was then given to Cathy, who would have to work out the number of each size, etc., that should be bought. She estimated that through talks with product sales personnel and the store owner they had visited previously.

Decorating the Store

This task completed, Mick, from the middle of January to the middle of March, turned his attention to decorating the store. Drawing from his experience as an industrial engineer and ideas he gathered from visiting other stores, he designed the layout himself and did most of the work. He hired others to do tasks such as the wiring and the counter and cabinet construction, but he was able to specify exactly what he wished done. He was also careful not to omit the special room in the back of the store for the baby.

Everything went very smoothly at the merchandise show for the two prospective merchants. They were able to meet the salespersons they wished and purchase clothing they liked. Deliveries of almost all articles were promised within six weeks.

February was spent working on the store, obtaining the necessary city and state licenses, selecting a full-time saleswoman, and becoming very nervous at the thought of actually opening the store. The person hired was an experienced saleswoman who had been recommended by a friend of Mick and Cathy's.

The Opening

By the beginning of March, almost all was ready for an opening. The only advertising that had been done up until this time was a large paper sign across the front windows. Also, Mick belonged to several civic organizations in town and informally passed the word about the store to other members. News traveled fast in town, and quite a few people knew about the proposed opening. Mick and Cathy decided that it might be better to hold other advertising until a few weeks after the store actually opened. This would give them some time to get a feel for operating the store. So it was decided to have the grand opening in mid-April, with newspaper and radio advertising to precede the opening by two weeks. The actual opening would be as soon as the store was completed and a majority of the inventory in stock. This turned out to be March 17—less than four months after Cathy's comments about the difficulty of finding attractive maternity clothes.

Questions for Discussion

1. How might the owners have changed their procedure in planning the business?
2. Do you think their method of researching the business was adequate? What changes would you have made?
3. Do you think adequate effort was devoted to determining capital requirements?
4. After some individual research on your part, would you accept their inventory allocation?
5. What weight would you give the special knowledge of the wife? The husband?
6. Do you think an adequate effort was made to determine the feasibility of the market? Give reasons for your answer.
7. What have you gained from studying this case?
8. Do you note any apparent personality characteristics that seem to indicate Mick to be the entrepreneurial type?

Source: Prepared by Curtis E. Tate, Jr., Robert Gatewood, and Walter Wilson, all of The University of Georgia.

CASE II–5

METAL FABRICATORS, INC.

Metal Fabricators, Inc., was a small firm engaged in the fabrication of metal products. Practically all its income came from small subcontracts from general contractors in the area. However, since its incorporation two years earlier, the two owner-managers had been attempting to develop and market a sandblasting machine with a new type of control mechanism, which they had conceived. Only two of the sandblasting machines, or "pots" as they are called, had been sold, although most of the company's efforts had been directed at this part of the business.

Ownership and Management

The two managers, Jerry Rogers and Joe Benson, had similar education and work experience, including about three years of college with several engineering courses. They were both competent welders, and both had served as construction superintendents on several medium-sized projects. Jerry's work experience had been much broader and more successful than Joe's, and he was still in demand as a construction superintendent. He had turned down several job offers during the last year. Jerry came from a low-income, small-town family, while Joe was from a relatively well-to-do family.

Larry Ford, who owned 51 percent of the stock in the firm, was a local businessman who devoted little of his time to Metal Fabricators. But it was Larry Ford's initiative that had brought Metal Fabricators into existence. Jerry and Joe were temporarily unemployed, as construction superintendents often are, when Larry asked them if they could build a special type of hopper for Ford's construction company. Jerry and Joe rented a building and a welding machine and constructed the hopper. This job led to others, and the firm was incorporated in March. Larry Ford, who purchased most of the stock, appointed Joe president and Jerry general manager, with the mutual consent of the two men.

Regardless of their titles, Jerry and Joe worked side by side to complete the small contracts they obtained. Within about a month there was more work than Jerry and Joe could do; they hired two or three welders on a part-time basis.

Organizational Problems

During its first 10 months of operation, the firm encountered difficulties similar to those normally encountered by small, new firms. Cash flow problems occurred, and there were times when Jerry and Joe felt obligated not to draw their salaries so that funds would be available to purchase required materials and to pay the welders. Organizational difficulties were also encountered. It didn't matter at first that Joe was president and Jerry was general manager, but when there were employees to be supervised, areas of responsibility and authority had to be established.

At first, Jerry and Joe discussed each new problem and usually arrived at a mutual conclusion as to what to do about it. Later on, though, Joe began to handle more and more of the business end of the operation, and Jerry began to run the shop. As the responsibilities of the two men became more clearly defined, they began to take unilateral action—often without informing each other.

The result of all these trends was that there were often disagreements as to whether the action taken was proper. When the men were together, they often argued about one or another. Several of the arguments were quite heated.

One day in November when Joe was at the shop for one of his almost daily visits, the following interchange took place:

Jerry: Joe, there are several things I'd like to talk to you about. I think we should get together for an hour or so right away.

Joe: What's bothering you, buddy? Looks like things are going pretty well on your end of the operation.

Jerry: I'd rather not discuss it now. Can we get together Wednesday night about seven?

Joe: Yes, I suppose that'll be all right.

When the men arrived for their meeting, each had made up a list of items he wanted to discuss. They went to the small, cluttered office that was built into one corner of the fabrication shop and started to talk:

Joe: We need to work out a plan and market our pots so that we can get them moving as soon as I get this valve ready. That should be within about two weeks.

Jerry: I don't want to discuss what we are going to do. I want to discuss what we have done and what mistakes we've made and how we are going to keep from making the same ones in the future.

Joe: Okay. Well, what's on your mind?

Jerry: Well, to begin with, you're handling the business end of this operation. You've prepared monthly financial statements, but you didn't seem to know that we had a shortage of cash until we had no money to pay our salaries. You should have anticipated the shortage so that we could do something about it.

Joe: You saw the financial statements, too, and you thought they were okay.

Jerry: Anyway, Joe, I wish you would try to have a little more foresight and let me know about these things before they get serious. Another thing, you've only been here about two hours a day recently. You spend the rest of the time working on our new control system. So I'd rather you not give the men any directions when you are here, without my approval.

Joe: Jerry, when I see the men doing something wrong I'm going to feel free to correct them with or without your approval. Anyway, the things that I've told them have been pretty obvious.

The conversation went on in this vein for about 30 minutes with Jerry bringing up points that had been bothering him and Joe commenting on those points. After Jerry had completed his list of items the session proceeded as follows:

Joe: Now I have several things that I'd like to mention. Particularly, you seem to be so concerned about my end of the business, I think you should pay more attention to running the shop.

Jerry: Running the shop! Why, everything is running perfectly in the shop. The men are happy and we get every job out within the estimated time. All we need is a little better financial management and a few more sales calls on your part.

Joe: Jerry, I've also been concerned because you keep pushing to make the company bigger. You want to hire more welders, and take on more of these humdrum little fabrication jobs. I'd rather we just do enough of that to get by. We are never going to be successful unless we do something really big. And if we can develop this sandblast machine and get just a few sales, I think we might really hit pay dirt.

Jerry: I'm not trying to make a killing, Joe, and I don't have a lot of faith in long shots anyway. I'd rather just sit back and build the things that we know how to build, and just do it a little cheaper and better than the next fellow.

Joe: Well, we are not going to settle that tonight! There was one other thing I wanted to ask you to do and that is to set up a wage allocation system so that we'll know how much of the men's wages are expended on each job. Several times in the past you haven't been able to tell me whether we even made money on a job or not.

Jerry: Sometimes we haven't made money, and that's because you keep changing the amount of the bids after we've agreed upon a figure. Last week on the Enjay job I spent an hour convincing you that we ought to bid $4,500 and you said okay. But yesterday I found out that you bid the job at $4,000. We are not going to make a cent on that contract, Joe. Sam said that he even called you and asked if you had left something out because our bid was so much lower than any of the others. But rather than admit that you had made a mistake, you stuck with the original bid.

Joe: We disagree about that, but I'm president of this company and I have to be able to make decisions.

Jerry: We've talked for 45 minutes and I don't think we've settled a thing.

Joe: Sure we have, you are going to set up a labor schedule for each job and I hope you are going to try to keep your nose a little more out of my business. I'm going to have the control system ready for the sandblast pot week after next. Also, I'm not going to give any more orders directly to the men.

Jerry: You said, too, that you would made 35 sales calls within the next 60 days.

Joe: Yes, I said that, and I will.

Jerry: Well I still don't think we've accomplished much, but I suppose we've talked it out. I'll see you tomorrow.

Personnel Problems

As the workload increased, Joe and Jerry soon found that they either had to hire some more welders or turn down some contracts. At first, students at a nearby trade school were hired on a part-time basis. Also, for a while two experienced welders who had full-time jobs elsewhere were hired to work evenings and weekends. Recently it became clear that the work load was sufficiently dependable to support at least three full-time employees, and the following conversation ensued between Jerry and Joe:

Joe: I'll call Mr. Smith who teaches over at the trade school tomorrow and ask him to recommend three of his new graduates.

Jerry: Joe, this is rather ticklish work, and these trade school boys just don't have the savvy to do the job. We have to watch them every second. And we are spending more time training them than we are actually performing the work.

Joe: Jerry, a good welder will cost us $10 an hour. We can get these boys from trade school for $5.

Jerry: Sure, we pay them about 50 percent as much as we would a good welder, but you give me one good, experienced welder and I can put out more work than I can with all three of those kids. Besides, when we get one of these kids halfway trained, we'll have to pay him $7.50 an hour to keep him.

Joe: We'll still save money while we're paying him $5. You and I can do the complicated work and, if we plan and schedule the work right, all the other men will have to do is weld.

Jerry: Well, I'm still not convinced, but I'll sure try to make it work. Go ahead and call Mr. Smith tomorrow.

Three young men who had been at the top of their class at the vocational-technical school were hired on the recommendation of Mr. Smith. They started at about 50 percent of the going rate for experienced welders. During the weeks that followed, one of the welders found a better job elsewhere and failed to show up for work one morning. Another decided he did not really like welding and quit his job to go to work on a pipeline. When the second welder left, Joe and Jerry had to decide how to obtain replacements.

Questions for Discussion

1.   What does the case indicate about the need for organization?
2.   What does it suggest about the need for planning?
3.   What does it imply about control?

4. How do you explain the shortage of finances? How could this problem be overcome?

5. What does the case show about the differing objectives of the two owner-managers? The silent partner, Larry Ford?

6. What do you think of the selection procedure of the firm? Explain your answer.

7. How would you improve the procedure?

8. What is your reaction to hiring students directly out of the vocational-technical school rather than recruiting experienced employees?

9. What is your analysis of the wage policy of the firm?

10. What would you do now?

Source: Prepared by Arthur D. Sharplin, McNeese State University.

III

SELECTING AND LEADING EMPLOYEES

Many management texts begin with a statement such as, "Management is getting things done through people." And the annual reports of most companies include statements such as, "Our people are our most important asset." Both of these statements are correct: whether the business is large or small, its success or failure depends on having a capable, well-trained, highly motivated work force. This part of the book presents some valuable insights that can help small business managers select, train, develop, and motivate employees.

In essence, all owners of small businesses are personnel managers. They must decide what work is to be done, determine what type and how many employees are needed, recruit those employees, train and develop them, reward them with adequate pay and benefits, and lead and motivate them to perform effectively. How well—or poorly—owners handle this important function determines the success or failure of their businesses. In summary, they must be capable of handling the personnel management function, or they must hire someone to do it for them.

Chapter 10 looks at the overall question of managing human resources in small firms and covers such topics as planning personnel needs, recruiting employees, selecting the right people for the jobs, training and developing managers, and complying with equal employment opportunity laws and immigration laws.

In Chapter 11, we discuss leading and rewarding employees, examining the need for good human relations in small businesses. Exercising managerial leadership, communicating with employees, motivating employees, compensating them with wages and benefits, and appraising employees' performance are discussed.

Chapter 12 deals with maintaining relationships with employees and covers topics such as protecting employee safety, environmental protection, counseling disturbed employees, handling employee grievances, exercising discipline, and dealing with labor unions.

10

MANAGING HUMAN RESOURCES IN SMALL FIRMS

Good ideas and good products are "a dime a dozen," but good execution and good management—in a word, good people—are rare.—Arthur Rock, venture capitalist

Small businesses must make wooing and keeping employees as high a priority as attracting and retaining customers.—John L. Ward, Loyola University of Chicago

LEARNING OBJECTIVES

After studying the material in this chapter, you will be able to:

1. Explain how small business managers plan personnel needs and develop sources from which to recruit personnel.
2. Discuss the methods used for recruiting personnel.
3. Describe the usual steps in the process of employee selection.
4. Explain the importance of personnel development and discuss some development methods.
5. Tell how selection of managers differs from selection of nonmanagerial personnel and describe some methods of manager development.
6. Discuss the laws that affect personnel recruiting, selection, and development.

SUPREME PLUMBING AND HEATING COMPANY: WHERE ARE THE WORKERS?

In the late 1950s, two friendly competitors formed the Supreme Plumbing and Heating Company as a partnership in a rapidly developing industrial area southwest of Houston, Texas. At first, the partners did most of the work themselves, including plumbing, heating, and wiring for both commercial and residential buildings. The business grew rapidly, and several craftsmen and other employees were added. This left the partners devoting almost full time to managing the business rather than doing the work themselves.

Supreme competed with six other companies within a 50-mile radius both for business and for the best craftsmen. This became difficult in the 1960s when the Lyndon B. Johnson Space Center was built nearby. Most of the area's skilled workers left their jobs with the companies to work at the center for better pay and benefits, causing a great shortage of craftsmen in the local area. At the same time, demand for plumbing, heating, and wiring was increasing in the area. It would have been a good opportunity for Supreme to expand its operations—if the needed workers could have been found.

The partners decided that the only way to have an adequate supply of trained craftsmen was to do their own training; so they started an apprenticeship program. The plan was to hire high school graduates or dropouts to work with some of the older craftsmen as apprentice plumbers and electricians, at the prevailing wage rate, until they learned the trade. When they finished their training, they would train others so there would be a continuous training program.

Although the program gave the young people an opportunity to learn a trade that would be valuable to them in future years, the plan didn't work. The trainees would work for Supreme just long enough to be trained, then quit to take

SCORE Card   by Nebesky

"Welcome aboard. You're just what we're looking for. Not too bright, no ambition, and content to stay on the bottom of the ladder and not louse things up!"

Source: *Savant,* February/March 1988. Cartoon courtesy of J. Nebesky.

another job, go into the armed services, or go back to school. The partners had to reduce the amount of construction work they bid on because of their limited work force. To compensate for this loss of revenue, they started a wholesale plumbing, heating, and electrical supply business.

The worker shortage at Supreme continued until there were only three plumbers, three plumber's helpers, two electricians, and two electrician's helpers left. As the craftsmen were nearing retirement age and the helpers weren't interested in learning the trade, the owners had to go on with the wholesale business, although they would have preferred to continue in construction.

Source: See Leon C. Megginson, *Human Resources: Cases and Concepts* (New York: Harcourt, Brace & World, 1968), pp. 8–10, for the original case. The name of this updated case has been disguised at the request of the business owners.

This Opening Focus emphasizes the importance of having capable, well-trained, and highly motivated employees. A small business must have a sufficient supply of human resources if it is to succeed. A young entrepreneur in the late 1800s, Andrew Carnegie, expressed this thought when he said, "Take away all our factories, our trade, our avenues of transportation, and our money, but leave our organization, and in four years, I will have reestablished myself." In other words, while physical and financial resources are important to a small business, human resources are the most vital. This need was emphasized in a recent SBA report, which concluded that if small firms are to succeed, they must "boost wages, increase benefits, hire marginal workers, and invest in labor-saving technology."[1] Thus, being able to identify and hire good employees can mean the difference between a successful and an unsuccessful business. This process involves (1) planning for, (2) recruiting, (3) selecting, and (4) training and developing employees, all of which are discussed in this chapter.

PLANNING FOR PERSONNEL NEEDS

Managers of small businesses can't wait until they need a new employee to think about their personnel needs. Like larger competitors, the small business manager must (1) determine personnel needs and (2) develop sources from which to recruit personnel.

Small businesses are finding it more difficult to carry out both these activities, as many of them are facing absolute labor shortages. According to the National Federation of Independent Business, 25 percent of small companies couldn't find the workers they needed in 1988.[2] Many small businesses face these labor shortages because of the declining work force, as the number of Americans aged 16 to 24 is expected to decrease by more than 7 percent by the year 2000. As small businesses employ two-thirds of these entry-level workers, they are the first to feel the shortage.

For example, Sue Ley, owner of CleanDrum, Inc. (Case III–1), had to limit her selling activities because she could not afford—or find—anyone to run the plant.

To meet this declining supply of potential employees, many small businesses are changing the way they operate. They are spending more and using new methods to attract more applicants, making their workplaces more attractive, and using employee benefits and other incentives to retain valued employees. Finally, small companies are also stepping up automation and even subcontracting out part of their work to reduce the number of employees needed.[3]

Determining Types of Employees Needed

When business owners want to construct a building, they obtain a set of blueprints and specifications. When they buy merchandise, materials, and supplies, they develop specifications for those items. In the same way, even small businesses should have **job specifications,** which are statements of the mental, physical, and other qualifications required of a person to do the job. Drawing up job specifications begins with a **job description,** a summary of the job in the form of a list of its duties, responsibilities, and working conditions, as well as relationships between that particular job and other jobs in the organization (see Figure 10–1 for an example). When the personal qualities, education, training, and experience needed to perform the job are added, the result is a set of job specifications that forms the basis for recruiting and selecting new employees.

Just a word of caution: Job descriptions should be flexible in very small firms to give the owner more freedom in assigning work to available employees, whether the work fits their job description or not.

Don't ask for more than is needed to do the job properly! Ask yourself: "Is a college education really needed, or can a high school graduate do the job?" Or again: "Are three years' experience required, or can an inexperienced person be trained to do the work?" Increasing education and experience levels raises the starting pay expected, and you may actually be better off training someone to do things your own way.

Developing Sources of Personnel

As with purchasing supplies for building and running the business, the owner needs sources from which to seek new workers. Some of these sources are shown in Figure 10–2. Not all of them will be appropriate for all small businesses.

Internal Sources

Filling job openings from among present employees rather than going outside the business makes good sense. This method raises morale and improves employees' motivation, since they know they can move up in your firm. It also saves time, effort, and money, since outside recruiting is time consuming and costly.

Burger King has estimated that it costs as much as $500 in time, training, and paperwork for each worker hired. Because of the shortage of qualified workers, it now pays above minimum wage; offers flexible hours, free meals, stock-purchase plan, and pension plans; and gives employees "lots of special attention."[4] After three months, employees can earn bonus money for college and receive gifts for good work and for recruiting new employees. Those who recruit management-level workers—in some areas—can earn substantial cash bounties.

Filling jobs from within is also more effective because the worker's performance has been observed and evaluated over a period of time, and this method also leads to stability. Employees can be upgraded, transferred, or promoted to fill job openings.

Figure 10–1   Sample Job Description

Job Title: Office and credit manager
Supervisor: Store manager
Number of Subordinates: Two

JOB SUMMARY

Responsible for all of the store's office and credit functions, as well as control of the store's assets and expenditures. Helps manager administer store's policies and methods by exercising mature judgment and initiative in carrying out related duties and responsibilities.

Duties	Approximate percentage of work time spent on each duty
1. Prepares bank deposits, listing checks and cash, and takes deposit to bank (daily).	5%
2. Inspects sales tickets for accuracy and completeness of price, stock classification, and delivery information (daily).	5
3. Keeps sales and expenses record sheets, posting sales and expenses and accumulating them for the month.	15
4. Processes credit applications: analyzes financial status and paying record of customers, checks references and credit bureau to determine credit responsibility (daily).	10
5. Sends collection notices to past-due accounts, using mail, telephone calls, and personal visits (if necessary) to collect (daily).	10
6. Checks invoices of outside purchases to verify receipt, quantity, price, etc. Gets store manager's approval (weekly).	5
7. Maintains inventories and their records.	10
8. Does all bookkeeping and prepares periodic financial statements.	20
9. Helps out on sales floor and in other areas when needed.	15
10. Miscellaneous duties.	5

Source: Personnel Management, Administrative Management Course Program, Topic 6 (Washington, D.C.: Small Business Administration, 1965), p. 56, updated.

Figure 10–2   Sources of Potential Employees

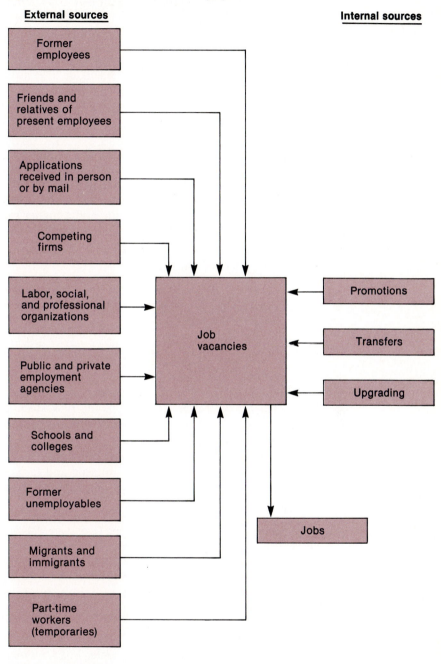

Upgrading occurs when an employee who is presently not capable of doing a job that has become more difficult receives training to enable him or her to do the work successfully.

A small service organization decided to replace its typewriter with a word processor. The present typist, age 52, had been with the firm for 20 years but knew nothing about using a word processor. Instead of hiring a new operator, management sent her to the manufacturer's school for training. She mastered word processing in a short time and was soon back at the company using her new skills.

Transferring is moving an employee from one location or department to another, without necessarily changing job title or pay. **Promoting** is moving a person to a higher position, frequently with increased responsibilities, greater status or prestige, a new title, and a higher salary.

Of course, one of the best internal sources is family members, which will be covered in detail in Chapter 24.

For example, Sue Ley's daughter ran CleanDrum's office, answered the phone, and did the booking. One son drove the tractor-trailer, and another one worked part-time while going to college.

External Sources

External sources are used as the business grows and needs to fill lower-level jobs. They may also be used to provide new ideas and perspectives and to obtain needed skills when necessary, especially for scientific, technical, and professional positions.

Many small firms keep a list of *former employees* as a potential source of trained workers. If a worker left voluntarily and for good reason, is in good standing, and seeks reemployment, rehiring may be a good idea.

Diane Allen worked for Bell Stained Glass and Overlay in Mobile, Alabama. When her husband started teaching in a small town 40 miles away, she resigned. Bell, while hating to lose a good artist, agreed because its business was slow. Later, when Bell moved to a new location and its business increased, Diane was asked to come back, and she agreed.

As will be shown later, *friends and relatives* of present employees may also be a good source of dependable people. But remember, if a friend or relative is hired but doesn't work out and must be terminated, you've lost a friend as well as an employee.

Small business owners should make it a habit to keep *mail or drop-in applications* that come in either through the mail or in person. In some areas (especially in shopping centers), workers change jobs frequently. So attracting workers from *other businesses*—even competitors—is another good source.

Managers, technical, and professional personnel may be found in various *social and professional organizations.* Also, *schools and colleges* can be good sources for skilled personnel and part-time employees. Contrary to popular belief, the occupations expected to grow most during this decade are not in the high-tech, sophisticated fields requiring a college education and years of experience. Instead, they will require skills taught in vocational and technical schools—places that train students for a specific career, such as legal assistant or computer service technician, the two fastest-growing areas.[5]

According to Robert Obenhaus, president of Houston's Microcomputer Institute, "After an intensive eight-hour-a-day, five-day-a-week program, students are qualified to enter an office and immediately start working as a computer programmer or computer maintenance technician."[6]

The recent influx of Southeast Asians, Haitians, and Latin Americans continues a long American business tradition. Historically, businesses have found *migrants and immigrants* to be good sources of workers.

More small companies are now filling part-time as well as full-time positions with *retirees.* Many small businesses (especially fast-food stores that can't find enough teenagers) are hiring workers who retired at age 65 or younger.

Sterile Design Incorporated, of Tampa, Florida, has taken advantage of this source. Personnel director Judy Steffens, who enlists the aid of community and local organizations to recruit older workers, said that more than half of the firm's work force is composed of "minishifters." These are older people who work short, four-hour shifts in a plant that packages medical and hospital supplies.[7]

Handicapped workers provide a good source of productive and highly motivated workers. A company can receive federal tax credit up to a maximum of $2,400 for each employee hired.

Jones Manufacturing Company, a Birmingham, Alabama, plumbing supplies plant, uses handicapped workers to inspect and box gaskets and couplings. During a recent 15-month period, these 160 employees—half of the total work force—were

25 percent more productive and had 40 percent fewer accidents than the other half.[8]

Part-time and temporary workers (temps) offer a small business flexibility and a way of reducing hiring (and benefit) costs. No longer is part-time employment only for students seeking summer jobs or homemakers supplementing the family income by doing clerical work. Instead, recent college grads, retirees, corporate dropouts (or those pushed out), and others seeking work are taking temporary jobs. Much in demand are accountants (or bookkeepers), factory workers, fast-food workers, retail clerks, secretaries, and even lawyers and systems analysts.[9]

When Michael Taranto, president of Norwich Togs Inc. of Forestdale, Massachusetts, needs help with production problems, he turns to his 78-year-old part-time adviser. For questions of employee benefits, Taranto calls his 66-year-old part-time personnel director, a retired insurance agent. And if it's a financial problem, he turns to his 67-year-old part-time controller.[10]

One group of part-time workers is made up of those who wish to work less than 40 hours a week, so they may be hired to work a few hours each day (e.g., as a clerk in a store) or a few days each week (as a bookkeeper or accountant).

For example, Leonard Grey, part owner of a small Birmingham, Michigan, accounting firm, hired Barbara Fitzpatrick as an accountant for $5,000 less than she was offered by a major accounting firm. Ms. Fitzpatrick, who has a young daughter and works in her husband's business on weekends, didn't want to work 70-hour weeks during tax season. She works four days a week—and up to 55 hours during tax time—and thinks it's worth giving up employee benefits and the higher salary.[11]

Another type of part-time employees is **leased manpower,** or employees obtained from some outside firm that specializes in performing a given service. These workers may work full time for the leasing firm and only part time for the small employer. This is an especially useful source of employees for clerical, maintenance, janitorial, and food service tasks.

Leasing saves labor costs for a business, as it doesn't have to pay leased workers health insurance and other benefits. Also, it permits greater flexibility to cut back on staff when business is slack. National Planning Associates, a research organization, estimated that there will be 4 to 5 million leased workers in the United States by 1995.[12]

The use of temporary workers in the United States is rising rapidly.

For example, it was estimated that in 1990, 1 of 12 U.S. workers was a "temp."

This estimate by Mary Ann Padilla was based on her experience in her firm, Sunnyside–Temp Side, Inc. This was an employment agency until the oil industry decline in Denver in 1984–85. Padilla found new permanent jobs for her clients but spent most of her time providing temporary help for the jobs that were still available. This transformed her business so that the temporary division is now her biggest revenue producer.[13] Her effectiveness in providing temporary workers, together with the prediction cited above, led to her being honored in 1987 by Avon Products, Inc., and the Small Business Administration as one of the "Women of Enterprise."

RECRUITING EMPLOYEES

Once the number, types, and sources of employees needed are known, the small business manager starts looking for them. Don't limit applications to people who drop in and ask for a job; instead, go out and recruit.

Recruitment, reaching out to attract a supply of potential employees, is usually done (1) by advertising, (2) from employment agencies, (3) by using employee referrals, and (4) by scouting.

By Advertising

Advertising includes "Help Wanted" signs in the window of the business and radio spots. And some enterprising fast-food restaurants use job application announcements and forms as tray liners. However, newspaper want ads are still the most common form of recruiting.

The ad in Figure 10–3 was placed in the Help Wanted section of the *Chicago Daily News* classified of April 11, 1887, by Richard Sears. Alvah Roebuck answered the ad, and Sears, Roebuck and Company was formed. Roebuck, a mild-mannered Indiana watchmaker, couldn't cope with Sears's frenetic personality and left the company after three years.[14] (Be aware that it's now illegal to ask an applicant's age.)

Figure 10–3

```
┌─────────────────────────────────────┐
│         WATCHMAKER WANTED           │
│  with references who can furnish tools. │
│   State age, experience, and salary  │
│               required.              │
│          T39. Daily News            │
└─────────────────────────────────────┘
```

From Employment Agencies

Private and state employment agencies serve as important means of recruiting personnel. **State employment agencies,** operated by the states in cooperation with the Department of Labor's U.S. Employment Service (USES), are sources of skilled and unskilled production and service workers as well as clerical and technical employees. There is no charge for this service. **Private employment agencies** charge a fee for finding an acceptable employee for a given position. These agencies do some screening, however, especially for the higher levels of skilled, clerical, technical, and professional occupations. They also serve as a good source of temporary workers.

By Using Employee Referrals

In one respect, small firms have an edge over larger ones in attracting workers. They tend to foster a secure, "family" feeling and do a fine job of filling openings by word of mouth. **Employee referrals,** whereby a present employee recommends a friend or acquaintance for a given job, are quite effective, especially for small firms. Present employees know the requirements of the job and the qualities needed in a person to fill the job successfully. Hence, they can assist in recruiting by suggesting possible employees. This method prevails particularly in high-technology companies. Judging by the experience of some businesspeople, employee referrals are the best source of *good* applicants.[15]

Codex Corporation, a maker of data communication equipment in Mansfield, Massachusetts, offers a hefty reward of $1,000 a head to any employee who helps fill a salaried position, and $500 for helping to fill a nonsalaried position. It promotes its recruitment efforts with posters advertising various needs, placed in appropriate places such as cafeterias and office hallways.[16]

Personnel Post, a New York firm providing temporary office workers, offers $50 finders' fees.[17]

While employee referrals are important as a means of recruiting by small business, they should be used with caution. First, care must be taken not to violate equal employment opportunity (EEO) guidelines. Second, if friends or relatives of employees are hired, there is a danger that cliques will develop or that off-the-job personal animosities will interfere with job performance. Also, chances of employee theft or embezzlement may be increased.

By Scouting

Scouting can take several forms. While *campus recruiting* isn't often used by small businesses, it is a helpful technique for recruiting scientific, technical, professional, and managerial personnel. Campus recruiting works best when the small business manager works closely with the placement officer at a local college, and they maintain a friendly relationship. Colleges and universities are a great source of part-time employees, who need to earn part of their school expenses.

Larger firms that are reducing their work force provide another recruiting area, especially where there are mergers or consolidations. Many of those firms provide **outplacement,** a service to help laid-off employes find new jobs. Not only do the laid-off workers benefit from this process, but enterprising small companies that take the trouble to use this service can find a rich source of seasoned, professional job candidates without having to pay heavy recruitment costs.

When Honeywell Inc. laid off several people at its small-computer division in Billerica, Massachusetts, Prospective Computer Analysts Incorporated, an engineering consulting firm in nearby Bedford, Massachusetts, listed openings with Honeywell for two engineering jobs and obtained the engineers at a savings of $6,000, the cost of an executive search firm.[18]

SELECTING THE RIGHT PERSON FOR THE JOB

Selection is the process of determining whether an applicant has personal qualities that match the job specifications for a given position. Figure 10–4 shows some qualities—such as hard work, ability, and high standards—that working men and women say got them ahead.

No potential employee is perfect! So don't expect to find someone with all the qualities shown. Instead, find people who have the qualities you need, and be willing to accept qualities you don't need or want—so long as those qualities don't harm the business.

Gathering Information about the Applicant

Many people applying for a job will not be qualified, so try to find out all you can about what they can—and can't—do. In general, what a person has done in the past best indicates future performance. The small business manager should therefore use the most appropriate technique(s) to help discover a person's past performance and future possibilities.

The amount of information you need to know about an applicant depends on the type of employee being recruited. Figure 10–5 shows some selection techniques that are frequently used, but not all are needed for every job. Unskilled labor may require only a check of aptitude for the job, physical health, and record of past performance—the items marked with an asterisk in the figure. Applicants for semiskilled positions, such as electricians, may need additional tests of ability to do the job. Usually, such low-level jobs are filled frequently, and so the selection process must be pared down to essentials. For technical, professional, or managerial positions, all the techniques shown in the figure might be used.

Figure 10–4 Working to Get Ahead

What working men and women say got them ahead:

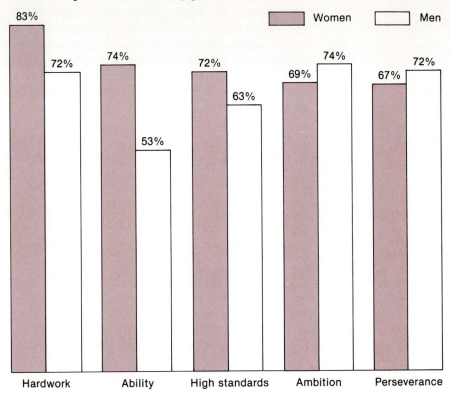

Note: Respondents could choose more than one.

Source: Working Woman, October 1985, as reported in *USA Today,* November 7, 1985, p. 1B. Copyright 1985, USA TODAY. Adapted with permission.

Whether formal or informal, some form of *preliminary screening* of applicants usually takes place early in the selection procedure. It can be done in an interview or through a letter of application, a résumé, or other methods. Most firms use some form of interviewing at this point. In general, you should look for such obvious factors as voice, physical appearance, personal grooming, educational qualifications, training, and experience. Many applicants are eliminated at this stage for reasons such as inappropriate dress, attitude, education, or experience.

Biographical information comes from application blanks, résumés, school records, military records, credit references, and so forth. You should look for solid evidence of past performance, concrete information on which to base the decision instead of depending on opinions or assumptions. Having prospective employees fill out an application blank in your presence—in

Figure 10–5   Selection Techniques for Gathering Information about Potential Employees

Techniques used to gather data	Characteristics to look for	Applicants who are available as potential employees
Preliminary screening*	Not obvious misfit from outward appearance and conduct	
Biographical information from application blank, resume, etc.	Adequate educational and performance record	
Testing Intelligence test(s)	Meets minimum standards of mental alertness	
Aptitude tests*	Specific capacities for acquiring particular knowledges or skills	
Proficiency or achievement test(s)	Ability to demonstrate capacity to do job	
Interest test(s)	Significant vocational interest in job	
Personality test(s)	Personal characteristics required for job	
In-depth interview	Necessary innate ability, ambition, or other qualities	
Verifying biological data from references	No unfavorable or negative reports on past performance	
Physical examination*	Physically fit for job	
Personal judgment*	Overall competence and ability to fit into the firm	

* Might be adequate to fill lower-level jobs.

Source: Adapted from Leon C. Megginson, *Personnel Management: A Human Resources Approach,* 5th ed. (Homewood, Ill.: Richard D. Irwin, 1985), p. 203.

longhand—serves as a simple performance test of their neatness and communications ability—or even simple literacy. No matter how good an applicant's record appears, don't base a decision on her or his unconfirmed statements. Unfortunately, there's a trend toward inflating résumés, and small business managers should make it a point to verify education and employment history and check references. In one study, over a fourth of

Figure 10–6   Résumé Inflation

Of 501 executives surveyed, 66 percent said their companies discovered instances of resume inflation after hiring employees in the past year. The executives said there were misrepresentations of:

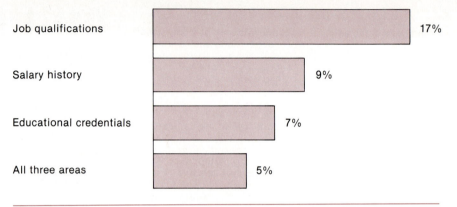

Job qualifications   17%

Salary history   9%

Educational credentials   7%

All three areas   5%

Source: Ward Howell International Inc., as reported in *The Wall Street Journal,* June 17, 1985, p. 1. Adapted with permission of *The Wall Street Journal,* © Dow Jones & Company, Inc., 1985. ALL RIGHTS RESERVED.

the respondents said they had hired employees in the past year who had misrepresented their backgrounds. As can be seen from Figure 10–6, the most common misrepresentation was in the area of job qualifications. Second was salary, and third was education. Adding a fancy title to a job status is a common misrepresentation, as is taking credit for someone else's work.

Several "red flags" may be indications of a phony résumé: gaps in dates or sequences that do not add up, such as the time between getting a degree and a job; degrees from unknown schools; vagueness; and listing accomplishments that don't make sense, such as years of education and experience that are greater than possible for the applicant's age. In most instances, an employee is not banished for stretching the truth, but it does depend on the degree of exaggeration.[19]

Since 1971, when the U.S. Supreme Court ruled that *employment tests* must be job related, most small firms have minimized their use because of the cost involved and the possible legal hassles. A word of caution is needed about the use of a special test, the **polygraph,** or "lie detector."

Before 1989, nearly half of all U.S. retail companies used the polygraph. Because the results were so debatable, Congress passed a law barring most private employers from using polygraph tests.[20] As a result, written and computerized tests for assessing employee honesty are increasingly being produced and sold, as shown in the Computer Update.

The declining use of polygraph testing is also leading to the resurrection of a century-old European method of job screening—handwriting analysis, commonly called **graphology.** About 350 graphologists are working full

Source: *USA Today,* August 7, 1985, p. 8A. Copyright 1985, USA TODAY. Reprinted with permission.

time to help U.S. companies select employees. They assess job candidates' aptitude and character by examining up to 300 personality traits. Companies must tell employees their handwriting is being analyzed.

Sheila Kurtz, a psychologist, owns A New Slant Inc., a New York firm with a branch in London. With more than 200 business clients, she says graphology is growing in importance for banks and other firms where employees' integrity is important.[21]

Interviewing can be an excellent means of getting information about a candidate's abilities, attitudes, and motivation. As the only two-way technique used in the selection procedure, it should be used not only to learn more about applicants but also to let them learn about the business. Brenda Ruello of Heidrick & Struggles warns that during a job interview "you don't learn by talking, you learn by listening." Ruello, who conducts in-house training programs in interviewing techniques, has observed four basic interviewing errors:[22]

- Judging too quickly.
- Talking too much.
- Not listening selectively.
- Not creating an atmosphere conducive to seeing interviewees as they really are.

COMPU-SCAN: AN EFFECTIVE TOOL FOR PREEMPLOYMENT SCREENING

With employers losing millions of dollars each year through employee problems such as theft and substance abuse, many of them are looking for efficient ways to identify potential problem workers. George E. Hunter and John B. Rucker, Jr., two former FBI agents, have developed an effective tool for screening employees and finding the ones most likely to rip off the company.

Hunter and Rucker started Hunter Security Inc. in 1978 to conduct polygraph tests and provide other investigative services. Most of their business was with retailers.

Since polygraph tests were becoming so unpopular, employers did not want to risk running off potentially capable employees by using the controversial test. So Hunter and Rucker developed Compu-Scan Pre-Employment Risk Analysis as an alternative screening tool that would be accurate, consistently effective, easily understood, thorough, available to employers at their location, and cost effective. After several revisions, Compu-Scan was approved by

some diplomates in industrial organizational psychology, who deem it as valid as the polygraph. The test takes about 20 minutes, and its 118 questions are easily understood by seventh graders.

The test, which is computerized, has questions with "yes," "no," or numerical answers recorded at four-second intervals, so that the person being tested has little time to ponder before responding. Instead, applicants are forced to give their first reaction, which tends to be more truthful. There are control—or validation—questions at random throughout the survey. A computer analyzes the information so that the operator can immediately tell the employer if hiring the person is risky. There are cutoff scores for certain categories, such as criminal history, theft history, and general attitude, which may indicate a potential problem that should be investigated further.

The agency's best customers are retail electronics stores, convenience stores, trucking companies, and fast-food chains.

John B. "Jack" Rucker, left, and George E. "Buddy" Hunter of Compu-Scan, Baldwin County, Alabama.

Source: Adline Clarke, "Screening Tool for Job Applicants Devised," *Mobile* (Alabama) *Press Register*, March 22, 1987, p. 1–D.

There is no generally accepted list of questions to ask potential employees, but Table 10–1 ranks, by prevalence of use, the most significant questions usually asked of college seniors. Be careful *not* to ask questions that violate EEO laws—as will be discussed later.

References play an important role in gathering information about an applicant. Essentially, there are three types of references: personal, academic, and past employment. For applicants with any work history, the most valued references are from former employers. Using a personal visit, a telephone call, or a personal letter, the manager can verify work history, educational attainments, and other information the applicant has presented. By law, former employers may, if they choose, limit their responses to information about dates and title of the most recent job and total period of employment. Be sure to get the applicant's permission before contacting the present employer, who may not know the employee is job hunting.

Table 10–1   Most Significant Questions Asked of Graduating Seniors, Ranked by Use

Most significant questions asked	Percentage of companies using
1. What are your long-range goals? Ambitions? Future plans? Basic objectives? What do you want to be doing 5–10–15 years from now? What are your immediate objectives?	93
2. Why did you choose your field of special study? How have you prepared yourself for work in your chosen field? What subjects have you enjoyed most? Least? Do you have plans for graduate study?	74
3. What type of work do you want to do? Why? Why do you think you qualify for this type of work? In what type of job would you like to start?	60
4. Why do you think you might like to work in our type of industry? Our company? Why did you select this company? What can you contribute to a company such as ours?	53
5. What were your extracurricular activities? What have you gained from your activities? What leadership office have you held? What are your hobbies—your interests out of school?	40
6. What is your scholastic record? Where do you stand in your class? Explain your academic record. In what courses have you earned your best grades? How well did you apply yourself in your studies?	37
7. Do you like to travel? Are you willing to travel? To relocate? Have you geographical preferences? Would you like to live in our community?	36
8. What are your major strengths and weaknesses? Your accomplishments to date? Major achievements in college? Any plans for improvement?	30
9. What work experience have you had? Summer jobs? Part-time work? What experiences did you like best? Why?	28
10. What do you know about our company? What questions would you like to ask? Is the size of a company important to you?	15

Source: Victor R. Lindquist, *The Northwestern Lindquist Report,* Northwestern University, Evanston, IL 60208.

Finally, most employers give some kind of *physical examination* to screen for: (1) communicable disease, (2) ability to do the work satisfactorily, and (3) probable high incidence of absenteeism, illness, or accident. As narcotics use and AIDS spread, employers—both large and small—are increasingly likely to require job seekers to take drug tests. The U.S. Supreme Court has approved drug testing of job applicants by private employers.[23]

Job Offer

Eventually you make a job offer to the person selected. It should include details of working conditions, pay, work hours, holidays, vacations, and other employee benefits, as well as the new employee's duties and responsibilities. Given the prevalence of lawsuits today, managers should put job offers in writing and get the applicants to sign indicating their understanding and agreement.

Orientation

Selection also should include orienting new employees to the job. A new job is usually a difficult and frustrating experience, even for the best-qualified people. The orientation process should include at least an introduction to co-workers; explaining the business's history, policies, procedures, and benefits; and working closely with the new employee during the first pay period. More employees leave a firm during that period than at any other time during their employment.

After more than 20 years as a full-time wife and mother, Elaine Reeves (name disguised) accepted her first job outside the home. When she reported for work on Monday morning, Elaine was greeted by the business's owner and shown the typewriter, other office machines, and supply cabinet. Then she was left on her own while the owner went to call on several contractors. In these unfamiliar surroundings, and with the other employees wrapped up in their own work—which made them seem unfriendly and unhelpful—she felt shaken and discouraged and was thinking of turning around and going home. The owner walked in just in time to stop her.

TRAINING AND DEVELOPING EMPLOYEES

The continued effectiveness of a business results not only from the ability of the owner but also from (1) the caliber of its employees, including their inherent abilities, (2) their development through training, education, and experience, and (3) their motivation. The first of these depends on effective recruiting and selection. The second results from **personnel development.** The third, motivation, which will be covered in the next chapter, results from the manager's leadership abilities.

Need for Training and Development

Not only must new employees be trained, but the present ones must be retrained and upgraded if they are to adjust to rapidly changing job requirements. Some of the results of training and developing workers include:

- Increased productivity.
- Reduced turnover.
- Increased earnings for employees.
- Decreased costs of materials and equipment due to errors.
- Less supervision required.

All these results contribute to profitability and employee satisfaction.

Bill Saul, chairman of Remmele Engineering, Inc. (a Minneapolis, Minnesota, automation-equipment manufacturer), firmly believes that it is profitable to train people. "Every time we bring in a new, well-trained employee, he can theoretically bring in $90,000 in sales. It doesn't take that long to recoup the cost of training."[24] While most companies train apprentices on the shop floor, Remmele has its own 6,000-square-foot training center.

Employees usually have a greater sense of worth, dignity, and well-being as they become more valuable to the firm through training and development.

Ways of Training Nonmanagerial Employees

To train nonmanagerial employees, small business managers can use many methods, including: (1) on-the-job training (OJT), (2) apprenticeship training, (3) internship training, and (4) outside help with training.

On-the-Job Training

The most universal form of employee development, **on-the-job training (OJT),** involves actual performance of work duties by the employee under the supervision and guidance of the owner, a manager, or a trained worker or instructor. Thus, while learning to do the job, the worker acts as a regular employee, producing the good or service that the business sells. Consciously planned or not, this form of training always occurs. While the methods used vary with the trainer, OJT usually involves:

- Telling workers what needs to be done.
- Telling them how to do the job.
- Showing them how it must be done.
- Letting them do the job under the trainer's guidance.
- Telling—and showing—them what they did right, what they did wrong, and how to correct the wrong activity.
- Repeating the process until the learners have mastered the job.

MARTY
Lowe

Source: Reprinted from *The Wall Street Journal;* permission
Cartoon Features Syndicate.

The primary advantages of OJT are that (1) it results in low out-of-pocket costs, and (2) production continues during the training. Also, there is no transition from classroom learning to actual production. On the other hand, the disadvantages are excessive waste caused by mistakes and the poor learning environment provided by the production area. While most OJT is done by owners and managers, they are not necessarily the best ones to do it, as their primary focus is on running the business. For this reason, another capable employee—or even an outside trainer—should be assigned this responsibility, if possible. Also, a specific follow-up procedure is necessary to evaluate the results of the training and to serve as a basis for improving future development.

Apprenticeship Training

For workers performing skilled, craft-type jobs, **apprenticeship training** blends the learning of theory with practice in the techniques of the job. If the job can best be learned by combining classroom instruction and actual learning experience on the job, this training method should be used. It usually lasts from two to seven years of both classroom learning and on-the-job training. Remmele Engineering's training center is an example of this type of training.

Internship Training

Internship training combines education at a school or college with on-the-job training at a cooperating business. It is usually used for students who are prospective employees for marketing, clerical, technical, and managerial positions. Co-op programs prepare students for technical positions, provide income to meet the cost of their education, and give them a chance to see if they would like to go to work for the company. This method also gives the small business owner a chance to evaluate the student as a prospective full-time employee.

Outside Help with Training

Many outside programs are available to help with the training of small business employees. For example, the **National Apprenticeship Act** of 1937, administered by the U.S. Labor Department's Bureau of Apprenticeship and Training, sets policies and standards for apprenticeship programs. Write to this bureau for help in conducting such a program.

Vocational-technical schools, business schools, junior colleges, and small private firms help small companies by conducting regular or special classes. Through such programs, potential employees can become qualified for skilled jobs such as machinist, lathe operator, computer service technician, and legal assistant.

The **vocational rehabilitation programs** sponsored by the U.S. Department of Health and Human Services (HHS) in cooperation with state governments provide counseling, medical care, and vocational training for physically and mentally handicapped individuals. One example of this, Jones Manufacturing Company, appeared earlier in this chapter.

The **Job Training Partnership Act (JTPA)** underwrites the most important public training programs currently being used to help small businesses. They're developed and effectively controlled by **private industry councils (PICs)** and funded by block grants to the states. The funds provided must go for training, including on-the-job training, and none can be used for stipends or wage supplements. In addition to getting cash reimbursement for hiring and training through PICs, small firms can also get an investment tax credit to offset the cost of hiring eligible workers.

One of the first employers to use the JTPA was Hilti, Inc., a Tulsa, Oklahoma, maker of fastening systems used in the construction industry. It received some $80,000 in federal assistance, through the Tulsa-area Private Industry Training Council, to help offset the $434,000 cost of retraining 50 employees in new skills. After six months of training, the workers became machine tool operators; worked in heat treating, plating, and inspection; and held various support positions.[25]

SELECTING AND DEVELOPING MANAGERS

Determining the job requirements for someone to be a manager is more difficult than filling other positions because managerial jobs differ so greatly. But one generalization usually applies: *The employee who is a good performer at the nonmanagerial level does not necessarily make a good manager, because the skills needed at the two levels differ drastically.*

Selecting Managers

In small firms, managers are usually promoted from within, but many businesses hire college graduates for management trainee programs. Dr. Whitt Schultz, business owner, consultant, and lecturer, has found that the characteristics to be developed to produce good managers are creativity, productivity, innovativeness, communication skills (including oral, written, nonverbal, and telephone), self-motivation, and the drive and energy to energize others to achieve consistently large amounts of high-quality work.[26] You can see that these tend to be the same qualities that lead to success as an entrepreneur (see Chapter 2).

Developing Managers

In addition to the usual methods used to develop all employees, some special techniques are used to develop managerial personnel. These include (1) coaching, (2) planned progression, (3) job rotation, and (4) executive development programs.

Coaching

In **coaching,** managers provide guidance to employees while the employees perform their regular job. Ideally, the junior executive absorbs some of the qualities that have made the owner or senior executive successful. Coaching therefore tends to be an informal rather than a formal procedure.

Planned Progression

Planned progression requires the company to outline the path of promotion that lies ahead of a new manager. One form of planned progression is an "assistant to" position, which may be a routine administrative position or one created specifically for training purposes.

Job Rotation

By means of **job rotation,** a young manager learns various operating procedures by temporarily performing many different jobs in different areas. The short-run inefficiencies are outweighed by the well-rounded development young executives get.

Executive Development Programs

A well-conceived, well-developed, and well-taught **executive development program** offers an effective way to develop managers. It is used for only a relatively few promising managers because of its cost. This type of program, taught outside the company, is among the most progressive and dynamic of all the developmental techniques, as it broadens the participant's perspective and provides contact with other promising managers.

COMPLYING WITH EQUAL EMPLOYMENT OPPORTUNITY LAWS

Federal and state laws and regulations affect almost all aspects of personnel relations. Since state laws vary so widely, only the federal ones affecting recruiting and selecting employees are discussed here. It should be strongly emphasized that a highly qualified person should be employed—either full time or part time—to see that you adhere to these laws.

Laws Providing Equal Employment Opportunity (EEO)

In 1964, Congress passed the **Civil Rights Act.** Title VII of this act, as amended, prohibits discrimination on account of race, color, religion, sex, or national origin in hiring, upgrading, and all other conditions of employment. As shown in Table 10–2, the smallest firms are exempt. Other groups

Table 10–2   Legal Influences on Equal Employment Opportunity (EEO) and Affirmative Action (AA)

Laws	Coverage	Basic requirements	Agencies involved
Title VII of Civil Rights Act of 1964, as amended	Employers with 15 or more employees and engaged in interstate commerce; federal service workers; and state and local government workers.	Prohibits employment decisions based on race, color, religion, sex, or national origin.	Equal Employment Opportunity Commission (EEOC)
Executive Order 11246, as amended	Employers with federal contracts and sub-contracts	Requires contractors who under-utilize women and minorities to take affirmative action, including setting goals and timetables; and to recruit, select, train, utilize, and promote more minorities and women.	Office of Federal Contract Compliance Programs (OFCCP), in the Labor Department
Age Discrimination in Employment Act of 1967	Employers with 20 or more employees.	Prohibits employment discrimination against employees aged 40 and over, including mandatory retirement before 70 with certain exceptions.	EEOC
Vocational Rehabilitation Act of 1973	Employers with federal contracts or subcontracts.	Prohibits discrimination and requires contractor to develop AA programs to recruit and employ handicapped persons.	OFCCP
Vietnam-Era Veterans Readjustment Act of 1974	Employers with federal contracts or subcontracts.	Requires contractors to develop AA programs to recruit and employ Vietnam-era veterans and to list job openings with state employment services, for priority in referrals.	OFCCP

Source: L. C. Megginson, *Personnel Management,* 5th ed. (Homewood, Ill.: Richard D. Irwin, 1985), Chapter 4, p. 97. Extracted from BNA's Policy and Practice Series, *Fair Employment Practices* (Washington, D.C.: Bureau of National Affairs).

affected by this type of legislation are older workers, the handicapped, and Vietnam-era veterans. All of these have special laws, rules, and regulations for their protection.

Some Special Aspects of Sex Discrimination

Generally, all jobs must be open to both men and women unless sex is a **bona fide occupational qualification (BFOQ)** necessary to the normal operations of the particular business. Therefore, "male only" or "female only" advertisements cannot be run by a company unless sex can be proved to be a BFOQ. Also, terms such as "bar-girl," "busboy," and "girl Friday" cannot be used. Disqualifying female employees from jobs requiring heavy lifting, night shifts, and dirty work is illegal unless justification exists for these restrictions. Automatic discharge of pregnant women and refusal to reinstate them after childbirth, requiring retirement at different ages, and not hiring women with small children constitute discrimination. Men and women must also receive the same rate of pay for the same work.

Some Laws Pertaining to Age

The **Fair Labor Standards Act** of 1938 and many state statutes prescribe the minimum age for employees. Typically, these laws specify a minimum age of 14 to 16 years, with a higher minimum often set for hazardous occupations. On the other hand, the **Age Discrimination in Employment Act** of 1967 prohibits—with certain exceptions—discrimination against present or prospective employees aged 40 and above. This includes not only hiring but also retirement and other aspects of employment.

The Immigration Reform and Control Act of 1986

This new law prohibits employment discrimination on the basis of national origin. Employers should not fire or fail to hire anyone on the basis of foreign appearance, language, or name. Under this law, employers, including small businesses, are required to verify that all employees hired after November 6, 1986, are U.S. citizens or aliens authorized to work. The law's purpose is to provide jobs only for those legally authorized to work in the United States.

Some Practical Applications of EEO Laws

In essence, all employees are entitled to equality in all conditions of employment. Hiring, training, promotions and transfers, wages and benefits, and all other employment factors are covered.

Hiring

In recruiting applicants for employment, managers cannot rely solely on walk-ins or word-of-mouth advertising of job openings, especially if their present work force is predominantly of one race. Friends or relatives of present employees cannot be recruited if a company has a disproportionate number of a certain class of employees. A company cannot set hiring standards with respect to test results, high school diploma, height, arrest record, manner of speech, or appearance if such standards result in discrimination on the basis of race, color, sex, religion, or national origin. Federal laws require you to retain all recruitment forms for at least one year after an employment decision has been made.

Promoting

Seniority systems should not result in locking minorities into unskilled and semiskilled jobs without providing them with lines of progression to better jobs. Training and performance appraisals should be conducted on a nondiscriminatory basis. Equal opportunity for promotions should be offered. Posting available job openings on a bulletin board to give present employees a chance to bid on them has been found to be a good method of complying with EEO laws and has been accepted by the Equal Employment Opportunity Commission if there are no evidences of discrimination.

Wages and Benefits

There must be no discrimination in hourly rates or deferred wages, including pensions or other deferred payments. Recreational activities—company sports teams, holiday parties, and the like—should be open to all employees on a nondiscriminatory basis.

Enforcing EEO Laws

The **Equal Employment Opportunity Commission (EEOC),** the primary enforcing agency, receives and investigates charges of employment discrimination. To stop violations, the commission may take action itself or go to a U.S. district court. The Labor Department's Office of Federal Contract Compliance Programs (OFCCP) requires employers with government contracts or subcontracts to have **affirmative action programs (AAPs)** to put the principle of equal employment opportunity into practice. The OFCCP can cancel a guilty firm's contract or prohibit it from getting future contracts if a violation is blatant.

Terminating Employees

While you still have the right to terminate employees for cause, the concept of "employment at will" is losing acceptance in courts and legislatures. **Employment at will** essentially means that employers may fire employees with or without cause at any time they choose. Courts and legislators are now applying instead the "good faith and fair dealing" concept, whereby terminations must be "reasonable" and not "arbitrarily" or "indiscriminately" applied. Violating this concept may lead to punitive damages, as well as actual damages that have been sustained by one of the protected employees.

Montana's Wrongful Discharge from Employment Act—the only one in the United States in 1989—protects employees from arbitrary dismissal. It forbids firing workers who don't belong to a union and don't have individual job contracts without showing "good cause," as determined by a court.[27]

WHAT YOU SHOULD HAVE LEARNED

1. The most important resource for a small business, as for any business, is people. Therefore, small business managers must determine the needed number and skills of employees and the sources from which to recruit them. Determining personnel needs begins with a job description and job specifications. These, added to the number of jobs to be filled, will tell the manager the number and types of people needed.

   New employees can be recruited from either internal or external sources. When feasible, it is best to fill job openings from inside the business, as it contributes to good employee morale and saves time and money, and employees' past performance is known. Employees can be upgraded, transferred, or promoted to fill job openings. External sources for employees include former employees, applications, friends and relatives of present employees, other businesses, social and professional organizations, schools and colleges, retirees, handicapped workers, and part-time and temporary workers.

2. Employees can be recruited through advertising, employment agencies, employee referrals, and scouting. Newspaper want ads are the most common method of recruiting. State employment agencies can supply, without charge, the required personnel. For higher levels of employees, private employment agencies, employee referrals, and scouting may be more effective.

3. Prospective employees must be evaluated to select the right one for the job. To do this, you must gather information about the candidate, with special emphasis on past performance. A preliminary screening interview or review of the candidate's application or résumé weeds out obviously unsuitable applicants. Biographical information is obtained from the application or résumé and from school, military, and other records. Sometimes, applicants are given some form of test, but this must be done cautiously because of legal restraints.

   Interviewing is one of the best ways to size up candidates, especially their attitudes and personalities. It also provides a good opportunity to give them information about the business and "sell" the job—important if the applicant pool is small and other employers are competing for well-qualified candidates.

   The applicants' references should be verified. A physical examination, often the last step of the selection process, checks on the candidate's health.

   Ultimately, the decision of whom to employ comes down to the personal judgment of the hiring manager. Once the decision has been made, a clear, preferably written job offer should be extended. Orientation can range from a simple introduction to co-workers to a lengthy training process.

4. After employees are hired, their effectiveness depends on personnel development, so all workers should be retrained and upgraded periodically. Training methods include on-the-job training (OJT), apprenticeship training, internship training, and outside training. Help with training can be obtained from the Bureau of Apprenticeship and Training, vocational-technical education programs, and private industry councils (PICs) operating under the Job Training Partnership Act (JTPA).

5. In selecting managers, employers should look for managerial qualities, which aren't the same as nonmanagerial competence. Techniques used especially for developing managers include coaching, planned progression, job rotation, and executive development programs.

6. Federal and state laws affect small business managers in their dealings with current and prospective employees. The equal employment opportunity provisions of the Civil Rights Act are especially important. Legislation has been passed to prevent discrimination on the basis of race, color, sex, age, religion, or national origin. Also all employees, once hired, must be treated equally in all terms and conditions of employment. The Equal Employment Opportunity Commission (EEOC) is charged with assuring this fairness, and the Office of Federal Contract Compliance Programs (OFCCP) requires government contractors to have affirmative action programs (AAPs) to guarantee it.

KEY TERMS

job specifications, 273

job description, 273

upgrading, 276

transferring, 276

promoting, 276

leased manpower, 278

recruitment, 279

state employment agencies, 280

private employment agencies, 280

employee referrals, 280

scouting, 280

outplacement, 281

selection, 281

polygraph, 284

graphology, 284

personnel development, 288

on-the-job training (OJT), 289

apprenticeship training, 290

internship training, 290

National Apprenticeship Act, 291

vocational rehabilitation programs, 291

Job Training Partnership Act (JTPA), 291

private industry councils (PICs), 291

coaching, 292

planned progression, 292

job rotation, 292

executive development program, 292

Civil Rights Act, 293

bona fide occupational qualification (BFOQ), 294

Fair Labor Standards Act, 294

Age Discrimination in
  Employment Act, 294
Equal Employment Opportunity
  Commission (EEOC), 295
affirmative action programs
  (AAPs), 295
employment at will, 295

QUESTIONS FOR DISCUSSION

1. What does personnel planning involve in the small company?
2. What external sources are usually used by small businesses for finding new employees?
3. What are some advantages and disadvantages of filling job openings from within the company?
4. Distinguish among upgrading, promoting, and transferring employees.
5. What are some arguments (*a*) for and (*b*) against using employee referrals in recruiting new employees?
6. What are some sources of references that the small business manager can use in investigating applicants?
7. (*a*) Why should a physical examination be required of an applicant? (*b*) Why not?
8. How should new people be introduced to their jobs?
9. How do EEO laws affect recruiting and selecting employees?
10. (*a*) What agencies enforce EEO laws? (*b*) How do they enforce them?

SUGGESTED READINGS

Bork, Robert H. "The Supreme Court and Civil Rights." *The Wall Street Journal,* June 30, 1989, p. A12.

Bowles, Jerry. "Resources for Small Businesses." *Fortune,* Fall 1987, pp. 192–96.

Brophy, Beth. "Find Your Job in Classifieds." *USA Today,* August 14, 1985, p. 6B.

Fader, Shirley Sloan. "When You Are Doing the Hiring." *Working Woman,* February 1985, pp. 48–49.

Halcrow, Allan. "Employees Are Your Best Recruiters." *Personnel Journal* 67 (November 1988): 42–49.

Hale, Ellen. "Your Work May Improve with Age." *USA Today,* March 19, 1986, p. 1D.

Harlan, Christi. "Written 'Honesty' Tests Attract Interest as Polygraph Ban Begins." *The Wall Street Journal,* January 3, 1989, p. B3.

Kohl, John P., and David B. Stephens. "Wanted: Recruitment Advertising That Doesn't Discriminate." *Personnel* 66 (February 1989): 18–25.

Nussbaum, Bruce. "Needed: Human Capital." *Business Week,* September 19, 1988, pp. 100–103; and various articles on pp. 104–41.

Schmidt, Peggy. "Women and Minorities: Is Industry Ready?" *The New York Times,* October 16, 1988, p. F25.

Szabo, Joan C. "The Job Machine Rolls On: Employment Growth in Small Business." *Nation's Business,* July 1988, p. 10.

ENDNOTES

1. Barbara Marsh, "Small Firms' Disadvantage in Hiring Likely to Grow," *The Wall Street Journal,* November 27, 1989, p. B1.

2. "A Shrinking Labor Pool Is Really Cramping Small Fry," *Business Week,* April 3, 1989, p. 82.

3. Udayan Gupta and Jeffrey A. Tannenbaum, "Labor Shortages Force Changes at Small Firms," *The Wall Street Journal,* May 22, 1989, p. 1B.

4. Annetta Miller, "Burgers: The Heat Is On," *Newsweek,* June 16, 1986, p. 53; Donald C. Bacon, "Firms Try Harder to Attract Workers," *Nation's Business,* December 1988, p. 6; and "Burger King to Cut 550 Jobs in Revamping," *The New York Times,* April 4, 1989, p. C5.

5. *USA Today,* August 24, 1984, p. 3B.

6. Constance Mitchell, "Vocational Schools Ready for New Jobs," *USA Today,* August 24, 1984, p. 3B.

7. Bill Crawford, "Older Workers Find They're Still Needed in the Corporate World," *AARP Magazine,* February 1986, p. 1.

8. Alan Alper, "Help from the Disabled," *Venture,* April 1985, pp. 21, 24.

9. Laura E. Chatfield, "Temporary Attractions: Workers Like Flexibility," *USA Today,* August 31, 1989, p. 8B.

10. "Recruiting-Hiring Experience," *Inc.,* December 1985, p. 54.

11. Marsh, "Small Firms' Disadvantage," p. B2.

12. Reported in "Leasing Workers Saves Money," *USA Today,* July 23, 1989, p. 7B.

13. "A Temporary Solution," *USA Today,* June 18, 1987, p. 9B.

14. Champ Clark, "Classified Ads That Click," *Money,* December 1975; and Eugene Carlson, "American Entrepreneurs: Upon a Little Book, Sears Built the Big Store," *The Wall Street Journal,* February 21, 1989, p. B1.

15. Correspondence with Professor Russell C. Eustice of Husson College.

16. John F. Persinos, "Big Name Hunting," *Inc.,* December 1984, p. 210.

17. *The Wall Street Journal,* April 14, 1989, p. 1A.

18. *Inc.,* November 1985, p. 159.

19. Based on Beth Brophy, "Companies, Beware: Resume Hype Rising," *USA Today,* April 12, 1985, p. 6B; "Job Applicants Might Not Be All They Claim," *USA Today,* June 27, 1985, p. 7B; and Malcolm Ritter, "Study Says Third of Workers Lied about Their Experience," *Mobile* (Alabama) *Register,* September 3, 1987, p. 28–A.

20. "Lie Tests Are Sharply Curbed," *The New York Times,* October 22, 1988, p. 16.

21. Shelley Liles-Morris, "Graphology Company Puts New Slant on Hiring," *USA Today,* December 8, 1989, p. 4B.

22. *Working Woman,* February 1985, p. 48.

23. Ted Gest, "Testing, Testing," *U.S. News & World Report,* March 13, 1989, p. 52; and "Green Light on Drug Tests for New Hires," *USA Today,* June 20, 1989, p. 1A.

24. "In Search of Survival," *Inc.,* November 1985, p. 80.

25. Frank Leslie, "Hilti First to Participate in Retraining Program," *Tulsa World,* April 3, 1983, pp. G–1, G–4.

26. Whitt N. Schultz, "How to Improve Your Career," *Southeastern Jobs Directory,* November 7, 1983, p. 12.

27. Amy Dockser, "Wrongful-Firing Case in Montana May Prompt Laws in Other States," *The Wall Street Journal,* July 3, 1989, p. 11.

11

LEADING AND MOTIVATING EMPLOYEES

The good boss selects people with demonstrated capabilities, tells them what results are expected, largely leaves them alone to decide the means by which they can be obtained, and then monitors the results.—Sanford Jacobs, entrepreneur

The key to . . . success is superior customer service, continuing internal entrepreneurship, and a deep belief in the dignity, worth, and potential of every person in the organization.—Tom Peters, coauthor of *In Search of Excellence*

LEARNING OBJECTIVES

After studying the material in this chapter, you will be able to:

1. Explain how managerial assumptions affect human relationships with employees.
2. Describe three leadership styles and discuss the factors affecting which one a manager uses.
3. List some barriers to effective communication and show some ways to improve communication.
4. Explain how to improve employee motivation.
5. Describe how to compensate employees with money and employee benefits.
6. Tell why personnel appraisals are used.
7. Explain how to improve productivity.

MURRY EVANS: DEVELOPING WINNING TEAMS

Murry Evans is both a franchisee and a franchisor. And he has succeeded at both because he developed winning teams. His secret of success: "If you get good people, train them well, work with them, and praise them for good work, you'll have a winning team." He then quotes one of the late Paul "Bear" Bryant's favorite sayings, "There ain't no fun in anything but winning."

Murry's career as a franchisee began in 1963, when, at age 24, he opened his first Burger King franchise in Mobile, Alabama, with $40,000 he had borrowed from his hard-working father-in-law, an Ohio farmer. His lifetime goal then was "to open five Burger King restaurants." In 1989, with 46 stores, he had far exceeded his goal, owning more franchises than any other individual franchisee in the United States.

Evans attributes much of the success of Midtown Restaurants Corporation to the hard work and dedication he and his wife, Marilyn, put into that first Burger King. After teaching school to support them so he could graduate from The Citadel, she did everything from cleaning tables and washing dishes to preparing the payroll.

As the owner of SIGNS NOW, the original one-day high-tech sign company, Evans is also a successful franchisor. Begun in 1983 to produce computer-generated vinyl signs and lettering in one day, it now has 48 franchises around the world—in addition to two company-owned stores in Mobile.

Evans believes SIGNS NOW is so successful because it is trying to give people—young and old, male and female—a chance to own a good, solid business, providing a needed service, while letting them earn a profit. Franchisees will

Source: Photo © 1989 by Thigpen Photography, provided courtesy of SIGNS NOW.

succeed, he says, if they have a good location, work hard, and are dedicated to the job.

Believing that "if our franchisees are successful, we're successful," he and his team are trying to help them succeed. Having been a franchisee himself for 25 years, Evans is sympathetic to their problems and can help them solve those problems.

Evans is living proof that having big ideas, a good team, motivation, and willingness to work hard leads to success.

Sources: Correspondence and discussions with John E. Carpenter, Director of Franchise Sales for SIGNS NOW; and others, including Ronaleen R. Roha, "The Elusive Affordable Franchise . . . and How to Find It," *Changing Times,* October 1989, pp. 60–68; and Judith A. Rogala, "SIGNS NOW and in the Future," *Business Age,* April 1989, pp. 18, 23, 24, and 56.

The opening quotations and Opening Focus illustrate the importance of leading and motivating people in small firms. These activities include:

- Practicing "good" human relations.
- Using enlightened leadership in dealing with them.
- Communicating openly and truthfully with them.
- Using positive motivation.
- Compensating them fairly.
- Evaluating their performance.

GOOD HUMAN RELATIONS IS NEEDED IN SMALL FIRMS

Defining the term *human relations* is difficult, for it means different things to different people. Dr. Alfred Haake, lecturer for General Motors, would begin his lectures on human relations by saying, "Some people say that good human relations is treating people as if it were your last day on earth." "Ah, no!" he would continue. "Good human relations is treating people as if it were *their* last day on earth." Regardless of the definition used, successful small business managers practice good human relations.

What Is "Good" Human Relations?

Human relations involves the interaction of people in an organization. Part of most aspects of working with people, it is particularly needed in the areas of leadership, communications, motivation, evaluating performance, and compensating employees. A survey of 252 personnel and marketing managers in New York and Hawaii emphasized this need for good human relations, especially for communicating and motivating.[1] The managers were asked to rank, in order of importance, the skills they felt every business graduate should have. Communicating, working with and using the skills of others, and motivating consistently ranked first, second, and third in importance for these managers. While this study did not distinguish between managers of small and large businesses, we feel that those areas are even more important in small firms than in large ones.

Ben Cohen and Jerry Greenfield, founders of Ben & Jerry's Homemade Inc., gourmet ice cream makers, try to run their company using good human relations. They use participative management, hold companywide employee meetings every eight weeks, limit top-paid employees to only five times the salary of the lowest-paid full-time worker, divide the company's profit-sharing pool—5 percent of pretax earnings—according to seniority, not rank, and give 7.5 percent of pretax profits to charity, especially to community self-help groups and children's rights programs.[2]

How Managerial Assumptions Affect Management Approach

Managers' actions toward their employees result from their assumptions about how those employees will react to them. Douglas McGregor, an early management writer, concluded that managers may be divided into two categories according to their assumptions about employees.[3] The first group of managers, on the basis of what McGregor called **Theory X** assumptions, expects employees to hate work, shun responsibility, and have little interest in their jobs. Such managers (sometimes called *hard-nosed supervisors*) therefore treat employees as if they really did not want to work: they do not give the workers responsibility, try to use coercion to motivate, and use discipline instead of positive motivation.

Other managers accept **Theory Y** assumptions that employees are ambitious, self-motivated, innovative, and creative. These participative-style supervisors therefore treat employees as if they would do more than is required of them, use time effectively, be interested in improving their job, seek satisfaction in their work, and seek and accept greater responsibility.

Keith Dunn started his own restaurant because of the poor treatment he'd received from his employers. After some motivational techniques—such as contests and benefits—failed, he started including his employees in managing the business. Now that they feel a vital part of the business, the annual turnover rate has dropped from 250 percent—normal for the industry—to 60 percent.[4]

What kind of manager—Theory X or Theory Y—do you think you'll be? What do you think you'll assume about the performance of your employees when you become a manager?

Sue Ley tried using the informal, participative style of supervision in CleanDrum, Inc. (Case III–1). She realized this style was working when employees came up to her and said, "Why don't we do it this way?"

EXERCISING LEADERSHIP

Management and leadership are similar enough to be easily confused, but there are some significant differences. Leading is an important part of management but not the whole of it. Leadership is the ability of one person to influence others, either formally or informally, to strive to attain goals or objectives. Management, while requiring the use of leadership, also includes the other functions of planning, organizing, staffing, and controlling. Leadership is especially important for small business managers: without it, they cannot get workers to strive to achieve their goals or the business's objectives.

Leadership Styles

Of the many leadership styles, the most commonly used are the autocratic, democratic, and laissez-faire. Using **autocratic leadership,** managers make most of the decisions themselves, with no input from their employees. This style is common in the military or in situations that allow little room for error and where time, quality, or money is an important factor. **Democratic (participative) leadership** involves employees, as individuals or a group, in setting the business's objectives, developing strategies, making job assignments, and arriving at other decisions. **Laissez-faire (free-rein) leadership** is a "loose" form of leadership whereby the manager lets employees do pretty much what they want.

Effective Managers Use Various Leadership Styles

It is tempting to say that one of these leadership styles is better than another for small business managers. Yet experience has shown that no one style is ideal at all times. Instead, the best approach depends on the situation and the people involved.

Most small business managers vary their leadership from one extreme of making decisions alone and announcing them to subordinates to the other extreme of setting limits and letting employees operate as they please within those limits. This approach is popular with managers because it gives them a range of leadership styles instead of only two or three.

Where a given manager operates at a given time depends on the relationship between: (1) the manager's traits, skills, and inclinations; (2) the employees' abilities, characteristics, and attitudes; and (3) the situation at the time when the manager must act.

COMMUNICATING WITH PEOPLE

Communication, the process of transferring meaning—ideas and information—from one person to another, is a small business manager's "number one job." Studies show that verbal communications take up about 80 percent of a manager's time.[5] Communication is important because people need

---

Table 11–1   What Employees Want to Know

Surveyed employees said the most important information to them at work concerns:

Employee benefit program	82%
Pay policies and procedures	78
Company's plans for the future	73
How to improve work performance	65
How my work fits into the total picture	61

Source: The Hay Group Research for Management Database, as reported in *The Wall Street Journal,* August 9, 1985, p. 19. Reprinted by permission of *The Wall Street Journal,* © Dow Jones & Company, Inc., 1985. ALL RIGHTS RESERVED.

and want to know what is going on so as to do their jobs properly. Owners, employees, customers, vendors, and others need to coordinate their work, so communication must be clear and complete. In addition, speaking pleasantly and persuasively makes people want to do good work. A Japanese proverb says, "One kind word can warm three winter months." Table 11–1 shows what one group of employees wanted to know, according to a survey by the Hay Group.

What Happens When You Communicate?

While explaining a process as complex as communication is difficult, Figure 11–1 shows that the process involves: (1) someone (the source) having an idea, thought, or impression that (2) is encoded or translated into words or symbols that (3) are transmitted, or sent as a message to another person (the receiver), who (4) picks up the symbols and (5) decodes, or retranslates, them back into an idea and (6) sends some form of feedback to the sender. Feedback completes the process, because communication cannot be assumed to have taken place until the receiver demonstrates understanding of the message. Since communication is an exchange of *meaning* rather

Figure 11–1   The Communication Process

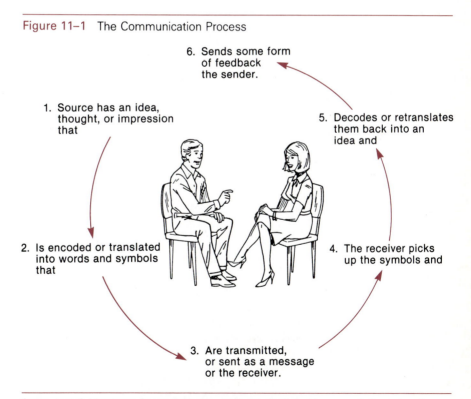

Source: Leon C. Megginson, Donald C. Mosley, and Paul H. Pietri, Jr., *Management: Concepts and Applications,* 2d ed. (New York: Harper & Row, 1986), p. 332.

than words or symbols, many forms of nonverbal communication convey meaning through signals, signs, sounds (other than words), and facial expressions.

Barriers to Effective Communication

Despite communication's importance and the amount of time managers spend doing it, it is not always effective. One study showed that up to 70 percent of all business communication fails to achieve the desired results.[6] This ineffectiveness comes from many factors, particularly some barriers erected by the business itself or by the people involved.

First, because of managers' position of authority, employees tend to believe what higher-level managers say, regardless of whether it is true or not. In addition, the status of the communicator either lends credibility to what is being said or detracts from it, for messages of higher-status people tend to carry greater credibility than those of lower-status people.

The imprecise use of language also serves as a barrier. Have you noticed how frequently people use the expression "you know" in daily communications or adopt "buzz words" (especially those from high-tech fields) without really knowing what they mean? On the other hand, **jargon**—complex, technical language—used by a specialist can also cause misunderstanding.

At William M. Mercer-Meidinger Inc., a New York consulting firm, a specialist in firing people is dubbed an expert in "structuring employee terminations." The expert uses such terms as *outplacement* and *replacement* to soften the impact on the employee being fired.[7]

Perhaps the greatest barriers to effective communication are simply inattention and poor listening. Managers are often so preoccupied with running their business that they may not pay attention to employee feedback.

How to Improve Communication

By clarifying ideas, considering the environment in which the communication occurs, considering emotional overtones as well as the message, following up on communication, and being good listeners, managers should be more effective communicators.

Changing Our Attitude toward Others

Communication can also be improved by changing our attitude and considering the other person when we try to communicate. Dr. Sylvia Sorkin, a practicing psychologist, told a group of managers in a development program that:

■ The five most important words you can use are "I am proud of you."
■ The four most important words are "What do you think?"

- The three most important words are "Will you, please?"
- The two most important words are "Thank you!"
- The one most important word is "You."

Becoming a Better Listener

As we have emphasized, communication is a two-way street. Even more important than getting your meaning across is really hearing and understanding what the other person says. To improve your listening skills, try these tips:

- You can't listen while you are talking. Be sure you give the other person plenty of opportunity to speak.
- You can't listen attentively if there are distractions. Find a quiet place where you can concentrate on what the other person says.
- You can't listen while thinking about something else. Give the other person your full attention, and don't doddle, write, or do other work. (You *can* take notes!)
- Ask questions. Not only do sensible (not nosy or rude) questions increase your understanding, they also encourage the other person to give more details.
- If you have been paying attention, you should be able to summarize what the other person has said. Such a summary will give the speaker a chance to correct misunderstandings right away.
- To really understand what another person says, you have to understand what it means to that person. Try to put yourself in his or her place.
- Try to listen with an open mind, without losing your temper or showing signs of being upset.
- Don't interrupt.
- After an important conversation or meeting, jot down notes to yourself about the main points discussed.
- Active listening techniques, such as reflective statements that merely paraphrase what the speaker has said (as you understand it), can encourage the other person to continue because you are not being judgmental.

MOTIVATING EMPLOYEES

Before reading the following material, complete the exercise in Figure 11–2. This exercise helps explain why motivation is so complex and why it is so difficult to motivate some employees. Managers must use different incentives to motivate different people at different times in their working lives. Yet it is difficult to know what a given employee wants at a given time. Understanding those needs, and understanding how to use the appropriate motivation, are the secrets of successful management.

Figure 11–2   What Do You Want from a Job?

Rank the employment factors shown below in their order of importance to you at three points in your career. In the first column, assume that you are about to graduate and are looking for your first full-time job. In the second column, assume that you have been gainfully employed for 5 to 10 years and that you are presently employed by a reputable firm at the prevailing salary for the type of job and industry you are in. In the third column, try to assume that 25 to 30 years from now you have "found your niche in life" and have been working for a reputable employer for several years. (Rank your first choice as "1," second as "2," and so forth through "10.")

Ranking of Selected Employment Factors

Employment factor	As you seek your first full-time job	Your ranking 5–10 years later	Your ranking 25–30 years later
Fair adjustment of grievances			
Good job instruction and training			
Effective job supervision by your supervisor			
Promotion possibilities			
Recognition (praise, rewards, and so on)			
Job safety			
Job security (no threat of being dismissed or laid-off			
Good salary			
Good working conditions (nice office surroundings, good hours, and so on)			

Source: Leon C. Megginson, Donald C. Mosley, and Paul H. Pietri, Jr., *Management: Concepts and Applications,* 3d ed. (New York: Harper & Row, 1989), p. 312.

What Is Motivation?

Motivation, the process used by managers to bring out the best in employees by giving them reasons to perform better, is not easy. First of all, managers are *always* motivating employees—either positively, to perform, or negatively, to withhold performance—even when not conscious of doing so. When the manager gives employees a reason to perform better, he or she creates positive motivation; on the other hand, if the manager says or does something that annoys, frustrates, or antagonizes employees, they will react negatively and either withhold production or actually sabotage operations, as shown in the following example.

Some time ago, a customer went into a Hopper's Drive-In in a college town and ordered a banana split. When it came, something was obviously wrong. There were five scoops of ice cream, double portions of fruit and nuts, and a huge serving of whipped cream, with several cherries on top. The customer asked the young employee, "What's wrong?" The young man didn't even pretend not to understand. "I'm mad at the boss," he promptly replied. A few months later, the drive-in went out of business.

Two ways to succeed in business are to increase employee productivity and efficiency and to improve employee satisfaction. While there is a limit to improvements in employee productivity—people are rarely totally satisfied—effective motivation can have a positive effect on both. However, *because there are many factors that affect productivity and satisfaction, motivation alone is not enough.*

In general, employee performance is a product of the employee's ability to do the job, the application of positive motivation, and the extent to which the job meets the employee's expectations; that is,

$$\text{Performance} = \text{Ability} \times \text{Motivation} \times \text{Expectations}$$

Most employees go to work for a company expecting to do a good job, receive a satisfactory income, and gain satisfaction from doing a good job. However, performance and satisfaction are dependent on being able to do the job satisfactorily. If employees are not performing as expected, they may be unsuited for the job, inadequately trained, or unmotivated. If unsuited, move them to a more suitable job, and if untrained, train them. If they are both suited and trained, try harder to motivate them. But you must be careful to keep employee expectations realistic so as not to lead them to make unwarranted requests.

Why Motivate Employees?

One reason managerial motivation is so difficult to use is that there are different purposes for motivating people, and each of these requires different incentives. Usually managers use motivational techniques (1) to attract potential employees, (2) to improve performance, and (3) to retain good employees.

Attracting Potential Employees

Managers wanting to encourage potential employees to come to work for them must find and use incentives that would appeal to a person needing a job. These incentives usually include a good income, pleasant working conditions, and promotional possibilities.

The exercise in Figure 11–2 has been used with junior- and senior-level business students since 1957. "Good salary" has been the primary consideration in looking for a first job—with very few exceptions—in over 200 surveys reviewed, with "promotion possibilities" and "good working conditions" a close second and third. How did you rate these factors?

Improving Performance

Managerial motivation is also used to improve performance and efficiency on the part of present employees. Employers can motivate workers by praising good work, giving more responsibility to employees, publicly recognizing a job well done, and awarding merit salary increases.

Notice in the Opening Focus that Murry Evans treated his people well in order to bring out the best in them. He gave them personal attention and helped them with their problems.

Retaining Good Employees

Motivation can also be used to encourage present employees to stay with the company rather than leave for another job. This is accomplished primarily through the use of employee benefits, most of which are designed to reward employees who stay with the company.

There may be occasions when, because of poor performance or for other reasons, a business may want to use incentives to get undesirable employees to leave. During economic downturns or other financial reverses, a company might find it less expensive to "pay off" workers with a cash settlement or early retirement than to continue to pay their salary and benefits.

To reduce payroll costs, Amos Press, Inc., a printing firm in Sidney, Ohio, offered 17 of its 350 employees (those 60 and over) cash incentives and a series of educational seminars to retire. Eight chose retirement. It cost Amos $250,000 over five years, but it resulted in a net savings of $175,000.[8]

How to Motivate Employees

The theory of motivation is relatively simple (as shown in Figure 11–3). An employee has a need or needs, and management applies some kind of incentive (or stimulus) which promises to satisfy that need. The employee responds with favorable behavior, which results in job satisfaction, so that his or her needs are satisfied and the company achieves productivity and efficiency. Management's problem in motivating employees, then, is to know them well enough to know what they need and what incentives will stimulate them to perform.

Figure 11–3   The Motivational Process

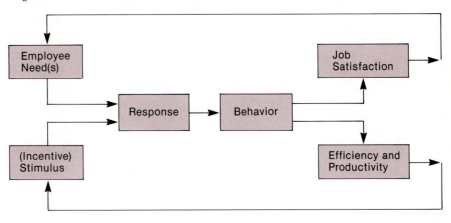

Source: Adapted from Leon C. Megginson, *Personnel: A Behavioral Approach,* 2nd ed. (Homewood, Ill.: Richard D. Irwin, 1972), p. 668.

Some Practical Ways to Improve Motivation

Some "tried and true" ways of improving motivation are:

- Quality circles.
- Zero defects programs.
- Job enrichment.
- Management by objectives.
- Variable work schedules.

These techniques offer promise for motivating people, especially in small businesses. Both quality circles and zero defects programs were originally developed in the United States, then were adopted and perfected by the Japanese, and now are being extensively used again in the United States.

Quality circles (QCs) are small, organized work groups meeting periodically to find ways to improve quality and output. They motivate by getting employees involved and taking advantage of their creativity and innovativeness.

The **zero defects** approach is based on getting workers to do their work "right the first time," thus generating pride of workmanship. It assumes that employees want to do a good job—if permitted to.

Job enrichment emphasizes giving employees greater responsibility and authority over their job, as the best way to motivate them. Employees are encouraged to learn new and related skills or even to trade jobs with each other as ways of making the job more interesting and therefore more productive.

As discussed in Chapter 6, the purpose of **management by objectives (MBO),** also called **goal-centered performance appraisals,** is for managers and employees to work together to set goals for the organization, their division, and themselves, and then to use those goals as guides to performance and as a means of evaluating it.

Variable work schedules permit employees to work at times other than the standard workweek of five eight-hour days.[9] Such schedules are being extensively used—especially by small firms—to motivate employees. **Flexitime** allows employees to schedule their own hours as long as they are present during certain required hours, called *core time.* This gives employees greater control over their time and activities. **Job splitting** is dividing a single full-time job into distinct parts and letting two (or more) employees do the different parts. In **job sharing,** a single full-time job is shared by two (or more) employees, with one doing all aspects of the job at one time and the other at another time, as the following example shows.

Cheryl Houser, burned out after selling ads for the *Seattle Weekly* for four years, wanted time to travel, do volunteer work, and, eventually, have a baby. Carol Cummins, a co-worker expecting a baby, also wanted to work part time. Being good salespeople, they talked their boss, Jane Levine, vice-president of advertising and marketing, into letting them share one full-time job. Houser works on Mondays and Thursdays, Cummins on Wednesdays and Fridays, and both come in on Tuesdays.

In exchange for lighter work duties, since they work only three days a week, the paper gets two seasoned workers for the price of one.[10]

Small business owners are faced with a dilemma when considering these motivational programs. They may believe that using the new methods will improve employee performance—and hence increase profits. But they may not have the knowledge, time, money, or personnel to implement them.

Does Money Motivate Employees?

As you will remember, most students say "good salary" is the first thing they will be looking for in their first job (see Figure 11–2). Also, several studies have indicated that money motivates. For example, one poll found that 69 percent of U.S. workers would work harder to earn more money if the added income were taxed at a lower rate.[11] Yet other studies found that psychic rewards may be more significant than monetary rewards.[12] We believe that money motivates, but so do many other factors, as indicated in the Opening Focus.

Research and practical experience indicate that, while money is a powerful motivator, it is not the only one. At our lower level of needs—physiological and safety-security needs—money is the primary motivator. But above that level, money (particularly day wages) tends to decline in significance, and the higher-level needs become more important. This position tends to be confirmed by a study of the most important factors in motivating employees.

While compensation is one of the top four, the other three are working conditions, job security, and self-actualization, which do not involve money.[13]

Motivation Is More than Mere Technique

Successful motivation of employees is based more on a managerial philosophy than using a given technique. Successful managers try to create an environment in their small firms in which employees can apply themselves willingly and wholeheartedly to the task of increasing productivity and efficiency. This thought was expressed by Clarence Francis, chairman of General Foods, when he said: "You can buy a man's time; you can buy a man's physical presence at a given place; you can even buy a measured number of skilled muscular motions per hour or day; but you cannot buy enthusiasm; you cannot buy initiative; you cannot buy loyalty; you cannot buy devotion of hearts, minds, and souls. You have to earn these things."[14]

APPRAISING EMPLOYEES' PERFORMANCE

Managers of small businesses need an effective system of **personnel appraisal** (also called **employee evaluation** or **merit rating**) to enable them to answer the question: How well are my people performing? Under such a system, each employee's performance and progress are evaluated, and rewards are given for above-average performance. Often, this method is used in determining merit salary increases.

If an MBO program (or its equivalent) is not being used, employee appraisals are usually based on such factors as:

- Quantity and quality of work performed.
- Cooperativeness.
- Initiative.
- Dependability, including attendance.
- Job knowledge.
- Ability to work with others.
- Safety.
- Personal habits.

Each of these factors can be evaluated as, for example, superior, above average, average, below average, or poor. The person's wage or salary is then determined from the evaluation.

Employee evaluations should be related to promotions and salary increases in addition to identifying marginal workers and designing training activities for them. They can also be used to motivate employees—if the evaluations are really translated into rewards.

As small businesses have felt increasing pressure to improve productivity, evaluating employee performance has become a vital concern for those who want to get the best output from their people. While most companies do it, few of them do it well.[15]

COMPENSATING EMPLOYEES

Another aspect of leading and rewarding employees is providing what employees consider "fair" pay for their activities. Their earnings should be high enough to motivate them to be good producers, yet low enough for the business to maintain satisfactory profits.

Legal Influences

There are many federal and state laws affecting how much small business owners pay their employees (see Figure 11–4 for the primary federal laws involved). According to the **Fair Labor Standards Act of 1938** (also called the wage and hour law), employees must be paid a **minimum wage** for all hours of work up to 40 hours a week.[16] Above 40 hours, they must be paid one-and-a-half times their hourly rate of pay (called *time-and-a-*

Figure 11–4   Legal Influence on Compensation and Hours of Work

Laws	Coverage	Basic requirements	Agencies involved
Public Construction Act (Davis-Bacon Act)	Employers with federal construction contracts or subcontracts of $2,000 or more.	Employers must pay at least the prevailing wages in the area, as determined by the Secretary of Labor; overtime is to be paid at 1½ times the basic wage for all work over 8 hours per day or 40 hours per week.	Wage and Hour Division of the Labor Department.
Public Contracts Act (Walsh-Healy Act)	Employers with federal contracts of $10,000 or more.	Same as above.	Same as above.
Fair Labor Standards Act (wage and hour law)	Private employers engaged in interstate commerce; retailers having annual sales of $325,000. Many groups are exempted from overtime requirements.	Employers must pay a minimum of $3.35 per hour and 1½ times the basic rate for work over 40 hours per week and are limited (by jobs and school status) in employing persons under 18.	Same as above.
Equal Pay Act	All employers.	Men and women must receive equal pay for jobs requiring substantially the same skill, working conditions, effort, and responsibility.	Equal Employment Opportunity Commission
Service Contracts Act	Employers with contracts to provide services worth $2,500 or more per year to the federal government.	Same as Davis-Bacon.	Same as Davis-Bacon.

Source: Leon C. Megginson, *Personnel Management,* 5th ed. (Homewood, Ill.: Richard D. Irwin, 1985), chap 4, p. 114. Extracted form the Bureau of National Affairs, Inc., BNA Policy and Practice Series: *Wages and Hours* (Washington, D.C.: Bureau of National Affairs).

half). Certain managerial and professional personnel—as well as part-time students—are exempt from the provisions of the act.

For most nonfarm jobs, 14 is the minimum working age for pay. Workers aged 14 and 15 can work on nonhazardous jobs for up to 3 hours on a school day and 8 hours on any other day, but no more than 18 hours per week from 7 A.M. to 7 P.M. during the school term. Those aged 16 and 17 can work an unlimited time on nonhazardous jobs. Both part- and full-time students can be paid at rates less than the minimum wage. Finally, certain retail and service businesses and service stations don't have to comply if their annual sales are less than $500,000. Laundry, fabric care, dry cleaning, and some construction firms also qualify for exemptions.

The **Equal Pay Act of 1963** requires that women be paid the same rate as men for doing the same general type of work. Also, EEO laws (discussed in Chapter 11) require that pay for minorities, older workers, handicapped workers, and veterans be the same as for others.

Since each state's laws vary so much from every other's and from the federal law, we won't try to discuss them.

Setting Rates of Pay

In addition to legal factors, many variables influence what employees consider a "fair wage." First, employees feel that they should be paid in proportion to their physical and mental efforts on the job. The standard of living and cost of living in the area also matter. And unions help set wages in a geographic area through collective bargaining, whether the company itself is unionized or not. The economic factors of supply and demand for workers help set wages. Finally, the employer's ability to pay must be considered.

In actual practice, most small businesses pay either the minimum wage or the same wages that similar businesses in the area are paying. A small business paying less than the prevailing wage will have difficulty finding employees. Also, it cannot afford to pay much more unless its employees are more productive. Finally, small business managers pay whatever they have to in order to attract the people they really need—and can afford.

For example, CleanDrum, Inc. (Case III–1), paid the minimum—$3.35 in 1989—to three of its unskilled workers, but $4.50, $5, and $6 to other, more skilled employees. One competitor paid similar wages, but another, which was highly automated, paid $10.

Using Money to Motivate

Many small business managers use some form of financial incentive to motivate their employees to use their initiative and to perform better. Some of the more popular financial incentives are (1) merit increases, (2) incentive payments, and (3) profit sharing. One study found that nearly a third of U.S. companies offer employees profit sharing or cash incentive awards

Figure 11–5   New Pay Programs Grow Popular

Pay raises are not the only way companies reward employees any more. Here's the percentage of U.S. companies using non-traditional forms of compensation:

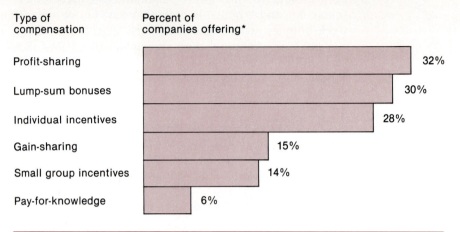

Type of compensation	Percent of companies offering*
Profit-sharing	32%
Lump-sum bonuses	30%
Individual incentives	28%
Gain-sharing	15%
Small group incentives	14%
Pay-for-knowledge	6%

* Some companies offer more than one plan.

Source: "Plans Become Labor's Latest Battleground," *USA Today,* November 7, 1989, p. 1B. Copyright 1989, USA TODAY. Adapted with permission.

in addition to regular merit increases and management bonuses.[17] Figure 11–5 shows the results of a survey of 1,598 small and large manufacturing and service companies by the American Productivity and Quality Center. Notice how popular profit sharing, lump-sum bonuses, and individual incentive payments are.

Merit Increases

Merit increases, which base a person's wage or salary on ability and merit rather than on seniority or some other factor, tend to be effective. By design, merit programs identify, appraise, and reward employees for outstanding contribution toward the company's profit. Thus, an employee's wage or salary relates directly to that person's efforts to achieve the employer's objectives.

Incentive Payments

Incentive payments can be paid in the form of (1) incentive wages, (2) commissions, (3) bonuses, (4) push money, and others.

An **incentive wage** is the extra compensation paid for all production over a specified amount. This type of compensation works in situations where a worker can control the volume of sales or production. Piece rates, commissions, and bonuses are forms of inventive wages. Under a **piece**

rate system, employees' earnings are based on a rate per unit times the number of units produced. Usually, some form of guaranteed base rate ensures that each employee earns a minimum amount. Piece rates are usually used in production- or operations-type activities.

A study of the effects of using piece rates in the corrugated shipping container industry found that 16 of 18 operations showed significantly increased productivity after use of such incentives. Productivity per employee increased around 75 percent on the average.[18]

Commissions, which consist of a given amount per sale or a percentage of sales, are used extensively to reward salespeople, especially in retailing. They particularly are used in door-to-door selling of items such as encyclopedias and magazine subscriptions but are also used by most department stores and similar retail outlets.

Bonuses are amounts given to employees either for exceeding their production quotas or as a reward on special occasions. Many production or sales personnel have work quotas and receive bonuses if they exceed that amount.

Delta Business Systems Inc., which sells, leases, and services office equipment, offers some 20 different incentive programs to its 315 employees. Of these programs, 13 are available to its 215 nonsales people. Secretaries and administrative assistants compete for a $50 monthly "Most Valuable Associate" award. Each dispatcher can earn up to $40 a month by scheduling preventive maintenance calls. The four warehouse workers can divide up to $400 every two months by functioning smoothly as a team. This bonus system has been effective because it "makes employees accountable for their own performance."[19]

A form of incentive pay that does not fall neatly into any of the categories is called **push money (PM).** Under this arrangement, employees have a given wage or salary. But if they sell a unit of some item that the business is pushing, such as a given brand of candy or music system, they receive a certain share—usually 10 percent—of the sale as push money.

Profit Sharing

In **profit sharing,** employees receive a prearranged share of the company's profits. Profit sharing can be quite effective in motivating employees by tying rewards to company performance. Not only does it reward good performance, but a good plan can reduce turnover, increase productivity, and reduce the amount of supervision needed.

In 1982, Sheeran Cleveland Architects had lost five of its seven full-time architects and designers in one year to larger, better-established firms. Peter Sheeran, the president, wanted to find a way to reward people so they would know that the harder they worked, the more money they would earn. He introduced a plan that paid out 50 percent of the firm's earnings to employees. Productivity jumped, people started working harder and assuming more responsibility, turnover slowed dramatically, and the firm could recruit able architects and designers from competing companies.[20]

Employee stock ownership plans (ESOPs) are a modification of profit sharing. In general, an ESOP borrows money, purchases a block of the company's stock, and allocates it to the employees on the basis of salaries and/or longevity. Each year, management places a portion of its profits in the ESOP fund, which in turn uses the money to pay off the loan. Since the workers do not actually receive their shares until they retire or leave the company, they do not have to pay taxes on them until they withdraw their shares. These plans are particularly attractive to small companies because they (1) provide a source of needed capital, (2) boost the company's cash flow, (3) raise employee morale and productivity, and (4) provide a lucrative new employee benefit.

There were around 9,000 worker-owned firms—employing nearly 9.3 million people—in 1988, and most of them were small firms employing fewer than 200 workers.[21]

People Express Airline Inc. was worker owned when it was formed in 1980. All employees owned some shares of the company, which they could buy at big discounts. This practice led to a "sense of mission" among the people who worked for the company.[22] Later, when People Express got into financial difficulty and began to lose money, the program was less popular.

Compensating Managerial and Professional Personnel

In general, managers of small businesses are paid on a merit basis, with their income based on the firm's earnings. Many small companies also use profit sharing, bonuses, or some other method of stimulating the interest of managerial and professional personnel.

Managers of Radio Shack stores receive a share of profits if their store's profit margin is 10 percent or more. For example, if a given store has an 11 percent profit margin, the manager gets 11 percent of those profits as a bonus; with a 15 percent profit margin, the manager takes home an extra 15 percent of profits.[23]

Employee Benefits

Employee benefits (sometimes called **fringe benefits**) are the monetary and other types of rewards and services provided to employees in addition to their regular earnings. Figure 11–6 shows some of the most popular employee benefits. In general, these benefits increase in importance as employees' lifestyles expand and it takes more than just wages to satisfy them.

Benefits are costly! And once given, they are difficult—if not impossible—to take back. Moreover, their cost is rising much faster than wages. For example, while wages increased 3.7 percent from 1987 to 1988, benefit costs rose 6.7 percent.[24]

Figure 11–6   Some of the Most Popular Employee Benefits

1. Legally required:
   Social security
   Unemployment insurance
   Workers' compensation
2. Voluntary, private:
   a. Health and accident insurance:
      Eye care and eyeglasses
      Chiropractic care
      Dental and orthodontic care
      Health maintenance—diagnostic
         visits/physical exams
      Major medical/hospitalization
      Psychiatric and mental care
      Accident and sickness insurance
   b. Life and disability insurance:
      Accidental death and
         dismemberment
      Group term life insurance
      Long-term disability
   c. Sick leave, including maternity leave
   d. Income maintenance:
      Severance pay
      Supplemental unemployment
         benefits (SUBs)
      Pensions
   e. Pay for time off:
      Holidays
      Personal time
      Sabbatical leaves
      Union activities
      Vacations

   f. Employee services and others:
      Alcohol and drug rehabilitation
      Auto insurance
      Child care and day-care center for other
         family members
      Christmas bonuses
      Clothing and uniforms
      Company car
      Credit unions
      Discount privileges on organization's
         products or services
      Loans and financial assistance
      Food services and cafeteria
      Group tours and charter flights
      Gymnasium and physical training center
      Legal assistance
      Liability coverage
      Matching gifts to charitable
         organizations or schools
      Matching payroll deductions and
         savings plans
      Moving and transfer allowances
      Personal counseling and financial advice
      Recreation center
      Service awards
      Stock purchase and profit-sharing plans
      Transportation and parking
      Tuition for employee and/or family
         members

Source: Leon C. Megginson, *Personnel Management,* 5th ed. (Homewood, Ill.: Richard D. Irwin, 1985), p. 521.

While the average employer pays about 35 cents on top of every dollar of a worker's basic earnings as benefits, small firms are not as free with their benefits. For example, while 91 percent of workers at larger firms are covered by pension plans, only 43 percent at companies with fewer than 100 workers are covered.[25]

Small firms have been hurt by Section 89, which Congress passed requiring that businesses offering tax-exempt employee benefits must offer the same benefits to lower-paid workers as to highly paid ones. In 1989, the law was amended to ease the paperwork required.

Legally Required Benefits

Small employers are legally required to provide Social Security, unemployment insurance, and workers' compensation.[26] Also, since 1986, employers with 20 or more employees must continue health insurance for up to 18 months for employees when they are terminated—either voluntarily or otherwise—and up to 36 months for widows, divorced or separated spouses, and dependents of employees.[27]

Under **Social Security,** employers act as both taxpayers and tax collectors. They must pay a tax on each employee's earnings and deduct a comparable amount from each employee's paycheck. In 1990, the tax rate was 7.65 percent, and the taxable wage base was $51,300; so employers *and* employees each had to pay a maximum of $3,924. Self-employed people must pay the entire cost themselves, which is twice the listed amount (15.3 percent in 1990, or a maximum of $7,849). Since Congress changes these figures periodically, check with the local Social Security Administration office for the latest figures.

Unemployment insurance was also provided for by the Social Security Act. State governments receive most of the tax, which can be as high as 4.7 percent of the first $8,000 of each employee's pay, while the rest goes to the U.S. government for administrative costs. If the business can lower its unemployment rate, the tax is reduced under a merit rating system. Using funds from the tax, the state pays unemployed workers a predetermined amount each week. This amount varies from state to state.

Employee losses from accidents and occupational diseases are paid for under state **workers' compensation** laws. Each employer's plans are required to pay insurance premiums to either a state fund or a private insurance company. The accumulated funds are used to compensate victims of industrial accidents or illnesses. A firm's premiums depend on the hazards involved and the effectiveness of its safety programs. The amount paid to an employee or to his or her estate is fixed according to the type and extent of injury.

Other Employee Benefits

As shown in Figure 11–6, there are many voluntary benefits in addition to the legally required ones. Health, accident, life, and disability insurance

Figure 11–7   General Provisions of the Employee Retirement Income Security Act

Coverage	Basic requirements	Agencies involved
All employee benefit plans of employers engaged in interstate commerce and with 25 or more employees.	Benefit plans must meet certain minimum standards for employee participation, vesting rights, funding, reporting, and disclosure. Plans must be funded on an actuarially sound basis. Vested benefits are to be insured through Pension Benefit Guaranty Corporation (PBGC).	Department of Labor Internal Revenue Service Pension Benefit Guaranty Corporation (PBGC)

Source: Extracted from F. Ray Marshall, Allan G. King, and Vernon M. Briggs, Jr., *Labor Economics,* 4th ed. (Homewood, Ill.: Richard D. Irwin, 1980), especially chap. 17.

are popular with small businesses and their employees. In trade and service businesses, discounts on the firm's goods or services are also well received.

Pension programs were common in small firms until the passage of the **Employee Retirement Income Security Act (ERISA)** in 1974 (see Figure 11–7 for its basic provisions). Because the law proved too complex and difficult for small businesses to conform to, many of them decided to give up their voluntary pension programs.[28]

For example, Ronald Turner, a third-generation lumber company owner in Clarksburg, West Virginia, dropped his employee pension plan when Congress modified ERISA in 1989. Saying that the changes made the benefit program too costly and complex to maintain, he gave the employees the cash due them from the fund. He had tried to obey the law, but quit after the required paperwork grew from 35 to 77 pages, and the IRS disqualified the plan "on a technicality."[29]

Many small firms have decided to let their employees establish private pension programs using **individual retirement accounts (IRAs).** Under the 1986 Tax Reform Act, a taxpayer who is not covered by a qualified employer retirement plan, who has a taxable income of less than $40,000 for a married couple filing jointly or $25,000 for a single taxpayer, may make a deductible contribution of $2,000 annually to a qualified IRA account (plus $250 to the spouse's account). As the requirements are so complex— and change frequently—check with your tax or financial adviser.

Another financial benefit permits self-employed persons and partnerships to set up tax-deferred retirement programs. Up to $30,000 a year—but no more than 25 percent of the person's eligible total earnings—can be put into a **Keogh retirement plan** and deducted from income taxes.[30]

COMPUTER UPDATE

COMPUTER SPECIALISTS, INC.: FLEXIBLE SPENDING ACCOUNTS

Computer software has made it technically and economically feasible for small companies to use cafeteria-style benefit programs. The employees at Computer Specialists, Inc., a contract programming business in Monroeville, Pennsylvania, have such a flexible-spending account. They can choose from a menu of benefits that includes the typical ones, such as medical and dental insurance and vacation days, and not-so-typical ones, such as car payments, adoption assistance, and a clothing allowance. One employee was "frightened to death" to drive; so the company picked up her $105 monthly cab bill, in addition to paying for her new eyeglasses, a pair of shoes, and a dress. Incidentally, she had to pay income tax on the last three items.

Source: Ellen Kolton, "Fringe Benefits: True Flexibility," *Inc.*, July 1985, p. 104.

A small business with employees may choose to establish a **simplified employee pension (SEP) plan** to help workers provide for their retirement. Employees open their own IRAs—at a place of their choice. Then the employer pays 15 percent of each employee's salary, or $3,000, whichever is less, into that employee's IRA account each year. In this way, workers can take their pensions with them if they leave their employers. There are some restrictions.[31]

Finally, some employers have **401(k) plans,** which permit workers to place up to $7,000 of their wages annually in tax-deferred retirement savings plans. Employers can match the employees' contributions (and often do) on a one-for-one basis. A 10 percent penalty results if the employee withdraws the money before age 59½.[32]

Flexible Approach to Benefits

Cafeteria-style benefit plans help reduce the 10 to 20 percent annual increase in benefit costs.[33] Under this system, all employees are told the dollar value of benefits they are entitled to receive. Each employee then tells the employer how to allocate the money among a variety of available programs. This system increases employee awareness of the value of the benefits and offers freedom of choice and a personalized approach (see Computer Update).

NEED FOR AN INTEGRATED APPROACH

We would like to end this discussion of leading and motivating employees by returning to the ideas expressed in the Opening Focus. The small business owner needs to use more than just financial rewards to get employees to perform. Instead, you need to hire good people, train them well, communicate with them, let them make suggestions, provide them with an equitable income, and offer innovative employee benefits. The following example incorporates most of these ideas.

Jim Miller, CEO of Intermatic, Inc., claims its personnel policies and programs have been the key to its growth, profitability, and survival. In fact, he thinks this philosophy saved the Spring Grove, Illinois, producer of timing devices and low-voltage lighting from disaster.

In 1970, when Intermatic was on the verge of bankruptcy, Miller, a former employee, was asked to return as president. To save the company, he reduced the work force by 50 percent, closed down one division, restructured the staff, consolidated positions, and instituted the employee relations policies and programs that have since assured the firm's success.

An incentive system for production workers earns them about 135 percent of their base pay, and some of the unusual employee benefits are:

- Programs that pay workers to shed pounds.
- Free eye examinations and glasses.
- Aerobics classes.

Jim Miller
Source: Photo courtesy of Intermatic, Inc.

- Golf lessons.
- An outside exercise course.
- An indoor track.
- Tennis courts.
- Membership in arts-and-culture clubs.
- Shopping at company-subsidized stores for items such as jeans, T-shirts, and baseball caps.
- Reimbursement for tuition for college courses.

In addition, Miller is quite open in his communications with employees, telling them what has to be done and why it must be done. He also is available to help people with their personal problems, knows them by name, and knows their family situations.

The payoff? Turnover is only 3 percent, compared to over 5 percent for similar firms, and it has become such a popular place to work that there's a waiting list of people seeking employment with Intermatic.[34]

WHAT YOU SHOULD HAVE LEARNED

1. To be successful, small business managers must provide the kind of leadership and compensation that will inspire workers to perform productively. Part of the secret lies in good human relations: working with people in a way that makes them feel useful, understood, and valued. A managerial philosophy based on Theory Y assumptions can be a step in the right direction.

2. Leadership, although an important part of management, should not be confused with it. Leadership is the ability to inspire others to reach objectives that are not necessarily their personal goals. The most commonly used styles of leadership are autocratic, democratic (participative), and laissez-faire (free rein). Effective managers use each of these styles at various times, depending on the characteristics of the situation and the people involved.

3. Managers spend around 80 percent of their time communicating. Communication, as an exchange of meaning, is completed only when the receiver demonstrates understanding of the message through some form of feedback. Barriers to effective communication include the status of the communicator (lack of credibility), imprecise use of language, jargon, and poor listening. Managers can become better communicators by (*a*) identifying the audience and environment of the communication, (*b*) considering the emotional overtones of the message, (*c*) following up on the communication, and (*d*) being good listeners.

4. Motivation is the process used to bring out the best in employees. Managers need to increase employee productivity and improve employee satisfaction through effective motivation. Management's problem in motivating employees is to know them well enough to know what incentives will stimulate them to perform. Different incentives must be used according to the purpose of the motivation. To attract potential employees, managers must offer a good income, pleasant working conditions, and promotional possibilities. To improve performance, they can use praise and public recognition of good work, merit salary increases, and added responsibility. To retain good employees, managers must also provide employee benefits.

   Some currently popular motivational techniques include quality circles, zero-defects programs, job enrichment, management by objectives (MBO), and variable work schedules.

   Although managers may use various techniques to improve employee motivation, they must realize that motivation is more than mere technique. The best motivators are based on a managerial philosophy that recognizes the worth of employees and expects the best from them.

5. Money is an important motivator to small business owners and employees. The small business must pay its employees enough to attract and keep them. Going beyond the minimum level of compensation required to get and keep employees—and conform to various laws—management can use wages to motivate through merit increases, incentive payments, and profit sharing. Merit increases publicly reward improved performance and serve to motivate others. Incentive payments, such as incentive wages, commissions, bonuses, or push money, reward performance more directly by tying compensation to productivity. Profit sharing rewards all employees of a firm when productivity increases; it may be more satisfactory where individual performance is hard to measure or a team spirit is desirable. Employee stock ownership plans (ESOPs), a modification of profit sharing, have been successful in some firms.

   Compensating managerial and professional personnel is sometimes more complex, but they can also be paid on a merit basis, with their income based on the firm's earnings.

   Employee benefits, which are increasingly important to both employees and employers, are quite costly. While Social Security, unemployment insurance, and workers' compensation are legally required, pension plans and various kinds of insurance have always been popular voluntary benefits. Now, however, many small companies encourage employees to set up their own retirement plans using individual retirement accounts (IRAs) or 401(k) plans. Individual employers also offer a variety of other benefits and sometimes let employees choose their own benefits.

6. Appraising employees' performance is an important part of small business management. Merit raises and promotions should be based on such performance appraisals, and employee evaluation can also point up possible training and development needs in specific areas.

7. In today's business environment, managers have felt increasing pressure to improve productivity. To do this, leadership and motivation are vital, compensation can provide a part of the motivation, and employee evaluation can show how well managers are succeeding in motivating employees to perform better.

KEY TERMS

Theory X, *303*

Theory Y, *303*

autocratic leadership, *304*

democratic (participative) leadership, *304*

laissez-faire (free-rein) leadership, *304*

communication, *304*

jargon, *306*

motivation, *308*

quality circles (QCs), *311*

zero defects, *311*

job enrichment, *311*

management by objectives (MBO) (or goal-centered performance appraisal), *312*

flexitime, *312*

job splitting, *312*

job sharing, *312*

personnel appraisal (employee evaluation, merit rating), *313*

Fair Labor Standards Act of 1938, *314*

minimum wage, *314*

Equal Pay Act of 1963, *315*

merit increases, *316*

incentive wage, *316*

piece rate, *316–17*

commissions, *317*

bonuses, *317*

push money (PM), *317*

profit sharing, *317*

employee stock ownership plans (ESOPs), *318*

employee benefits (or fringe benefits), *319*

Social Security, *320*

unemployment insurance, *320*

workers' compensation, *320*

Employee Retirement Income Security Act (ERISA), *321*

individual retirement accounts (IRAs), *321*

Keogh retirement plan, *321*

simplified employee pension (SEP) plan, *322*

401(k) plan, *322*

cafeteria-style benefit plan, *322*

QUESTIONS FOR DISCUSSION

1. How would you define (or explain) "good human relations"?
2. (*a*) List and describe the three most commonly used leadership styles. (*b*) Which one does your instructor most often use in this course?
3. (*a*) Why is communication so important in a small business? (*b*) What are some barriers to effective communication? (*c*) How can these barriers be overcome?
4. (*a*) What is motivation? (*b*) Why is it so important to a small business manager?
5. What are some practical ways to improve employee motivation?
6. How would you explain the role of money in employee motivation?
7. (*a*) What is the purpose of personnel appraisals? (*b*) Why are they so important?
8. What are some legal restraints that affect how much a company pays its employees?
9. What are some of the other factors that affect the amount and form of compensation paid to employees?
10. How can wages be used to motivate employees to perform better?
11. (*a*) Explain the three legally required employee benefits. (*b*) What are some of the other benefits frequently used by small businesses?

SUGGESTED READINGS

Alvarez, Elizabeth. "How to Delegate When There's No One to Delegate to." *Working Woman,* February 1987, pp. 51–52.

Garland, Susan B., and Howard Gleckman. "Health Insurance: A Tax-Reformed Footnote Trips Up Small Business." *Business Week,* January 30, 1989, p. 45.

Hannon, James P. "Should Your Company Adopt an ESOP?" *Management Accounting,* January 1989, pp. 31–35.

Labich, Kenneth. "Hot Company, Warm Culture." *Fortune,* February 27, 1989, pp. 74–76.

Nelton, Sharon. "Motivating for Success." *Nation's Business,* March 1989, pp. 18–24.

"One Size Doesn't (Bene)fit All." *Nation's Business,* December 1988, pp. 35–36.

"Pocket Guide to Money: Retirement Plans." *Consumer Reports,* January 1990, p. 16.

Randall, Robert F. "The Coming Crunch in Employee Benefits." *Management Accounting,* January 1989, pp. 18–22.

Ricklefs, Roger. "Health Insurance Becomes a Big Pain for Small Firms." *The Wall Street Journal,* December 6, 1988, p. B1.

Saltzman, Amy. "One Job, Two Contented Workers." *U.S. News & World Report,* November 14, 1988, pp. 74–76.

Williams, Kathy. "Small Business (Unemployment Compensation Fund Reform Is No. 1 Issue)." *Management Accounting,* April 1989, p. 37.

ENDNOTES

1. Alfred G. Edge and Ronald Greenwood, "How Managers Rank Knowledge, Skills and Atttributes Possessed by Business Administration Graduates," *AACSB Bulletin* 2 (1974): 32.

2. "Ben & Jerry's Homemade Inc.," *The Wall Street Journal,* Centennial Edition, 1989, p. A28.

3. Douglas McGregor, *The Human Side of Enterprise* (New York: McGraw-Hill, 1960).

4. Joshua Hyatt, "The Odyssey of an Excellent Man," *Inc.,* February 1989, pp. 63–69.

5. For more information on this topic, see Rosemary Stewart, *Managers and Their Jobs* (New York: Macmillan, 1967); and Henry Mintzberg, *The Nature of Managerial Work* (New York: Harper & Row, 1973), p. 38.

6. Ralph W. Weber and Gloria E. Perry, *Behavioral Insights for Supervisors* (Englewood Cliffs, N.J.: Prentice-Hall, 1975), p. 138.

7. *The Wall Street Journal,* February 5, 1985, p. 1.

8. Ellen Kolton, "An Offer They Couldn't Refuse," *Inc.,* April 1985, pp. 155–56.

9. See Beth Brophy, "Time Clocks Keep More Varied Beats," *USA Today,* April 16, 1986, p. 1A.

10. Amy Saltzman, "One Job, Two Contented Workers," *U.S. News & World Report,* November 14, 1988, pp. 74 and 76.

11. William Giese, "Losing Incentive to Work," *USA Today,* March 13, 1984, p. 3B.

12. Stanley Sloan and David E. Schrieber, "Incentives: Are They Relevant? Obsolete? Misunderstood?" *Personnel Administrator,* January–February 1970, pp. 25–27.

13. William E. Rief, "Intrinsic versus Extrinsic Rewards: Resolving the Controversy," *Human Resource Management* 14 (Summer 1975): 7.

14. Speech on "Management Methods," 1952; reprinted in *Management Methods Magazine,* 1952.

15. Berkeley Rice, "Evaluating Employees," *Venture,* September 1985, pp. 33–34.

16. The rate was $3.80 an hour at the time of publication and was scheduled to be raised to $4.25 in April 1991. Since this rate is subject to change, however, check with the Wage and Hour Division of the Department of Labor for the latest information. See also Barbara Marsh, "Effects of Minimum Wage Increase Seen as Manageable," *The Wall Street Journal,* November 11, 1989, p. B2, for a history of how the minimum wage has increased from the original rate of $0.25 in 1938.

17. "Added Incentives," *The Wall Street Journal,* November 20, 1985, p. 1.

18. Donald L. McManis and William G. Dick, "Monetary Incentives in Today's Industrial Setting," *Personnel Journal* 52 (May 1973), pp. 387–89.

19. Ellen Kolton, "Paddling for Profits," *Inc.,* March 1985, pp. 137–38.

20. Donna Sammons Carpenter, "We're in the Money," *Inc.,* November 1984, pp. 183–84.

21. Anne Zidonis, "Avis Puts Workers in Driver's Seat," *USA Today,* December 15, 1988, p. 1B.

22. *The Wall Street Journal,* July 26, 1983, p. 1.

23. For more details, see "At Radio Shack, Six-Day Weeks and Six-Figure Bonuses," *Business Week,* September 15, 1983, p. 95; and Margaret Magnus, "Personnel Policies in Partnership with Profit," *Personnel Journal* 66 (September 1987): 102–9.

24. "Benefit Costs Are Surging," *USA Today,* December 15, 1989, p. 1A.

25. "Pension Coverage Eludes Most Workers at Small Firms," *The Wall Street Journal,* September 13, 1989, p. 1.

26. See David W. McFadden, "Employee Fringe Benefits Expense," *Management Accounting,* January 1989, pp. 24–30, for details on these programs.

27. Steven P. Galante, "Employees Face Higher Costs as Congress Mandates Benefits," *The Wall Street Journal,* June 16, 1986, p. 37.

28. Bryna Brennan, "Small Firms Dropping Pension Plans; Laws Too Complex," *Birmingham* (Alabama) *News,* December 17, 1989, p. 2D.

29. Ibid.

30. See "Retirement," *U.S. News & World Report,* November 18, 1985, p. 55, for a fuller explanation of IRAs and Keogh plans.

31. Carol Lee Morgan, "You *Can* Take It with You," *Parade Magazine,* May 7, 1989, pp. 22–23.

32. The IRS has tightened the rules so that before you can withdraw those funds, even for emergencies, you may have to prove that they are your only source of funds and that you can't raise cash by borrowing or selling assets, including investments and property owned by your spouse or children. For more details, see Leonard Wiener, "A New Clamp on 401(k)'s," *U.S. News & World Report,* November 14, 1988, p. 76.

33. Daniel Cohen, "A Flexible Approach," *Venture,* June 1985, pp. 34–35.

34. Correspondence with Intermatic, Inc.

12

MAINTAINING RELATIONSHIPS WITH EMPLOYEES

The highest and best form of efficiency is the spontaneous cooperation of a free people.— Woodrow Wilson

*You can't manage people—you can only work with them. For your business to succeed, you must work closely with them and take exceedingly good care of them.—*Paul Hawken, *Growing a Business*

LEARNING OBJECTIVES

After studying the material in this chapter, you will be able to:

1. List some factors influencing employee safety and tell how the Occupational Safety and Health Administration operates to safeguard employees in small firms.
2. Discuss ways in which efforts to protect the environment can affect small business.
3. Define *counseling,* describe its benefits to small business, and list some of the areas in which counseling may be needed.
4. Outline a procedure for handling employee complaints.
5. Outline a procedure for disciplining employees who cannot discipline themselves.
6. Discuss some of the complexities of dealing with unions.

MARY H. PARTRIDGE AND MICHAEL LEVY: "HIS AND HERS" BUSINESSES

Michael Levy and Mary H. Partridge, of The Woodlands, Texas, are married to each other but have separate businesses, using the same office and telephone. He owns and operates Michael Levy & Associates, consultants in training and organization development; she owns and is president of The Woodlands Consulting Group, consultants in personnel administration and human resource development.

Having separate businesses allows each of them to have his or her own sense of ownership and direction. It also permits each to develop her or his own clients and expertise. When they choose, or need, to use each other's specialized abilities, they collaborate. But when they do this, they try to keep clear who the decision maker is. In those instances, the decision maker remains practical, while using the other one as a creative resource. They find it "a nice mix."

Their traditional activities include training trainers for both small and large companies. They do this through formal group seminars or by working "one-on-one" to coach a company's supervisors or other persons responsible for training personnel. They also conduct seminars on training and development for middle managers.

As the environment has changed, the couple have adjusted their activities. The "fat trimming" of the oil industry, their primary clients, has led to an emphasis on developing the team after the layoffs, transfers, and terminations. They also help the remaining employees adjust to the need to do more and varied work with fewer employees. They refocus the managers' and employees' emphasis on the mission, objectives, and values of the business.

Photo courtesy of Michael Levy and Mary H. Partridge.

Much time is now spent on executive coaching. This involves "one-on-one" consulting with managers to improve their management approach, communication abilities, and leadership style.

"Practicing what they preach," the two consultants avoid hiring staff and incurring lots of overhead. Instead, when needed, they use a network of consultants whom they know well as independent contractors.

Levy and Partridge do very well with their his and hers personnel consulting businesses.

Source: Correspondence and discussions with Mary H. Partridge and Michael Levy.

The previous two chapters showed how to plan personnel requirements, recruit applicants, select capable people, train and develop employees, compensate them, motivate them, and appraise their performance. Now you should become familiar with some other important phases of the personnel function, such as protecting employee safety, cleaning up the environment, counseling disturbed employees, handling employees' grievances, exercising discipline, and dealing with labor unions. As the Opening Focus shows, there's a need to counsel and retrain the managers and employees left after a small business must lay off and terminate employees.

PROTECTING EMPLOYEES' SAFETY

Employee safety is a condition involving *relative* freedom from danger or injury. Totally safe working conditions, while theoretically possible, are impractical to provide in actuality. Part of this chapter looks at how small business owners and managers can maintain working conditions in which employees not only *are* safe but also *feel* safe. In other words, employees need to know that management cares about their safety.

Factors Influencing Safety

Many factors influence the existence of safe working conditions. These factors are too numerous for individual discussion. However, the most significant ones are covered here.

Organization Size

The smallest and largest firms tend to be the safest places to work. Statistically companies with under 20 or over 1,000 employees are considerably safer than those in between. By the same measure, the most dangerous places to work are those with 50 to 1,000 workers.[1]

Type of Industry and Occupation

The type of industry to which the business belongs influences the health and safety of the work area. Although their safety records change periodically, the least safe industries usually include longshoring, meat and meat products, roofing and sheet metal, lumber and wood products, and miscellaneous transport.[2]

The type of occupation also affects safety. Workplace dangers and injuries that were once considered likely only in construction and factories have now invaded offices and stores. For example, wrist injuries triggered by repeated motions—often called *carpal tunnel syndrome*—now affect telephone and computer operators, checkout clerks using scanners in supermarkets, and others. Back injuries are now prevalent among hotel and motel workers, as well as health care workers who must frequently lift patients or mattresses.

According to the Bureau of Labor Statistics, the illness and injury rate, on the average, in the private sector is 8.3 per 100 workers. Conversely, it is 10.7 for hotel and motel workers, and 14.2 for nursing and personal-care home workers.[3]

Human Variables

As Figure 12–1 shows, many human variables also influence safety. The most important of these variables are job satisfaction, personal characteristics, and management styles and attitudes. Studies indicate a close relationship between safety and employees' satisfaction with their work. It appears from progress made thus far that a short test to determine accident proneness is possible, but it might violate the Vocational Rehabilitation Act.

The Occupational Safety and Health Act

The **Occupational Safety and Health Act (OSHA),** which created the **Occupational Safety and Health Administration (OSHA)** to administer it, is intended to assure, so far as possible, safe and healthful working conditions for every employee and to preserve our human resources. The law covers most businesses that are engaged in interstate commerce and have one or more employees, except those covered by the Atomic Energy Act or the Federal Mine Safety Act.

Figure 12–1   Safety Is No Accident

Accidents don't just *happen;* they are caused. Among the many causes are human, environmental, and technical factors. In fact, safety engineers are convinced that accidents often result from individual personal qualitities. Patterns of accident frequency have shown that there are accident-prone people who can be identified during the selection procedure.

Several characteristics have been identified with "injury repeaters," as they are usually called. In general, they are: (1) blunt, abrupt, and impatient people who are quick to translate enthusiasm—or irritation—into physical reaction; (2) instinctive mavericks, compelled to cultivate a feeling of superiority over the people and institutions around them, as shown by a contempt for most of the prohibitions and warnings they encounter, including counseling concerning safety; and (3) generally given high scores on tests intended to measure "introversial and extroverisal distractibility."

Moreover, they react to pain differently from workers whose records are relatively accident free. While it cannot be said that accident-prone employees enjoy pain, it can be stated that they do not fear it, nor does it bother them nearly as much as it does other workers.

Another study found that accidents are caused by individuals who show tendencies toward emotional insecurity, low motivation, and aggressiveness directed toward themselves. This study corroborated an earlier one that concluded that accident-prone individuals showed hostility toward themselves.

Most industrial injuries occur in persons between the ages of 20 and 24. Above that age, the injury rate becomes progressively lower. A study of firms with low accident rates found that in firms where a high percentage of the employees were married, the accident rate was lower.

There is also a relationship between job satisfaction and safety. In fact, a study at one plant showed a close link between job satisfaction and a low injury rate.

Source: Extracted from Leon C. Megginson, *Personnel Management: A Human Resources Approach,* 5th ed. (Homewood, Ill.: Richard D. Irwin, 1985), pp. 407–9.

Employee Rights

Employees have several important rights under the act. First, if they believe that their employer's violation of job safety or health standards threatens physical harm, they may request an OSHA inspection. Employees may not be discharged or discriminated against for filing the complaint. Second, employees can participate in hearings when OSHA cites an employer and can protest if they think the penalty is too light. Third, they are entitled to information about the company's monitoring process for toxic and other hazardous materials. Finally, employee representatives can request the Department of Health and Human Services to determine if any potentially toxic substance is found in the place of employment and have safe exposure levels set for that substance.

Employer Obligations

Even though many accidents result from the employees' own carelessness and lack of safety consciousness, employees usually do not receive citations. Instead, OSHA holds employers responsible for making employees wear safety equipment.

For example, Sam Sawyer, a top-rated operator handling caustic soda, would wear his company-provided goggles only when his supervisor was around. His supervisor, Dave Watts, had caught him without them four times during the past six months (see Case III–4 for further details).

Employers are subject to fines for unsafe practices *irrespective* of whether any accidents actually occur. The small business owner or manager should provide safety training for supervisors and employees, encourage and follow up on employee compliance with safety regulations and precautions, and discipline employees for noncompliance. The act encourages increased examination and questioning of management's staffing decisions and equipment selection. To illustrate, employees may claim that a crew size is unsafe or that a machine is potentially dangerous.

Management Rights

Management can request a free health hazard evaluation by the National Institute of Occupational Safety and Health in HHS. Training may be obtained from OSHA and National Safety Council chapters. However, "dry runs" by OSHA inspectors are not permitted. If they do inspect a place of business, they must inspect fully and, if violations are found, cite and fine. The firm's workers' compensation insurance carrier may be helpful in suggesting ways to improve safety and employees' health. However, its approval does not guarantee the same from OSHA. Information useful to management may also be obtained from equipment manufacturers, other employers who have had an inspection, trade associations, and the local fire department. Management should provide effective coordination among managers and employees responsible for manufacturing, safety, medical care, industrial relations, and so forth.

Small business managers also may turn to a consultative service, paid for by OSHA. This service provides experts, who come in on request and make recommendations for improving the work area. If the business is cited by an inspector on a routine inspection and corrects the violations, these consultants can come in and inspect the improvements. If the improvements meet all inspection requirements, the consultant can give management a certificate of immunity from another inspection for one year.

Improvements in OSHA Enforcement

From management's point of view, many improvements in enforcement have occurred during recent years. For example:

- Businesses with fewer than eight employees no longer need to maintain injury and illness records. However, special reports are required for fatalities and accidents that hospitalize five or more persons.
- Inspectors must present a search warrant if management requests one, though few employers do.
- OSHA does not inspect firms with 10 or fewer employees in "relatively safe" industries. Nearly 80 percent of American firms are thus exempt from inspections.
- OSHA tries to stretch its limited number of inspectors by concentrating on workplaces with unsatisfactory records.

What are the results of these improvements? Although OSHA usually inspects fewer than 4 percent of the workplaces each year, injury and fatality rates declined between 1979 and 1983, after which the rates began to climb again. Because of a large increase in these rates in 1984, however, OSHA changed its inspection policy to make spot checks of companies generally exempt from full-scale inspections.[4]

The importance of the inspection program and its technical nature will keep it in a state of transition. Therefore, small firms are advised to use the resources suggested previously, as well as local chambers of commerce, area planning and development commissions, and local offices of the Small Business Administration. As indicated in Chapter 8, Small Business Administration loans could be available to help meet safety and health standards.

Since 1988, small businesses have found that the paperwork burden makes it especially difficult for them to comply with OSHA's Hazard Communications Standard. It requires *every* employer in the country to identify hazardous substances in the workplace, list them, and train employees to use them safely. At first, the law applied only to manufacturers, but now the rule applies to all—"from accountants to zookeepers."[5] Contact OSHA for further details.

ENVIRONMENTAL PROTECTION

In 1970, the **Environmental Protection Agency (EPA)** was created under an act of the same title to help protect and improve the quality of the nation's environment. The act covers solid waste disposal, clean air, water resources, noise, pesticides, and atomic radiation.

Industrial pollution can be prevented or controlled through use of waste treatment, process changes, or both. Builders, developers, and contractors—many of them small businesses—can help prevent and control water pollution. Soil erosion, wastes from feedlots, improper or excessive use of pesticides and fertilizers, and careless discarding of trash and junk are among the causes of water pollution.

Environmental protection, though beneficial to society, can be hard on business, especially small business. Because of agency requirements that pollution control equipment be installed in marginal plants, many of these plants have closed, and employees have lost their jobs.

COUNSELING DISTURBED EMPLOYEES

Counseling is designed to help people do a better job and provide them with an understanding of their relationships with their supervisors, fellow workers, and subordinates. Counseling operates at all levels and with all employees, without restriction to any one level of supervision.

While most small firms don't have formal counseling programs, they do counsel employees on a day-to-day basis. The informality of small firms leads naturally to seeking and receiving advice and counsel.

Benefits of Counseling

No organization operates without systematic interpersonal relationships. Counseling may improve these relationships and make the interactions more pleasant. It at least provides a way to sit down and talk to other people and let them know where they stand. It tends to reduce anxiety, fear, and distrust. Thus, it helps to develop and strengthen good working relationships so that areas of misunderstanding and apprehension can be cleared up.

What Counseling Involves

How does **counseling** operate? In the first place, it operates in a conversational setting between two people. You can talk with another person and draw that individual out; you can "set the other straight" and pointed in the right direction. Counseling is always a bilateral relationship.

Counseling and guidance involve two-way communication. Conveying meaning to subordinates is desirable, but it is likewise important to learn from them what the manager needs to know in order to be of assistance. If managers do not feel qualified to perform these jobs, specialized employees may be used.

An in-plant counseling program at Norton Company relies on "faithful and trustworthy" employees who understand the business. They are available at any time during the day to help their fellow employees solve their problems. The aim is to take the burden off managemeet's shoulders and to increase the workers' efficiency by settling worries quickly and in a private and confidential manner. Although these "counselors" do not have authority to settle problems themselves, they are trained to see that the problem gets to the person who can.[6]

Areas Needing Counseling

Counseling involves all aspects of employee relations. It begins with the employment procedure and does not stop until the worker leaves the company—if then. Yet counseling is practiced in certain areas more frequently than in others. These areas include: (1) job-related activities and (2) personal problems. As shown in Figure 12–2, a survey of 293 companies found that counseling was most frequently given for substance abuse, nervous disorders, marital and family conflicts, stress, financial problems, termination, and retirement.

Job-Related Activities

While all aspects of job performance are subject to counseling, the most prevalent ones are performance, discipline, safety, and retirement.

Performance appraisal.   Management is responsible for informing employees of their progress in the area of performance and for motivating them. Motiva-

---

Figure 12–2   Companies Invest in Counseling

Nearly half of companies surveyed sponsor an Employee Assistance Program— usually free of charge. EAPs provide counseling for:

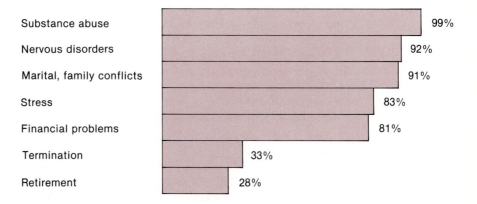

Substance abuse	99%
Nervous disorders	92%
Marital, family conflicts	91%
Stress	83%
Financial problems	81%
Termination	33%
Retirement	28%

Source: Hewitt Associates survey of 293 companies, as reported in *USA Today,* January 15, 1987, p. 1A. Copyright 1987, USA TODAY. Adapted with permission.

Source: Reprinted from *The Wall Street Journal;* permission Cartoon Features Syndicate.

tion is based on setting goals, stimulating employees to achieve those goals, and apprising them of their progress. The manager, after appraising the performance of individual subordinates, should discuss the results with them to help each see his or her strengths and weaknesses more clearly. The whole appraisal procedure should motivate the worker to build on the strengths and eliminate the weaknesses.

Discipline.   One important part of discipline is counseling the involved workers to improve output. As counseling does not always work, disciplinary action is sometimes needed. Some loss of work is unavoidable for numerous reasons. Yet the substantial avoidable part needs to be controlled. If the poor work results from negligence or lack of responsibility on the part of the employee, the manager may be able to correct it through counseling. If the loss of work is caused by physical or mental illness, it may require outside professional treatment.

Safety.   As was shown earlier in this chapter, the entire area of safety requires considerable counseling and guidance. Because safety is largely a matter of attitudes, your role as a small business manager is to counsel employees on the need for safe operations.

Retirement.   Employees need considerable preparation for retirement, especially with regard to the benefits coming to them. The top manager of small firms bears primary responsibility for this type of counseling.

Termination.   Now that much of business is more concerned with cost saving, primarily because of foreign competition, terminations are more frequent. When an employee just cannot produce, or when the business cannot afford to keep the employee, termination is often the only option. But, as shown in Chapter 10, both large and small employers are now providing outplacement assistance, which is a service to help laid-off workers find new jobs. Even with such help, though, termination is still traumatic for the worker, and counseling is needed, as shown in Figure 12–2.

Personal Problems

According to an article in *Personnel Journal,* almost a fifth of any company's employees suffer personal problems, which affect on-the-job performance. It is estimated that productivity is reduced by as much as 25 percent and that "astronomical" dollar losses result.[7] Two-thirds of those problems are drug and alcohol related, while the others are emotional problems. One way employers are coping with these problems is through counseling, referral to trained professionals, and employee-assistance programs.

We discuss these personal problems under the headings of (1) illness, (2) mental and emotional problems, and (3) substance abuse.

Illness.   Physical health is one area often needing counseling. Counseling may result from loss of work due to illness, low productivity, or personal health problems. Also, managers should advise workers when off-the-job activities interfere with job performance. Even the smallest firms should have some policies and standards for handling illness problems.

Mental and emotional problems.   The American Medical Association recognizes mental illness, one of the top four diseases, as among the most complex and pressing health problems in the nation. An indication of the severity of work and environmental pressures comes from the following statistic: Of the four primary causes of illness—heart trouble, mental illness, cancer, and alcoholism—three are directly attributable to stress and strain, and even the fourth one—cancer—may be indirectly caused by these factors.

When emotional problems interfere with job performance, they are subject to managerial counseling. Managers may counsel employees as to possible improvements in their behavior or toward seeking professional advice. One research study has shown counseling to be an effective method of aiding emotionally disturbed employees. Counseling tends to result in reduced absenteeism and tardiness, while increasing morale and productivity.[8]

Substance abuse.   A mushrooming health problem for managers today—even in small businesses—is alcohol and drug addiction, which the federal government now calls **substance abuse. Alcoholism** and **drug addiction** have recently received wide attention in the business community, government agencies, and the media because of their detrimental effects on job performance and because they are so widespread and growing in severity.

The National Council on Alcoholism estimates that 5 to 10 percent of employees have a drinking problem.[9] According to the National Institute on Alcohol Abuse and Alcoholism, 45 percent of employed alcoholics are professional or managerial, 30 percent are blue collar, and 25 percent are white collar.[10] These problem workers have around three times as many accidents, are absent around three times as often, and require almost three times as much in sickness payments as average workers.[11] Other inestimable losses stem from inefficiencies and slowdowns, interpersonal problems, and the necessity to discharge highly trained and skilled employees. Figure 12–3 lists early signs that may identify an alcoholic.

Drug addiction increasingly poses a problem for small businesses. A

Figure 12–3   Early Signs of Alcoholism

1. Excessive tardiness for work, with invalid or improbable excuse.
2. Increasing frequency and length of absences, especially on Mondays.
3. Slackening work pace.
4. Declining quantity and quality of performance.
5. Increasing frequency and intensity of arguments with colleagues.
6. Poor, "fuzzy," or irrational decisions.

study by Hoffmann-La Roche Inc. of 102 companies indicates what problems drugs cause in the workplace. The results, shown in Figure 12–4, show that 54 percent of absenteeism results from drug use. It also causes accidents, increased medical expenses, insubordination, thefts, and quality and service problems.

How can small firms attack this problem? They can increase their security activities, test applicants for drugs in blood or urine, institute education programs, help those discovered to be on drugs, and hire or rehire certified ex-addicts. Yet many of these procedures are not proving very effective.

Since March 18, 1989, small businesses with federal contracts and grants must have a substance abuse policy that conforms to federal guidelines. The **Drug-Free Workplace Act** and the Department of Defense's **Drug-Free Workforce Rules** now impose sweeping new obligations on contractors and grantees, requiring them to develop a new substance abuse policy.[12] The cost of such a drug-free environment is unknown, but small firms may be unable to bear the cost of these obligations.

Figure 12–4   Drug Problems in the Workplace

Percentage of problems caused by drugs at 102 companies:

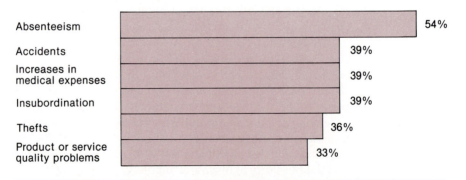

Source: "Drug Problems in the Workplace," *USA Today,* December 7, 1989, p. 1A. Copyright 1989, USA TODAY. Adapted with permission. (Original source: Hoffmann-La Roche Inc., October 1989.)

DEALING WITH EMPLOYEE COMPLAINTS

Complaints will inevitably occur, even in small firms. Therefore, managers should encourage employees to inform them when they think something is wrong and needs to be corrected. Also, supervisors should be told how to handle the complaints. An effective procedure should provide; (1) assurance to employees that expressing their complaints will not jeopardize their relationships with immediate supervisors, (2) a clearly understood method for presenting their complaints, and a description of how those complaints will be processed, and (3) a minimum of red tape and time in processing complaints and determining solutions.

Unresolved complaints can lead to more problems. So managers should listen patiently and deal with them promptly even if they seem to be without foundation. Managers should analyze the complaint carefully and gather pertinent facts. After making a decision, management should inform the employee of it and later follow up to determine whether the cause of the problem has been corrected.

Detailed, written records of all complaints (and disciplinary actions) should be maintained in employees' files. Such records are beneficial in defense against any charges of unfair labor practices that may be brought against a manager.

IMPOSING DISCIPLINE

Behavioral scientists have found that employees like to work in a disciplined environment—in the sense of having a system of rules and procedures and having them enforced equitably. Two ways of obtaining such an orderly, disciplined environment exist: either motivate employees to exercise self-control or impose external discipline.

Encouraging Self-Discipline

Employees should have confidence in their ability to perform their job, see good performance as compatible with their own interests, and know that their boss will provide support if they run into difficulties. Consequently, managers should encourage self-discipline among employees rather than rely on direct control. The personal example of owner-managers will be important in influencing employee discipline.

The owner of a small firm selling and installing metal buildings had a problem with his employees' taking long lunch breaks. When he asked his crew supervisors to correct this practice, one of them had the courage to say, "We would find that easier to do if you didn't take two-hour lunches yourself."

How to Discipline Employees

Probably 95 percent of employees conduct themselves reasonably; they rarely cause any problems. Yet, if the owner of a small company does not deal effectively with the few who violate rules and regulations, employees' disrespect will likely become widespread. In order to be effective in administering discipline, management needs a system that involves:

- Knowing the rules and seeing that employees know them.
- Acting promptly on violations.
- Gathering pertinent facts about violations.
- Allowing employees an opportunity to explain their position.
- Setting up tentative courses of action and evaluating them.
- Deciding what action to take.
- Taking disciplinary action, while observing labor contract and EEO procedures.
- Setting up and maintaining a record of actions taken, and following up on the outcome.

The procedure should distinguish between major and minor offenses and consider extenuating circumstances, such as the employee's length of service, prior performance record, and duration of time since the last offense. Figure 12–5 shows an effective disciplinary procedure that considers most of these variables.

Employees fired for misconduct will probably be denied unemployment benefits in most states. But what constitutes an offense varies by state. In general, it involves (1) willfully disregarding company interests or the duties and obligations of the job, (2) deliberately violating company rules, or (3) being grossly or repeatedly negligent after being warned. Inefficient performance, inability to do the work, occasional carelessness that does not result in major losses, and good-faith errors in judgment usually are not considered misconduct.[13]

Managers of small firms have been heard to say that traditional discipline does not work for them. Instead, some are using **positive discipline** to improve morale and lower turnover. Under this approach, employees who come in late, do a sloppy job, or commit some other breach of conduct receive an oral "reminder," not a "reprimand." Then comes a written reminder, followed by a paid day off to decide whether they really want to keep their job. If the answer is yes, the employee agrees in writing (or usually orally if a union is involved) to be on his or her best behavior for the next year. The employee who does not perform satisfactorily after that is fired. Since the cases are *fully documented*, employees usually have little recourse.

Figure 12–5 An Example of Disciplinary Procedure Using Graduated Penalties

		Enforcement		
Offenses	First action step	Second action step	Third action step	Fourth action step
Minor — Infractions that do not do great damage or have serious consequence when viewed individually but may be considered serious when accumulated.	Education and informal warning or warnings by first-line supervisor.	Warning in presence of union representative by first-line supervisor.	Warning or written reprimand by higher supervision in presence of union representative and/or suspension up to two days.	Becomes a major offense and is handled accordingly (does not necessarily involve immediate suspension).
Major — Violations that substantially interfere with production or damage morale; or when seriousness of offense is apparent to a reasonable mind; or an accumulation of minor offenses.	First offense — *Step 1:* Immediately remove employee from job and have report to higher supervision. *Step 2:* Suspension up to five days, plus a written reprimand or written final warning, if necessary.	Second offense — *Step 1:* Immediately remove employee from job and have report to higher supervision. *Step 2:* Written final warning. Suspension up to 10 days, or discharge if final warning was given for first offense.	Third offense — *Step 1:* Immediately remove employee from job and have report to higher supervision. *Step 2:* Discharge.	
Intolerable — Offenses of a criminal or drastic nature that strain employee relationship or would be outrageous to most people.	First offense — *Step 1:* Immediately remove employee from job and have report to industrial relations department. *Step 2:* Discharge.	Pointers: 1. Economic penalties (such a suspensions, transfers, discharges) should be imposed only by higher supervision after consultation with industrial relations department. 2. Written final warnings should always be accompanied by an economic penalty. 3. To be considered a *second* offense, violations should occur within a year of the first offense.		

Source: Walter Collins and Herman Harrow, ''Does the Penalty Match the Offense?'' *Supervisory Management 3* (September 1958): 20. Reprinted by permission of the publisher. © 1958 by American Management Assn., Inc.

Tampa Electric Company uses a system of giving problem employees a day off—with pay—to think over their behavior. When a lazy mechanic was recently given a day off to decide if he wanted the job, he turned around on his own. At first, he thought it was great to have a paid day off. Then, however, it dawned on him that whatever happened to his job was his own responsibility.[14]

DEALING WITH UNIONS

In the past, union organizers have tended to concentrate their organizing efforts on larger firms as they are easier to unionize. This tendency is now changing. Union organizers are trying to organize small firms because that's where the potential new members are. Also, small business owners are more active in lobbying Congress and state legislatures for laws and regulations the unions oppose.[15] Dealing with the union is important not only to the small company but also to other businesses in the area.

Laws Governing Union-Management Relations

The **National Labor Relations Act of 1935 (NLRA),** as amended, requires management to bargain with the union if a majority of a company's employees desire unionization. (See Figure 12–6 for the provisions of this and related laws.) Managers are forbidden to discriminate against employees in any way because of union activity. The purpose of the NLRA was to facilitate the process of collective bargaining, not necessarily to prevent or settle disputes. Under the act, both the company and the union are required to bargain in good faith to resolve difficulties and reach an agreement. The **National Labor Relations Board (NLRB)** serves as a labor court, and its general counsel investigates charges of unfair labor practices, issues complaints, and prosecutes cases. The union or management can appeal a ruling of the board through a circuit court all the way up to the U.S. Supreme Court.

In some states a **union shop clause** provides that employees must join the recognized union within 30 days after being hired. Under **right-to-work laws** in effect in 21 states (see Figure 12–7), the union shop is not legally permitted.

What Happens When the Union Enters

Unions exist to bargain on behalf of their members, as a counterbalance to the economic power of the employer. Employees, through their elected representatives, negotiate with the company for wages, fringe benefits, working conditions, security, and so forth. The union's principal role is to be the **exclusive bargaining agent** in employees' relationships with management, especially in collective bargaining. To do this, the union must first organize the company's employees. In this process, the manager can and cannot do certain things. Appendixes F and G at the end of this book give abridged versions of these restrictions.

Figure 12–6 Some Laws Governing Union-Management Relations

Laws	Coverage	Basic requirements	Agencies involved
National Labor Relations Act of 1935, as amended (also called the Wagner Act)	Nonmanagerial employees in nonagricultural private firms not covered by the Railway Labor Act, and postal employees.	Employees have right to form or join labor organizations (or to refuse to), to bargain collectively through their representatives, and to engage in other concerted activities such as strikes, picketing, and boycotts; there are unfair labor practices in which the employer and the union cannot engage.	National Labor Relations Board (NLRB).
Labor-Management Relations Act of 1947, as amended (also called the Taft-Hartley Act)	Same as above.	Amended NLRA; permits states to pass laws prohibiting compulsory union membership; sets up methods to deal with strikes affecting national health and safety.	NLRB; Federal Mediation and Conciliation Service.
Labor-Management Reporting and Discourse Act of 1959, as amended (also called the Landrum-Griffin Act)	Same as above.	Amended NLRA and LMRA; guarantees individual rights of union members in dealing with their union; requires financial disclosures by unions.	U.S. Department of Labor.

Source: Extracted from F. Ray Marshall, Allan G. King, and Vernon M. Biggs, Jr., *Labor Economics,* 4th ed. (Homewood, Ill.: Richard D. Irwin, 1980), chap. 4.

The first thing you should do if your employees try to form a union is to recognize that it is because they believe they need the protection the union offers. You should ask yourself such questions as: "Why do my employees feel that it is necessary to have a union to represent them?" "Is it a lack of communication or failure to respond to their needs?" "Am I treating them arbitrarily or unfairly?" Studies of successful nonunionized companies find that management and employees participate in the business process as a team rather than as adversaries.

The second thing you should do is call in a competent consultant or labor lawyer. Small firms are increasingly turning to advisers to deal with unions.

When employees tried to organize Persona Inc., a Watertown, South Dakota, manufacturing firm, Dennis D. Holien, its president, called in a consultant, Henry N. Teipel of St. Paul, Minnesota. With his help, the personnel manager even wrote

Figure 12–7   States with and without Right-to-Work Laws

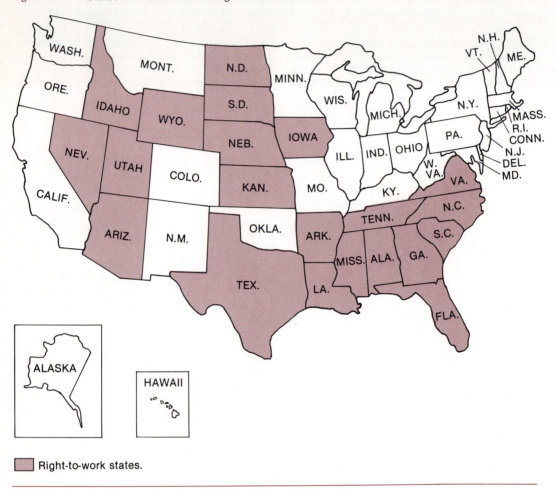

Right-to-work states.

Source: Adapted from information furnished by the National Right-to-Work Foundation.

scripts to prepare for employee meetings. The advice, which cost $4,000, "saved a tremendous amount of money . . . by keeping the battle short and the union out."[16]

If your company is unionized, you should be prepared for certain changes. Many of your actions and statements may be reported to union officials, and the union may file unfair labor practice charges with the NLRB. Your best defense is to know your rights under the prevailing laws—and to maintain favorable relationships with employees.

Negotiating the Agreement

Bargaining with the union for an agreement requires preparation, the actual negotiation, and then living with the contract. All these require special expertise, as well as patience and understanding, so again it is advisable to consult your labor lawyer.

Preparation

Preparation may well be the most important step in negotiating the agreement. Obtaining facts about wages, hours, and other terms and conditions of employment before sitting down at the bargaining table should improve your position. You should collect information on other contracts in the industry and in the local area. Disciplinary actions, complaints, and other key matters that arose before the union's entry should be studied. Current business literature concerning business in general and the status of union-management relations in the industry can be useful. A carefully researched proposal should be developed well in advance of negotiation sessions.

Negotiating

Good preparation should put you in a positive negotiating position instead of a defensive stance against the union's proposals. The "I don't want to give away any more than I have to" attitude generally leads to poor union-management relationships. All too frequently, however, fear seems to overcome the owner's or manager's willingness to develop in advance a proposal with attractive features that will appeal to employees.

You should recognize the negotiation step as critical: it must be handled properly, preferably with outside assistance. The effects on the company of not only wages but also seniority, discharge rules, and sick leave should be considered, with the understanding that anything given away can probably never be taken back.

What Is Included

The agreement between the company and the union usually consists of at least 10 clauses covering:

- Union recognition.
- Wages.
- Vacations and holidays.
- Working conditions.
- Layoffs and rehiring.

- Management prerogatives.
- Hours of work.
- Seniority.
- Arbitration.
- Renewal of the agreement.

Specific details are set forth in each of these areas, and rules are established that should be obeyed by the company and the union. The management prerogatives clause defines the areas in which management has the right to act freely as an employer, without interference from the union.

Living with the Agreement

Once the agreement is signed, you must learn to live with its provisions until the time for renegotiation. All management personnel should be thoroughly briefed on its contents and implications. Meanings and interpretations of each clause should be reviewed and the wording of the agreement clearly understood. Supervisors' questions should be answered to better prepare them to deal with labor matters.

A small firm's labor relations and personnel practices should be consistent, uniform in application and interpretation, and based on a sense of fair play. In numerous instances, owners have pursued policies that could be labeled selfish and greedy; the end product has been unionization, bankruptcy, or both.

To be prepared to act properly in a specific labor relations situation, you should obtain advice and reliable information from numerous private groups and government agencies. Government sources include federal and state mediators, wage and hour investigators, National Labor Relations Board regional offices, state industrial relations departments, and business executives working with SCORE (Service Corps of Retired Executives). Some private sources are employers' associations, trade associations, labor relations attorneys, and labor relations consultants.

WHAT YOU SHOULD HAVE LEARNED

Effective personnel management includes the functions of protecting employee safety and health, preserving the environment, counseling employees, handling employees' complaints, exercising discipline, and dealing with labor unions. All of these complex subjects were covered in this chapter.

1. It is not possible to ensure complete safety for employees at work, but employers should work to eliminate hazards and to create a feeling of concern for safety. Employee safety varies with the size of the organization, the industry and occupation involved, and personal characteristics of employees. Employers, who are ultimately responsible for safety, have certain rights and obligations. To promote safe and healthful working conditions in industry, OSHA concentrates on the businesses most likely to be unsafe or unhealthy. However, employees of any business who are aware of hazardous conditions can report them to OSHA and request a safety inspection without jeopardizing their jobs.

2. Environmental protection is also a concern of small firms. Although prevention of water and air pollution, soil erosion, pesticide contamination, atomic radiation, and other threats to the environment is undoubtedly beneficial to society, the costs of required equipment

or procedures can be a special hardship for small businesses with limited resources.

3. All managers must perform counseling at some time or other. It may amount to simply being willing listeners when employees gripe about their problems at home, or it may be needed to correct a work problem. Specific counseling, however, is usually called for in the job-related areas of performance appraisal, discipline, safety, and retirement, as well as the personal areas of illness, mental and emotional problems, and substance abuse.

4. While some complaints from employees are inevitable, they can often be handled informally in a small firm. But an established procedure helps when problems cannot be easily talked out or when employees find it difficult to express themselves to management. Dissatisfaction with the way complaints are handled can result in unionization.

5. Employees want to know what to expect and what management expects of them. In the ideal work situation, employees discipline themselves, especially if managers set a good example. For those employees who need external discipline, counseling may be ineffective. Therefore, a discipline procedure should be established that takes into account the severity of the offense and the number of times it has been committed, as well as other factors and extenuating circumstances. Positive discipline, which challenges employees to discipline themselves, is being used in many small firms.

6. Dealing with unions is a challenge most owners and managers of small businesses would rather not face, and most will try to keep a union out of their business. Their efforts have often been successful, for, until recently, unions did not focus on small businesses. Also, a small company where employees are treated as individuals, where communication and working relationships between management and employees are good, and where production is seen as a team effort is less vulnerable to unionization than a large, seemingly impersonal organization.

    When a union does enter, however, many things change. Many laws govern labor-management relations, so be sure to have a good consultant to help you. Negotiating an agreement with the union requires much preparation. Generous proposals from management will make negotiations easier and more pleasant, but managers should consider possible effects of their concessions and realize that anything given away can probably never be taken back. After agreement is reached, supervisors should be briefed on the terms of the contract so that they will be prepared to deal with labor matters. Managers inexperienced in dealing with a union can get help from a variety of sources, both government and private.

KEY TERMS

Occupational Safety and Health Act (OSHA), *333*

Occupational Safety and Health Administration (OSHA), *333*

Environmental Protection Agency (EPA), *336*

counseling, *336*

substance abuse (alcoholism, drug addiction), *339*

Drug-Free Workplace Act, *340*

Drug-Free Workforce Rules, *340*

positive discipline, *342*

National Labor Relations Act of 1935 (NLRA), *344*

National Labor Relations Board (NLRB), *344*

union shop clause, *344*

right-to-work laws, *344*

exclusive bargaining agent, *344*

QUESTIONS

1. *(a)* Discuss the most significant factors that influence safe working conditions. *(b)* What can a small business manager do about them—if anything?

2. Discuss briefly the Occupational Safety and Health Act and OSHA.

3. What are an employer's obligations under this act?

4. List the areas covered by the EPA.

5. *(a)* Discuss the areas requiring counseling. *(b)* What—if anything— can a small business manager do to improve counseling in those areas?

6. List the four characteristics that should be included in a complaint procedure.

7. Explain the differences between discipline through self-control and externally imposed discipline.

8. *(a)* Discuss the laws governing union-management relations. *(b)* Should you, as a small business owner, favor or oppose your employees' unionizing? *(c)* Defend your answer.

SUGGESTED READING

Bennett, Amanda, Jolie Solomon, and Allanna Sullivan. "Firms Debate Hard Line on Alcoholics." *The Wall Street Journal,* April 13, 1989, p. B1.

Brophy, Beth, et al. "You're Fired!" *U.S. News & World Report,* March 23, 1987, pp. 50–54.

Fenn, Donna. "Benefits: Keeping Fit." *Inc.,* February 1986, pp. 101–2.

Geyelin, Milo. "Study Faults Federal Effort to Enforce Worker Safety." *The Wall Street Journal,* April 28, 1988, p. B1.

Holtzman, Elizabeth. "States Step In Where OSHA Fails to Tread." *The Wall Street Journal,* March 31, 1987, p. 36.

Jacobs, Stanford L. "They Say Things to the Boss That Others Wouldn't Dare." *The Wall Street Journal,* November 25, 1985, p. 27.

Karr, Albert R. "Small Business Scores Big in Congressional Lobbying." *The Wall Street Journal,* October 3, 1988, pp. B1, B2.

Lynch, Lorrie. "Unions Step Up Recruiting." *USA Today,* February 11, 1985, p. 3A.

Megginson, Leon C. *Personnel Management: A Human Resources Approach.* 5th ed. Homewood, Ill.: Richard D. Irwin, 1985. Especially chapters 10, 12, 13, 18, and 19.

"Work-Related Injuries Higher for Whites." *The Wall Street Journal,* April 6, 1989, p. B1.

ENDNOTES

1. New York (state), Department of Labor, Division of Research and Statistics, *Injury Rates in Factories* (New York, 1966).

2. *Accident Facts* (Chicago: National Safety Council, 1979).

3. "Job Hazards Are a Mounting Threat to Service Workers," *The Wall Street Journal,* March 28, 1988, p. 1.

4. Cathy Trost, "OSHA to Check Safety at More Firms in an Expansion of Inspection Policy," *The Wall Street Journal,* January 8, 1986, p. 11A.

5. Sanford L. Jacobs, "Small Business Slowly Wakes to OSHA Hazard Rule," *The Wall Street Journal,* November 22, 1988, p. B1.

6. "Norton Delegates Personnel Affairs to the Workers," *International Management* 30 (June 1975): 48–50; and Graham D. Taylor, "Modern Firm to Multinational: Norton Company, a New England Enterprise," *Journal of American History,* September 1986, pp. 487–88.

7. Stuart Elliott, "Workers' Woes Give Firms Financial Fits," *USA Today,* June 13, 1988, p. 1B.

8. Gerald H. Graham, "Recognizing Emotional Disturbance Symptoms," *Personnel Administrator* 15 (July–August 1970): 3–7.

9. See "Alcoholism: Everybody's Business," *Bell Telephone Magazine,* January–February 1975, pp. 7–9, for further details.

10. David W. Hacker, "Did His Job Make Him Drink?" *National Observer,* November 1975, pp. 1, 20.

11. "Alcoholism: A Growing Medical-Social Problem," *Statistical Bulletin* (Metropolitan Insurance Company), April 1967, pp. 7–10.

12. Contact your nearest Small Business Administration office for more information on these laws.

13. Beth Brophy, "What Boss Calls Bad Conduct Must Fit Law," *USA Today,* March 6, 1985, p. 5B.

14. Laurie Baum, "Punishing Workers with a Day Off," *Business Week,* June 16, 1986, p. 80.

15. Albert R. Karr, "Small Business Scores Big in Congressional Lobbying," *The Wall Street Journal,* October 3, 1988, pp. B1, B2.

16. Jeffrey A. Tannenbaum, "Consultants, Small Business Come to Need One Another," *The Wall Street Journal,* Steptember 28, 1989, p. B1.

CASE III–1
CLEANDRUM, INC. (C)

CASE III–2
OUR HERO RESTAURANT (C)

CASE III–3
THE BEARY BEST COOKIES

CASE III–4
THE CASE OF SAM SAWYER

CASE III–5
THE PEPPER BUSH

CASE III–1

CLEANDRUM, INC. (C)

CleanDrum, Inc. (CDI), formed by Sue Ley three years ago, buys, straightens, cleans, paints, and sells used 55-gallon steel and plastic drums for transporting and storing oil, chemicals, and similar products. The company employs six workers in the plant. In addition, Sue's daughter and two sons have worked for CleanDrum at various times. Her daughter performs the office, telephone, and bookkeeping duties.

One son, who has left CDI several times for better-paying jobs, now drives the company's tractor-trailer. Sue says, "He's excellent because he has long arms for speedy loading and unloading, as well as a personable way with customers. But he doesn't want to take on the responsibility of selling."

Sue's other son works part time for a utility company while going to college. Recently, his employer increased his hours—at the same time his class load increased. He wants to work part time for CDI. On the basis of previous work around the plant, Sue thinks he might make a good sales rep because "he's very personable." But she doesn't know what kind of flexible way to pay him. Should she put him on commission?

Sue co-owns and manages CDI. Among her many duties, she supervises production, trains workers, and buys drums, in addition to spending two days on the road selling the drums. The plant workers move, lift, turn, paint, and inspect drums and control the operations of the machines.

Drums are delivered by trailer to the plant, where workers unload them, remove bungs (stoppers screwed in the top of the drums), and store the drums near the first operation or in the storage area. The steel drums are turned over for steam jet flushing, inspected for rust that needs to be removed, rolled into a straightener, and picked up and rolled into a cleaning vat. The workers watch the rinsing and pressure testing machines for timing, remove the drums, and lift and turn them for flushing, drying, and inspection. After a painter spray-paints the drums, they are moved either to a trailer for shipment or to storage. The plant operates 40 hours per week.

Shortly after the plant started operating, the partners became concerned about CDI's losses. Edie Jones, a financial partner, felt that labor costs could be reduced, but Sue argued that employees were producing effeciently, and at minimum wage. (Note: At that time, the minimum wage rate was $3.35 per hour.) Then Edie suggested that workers be classified as "contract" workers, thereby eliminating the need for payroll taxes and IRS W–2 forms. This was tried during the year, but U.S. Department of Labor officials declared that this procedure was incorrect. Because of high turnover in the six full-time jobs, 104 W–2 forms had to be completed during the year, one for each worker employed, regardless of the length of employment. One hiree lasted half an hour, others for a day or so, while only two workers stayed the full year.

"Now I have a pretty good crew," says Sue. "Two of the guys have been with me for three years. They were trained by a greenhorn—me. One man is a good lead man: he knows what to do. If not, he has the telephone number of the person to call for help. When I leave him in charge of the plant while I visit customers, I feel more confident than before. I have good guys out there who are interested in the work, who come up to me and say, 'Why don't we do this this way?' "

The workers' pay has improved because of the stability of the work force. Until this past year, all the workers had been paid the minimum wage. "None of them had families dependent on them. Now, the group leader's pay is over $6 per hour, the other long-timer earns $5, a skilled worker makes $4.50, and the rest earn minimum wage. One competitor in another city is paying only minimum wages, but another one, a mechanized plant in another area, is paying over $10 an hour."

Social Security, workers' compensation, and unemployment insurance are the only employee benefits provided, but two of the workers are making health insurance payments on their own.

The stable work force also has made it easier to maintain a high quality of output. (Remember, the company was formed on the basis that there would be a demand for high-quality drums.)

Sue says that the company has not had enough money to pay someone to supervise the shop or to go out selling. Instead, "in the past, when I came to work, I often found a breakdown, a lack of materials, or that an employee hadn't shown up. It was as if my hands were tied and I couldn't get out and sell. Now I have someone who can run the shop, and I can be on the road two days a week."

Questions for Discussion

1. What grade(s) of employees are needed in the plant? Discuss. Comment on the training.
2. How did CDI obtain the high quality of product needed with the high labor turnover and with Sue gone so much of the time? Comment.
3. What do you think of Edie's ideas about reducing costs? Explain.
4. Was the pay program good at that time, when the minimum wage was $3.35? Explain.
5. What type of relationship does Sue appear to have with the workers?
6. Do you have any recommendations for Sue?

Source: Prepared by William M. Spain, SCORE, and Charles R. Scott, University of Alabama.

CASE III–2

OUR HERO RESTAURANT (C)

From its beginning, Our Hero Restaurant faced the problem of the roles Steve and Barbara Chappell were to play in the management and operation of their venture. The difficulty faced by two co-owners, each fully responsible and able to supervise the other workers, was deepened by Barbara Chappell's particular concern as a "liberated woman" to be an equal in the management. Moreover, the two recognized that the male-female/husband-and-wife relationship often brought emotional involvement in place of objectivity. The arguments over who should make decisions and the lack of communication were solved by two principal means:

1. Incorporation with only Barbara and Steven Chappell as shareholders.
2. Explicit division of labor and delegation of duties.

In the latter, the Chappells were lucky to have Pete Sherman, who had been the part-time assistant manager of the store from its first day of operation. Sherman was earning an undergraduate degree in business administration at NEU and, as Steve Chappell testified, had learned the Our Hero operation inside out. He had been instrumental in keeping the business going in its volatile first six months and hence was so well thought of by the Chappells that they later were to turn the entire operation over to him for weeks at a time.

Early on, however, it had been decided that, while Barbara and Steve Chappell would take turns at paying bills, Barbara would handle the personnel and payroll matters; Steve the ordering, accounting, and long-term planning; and Pete Sherman the scheduling and inventory. Basically, this arrangement was worked out according to the personal preferences of each of the three.

In the process of discussing his problems over the two years of operations, Steve Chappell indirectly underlined the two main reasons for Our Hero's success: the store's access to a large market for fast food, and the lack of excessive competition. As for the basic market, literally thousands of students (to say nothing of large numbers of faculty and staff during the daytime hours) were within easy walking distance. These groups not only enjoyed fast food on its merits but also were often rushed for time.

As for direct competition, none of the four other private food outlets in the immediate area served quite the same specialized sandwiches. From another angle, observation indicated that two patterns prevailed in the competitive division of the campus market. First, the many alternative food sources off campus—none closer than a mile from the campus—were no real threat to Our Hero and other on-campus restaurants; second, the students tended to gravitate to restaurants according to location without much cross-campus interchanging. Our Hero and the cluster of food sources around it largely held the trade of the students on the south side of the campus, especially those in the southeast quadrant; while the only other cluster of private restaurants, on the northwest side, mainly commanded the student market in that sector.

Although Chappell did not stress it, a fair appraisal of Our Hero's product would have shown it to be an additional competitive advantage. In addition to the food's quality and quantity for the price, the service was quick, the surroundings were neat and attractive, and the restaurant's personnel were clean and attentive. Moreover, the hours of service—11 A.M. until 2 A.M. Sundays through Thursdays and 11 A.M. until 3 A.M. on Fridays and Saturdays—were certainly accommodating. Finally, some credit had to be given to the Our Hero trademark, which was becoming better known.

Two further features of Our Hero's experience were also worth weighing in favor of its success. The more unusual of the two was the labor supply. The Chappells had found, on the one hand, that the availability of part-time help paralleled the size of the product market—both peaking in September through December and late January through early May, which constituted the school year. On the other hand, unlike some other Our Hero restaurants, they had also been exceedingly well satisfied with the ability, enthusiasm, and honesty of their workers. As a consequence of both these factors, no worker had ever been laid off or fired.

Last of all, the Chappells were not absentee owners. Typically, they both worked at lunchtime[1] alongside the part-time student labor, and Steve Chappell remarked, "Barbara and I make the best heroes." Also, Steve

---

[1] There was also another reason for the focus on lunchtime: Steve Chappell claimed that the most discriminating customer came at the lunch hour, adding that "taste buds deteriorate during the day."

Chappell indicated that he spent weekly, in addition to 20 hours in the store, 10 to 15 hours on bookkeeping and 5 on management analysis.[2]

Questions for Discussion

1. Evaluate the Chappells' organizational structure and division of labor. Would you suggest any changes? What? Why?
2. Would you concur with Steve on the reasons given for the success of the business? Why?
3. Do you consider the Chappells' success the result of:
    a. Their planning?
    b. Their implementation?
    c. Their willingness to expend the amount of time required?
    d. The image of the franchise?
    e. Each of these contributing to the total success of the firm? Explain the rationale of your choice.
4. To what extent did their personnel contribute to their success?
5. Evaluate their policy of not firing or laying off their employees.

Source: Adapted from a case prepared by John Clair Thompson, University of Connecticut.

THE BEARY BEST COOKIES

Jeanne Parnell faced a crossroads. Previously, her small sole-proprietorship cookie business had met her needs adequately. As a mother of three children under the age of six and an active member of her church, she needed something to do that would not consume a large amount of her time. As the wife of a husband trying to establish himself in the insurance business, she needed something that would earn enough money to contribute significantly to the family income. Selling oatmeal chocolate chip cookies to health clubs and small restaurants in Baton Rouge, Louisiana, had met both requirements. Realizing that there might be a significant opportunity to expand her business beyond its present base of 16 stores, she also recognized that growth would necessitate changes in the way she did business.

When she discussed this with her husband, he replied, "You go ahead and make as much money as you can; we could use it! But it will have to be *your* project, as it's been from the start. You know I'm too busy with work at the office to be able to help out much." It was obvious that, while

---

[2] Like many chain fast-food managers, Steve Chappell kept close track of seemingly mundane matters, and he used them actively in managing, especially in ordering bread: same day, last year; running totals for the year; weather; and so forth.

he wasn't going to stand in her way, neither was he going to get behind her and push. It was going to be her decision and her effort.

History of the Business

In 1986, the Parnells realized that, with two children and another on the way, they needed some additional income. Rick was just starting out in the insurance business, and, while he knew that his business would earn enough for them to live comfortably, it would be several years before he was fully established.

After the kids were asleep one night, they sat down and discussed the possibilities. It was agreed that Jeanne wouldn't go out and work full time, and that even a part-time job would cause too much inconvenience and would probably require leaving the younger kids with someone else. That was a trade-off that both were unwilling for Jeanne to make. Rather than go to work for someone else, they decided, Jeanne should go into business for herself baking cookies.

There were many advantages to this alternative. First, Jeanne loved to bake cookies and experiment with different recipes. She had developed one that she particularly liked and her friends raved about—a recipe for oatmeal chocolate chip cookies. Another advantage was that Jeanne's father owned a restaurant in town and was willing to let her use the kitchen during off hours at no cost. The Parnells also had some accountant friends who they thought could lend advice as Jeanne might need it.

The business was registered as "The Beary Best Cookies," with a teddy bear as the logo, as shown in Exhibit 1. They spent $200 on attorney and registration fees and $75 to register the logo as a trademark.

Marketing

The Beary Best Cookies had a product but no market! One attribute of Jeanne's cookie was its high-quality ingredients. She felt that this, together with the low amount of starch, made the cookie not only better-tasting but also more healthful than cookies sold in supermarkets. Following up this health angle, she spoke with the manager of the health club where she worked out, and ended up with all four of the chain's local franchises as customers. She purchased four large, old-fashioned glass jars in which to put the cookies and replenished the supply every week, rotating the old ones to the top. The jar held around 50 of the large cookies. She labeled each jar with the Beary Best Cookies logo to identify the product in the consumer's mind. Her wholesale price was 30 cents, and the health clubs sold the cookies for 50 to 60 cents.

On the basis of some rough calculations, Jeanne had determined that her cost of goods sold per cookie was five cents, which represented only 16.7 percent of her selling price, giving a 500 percent markup. Her retailers benefited also, enjoying up to a 100 percent markup with no additional effort on their part.

Sales at the clubs were so good that Jeanne had to replenish the jars

Exhibit 1   The Beary Best Cookies Logo

twice a week. This was such an encouraging beginning that, since she had enough time available to service additional stores, Jeanne decided to expand. She had noticed that some restaurants around town had been selling candy and other snacks and sweets at the cash register, as an impulse item. Cookies were not, however, an item generally sold in this fashion. Since she saw her cookie as not only healthful but also of high quality, she sought out restaurants with the same quality image. She also reasoned that customers at these restaurants were more likely to spend 60 cents on a cookie because it represented a small portion of their total bill. Using the same marketing approach as before (cookies in a glass jar by the cash register), she added four new customers in 1987 and was servicing 16 establishments by the middle of 1988.

Jeanne had also once supplied the cookies to her oldest child's school for a fund-raising project. She had given the cookies to the school as an act of charity, and the school sold them for 50 cents apiece. The school was pleased with the results and indicated interest in conducting similar fund-raisers in the future.

Jeanne did no advertising, and the only places she contacted were establishments she selected. Consumers would find out about the product when they were paying their bill, and Jeanne and her customers saw the cookies as an impulse item.

Production and Distribution

On Mondays and Thursdays, Jeanne would get up about 4 A.M. and go to her father's restaurant to bake cookies. She would bake batches of several hundred each of those days, and she would usually be gone by the time the cooks started to arrive. She hand-mixed the dough and usually added ingredients to taste rather than by measuring. She then baked the cookies until they appeared brown enough; she didn't use a timer because the ideal time seemed to be different for different batches. She took the cookies home with her in airtight plastic containers to preserve their freshness, arriving home in time to get her oldest child up and off to school and to spend time with her husband before he left for work. She would then get her other two children up and dressed and take them with her on her midmorning delivery route. Most of the employees and managers of the stores enjoyed seeing her deliver the cookies, talking with her for a while, and seeing how the kids were doing. Jeanne, feeling that this personal touch was an important part of her business, valued the relationships she had developed over the months.

By early afternoon she was finished and had the rest of the day to spend as she pleased. Once a week she went to the supermarket and purchased the ingredients she needed, storing them at her father's restaurant.

Once, when she took an out-of-town vacation for two weeks, she had a friend run the business for her. The friend, Joe, who was partially disabled and mostly confined to a wheelchair, was allowed to keep whatever profits were made, and Jeanne left town feeling satisfied that her business was taken care of and also that she had helped out a friend by giving him something to do and a way to make some extra money. All did not turn out well, however, as she lost a customer who was apparently not satisfied with the cookies or with the service Joe had provided. Some of the other customers were also disgruntled, and it was then that Jeanne decided it was better to do everything herself. She never did get in touch with Joe about it, preferring not to tell him she thought he had done poorly. That was the only time her business had lost a customer.

Although she had had good results with her oatmeal chocolate chip cookie, she had toyed with the idea of offering a second variety: plain chocolate chip. She had even created a character in her mind to represent this potential new product: Chipper, a chipmunk.

Financial and Business Arrangements

The Parnells filed a joint tax return and included the profits from The Beary Best Cookies with his earnings. Their recordkeeping was very haphazard (they had not used the help of their accountant friends very much), so they really weren't sure of their profit. For the sake of simplicity, Jeanne counted the gross sales figures as profits, and the sales figure was used for tax purposes. This didn't disturb them greatly since their costs were so low. They were able to estimate, however, that their profit from Jeanne's 16 stores was in the neighborhood of $800 per month.

A friend had recently mentioned the subject of insurance, especially product liability insurance. Jeanne had not given much thought to this before and had made no arrangements covering it. She had assumed that she would be covered in all insurance matters through her father since she used his restaurant kitchen for her baking. Rick had never been deeply involved in the business and had never thought about the oversight. The friend had advised Jeanne to have Rick arrange a policy because of the risk involved in not having one, and she had mentioned the idea to him.

The Beary Best Cookies was debt free, and Rick preferred it to remain that way. Not that he was ready to provide a great deal of money for the firm's operations or expansion: in his mind, Jeanne had started the business to make money, not use it. He was satisfied with the way Jeanne had conducted the firm's business, since there were no additional cash requirements, and he was hoping it would stay that way.

Market Niche and Competition

The Beary Best Cookies faced no significant competition within its market niche of health clubs and fine restaurants. Jeanne knew that there were other restaurants in the Baton Rouge area that she could service, and that it might be wise to think of other markets as well. Some suggestions she received from her husband and friends were: drugstores, sporting goods stores, food stores (large supermarkets or small specialty shops), gas stations, and even taverns. They all sounded like good possibilities, but Jeanne had some aversion to the last idea due to her religion. She also had doubts about some of the categories because they didn't really fit in with the high-quality, health-oriented image she envisioned for her business.

The thought of franchising her operation had occasionally crossed her mind, but she made no effort to explore this further and was completely unfamiliar with the legal procedures, although her husband had some useful contacts. She did have a friend in Jackson, Mississippi, to whom she had given her recipe and marketing concept at no charge. She had heard that the friend was doing rather well with it.

Expansion Issues

Since Jeanne was already devoting the greater part of two days a week to her business, she realized that any attempt at a major expansion of her business would no doubt require a significantly greater time commitment. The alternative was to hire workers to do some of the activities she performed, such as purchasing the ingredients, baking the cookies, or delivering the cookies to customers. Her experience with Joe caused her to resist the idea; she had been observing the old adage: "If you want something done right, do it yourself."

A friend of hers didn't think this was too smart, and told her, "If you're going to expand the business, you will reach a point where you can't do everything yourself; you just won't have the time. You'd really need to hire a person or two." That made sense to Jeanne. When she mentioned it to her husband over dinner, she further remarked, "You know, Rick, it would be a good chance to help out a few friends of ours by giving them some part-time work."

"Would you hire Joe?" he responded.

"Well, no, he didn't seem to do very well," she replied.

"And you never told him that because he was a friend. What if some of the friends you hire do poorly and you have to get on their back or even fire them? That could cost some lost relationships. Hiring friends might put you in a tough position, Jeanne."

Jeanne thought her husband had a good point. It was becoming clear to her that the issues involved with this expansion were numerous and more complex than she had thought they would be. For instance, if she didn't hire friends, whom would she hire, and how would she get in touch with them?

If she did hire people, she realized that her business would be changed drastically, and her duties would evolve from those of a baker, delivery person, and marketer to those of a manager. She was unsure whether she wanted to make this transition since she really didn't like to come down hard on people when they didn't do well, and she had the idea that was what a manager did most of the time. Were there any ways to make this part of the business easier?

Another concern was training: She knew how she wanted the job done, but what was the best way to assure that her employees would know this and perform according to expectations? This was a significant concern for her, as it addressed the issue of product quality and service, areas in which Joe had performed poorly.

Jeanne was also aware that there were legal and tax issues that would have to be faced if she hired employees, and she was concerned about biting off more than she could chew. She would probably have to retain one of their accountant friends to keep the books, since the recordkeeping would need to be done on a more professional basis. Jeanne was also unclear as to whether any state or federal labor laws might significantly affect her business were she to expand in that fashion. The same friend she had talked to before mentioned that the local Department of Health should approve the containers that she used to transport her cookies, something which she hadn't yet taken care of. She wondered if there were any other regulatory issues that needed to be resolved.

Jeanne's father assured her that she could use the ovens at his restaurant every morning if she needed to, so increasing production wouldn't be a problem. He had suggested to her that a small advertising effort in a local restaurant trade magazine would probably yield good results and even thought that a radio advertising campaign, to support her retailers, would be a good idea once she had added more stores. Jeanne had also considered the supermarket option, but her father didn't think this was a good idea. "They'll probably make you pay some money up front to buy shelf space; they do that these days." That would be a problem since Rick had told her that one of the things he liked best about her business was that it didn't take much of an investment or require a lot of cash. Jeanne had had her doubts about supermarkets, anyway, since she would have to develop some kind of packaging and price the cookies competitively, as well as reduce the size.

Decision Time

Jeanne sat on the decision for several weeks until her husband came home one evening and asked, "What did you decide about the business, honey?" She admitted she still didn't know, and Rick agreed to take a few hours that evening and discuss it to help her arrive at a decision. She had decided that she did want to expand but needed answers to quite a few questions before she could proceed. These questions were:

Whom should she hire, and how should she get in touch with them? How many employees did she need? Should she hire them all at once or one at a time? What positions should she create, and what should be their duties? Which position should she fill first? What procedures would she need to institute? Where should she expand her market? Were supermarkets worth the bother? What other locations besides her present customers might be interested in her product? What would be the best way to contact these potential customers—through a trade journal or through personal contacts, as she had been doing? What was the best medium to use to support her customers with product advertising? Should she expand her product line and offer a second kind of cookie? Was franchising a viable—or desirable— option? What other issues needed to be resolved before she could proceed with confidence?

Jeanne and Rick were going to be in for a long evening.

Questions for Discussion

1. Evaluate the performance of The Beary Best Cookies up to this point.
2. (a) Should Jeanne expand? (b) Why or why not?
3. What new markets should The Beary Best Cookies pursue?
4. (a) Where should The Beary Best Cookies look for its new employees? (b) Why?
5. What duties should be performed by others immediately, and which should Jeanne Parnell continue to perform?

Source: Prepared by Scott D. Julian and Bob Justis, Louisiana State University.

THE CASE OF SAM SAWYER

Sam Sawyer was a top-rated operator in a building devoted to a five-stage batch process involving material with a high percentage of caustic soda. The five stages in the process were located on five separate floors. In addition to controlling temperatures carefully on various pieces of equipment and making sure that the time cycles were closely controlled, the operators moved the material in open buggies from one stage to the proper chute located in the floor and dumped the material through the chute to equipment on the floor below, where the next stage took place.

Because of the corrosive nature of the material, eye protection in the form of close-fitting goggles had been provided for a number of years. Until a year ago, the safety rules required only that goggles be worn when removing material from equipment, since it was during the unloading operations that the greatest possibility of injury existed. The wearing of goggles at other times was up to the discretion of the operator.

At two stages in the process, the material was light and fluffy, and there were occasional backdrafts through the chutes causing it to fly. There had been three cases of minor eye irritations from this cause. Consequently, the safety rule had been changed about a year earlier, and operators were required to wear goggles whenever they were near exposed material.

Dave Watts, who had been supervisor for two years, had come to the plant three years ago directly from engineering school. Before becoming supervisor, he had worked on all stages of the operation and had gotten along well with all the men. He felt very kindly toward them because they had taught him the "tricks of the trade" so that by the time he became supervisor he had a thorough knowledge of the operations.

Watts' shift supervisor was very safety-minded, often saying that "all personal injuries can be prevented." He was quite insistent that safety rules be followed to the letter.

Sam Sawyer, the oldest operator in point of service, had been working on this particular operation for 20 years and was an outstanding operator on all five stages. Because of his years of experience and his excellence as an operator, he was looked up to by the rest of the men. He had an outstanding safety record, which was one of the best in the plant, as he had had only one minor injury in all his years of service.

When the new safety rule went into effect earlier, Dave was bothered because everyone went along with it except Sam, who resisted the change in the rule. This caused some difficulty in selling the rule to the other men because they respected his opinions. His main contention was that it was unnecessary to wear goggles except when unloading equipment. After much discussion however, he agreed to go along with the rule.

During the past six months, Dave had caught Sam without his goggles on four occasions. He had a strong feeling that Sam was not complying with the safety rule fully and that his opinions were unchanged. Dave suspected that Sam was complying with the rule only while he was around. On half a dozen occasions he had had the feeling that Sam had put the goggles over his eyes when the supervisor came on the floor. Before the rule change, Sam had worn his goggles around his neck when they were not needed, but he had started wearing them pushed up on his forehead. The supervisor's doubts were confirmed three days ago when he came upon Sam unexpectedly and saw him bob his head to shift the goggles from his forehead to his eyes.

Questions for Discussion

1. What does the case show about the need for emphasis on safety by management?
2. How can you explain the workers' lack of interest in their own safety?
3. What would you do if you were the supervisor?

Source: Prepared by Bruce Gunn, Florida State University.

CASE III–5
THE PEPPER BUSH

Sherman Kent, an electrical engineer and a graduate of one of the foremost universities in the Southwest, determined that his future lay in operating a restaurant. This idea evolved by accident over a period of time when Sherman did the cooking for hunting and fishing trips with friends. He used jalapeño pepper liberally to flavor the food and combined it with cheese to form a spread to enhance the flavor of the meat.

His hunting and fishing companions suggested that he should market his product. As the discussions became more serious, they agreed to back him financially if he would establish and manage a restaurant specializing in hamburgers with the special-recipe jalapeño cheese sauce. Thus, the Pepper Bush was born.

Three years ago, in the spring, Sherman opened the small restaurant in a suburban community of approximately 15,000 near a large metropolitan area. He was the operating partner, and two other partners helped finance the business by securing a small loan from a local bank. He secured a building with a seating capacity of 50 and equipped it to serve the usual line of short-order food items. Though he specialized in hamburgers with the special jalapeño and cheese sauce, he also served other kinds of hamburgers, french fries, beverages, and so forth. His principal competition was franchise food operations such as McDonald's and Burger King.

The personnel policies of the Pepper Bush could be described as highly unstructured. When Sherman opened the restaurant, he hired a cook, three waitresses, and a dishwasher by running ads in the local papers. He did much of the cooking himself and performed all of the management functions. This past year, his employees consisted of two cooks, five full-time waitresses, two part-time waitresses, and three dishwashers.

One of the cooks, Alvin Marsh, also served as assistant manager. Alvin was one of the first employees hired and had been with Sherman throughout the two-and-a-half-year existence of the Pepper Bush. He served as manager in Sherman's absence and for the previous six months had been actively involved with Sherman in hiring new employees. When a vacancy occurred, one of the employees would bring a friend to Sherman to be interviewed, or Sherman would run an ad in the local paper.

The interview was relatively brief, no formal application was required, and the applicant was either hired on the spot or told immediately that he or she would not be hired. Turnover of employees had been remarkably small. Two of the waitresses had been at the Pepper Bush since it opened. Sherman stated that the low turnover rate was due to the fact that he took a personal interest in each of his employees and took into account individual differences. For example, he did not require any uniform dress. Most of the waitresses wore jeans and a blouse, and the male help could wear their hair as long as they desired. He also allowed a "very flexible schedule of work," with the various classes of employees working out their own substitutions, as long as each category was covered during the appropriate hours.

Sherman had no formal job descriptions, and his training consisted of on-the-job training. For example, all waitresses were expected to be able to work the cash register, wait tables, clean the tables, and, if on the last shift, clean up for the night. But if the waitresses were too busy, the cook might also work the cash register or clean the tables. All employees were expected to do whatever needed doing.

By this past summer, business had increased to a gross of $250,000, and Sherman was thinking of expanding. Financing could be secured from the bank, and a newer and larger site could be found in the vicinity of the present restaurant.

The proposed expansion would complicate Sherman's personnel problems. The "personal touch," the paternalistic attitude that Sherman had taken toward his employees (the average age of the 10 full-time employees was 21), was a luxury he could afford. But if he expanded—and he expected at least to double the number of employees within the next six months—would he need a more formalized organizational structure? Sherman and Alvin also discussed the overall personnel problems.

Questions for Discussion

1. Should Sherman and Alvin continue the present unstructured informal personnel policy if they did not expand?
2. How would the proposed expansion affect this policy?

Source: Prepared by William V. Rice and Robert McGlashan, The University of Houston at Clear Lake City.

IV

OPERATING THE BUSINESS

Up to this point, we have been concerned with the challenge of owning and managing a small business: planning for, organizing, and managing the business and selecting and leading the work force. Now it is time to look at the process of actually operating the business.

Many and diverse activities are required to carry on operations. Your business must determine what products to sell; decide whether to purchase them from someone else or produce them; plan, acquire, lay out, and maintain the physical facilities needed for operations; procure and produce the right quality of the right products, at the right time and at the right cost; control the quality and quantity of inventory; control the quality of your output; maintain a work force; and *do all of this as efficiently and economically as possible!*

All these activities make operations interesting, challenging, and rewarding—but also quite frustrating. To help meet this challenge, this part will cover designing operating systems for production and service. Locating and laying out facilities are discussed in Chapter 13. Chapter 14 covers purchasing, operations, and quality control.

13

LOCATING AND LAYING OUT FACILITIES

Production is not the application of tools to materials, but logic to work.—Peter F. Drucker

You know your company is ready for robots when you recognize that automating is cheaper than relocating in South Korea or Taiwan.—Bruce H. Kleiner, management professor

LEARNING OBJECTIVES

After studying the material in this chapter, you will be able to:

1. Explain what an operating system is and how it functions.
2. Discuss how to determine the right location for a small business.
3. Describe the important factors involved in choosing a retail site.
4. Describe the most important factors involved in choosing a manufacturing site.
5. Go through the steps in planning the layout of physical facilities.
6. Explain how to set and use performance standards.

TEAGUE BROTHERS RUG AND CARPET CLEANERS: CLEANING PERSIAN CARPETS

"We are in business to provide a needed service," said Joe Teague, who, with his wife, Margaret, owns and operates Teague Brothers Carpet Sales and Service. "First we sell carpets, and then we clean them."

Joe Teague operated a moving company before opening the carpet business in 1959. His wife joined him in 1962, when their children were in school. Business declined sharply in the mid-1960s and early 1970s, when wall-to-wall carpeting became popular, but has since recovered. The Teagues' daughter and son-in-law now run the family moving business, while the parents concentrate on the carpet business.

The Teagues operate in a building containing a sales showroom, an office, two production rooms where the carpets are cleaned, and a warehouse. The two activities require two different operating systems. The new carpets are on display in the sales showroom, along with chairs and desks for customers and sales personnel. After purchase, the carpets are delivered, or the carpeting and runners are installed. When customers bring carpets—bought from the Teagues or others—for

cleaning, that operation takes place in the two production rooms. While cleaning Oriental carpets may seem simple and easy, it is really quite complicated and difficult, according to Mrs. Teague.

The process starts on one of the major pieces of equipment: a long cylinder called a beater vacuum. The rug, inserted upside down, literally has the dirt beaten out of it by a series of leather "fingers." The vacuum then sucks the dirt away.

Next, the carpet is laid flat on the sloping floor, spot-sprayed with cleaning fluid, and thoroughly doused with a mixture of cleaner and water from a wooden container 15 feet above the floor. An electric cleaning machine is repeatedly passed back and forth by one of two men; then the carpet is rinsed clean, and the cleaner and water are drained into a gutter around the edge of the floor.

Next, the two men pick up the carpet and feed it into slots on the second major piece of equipment: the rolling machine (see photo). Rollers feed the rug through while it is rinsed to get out any remaining dirt or cleaning mixture; the rollers squeeze it to extract excess water. The

Willie Autry and Archie Lawson remove a carpet from the machine after the final rinse of cleaning. The rug is ready to go into the drying room.

Source: Mobile (Alabama) *Press Register*, August 24, 1986, Photo by Jay Ferchaud. © 1986, The Mobile Press Register, Inc. All rights reserved.

carpet then is hung up on a pole and dried at a constant temperature of 140 degrees. While only 1 carpet can be cleaned at one time, up to 40 can be dried simultaneously.

This washing process may seem a peculiar way to clean a valuable carpet, but that is the way they are cleaned after being woven in Iran, Turkey, Pakistan, and Afghanistan.

Sources: Visits to Teague Brothers; Marion Valentino, "Taking an Old Favorite to the Cleaners," *Mobile* (Alabama) *Press Register,* August 24, 1986, p. 14-F; and Carol Cain Lynn, "Business All in the Family," *Mobile* (Alabama) *Press Register,* August 6, 1989, p. 3-E.

As the Opening Focus illustrates, all businesses produce some product, either selling a good or providing a service. A retailer forecasts demand and then purchases merchandise and displays, sells, and delivers it to customers. A producer forecasts demand and then purchases material, processes it into products, and sells and delivers the products to customers. A service business tries to satisfy the needs of customers by providing a needed service. This chapter examines what is involved in producing the firm's product, how to choose the right location to produce it, how to plan and lay out physical facilities, and how to constantly improve operations.

DEVELOPING OPERATING SYSTEMS

The steps required to start a business were discussed in Chapter 5. Among those steps are:

1. Searching for a product.
2. Studying the market for the product.
3. Deciding how to get into business.
4. Making strategic plans.
5. Making operational plans, including planning the many aspects of operating the business once it's started.

As shown in Figure 5–1, once the idea for the business is found, the ownership-management question settled, and the money obtained, then operating systems can be set up, including providing building(s), materials, equipment, and people to produce the product.

These operating systems are really quite similar. The sequence of events and activities may vary because each business adjusts the system to fit its own needs. At the same time the main system is operating, support systems, such as accounting, personnel, and cash flow systems, must be integrated into the overall producing system.

What Are Operating Systems?

An **operating system** consists of inputs, processes, and outputs. The **inputs** include materials, people, money, information, machines, and other factors. The **process** involves converting these inputs into the goods or services the customers want, using the employees, machines, materials, and other

Figure 13–1   Examples of Inputs Transformed to Outputs

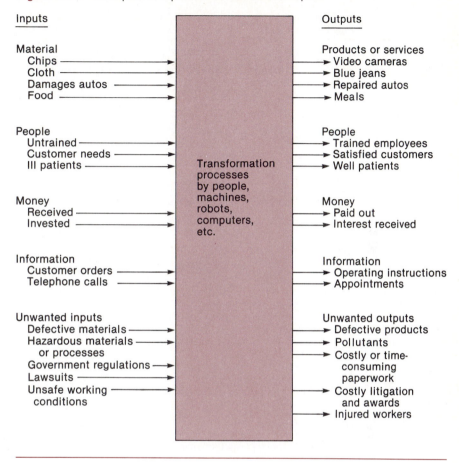

Inputs

Material
  Chips
  Cloth
  Damages autos
  Food

People
  Untrained
  Customer needs
  Ill patients

Money
  Received
  Invested

Information
  Customer orders
  Telephone calls

Unwanted inputs
  Defective materials
  Hazardous materials
    or processes
  Government regulations
  Lawsuits
  Unsafe working
    conditions

Transformation
processes
by people,
machines,
robots,
computers,
etc.

Outputs

Products or services
  Video cameras
  Blue jeans
  Repaired autos
  Meals

People
  Trained employees
  Satisfied customers
  Well patients

Money
  Paid out
  Interest received

Information
  Operating instructions
  Appointments

Unwanted outputs
  Defective products
  Pollutants
  Costly or time-
    consuming
    paperwork
  Costly litigation
    and awards
  Injured workers

factors. The **outputs** consist of the goods and services required by the customers; desired outputs also include satisfying the needs of employees and the public. Figure 13–1 provides a few examples of how inputs are transformed into outputs.

How Operating Systems Work

Production, or **operations,** includes all the activities from obtaining raw materials through providing the good or service to the buyer. Thus, *operations* refers to those activities necessary to produce and deliver a service or good. Figure 13–2 shows examples of the processes and operations used in different types of businesses. Note that each conversion of inputs to outputs represents a major activity and involves some type of transformation: cloth, thread, and buttons are sewn into shirts; dirty carpets (as shown in

Figure 13–2 Examples of Operating Systems

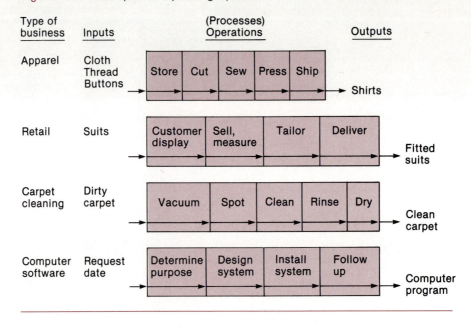

Type of business	Inputs	(Processes) Operations					Outputs
Apparel	Cloth Thread Buttons	Store	Cut	Sew	Press	Ship	Shirts
Retail	Suits	Customer display	Sell, measure	Tailor		Deliver	Fitted suits
Carpet cleaning	Dirty carpet	Vacuum	Spot	Clean	Rinse	Dry	Clean carpet
Computer software	Request date	Determine purpose	Design system	Install system		Follow up	Computer program

Figure 13–3 Examples of Productive Elements, as Applied to Carpet Cleaning

Productive Elements	Example
1. System(s) for changing form, place, or time.	System for cleaning Oriental carpets.
2. Sequence of steps to change the inputs into outputs.	*a.* Beating dirt out. *b.* Dousing with cleaning fluid. *c.* Cleaning with an electric cleaning machine. *d.* Rinsing. *e.* Drying.
3. Special skills, tools, and/or machines needed to make the change.	*a.* Beater vacuum. *b.* Electric cleaning machine. *c.* Rolling machine.
4. Instructions and goods specifications.	*a.* Workers are trained in the approved cleaning method. *b.* Cloth tags are attached to carpets for identification.
5. Time frame in which work is to be done.	Each step is done at a specified time.
6. Controls for exceptions and errors.	One of the owners supervises the entire operation to detect and correct errors.

the Opening Focus) are cleaned; or a request for data is converted into a computer program.

The Opening Focus is a good illustration of the productive elements that are common to all processes of changing inputs to outputs. Figure 13–3 lists some of these elements and gives an example of each.

A business usually has systems other than the production system, as the following example shows.

Domino's Pizza became the nation's second-largest pizza peddler by putting speedy service ahead of a wide selection of products. According to its founder, Thomas S. Monaghan, "Basically, we're a delivery company, and it just so happens that people want us to bring them pizzas. If you have too many items, you can't operate a delivery system effectively."[1]

In essence, Domino's has three systems: (1) an order-taking system, which is marketing, (2) a production system, which involves preparing the pizza, and (3) a delivery system. While these systems must be coordinated, the delivery system is the most important one.

Systems Must Be Coordinated

As indicated, there is usually more than one operating system in a business. These systems must be coordinated for best production.

For example, the objective of fast-food operations is to supply food quickly and with little customer effort. At Burger King, for example, there are three systems:

1. *Marketing system.*   The order for a Whopper is taken from the customer and money received to pay for it.
2. *Production System.*   The order is given to the cook, who prepares the hamburger and packages it, while other employees prepare drinks.
3. *Delivery system.*   The completed order is handed to the customer.

These three systems are coordinated to provide quick service and to keep the line moving. Figure 13–4 shows how the production system operates. Notice the inputs, processes, and outputs. The inputs, such as rolls, meat patties, mayonnaise, lettuce, onions, and pickles, are processed by cooking, assembling, and wrapping into the output a double-meat hamburger, which is then delivered to the customer.

How to Begin Operations

You are now ready to begin operations, which involves choosing the right location, planning physical facilities, deciding on a layout, and implementing your plans.

Figure 13–4   Operations Involved in Producing a Hamburger

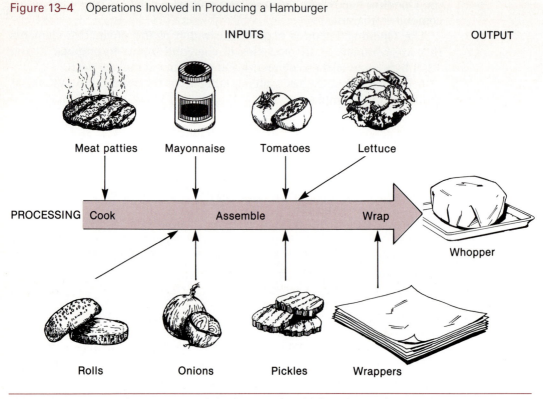

Source: Adapted from Leon C. Megginson, Lyle R. Trueblood, and Gayle M. Ross, *Business* (Lexington, Mass.: D. C. Heath, 1985), p. 202.

CHOOSING THE RIGHT LOCATION

As shown in Chapters 6 and 7, you must define the character of your business and establish your business strategies before you begin to investigate available locations for your business. You must then ask yourself such questions as: Do I plan to have just one store or to grow regionally or nationwide? Do I intend to concentrate on one product area or expand into several? The answer to these questions will focus your search.

Why Choosing the Right Location Is So Important

Location is one of the factors that can make the difference between success and failure for a small business. Sales come from customers who find it advantageous to buy from you rather than someone else. These advantages can include convenience, cost, reliability, and good service. All of these are influenced by location. Therefore, each business should evaluate its specific location requirements very carefully.

When a business chooses a location, it usually expects to stay there for some time. It is very expensive to move to another location; customers follow established patterns of activity and do not like changes; and employees are affected in the same way. These are good arguments for choosing the right location from the start.

Changes are difficult to predict, however. The introduction of a new highway or repair work on an existing road can isolate a business. The movement of a large store into the area can change the patterns of traffic and the buying habits of the public. Increased eating out has decreased the per capita purchase of food items in food stores while escalating those in restaurants and fast-food outlets. Changing technology, such as the introduction of prerecorded video tapes, has drastically changed the way stores operate—and spawned a new industry, video sales and rental shops, such as the Maine Line Company (see Chapter 2). Predicting changes that will affect a business, therefore, is part of the thorough study required for locating the business.

Collecting Information about Potential Locations

Information on which to base a decision can come from a wide variety of sources, as we discussed in Chapter 5 and will cover in more detail in Chapter 17.

At some point, the data collected must be analyzed to provide the information necessary for a decision. A score sheet like that in Figure 13–5 can

---

Figure 13–5 Rating Sheet on Sites

Grade each factor: 1 (lowest) to 10 (highest)
Weigh each factor: 1 (least important) to 5 (most important)

Factors	Grade	Weight
1. Centrally located to reach my market.	_____	_____
2. Raw materials readily available.	_____	_____
3. Quantity of available labor.	_____	_____
4. Transportation availability and rates.	_____	_____
5. Labor rates of pay/estimated productivity.	_____	_____
6. Adequacy of utilities (sewer, water, power, gas).	_____	_____
7. Local business climate.	_____	_____
8. Provision for future expansion.	_____	_____
9. Tax burden.	_____	_____
10. Topography of the site (slope and foundation).	_____	_____
11. Quality of police and fire protection.	_____	_____
12. Housing availability for workers and managers.	_____	_____
13. Environmental factors (schools, cultural, community atmosphere).	_____	_____
14. Estimate of quality of this site in years.	_____	_____
15. Estimate of this site in relation to my major competitor.	_____	_____

Note: Copies of this *Aid* and other publications are available from SBA for a small processing fee. Order forms 115A and 115B can be obtained free from SBA, P.O. Box 15434. Forth Worth, TX 76119. *Aids* may be condensed or reproduced. They may not be altered to imply approval by SBA of any private organization, product or service. Material courtesy of Small Business Administration.

Source: U.S. Small Business Administration, *Locating or Relocating Your Business,* Management Aid No. 2.002, p. 6.

be valuable in comparing possible locations. Evaluations can sometimes be quantitative, such as number of households times median income times percentage of income spent on store items times some special factor for this store. Others are ratings, grading factors from 1 for the lowest to 10 for the highest.

Some factors are very important and should be given more weight than others. In fact, one factor in a given site might be so intolerable that the site must be eliminated from consideration.

Some Important Factors Affecting Location Choice

Two sets of factors should be considered when choosing a location for your small business. Some general factors affect all types of businesses, but there are also some factors that pertain to specific types of businesses.

General Factors Affecting All Businesses

The more important general factors are (1) access to the work force, (2) availability of utilities, (3) availability of vendors, (4) access to transportation, and (5) taxes and government regulations.

Access to work force.   The number of people with the necessary characteristics and skills must be available. And availability depends on the distance to and from work, congestion, accessible public transportation, and the people's employment and income level. If you locate your business where people can walk to work and possibly even go home for lunch, there may be an advantage in pay negotiations, worker loyalty and interest, and better job attendance. Proximity to child care is becoming increasingly important for small firms.

Availability of utilities.   Access to utilities, such as electric power, gas, water, sewerage, and steam, is important. Increasing use of machines and problems in waste disposal can make utilities a major factor in location.

Availability of vendors.   A sufficient number of vendors must be available to supply the inventory needs of the business. When selecting vendors, you must determine the types of supportive service each seller provides, such as help in: (1) designing a product or products, (2) selecting machinery and plant, (3) solving technical problems, and (4) pricing and formulating trade credit practices.

You may be unable to find a satisfactory vendor if there are no parts or tools available for the product you want to produce or sell. Or a service firm, unable to find the part or equipment needed to perform its service, may have to make its own, as in the following example.

In 1984, Phil Hardy founded Telecommunications Technology Inc. to market new "intelligent" pay phones—ones with chips for switching. "We had no idea we would be manufacturing phones, as we wanted to have a vending phone business," says Hardy. But, unable to find a high-quality, coin-operated phone, and faced with steep tariffs to use Bell Telephone lines, the company designed and now makes its own phones.[2]

Phil Hardy, founder and marketing director for TTI, makes a call on one of the company's TTI Model 400k pay phones.

Access to transportation.   The success of a location can hinge on the availability, type, use, and cost of transportation. Questions you need to ask are:

- Can the most economical type of transportation be used for both incoming and outgoing shipments?
- Are there railroad spurs to the location? Truck lines? Buses?
- Does the site allow for enough parking?

Taxes and government regulations.   A firm's location is influenced by rates and types of taxes, licenses, zoning, waste disposal, government services, and other restrictions, as well as by government attitude toward business at the state and local levels. The value of available state and municipal services, such as recreation and education, should be balanced against the costs. The best location is one that provides optimum benefits with optimum costs.

Specific Factors to Consider for Various Businesses

The type of business influences most location decisions because it determines the relative importance of the general factors mentioned above; for example, location of customers may be more important to a large department store, while location of employees will be more important to a manufacturing plant. We will discuss the basic considerations for (1) retailers, (2) producers, and (3) service businesses.

The lines between these types of business can be fuzzy, so the locational analysis will depend on the primary emphasis of the business. **Retailers** are firms or people who obtain goods from wholesalers, brokers, and agents and sell them to the ultimate consumers for personal, nonbusiness use.[3] But some stores personalize the items they have bought, which may be a producing activity. **Producers** change raw material or parts into finished products for sale through agents or representatives, but some small producers may also sell their goods at retail. **Service businesses** provide for the nonproduct needs of customers. Some companies perform retail, production, *and* service activities, but tend to emphasize one of them. However, location analysis should apply to the major activity of the firm.

Retailers are concerned with people who come to—or are drawn into—the store for the purpose of making a purchase. The major emphasis is on the store and the people. Location is concerned with people's movement, attention, attitudes, convenience, needs, and ability to buy. In other words, which location will provide sales at a reasonable profit?

Producers are not usually concerned with the flow of people coming in to buy goods. Usually sales are made by salespeople or through other promotion for delivery at some future date. The plant and customer can be some distance apart, so other factors become more important. Still, nearness to customers and suppliers is beneficial to keep costs down and permit satisfactory service. Primary emphasis in locating, though, is placed on cost and service.

Service companies have some of the characteristics of both retailing and producing. These companies perform specialized services to individuals and organizations. Services requiring customers to come to the business location, such as a hairdresser, have considerable latitude within convenient travel. Services going to the home of a customer may have even more latitude, but try to be within an area where customers are clustered. In fact, service businesses that cannot attract enough customers to a central location may acquire more by taking their show on the road.

For example, after grooming dogs for 27 years from a fixed location, Ronnie and Martell White now use a "grooming van." They are the owners of On the Spot Dog Grooming. With a small office in their home, they cover an area of about 100 square miles. The van is fully loaded with an extensive unit for all aspects of dog grooming, including a built-in bathtub. On an average day, the Whites service eight dogs or more at a cost of $15 or $20 each.[4]

Many small service businesses start and continue to operate out of the owner's home. This is a logical arrangement since the owner may be tentative about going into business and not want to have the fixed expense of an office. Also, the owner tends to go to the clients to perform the service. Finally, as will be shown in Chapter 23, there are tax benefits.

Notice in Case III–3, The Beary Best Cookies, that Jeanne Parnell did most of the work out of her home. She even took her children with her to deliver her cookies.

Figure 13–6 lists some of the many factors to be considered in making location decisions. Although the factors have been separated into retail and producing, many of them apply equally to retailing, producing, and service organizations.

LOCATING RETAIL STORES

In choosing a site for a retail store, there are two important factors, which are interrelated. One is the type of store (i.e., the type of goods sold), and the other is the type of location.

Figure 13–6 Some Important Location Factors

	Factors affecting selection of	
City	Area in city	Specific site
Retail:		
Size of trade area	Attraction power	Traffic passing site
Population trends	Competitive nature	Ability to intercept
Purchasing power	Access routes	traffic
Trade potential	Zoning regulations	Compatibility of
Competition	Area expansion	adjacent stores
Shopping centers	General appearance	Adequacy of parking
		Unfriendly competition
		Cost of site
Producing:		
Market location	Zoning	Zoning
Vendor location	Industrial park	Sewer, effluent control
Labor available	Transportation	Transportation
Transportation		Terrain
Utilities		Utilities
Government, taxes		Labor available
Schools, recreation		

Source: U.S. Small Business Administration, *Choosing a Retailing Location,* Management Aid No. 2.021 (Washington, D.C.), p. 2.

Types of Stores

Customers view products they buy in different ways when selecting the store from which to buy. Therefore, stores can be grouped into (1) convenience, (2) shopping, and (3) specialty stores, according to the type of goods they sell.

Convenience Goods Stores

Convenience goods are usually low-priced items that are purchased often, are sold in many stores, are bought by habit, and lend themselves to self-service. Although the term *convenience goods* may make you think of **convenience stores,** small markets with gas pumps out front, convenience goods stores are better typified by the grocery and variety stores where you shop regularly for consumable items. Convenience goods stores are interested in having a high flow of customer traffic, so they try to get people to remember their needs and come in to purchase the items currently on display. The quantity of customer flow seems more important than its quality. These stores are built where the traffic flow is already heavy.

When consumer needs are recognized at home, the convenience of location and ready availability of these items are quite important. Nearly 70 percent of women have been found to patronize stores within five blocks of their residence. Store hours are also very important.

Shopping Goods Stores

Shopping goods are usually higher-priced items, which are bought infrequently, and for which the customer compares prices. People spend much time looking for these items and talking to sales personnel. Therefore, capable salespeople with selling ability are required (see Chapter 16 for more detail). Examples of these goods are suits, automobiles, and furniture.

Not all people buy the same quality or type of shopping goods, so a shopping goods store must be located where its particular customers can find it easily. For example, a downtown store, close to the traffic flow of higher-income people, used to be best for quality clothing. Now such stores gravitate to large shopping malls in the suburbs, while the stores in the center of most cities cater to the needs of the inner-city residents. Discount stores tend to be located near highways or at major traffic intersections. Comparison shopping, as is done for automobiles, sometimes impels competitors to locate near each other. Also, a theater tends to promote traffic for eating places.

Care should be exercised not to locate too far away from potential customers. Studies have indicated that the majority of shoppers live within five miles of the stores they patronize.

Specialty Goods Stores

Specialty goods are high-priced shopping goods with trade names that are recognized for the exclusive nature of the clientele for the goods. By their very nature, specialty goods stores often generate their own traffic, but customer flow can be helped by similar stores in the vicinity. Some examples of specialty goods are quality dresses, precious jewelry, and expensive video and sound equipment. In essence, people do not comparison shop for specialty goods, but just buy the name on the item.

Types of Locations

In general, the types of locations for retail businesses are (1) downtown, (2) a free-standing store, and (3) community shopping centers or malls.[5]

Downtown Location

Changes in retail locations have occurred as discounters have located their stores outside the downtown area. Now, governments, financial businesses, and the head offices of large firms provide most of the downtown business for retail establishments. Those businesses planning to locate in the downtown area need to watch for changes in trends.

A downtown location has many advantages, such as lower rents, better public transportation, and proximity to where people work. But the disadvantages include limited shopping hours, higher crime rates, poor or inadequate traffic and parking, and deterioration of downtown areas.

Free-Standing Locations

A free-standing location may be the best for customers who have brand or company loyalty, or those who identify with a given shop, where a business has an edge over its competition, where the character of customers and growth objectives blend well. The low costs, good parking, independent hours and operation, and restricted competition in these locations tend to fit the more entrepreneurial types of businesspeople. However, in order to attract customers, especially new ones, you may have to do considerable advertising. Moreover, acquiring a suitable building and land may be difficult.

For example, Steve and Barbara Chappell had great difficulty finding a building for their Our Hero Restaurant (Case II–2) after buying the franchise. The local university wasn't interested in either selling or leasing property for it.

Steve got the names of adjacent property owners from the town hall, wrote to them, and then called them. He found one owner just completing a building and was able to negotiate a lease—but only because of his extraordinary efforts.

Shopping Centers

Shopping centers are planned and built only after lengthy and involved studies. These centers vary in size from small neighborhood and strip centers, to community centers, to the large regional malls.

Why shopping centers are so popular.   Shopping centers are designed to draw traffic according to the planned nature of the stores to be included in them. The design of the centers ranges from small, neighborhood convenience goods stores to giant regional centers with a wide range of goods and services, which may or may not be specialized. A current trend is for large "power centers" to compete with one another to be the largest. For example, the center that is called "the largest mall in the world" is located in Edmonton, Canada.

The typical shopping center has two **anchor stores.** These stores, often large department stores, are located at the ends of the mall and are strategically located to generate heavy traffic for themselves and for the small stores between them. These shopping centers offer many services, such as specialized activities to bring in traffic, merchant association activities, parking, utilities, and combined advertising.

Enclosed malls have eliminated weather problems for big stores themselves as well as for their customers. Also, older and handicapped people are encouraged to use the mall to exercise in a controlled climate.

Some centers may have a "theme" that stores are expected to conform to. The purpose of the theme is to pull the stores together and have them handle products of similar quality. For example, the center may have regulations on shopping hours, how to use the space in front of the store (what to display and how), and so on. Usually, shopping centers can provide most of the information needed when someone is considering them as a site location for a retail or service business.

Drawbacks of shopping centers.   Although the above advantages are considerable, there are also disadvantages to locating in a center. Some of the most significant of these are cost, restrictions imposed by the center's theme, operating regulations, and possible changes in the center's owners and managers, which could bring policy changes. There is now a "total rent" concept for cost that must be considered in evaluating the costs of renting space in a shopping center. Costs may include dues to the merchants' association, maintenance fees for the common areas, and the cost of special events or combined advertising. The usual rental is a basic rent, usually based on square footage, plus a percentage of gross sales (usually 5 to 7 percent). These costs tend to be high and often discourage tenants, as the following example shows.

Kitty operated her medium-priced ladies' wear shop in the same location for a number of years. It was in a small shopping area across from one of the community's larger shopping malls. A representative of the mall tried to persuade Kitty to move to the mall.

After inquiring about the rental terms, Kitty was appalled. The basic rent was $21.75 per square foot, with an additional charge of 5 percent of the gross sales. Later, Kitty told a friend: "Do you know that just the basic rent would have cost me $1,200 a month? Then I would have had to add on that 5 percent. Can you imagine what I would have had to charge for my clothes in order to make a profit after paying that kind of rent? I think I'd better stay put."

Also, shopping centers can decline in sales and popularity until they are "dead." This hurts the small businesses more than large ones, which can share the loss with their stores in other locations.

Connie's Confections (Case IV–2) ran into this problem and must consider moving to another location.

LOCATING MANUFACTURING OPERATIONS

Manufacturing usually involves making, or processing, a raw material into a finished product. The raw materials may be those extracted from the ground, or they may be outputs of other companies (such as metal plates, silicon chips, or ground meat for hamburgers), which are changed in form or shape, or assembled into a different type of product. The location of a manufacturing plant is usually selected with the aim of serving customers properly at the lowest practical cost. Figure 13–6 shows some of the factors to consider in locating a manufacturing plant. Only two of the more important of these, (1) nearness to customers and vendors and (2) availability and cost of transportation, are discussed.

Nearness to Customers and Vendors

Of considerable importance to manufacturers is the time and cost of transporting finished goods to the customers and acquiring raw material from vendors. A central location among customers and vendors tends to minimize this time and cost factor. Distances, methods of movement, speed of delivery, and cost are also important. In making the locational decision, a map with pins and strings on it, or a computer with appropriate software, helps find the best location for the movement of materials and finished goods.

Availability and Cost of Transportation

The success of a given location can hinge on the availability and cost of the proper mode(s) of transportation. **Transportation modes** are the methods used to take products from place to place. A small producer has many choices of ways to move goods to and from its plant and/or warehouse. As will be shown, each mode has advantages and disadvantages.

Selection of the mode of transportation depends on speed, frequency, dependability, points served, capability (which includes capacity, flexibility, and adaptability to handle the product), and cost. As shown in Figure 13–7, the various modes can be evaluated as to their effectiveness on each of these variables.

Rail, truck, water transport, and pipelines are popular means of transporting bulky and heavy materials. Although the modes of transportation are changing, these tend still to be the primary modes used by small producers. The use of containers can also affect the transportation system used.

Figure 13–7   Comparison of the Basic Modes of Transportation

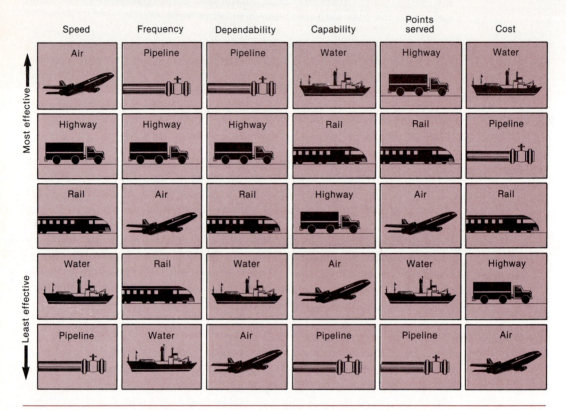

Source: Adapted from J. L. Heskett, Robert M. Ivie, and Nicholas A. Glaskowsky, Jr., *Business Logistics: Management of Physical Supply and Distribution* (New York: Ronald Press, 1964), p. 71. Copyright © 1964 by Ronald Press. Used by permission of John Wiley & Sons, Inc.

Trucks play an increasing part in shipping because of their flexibility and improved highway systems. However, changing traffic and government rules and regulations also affect location decisions.

A Nebraska feed and seed store owner has begun a campaign to get a recent city ordinance rescinded. The ordinance prohibits tractor-trailers from unloading in front of his store. The extra cost of unloading on the edge of town and transporting sacks of feed and seed to the store, says the store owner, will force him out of business.

While these modes of transportation are important, the use of air transport is increasing, particularly for items and information that must be delivered in a hurry, as well as for products with a high unit value and low weight and bulk. In such cases, a site near an airport should be considered if the costs are not too high.

PLANNING PHYSICAL FACILITIES

Once the location is determined, the business owner must begin planning, acquiring, and installing the facilities. These facilities, which include the building, machines and equipment, and furniture and fixtures, must be designed or selected to produce the desired product at the lowest practical cost. As the next Computer Update shows, computers are now being used in this type of design operation.

These various activities can be reduced to four steps: (1) determine the product to be sold and the volume in which it is to be produced, (2) identify the operations and activities required to process the product to the purchaser, (3) determine space requirements, and (4) determine the best arrangement of the facilities; that is, an effective layout.

Determine Product to Be Produced

This step was discussed in earlier chapters, especially Chapters 5 through 7. It is important, though, to review these discussions, particularly the matter of volume. Facilities should be planned for the future so as to avoid early major changes. However, planning too far into the future can result in heavy initial expenses for facilities that are too large. Projections for five years are normal, and industry standards for the space required for planned sales or production volume can be a good start in planning. Next, a detailed study is needed.

Identify Operations and Activities

Assuming that your business plans either to produce a product or to sell it to the ultimate consumer, the operations and activities can be broken down into three steps: (1) purchase materials and parts for production or goods to sell, (2) perform operations to produce or sell, and (3) carry out support activities.

The central activity, **operations,** comprises the steps or segments of work performed to accomplish the conversion of inputs into outputs. Operations such as selling and assembly are performed by trained workers, as are other operations such as drilling, word processing, and operating specialized machines. Some operations, such as selecting items and placing them in a cart in self-service stores, are performed by the customer.

Activities, such as moving materials and displaying goods, are necessary for servicing production and/or selling operations. Nonactivities, including delays, are caused by an imbalance of the times of the operations. Except when planned for, as in the case of browsing while shopping, the number and extent of nonactivities should be minimized.

Sequences of operations may be fixed (e.g., producing the hamburger in Figure 13–4) or may change from order to order, as happens in retail stores or service businesses. Planning emphasizes typical, high-volume products and is vital when designing a system for efficient use of the facilities and for maximization of sales.

COMPUTER UPDATE

AUDODESK, INC.: DESIGNERS GET INTO THEIR DESIGNS

A few years ago, designers found that with computers they could tinker with, test, and perfect their work on screens before going into costly prototypes. Some of the fancier systems even showed animated designs in three dimensions. Now, a Sausalito, California, company, Autodesk, Inc., believes engineers will want to go even further—getting inside their designing.

The company, which sells software to mechanical designers, is working on a product that creates a design "Never-Never Land" called *Hyperspace.* When the software is coupled with a high-powered computer, and special electronic eyeglasses and gloves are used, the designer has the impression that he or she is walking inside the project being designed. With this system, engineers can design not only a building but also its environment, and explore it while the designing is still being done.

Source: G. Pascal Zachary, "New Software Invites Designers into Designs," *The Wall Street Journal,* August 4, 1989, p. B1. Reprinted by permission of The Wall Street Journal, © Dow Jones & Company, Inc., 1989. ALL RIGHTS RESERVED.

Determine Space Requirements

Space is required for workers, customers, materials, equipment, and machines, as well as their movement, in stores, plants, and offices. It is needed to provide the environment desired (as in stores) and to foster or deter browsing. Space is needed for carts and trucks, inventory, displays, waiting, personal facilities, maintenance and cleaning, and many other services. The number and size of all these areas is dependent on the volume of output planned. If 1,000 widgets are needed per hour and a machine can perform one operation at the rate of 200 per hour, five machines are needed to obtain that volume. Space must be provided for these machines, their operators, inventory, and movement around the area.

Decide on the Best Layout

The objective in layout planning is to obtain the best placement of furniture and fixtures; tools, machines, and equipment; people, including employees and customers; storage and materials handling; and service activities such as cleaning and maintenance. There are many ways to plan layouts. One way used by professionals is to prepare a diagram of the floor and wall space of the building and then use templates, or models, of the items that are to go into the space. Then the templates are placed on the drawing to see if there is a smooth flow of operations or if the arrangement of facilities and people is illogical. This is similar to using cutouts of furniture to plan the arrangement of furniture in your home.

There are three aspects of layout that we will discuss—types of layouts, determining the general layout, and determining the detailed layout.

Figure 13–8   Product and Process Layout Comparison of Cafeterias

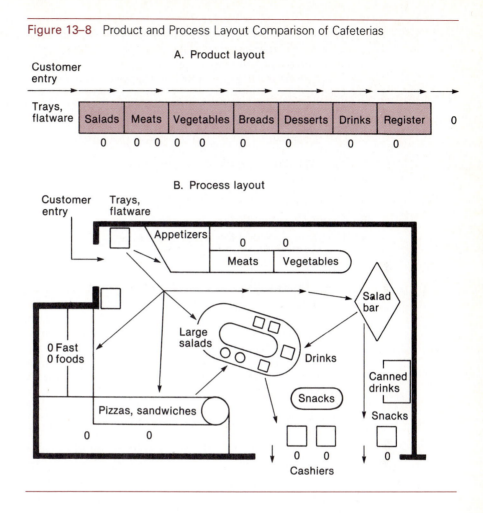

Types of Layout

The three general types of layout are product, process, and a combination of these two.

Product layout.   In a **product layout,** the arrangement follows the sequence of operations to be performed. In this type of layout, materials, workers, and/or customers move forward from one operation to another with little backtracking. The best-known type of product layout is the automobile assembly line, where the car moves forward from the first operation until it is driven off the line. Cafeteria lines, as shown in Figure 13–8(A), are also set up according to this type of layout, with the customer moving forward in a set sequence. This arrangement tends to improve efficiency and maximize sales.

The fast-food industry has adopted the product layout, with some variations. For example, if you order a Whopper from a Burger King franchise, notice (in Figure 13–4) that its production moves in a forward motion from cooking the meat to assembling the hamburgers and then to wrapping them and presenting them to the customer.

The advantages of the product layout plan include:

- Specialization of workers and machines.
- Less inventory.
- Fewer instructions and controls.
- Faster movement.
- Less space needed for aisles and storage.

Robots, like factory workers, depend on conveyor belts and other machines to bring them parts to work on. While conveyor systems are ideal for robotics, they cannot be changed easily when robots do different tasks. But ProgramMotion Inc., of Paoli, Pennsylvania, has designed flexible systems to move work from robot to robot. Its first product was a programmable conveyor system for semiconductor manufacturers. The system operates like a model railroad, moving parts around a track to the robots. Switches change the direction of the flow and can be reprogrammed to form different systems.[6]

Process layout.   The second type of layout, the **process layout,** is based on grouping together machines performing the same type of work and workers with similar skills. In stores, similar items are grouped together in a process layout so that customers can find and select items they want. Examples of this type of layout include printing presses grouped together so that each press can stay busy, typists put in a "pool" to perform typing for many offices, and toys located together in a store. The process layout increases the movement of material or people, as is shown in Figure 13–8(B), but requires having a larger inventory. The advantages of a process layout include:

- Flexibility to take care of change and variety.
- Use of general-purpose machines and equipment.   More efficient use of machines, time, and personnel.
- Ease in finding and evaluating merchandise.
- Grouping workers with like skills together.

Combination layout.   Few layout plans are totally product or process layouts. Instead, most layout plans combine the two to obtain the advantages of both. For example, a change from a product layout to a process layout increases inventory costs and decreases idle time costs. At some point, there is a balance.

Determining the General Layout

The next step in the design process is to determine the general layout, using blocks for sections of the layout. A **block** can be a machine, a group of machines, a group of products on display, or a department. The use of these blocks helps to establish the general arrangement of the plant, store, or office before spending much time on details. Using similar layouts as an example, and estimating the space needed, you can estimate the space needed in each block.

In Figures 13–9 and 13–10, the broken lines outline the spaces set aside for particular operations and activities. Space is also provided, where appropriate, for maintenance, planning, food service, personal needs, and other needed services. Each service should be placed conveniently near the units that use it.

If the layout of an existing building is being planned, the location of outside walls is predetermined. For example, Figure 13–9 shows an odd-shaped building in which it was difficult to plan a good layout for customer selling. On the other hand, planning a new building offers greater flexibility, since the building can be designed from the inside out.

Entrance locations are important in the layout of retail establishments, as shown in Figure 13–9. Customers usually enter downtown stores from the street, parking lot, or corridors, and goods usually enter from the back—setting the flow of goods from back to front. A number of producing plants use a U-shaped flow, as shown in Figure 13–10. External factors to consider include: entrances for employees, parking for customers, connections to utilities, governmental restrictions, and weather factors.

In manufacturing, many devices, such as conveyors, carts, hand trucks, and cranes, are used to move materials. Wholesale warehouses also face many types of materials-handling problems. The objective is to move the items as quickly as possible, with a minimum of handling, and without increasing other costs.

Determining the Final Layout

If performance is to be efficient, the final layout must be planned in detail. An understanding of methods study is helpful in planning workers' activities. Each operation should be examined to assure easy performance of work. If workers spend too much time in walking, turning, twisting, or other wasted motion, the work will take longer and be more tiring. Tools and other items to be used should be located close at hand for quick service. A short study of location of tools in a garage illustrates this point.

Some specific factors to be considered when doing your final layout are:

1. *Space for movement.* Is there enough room if a line forms? Can shelves be restocked conveniently? Are aisles wide enough for one- or two-way traffic?

Figure 13–9   Block Layout of a Fabric Store

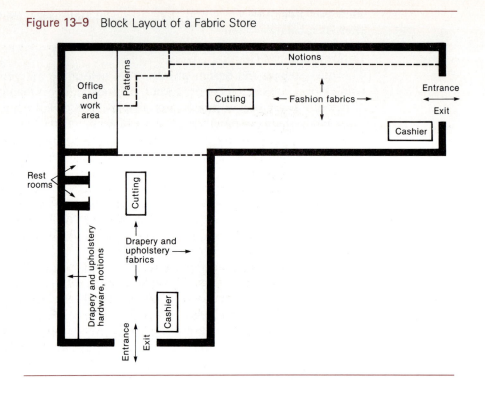

For example, grocery store aisles are designed to allow passage of two carts, but they often become blocked by special displays of new or sale items. Similarly, it may be difficult to squeeze between the display racks in department stores, and office planners often fail to allow enough space for storage of accumulated files.

2. *Utilities.*   Has adequate provision been made for incoming wiring and gas at each machine? Will any future moves of utilities be necessary? Are EPA standards for waste disposal being met?

3. *Safety.*   Is equipment using flammable material properly isolated, and is proper fire protection provided? Are moving parts and machines guarded and the operators protected from accidents?

4. *Working conditions.*   Do workers have enough working space and light? Are there provisions for low noise levels, proper temperature, and elimination of objectionable odors? Are workers safe, and can they socialize? Are personal needs provided for?

5. *Cleanliness and maintenance.*   Is the layout designed for good housekeeping at low cost? Can machinery, equipment, and the building itself be maintained easily?

Figure 13–10   Plant Layout for a Metal Sign Company

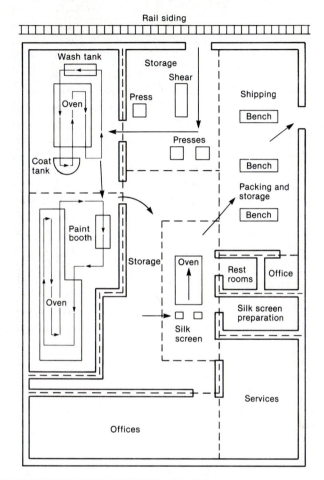

6. *Product quality.*   Are there provisions for protecting the product as it moves through the plant or stays in storage?

7. *Aesthetics.*   Are the layout and surroundings attractive to workers and customers?

The Gloucester, Virginia, ServiStar Hardware Store, patronized primarily by men, was dank, dark, and ugly. With more women becoming do-it-yourselfers and hence buyers of more hardware store items, ServiStar decided to change its image. It installed bright lights, chrome gridwork, and even murals. "Some of the old guys come in and kid us about being a disco," says Robert Fitchett, whose family owns the store, "but our sales are up 33 percent from last year."[7]

Implementing Your Plans

Finally, you should test your layout plans to see if they are sound. One way to do this is to have employees, customers, or other knowledgeable people review the plans and make suggestions. Another method is to move the templates or models of the goods or people through the process to analyze their movements.

Mick McGregor drew on his experience as an industrial engineer, plus ideas gathered from visiting competitors, to design The Mother and Child Shop (Case II–4). He used his engineering concepts to find the most effective layout for customer movement.

Finally, construction of a new building requires consideration of at least the following factors: (1) type and method of construction, (2) arrangements for vehicular movement and parking, (3) provision for public transportation, if available, and (4) landscaping.

HOW TO IMPROVE OPERATIONS

Products and methods of operation are constantly changing, and competition pushes out obsolete or inefficient businesses. However, there are some tools available in the disciplines of work simplification and industrial engineering to help you keep up to date and constantly improve your operations.

The objective of **work simplification,** or **industrial engineering,** is to record present activities in such a way as to highlight inefficiencies, and then to find ways to improve the process. Self-service in retail stores resulted from such studies, which showed that part of the service could be transferred to the customer, with improved operations and reduced costs. Computers are now used to help improve operations, particularly through the use of software that simulates operations.

The steps used in designing and improving work are: (1) state the problem, (2) collect and record information, (3) develop and analyze alternatives, and (4) select, install, and follow up on the new work method.

State the Problem

As usual, it is best to begin by clearly stating the problem, not a symptom of it. Ask questions such as: Is the cost of the work too high? Is the quality of the service low? Is the service to customers delayed? The reason(s) for making such a study should be clearly stated and understood in order to provide direction, reduce confusion, and ease employee fears. For example, one reason might be to reduce time so that customers receive better (faster) service.

John needed to have a gear replaced on his lawn mower. The repairman, Al, said to bring the mower to his shop at 8 A.M. John arrived at 8 A.M., Al at 8:30. Al said he couldn't replace the gear right away and to come back at 11. At 11 John came back; Al was talking on the phone, and the mower was not repaired. Al talked a while longer, hung up, then took a few more minutes to put the gear on. John said he will not go back because of Al's lack of interest.

Collect and Record Information

This step consists of collecting information for the what, how, where, who, why, and when of the work being done. Observing the work being performed, talking with knowledgeable people, and studying available data are methods of obtaining information. Information is recorded in chart form for easier study. The forms can be designed on paper or programmed into a computer.

Figure 13–11 illustrates a process flowchart for the first and second operations in making a metal sign, as shown in Figure 13–10. Not only does the chart show the operations (○) of cutting sides and corners, but it also shows transportation (→), inspections (□), delays (D), and storage (▽) of the work in progress. (Symbols are used to simplify your understanding of the process.) Observe the number of delays and transportations that

Figure 13–11   Process Flowchart for Making Metal Signs

Item description	Operation / Transportation / Inspection / Delay / Storage	Distance in feet	Pickups Lay-Downs	Time in Minutes	Quantity	Analysis (Why? What? Where? When? Who? How?)	Notes
IN STORAGE AREA	○ ⇨ □ D ▽						
TO SHEARS BY CART	○ ⇨ □ D ▽	15	1	2	1	Where? ✓ How? ✓	Fork truck conveyor
IN STACK	○ ⇨ □ D ▽			10	1	Why? ✓	
CUT SIDES, SHEAR	○ ⇨ □ D ▽		1	2			
IN STACK	○ ⇨ □ D ▽			10	3	Why? ✓	Conveyor roll to press
TO PRESS, CART	○ ⇨ □ D ▽	10	1	6		Where? ✓ How? ✓	//
IN STACK	○ ⇨ □ D ▽			3	3		
CUT CORNERS, PRESS	○ ⇨ □ D ▽		1	1	1		

occur, and then try to reduce these, because they are costly. Delays and transportation usually consume more than half the labor time.

Develop and Analyze Alternatives

Listing the available alternatives is basic to any type of analysis and a critical step in decision making. All work and services can be performed in many ways, and products can be made from many different materials. For example, a pencil might be made of wood, metal, plastic, or a combination of these; it can have an eraser and clip or not have them; and it may be cylindrical, hexagonal, or some other shape. A hole can be punched, drilled, burned, or cut. Products can be sold through a catalog, a personal-service store, a self-service store, a vending machine, or a computer kiosk (see Chapter 16). A whole process, each part of the process, and each individual activity should be questioned by recording all the alternatives.

One method of generating a large number of ideas is called **brainstorming,** which brings together several people in a small group where everyone is encouraged to make suggestions. No limits are placed on the number and quality of suggestions; no "put-downs" are permitted; and "farfetched" ideas are encouraged and recorded for consideration. The following are some questions that might be used in improving work performance:

- Who performs the activity, what is it, and where is it being done?
- Why is the activity/operation being performed?
- Can the activity be performed in another way?
- Can it be combined with another operation or operations?
- Can the work sequence be changed to reduce the volume of work?
- Can it be simplified?

Select, Install, and Follow up on New Method

Using your objectives, such as lower costs or better service, as a guide, pick the method that best suits your goals. Consultation with people who are involved can help to avoid surprises and gain the support of those affected. Installing this new method includes setting up the physical equipment, gaining acceptance, and training workers. Test the method to see that it works and follow up to see that workers are satisfied with it and are following procedures.

SETTING AND USING PERFORMANCE STANDARDS

One of the most difficult problems for managers of small firms is measuring the performance of employees, as there are few precise tools for establishing standards against which to measure performance. Instead, we must rely heavily on the judgment of people. Physical work can be measured more precisely than mental work, but doing so still requires judgment.

Managers must develop standards, budgets, or just rules of thumb by which to measure performance. If all a manager can say is that "the level

of output is not enough," a worker does not know how to improve performance, as the following example shows.

Dennis Kidder, president and founder of Kidder International, Inc., a water ski
company, stamps his will on his 35 production workers at every opportunity. He'll
ask how many pieces they have handled so far and then say, "Is that all?" regardless
of their replies. When workers said they couldn't meet a production speedup to
100 skis a day from 75, Kidder took over a workbench and passed through 125.
He designed and built most of the manufacturing equipment in the shop, often
after brainstorming with a local machine shop owner who makes fireworks on the
side.[8]

Time standards can be used to:

- Determine the number of people and the amount of facilities needed for a desired output.
- Estimate the cost of sales and other orders.
- Determine the standard output for incentive systems.
- Schedule production.
- Measure performance.

These standards can be set up by (1) estimates by people experienced in the work, (2) time studies, using a watch or other timing device, and (3) synthesis of the elemental times obtained from published tables.

Most small businessmen use the first method, using estimates of experienced people. These estimates should be recorded and given to workers for their guidance. The standards should allow for the time needed to do the work at normal speed, plus time for unavoidable delays and personal requirements. A good set of standards can be set this way at a minimal cost.

WHAT YOU SHOULD HAVE LEARNED

1. This chapter has explained what an operating system is and how it operates. All businesses have operating systems, which transform inputs of people, money, machines, methods, and materials into outputs of goods and/or services. These operating systems help the business achieve the goal for which it was established.

   All operating systems have certain productive elements. They include: (a) a system for changing form, place, or time, (b) a sequence of steps to change the inputs into outputs, (c) special skills, tools, and/or machines to make the change, (d) instructions and goods identification, and (e) a time frame within which the work is to be done.

2. The method and importance of choosing the right location for a business were also discussed. Some general factors that must be considered in locating any business are access to: (*a*) the work force, (*b*) utilities, (*c*) vendors, and (*d*) transportation, as well as (*e*) taxes and government regulations. In choosing the location, these factors, along with specific factors depending on the type of business, are collected and evaluated using some kind of evaluation system.

3. The two most important factors involved in choosing a retail site are the type of business and the type of location. The type of business—convenience goods, shopping goods, or specialty goods—largely determines the location. Convenience goods stores are usually located where the traffic flow is high. Shopping goods stores are located where comparison shopping can be done. Specialty goods stores, selling high-priced items with recognized names to exclusive clientele, often generate their own traffic but are helped by having similar stores in the vicinity.

    The types of locations for retail establishments include downtown, freestanding stores, neighborhood or strip shopping centers, community shopping centers, and regional shopping centers.

4. Among the most important factors in choosing a manufacturing site are locating near customers and vendors and the availability and cost of transportation. A variety of transportation modes is available to choose from.

5. The steps involved in planning physical facilities are (*a*) determining the desired product and volume to produce, (*b*) identifying the operations and activities required to process it, (*c*) determining the space needed, and (*d*) determining the best physical arrangement and layout of those facilities.

    Once the product is determined and the operations and activities decided upon, the total space requirements can be estimated. Once this is done, the actual layout begins. The three types of layout are product, process, and a combination. In the product layout, there is a flow according to the sequence of operations. The process layout groups together activities of a similar nature.

    Next, the physical facilities must be laid out in the building to provide for a smooth flow of work and activities. An effective layout will provide space for movement, adequate utilities, safe operations, favorable working conditions, cleanliness and ease of maintenance, product quality, and a favorable impression.

6. The importance of, and the method of, improving performance standards was explained. In general, improving performance includes: (*a*) stating the problem, (*b*) collecting and recording information, (*c*) developing and analyzing alternatives, and (*d*) selecting, installing, and following up on the new methods. Also included is setting and using these performance standards, including time standards.

KEY TERMS

operating system, *370*

inputs, *370*

process, *370*

outputs, *371*

production (operations), *371*

retailers, *378*

producers, *378*

service businesses, *378*

convenience goods, *380*

convenience stores, *380*

shopping goods, *380*

specialty goods, *380*

anchor stores, *382*

transportation modes, *383*

operations, *385*

activities, *385*

product layout, *387*

process layout, *388*

block, *389*

work simplification (industrial engineering), *392*

brainstorming, *394*

QUESTIONS FOR DISCUSSION

1. (*a*) What are the characteristics of an operating system? (*b*) What are some of the inputs into a business operating system? (*c*) What are some of the outputs resulting from the business processes?

2. What is the basic operating system for (*a*) making apparel? (*b*) A retail store? (*c*) Carpet cleaning? (*d*) Developing computer software?

3. What are the elements found in all operating systems?

4. Explain some of the more important general factors affecting location choice?

5. How do (*a*) retail stores, (*b*) producing plants, (*c*) service companies go about choosing a location?

6. (*a*) What are the two most important factors in choosing a retail site? (*b*) Explain each of them.

7. What are two important factors in locating a manufacturing site?

8. Why is planning the layout of physical facilities so important?

9. What are the steps involved in planning facilities?

10. Explain the three different types of layout.

11. What are some of the characteristics of an effective layout?

12. What are the four activities involved in improving operations?

13. (*a*) Compare the two cafeteria layouts in Figure 13–8. (*b*) Which do you think would be more efficient? (*c*) Why?

14. (*a*) Record your movements when you registered the last time. (*b*) What improvements could you make in the process?

SUGGESTED READINGS

Crocker, Olga L., and Richard Guelker. "The Effects of Robotics on the Workplace." *Personnel* 65 (September 1988): 26–33.

Emshwiller, John R. "Industrial Parks Sprout for Small Firms." *The Wall Street Journal,* March 13, 1989, p. B2.

Galante, Steven P. "Distributors Bow to Demands of 'Just-in-Time' Delivery." *The Wall Street Journal,* June 30, 1986, p. 27.

Gupta, Udayan. "At the Mall, Tenants Press Grievances as Never Before." *The Wall Street Journal,* June 12, 1989, p. B2.

Holland, Max. *When the Machine Stopped: A Cautionary Tale from Industrial America.* Cambridge, Mass.: Harvard Business School Press, 1989.

McCarthy, Michael J. "Small Businesses Blossom Near Atlanta." *The Wall Street Journal,* March 28, 1989, p. B1.

Ricklefs, Roger. "Regional Variation in Small Firms' Success Is Striking." *The Wall Street Journal,* July 12, 1989, p. B2.

Rundle, Rhondal. "Oxford Scientist Finds U.S. More Fertile for Start-ups." *The Wall Street Journal,* May 17, 1989, p. B2.

Shellenbarger, Sue. "Rural Enterprise: Tough Row to Hoe." *The Wall Street Journal,* September 12, 1989, p. B1.

Wysocki, Bernard, Jr. "The New Boom Towns." *The Wall Street Journal,* March 27, 1989, p. B1.

ENDNOTES

1. Bradley A. Stertz, "Domino's Beefs Up Menu to Keep Up with Rivals," *The Wall Street Journal,* April 21, 1989, p. B1.

2. Adline Clarke, "TTI of Mobile Manufacturing Smart Phones," *Mobile* (Alabama) *Press Register,* October 12, 1986, p. 1–C.

3. Leon C. Megginson, Lyle R. Trueblood, and Gayle M. Ross, *Business* (Lexington, Mass.: D. C. Heath, 1985), p. 404.

4. Jeffrey Theodore, "They Groom Dogs 'On-the-Spot,'" *Baldwin* (County, Alabama) *Press Register,* June 12, 1989, p. 4.

5. Joseph B. Mason, et al., *Modern Retailing* (Plano, Tex.: Business Publications, 1987), pp. 2–4.

6. Virginia Inman, "Upstairs," *Inc.,* April 1986, p. 24.

7. Scott Kilman, "Retailers Change Their Stores and Goods, Looking to Cash In on New Buying Habits," *The Wall Street Journal,* September 8, 1986, p. 23.

8. "A Special Report: Small Business," *The Wall Street Journal,* May 20, 1985, p. C5.

14

PURCHASING, OPERATIONS, AND QUALITY CONTROL

With the automation we have today, an agent can do five times the work he could do only six years ago.—William Quartermaine, business leader, in 1885

Resources must be employed productively and their productivity has to grow if the business is to survive.—Peter F. Drucker

LEARNING OBJECTIVES

After studying the material in this chapter, you will be able to:

1. Give reasons for the importance of purchasing.
2. Explain the need to choose vendors carefully.
3. Describe how to establish an effective purchasing procedure.
4. Discuss how to establish and maintain effective inventory control.
5. Explain what is involved in operations planning and control.
6. Describe how to maintain quality control.

ANDERS BOOK STORES: DEALING WITH HUNDREDS OF VENDORS

Bob and Kathy Summer find owning and managing Anders Book Stores (ABS) "frustrating—but fun!" They should enjoy it, for they've been associated with ABS for a long time. Bob's mother was a part-time bookkeeper for Jim Anders, the founder and former owner, for 25 years. Bob and Kathy clerked there part time while attending college. Upon graduating in 1973, they expressed an interest in buying the store, but Anders was saving it for his two sons. So Bob went into the military as a fixed-wing and helicopter pilot, and Kathy went to work teaching math.

In May 1982, when Bob was home on leave, Anders called to see if he and Kathy were still interested in ABS, as neither of his sons was interested in running it. Although Bob was still in the military, and they had little savings, they said yes. Within two weeks, Bob had left the service, they had obtained financing from Anders and a bank, and they were the owners of the corporation. Anders promised to help them make the transition, but he died just four months later. Still, with Kathy's knowledge of the education system, Bob's administrative experience in the military, and his mother's financial expertise, they were able to run the business successfully.

The Summers have divided the administrative responsibilities for ABS, which sells books and supplies from preschool through graduate school. Bob specializes in college-level books; Kathy handles everything associated with textbooks and supplies for 12 private schools. She orders the books, receives them and sorts them by grade, sells them, and returns unsold copies to publishers. In handling these activities, as well as being responsible for materials and supplies, she deals with "over 1,000 vendors each year," without the benefit of a computer, as there are no software systems yet available to handle those diverse activities.

On the college level, Anders sells to students of the University of South Alabama, which has its own bookstore a few blocks away, and other colleges in the area. In addition to the main store, there is a branch on the Mobile College (MC) campus, about 15 miles away, which handles all

Source: Mobile (Alabama) Register, November 28, 1989, p. 7–A. © 1989, The Mobile Press Register, Inc. All rights reserved.

sales of textbooks, materials, and supplies for 1,200 students. Bob receives the book orders from MC; buys, receives, and sells the books; reorders if necessary; and returns unsold books to the publishers.

There are several problems faced by Anders in its sales of textbooks. A major problem is estimating how many copies of each text to order. The book order for each course states the name(s) of the author(s), title, publisher, edition and year of publication, and the estimated number of students in the class. Bob then estimates how many copies of each text to order, taking into consideration that some students will share a book, and some will not buy a text.

Bob has three sources for the books: (1) students who sell him used books, (2) used-book wholesalers, and (3) original publishers for new textbooks. An indication of the problem involved is that ABS has 1,200 publishers listed in its computer, although it regularly buys from "only" about 300 to 400 in any one year. When you consider that Kathy also buys from "over 1,000" vendors, you can understand why they say that "buying and bookkeeping problems are horrendous."

Bob groups together all orders for texts from the same publisher and sends them in at one time. This is done six to eight weeks before school starts in order to have books on the shelf for students when classes begin. Publishers then ship the books, sometimes as much as six weeks before they are needed. For up to eight cases of books from one publisher, Bob has the books shipped by UPS; freight is used for larger shipments.

A related problem is not having enough copies of a text to meet student needs. Then Bob has to reorder. When he sees that more texts are needed, he calls the vendor to have them sent by UPS. (If the book is needed immediately, and the student is willing to pay up to $10, the book can come by second-day express.) The vendor usually ships the books one to seven days after the order is received. Enrollment increased so rapidly at Mobile College in the fall of 1989 that Bob had to place over 50 reorders, for about 25 percent of the textbooks sold.

Another problem is the low profit margin. On state-adopted elementary and high school books, there is a gross profit of only 15 percent, and ABS has to pay the cost of returning books. On college texts, there is a 20 percent profit margin, with ABS paying *all* the transportation costs.

A third problem is paying for the books and returning unused copies. The invoice, which comes with the books, is payable within 30 days, even though the schools may not be open and the books not sold. Unsold books also pose a problem. Until a few years ago, some publishers permitted only a limited refund for a limited time on returns—say 75 percent if the books were returned after six months, and nothing after a year. Now, most publishers would give a full refund for returns up to a year, but there is a "restocking fee" that Anders must pay.

A related problem is caused by the rapid merger of publishers. When books are ordered in the summer from one publisher, which is then acquired by another publisher before the end of the year, to which company are the books returned for a refund?

Poor-quality books pose another problem. The Summers showed the casewriter some books with the first 78 pages glued together. When an attempt was made to unstick them, the pages tore. Some other books had sections and pages that had come unglued and were falling apart. Although the publisher replaces these books, it is inconvenient and time consuming.

Shoplifting and vandalism are other problems. Paint has been smeared over books and merchandise, covers have been slashed, and so forth, so that a guard has had to be hired during peak periods.

Most of the large publishers send out an annual evaluation form for their dealers to complete. Since doing this, Bob and Kathy have noticed an improvement in service from the publishers.

Despite the challenges and problems offered by their business, the Summers say they enjoy their work.

Source: Discussions with Kathy and Bob Summer.

The Opening Focus illustrates that the profitability of a small business depends largely on effective purchasing, inventory, operations, and quality control. Most small firms have many potential sources of supply of goods and services. Each of these sources requires close study to secure the proper quality, quantity, timing, price, and service needed. This chapter emphasizes the strategies and procedures needed for effective purchasing, as well as inventory, operations, and quality control.

THE IMPORTANCE OF PURCHASING

Every small business needs products or services that are provided by someone else. The wide variety of items available requires careful study to ensure that the proper selection is made. Some items, such as electricity, come from only one supplier, which requires a careful analysis of use in order to obtain them at the lowest cost. Others, such as insurance, machines, and equipment, also require special attention, as they are often expensive and are purchased infrequently. Still other items, such as paper clips and welding rods, are relatively inexpensive, and their purchase is usually routine. Finally, materials that are part of the company's main product and have a high cost relative to revenue take up a large share of the manager's time. This chapter is primarily concerned with the latter items, those that are an important part of the firm's main product.

What Purchasing Involves

Obtaining all items, including goods and services, in the proper form, quantity, and quality, and at the proper place, time, and cost, is the main objective of **purchasing.** Purchasing identifies the needs of the company and finds, negotiates for, orders, and assures delivery of those items. In order to do this, the manager responsible for buying should maintain a list of reliable vendors and keep effective records of each one's performance. In short, buyers should coordinate the needs of their companies with the operations of suppliers, establish standardized procedures, and set up and maintain controls to ensure proper performance.

Notice that Bob and Kathy Summer do all of these things in buying for Anders Book Stores.

In retail stores, buying requires close attention to consumers' changing demands and to the level of stock of many items, which change as factors such as styles, colors, technology, and personal identification change. Yet customers expect those items always to be in stock. Each type of item may be handled differently, so the person(s) doing the buying must work closely with those doing the selling to satisfy these differing needs.

Purchasing in manufacturing is concerned with getting the proper materials and processing them into finished goods, while maintaining inventory and quality control. Thus, those doing the purchasing must work closely with those doing the production and selling.

Why Purchasing Is So Important

The amount spent on goods and services represents the largest single cost to most small firms. Thus, a high percentage of total revenue is needed to purchase these items. Because the percentage is so great, a small variation in purchasing costs creates a large change in profits (or losses).

For example, if the cost of purchasing goods is 50 percent of revenue, and if profits are 5 percent, a 1 percent increase in purchasing costs reduces the profits by 10 percent. Likewise, a 10 percent increase in costs wipes out the entire potential profit. Reductions in cost, a much more difficult achievement, results in comparable percentage *increases* in profits.

The price of purchases is important, but other aspects can be just as critical. For example, obtaining **just-in-time delivery**—where the materials are delivered to the user just at the time they are needed for production—can save on inventory costs. Close coordination between supplier and user can greatly improve efficiency.

Although neither is small, Wal-Mart Stores has an agreement with Procter & Gamble (P&G) that is expected to revolutionize the way manufacturers deal with even small retailers. P&G already shares a computer-to-computer inventory system with Wal-Mart. Now it is making changes to more efficiently move the flow of goods from raw materials through manufacturing to the product supply division in order to expedite deliveries and drive down costs to the retailer.[1]

Having the appropriate stock—the right style, at the right price, at the right time—properly displayed for customers can result in higher sales—and profit.

MAKING SOMEONE RESPONSIBLE FOR PURCHASING

While capable subordinates, such as specialty buyers, may be delegated the authority to order in their areas of expertise, in general, one person should be given the responsibility for ordering all goods and services. But that person, of course, should ask for—and get—the help of people knowledgeable in the area where the items are needed. By having a single person responsible:

1. Duplicate orders for the same items are avoided.
2. Specialized skills needed for purchasing are used.
3. Responsibility for improvements in the buying process is centralized.
4. Better relations can be maintained with vendors.

Those doing the purchasing should be aware of trends and special situations that can affect a small company's operations. And they should call situations such as the following to the attention of the owner or top manager:

1. *Expected changes in price.* Buying later for expected decreases in price or buying increased quantities for expected inflation in price can result in savings. However, **stockouts,** which are sales lost because an item

is not in stock when customers want it, or too heavy inventory costs should be guarded against. They may cancel out expected savings.

For example, high inventories in the computer industry threatened the earnings of many companies near the end of 1984. Apple had 71 days of inventory on hand, worth $261 million, yet its pretax profits for the entire year were only $231 million. So it entirely shut down production for a week. IBM had 162 days of inventory, worth over $6 billion, while its yearly profits were less than $12 billion.[2]

---

2. *Expected changes in demand.* Seasonal products and high-fashion items fall into this category.
3. *Orders for specialty goods.* The quantity ordered should match expected demand, so that no material is left over. When the quantity of the demand is known, estimates of losses expected to occur during the production process are added to the order. With an unknown demand quantity, forecasts plus the estimates of losses are used.
4. *Short supply of materials.*

In the Salaminder, Inc., example in Chapter 6, you learned that the demand for high-quality (and high-priced) western clothing skyrocketed because of the popularity of the movie *Urban Cowboy.* But demand plummeted in just a few months. The small producer had to overcome the short supply by rapidly expanding operations— only to have to cut back severely the next summer.

Speculative buying should be avoided by a small business unless that is its primary business. While all business decisions have a certain element of speculation, small firms cannot afford to gamble with money required for normal business operations.

SELECTING THE RIGHT VENDORS

You will be more successful in purchasing if you can find several acceptable sources of supply of goods and services because (1) reliability in delivery and quality affects nearly all operations, (2) vendors can be valuable sources of information for various aspects of operations, and (3) vendors can provide valuable service.

Because they purchase only small amounts, small companies need to maintain a good relationship with vendors in order to obtain good service. Therefore, as long as it's to your advantage to buy from a given supplier, continue to do so. However, if you are just starting your business, or are dissatisfied with a current supplier, you must search for one that satisfies your needs. You can find many good sources by consulting the Yellow Pages of telephone directories, the *Thomas Register of American Manufacturers,* the *McRae Bluebook,* newspapers, trade journals, and publications of

COMPUTER UPDATE

THE INDEPENDENT INSURANCE AGENTS ASSOCIATION

About 1,000 U.S. independent insurance agents are hooked up to a free electronic bulletin board provided by the Independent Insurance Agents Association. This free service permits the agents to swap business tips.

For example, Chuck Allen, who has a one-man agency in Oklahoma City, had trouble finding a company to insure a local group of anesthesia nurses. After contacting around 20 to 25 companies without finding one willing to insure such an extremely limited market, he put a note on the association's computer bulletin board explaining his predicament. Within a week, he had heard from two people in Georgia and Washington, one of whom suggested a company for him to contact. Although the insurance company had stopped insuring anesthetists, it did know of another firm that still did. The result was that Allen wound up selling the nurses a policy with the second company.

Source: Michael W. Miller, "Technically Speaking," *The Wall Street Journal*, May 20, 1985, p. 84C.

research organizations. In addition, visits to trade shows and merchandise marts give you an opportunity to view exhibits and talk with salespeople. Electronic networks can be set up and used to obtain information on possible sources (see the next Computer Update).

Types of Vendors

As will be discussed in Chapter 16, the vendors from whom you buy may be brokers, jobbers, wholesalers, producers, or others. Each provides a particular type of service. For example, wholesalers stock large quantities of many items in order to give fast delivery of a wide variety of items to retailers. A producer can ship directly to you, with no intermediate handler, or sell through sales representatives or agents who can help the small business.

Anders Book Stores buys new textbooks from the producers (the publishers), but buys used texts from wholesalers (used-book companies). Also, supplies and other items are ordered from a variety of sources.

Regional and national trade shows and private trade associations can keep firms up to date on sources and their products and services.

Use Few or Many Vendors?

Should you buy from one, a few, or many vendors? A single source of supply can result in a closer and more personalized relationship. When shortages occur, this relationship can result in better service than when many sources are used. Also, discounts may be obtained with larger volume buying. If one seller can supply a wide assortment of the items needed, the cost of ordering is reduced. On the other hand, multiple sources provide a greater variety of goods and often better terms. Most small firms use several sources.

For example, Connie's Confections (Case IV–2) buys its basic ingredient, chocolate, only from Nestlé. But the other ingredients are bought from various suppliers, depending on price, quality, and assured delivery.

Notice also that Anders Book Stores buys from some 1,300 to 1,400 different vendors.

Some companies put out requests for bids, and negotiations result in better arrangements. Sometimes it is desirable—or even necessary—to use a single source for specialized items, as the example about the Blounts (at the top of the next page) illustrates.

Investigating Potential Suppliers

The search for suppliers usually results in identifying many sources from which to choose. Potential sources can be checked for factors such as quality of output, price, desire to serve, reliability, transportation, terms of payment, and guarantee and warranties. All of these factors affect a company's performance; therefore, a minimum standard must be set for each.

For example, Ron Turken, of Cabinet Wholesalers, believes that "Vendors . . . should want to help us. I am looking for suppliers who understand our business and want to be part of it."[3]

Vendors should not be chosen on the basis of price alone, for quality and/or service may suffer if the supplier has to lower prices to obtain your order. Instead, vendors should be chosen to meet carefully set quality and service standards. These standards can be used to ensure acceptable quality without paying for quality higher than needed. Some suppliers aim their output toward the low-price, low-quality market; others aim at high-quality markets.

Ariane Daguin and George Faison, of D'Artagnan Inc., pick up fresh game twice a week and deliver it, along with homemade paté de foie gras and imported New Zealand venison, to gourmet stores and restaurants daily. According to one customer, "The foie gras is fantastic, better than all others."

Foie gras, a rich duck liver paté, is usually imported. Daguin, however, learned to make it from her father, a chef in France. She also found a source of supply in an upstate farmer who fattens mallard duck livers, used to make the delicacy.[4]

Several years ago, Winton M. and Carolyn Blount donated the land and money to build the Wynton M. Blount Cultural Park in Montgomery, Alabama, where the Alabama Shakespeare Festival is held. As they were great admirers of Queen Elizabeth II's beautiful black swans, they inquired as to where she had found them. The answer came back from England that they had been bought at a farm just a few miles from Montgomery—the only known source of supply of the beautiful birds shown here.

Source: Photo by Alabama Shakespeare Festival photographer Phil Scarsbrook. Used with permission.

Prices from different vendors are rarely the same. Higher prices are justified for more reliable and faster delivery; better terms for returning goods; more services, such as advertising, type of packaging, technical assistance, and information; and better, or delayed, payment plan. And, of course, higher prices must be paid for higher quality.

The farmer in the previous example sold the duck livers to D'Artagnan for well
over the going price for ordinary duck livers.

Small manufacturers must consider their total cost of production when
purchasing goods. They may be able to purchase parts at low prices, but
must add processing costs, which might result in a higher-cost finished
product. For example, the price plus transportation cost to buy items from
a distant source may be less than from a local one, but the faster service
from the local supplier may permit smaller inventories. The cost savings
resulting from reduced inventory may more than compensate for the higher
local price. Also, one source may be able to supply a wider assortment of
the goods needed, thus reducing the expense of ordering from many sources.

Evaluating Vendors' Performance

Just as you investigate potential suppliers, you should also evaluate their
performance after you have chosen them. While it requires some time
and effort, small businesses should develop some type of rating system to
use in selecting, evaluating, and retaining vendors. Some such rating systems pick out the factors the small business considers important, such as
quality, quick service, and reliability, as well as price, and then rate them
according to their importance to the firm.[5]

Sharp Corporation uses this kind of rating system in its Memphis Plant to evaluate
its 70 suppliers, who tend to be small businesses. A copy of its creed, "Practice
Sincerity and Creativity," is submitted to potential vendors with a statement that
Sharp expects "100% quality parts," precisely on schedule. Vendors who agree to
this stipulation become suppliers and receive a periodic report card showing how
they rate on satisfying quality, price, prompt delivery, and other standards.[6]

Notice in the Opening Focus that many textbook publishers ask their customers
to evaluate them.

Maintaining Good Relations with Vendors

Because vendors are so important, you should make an extra effort to maintain pleasant relationships with them. You and your vendors can foster
good relations by helping each other solve problems.

For example, when Polaroid Corporation introduced its SX-70 instant cameras a
few years ago, some of them spat out pictures before they were developed.
Something had to be done before the new product got a reputation for unreliability.
Polaroid turned to International Components Corporation, a small Chicago company,

Source: Photo courtesy of Polaroid Corporation, Cambridge, Massachusetts.

for help because of its reputation as a knowledgeable designer and manufacturer of small, special-purpose motors. The SX-70's problem was traced to a signal generated when the print-delivery motor ran. While most motors do create such signals, they normally do nothing more serious than distort the picture on a TV set, as a hair dryer does. But in the SX-70, the signal sometimes matched the frequency that triggers the "print done" circuit and prematurely switched on the ejection mechanism. International Components solved the problem by designing and making part of the motor with a different metal alloy so that the signal it produced did not disrupt the camera's electronic circuitry.[7]

If you are argumentative and try to drive too hard a bargain, you may spoil a good working relationship. This, in turn, may result in extra cost and/or poor service to you in the long run. Thus, mutual respect can work to the benefit of both buyer and seller, as the following example shows.

Our Hero Restaurant (Case II–2) had trouble finding a bakery to furnish preservative-free high-quality bread for its sandwiches. One was found 30 miles away, and it agreed to deliver the bread fresh six days a week. In turn, the restaurant agreed to buy bread only from that bakery.

ESTABLISHING AN EFFECTIVE PURCHASING PROCEDURE

After deciding on the vendor(s) to use, you must establish a purchasing procedure to ensure effective purchasing. While there is no "one best way," Figure 14–1 presents a computer flowchart of a well-designed purchase

Figure 14–1 Purchase Order Process Flowchart

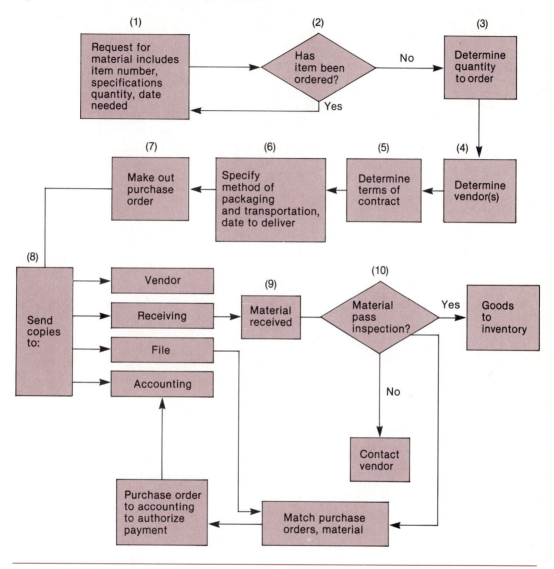

order system. The diagram shows the basic process but does not include the many variations needed for special conditions. For example, some companies order standardized units, while others order specially designed ones; some items can be stored, while others cannot; some companies' needs change rapidly and often, while some are quite stable. Taking these variations into consideration, though, a good purchasing agent will standardize

Figure 14–2   Purchasing and Retailing Schedule for Style Goods, 1990–91

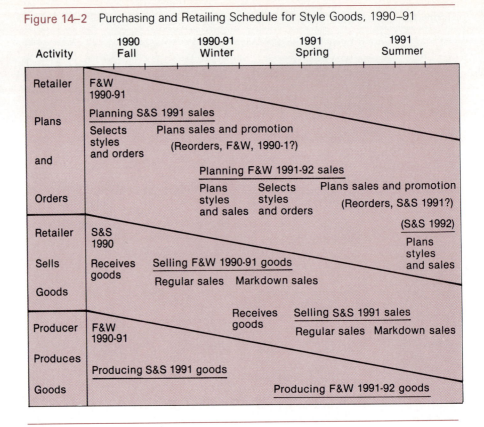

Legend: S&S = Spring and summer; F&W = Fall and winter.

as many of the purchasing activities as possible in order to give the necessary attention to special conditions.

How Purchase Orders Originate

The request to purchase goods or services (item 1 in Figure 14–1) can originate from many sources. If a service is needed, the request usually comes from the user of that service, as when the accounting manager requests an outside audit, the personnel manager needs to install or change an insurance program, or the marketing manager needs to place an ad with an agency. But when goods are needed, the request can originate in any of several ways, such as:

■ Observation of a low level of inventory.

■ The need to order at a prescribed time.

■ Operating management requests.

■ Customers' requests for a given item.

■ The purchasing manager's observation of special external conditions that indicate the need to purchase an item.

Based on Inventory Level

The first of these methods, observing a low level of inventory, results from an effort to carefully control inventory. To this end, reorder points and order quantity standards are established for each item. Then, when the level of that item in inventory drops to its reorder point or below, a notation is made to reorder. The reorder quantity is usually a standard **economic order quantity (EOQ),** which is the best quantity to order, taking into account ordering costs and carrying costs for items. These standards will be discussed later.

Using Purchasing Schedules

Purchasing by retailers poses different problems from purchasing by a producer. Figure 14–2 shows a suggested schedule for buying style goods.

The retailer visits a trade show in August, or consults vendors, and places orders based on evaluation of styles and plans. Between August and February, plans for the spring and summer are completed. Goods are received in time for the selling seasons; inventory and sales are checked to consider placing orders to replenish stock. End-of-season sales are run to remove stock from inventory. Planning is started during this latter time in preparation for the fall and winter seasons.

Another scheduling scheme is used for staple items that need to be kept in stock all the time. The orders can be issued: (1) when stock reaches a level at which a reorder is needed, (2) at fixed intervals, or (3) when the vendor visits the buyer. The objective is to schedule purchasing for good service and low cost. The systems are used in retailing, manufacturing, and service businesses.

Placing the Purchase Order

There are many ways of actually placing orders for needed goods (item 7 in Figure 14–1), depending on the company's needs and the supplier's demands. **Purchase orders** are very common, as they become legal records for the buyer and vendor. **Standing orders** simplify the purchasing procedure and allow for long-range planning by setting schedules for delivery of goods in predetermined quantities and at agreed-to terms. Variations on each of these methods include making the purchase order a draft on the buyer's bank for quick payment and negotiating contracts under which the vendor carries inventory for the buyer. Some companies—even small ones—work out barter agreements for exchange of goods, as in international trade.

Receiving the Items

Receiving items and forwarding them to inventory (item 9 in Figure 14–1) is the last step in the purchasing procedure. A copy of the purchase order, including the desired specifications, has been sent to those receiving the goods. Upon arrival, the goods are checked for damage in transit; for specified quality characteristics such as color, size, and whether or not they are the items specified; and for the correct quantity and price.

The person who ordered the items, as well as the accountant, is informed that the items have been received and are ready for processing. Proper receiving procedure can detect deviations from these standards.

The items can be stored in the containers in which they are received, in different containers, or by individual item. The receiving agent prepares the goods for storage.

Using Computers to Aid Purchasing and Inventory Control

Small companies are increasingly using computers to keep track of inventory items, spot replenishment needs, identify sources of supply, and provide information needed for ordering. In most cases, computers provide information needed by the purchaser to use in the order process. Sometimes items are of such a nature that an order can be more fully prepared for mailing by the computer.

Information used to decide variables such as what to purchase, who does the purchasing, and when it is done can be stored in the computer. Then, using specialized programs, the computer searches for and processes data to provide information needed for ordering. For items in stock, a program directs the computer to identify the need for a reorder and to compile information on important data such as price, specifications, sources, delivery time, and quantity needed for ordering. For specialty items, the computer files can be searched for similar items that have been ordered in the past. Ordering specialty items requires much more of the purchasing agent's attention than is needed for standardized items.

The instant availability of updated computer information reduces errors and processing time compared to manual systems. The computer also expands the types and amount of information for potentially better and faster processing of orders. For example, many computer installations are designed to perform automatically, for selected items, the purchasing steps numbered 1 through 7 in Figure 14–1. Thus, the computer can increase the number of routine purchases made. Also, information can be easily updated at frequent intervals using the computer.

CONTROLLING INVENTORY

As shown earlier, purchasing involves obtaining the right quantity of materials, of the right quality, at the right time and place, and at the right price. However, purchases are made in advance of use, creating inventory, and the costs of inventory must be controlled.

Why Carry Inventory?

The reason for carrying inventory is to disconnect one segment of the operating process from another so that each part can operate at its optimum level. For example, if you did not have an inventory of food in your home,

Figure 14–3   Diagram of Material Flow and Inventory

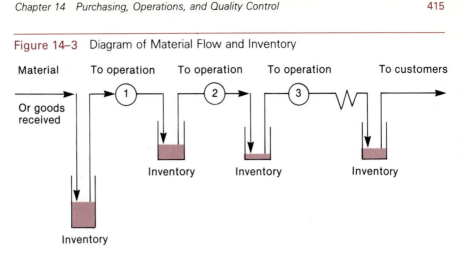

you would have to go out, find some, buy it, bring it home, and prepare it every time you were hungry. But by having food in your pantry or refrigerator, you buy it at your convenience, keep it as inventory, and then process it when you get hungry.

The same holds true in a manufacturing plant. Figure 14–3 shows what happens from the receipt of raw materials, through each of three operations, to final sale to customers. Notice that inventories are shown at different levels at different stages of the operation, and the inventory level at a given stage depends on what activities have occurred in the operations process. For example, Operation 1 may have been running recently, while Operation 2 may have been shut down for a while. Also notice that Operation 3 may not have enough material if Operation 2 does not start up soon.

A similar situation occurs in a retail store. Retailers receive goods, store them, display them for sale, sell them to customers, and then reorder more of the goods. The level of inventory at any given time depends on the amount of goods bought relative to the quantity sold. Thus, a retailer must have enough goods in inventory after an order is received to last until the next order is placed and received. Figure 14–4 illustrates this process. Notice that the goods on the left are ordered and are in transit. When received, they are put in storage with other, similar goods, as inventory. They are then put on display and gradually sold, and more goods are ordered.

Types of Inventory

Inventories exist in small firms at all times in one or more of the following forms:

- Finished items on display for sale to custommers.
- Batches of goods, such as materials, parts, and subassemblies awaiting processing or delivery.

Figure 14–4   Goods Flow and Inventory in a Retail Firm

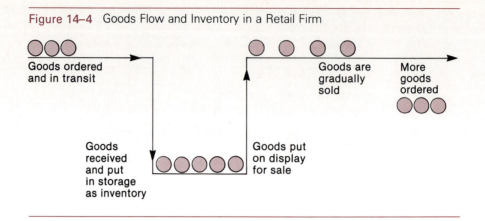

- Repair parts awaiting use.
- Supplies for offices, stores, or shops, or for use in packaging.
- Miscellaneous items, such as tools placed in a toolroom.

These inventories—especially the first two kinds—represent a high investment in all businesses. Many companies have failed because their inventory tied up too much money, or the items in inventory became obsolete, damaged, or lost.

For example, Chris Hoelzle seemed to be a technological whiz in the mid-1980s. His two Los Angeles businesses, a computer repair store and a computer salvage operation, had 35 employees and annual revenues of $1.4 million. Then, with the computer "bust" of 1985 (mentioned earlier), profits turned to losses. Hoelzle reacted by spending "like mad" to buy inventory and hire employees in order to maintain profits by increasing volume. Soon he was bankrupt—without declaring bankruptcy.

Then he went back to basics: he sold computer printer parts to large companies, slashed staff, sold inventory, and closed his stores. He sold "200 tons of electronic junk" at bargain prices and started again from the ground up. By 1988, he had 15 employees, $3 million in annual revenues, and three times his pre-1986 profits.[8]

Appropriate policies concerning the items to carry in inventory, the level of inventory, and control of the stock can reduce the number of such small business casualties.

Another problem with purchasing and inventory control is that most income comes from a small percentage of products or services; some materials have high value, and some have lower value. About 80 percent of the average firm's income comes from about 20 percent of its products. Therefore, inventory planning and control should be directed mainly toward that 20 percent. For that main 20 percent, standards and procedures may be set for *each item*; for the next, say, 30 percent, items may be handled in *individual groups*; and the last 50 percent of items might be considered as *one group*. To find the best groupings, a company's product line must be analyzed in the light of the procedures discussed in the remainder of this chapter.

Cost of Carrying Inventory

Having inventory on hand costs a small business more than most people realize. These costs consist of:

- Cost of providing and maintaining storage space.
- Insurance and taxes.
- Profits lost because money is tied up in inventory (opportunity cost).
- Theft and destruction.
- Obsolescence and deterioration of the items.

Notice in the previous example how Hoelzle's inventory turned into "200 tons of electronic junk."

Estimates of these and other costs of carrying inventory for a year range from 15 to over 100 percent of the average inventory investment.

Determining When to Place an Order

Figure 14–5 shows the changing inventory levels of an item as the goods are ordered, sold, and reordered. Notice that at the left the inventory level is low, down to the margin of safety. When the new shipment is received, the inventory level immediately increases. Next, as the item is sold, the

---

Figure 14–5   Changing Level of Inventory of an Item

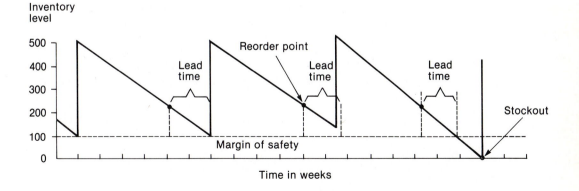

inventory level declines to the safety margin. Before it gets there, however, it reaches the **reorder point,** where new goods are ordered.

The level of inventory at which an order should be issued is based on (1) the quantity to be used between the time an order is issued and the time the items are received, plus (2) the quantity needed to provide a margin of safety. **Lead time** is the amount of time that must be allowed between ordering and receiving the goods. The small business must anticipate the use of an item and order it far enough in advance to allow time for the order to be processed and received.

The optimum inventory level at which to order goods can be estimated or actually calculated. It is the point where the sum of the costs of carrying inventory and the costs of stocking out is the lowest. Too low a level causes excessive stockout costs; too high a level causes excessive inventory carrying costs and even financial difficulties. Figure 14–5 shows the results of a delay in delivery in the last period, causing a stockout, as there is a complete depletion of the inventory.

Determining How Much to Order

The order quantity is determined by the level of inventory and the order interval. When orders are placed at certain intervals, the order quantity should be set to bring the inventory level up to a predetermined amount. When inventory level determines the time to order, the order quantity is a fixed amount called the economic order quantity (EOQ), mentioned earlier. The EOQ is determined by balancing (1) the cost of an order, which includes the costs of processing and handling the order, the costs of the item (realizing that larger orders usually warrant price discounts), and transportation costs, with (2) the costs of carrying the inventory.

Figure 14–6 shows the way costs per unit vary as the quantity ordered changes. The point of lowest cost is the EOQ, which can be found by using a standard formula,[9] or by comparing the unit costs for different order quantities. Note how a discount affects the curve and that quantities in a range near the EOQ have approximately the same low cost.

Determining How to Order

Many items, especially the 50 percent with lower value and/or volume, can be ordered on a routine basis. The procedure starts with the need, as reflected by the reorder point, and requires one of the following methods:

1. Maintaining perpetual inventory, which records when the inventory has reached the reorder point. Figure 14–7 shows a perpetual inventory card. This can be easily computerized by using bar codes.
2. Setting aside a given quantity of the item in the stockroom that will not be used without making a new purchase order.
3. Some physical method of calling attention to the need for the order, such as the gauge for a tank of oil.

4. A count of items in stock on a regular basis, as in retail stores. The amount to reorder, the vendor, and the method of packaging and transporting can be recorded on the inventory form or in the computer.

Figure 14–6   Changes in Purchase Unit Costs

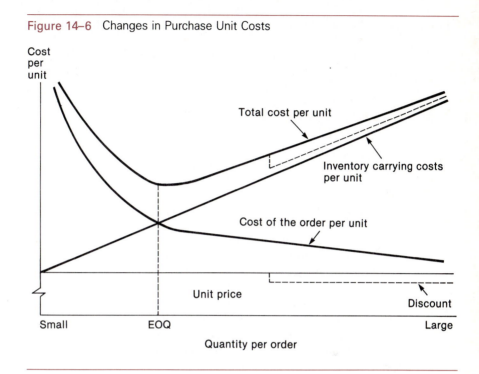

Figure 14–7   Inventory Record Form

| Date | Received | | Issued | | Balance on hand |
	Order no.	Units	Reg. no.	Units	
7/13	3401	400			450
7/17			1075	10	440
7/22			1090	10	430

Reorder point: 70 bags   Reorder quantity: 400 bags

Item no.   Description   Unit
315   Zinc oxide (3Z33)   50# bags

OPERATIONS PLANNING AND CONTROL

As shown in Chapter 6, operations planning and control begins when you determine what business you're going into, what product(s) you will sell, and what resources are needed to produce the quantity you expect. As the operations of any business are based on expected sales during a given period of time, estimates of future sales are quite important. From these estimates, you can estimate the facilities needed, how they should be laid out, what number and types of employees to hire, what items—and how many—to purchase, what inventory level to maintain, and other such factors.

If they are to have products available when demanded, small firms must do careful forecasting and planning for sales. Predicting the sales of a small company with any degree of accuracy is difficult, but even crude estimates are better than none. Considerable cost is involved in serving customers if items are not in stock.

Handling Variations in Demand

If sales were to remain constant, operations planning and control would be simple, changes would not be needed, and planning would be at a minimum. However, as will be shown in Chapter 15, customer demand for goods and services varies from one period to another for such reasons as changing seasons, lifestyles, and economic conditions.

In fact, most sales of goods have seasonal variations. Some examples of complementary seasonal goods are summer and winter clothing, furnaces and air conditioners, footballs and baseballs, sweaters and swimsuits, and many types of construction items. If a small business chooses a narrow marketing niche for one of these products—as is often recommended to small businesses—sales will probably vary considerably during the year. Therefore, the business may be faced with hiring, training, and laying off employees, not using facilities efficiently, and facing cash flow problems and product shortages.

There are several operating plans that may be used to cope at least partially with these seasonal variations. The most popular such plans are these:

1. *Allow operations to rise and fall according to changing sales demands.*   While employment costs for hiring, layoffs, overtime, and severance pay tend to be high, the risk of overstocking is quite low. The current trend among small businesses, however, is to use one of the other methods, if feasible.

2. *Use self-service to reduce the number of employees and hire temporary or part-time workers during peak periods.*   This plan can partially overcome the employee problems of Plan 1.

3. *Use inventory buildups—or drawdowns—to level operations.*   This plan tends to be used by small producers whose goods can be placed in inventory and kept for future use. During slow sales periods, the plant

produces more than it sells, placing the excess in inventory so that, when demand rises, inventory can be used to meet it. While the cost of carrying inventory tends to be high, other costs should be low—especially the cost of stockouts. Some service businesses try to use variations of this method. For example, hospitals ask surgeons to schedule elective surgery during slower periods of activity.

4. *Carry complementary products.*   While some small firms carry only one product, most carry enough of a variety to reduce seasonal and cyclical variations in sales. This is also a hedge against customers' changing demands. For example, sporting goods include enough seasonal products to balance demand during the year.

5. *Subcontract out production during maximum demand periods.*   This method reduces the cost of inventory, overtime, added capacity, and hiring. Yet it does incur the extra cost of paying another producer, and some control of the process is lost.

6. *Decide not to expand operations to meet increased demand, thus losing sales.*   This method results in selling fewer units throughout the year. Many times, the cost of expanding capacity and/or overtime pay exceeds the benefit of the added sales. In fact, firms have expanded and later gone bankrupt as sales fluctuated.

Do you remember in our earlier example that Chris Hoelzle started buying inventory and hiring people as his sales and profits declined?

---

7. *Use special inducements to stimulate sales during periods of low demand.*   Lowering prices, advertising more heavily, or using sales promotions during the off season, as discussed in Chapter 16, are common ways of minimizing the effect of seasonality.

For example, most of us have taken advantage of special sales at the end of a season, such as buying Christmas lights, wrapping, or cards after December 25, or buying summer or winter clothes at the end of the season.

Scheduling Operations

Scheduling is setting the times and sequences needed to perform specialized activities. It usually includes when to do something and the time allowed for doing it. You are often faced with this problem of scheduling. For example, you *try* to schedule your classes to minimize inconvenience and for your greatest benefit. Then you have to schedule appointments with the doctor or dentist around them. And what is it but scheduling when you plan a date with a special friend? Figure 14–2 showed a schedule of the steps involved in selling style items. The production of goods is scheduled not only to be able to serve customers, but also for most efficient operation. As orders are received, they are either filled from inventory or ordered into production. Standard items, which are often sold from inventory, can be scheduled into production as needed to eliminate idle time on the part of workers and machines. In fact, many companies make standard products in order to obtain flexibility in their operations, even if they also produce specialized products.

Scheduling Specialty Items

Specialty items, on the other hand, are produced in **job shops,** where each job is scheduled for specific machines and employees according to the sequence needed to produce the item. The objective is to process orders through the plant with as little idle time as feasible, and at the lowest cost.

The complexity of setting schedules varies. A simple schedule is shown in Figure 14–8. Two parts, A and B, are to be assembled into a finished product, AB, with a shipping deadline of June 7. It takes six days to assemble and ship AB, so assembly needs to be started June 1. Parts A and B are therefore needed by June 1. Since it takes three weeks to make part A, its production must start no later than May 10. In the same way, part B must be started on May 24. Note the absence of idle time and the just-in-time delivery of materials and parts as they are needed for assembly and shipping.

This is a basic type of scheduling, and variations can be, and often are, made by small businesses. For example, the scheduling of the design and creation of clothing and costumes for major entertainment events poses such scheduling problems.

Figure 14–8   Scheduling Assembly AB, Using a Bar (Gantt) Chart

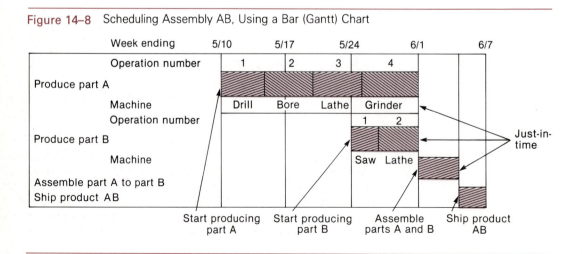

The 1989 Miss USA Pageant was such an event. As you saw in the Opening Focus for Chapter 3, the contestants' evening gowns were designed by Sherri Hill, of Norman, Oklahoma.

Some of the other costumes were designed and produced by Los Angeles costume designer Pete Menefee. In addition, he took 12 to 14 of Mrs. Hill's dress designs and made them in different fabrics. Since each contestant required a different pattern, they made 120 different dresses for the girls to choose from.

The dresses, made in Los Angeles, were shipped to the contest site in Mobile, Alabama, where Menefee altered them with the help of local seamstresses. In addition, he saw that each girl had the proper hosiery, shoes dyed to match, and costume jewelry to go with the gowns.[10]

Source: Mobile (Alabama) *Register,* February 20, 1989, p. 1-B. © 1989, The Mobile Press Register, Inc. ALL RIGHTS RESERVED.

Figure 14–9   PERT Chart for Planning the Installation of a Pipeline

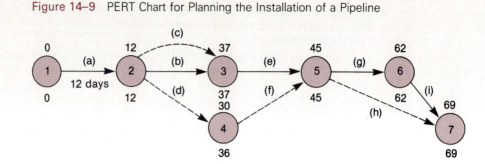

	Estimated	Completion date		
Activities	Days	Earliest	Latest	Slack
(a) Survey ditch	12	12	12	0
(b) Dig ditch	25	37	37	0
(c) Order and receive rock	3	15	37	22
(d) Order and receive pipe and fittings	18	30	36	6
(e) Rock ditch	8	45	45	0
(f) Assemble valves and fittings	9	39	45	6
(g) Lay pipe	17	62	62	0
(h) Install fittings	13	58	69	11
(i) Cover ditch	7	69	69	0

Figure legend:
Earliest day estimated to be completed	12
Start or end of activity	O
Latest day can be completed	12
Critical path ———————►	(Slack = 0; solid line in chart)

Critical Path Scheduling

A chart has been developed for scheduling a sequence of operations, each of which may be dependent on the completion of several other activities. This type of chart, using the **critical path method (CPM)** or **program evaluation and review technique (PERT),** is used by many companies, especially in the construction industry.

Figure 14–9 shows a chart for the installation of an underground pipe. Circles represent the start and end of activities, while the lines show activities (the length of the line has no significance).

The times required to perform activities are usually the best estimates of knowledgeable people. The times above and below the circles give the earliest and latest times for the end of the prior operation and the beginning of the next one; the difference is called **slack time.** The circles with zero

---

COMPUTER UPDATE

LUCINDA GRAY, TRAVEL AGENT: LET HER FINGERS DO YOUR SCHEDULING!

Lucinda Gray, a Raymond & Whitcomb agent, punches the blinking light on her 22-button phone and reaches for the keyboard of her Sabre computer. "I never write anything down any more," she says.

The Sabre, marketed by American Airlines, and similar systems offered by four other airlines are the nerve system of the modern travel industry. Each contains the schedules of the others; Gray's computer gives her access to 650 airlines flying 150,000 routes, 9,000 hotels, and 19 rental companies.

A client is calling the agency, wanting to fly to Houston, San Francisco, and home again. He needs hotel rooms and rental cars, prefers nonsmoking aisle seats and midsized cars. Fingers flying, Gray checks schedules and inventories in the computer and makes the reservations. As she books seats, rooms, and cars, the computer automatically removes them from inventories.

Once the confirmations come back and the tickets are buzzing out of her printer, Gray thanks her client. Total time spent booking the trip: about five minutes.

Source: Dan Baum, "A Matter of Time," *The Wall Street Journal,* May 20, 1985, p. 91C. Reprinted by permission of The Wall Street Journal, © Dow Jones & Company, Inc., 1985. ALL RIGHTS RESERVED.

---

slack time are on the critical path. The estimated number of days required for the job to be completed equals the sum of the times required for all the activities on the critical path. Activities *(a)*, *(b)*, *(e)*, *(g)*, and *(i)* in Figure 14–9 make up the critical path of 69 days (12 + 25 + 8 + 17 + 7). Therefore, they are the activities to be watched most closely.

Computers are now being used effectively by small businesses to perform scheduling operations. The Computer Update above shows what happens when a small travel agency books a traveler.

Controlling Operations

Even if the best of plans are made, the information is communicated effectively, and the best workers perform the work effectively, controls are still needed. Without the exercise of adequate control over the operations, the process will fail.

In simple systems, the comparison of planned performance with actual performance can be made informally by personal observation. Usually, though, a system of formal checks is needed. Standards are set, data on actual performance are collected, standards and actual data are compared, and exceptions are reported. For example, if part A (Figure 14–8) has not been drilled by at least May 17, an exception report would be given to the supervisor responsible.

QUALITY AND ITS CONTROL

In recent years, American consumers have shown increasing concern about the quality of U.S. goods and services, as foreign companies produce and sell to Americans products of increasingly superior quality. In the past, Japanese companies imitated American production, but "Made in Japan" was a byword for poor quality. Now this has changed drastically. Japan has developed its own products and methods and leads American companies in many areas, especially quality and reliability. An American, W. E. Deming, introduced modern quality control techniques into Japan in the 1950s.[11] Many American companies are now taking steps to improve the caliber of their products.

Small Businesses Need Quality Output

Small businesses must compete in the market with large companies. Although they can try to compete in many areas (for instance, with lower prices, higher quality, catering to customer needs, and/or added services), many small businesses find that emphasizing quality and reliability and designing output to match customer needs are better tactics than lowering prices. These objectives are becoming increasingly obvious as foreign companies that are very competitive in price because of lower labor costs also emphasize quality, reliability, and customer service.

A quality product and good service create (1) satisfied customers, (2) a reputation as a quality producer, and (3) growing markets. Poor quality reverses this situation and can result in lawsuits as well as paperwork and rework costs on returned goods.

Quality can have at least two meanings. First, it refers to characteristics of products being judged. (This is our definition of the term *quality* in this chapter's discussion.) Second, it means the probability that products will meet established standards. In the discussion that follows, we will use the term *reliability* to cover this meaning.

What Is Quality?

Assessment of the quality of a product is relative; it depends on the expectations of the evaluator—the customer. Customers who are used to high-grade goods and services tend to be much more critical of purchases than those accustomed to lower grades. Because small companies usually cannot cater to all quality levels, they must set their sights on the level demanded by their customers.

Quality involves many characteristics of a product: dimension, strength, color, taste, smell, content, weight, tone, look, capacity, accomplishment, creativity, and reliability, among others. Part of the quality of service are such activities as salespersons' smiles, attentiveness, friendly greetings, and willing assistance. Standards to meet the desires of customers must be established for each characteristic.

Customers desire high quality but often want to pay only a limited price for a product. Some qualities, such as a friendly greeting, cost little; others, such as precision jewelry settings, cost much. Quality-level analysis is thus based on the value of quality to the customer and the cost of producing that level of quality. The following questions must be answered in serving customers: Who are my customers? What quality do they want? What quality of product or service can I obtain, and at what costs?

How does a company determine where to set the quality level? Market research, questionnaires, talking to customers, comparison with competitors' products, and trial and error are a few of the methods.

Improving and Controlling Quality

There are many ways a small business can improve quality, but we will discuss only three: (1) setting up quality circles, (2) designing quality into the operations processes, and (3) installing a good quality control process.

Establishing Quality Circles

Companies in America and Japan report good results from their use of quality circle programs. In **quality circles,** a small group of workers led by a senior worker meets regularly to identify and develop ways to solve company problems—one area of which is quality. The members, who are usually not supervisors, receive training in areas such as problem identification, communications, and problem solving. Also, as they meet, they may have access to resource people who can provide further expertise.

Quality circles and similar programs have been instrumental in improving quality, reducing paperwork costs, improving job methods, and bettering communications. Quality circles appear to have their greatest success when top management gives them unrestricted support.

Designing Quality into the Process

Since quality is achieved during the production of goods or the performance of services, the processes must be designed to produce the needed quality of output. Machines must be capable of turning out the product within set tolerances, workers must be trained to produce that level of quality, and materials and goods must be purchased that meet the stated standards. In service companies, employees must be trained to understand a customer's needs and to perform the work to the customer's satisfaction. If the process or employees cannot produce the proper quality of output, no type of control can correct the situation.

Installing a Quality Control Process

Quality control, or **quality assurance,** is the process by which a producer ensures that the finished goods or services meet the expectations of customers. Therefore, quality control focuses on the reliability of the product or service to conform to standards, and involves at least the following steps:

1. Setting standards for the desired quality range.
2. Measuring actual performance.

"We removed all the sugar, caffeine, fats and carcinogens, and there wasn't anything left."
Source: Reprinted from *The Wall Street Journal*; permission Cartoon Features Syndicate.

3. Comparing that performance with established standards.
4. Making corrections when needed.

Some standards may be measured by instruments, such as rulers or gauges for length; but color, taste, and other standards must be evaluated by skilled individuals. Measurement may be made by selected people at selected spots in the process—usually upon receipt of material and always before the product goes to the customer. Inspection methods include spot checks (statistical analysis or sampling) and checking every item (100 percent inspection).

Inspection reduces the chances that a poor-quality product will pass through the process and to customers. By recording the number of defective units per 100 units, the quality of performance of the process or person can be observed and needed corrections made. A final quality check might be to record the number of complaints received per 100 sales made.

WHAT YOU SHOULD HAVE LEARNED

1. The purchasing function accounts for a small company's largest single type of cost. Goods and services must be obtained at the proper price, quality, and time, and in the proper quantity, and with the proper service. A company has a wide variety of items to purchase. Therefore, it should assign the responsibility for this function to one person.

2. Sources of supply must be found and investigated and one or more vendors selected. Reliability in delivery and quality affect nearly all operations. Vendors can be valuable sources of information and can provide valuable services. You must decide whether to use one (or a few) source(s) or many. Using one or a few will give you better relationships and often better prices, but it may not provide the variety, of items you need. Vendors should be evaluated to see that they have

acceptable quality and price. Periodically, the vendors' performance should be appraised and rated.

3. An effective purchasing procedure consists of (a) determining the items needed, in what quantity, from whom to purchase, and the terms of the contract, (b) sending the purchase order, (c) receiving the goods, (d) inspecting them, and (e) paying for them. Purchases can be made on the basis of a predetermined inventory level, using purchasing schedules, or by some other method.

4. Inventory is carried in order to disconnect one part of the operating process from another so that each part can operate effectively. Inventory takes many forms, such as items on display for sale; batches of goods awaiting processing or delivery; repair parts awaiting use; supplies for use in offices, stores, or shops; and miscellaneous items. The cost of carrying inventory consists of providing and maintaining storage space, insurance and taxes, profits lost from money tied up in it, obsolescence and deterioration, and theft and destruction.

    Determining the level of inventory at which to order more is tricky. Too low a level of inventory causes stockouts, while too high a level causes excessive inventory carrying costs. Therefore, the optimum inventory level at which to order goods is the point where the sum of the cost of carrying inventory and the cost of stocking out is the lowest.

    Orders may be placed (a) at certain time intervals, (b) when inventory reaches a certain level, or (c) when a customer orders special items. The quantity to be ordered can be obtained by balancing the costs of carrying inventory against the costs of ordering it.

5. Operations planning and control start with a forecast of sales from which operating plans are developed. Alternative plans for seasonal sales include producing to demand, producing at a constant rate and inventorying for future demand, carrying complementary products, subcontracting high demand, not meeting high demand, and using off-season sales inducements. Each plan has advantages and disadvantages, so cost formulas involving costs of inventory, overtime, changing level, and the like are used by planners.

    Day-to-day scheduling involves deciding whether to fill a customer's order from inventory or to order it into production. Most companies stock some standard items and regulate production on the basis of a preplanned schedule or customer needs. Schedulers can use CPM or PERT charts, as well as computers, to aid in planning schedules.

    Control of operations is obtained by reacting to exceptions to plans. As work is performed, plans are completed, events are recorded, exceptions are reported, and corrective action is taken.

6. In small businesses, the preferred emphasis is on quality of goods and services rather than on low price. The term *quality* refers both to acceptable product characteristics and to reliability of units. Quality includes a wide range of characteristics (dimension, taste, tone, and

so forth), some of which can be measured, while others require the use of judgment. Quality circles have been used beneficially by companies for improvement in many areas, especially in maintaining acceptable quality standards.

Quality control steps include setting standards, measuring performance, comparing actual performance with standards, and making corrections. Sampling (spot checking) and 100 percent inspection are used to check performance or quality.

KEY TERMS

purchasing, *403*

just-in-time delivery, *404*

stockouts, *404*

economic order quantity (EOQ), *413*

purchase orders, *413*

standing orders, *413*

reorder point, *417*

lead time, *418*

scheduling, *421*

job shops, *422*

critical path method (CPM), *424*

program evaluation and review technique (PERT), *424*

slack time, *424*

quality, *426*

quality circles, *427*

quality control (quality assurance), *427*

QUESTIONS FOR DISCUSSION

1. Discuss the advantages and disadvantages of buying locally versus buying from a distant seller.

2. What are the advantages and disadvantages of shopping at a single store rather than at several?

3. *(a)* How would a hardware store be affected by running out of a stock item (stocking out)? *(b)* A drugstore?

4. *(a)* In what ways can inventories serve to reduce costs? *(b)* To increase costs? *(c)* To change income?

5. *(a)* How would you make an economic study to determine the quantity of a food item to buy for your family on each trip to the store? *(b)* How often should purchases be made?

6. In some parts of the country, building construction varies seasonally. *(a)* Is this a problem for company management? *(b)* What decisions must management make concerning these variations?

7. Question a buyer or purchasing manager about his or her system of purchasing. Compare it with the text.

8. Many times, sales personnel do not practice good selling relations. How would you control the quality of this type of service?

9. *(a)* What is quality? *(b)* How can it be measured? *(c)* How can it be controlled?

10. Outline instructions for installing a new quality circle.

11. How can just-in-time scheduling be used in a print shop?

SUGGESTED READINGS

Candler, Julie, "The Leased Advantages." *Nation's Business,* May 1989, pp. 40–43.

Foster, Richard N. "A Call for Vision in Managing Technology." *Business Week,* May 24, 1982, pp. 24–33.

Frazier, Gary L., Robert E. Spekman, and Charles R. O'Neal. "Just-in-Time Exchange Relationships in Industrial Markets." *Journal of Marketing* 52 (October 1988): 52–67.

Koten, John. "Auto Makers Have Trouble with 'Kanban'." *The Wall Street Journal,* May 7, 1982, p. 35.

Mandel, Michael Schroeder, and James B. Treece. "Are Inventories Really under Control?" *Business Week,* July 31, 1989, p. 71.

Megginson, Leon C., Donald C. Mosley, and Paul H. Pietri, Jr. *Management: Concepts and Applications.* 3d ed. New York: Harper & Row, 1989. Especially Chaps. 14–16.

Waters, Craig R. "Quality Begins at Home." *Inc.,* August 1985, pp. 68–71.

Wearenberg, Stephen B. "The Future Just-in-Time Workforce." *Personnel Journal* 68 (February 1989): 36–40.

Winninghoff, Ellie, and Sal Ruibal. "He's Unhampered by a Dirty Business." *USA Today,* March 24, 1989, p. 9B.

ENDNOTES

1. "Wal-Mart Plans 'Just-in-Time' Delivery System," *Birmingham* (Alabama) *Post-Herald,* February 14, 1989, p. B1.

2. Stuart Weiss, "How Inventories Could Bury 1985 Computer Profits," *Business Week,"* April 8, 1985, pp. 82–83.

3. "Evaluating Suppliers," *Small Business Report* 13 (December 1988): 62.

4. "As American as Homemade Foie Gras," *Venture,* August 1985, p. 8.

5. Joseph B. Mason et al., *Modern Retailing* (Plano, Tex.: Business Publications, 1987), pp. 530, 531.

6. Leon C. Megginson, Lyle R. Trueblood, and Gayle M. Ross, *Business* (Lexington, Mass.: D. C. Heath, 1985), p. 213.

7. Sanford L. Jacobs, "Small Concerns Find a Niche Solving Problems of Big Firms," *The Wall Street Journal,* April 21, 1986, p. 25. Reprinted by permission of The Wall Street Journal, © Dow Jones & Company, Inc., 1986. ALL RIGHTS RESERVED.

8. David E. Gumpert, "Lighten Load, Trim Sails to Ride out the Storm," *USA Today,* May 8, 1989, p. 10E.

9. This formula can be found in any production management text.

10. Kathy Jumper, "Menefee Wants His Clients to Be Happy, Look Good," *Mobile* (Alabama) *Register,* February 20, 1989, p. 1–B.

11. Jeremy Main, "Under the Spell of the Quality Gurus," *Fortune,* August 18, 1986, pp. 30–34.

CASE IV–1
CLEANDRUM, INC. (D)

CASE IV–2
CONNIE'S CONFECTIONS

CASE IV–3
PLASTIC SUPPLIERS INC.

CASE IV–1

CLEANDRUM, INC. (D)

Sue Ley, founder, co-owner, and manager of CleanDrum, Inc. (CDI), concerned about the losses it has been incurring, is contemplating expanding the company's plant. She says, "The men in the shop need 'breathing room.'"

CDI's product line includes cleaning and selling steel and plastic drums. About 85 percent of the drums are steel. CDI either receives or buys drums to be cleaned and then returns or sells them to customers. Drums not meeting customers' standards have holes drilled in their tops for use as waste receptacles, or the tops are removed so the drums can be used to store parts; these are processed and sold to other customers.

When Sue started the company, she rented a 10,000-square-foot building and installed the necessary cleaning equipment. Later, to reduce costs, she moved production to a 4,000-square-foot building, where operations are now conducted. (See Exhibit 1 for current plant and equipment layout.) Sue estimates that the machinery can process about 5,000 drums a month and that current production averages about 3,000 drums per month. Machines are not fastened to the floor, but have electrical and pipe connections.

The drums are brought in by trailer; about 250 drums make up a trailer load. The company has three trailers so that two can stay at the plant to be unloaded and loaded while the other is delivering clean drums to customers.

The operations and their sequence for processing a drum are shown in Exhibit 2. The production process involves the following steps. First, the drums are received and unloaded over a period of several days. The bungs are removed and the drums checked for quality. The drums are stacked, moved to a waiting area, or moved to first flush. About 300 drums are in each of the receiving and shipping areas.

Exhibit 1   Layout of CleanDrum Plant

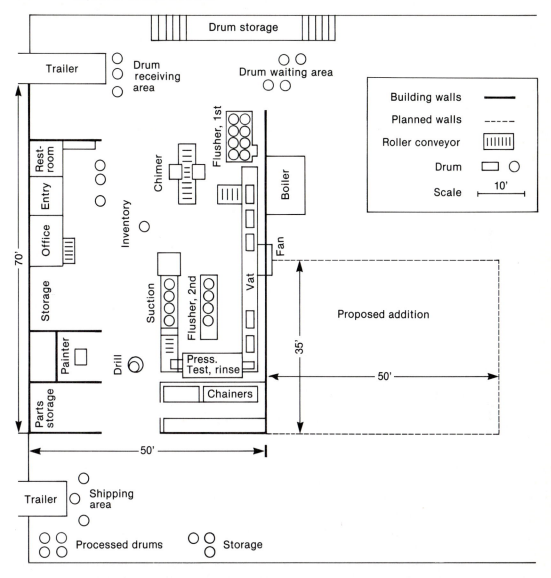

Second, each steel drum is upended on a pipe and flushed with steam and a chemical.

Third, when finished, the drum is righted, a light is lowered into it, and it is inspected for rust. Rusty drums are rolled to chainers in a separate room where chains are inserted in each drum and the drum is rotated until the rust is removed. Then the drums are returned to the main area for further processing.

Exhibit 2   Sequence of Operations at CleanDrum

Operations			Time in	
Steel drums	Plastic drums	Machines	drum	Handling
1. Receive	1. Receive	Trailer		L 5 T
2. First flush	2. First flush	Flusher	3 minutes	L 2 T
3. Inspect for rust;		Visual	3 minutes	L 2 T
if so, clean with chain		Chainer*	15 minutes	L 3 T
4. Straighten		Chimer	1 minute	T
5. Clean		Vat	10 minutes	L 3 T
6. Outside rinse		Rinser	3 minutes	M
7. Pressure test;		Forced air†	20 seconds	M
if not passed;		Hand cutter	10 minutes	L 2 T
cut out top	3. Pressure test	Hand tester	2 minutes	L 4 T
8. Last flush	4. Flush	Flusher	4 minutes	L 4 T
	5. Wash outside	Hand washer	3 minutes	T
9. Dry		Suction	2 minutes	L 4 T
10. Inspect for rust;		Visual‡	2 minutes	—
if not passed,				
cut 9″ hole		Drill press	10 minutes	L 2 T
11. Paint (90%)		Paint booth	4 minutes	L 2 T
12. Ship		Truck		L 5 T

* About 5 percent.
† When a drum does not meet pressure testing standards, the top is cut out and the drum is sold for storage of foundry parts.
‡ When a drum does not meet rust and straightening standards, a 9-inch hole is cut in the top and the drum is sold for waste.
L = Lift; Number (5,2, etc.) = Distance moved up or down, in feet; T = Turn; M = Mechanically lifted, turned, and rolled into outside rinses.

Fourth, drums needing straightening are run through the chimer.

Fifth, the drums are lifted onto a conveyor and rolled into the vat for soak cleaning. Six drums can be cleaned at the same time.

Sixth, after cleaning, drums are mechanically lifted, turned, and rolled into the outside rinser.

Seventh, they are pressure tested. Those not meeting the pressure test are moved from the process.

Eighth, the good drums roll down the conveyor, where a worker lifts and upends each onto a steam pipe for the last flush.

Ninth, after flushing, each drum is righted and placed on the floor, where a suction pipe is inserted to dry the inside (see Exhibit 3).

Tenth, the final inspection for rust is made.

Eleventh, the good drums are rolled to the paint booth for individual spray painting while being turned. When each drum is dry, a label is affixed to signify to the customer that the drum has gone through the entire cleaning process and conforms to established standards.

Finally, the drums are put into a waiting trailer for delivery or are moved to storage.

Exhibit 3   The CleanDrum Flushing and Drying Operation

Plastic drums follow a separate path that causes "some confusion." After the first flush, they are manually pressure tested, flushed again, and washed on a mobile cradle.

Sue has found some businesses that will take a few steel drums that do not meet the standards of regular customers. By further processing certain defective drums, CDI receives added income. Some drums are sold for scrap.

At times, space around the machines is crowded with drums (some stacked) awaiting the next operation. During the summer, the plant is extremely hot even with the draft through the open ends of the building, augmented by a six-foot-diameter fan placed in the wall by the vat. In rainy weather, workers in receiving and shipping wear raincoats or other protective wear.

Sue and the owner of the building have decided to enlarge it by 50 percent to provide more room for the workers. The additional space will raise the rent 50 percent from $600 to $900 per month. The building is of steel construction with a corrugated steel roof. The landlord says that the floor will be designed for good drainage. Currently, the drainage from the second flusher and rinser runs off into the sewer. The fluids in the first flusher and vat are recirculated. Every two or three months, the fluids are diluted enough to run into the sewer. The city authorities have approved these processes.

The owner of the building has made available some lengths of roller conveyor totaling about 100 feet for moving the drums. These have been stacked in the open in the back of the lot for several years.

Questions for Discussion

1. Evaluate the production system.
2. (a) What are the advantages and disadvantages of the expansion?
    (b) What costs must be considered?
3. (a) Is drum handling a problem? (b) How can handling be reduced?
4. (a) Do you recommend a rearrangement of the current layout?
    (b) Explain.
5. (a) How would you lay out the expanded plant? (b) List the advantages
    and disadvantages of your layout.
6. (a) Does the enlargement decision appear to be sound? (b) What do
    you recommend that Sue do?

Source: Prepared by Charles R. Scott, University of Alabama, and William M. Spain, SCORE.

CASE IV–2

CONNIE'S CONFECTIONS

The sound of bells jingling as the door opens, the aroma of freshly cooked chocolate, the air circulating from the wooden ceiling fans—all are part of the distinctive image characteristic of Connie's Confections. Connie's, which produces "quality chocolates," is the brainchild of Connie Prince, who established the business in 1980. Now, Connie is faced with a dilemma.

"Here I sit with my main store in a dead shopping center—supposedly the anchor for the entire center. How can that be? I'm a candy store. When I set up here six years ago, this place was flourishing. Then the post office left, followed by the grocery store and half the other shops. All that's left are a bike shop, a barbershop, a laundry, and a computer store. That leaves me in a predicament. Do I pull up roots and leave this neighborhood environment that has supported me so well, or do I try to stay here?"

Beginnings

Connie had worked for a candy store in Houston, Texas, while she was in high school and decided to seek advice from her former employer before starting her business. "After one week in Houston," Connie says, "I was convinced that manufacturing my own candy was the best way to go. Securing the formula and process for making the chocolates from my former employer as a gift, I was ready to open my candy store."

Connie's Confections opened its doors in October 1980. The building leased by Connie's had previously been a restaurant, so Connie was able to use some of the existing facilities. Four years later, Connie opened another retail store in the heart of the city's business and government complex. Later, she expanded further by opening a retail store in one of the exclusive areas of the city—an area that Connie described as having "snob appeal." This store, however, never became profitable and was closed. "Part of that failure was attributable to road construction immediately in front of the facility. Choosing that location was, to say the least, not a wise decision," Connie lamented.

Three Businesses in One

Connie's Confections is a manufacturer, wholesaler, and retailer of quality chocolates. Its products include cherry cordials, truffles, fudge, toffee, ice cream, cones, and a variety of molded chocolate items. Doing its own manufacturing gives Connie's the ability to customize its products. Not only can the products be personalized, but custom molds, which are very attractive to businesses looking for unique advertising, are also available for large purchases.

As a manufacturer, Connie's produces candy from scratch and acts as a subassembler. In either case, the primary raw material is chocolate, which is bought from Nestlé. Though usage varies seasonally, Connie's buys approximately 1,500 pounds of chocolate per month. As a subassembler, it buys candy components, such as cherries and nuts, using them to build specialized confections. In any case, the manufacturing process involves a great deal of heavy labor. As Connie noted, "In order to make one type of candy, 13 pounds of peanut brittle is cooked in a 20-pound kettle at 349 degrees and carried from one place to another. Specialized equipment, such as an enrober—which costs $16,000—is essential. Producing candy is not a simple, inexpensive process."

Inventory is labeled and shelved in the manufacturing area. The label indicates the product name, type, and production date. The shelf life of an item depends on the type of item, the season, and the quantity produced in a "run." Bulk chocolate will last an indefinite time without spoiling when stored in very low humidity at 68°–75° F. Connie's has equipment to store materials under such conditions. This allows larger production runs, which reduces the per-unit manufacturing costs.

Connie's also makes its own ice cream and cones. Ice cream is made in 16 flavors at the suburban location, which is Connie's main store. Connie's also sells a few specialty flavors made by others. An innovator, Connie's was the first candy store in the Jacksonville area to offer homemade "waffle" cones.

Connie's retail operation is currently confined to the two Jacksonville stores. The suburban main store is set up to cater more to the gift market. The products offered include chocolate candies, ice cream, and an assortment of complementary goods, including boxes, tins, cards, stuffed animals, baskets, and many decorative items. The store's sales are highly seasonal, with major sales occurring around Valentine's Day, Easter, Christmas, and—to a lesser degree—Mother's Day, Secretary's Day, and Halloween. Candy accounts for approximately 73 percent of sales at the suburban store, with ice cream adding 6 to 7 percent and the complementary items composing the remainder. The main store, which has been expanded from 750 square feet to its present 1,900 square feet, is open from 9 to 6 Monday through Saturday and 9 to 1 on Sunday. Because the store has very little seating, most of the sales are carry-out trade.

Relocate?

Connie explains her problem this way:

My present landlord has threatened to bulldoze one end of the building I'm in as soon as the tenants occupying that space leave in January. He feels it would give passing traffic a better view of the shopping center. He's trying to intimidate me because I still have four years to run on my lease, and he's hoping I'll simply leave on my own. I can stay and probably be a real thorn in his side, or I can—I hope—get him to buy me out of my lease.

One of the new malls has just contacted me regarding retail space. They've made me quite an attractive offer in a prime location. Since this mall is located in the yuppie area of town, it would be ideal for the image I like to create. Now I've got to figure out how to play the game with the lessor in the unit I'm now in and perhaps relocate in the mall.

But that relocation leaves me with another problem. In my present store, my manufacturing facilities are on-site. That is, in fact, one of my claims to fame with my product. If I move to the new mall, it is not practical to pay retail rates for a partially manufacturing facility. The question is: Where do I put my manufacturing, keeping in mind that just any place won't do? Because of the quality chocolates we use, I've got to maintain my inventory of raw materials and finished goods at 68 to 75 degrees and a humidity of 60 percent. With the climate here in the South, that's not an easy task. My electric bill for the main facility alone is over $1,200 a month in the summer—and keep in mind that our summer lasts at least five months, and sometimes six.

Unlike the suburban store, the downtown location is designed to cater to the heavy pedestrian traffic of the area. Half of the store's 1,900 square feet has been sublet to The Sandwich Shoppe, which complements Connie's products, especially for the lunchtime crowd. Ice cream accounts for 60 percent of sales, with candy and extras making up the rest. The store has a small seating capacity. The store is open Monday through Friday from 8 to 5 and staffed by only one full-time employee, though two part-time workers are added in the summer.

Questions for Discussion

1. Analyze the downtown location, the suburban operation, and the proposed new mall location.
2. What alternatives might Connie have for the suburban location?
3. What is "on-site," and is the "on-site" claim to fame important?
4. Discuss the problem of the location of the manufacturing facility.
5. What steps should Connie take to determine her future course of action?

Source: Prepared by Shirley Olson and Patrick Taylor, Millsaps College.

CASE IV–3
PLASTIC SUPPLIERS INC.

Company History

Plastic Suppliers Inc. (PSI) commenced operations in April, two years ago. The company was an offshoot of its founder's lifelong dream of owning his own business. Mr. Edmunds, the founder, had 16 years' experience working at IBM, where he had started at the bottom and worked his way up until he became head of the New Products Division. After that experience, he and five of his friends with the same technical background invested their lifetime savings in a small company, PSI, and started operations in McAllen, Texas.

PSI supplies plastic parts to plants in Mexico for assembly with other items. About 80 percent of the products are returned to the United States for sale or further processing. Some typical parts are luggage handles and auto seat belts.

Edmunds states that he is "concerned about the delays in the plant, the need for additional capacity, and the lack of profits in the company's operations."

Products and Services Provided

PSI has three profit-generating departments: engineering, tooling, and production. The engineering department creates mold designs; the tooling department makes the actual molds and mold repairs; and the production department runs the mold to produce the various plastic parts.

Although each department's function can be considered a continuous flow from mold design to parts production, clients come in needing one or two or all of the services that PSI offers. Some clients have their own molds (which they bring down from northern locations so that delivery will be faster) so all that PSI has to do is produce the plastic parts and maintain the molds. Other customers come in with specifications for the part they want to produce, so that PSI has to design and make the molds, then produce the parts. Added to all these functions, PSI, is also capable of rendering local delivery services.

The engineering department is responsible for designing the molds that are used to make the parts. Drawings are prepared showing all details of the mold. The drawings are facilitated by use of a computer with CAD/CAM (computer-assisted design/manufacturing) software. Designing the molds requires highly skilled people, who are unavailable in the local job market area.

The tooling department makes molds based on the drawings and specifications. Making a mold takes anywhere from a couple of weeks to three months. Skilled personnel must be used in this department also, because of the complexity of the tasks involved. Again, skilled personnel are unavailable in the local job market. After the molds are built, they are moved to the production floor for preliminary testing. If any flaws are discovered, the molds are sent back to tooling for adjustments.

Adjusted and tested molds are turned over to the production department, primarily staffed with semiskilled operators. The only skills required in this departrment are in setting up machines to specifications to turn out the right number of plastic parts. Knowledge of cycle times, water levels, and so forth is an important factor. Each machine is run by one worker. This task does not require any special skills. Second- and third-shift operations are needed in the production department when there are large production schedules.

Quality Controls and Problems

Edmunds realizes that quality control (QC) is of the highest priority with *maquiladora* (assembly plant) operations (discussed in the next section). Since PSI produces plastic parts that must be integrated into other products, all parts must fit perfectly. A large portion of PSI capacity is sent to a plant assembling plastic parts for automobile seat belts. This requires strict measurement and materials quality control. Therefore, a quality control department has been added.

Frequently, problems arise concerning a specific job. Usually time schedules are set up to ensure that the parts get to the customer on time and to maximize the utilization of personnel and machines. However, delays can—and often do—occur, caused by any of the following factors:

1. Too much time spent on designing the molds (engineering), or in making the molds (tooling), or in producing the parts (production).
2. Sometimes parts do not conform to QC standards, and then each department blames the other for the failure.
3. Sometimes the molds break or do not work correctly even if they have passed QC checks.
4. Finally, machine breakdowns are a much too frequent problem.

Location

The founder, Mr. Edmunds, is a native of south Texas. Most of the existing plastic injection molding outfits are located in the Northeast or Midwest, and the nearest (a very small facility) is in Dallas, Texas, some 550 miles to the north of McAllen. McAllen is located in Hidalgo County, which has an unemployment rate of about 17 percent and an average annual income of $3,300. A *maquiladora* program is located just across the border in Mexico, some 12 miles away. *Maquiladora* plants, established by Mexico to alleviate unemployment problems, are usually one-half of twin plant operations, normally U.S. owned and run, with one plant on each side of the U.S.–Mexican border. Parts and technical operations are performed on the U.S. side, while manual operations are performed on the Mexican side by non-skilled workers, paid less than $5 per day. The U.S. plant provides components duty free to its sister plant in Mexico for assembly, semi-processing, and/or repair, and subsequently to be reexported to the United States for further processing or as completed goods. A U.S. duty is levied on the returning products only to the extent of the value added in Mexico.

Fast Expansion

Rapid expansion during PSI's first two years was triggered by the increased demand from *maquiladora* operators. At the outset, PSI was doing several small jobs, but only one big project, manufacturing bag handles. One machine was devoted entirely to the plastic handles. The other three machines were almost always idle because of small production runs. Then, two *maquiladora* plants, Zenith (televisions) and TRW (seat belts), alone took practically all of the original capacity. Expansion was inevitable, and four months ago, four additional machines were installed.

The production department's capacity more than doubled over its first two years, and the personnel complement increased from 6 to 86 employees. The number of machines has grown from four to seven 150-ton, plus one 500-ton, plastic injection molding machines. Raw materials are stacked in boxes alongside the machines due to lack of storage space. A small warehouse nearby has been leased for extra storage space. A small office for the engineering department has been added due to overcrowding in the administrative office.

Financial Problems

During the first 20 months, no accurate financial reports were maintained. The new stockholders were concerned about the losses and the lack of accounting information to support decision making. About seven months ago, a CPA with consulting experience was hired and a consulting team brought in to determine the standard costs for labor, raw materials, and overhead, and also to set up a system to monitor expenses on a per-job basis. The study was finished three months ago; the resulting cost accounting system was not implemented, however, because Edmunds, the CEO, was too busy searching for more sales and financial sources to borrow from. The CPA developed financial statements for the past year (see Exhibit 1 for the income statement) and then left. With the existing plant filled to capacity, management has plans for a bigger facility.

Exhibit 1

Plastic Suppliers Inc.
Income Statement
For the year ended December 31

	Department			
	Production	Mold build	Repairs	Total
Sales	$120,000	$140,000	$34,000	$294,000
Cost of sales:				
Materials used	68,345	20,496		88,841
Direct labor	32,492	123,932	566	156,990
Overhead	31,433	26,058	3,515	61,006
Total cost of sales	132,270	170,486	4,081	306,827
Gross profit	(12,270)	(30,486)	29,919	(12,838)
General and administrative expenses:				
Payroll				108,232
Maintenance				24,289
Depreciation				36,114
Amortization				1,213
Rents and leases				311
Insurance—assets				7,887
Travel and entertainment				11,546
Shipping				507
Taxes				741
Consulting fees				30,428
Office supplies				7,324
Telephone and telegraph				5,622
Mail/postage/courier				2,596
Electricity and water				19,835
Fuel and oil				122
Contributions and donations				51
Licenses and permits				491
Memberships, dues, and subscriptions				1,418
Total general and administrative expenses				258,727
Operating income				(271,565)
Less other expenses (Revenues)				
Financial expenses				42,083
Other expenses				3,824
Net income (loss)				($317,471)

Questions for Discussion

1. List problems for management that are indicated in the case.
2. (a) List the advantages and disadvantages of the location of the PSI plant. (b) Would you have located the plant in the McAllen area? (c) Why or why not?
3. (a) What types of problems does the company have in balancing operations? (b) How might these be resolved?

4. *(a)* What are some possible approaches to the delay problems? *(b)* What do you recommend?
5. *(a)* Analyze the profit picture. *(b)* What can be done about it?
6. What steps do you recommend that management take to obtain a more favorable future?

Source: Prepared by Dr. Walter E. Greene of the University of Texas–Pan American.

V

MARKETING GOODS AND SERVICES

As staffing, operations, marketing, and financing are all essential business functions, each should be performed effectively if the small business is to be successful. The first two functions were covered in Parts III and IV, and the last will be covered in Part VI. The material in this part concentrates on the marketing function.

Marketing involves determining customers' needs, developing goods and services to satisfy those needs, and distributing those products to customers. It is an essential function because, unless the firm has a market—or can develop one—for its product, performing the other business functions is futile.

Chapter 15, "Developing Marketing Strategies," covers the marketing concept; strategy development, including marketing objectives, targets, and mix; types of products and their life cycles; marketing strategies for services; packaging; pricing strategies; credit; and transportation.

In Chapter 16, "Selling and Distributing the Product," determining channels of distribution, using intermediaries, using one's own sales force and supporting and controlling sales personnel, and promoting the product (including personal selling) are covered.

Chapter 17, "International Marketing and Marketing Research," rounds out the discussion of the marketing function. It covers the role of international marketing, importing, exporting, and doing marketing research.

15

DEVELOPING MARKETING STRATEGIES

The buyer needs a hundred eyes, but the seller needs none.—Anonymous

---

We don't focus enough attention on adequate product differentiation, much less on distribution channels, service organizations, or the reputation of vendors. We tend to forget that those things tremendously influence what someone buys.—William H. Davidow, venture capitalist and author of *Marketing High Technology*

Packaging is the last five seconds of marketing.—John Lester, vice president, Lester Butler Inc.

LEARNING OBJECTIVES

After studying the material in this chapter, you will be able to:

1. Describe the marketing concept, and explain how it can be used by a small business.
2. Explain how to develop a marketing strategy.
3. Distinguish between consumer and industrial products.
4. Explain how the product life cycle affects marketing strategies.
5. Explain how packaging affects marketing.
6. Describe how prices are set and administered.
7. Explain how physical distribution affects the marketing strategy.
8. Discuss some of the problems involved in granting and administering credit.
9. Show how the marketing of services differs from marketing goods.
10. Explain how marketing strategies can be implemented.

JUDY PUGSLEY: MARKETING A SERVICE

Judy Pugsley's advertising agency, Try J. Advertising, of Carlsbad, California, sells service! It specializes in the automotive field, with automobile dealerships as its target market. In 1989, it served GMC, Pontiac, Mazda, Toyota, and Lexus—the new luxury-car division of Toyota.

Pugsley and her people perform the following services:

- Provide for clients' printing needs by acting as their agent.
- Prepare items such as business cards, letterheads, and stationery.
- Write, photograph, print, and distribute newsletters to clients' employees and customers.
- Write and print direct mail pieces.
- Produce training videos.
- Write and produce radio, newspaper, and television ads.
- Plan special events, such as grand openings and new model introductions.

Try J. Advertising, Inc., was created as an advertising agency in 1981. It was incorporated with Pugsley as president and equal shareholder with Louis V. Jones, president of Toyota Carlsbad, who serves as secretary-treasurer.

When asked how she got started in business, Ms. Pugsley gave the following account:

Judy Pugsley
Source: Photo courtesy of Judy Pugsley.

I was attracted to creative writing by my father, Scott W. Irwin, who was an announcer, copywriter, advertising manager, and later manager of a radio station in Baton Rouge, Louisiana. My mother's career, library work, also influenced my career, but I found creating communication through words was more satisfying than putting someone else's words into the Dewey decimal system. I studied advertising in the School of Journalism at Louisiana State University. Not knowing if I would be a copywriter in an advertising agency or doing obituaries in the "Town Crier," I tried to cover all bases, including taking extra courses during summers to achieve a certificate of specialization in public relations.

After graduating in 1976, I became a field reporter for the *Louisiana Contractor Magazine,* which led to my first pair of work boots and a hard hat. After three years, I was transferred to the *San Diego Contractor Magazine.* My stay there was very brief, as I had to

sell ads in Los Angeles two weeks out of every month. Smog, people, and crowded freeways started me on the road to my own business in Carlsbad.

During 1979 and 1980, I was marketing director for the Wendy's Old-Fashioned Hamburgers San Diego County Region. Next, I was an account executive for the Ad Group, an advertising agency. I became the account executive for one of its main accounts, the San Diego Toyota Dealers' Advertising Association. One of the dealers appreciated my work and offered an in-house position at his store, Toyota Carlsbad. This led me to start my own agency in 1981.

Many factors have led to Pugsley's success, including the ability to handle responsibility, the skill and expertise needed to handle the technical aspects, and the ability to communicate. She attributes her ability as an effective communicator to her education. She also says that membership in Women in Communications and the Carlsbad Rotary Club have been invaluable in teaching her the ways of the business world.

Try J. Advertising's income is derived from two sources. First, it receives a 15 percent commission on the purchase of media time and advertising space for its clients. Second, copywriting, public relations, and art design are charged at a competitive hourly rate, which was

$30 per hour in 1989. The rate is determined by studying competitors' rates and estimating the level of skill Try J.'s people bring to the work. Try J.'s gross billings are around $900,000 per year. In addition to Pugsley, the agency's staff consists of an account executive, an art director, and a copywriter—all full-time employees—as well as a receptionist and bookkeeper who work part time. The bookkeeper has her own independent business.

Source: Discussions and correspondence with Judy Pugsley.

This Opening Focus illustrates several aspects of the marketing function. It gives a broad overview of marketing—such as the importance of the marketing concept, pinpointing specific target markets, pricing, product development, and customer service. This chapter is all about those and other related marketing activities.

THE MARKETING CONCEPT

The **marketing concept** helps a firm focus its efforts on satisfying customer needs in such a way as to make a satisfactory profit. The concept comprises three basic elements: a customer orientation, a goal orientation, and the systems approach. This concept is based on the truth that the survival of a small business depends on providing service.

With a customer orientation, small firms strive to identify the group of people or firms most likely to buy their product (the target market), and to produce goods or services that will meet the needs of that market.

For example, New York's Nailphile, Inc., which advertises, "Let our walking do your fingers," offers manicures at the office. And Gino's East sells pizzas at construction sites and train stations in the Chicago area, using oven-equipped delivery trucks.[1]

Being consumer oriented often involves research to explore consumer needs or to obtain reactions to new product ideas. But it should also be a philosophy practiced throughout the business.

In 1982, Pamela Swenson bought Sanitary Dry Cleaners in Laconia, New Hampshire. Not only does she make a living from this business, but she has some very satisfying moments. For example, "a little lady about 75 years old" drives half an hour to trade with her because "she likes spending a little time with us." Another customer said that although he had been trading with a cleaner nearer his home, he changed to Sanitary because "you know my name."[2]

In focusing on consumer orientation, however, the small firm must not lose sight of its own goals. Goals in profit-seeking firms typically center on financial criteria such as a certain level of profit and a given percentage return on investment, or on a stated share of the market.

The third component of the marketing concept is the systems approach. A **system** is an organized group of individual parts working together in unison to achieve a common goal. Using the systems approach, all parts of the business work together. Thus, consumer wants and needs are identified, and internal procedures are set up to ensure that the right goods and services are produced, distributed, and sold to meet the needs of the target market.

Understanding the Consumer Decision Process

Successful marketing results from understanding **consumer behavior,** which can be viewed as a decision process, as shown in Figure 15–1. The mental and physical steps in the **consumer decision process** are:

1. Recognizing the problem.
2. Searching for a solution to the problem.
3. Evaluating available alternatives.
4. Making the purchase decision.
5. Purchasing the product.
6. Making a postpurchase evaluation of the product and the decision to buy it.

By studying these steps, you should be better able to influence the consumer's decision.

Figure 15–1 The Consumer Decision Process

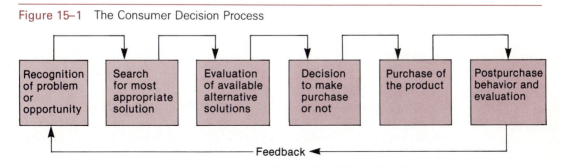

Source: Adapted from C. Glenn Walters and Gordon W. Paul, *Consumer Behavior: An Integrated Framework* (Homewood, Ill.: Richard D. Irwin, 1970), p. 18.

Determining Customer Needs

Understanding customers' needs starts with the realization that they purchase benefits as well as goods or services. Consumers do not simply choose a toothpaste, for example. Instead, some want a decay preventive, some seek pleasant taste, others desire tooth brighteners, and still others will accept any formula at a bargain price. Similarly, industrial purchasing agents are not interested in drills but, rather, in making holes. So they seek quality appropriate for their purposes, reliable delivery when needed, safe operation, and reasonable prices. Sometimes consumers' reasons for buying are trivial.

For example, one man chose an $18,000 car simply because its upholstery was more attractive than that of other cars he had test driven.

Understanding customers includes awareness of the time of the purchase and the use to be made of the product. Thus, small businesses should learn what customers like and dislike, or what "turns them on."

The owner of a ladies' dress shop in a small town had a good business. Many of her customers lived in a city 50 miles away. She knew her customers by name, understood their needs, and bought with them as individuals in mind. "This dress would suit Mrs. Adams" (name disguised) she would think as she chose a sample. And she would call Mrs. Adams when that dress came in.

Understanding customer needs requires insight into their buying roles. In the purchase decision process, each person may play only one or a few of the following roles:

- User—the person who consumes the product or service.
- Buyer—the person who actually makes the purchase.
- Decider—the person who decides what to buy.
- Influencer—a person who influences the buyer.
- Informer—a person who controls the flow of information about the product.

In a household, different roles in the selection of various goods and services are played by the various members. Therefore, salespeople should identify not only the specific needs of customers but also their roles. It may be necessary to make one presentation to those who will use a product and another to those who will make the buying decision. Some car salespeople still violate this principle by trying to sell a car to the man, even though the woman is choosing—or even buying—the car.

Figure 15–2   Customer Service

Some of the factors affecting good services

Employees:
  They should be courteous, helpful, and knowledgeable but not intrusive. There should be
  an adequate number of salespeople and cashiers. Some retailers, including Wal-Mart Stores
  Inc., make customer satisfaction part of the employees' job description.

Commissions:
  If making it a part of their jobs isn't enough, some retailers will offer commission payments
  to workers who serve their customers well.

Store design:
  Store layout should promote shopping efficiency. Merchandise should be in stock and easy
  to find. Cash registers should be reliable and fast.

Feedback:
  Keeping in touch with customers is crucial, especially for mail-order retailers. Toll-free hotlines
  are effective. Some retailers call or write their customers to solicit their suggestions.

Source: Adapted from Joyce M. Rosenberg, "Keeping the Customer Satisfied Is Much Easier Said than
Done," AP report in *Mobile* (Alabama) *Press Register,* August 21, 1988, p. 1-D.

Meeting Customers' Needs

The marketing concept should guide the attitudes of all employees in the firm. Salespeople should be encouraged to build personal followings among customers.

One retail salesperson, to build a following, wrote 20 letters every day, each describing new stock that would appeal to the specific customer.

Small firms should do little favors for customers. Although people dislike receiving big favors that they cannot repay, small acts of thoughtfulness make them feel that the business cares about them. Customers want a business to be helpful, and outstanding service will often generate good word-of-mouth advertising. On the other side of the coin, failure to render expected service can result in loss of customers. One service that harried shoppers especially appreciate is a liberal return policy.

Meeting customer needs and keeping them satisfied is more difficult than it seems, for it involves all aspects of the business. As shown in Figure 15–2, customer satisfaction involves not just employees and customers but other factors as well, such as store design and upkeep, method of employee payment, and methods for providing feedback to and from customers.

Implementing the Marketing Concept

In implementing the marketing concept, the systems approach should be followed. As shown in Figure 15–2, all parts of the business must be coordinated and marketing policies understood by all personnel, from the salespeople to the billing department, in order to avoid problems such as the following example.

A store sent its customers a flyer urging them to use its credit plan. Yet one customer got it in the same mail with a harsh letter threatening repossession of earlier purchases if the customer's account was not paid up within 24 hours. How might the customer be expected to react?[3]

Management should make a concerted effort to improve the application of the marketing concept by the following methods.

Be Conscious of Image

The small business manager should evaluate the business periodically to see what kind of image it projects, from the customers' point of view. Management should ask: Can customers find what they want, when they want it, and where they want it, at a competitive price?

Practice Consumerism

The major concerns of the consumer movement are the rights of consumers to buy safe products, to be informed, to be able to choose, and to be heard. **Consumerism** recognizes that consumers are at a disadvantage and works to force business to be responsive in giving the public a square deal. The movement relies on publicity, regulation, and lawsuits to correct poor performance. Small businesses can practice consumerism by doing such things as performing product tests, making clear the terms of sales and warranties, and being truthful in advertising.

Look for Danger Signals

There are many danger signals that can indicate when the marketing concept is not being followed. A business is in trouble if, over time, it exhibits one or more of the signs listed in Table 15–1.

Thomas Shoemaker was hunting for some Con-Tact paper in a Peoples Drug store in Washington, D.C. He finally gave up the search and was walking out when he saw a man with a Peoples ID badge adjusting some stock on a shelf. When Shoemaker asked him if the store carried Con-Tact paper, the man replied, "I don't know. I don't work here. I'm the manager."[4]

Table 15–1   Danger Signals Indicating Marketing Problems

Indicator	Indication
Sales	Down from previous period
Customers	Walking out without buying
	No longer visiting store
	Returning more merchandise
	Expressing more complaints
Employees and salespeople	Being slow to greet customers
	Being indifferent to or delaying customer
	Not urging added or upgraded sales
	Having poor personal appearance
	Lacking knowledge of store
	Making more errors
	(Good ones) leaving the company
Store image	Of greed through unreasonable prices
	Inappropriate for market area
	Unclear, sending mixed signals

Seeking a Competitive Edge

There is a close relationship between key success factors and the competitive edge that the small firm should seek. Some of these factors, based on industry analysis, were discussed in Chapter 3. Using current and appropriate factors, the small business must seek a **competitive edge.** This edge is based on having something that customers want, which gives the business an advantage over its competitors. Some factors that might provide such an advantage are quality, reliability, integrity, and service, as well as lower prices. In some industries, such as electronics or toys, novelty and innovation provide the most important competitive edge; in many small businesses, however, it can be as simple a thing as friendliness.

DEVELOPING A MARKETING STRATEGY

Small business owners should develop a marketing strategy early in the business operation. Such a strategy consists of: (1) setting objectives, (2) choosing target market(s), and (3) developing an effective marketing mix.

Setting Objectives

Marketing objectives should be tied in with the competitive edge. For example, an image of higher quality than competitors', at comparable prices, may be an objective. To achieve this objective and still make planned profits requires aligning all operations, including the added costs of improved quality, adequate capital, and so forth. Objectives must consider customers served and company survival. To attain objectives, a market must be identified and served.

Choosing Target Market(s)

The **target market** of a business should be the consumers or firms most likely to buy or use its product(s). Only when a clear, precise target market has been identified can an effective marketing mix be developed.

Medical Services, Inc. (Case V–2) pinpointed three groups as its target market. They were students at a nearby university, small businesses, and townspeople within a two-mile radius.

Use Market Segmentation

To define a target market requires **market segmentation,** which is the process of identifying and evaluating various layers of a market. Effective market segmentation requires the following steps:

1. Identify the characteristics of two or more segments of the total market. Then, differentiate among the customers on the basis of characteristics such as their habits, age, sex, buying patterns, or income level. For example, adults desire a table-service restaurant more than do teenagers and young children, who generally prefer a fast-food format. Some groups prefer even greater service.
2. Determine whether any one of those market segments is large enough and has sufficient buying power to generate profit for your business.
3. Align your marketing effort to reach that segment of the market profitably.

For example, Ryka Inc., a 25-employee firm in Weymouth, Massachusetts, intends to take a segment of the $4 billion-a-year athletic shoe market away from giants such as Nike, Reebok, and L.A. Gear. It plans to concentrate on athletic shoes for women.[5]

A firm's best strategy is to identify a target market that is not well served by other firms. Important considerations in choosing a target market include: (1) behavioral needs and attitudes, and how present and potential goods and services fit into consumers' consumption patterns, (2) customers' urgency to satisfy their needs, plus desire and willingness to compare and shop, and (3) geographical location and other demographic characteristics.[6]

Figure 15–3   Shrinking Households

The average size of households has declined
steadily for decades. Average number of persons
per household over the years:

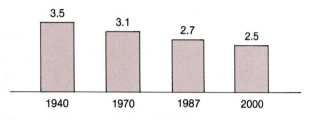

Source: U.S. Census Bureau statistics, as reported in *USA Today,*
November 28, 1988, p. 1A. Copyright 1988, USA TODAY.
Adapted with permission.

For example, CleanDrum, Inc. (Case V–1), has set the limits of its target market to
a 200-mile radius. It uses its own trucks to deliver its drums, and that is the optimum
distance for servicing customers.

Shifting Target Markets

Choosing and maintaining a target market is becoming more difficult because
of changing consumer characteristics. Therefore, the small business manager should evaluate the external environment for shifts in such factors
as population patterns, age groups, and income levels, as well as geographical
and regional patterns of consumption.

Population, age, and income shifts.   The underlying market factor determining consumer demand is the number and type of people with the purchasing
power to buy a given product. In general, the U.S. population is shifting
away from the North and to the West and South. Other important population
characteristics are household size and formations and education, as well
as the numbers of married couples, singles, single-parent families, unmar-
ried couples, and children. According to the U.S. Census Bureau, the average
size of U.S. households has declined from 3.5 in 1940 to 2.7 in 1987 and
is expected to be only 2.5 by the year 2000. Figure 15–3 reflects these
changes.

Age groups also change. The average age of Americans has been rising
and is expected to continue to rise in the foreseeable future, according to
the Census Bureau. The percentage of young people and young adults is
declining, while the 35-and-over group—especially the 45-to-64-year
group—is increasing rapidly (as can be seen in Figure 15–4) and is expected
to continue to do so. People in each age group differ in their consumption
patterns; so different marketing strategies are needed.

Figure 15–4   Selling to Older Consumers

The growing ranks of older consumers and a decline in the size of the youth market are leading companies to redesign products and sales appeals to capture the increasingly influential senior citizen market.

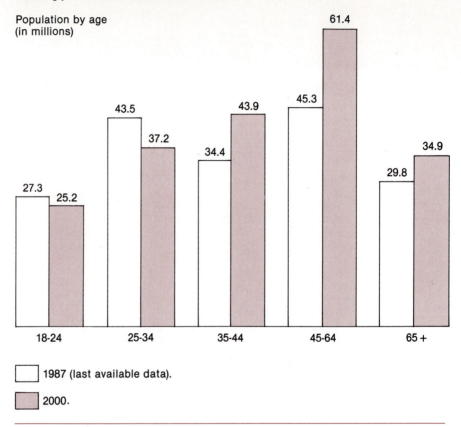

Population by age
(in millions)

	18-24	25-34	35-44	45-64	65 +
1987 (last available data).	27.3	43.5	34.4	45.3	29.8
2000.	25.2	37.2	43.9	61.4	34.9

☐ 1987 (last available data).

▨ 2000.

Source: U.S. Census Bureau data, as reported in a Newhouse News Agency graphic, *Mobile* (Alabama) *Press Register,* March 5, 1989, p. 1–D. Adapted with permission.

The two most dramatic shifts are the aging of the "baby-boomers" and the need to use and conserve the skills and work ethic of older workers. According to one author, the aging of the "boomers" is coinciding with a change in their work ethic. Joe Cappo says that, upon entering their 40s, they're taking stock of their lives and deciding they'll "pull back from the fast lane."[7] Like others, he feels that members of this group will look for more personal fulfillment, including more time with family and friends— and more time alone. This trend may cause a change in their spending habits.

For example, by the year 2000, as the baby-boomers age, increases in spending for food, owned dwellings, and insurance and pensions will grow about three times as fast as for home furnishings, health care, sports cars, and cash contributions. Also, spending increases for food will grow almost nine times as much as for education.[8]

Baby-boomers have really grown up: they now have their own organizations—the American Association of Boomers (AAB) and the American Association of Baby Boomers (AABB). The AAB was founded in June 1989 and the AABB three months later. The organizations try to get discounts on travel, drugs, movies, and group insurance similar to those obtained by the American Association of Retired Persons (AARP) for senior citizens.[9]

The second trend—the need to use and conserve the skills of older workers—is forcing employers to find productive ways to use those who want to keep on working. During the 1990s, employers will have to choose from an aging work force, as shown in Figure 15–4. There will be a crunch for younger workers with both basic and technical skills. In fact, the number of 18 to 35 year olds will decline. This will require redesigning jobs (as shown in Chapter 11); rehiring retirees as consultants, advisers, or temporaries; using phased-in retirement programs; and aggressively recruiting older workers.

For example, the Boston area's Bay Bank Middlesex is targeting senior workers through direct mailings and informal meetings at the bank in conjunction with senior groups such as Ability Based on Long Experience (ABLE). Over the last two years, it has hired about 40 people over 65, including secretaries, tellers, managers, and executives.[10]

One of the most important sources of consumer purchasing power is personal income. The total personal income of Americans has increased more than 12-fold since 1940, and, by the year 2000, household income of those earning over $35,000 should increase to 43 percent of the total, while those earning $15,000 to $35,000 should drop to 33 percent. These increases are partly explained by the large increases in the number of two-income married couples as a percentage of all married couples, as shown in Figure 15–5. Income also varies considerably by region and state, and these variations affect a small firm's marketing plans.

Regional differences in consumption.   Buying habits and purchasing patterns also vary by region. These patterns are significant, for where people live is one of the best clues as to what they want to buy.

Figure 15–5   More Two-Income Couples

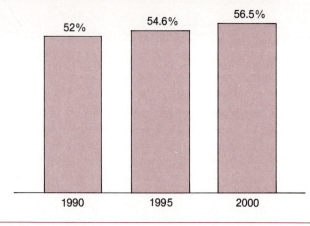

Two-income couples, as a percent of all married couples in the USA, rose from 28.5% in 1960 to 49% in 1985. Projected growth of two-income couples:

| 52% | 54.6% | 56.5% |
| 1990 | 1995 | 2000 |

Source: World Future Society data, as reported in *USA Today,* December 2, 1988, p. 1A. Copyright 1989, USA TODAY. Adapted with permission.

For example, Detroit automakers tailor cars to specific regions to exploit regional differences in taste. In the Northeast, which has crowded freeways, drivers are highly concerned about safety. But in wide-open, less crowded states such as Wyoming and Nebraska, car owners want to be sure that parts and service will be available. Drivers in Texas like lots of power and acceleration, while California drivers look for dependability and passenger comfort.[11]

Developing an Effective Marketing Mix

A **marketing mix** consists of controllable variables that the firm combines to satisfy the target market. The basic variables in this mix are the Four Ps: product, place, promotion, and price.

The right *product* for the target market must be developed. *Place* refers to the channels of distribution. *Promotion* refers to any method that communicates to the target market. The right *price* should be determined to attract customers and make a profit.

TYPES OF PRODUCTS AND THEIR LIFE CYCLES

The small firm often finds its most effective weapon in the field of product strategy. It may concentrate on a narrow product line, develop a highly specialized product or service, or provide a product-service "package" containing an unusual amount of service. In setting strategy, competitors' products, prices, and services should be studied carefully.

Types of Products

Most products can be classified into one of two general categories: consumer products and industrial products. **Consumer products,** including both goods and services, are purchased for ultimate satisfaction of personal and/or household needs. **Industrial products,** again both goods and services, are bought for use in a firm's operations or to make other products. As shown in Chapter 13, the type of product also largely determines the location of retail businesses.

Sometimes the same item can satisfy both consumer and industrial needs. The buyer's intent—or the ultimate use of the product—determines the classification of an item as either a consumer or industrial product. For example, a refrigerator light bulb is a consumer product if a householder buys it as a replacement but an industrial product if factory installed.

Consumer Products

As discussed in Chapter 13, the usual categories of consumer products are convenience goods, shopping goods, and specialty goods. Location, design, and operations of stores are based on the characteristics of buyers' purchasing behavior. You should consider how buyers *generally* behave when they purchase a specific item.

Industrial Products

Industrial products are used in producing other goods or in providing services to customers. Buyers include manufacturers, utilities, government agencies, schools, contractors, and other groups. These buyers usually provide prospective suppliers with a description of the product and request that bids or price quotations be submitted. Examples include semi-manufactured goods and parts; maintenance, repair, and operating supplies; capital equipment used in manufacturing the goods; and expendable items such as light bulbs and lubricating oil.

Product Life Cycle

Products are much like living organisms: they are brought into the world, they live, and they die. When a new product is successfully introduced into the firm's market mix, it grows; when it loses appeal, it is terminated. A new product may have a striking effect on the life cycle of other products as well.

Phonograph records are a good illustration of the product life cycle. Although 78 RPM records coexisted with the later 45s, they gave way to the long-playing 33s. Now the compact disc (CD) is threatening all records, even the 45s, which had maintained their hold on jukeboxes. A new jukebox that will play CDs offers vastly superior quality, along with lower maintenance costs. By 1989, cassettes had about 50 percent of the market, CDs had 35, and vinyl records had only 10.[12]

Figure 15–6   Life Cycle of a Typical Product

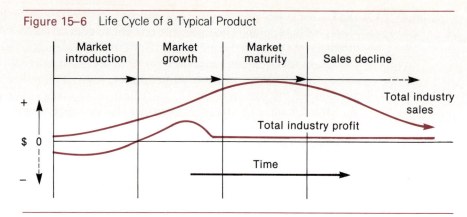

Source: E. Jerome McCarthy and William D. Perreault, Jr., *Basic Marketing,* 8th ed. (Homewood, Ill.: Richard D. Irwin, 1984), p. 330.

As shown in Figure 15–6, a **product life cycle** has four major stages: introduction, growth, maturity, and decline. As a product moves through its cycle, the strategies relating to competition, promotion, distribution, pricing, and market information should be evaluated and possibly changed. You can use the life-cycle concept to time the introduction, alteration, and maintenance of profitable products and the dropping or recycling of unprofitable ones.

Introduction Stage

The introduction stage begins when a product first appears on the market. Prices are usually high, sales are low, and profits are negative because of high developmental, promotion, and distribution costs. In this stage, it is vital to communicate to potential buyers the product's features, uses, and advantages. Only a few new products—such as home robots (see Computer Update)—represent major innovations. More often, a "new" product is an old one in a new form: a convenience food in a more convenient package, a new appliance model with innovative features, or a new fashion in clothing.

Many products never get beyond the introduction stage. The leading causes of new-product failure include insufficient or poor marketing research, technical problems in design or production, and errors in timing the product's introduction.

Growth Stage

During this stage, sales rise rapidly, and the innovator usually begins to make substantial profits. Competitors enter the market, and each attempts to develop the best product design (the robot in Computer Update shows an example of this tendency). Sales in the industry rise fairly rapidly as more customers buy the product.

Competitive reactions to the product's success during this period will affect its life expectancy. The entry of more firms into the market increases

COMPUTER UPDATE

YOUR PERSONAL ROBOT

People are getting ready to buy the next household appliance, a personal robot. What is now available may seem crude compared to R2D2 and the other *Star Wars* androids; but with steady advancements in robotics, the ultimate personal robot comes closer to reality than one likes to think.

Several home robots are already on the market. Some popular models include R5BX, sold by RB Robot Corporation of Colorado;

Hubot, sold by Hubotics; Stereobot, from Superior Robotics; HERO 2000, from Heath Electronics; Topo and FRED, from Androbot; and GENUS, from Robotics International. Many of them have an IBM-compatible computer, a telescoping arm, a CRT screen in their head, a speech-recognition circuit to respond to voices, built-in sonar for navigation, and a security system to detect intruders, smoke, or fire.

competition, drives prices down, and requires heavy promotional expenditures. This trend is readily seen in the case of electronic innovations, especially computers. As new models are introduced, prices on older models drop, at the same time that imitators provide more competition.

During this stage, marketing strategy typically encourages strong brand loyalty. The product's benefits are identified and emphasized in order to develop a competitive niche. This is the time of peak profitability.

Maturity Stage

Many competitors have entered by this stage. Competition becomes more aggressive, with declining prices and profits. Promotion costs climb, and some competitors begin to cut prices to attract business. New firms may enter, further increasing competition. Weaker competitors are squeezed out. Those who remain in the market make fresh promotional and distribution efforts.

Decline Stage

Sales fall rapidly during this stage, occasionally because of new technology or a social trend. The firm's management considers pruning items from the product line to eliminate unprofitable ones. Promotion efforts may be cut and marginal distributors eliminated. Furthermore, plans may be made to phase out the product.

For example, the Swanson TV Dinner, with food to be cooked in an oven on an aluminum tray and eaten while watching TV, was developed in 1955, the height of television's Golden Age. Now it is in the Smithsonian Institution, for possible display at the National Museum of American History. Now that VCRs have facilitated "time-shifting" of dinner-hour TV programs, the TV Dinner has been replaced by food in a plastic dish, to be popped into a microwave for instant cooking.[13]

Need for a Wide Product Mix

The life-cycle concept indicates that many, if not most, products will eventually become unprofitable. Hence, firms should investigate and evaluate market opportunities to launch new products or extend the life of existing products.

If the small firm has a wide product mix, a composite of life-cycle patterns is formed, with various products in the mix at different life-cycle stages: as one product declines, other products are in the introduction, growth, or maturity stages. Some fads may last only a few weeks or months (e.g., refer again to the western clothes example in Chapter 6), while other products may last for decades (automobiles, for example).

PACKAGING

Packaging involves protecting and promoting the product. It is important both to small firms and to their customers. Packaging can make a product more convenient to use or store and can prevent spoiling or damage. Good packaging makes products easier to identify, promotes the brand at the

Figure 15–7   Factors Influencing What Women Buy

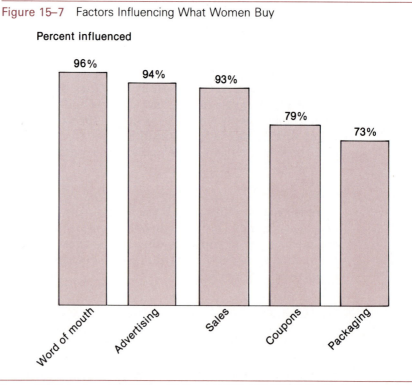

Percent influenced

Source: *USA Today,* August 13, 1985, p. 1D. Copyright 1985, USA TODAY. Reprinted with permission. (Original source: *Mademoiselle* magazine survey of 1,000 women in December 1984. Respondents could choose more than one answer.)

store and in use, and influences customers in making buying decisions (see Figure 15–7).

A better box, wrapper, can, or bottle can help create a "new" product or market: a small manufacturer introduced a liquid hand soap in a pump container, and it was an instant success. Sometimes, a new package improves a product by making it easier to use, such as motor oil sold in reclosable plastic containers with a built-in pouring spout. Packaging can also improve product safety, as when drugs and food are sold in child-proof bottles and tamper-resistant or tamper-evident packages.

Packaging can relate the product to the rest of the marketing strategy, as when expensive perfume is sold in a cut-glass bottle. Or a product line may be packaged using recognizable colors and shapes for all the items in the line, as is done with cosmetic lines such as Revlon. Package design can also reinforce popular advertising messages: L'Eggs pantyhose packages are illustrative.

Especially for small manufacturers and wholesalers, packaging can help reduce total distribution costs, both by providing better protection and by reducing or eliminating delays and lost sales. Retailers also benefit from reduced breakage, less discoloration, and decreased theft. Easy-to-handle packages can reduce their costs by speeding price marking, improving handling and display, and saving space. Increased total distribution costs that may rise because of packaging may be offset by improved customer satisfaction due to product improvements, greater convenience, or waste reduction.

HOW TO PRICE YOUR PRODUCT

There are three aspects of pricing that must be considered.

First, the price must be set so that the product is accepted by customers. Regardless of the desirability of the product, the price must be such that customers are willing—and able—to pay for it.

Second, the business would like to maintain—or increase—its market share as competition grows. If the new product is successful, competitors will introduce either a better product or a cheaper one. Therefore, the small business must set its price to try to maintain or expand its market share and/or profit.

Third, the business wants to make a profit on the new product. Therefore, the price must be sufficiently greater than cost to cover developmental, introductory, and operating costs—and make a profit.

In addition, product pricing should be based on the business's overall objectives, such as to achieve a certain (1) rate of return on investment, (2) level of sales, (3) company image, or (4) cash flow.

Establishing Pricing Policies

As shown in Table 15–2, there is a large variety of pricing policies a small business can adopt. The first three deserve particular attention: product life cycle, meet the competition, and cost-oriented pricing.

Table 15–2 Potential Pricing Policies for a Small Business

Policy area	Description
Product life cycle:	
Skimming price	Aimed at obtaining the "cream" of the target market at a high price before dealing with other market segments.
Penetration price	Intended to try to sell the entire market at a low price.
Meet the competition	Below the market price.
	At the competitors' price level.
	Above the market price.
Cost-oriented pricing	Costs are accumulated for each unit of product, and a markup is added to obtain a base price.
Price flexibility:	
One price	Offering the same price to all customers who purchase goods under the same conditions and in the same quantities.
Flexible price	Offering the same products and quantities to different customers at different prices.
Suggested retail price	Manufacturers often print a suggested price on the product or invoice or in their catalog.
List prices	Published prices that remain the same for a long time.
Prestige pricing	Setting of high prices used, say, by fur retailers.
Leader pricing	Certain products are chosen for their promotional value and are priced low in order to entice customers into retail stores.
Bait pricing	An item is priced extremely low by a dealer, but the salesperson points out the disadvantages of the item and switches customers to items of higher quality and price. (This practice is illegal.)
Odd pricing	Prices end in certain numbers, usually odd, such as $0.95—e.g., $7.95, $8.95
Psychological pricing	Certain prices for some products are psychologically appealing; there can be a range of prices that customers may perceive as being equal to each other.
Price lining	Policy of setting a few price levels for given lines of merchandise; e.g., ties at three levels: $8, $16, and $25.
Demand-oriented pricing	Potential customer demand is recognized, and prospective revenues are considered in pricing.

Notice the role played by the product life cycle, as discussed earlier. Most small business owners are apprehensive about introducing and pricing a new product. The owner has two alternatives: (1) to set a **skimming price,** which will be high enough to obtain the "cream" of the target market before dealing with other segments of the market, or (2) set a **penetration price,** which will be low enough to obtain an adequate and sustainable market. Manufacturers sometimes use a combination approach for a new product, setting a realistic price but encouraging customers to try the product by issuing discount coupons to make the price more attractive.

As the second item in Table 15–2 indicates, small businesses often handle pricing by "meeting the competition"; that is, following the pricing practices of competitors (see Computer Update). This practice can lead to severe losses if cost and volume of sales are not taken into account. Small firms

---

COMPUTER UPDATE

TELEDATA GUIDE INC.

Jeffrey Guide, a press staffer for the Small Business Administration, wanted to open a nationwide résumé service as a sideline. Having no idea how much to charge for the new service, he left a message on the Work-At-Home Forum (an "electronic billboard" computer network) describing his plans and asking for information about prices charged for similar services. He also left a message on H&R Block's CompuServe. Numerous responses from around the country told him the going rate was between $10 and $25 a page. On the basis of this information, his company, TeleData Guide Inc., based its charges on the lower figure.

Source: "A Special Report: Small Business," *The Wall Street Journal,* May 20, 1985, p. 89C.

---

with an attractive, possibly unique product should not be afraid to charge what the product is worth, taking into account not only what it costs to provide the product but also "what the market will bear."

Wilson's Used Cars (Case I–6) is an interesting example of this. When Kevin Wilson, its president, was in college, he worked part time selling used cars. His boss gave him a price list with the "asking price" and "minimum price" of each car. Being idealistic, he would take the list out and show it to a customer, explaining that the lower price was a fair one. For the first few weeks, he said, he didn't sell "one lousy car." People didn't believe him and made counteroffers he couldn't meet because he'd already given them the rock-bottom price. When he started playing the game—quoting the "asking price," letting them make a counteroffer, taking it to the boss, who "reluctantly" accepted it—then he "began to sell cars."

Cost-Oriented Pricing

Cost-oriented pricing is basic for all pricing policies. Total costs provide a floor below which prices should not be permitted to go, especially for long periods of time.

Cost-oriented pricing involves two aspects; namely, *markup* and *markon*. Markup is the more important of these processes, but both will be discussed.

Markup

Markup is the amount added to the product's cost to determine the selling price. Usually, the amount of the markup is determined by the type of product sold, the amount of service performed by the retailer, the rate at which the inventory turns over, and the amount of planned profit. Other things being equal, the greater the number and variety of services provided by the retailer, and the more slowly the item sells, the larger the markup required to cover costs. If the markup is inadequate, it may not generate enough funds to cover the costs of operations, resulting in a loss; if it is excessive, you may lose existing customers or be unable to attract new ones.

Markup may be calculated for each item carried, or it may represent the average markup of all goods. It may be expressed in terms of dollars and/or cents, or as a percentage. If the latter, you may calculate it either on cost or on the retail price. In either case, the formula is:

$$\text{Dollar markup} = \text{Retail price} - \text{Cost of the item(s)}$$

The way to figure markup percentage on cost is:

$$\text{Markup as percentage of cost} = \frac{\text{Dollar amount of markup}}{\text{Cost of the item}}$$

For example, assume that a retailer is pricing a new product that costs $6. The selling price is set at $10. Therefore, the total amount of markup is $4 (selling price [$10] less cost [$6] equals markup [$4]). The markup percentage, then, is:

$$\text{Markup percentage (cost)} = \frac{\$4}{\$6} = 66\tfrac{2}{3} \text{ percent}$$

The way to compute percentage markup on selling price is:

$$\text{Markup as percentage of selling price} = \frac{\text{Dollar amount of markup}}{\text{Selling price of item}}$$

Using the same assumptions as before, the calculation of the markup on selling price would be:

$$\text{Markup percentage} = \frac{\$4}{\$10} = 40 \text{ percent}$$

Markon

Realizing that all of the stock may not be sold at full price, but must be reduced in price to sell it, many retailers also compute a **markon,** which is an amount added to the price of an item that will later be marked down. This markon, which is added to the initial markup, is usually also used for merchandise that can be easily damaged or stolen, or for items for which employee discounts will be allowed.

How Prices Are Set by Small Businesses

Differing pricing practices are used by small service firms, retailers, wholesalers, producers, and building contractors. Some of the more popular ones are described here.

By Service Firms

Service firms particularly need to have a logical method of pricing because of the intangible nature of their product. The usual method, however, is to charge the "going rate," or to price according to individual circumstances.

Such firms should establish a price based on the cost of labor employed, materials used to provide the service, direct charges—such as transportation cost—and a profit margin. This technique requires a reliable accounting system to determine the cost of providing the service. Many firms charge customers an hourly rate, based on services performed, including the actual number of hours required to perform the services, plus any travel expenses. Others incorporate the labor, materials, and transportation costs into an hourly rate, or a rate based on some other variable, as the following example shows.

Lynne Brown's Mini Maid franchise charges according to the size of the house to be cleaned. Brown's team (usually four people) takes from 30 to 90 minutes to complete the job. Her service includes making beds, scouring sinks, general pickup, cleaning glass doors, sweeping and mopping/waxing floors, vacuuming carpets, cleaning bathrooms, polishing furniture, loading the dishwasher, wiping cabinets, shining counters, changing bed linens, removing garbage, and freshening the air.

Brown furnishes all the cleaning supplies needed, as well as the labor. Depending on the size of the house, her prices range from approximately $25 to $50. Also, in

Source: Baldwin (County, Alabama) *Press Register,* July 10, 1989, p. 5. © 1989. Mobile Press Register photograph. © 1989. All rights reserved.

estimating the price—which Brown does on the phone—she considers the frequency with which customers use the services. The more often they use Mini Maid, the better their rate.

Brown has a small office in her home with a 24-hour-a-day answering service, but most of her workweek is spent in her minivan. Her biggest expenses are payroll, telephone, transportation, advertising, her answering service, and cleaning supplies.

Brown attributes her success to doing specific activities, in a specific way, for a specific price—which, as she says, is the Mini Maid way.[14]

By Retailers

Different types of products are priced differently. Staple convenience goods, such as candy, gum, newspapers, and magazines, usually have customary prices or use the manufacturer's suggested retail price. **Customary prices** are the prices customers expect to pay as a result of custom, tradition, or social habits.

For example, Hershey Chocolate Company sold candy bars for five cents in 1940. As cocoa and sugar became scarce and more expensive because of World War II, the price of Hershey's candy bars didn't rise for a while. Instead, the size of the bars was cut in half by the end of 1942.

Some discount and food stores discount candy, gum, magazines, and other prepriced items a set percentage across the board—say 10 or even 20 percent. In fact, Food World discounts all prepriced items 10 percent, and Wal-Mart discounts greeting cards 20 percent and sewing patterns nearly 50 percent.

Fashion goods, by contrast, carry high markups (skimming prices) and are marked down if they do not sell well. High markup also characterizes novelty and specialty goods. When the novelty wears off, or the selling season ends, the price goes down.

The day after Christmas, Easter, and other holidays, early bird shoppers expect to find markdowns up to 50 or even 75 percent not only on Christmas and Easter candy, Christmas wrap and stuffed rabbits, but also on novelty items marketed as "stocking stuffers," holiday party clothes, and extravagantly priced "coffee table" books and other items intended as gifts.

Most grocery stores use **unit pricing** for meats, produce, and deli items, charging so much per ounce or pound for each item. Information about unit prices of other items facilitates comparison shopping by customers.

Although influenced by competitors', vendors', and customary prices, retailers still determine prices for many or most of the products they sell.

In any case, the retailer's selling price should cover the cost of goods, selling and other operating costs, and a profit margin. In some cases, however, a store might use **loss leaders,** or items sold below cost, to attract customers who may also buy more profitable items.

By Wholesalers

Wholesalers buy in large lots, sell to retailers and others in small lots, and perform many services for their clients (as will be discussed in Chapter 16). Their prices are usually based on a markup set for each product line. Since wholesalers purchase in large quantities and cannot always immediately pass along price increases, price drops can cause heavy losses. Therefore, they may sometimes quote different prices to buyers for the same products. Factors affecting these prices are (1) the size of the retailer's order, (2) the retailer's bargaining power, and (3) services extended.

By Producers

While meeting competitors' prices is common among small producers, many of them set their prices relative to the cost of production, using a break-even analysis. As shown in Chapter 18, their costs comprise purchasing, inventory, production, distribution, selling, and administrative costs, as well as a profit margin. Those figures are totaled to arrive at a final price. With weak competition or strong demand, the producer may raise this price, as the following example shows.

The Beary Best Cookies (Case III–3) sells a unique product—oatmeal chocolate chip cookies—to health clubs and fine restaurants in Baton Rouge, Louisiana. Facing no significant competition in its market niche, it charges 30 cents for a cookie that costs 5 cents to make (a 500 percent markup); the clients sell them for 60 cents, a 100 percent markup.

By Building Contractors

Most building contractors use **cost-plus pricing.** They start with the cost of the land; add expected construction costs for items such as labor, materials, and supplies; add overhead costs; add on financing and closing costs and legal fees; and add the real estate broker's fee. Then they total the costs and add on a markup for profit. Figure 15–8 shows how this formula would apply to a $100,000 house being constructed in a big-city suburb.

Discounts and Allowances

Small businesses use discounts extensively. These reductions from the list price are granted by a seller to a buyer who forgoes the performance of some marketing function. Allowances are provided to customers for accepting less of something or as adjustments for variations in quality.

Figure 15–8   Pricing the $100,000 House

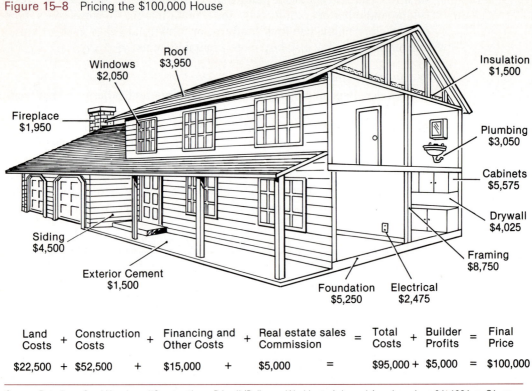

Land Costs	+	Construction Costs	+	Financing and Other Costs	+	Real estate sales Commission	=	Total Costs	+	Builder Profits	=	Final Price
$22,500	+	$52,500	+	$15,000	+	$5,000	=	$95,000	+	$5,000	=	$100,000

Source: Data from Carol Nanninga, "Constructing a Price," (Bellevue, Washington) *Journal-American*, June 24, 1984, p. G1, as adapted by Louise E. Boone and David L. Kurtz, *Contemporary Marketing*, 5th ed. (New York: Dryden Press, 1986), p. 478.

Notice that Mr. Simmons, of Simmons Mountainside Satellite Sales (Case II–3), received a 10 percent discount on purchases of 10 or more satellite dishes.

Some important discounts and allowances appear in Table 15–3. Trading stamps and coupons, which can reduce prices, are covered under sales promotions in Chapter 16. Transportation costs and allowances also affect list prices.

Other Aspects of Pricing

Product, delivery, service, and fulfillment of psychological needs make up the total package that the customer buys. A price should be consistent with the image the business wants to project. Since customers often equate the quality of unknown products with price, raising prices may actually increase sales, as the following example indicates.

Table 15–3   Discounts and Allowances Provided by Small Businesses

Reduction	Description
Cash discounts	Given as a reduction in price to buyers who pay their bill within a specified period of time (e.g., 2/10, net 30 days).
Functional or trade discounts	List price reductions given to channel members for performance of their functions.
Quantity discounts	Reduction in the unit price granted for buying in certain quantities.
Noncumulative	Apply to individual shipments or orders only.
Cumulative	Apply to purchases over a given period (e.g., a year).
Seasonal discounts	Induce buyers to stock earlier than immediate demand would dictate.
Promotional allowances	Provided by manufacturers and wholesalers to retailers for promotion (e.g., point-of-purchase display materials, per-case discounts, and cooperative advertisements).
Trade-ins	Allowance provided to customer by retailer in the purchase of, say, a major electric appliance.
Push money or prize money	Allowances provided retailers by manufacturers or wholesalers to be given to salespersons for aggressively selling particular products.

The Zimmer Corporation serves the sparsely supplied ultraluxury car market in Boca Raton, Florida. Sales of their $65,000 Golden Spirit neoclassic auto, which emulates the Packards and Duesenbergs of the 1930s, have consistently been 250 cars annually. Sales of their $45,000 Quicksilver, a sleek sports coupe priced in line with some sports cars made by Fiat, Jaguar, Porsche Enterprises, Inc., and Daimler-Benz, are expected to hit 1,000 cars a year.

Zimmer's clients are lured by the flashy glamour of the cars and the obscure name of their designer as much as by their rarity. The Golden Spirit buyer is a very, very affluent man, 60 to 65 years old, who already owns four or five cars. The Quicksilver customer will be similar, though perhaps a bit younger.[15]

However, the reverse might also be true: selling at a low price might lead customers to think the product was of low quality. Sometimes, cheap can be too cheap, especially when compared to nationally advertised products.

Pathmark's Premium All Purpose Cleaner seemed a clear "winner" when it was introduced in 1980. It was packaged to resemble Fantastik, the top seller in the field. Its contents exactly duplicated the other national brands. And it was priced to sell at only 89 cents, as opposed to $1.79 for Fantastik. It did not sell well. In 1986, Day-Glo stickers saying "If you like Fantastik, try me" were stuck on each package. As customers still did not respond to the low price or the promotion efforts, Premium was removed from the shelves in 1988. A spokesman said, "We believe the price was so low it discredited the intrinsic value of the product."[16]

In summary, small business owner-managers commonly make two errors in setting prices for their products, namely:

1. Charging less than larger businesses and considering themselves price leaders. Because of their relatively small volume of sales, product costs per unit tend to be higher for a smaller business than for a larger one. Also, small firms cannot take advantage of large-volume discounts on their purchases. Therefore, *small firms generally should not consider themselves price leaders.*

2. Undercharging during the early period of operation, particularly in firms offering services performed personally by the owner-manager. He or she mistakenly believes that prices can be raised later as more customers are secured. However, it is easier to lower prices than to raise them, and raising them usually creates customer dissatisfaction.

Price cutting should be considered a form of sales promotion. Price should be reduced only when the added volume resulting from the reduction produces sufficient sales revenue to offset the added costs. The probable reactions of competitors should be considered in determining whether to reduce prices.

PHYSICAL DISTRIBUTION

Because of its many cost-saving potentials, distribution is quite important to small businesses. **Physical distribution** includes the whole range of activities concerned with the efficient movement of a product from the production line into the hands of the final customer. To perform the activity effectively, you must make decisions in such important areas as protective packaging, materials handling, inventory control, transportation (internally and externally), order processing, and various aspects of customer service. Because of space limitations, only storing, order processing, and transportation are discussed.

Storing

Until sold or used, goods must be stored by manufacturers, wholesalers, and retailers. While some small manufacturers and wholesalers have their own warehouses, more of them use **public warehouses,** independently owned facilities that often specialize in handling certain products, such as furniture or refrigerated products. Public warehouses are particularly useful to small firms wanting to place goods close to customers for quick delivery. This practice avoids investing in new facilities, increases flexibility when entering a new market, and provides temporary storage of products to meet seasonal demands. Materials-handling activities and equipment such as forklifts, special containers, and packages are frequently used.

Order Processing

Effective order processing reduces or eliminates customer dissatisfaction due to slow shipment and incorrectly or incompletely filled orders. It begins the moment a customer places an order with a salesperson. The order goes to the office, often on a standardized order form. After the order is filled, the goods are sent to the customer.

Transportation

Transportation involves the physical movement of a product from the seller to the purchaser. Since transportation costs are the largest item in distribution, there are many opportunities for savings and improved efficiency. The two most important aspects are choosing the transportation mode to be used and understanding delivery terms. Since these subjects were discussed in Chapter 13, they will not be reviewed here.

CREDIT MANAGEMENT

Credit management involves (1) deciding how customers will pay for purchases, (2) formulating credit policies and practices, and (3) administering credit operations. The objectives of each of these activities are to increase profits, increase customer stability, and protect the firm's investment in accounts receivable, which is often the largest single asset on the firm's balance sheet.

Methods of Payment

Customers can pay for purchases in a number of ways, and small business managers must decide early in the life of the business which method(s) will be used. Payment methods include cash, checks, and various kinds of credit.

Cash

Given a choice, every business owner would prefer to make all sales for cash. Recordkeeping would be easier, and there would be no bad debts. But we live in a "cashless society," and it is unrealistic to expect buyers to carry cash for every purchase, especially large ones.

Checks

Accepting checks for payment increases sales, and most retailers find it unavoidable. With proper verification procedures, there are few bad-debt losses, making checks virtually equivalent to cash. Checks can be treated the same as cash in recordkeeping, and they are safer to have on hand than cash and easier to deal with in making bank deposits.

Credit

To stimulate sales, various forms of credit may be used, including a retailer's own credit plan, installment payment plans, and bank credit cards. *Store credit* allows a business to choose its own customers and eliminates fees to banks and finance companies. Accounts can be paid off every month or can be revolving charge accounts such as those used by large department stores. For major purchases, a retailer may give the buyer three months to pay before interest is charged or the account is turned over to a finance company. To extend credit even longer, the seller may offer an *installment payment plan* that gives the buyer a year or more to pay for the purchase. Buyers make a down payment, make regular weekly or monthly payments, and pay interest charges on the unpaid balance.

Whenever a seller extends credit, recordkeeping becomes more complex. Small firms can use manual or computer methods to maintain their charge accounts internally. Or they can turn the accounts over to a service firm that handles billing and collecting. Either way, there are costs for billing and collections, as well as bad-debt losses. Moreover, the seller is responsible for investigating prospective customers' creditworthiness. Some of these responsibilities and costs can be avoided by accepting *bank credit cards*.

Today's consumers have come to expect most retailers of any size to accept at least Visa and MasterCard, if not also American Express and Discover (and Diners Club for restaurants). This may be especially necessary in resort areas or other places where customers are less likely to have large amounts of cash, local checking accounts, or a store charge account. Some small business owners have found that the association with big names, such as American Express and Citicorp, gives their firms a certain cachet that attracts buyers.[17]

Although merchants pay a fee to join, a fee on sales, and other fees, many find it worth the expense. Provided they follow required verification procedures (usually a phone call to get an authorization number or a check of the card number against a list of current bad accounts), sellers are guaranteed payment, entirely eliminating bad-debt losses. The seller reports sales, sales returns and allowances, and other credits to the card's issuing bank, which credits and charges the seller's deposit account.

Setting Credit Policies

While the credit department of a small business can contribute heavily to increased sales and profit, several factors should be considered in formulating a credit policy; some are beyond the firm's control. Any credit policy should be flexible enough to accommodate these internal and external factors.

Typical credit policies used by small firms are (1) liberal extension of credit with a liberal collection policy, (2) liberal extension of credit with a strictly enforced collection policy, and (3) strict extension of credit with a collection policy adjusted to individual circumstances. Generally speaking, liberality in extension of credit or in collections tends to stimulate sales but to increase collection costs and bad-debt losses. Strict policies have the reverse effect. Whatever policy is chosen, a firm, businesslike attitude should be maintained toward both the sales department and customers.

Carrying Out Credit Policies

The person performing the credit management function should have ready access to the accounts receivable records and be free from interruptions and noise. Several tools this person can use in performing the function include the accounts receivable ledger or computer printout, invoices and other billing documents, credit files, account lists, credit manuals, reference material, and various automated aids.

Classification of Credit Risks

In granting credit, the firm's present and potential customers should be grouped according to credit risk: good, fair, or weak. These risks can be determined from information in the customer's file, trade reports, financial reports, and previous credit experience.

Good credit risks may be placed on a preferred list for automatic approval within certain dollar limits. Periodic review of these accounts usually suffices. Fair credit risks will require close checking, particularly on large amounts or in case of slowness of payment. While weak credit risks may be acceptable, they should be closely watched. Credit managers spend most of their time with them. Owners of retail and service firms can face many problems when they get involved in overextension or unwise extension of credit.

Mr. Neely (name disguised) and his wife had invested almost $6,000 of their savings in a venture. They had paid $4,000 cash for equipment and allocated the balance for working capital needs.

Sales increased during each of the 13 months they were in business, and all bills were paid. Much capital, however, was tied up in uncollectable accounts receivable. The trouble was that Mr. Neely was soft-hearted. He said: "I really don't want to extend credit to anyone, but the problem is finding a way to tell my customers that without losing their business."

The owners stopped giving credit altogether, but the firm's gross profits dropped by almost one-half. Mr. Neely was so discouraged that he sold the firm for $2,500.

Investigating Customers' Creditworthiness

One important cause of bad-debt losses is credit decisions based on inadequate credit investigation. Yet prompt delivery of orders is also important. The firm's credit-checking method should be geared to need and efficiency to improve the sales and delivery of its product. For new accounts, a complete credit application may be desired. Direct credit inquiry can be effective in obtaining the name of the customer's bank and trade references. Many suppliers and banks cooperate in exchanging credit information, but they should be assured that the information obtained will be treated confidentially. Outside sources of valuable credit information include local credit bureaus, which are linked together nationally through Associated Credit Bureaus, Inc., and TRW Credit Data, Inc., each of which provides guidelines and mechanisms for obtaining credit information for almost any area in the United States.

Collection Procedures

The collection of unpaid accounts is an important part of credit management. The collection effort should include systematic and regular follow-up, which is vital to establish credibility with the customer concerning the firm's credit terms. The follow-up should be timely. Most businesses, as well as professionals, now have computer capacity to show the age of a bill. For example, a statement sent to a customer may indicate that payment was due on a certain date, but that the bill is, say, 30, 60, or 90 days past due.

Holding customers' orders when an account is past due can be quite effective. Prompt contact with the customer, tactfully and courteously made, generally produces results. The firm should respond rapidly if and when the customer clears the account so that unnecessary delays in shipping are avoided. Therefore, the credit department and accounts receivable bookkeeper should be in close communication.

Pacific Envelope Company of Anaheim, California, manufactures and prints envelopes for around 1,200 customers. Bob Cashman, its CEO, claims the company has a strategy that eliminates 90 percent of collection problems.

First, Pacific offers a 10 percent discount for payment within 10 days. If the account isn't paid 8 to 10 days after it is due, Jean Smith, the office manager, calls the customer's accounts payable department to see if it has the delivery sheet showing receipt of the order and Pacific's invoice for it. If so, Smith asks when she can expect payment. If, however, the documents have not been received, Smith sends a duplicate and then calls a week later to ask when the payment will be received.

Cashman says the procedure works because "we have totally disarmed them. They have agreed that they have our merchandise and have obligated [themselves] to pay on a certain date."[18]

STRATEGY FOR MARKETING SERVICES

Since the service sector of the economy is so important and has certain unique features, we will cover the performance of the marketing function in service-oriented firms.

Nature of Service Businesses

Services can be classified into two categories: personal and business. **Personal services** include activities such as financial services, transportation, health and beauty, lodging, advising and counseling, amusement, plumbing, real estate, and insurance. **Business services** may include some of these, plus others that are strictly business oriented, such as advertising agencies, market research firms, and economic counselors.

ProServ Inc., a Washington-based sports marketing firm, performs various services for professional athletes, such as representing them in salary talks with management, negotiating the contract, handling all the player's investment and legal needs, and lining up product endorsements.[19]

Personal services can be performed by individuals or by automated equipment. Two examples of the latter are automatic car washes and computer timesharing bureaus.

There are good opportunities for small businesses in service industries, as the demand for services is expected to grow faster than for most other types of businesses. Factors accounting for increased spending for all kinds of services include rising discretionary income, services as status symbols, more women working outside the home—and earning more—and a shorter workweek and more leisure time.

On the other hand, service businesses have severe competition. It comes not only from other service firms but from potential customers who decide to perform the services themselves and from manufacturers of do-it-yourself products.

How Services Differ

Since many services, such as sign making (see Chapter 11, Opening Focus), an insurance company, and carpentry, are not regularly used, and since the firm must be chosen on the basis of its perceived reputation, a good image is of utmost importance. Because there are few objective standards for measuring the quality of services, they are often judged subjectively. Not only is a service usually complete before a buyer can evaluate its quality, but defective services cannot be returned.

Price competition among businesses offering standardized services is quite severe, since each firm offers essentially the same product. It is difficult, too, to demonstrate dependability, skills, and creativity. Some firms have attempted to overcome this difficulty by offering low introductory rates to new customers. But it cannot continue operating with rates set too low. Hence, the managers of a service business should stress quality control in an attempt to demonstrate superior performance.

Services also cannot be saved. This is particularly important for firms providing amusements, transportation services, and room accommodations. Special features or extra thoughtfulness that create a memorable experience will encourage repeat business.

The level of customer contact required to provide the service also varies. Customer contact refers to the physical presence of the customer in the system: the longer a customer remains in the service system, the greater the interaction between the server and customer. Generally, economies of scale are more difficult to achieve in high-contact services.

A beauty salon is a high-contact system, with the receptionist, shampoo person, and stylist all interacting with the customer. On the other hand, an automated car wash may have little contact with a customer.

Developing Service Marketing Strategies

Marketing strategies differ radically, depending on the level of customer contact. For example, the facility in low-contact services does not have to be near the customer's home or work. On the other hand, a high-contact service, such as a plumbing firm, must meet the customer's needs. Quality control in high-contact services consists basically of doing a good job and maintaining an image and good public relations. If employees have a poor attitude, the firm may lose customers.

Importance of the Marketing Concept

The marketing concept is more important for service businesses than for other types of small businesses. Customers or prospective customers often have the option of performing the services themselves. The business must demonstrate why it is to the customer's advantage to let the service firm do the job.

Pricing Services

The price of a service is often called *a fee*. The firm's price reflects the quality, degree of expertise and specialization, and value of its performance to the buyer. As shown earlier in the chapter, a high price tends to connote quality in the mind of the customer. For this reason, lower prices and price reductions may even have a negative effect on sales, particularly in people-based businesses.

The pricing of services in small firms often depends on value provided rather than on cost. Customers will pay whatever they think the service is worth, so pricing depends on what the market will bear. Pricing decisions are also affected by the nature of the purchase—routine, contractual, or occasional.

Notice in the Opening Focus that Try J. Advertising uses two methods of pricing its services to its regular clients. First, it applies a standard percentage (15 percent) to media sales; then it sets a dollar figure for other services. This figure is based on the level of expertise and client relationships.

Sometimes a multiplier approach is used for setting prices. For example, an automobile dealer's service department may set $20 an hour for the mechanic. Additionally, it considers the cost of using the equipment and facility, administrative overhead, and profit, and uses a multiplier to cover these factors. For a five-hour job and, say, a multiplier of 3, the price becomes $20 \times 5 \times 3 = \$300$.

Promoting Services

Word-of-mouth advertising, personal selling, and publicity are usually used by small firms to promote their service. Quite often, the message will have a consistent theme, related to the uniqueness of the service, key personnel, or the benefits gained by satisfied customers.

Effective media typically include the Yellow Pages of the telephone directory, direct mail, and local newspapers. Specialty advertising, such as calendars with the firm's name, may be considered. Referrals are also an effective form of promotion for small service firms, which ask satisfied customers to recommend the service to friends. Businesses that rely on phone contacts with customers find business cards useful. Making presentations before associations and sponsoring public events are also important in building a firm's revenues and profitability, as the following example illustrates.

Byrd Surveying is a small land surveying corporation established in 1974 that employs between 20 and 25 people. Their primary business is mortgage loan and boundary surveys; however, the firm also does engineering, subdividing, percolations, and construction layout work.

Source: Photo courtesy of Gerald Byrd.

Gerald Byrd is the president, CEO, and the only registered professional on the staff. He is licensed in Alabama, Florida, and Mississippi. As with any professional service organization, ethics is a main concern, and many forms of advertising are not considered ethical for this industry. Opportunities for marketing the services are few because professional associations are used to get the word out. Byrd belongs to the Mortgage Bankers Association, the Home-builders Association, and the Realtors Association and is very active in all of them.

In order to maintain an image of friendly professionalism, Byrd also hand-delivers many of his finished jobs. This is a follow-up prospecting function. It is also very important that all phone calls and "drop-ins" be treated individually with courtesy and respect. "Let's not forget the quality of the finished product," Byrd says. His motto is: "A satisfied client is a continuing client."[20]

IMPLEMENTING YOUR MARKETING STRATEGY

Now that you have developed your marketing strategy, how do you implement it? Implementation involves two stages, (1) the introductory stage and (2) the growth stage.

The Introductory Stage

When introducing a new product, the small business should (1) analyze present and future market situations, (2) shape the product to fit the market, (3) evaluate the company's resources, and (4) keep informed about competitors.

Analyze Market Situations

This step determines the opportunities that lie in present and future market situations, as well as problems and adverse environmental trends that will affect your company, as shown in Chapter 3. Because market size and growth are vital, potential growth rate should be forecast as accurately as possible. For example, the market growth rate for a new business should be at least 15 to 20 percent per year. Factors that affect this growth, such as actions of the federal government, should be evaluated. Relevant questions covered earlier include: Who are the firm's customers? What are their needs? What is the buying process?

Fit Product to Market

Management should shape its products to fit the market and then find other markets that fit its products. A market niche too small to interest large companies may be available.

A small firm manufactured and sold truck springs but found that this product was a standard item produced by larger firms that could benefit from economies of scale. Competition was too severe for the small business, and so management decided to specialize in springs for swimming pool diving boards. This change in product strategy proved to be highly profitable.

Evaluate Company Resources

A business's strengths, as well as its limitations, should be determined overall and at each stage of the marketing process. Financial, cost, competitive, and timing pressures must be viewed realistically, and successes and failures need to be understood and regarded as important learning experiences.

Understand Competitors

As repeatedly mentioned in this and previous chapters, a small business must stay informed about the competition and understand competitors' business situations. What are their strengths, limitations, pressures, costs, profitability, market strategies, and corporate strategies?

The Growth Stage

Once in operation, the small business can adopt one of three strategies: (1) expand sales to reach new classes of customers, (2) increase penetration in the existing target market, or (3) make no marketing innovations but copy new marketing techniques and attempt to hold the present market share by product design and manufacturing innovations. The strategy selected should be used by personnel in all areas, such as sales, advertising, production, and finance.

Expand Sales into New Markets

To reach new markets, you may (1) add related products within the product line, (2) add products unrelated to the present line, (3) find new applications in new markets for the firm's product, or (4) add customized products, perhaps upgrading from low-quality to medium-quality goods.

In introducing new and improved products, management needs to recognize their relationship to the existing product line, established channels of distribution, cost of development and introduction, personnel and facilities, competition, and market acceptance. Diversification, or product line expansion, should be examined, since it tends to increase profits, contribute to long-range growth, stabilize production, employment, and payrolls, fill out a product line, and lower administrative overhead cost per unit. The major pitfall of diversification is that the firm may not have the appropriate internal resources to compete effectively.

A small distributor of custodial equipment and supplies considered the attractive profit margins its suppliers were making and decided to manufacture certain items. Within a year, the manufacturing operation was discontinued, having incurred a sizable loss. Management admitted it had not realized that manufacturing was a different ball game from distribution.

Increase Penetration of Present Market

Perhaps a small manufacturing firm has been selling replacement parts primarily but wants to expand by selling to original-equipment manufacturers. Or a company may reduce the variety of products and models in order to produce substantial operating economies.

Make No Marketing Innovations

The strategy of retaining current marketing practices without trying to innovate suits a small business particularly well if its strength lies in its technical competence. In retailing, it is often advisable for store managers to follow this strategy.

Over the long term, a firm may follow one strategy for several years with the intent to change after certain marketing goals have been reached. But the change should take place if progress is desired.

WHAT YOU SHOULD HAVE LEARNED

1. Managers of small firms should insist that their firms follow the marketing concept. That is, they should focus all their efforts on satisfying their customers' needs at a profit. Consumer needs and market opportunities should be identified, and the target market(s) most likely to buy their products should be determined. Customers' buying roles should be understood and danger signals looked for. A competitive edge, something that sets the firm apart from and gives it an advantage over competitors, should be sought.

2. In developing a marketing strategy, managers should first set the firm's marketing objectives, such as the number of units of sales and the market share for each product. Then the target market(s) should be set, based on market segmentation. In addition to consumers' needs, attitudes, and buying behavior, managers should understand the following market dimensions: population patterns, age groups, income levels, and regional patterns. Finally, the marketing mix, which consists of controllable variables, should weigh heavily in decision making. The four basic variables in this mix are product, place, promotion, and price.

3. Products are classified as consumer products and industrial products. The former are subclassified into convenience, shopping, and specialty

goods. Product line classification is important because certain classes of products are aimed at particular target markets, and the classification affects determination of the appropriate kinds of distribution, promotion, and pricing.

4. A product life cycle has four major stages—introduction, growth, maturity, and decline. Strategies related to competition, promotion, distribution, and prices differ depending on the pertinent stage of the cycle.

5. Packaging, which involves protecting and promoting the product, can make it more convenient and can prevent spoiling or damage. It also makes products easier to identify, promotes the brand, and facilitates the purchase decision process.

6. Guided by the firm's objectives, pricing objectives should be formulated. The "best" selling price should be cost and market oriented. A few potential pricing concerns for small businessses are product life cycle, meeting the competition, and cost orientation.

   Most small businesses use cost-oriented pricing methods, usually using markups and markons. Discounts and allowances are also part of pricing. Differing pricing practices are used by different types of small firms.

7. Physical distribution, which involves moving the product from the seller to the buyer, is important in many small firms. Physical distribution includes the vital functions of storing, order processing, and transportation.

8. Credit management includes deciding on customer payment methods, formulating credit policies and practices, and administering credit operations. The firm's credit policy should be flexible and help increase revenues and profits. The firm's customers should be classified according to their creditworthiness—that is, good, fair, or weak. Credit investigations should be conducted. The collection of outstanding receivables should be systematic and include regular follow-up. The overall results of the credit functions and collection efficiency should be evaluated to see that they are achieving their objectives.

9. Service businesses are classified into personal and business. The marketing of services differs from the marketing of goods. Few objective standards have been formulated for measuring service quality, but quality should be emphasized. Also, price competition in standardized services is quite severe, output of service firms is difficult to standardize, and services cannot be saved.

10. Marketing strategies need to be implemented when formulated. One or more of these strategies can be adopted: expand sales to reach new classes of customers, increase penetration in the existing target market, or make no marketing innovation, but copy new marketing techniques instead.

KEY TERMS

marketing concept, 448

system, 449

consumer behavior, 449

consumer decision process, 449

consumerism, 452

competitive edge, 453

target market, 453

market segmentation, 454

marketing mix, 458

consumer products, 459

industrial products, 459

product life cycle, 460

skimming price, 464

penetration price, 464

markup, 465

markon, 466

customary prices, 468

unit pricing, 468

loss leaders, 469

cost-plus pricing, 469

physical distribution, 472

public warehouses, 472

transportation, 473

credit management, 473

personal services, 476

business services, 476

QUESTIONS FOR DISCUSSION

1. Why is the marketing concept so important to small firms?
2. Describe or outline the consumer decision process.
3. How are the key success factors for a firm related to a competitive edge that its management should seek?
4. (a) What is market segmentation, and (b) how can it be made more effective?
5. (a) Discuss some of the characteristics that should be considered in selecting a target market. (b) What are some changes affecting these?
6. What controllable variables are combined in a marketing mix to satisfy the target market?
7. Distinguish between consumer products and industrial products.
8. (a) Describe the major stages of the product life cycle. (b) How do marketing strategies differ depending on the stage of the product's life cycle?
9. In what ways is packaging important to small firms and their customers?
10. (a) What are the three basic aspects that should be considered in pricing products? (b) Explain cost-oriented pricing. (c) What is markup? (d) Explain how service firms, retailers, wholesalers, manufacturers, and building contractors actually set prices.
11. (a) What is the role of physical distribution in marketing? (b) Describe the three components of physical distribution discussed in this chapter. (c) Show how each applies to marketing.

12. *(a)* What is credit management, and why is it so important to small business? *(b)* Why is the acceptance of credit cards by small businesses increasing?

13. Discuss how the marketing of services differs from the marketing of goods.

14. How does the implementation of marketing strategies differ during the *(a)* introductory and *(b)* growth stages?

SUGGESTED READINGS

Anderson, Carol H., and Mary Kaminsky. "The Outshopper Problem: A Group Approach for Small Retailers." *American Journal of Small Business* 9 (Spring 1985): 34–43.

Boag, D. A., and A. Dastmalchian. "Market Vulnerability and the Design and Management of the Marketing Function in Small Firms." *Journal of Small Business Management* 26 (October 1988): 37–43.

"A Little Plastic Can Help Small Companies, Too." *Business Week*, May 22, 1989, p. 180.

Otten, Alan. "Portrait of Young Consumer as Wastrel." *The Wall Street Journal*, October 3, 1989, p. B1.

"Question Marks Surround the Opportunities (Marketing to Small Business)." *Sales Marketing Management*, February 1988, p. 23ff.

Robichaux, Mark. "Dealing with Deadbeats: Call Early and Often to Collect." *The Wall Street Journal*, July 18, 1989, p. B2.

"Shoestring Marketing." *Executive Female*, November/December 1988, p. 65ff.

"Small Businesses Should Check Credit." *USA Today*, September 28, 1989, p. 7B.

Stone, Andrea. "Lowering the Baby Boom: 2 Groups Demand Equity." *USA Today*, December 27, 1989, p. 8A.

Swasy, Alecia. "Sales Lost Their Vim? Try Repackaging." *The Wall Street Journal*, October 11, 1989, p. B1.

Szabo, J. C., and N. C. Baker. "Hot New Markets of the 1990s." *Nation's Business*, December 1988, pp. 20–24.

ENDNOTES

1. *The Wall Street Journal*, April 1, 1986.

2. "You Know My Name," *Forbes*, October 21, 1985, p. 94.

3. William M. Pride and O. C. Ferrell, *Marketing*, 3d ed. (Boston: Houghton Mifflin, 1983), pp. 14–15.

4. Bob Levy, "The Prime Offender: Business Itself," *Washington Post*, May 12, 1988, p. D20.

5. Suzanne Alexander, "Tiny Ryka Seeks a Foothold with Sneakers for Women," *The Wall Street Journal*, July 31, 1989, p. B2.

6. Julie L. Erickson and Marcy Magiera, "Pawing for Position," *Advertising Age*, April 4, 1988, p. 22.

7. Anita Manning, "Boomers Are Ready to Loll into Decade," *USA Today*, December 13, 1989, pp. 1D, 2D.

8. Thomas R. King, "Catering to the Maturing Baby-Boom Generation," *The Wall Street Journal*, Centennial Edition, 1989, p. A7.

9. Shelley Liles-Morris, "Firms Value Experience, Skill of Seniors," *USA Today*, December 20, 1989, pp. 1B, 2B.

10. Andrea Stone, "Lowering the Baby Boom: 2 Groups Demand Equity," *USA Today,* December 27, 1989, p. 8A.

11. *The Wall Street Journal,* October 14, 1982, p. 1; and "Targeting You by ZIP," *USA Today,* March 16, 1989, p. B1.

12. Jefferson Graham, "The Vinyl-Record Era May Sing Its Swan Song," *USA Today,* March 2, 1989, p. 1D.

13. Tom Shales, "It Came, It Thawed, It Conquered," *Washington Post,* April 16, 1987, pp. C1, C6.

14. Discussion and correspondence with Ms. Brown; and Susan French Cone, "Business Circle: Their Housework Not Just Routine; They Find No Two Days the Same," *Baldwin* (County, Alabama) *Press Register,* July 10, 1989, p. 5.

15. Jack Hayes, "Ostentatious—and Priced Accordingly," *Venture,* July 1986, pp. 96–97.

16. Alix M. Freedman, "A Price That's Too Good May Be Bad," *The Wall Street Journal,* November 15, 1988, p. B1.

17. Jeffrey A. Tannenbaum, "Small Firms Increasingly Say 'Charge It,'" *The Wall Street Journal,* April 7, 1989, p. B23.

18. Robert Shell, "Receivables: The Right Touch," *Inc.,* October 1985, p. 133.

19. "ProServ Inc.," *New York Times,* February 21, 1989, p. C8.

20. Prepared by Mary Jane Byrd, Mobile College.

16

SELLING AND DISTRIBUTING THE PRODUCT

Don't sell the steak; sell the "sizzle."—Dale Carnegie sales slogan

Sales-management skills are very different from selling skills, and talent in one area does not necessarily indicate talent in the other.—Jack Falvey, management consultant, speaker, and writer

LEARNING OBJECTIVES

After studying the material in this chapter, you will be able to:

1. Describe what is involved in promoting the sale of a product.
2. Describe different channels of distribution used for marketing products and discuss factors to consider in choosing an appropriate channel.
3. Describe the functions of intermediaries used in selling a product.
4. Discuss what is involved when a small business uses its own sales force.
5. Distinguish the types of salespeople and describe the creative selling process used in personal selling.
6. Describe the use of advertising to promote the sale of a product.
7. Explain the role(s) of merchandising, sales promotion, and publicity in a small business.
8. Discuss some of the opportunities and problems involved in selling to ethnic groups.

MEL FARR: SALES SUPERSTAR

Mel Farr was consensusal All-American when he played football for the UCLA Bruins from 1963 to 1967. The number one draft choice of the Detroit Lions in 1967, he was named the NFL's "Rookie of the Year." After being on the All Pro Team in 1967 and 1972, he retired from the NFL in 1974 because of extensive injuries. He was inducted into the prestigious UCLA Sports Hall of Fame in 1988.

Before retiring from the NFL, Farr started preparing for his post-football career. He worked in Ford's Dealer Development Division, played football, and finished his college degree from the University of Detroit in 1971. After retiring from the NFL in 1974, he remained with Ford to help set up its training program for minority dealers.

In 1975, Farr and a partner bought a bankrupt Ford dealership in Oak Park, Michigan. After he bought the partner out in 1978, Farr came up with a brilliant and successful marketing coup for his dealership. For years, he starred in a series of TV ads, dressed in a crimson cape and asking viewers to "See Mel Farr, Superstar, for a Farr better deal." They did! He became the youngest honoree in the Top 100 Black Businesses in America when it was first published by *Black Enterprise* magazine in 1978, and he's been listed

Source: Photo courtesy of Mel Farr Enterprises.

every year since. He was cited for outstanding achievements in business by President Carter in 1978 and has received numerous other awards and recognitions.

Source: Correspondence with Charlene Mitchell of Mel Farr Enterprises, and other sources, including Harriett C. Johnson, "The USA's 100 Biggest Black-Owned Businesses," *USA Today,* May 6, 1987, p. 4B.

This Opening Focus illustrates much of the material covered in this chapter. Mel Farr was creative in his advertising, sales promotion, and personal selling. This chapter deals with those subjects and also covers the channels of distribution to be used, the use of intermediaries for selling your product, using your own sales force, personal selling, advertising, and other forms of promotion. It also emphasizes the growing importance of ethnic groups in selling products.

PROMOTING THE SALE OF PRODUCTS

The process of developing marketing strategies was covered in detail in Chapter 15. It was shown that a marketing strategy is based on the marketing mix, consisting of the controllable variables that a small business must consider in carrying out its marketing strategy. This marketing mix, called the Four Ps of marketing, involves having the right *product* in the right *place* at the right *price,* to be sold through *promotion.* The first three of these variables were covered in the preceding chapter, and the last one is discussed here.

A well-planned and continuing program of communicating with customers and the public should be tailored to a target market in order to gain a competitive edge. Such communication develops awareness of, interest in, and desire for a product. The small business owner-manager will include advertising, merchandising, sales promotion, publicity, and personal selling in any promotional strategy.

Promotional specialists have four promotional objectives: (1) get *attention,* (2) hold *interest,* (3) arouse *desire,* and (4) obtain *action.* (The first letters of these four key words spell **AIDA,** the well-known opera. Remembering that title can help you remember these four key objectives.)

Getting attention is obviously necessary if potential customers are to become aware of the firm's goods or services. *Holding interest* gives the communication a chance to build the prospect's interest in the product and liking for it. *Arousing desire* favorably affects the evaluation process, perhaps building preference. And *obtaining action* includes building conviction or obtaining a trial of the product, which may then lead to subsequent purchase or adoption of the product. Neither this model nor any other will solve all promotion problems; different promotional plans may be needed for different market segments.

CHOOSING A DISTRIBUTION CHANNEL

One of the first things a small business must do in promoting sales of its product is choose a distribution channel. A **distribution channel** consists of the various marketing institutions and interrelationships involved in moving the flow of goods and services from producer to user. The distribution channel acts as the pipeline through which a product flows. While the choice of distribution channels is quite important, it is not a simple one because of the many variables involved.

A small manufacturer added an infant cereal to its product line and tried to distribute the cereal through its existing marketing channel of drugstores. Unfortunately, consumers considered cereal a food item and expected to buy it at food stores. When the manufacturer started using food brokers as a channel, sales improved.

Distribution Channels for Consumer Goods

As shown on the left of Figure 16–1, the traditional channels for distributing consumer goods are: (1) producer → consumer, (2) producer → retailer → consumer, (3) producer → wholesaler → retailer → consumer, and

Figure 16–1   Distribution Channels for Consumer and Industrial Goods

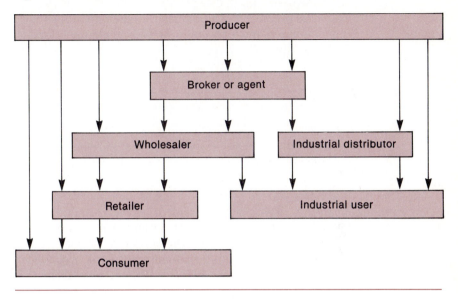

(4) producer → broker or agent → wholesaler → retailer → consumer. As you can see, the small business has essentially only two choices: (1) to sell directly to the consumer or (2) to sell through one or more intermediaries. This decision is usually made (at least initially) when choosing what type of business to enter. The first channel is the most frequently used by small firms, probably because it is the simplest.

As shown in Chapter 15, small firms performing services usually deal directly with consumers. Also, as will be shown shortly, retailers deal directly with customers. Most of our discussion will therefore concentrate on the remaining channels, which use intermediaries.

Louisiana strawberries are an interesting example of using channel 4. Because strawberries are so perishable, they must be sold quickly. So they are picked and placed in refrigerated railroad cars before they are sold. As they travel north, agents or brokers are contacting wholesalers in cities such as Chicago. As the berries are sold, the car(s) carrying them are diverted to the appropriate city, where the wholesaler picks them up and sells them through the remainder of the channel.[1]

Distribution Channels for Industrial Goods

Distribution channels for industrial goods, as shown on the right of Figure 16–1, differ from those for consumer goods. They are (1) producer → industrial user, (2) producer → wholesaler or industrial distributor → industrial user, and (3) producer → broker or agent → wholesaler or industrial distributor → industrial user. As with consumer goods, the first channel is the most frequently used, except in the case of supplies, accessories, and equipment. In general, items produced in large quantities but sold in relatively small amounts move through the second channel. Large, bulky items that have relatively few buyers, whose demand varies, flow through the third channel.

CleanDrum, Inc. (Case V–1), is a good example of a producer using the first channel. It sells its cleaned oil drums directly to oil and chemical companies.

The previous example of selling strawberries is an example of the third channel, if the berries are sold to a processor or an institution.

Factors to Consider in Choosing a Distribution Channel

Small business owners should design their own distribution channels, if feasible, in order to provide the optimum income. In doing so, they need to seek a balance between maintaining control over the flow of the product and minimizing the cost involved. The primary factors to consider include:

- Geographical markets and consumer types arranged in order of importance.
- Whether the product will be distributed through many outlets, selected outlets, or exclusive distributors.
- Kind and amount of marketing effort the producer intends to exert.
- Kind and amount of marketing effort expected of each outlet.
- Need for receiving feedback about the product.
- Adequate incentives to motivate resellers.

New products commonly require distribution channels different from those used for well-established and widely accepted products. Thus, a small business may introduce a new product, using one channel, then switch to another if the product does not sell well. Also, a new channel may be required if the company seeks new markets for its products.

When Wendell Ward and Percy Hale bought Bellville Potato Chip Company, a small firm in Bellville, Texas, near Houston, in 1985, its annual sales were $275,000, but it was losing $12,000 a year. One year later, the partners had made a profit of over $9,000 on sales of $1 million. Their success was based mainly on selling through distributors instead of directly to retailers, and the number of accounts increased from 12 to more than 700.[2]

A problem a small manufacturer may face is whether to ship directly from the factory to the intermediary or to establish regional warehouses. The latter choice provides more rapid service but probably at higher inventory carrying costs. However, transshipments between warehouses may permit lower inventories.

Finally, multiple distribution channels can create conflicts, and distribution can be adversely affected unless these conflicts are resolved. This problem should be anticipated and provided for.

Choosing the right channel permits a difference in pricing, too. Science Diet dog and cat foods are so expensive that they could never compete with other pet foods in grocery stores, but they are sold in pet stores and by veterinarians to people who are evidently willing, on the vet's recommendation, to pay the premium price.

SELLING THROUGH INTERMEDIARIES

The usual intermediaries are brokers, independent agents, wholesalers, and retailers; each is discussed below.

Brokers

A **broker,** without physically handling the goods, brings the buyer and seller together, for a fee, to negotiate purchases or sales. Each broker usually specializes in a limited number of items and sells by description or sample. The broker has only limited authority to set prices and terms of sale. Firms using brokers usually buy and/or sell highly specialized goods and seasonal products not requiring constant distribution, such as strawberries or crude oil. Also, canned goods, frozen-food items, petroleum products, and household specialty products are often distributed through brokers.

Independent Agents

Because brokers operate on a one-time basis to bring buyers and sellers together, a small business may choose to use an independent agent to develop a more permanent distribution channel[3] and to perform the marketing function. These **independent agents,** who market your product to others for a fee, are variously called *sales* or *manufacturers' agents* or *representatives (reps)*. Manufacturers' agents are used extensively in construction and building materials, hardware, and highly technical products; selling agents are used in textiles, lumber, and coal industries.

Factors to consider in choosing between using your own in-house sales force and independent agents are:

1. *Management.*   The agents can perform all the marketing activities with general guidance; an in-house sales force requires hiring, training, supervision, and doing the paperwork that goes with those activities.
2. *Cost.*   A single fee is charged by an agent, while many costs are associated with a sales force. The total cost of each depends on the other factors.

3. *Control.*   What degree of control do you need to achieve the firm's sales objectives? Products requiring special training, a personal touch, special services, and close control might best be handled by company personnel. If less control is needed, agents might be best.

4. *Territory.*   Agents handling many companies' products can usually cover larger territories, at a lower cost, than a small company's sales force can. The concentration of customers and size of order per contact have a bearing on the choice.

5. *Product.*   The type of product determines the character of the sales effort. Those products needing personal attention, such as in personal services, lean toward in-house sales personnel. Standardized products tend to be sold by agents.

6. *Market knowledge.*   Company salespeople tend to be strong on product knowledge; agents tend to be strong on territory and buyer knowledge.

Wholesalers

Wholesalers take actual physical possession of goods and distribute them to retailers, other channel members, or industrial users. They maintain a sales force and provide services such as storage, delivery, credit to the buyer, product servicing, and sales promotion.

Independent wholesalers may be either merchant wholesalers or agent wholesalers. **Merchant wholesalers** take legal title to the goods as well as possession of them. **Agent wholesalers** take possession of the goods but do not take legal title, and they usually perform fewer services than merchant wholesalers do.

Retailers

Retailers sell goods and services directly to ultimate consumers. They may sell through store outlets, by mail order, or by means of home sales. Included in this category are services rendered in the home, such as installing draperies and repairing appliances.

Some Services Performed by Retailers

Retailers, who purchase from wholesalers, agents, and/or manufacturers, must determine and satisfy customer needs. They deal with many customers, each making relatively small purchases. Some major decisions of retailers concern what goods and services to offer to customers, what quality of goods and services to provide, whom to buy from and sell to, what type of promotion to use and how much, what price to charge for goods and services, and what credit policy to follow.

Some Current Trends in Retailing

The more traditional retail outlets are department stores, mass-merchandising shopping chains, specialty stores, discount stores, factory outlets, supermarkets, and mail-order selling.

Figure 16–2   Using a "Refueling Stop"

Source: Photo courtesy of Southland Corporation.

A newer version of the discount house is **off-price retailers,** such as T. J. Maxx and Hit or Miss. They buy designer label and well-known brands of clothing at less than wholesale prices and pass the savings along to the customers, using mass-merchandising techniques and providing reduced services.

Another new development is self-service fast-food restaurants. Many of these are now following the gasoline companies' move to cheap, self-help "refueling stops."

One such fast-food operation is Circle Ⓚ. At many of its stores, customers can select the food they desire, heat it in a microwave oven, pay the cashier, and either eat the food there or carry it with them (see Figure 16–2).

Even supermarkets now use this approach. First came self-service, with the customers selecting their own items, taking them to the checkout counter, and paying the checker-cashier. Now customers in some stores can ring up their own groceries.

In 1985, Ream's Superstore, of American Fork, Utah, started giving customers this opportunity. It installed four U-Scan terminals along a counter in the front of the store. Customers carry their purchases to the counter, pass them over the scanner, and see the items listed on a monitor screen. The subtotal of the bill is registered on the monitor so the customer knows how much is being spent. Then the customer goes to a cashier, who has a receipt waiting, and pays for the goods.

Almost half the customers use the U-Scan, for which they get 1 percent off their grocery bill. The store expected to save more than $150,000 in labor costs the first year.[4]

The second new development is the use of video and computerized shopping. Computers are being used for simple **telemarketing:** they answer the phone, deliver a short prerecorded message, and take a message requesting more information.

One computer system is the Smart Answering Machine (SAM), sold by Dialectron, Inc., of Mountain View, California. It allows the computer, which has voice capabilities, to take on its owner's personality.[5]

The latest innovation is similar to automatic teller machines (ATMs); namely, computerized video kiosks in shopping malls that replace salespersons. Many retailers are now installing these devices, which utilize existing technologies, such as computer science, video display, laser disks, voice recognition, and sophisticated graphics (see Computer Update).

USING YOUR OWN SALES FORCE

Producers and retailers differ in their use of internal salespeople. Therefore, we treat these two users separately.

Producers

Producers who have their own sales representatives require a greater investment than those using intermediaries. Yet, in the case of selling a highly specialized, technical product, this course is probably the most effective.

Selecting Salespeople

When you need good salespeople, look at those who call upon your small business. You have an excellent opportunity to see them in action before deciding to hire them. Another source is the sales personnel on whom your salespeople call.

Whenever possible, in advertising for personnel, the opportunities the small business can offer salespeople should be emphasized rather than the qualifications desired; prospective salespeople want to know how the business can fulfill their needs. And since good salespeople are hard to

---

COMPUTER UPDATE

INTERAC CORPORATION: "YOUR ORDER, PLEASE?"

Interac Corporation, of Woodland Hills, California, has devised a new computer system to aid retailers. The system displays, on a laser disk in short segments, information customers can use to decide which product to purchase. For example, the disks display and explain the texture, color, and quality of 2,500 Monsanto Corporation carpets at J. C. Penney stores in the Chicago area. Also, Interac has just installed jukebox-like CD devices in record shops. Customers can hear three 40-second snippets from a selection of 60 to 120 albums, ranging from country to heavy metal. Customers use a touch screen to view and hear selections and then select the one(s) desired.

Source: Kevin Farrell, "Your Order, Please," *Venture*, January 1986, pp. 58 and 60; and Mimi Bluestone, "Thanks to CDs, Listening Booths Are Making a Comeback," *Business Week*, May 9, 1989, p. 107.

---

find, you may have to overlook some negative qualities. But a mutually agreeable probationary period (perhaps six months to a year) should be set.

Compensating Salespeople

To develop and maintain a highly productive sales force, a firm must formulate and administer a compensation plan that attracts, motivates, and holds the most effective salespeople. A compensation plan should give a sales manager the desired level of control and provide salespeople with an acceptable level of freedom, income, and incentive. The sales compensation program should be flexible, equitable, easy to administer, and easy to understand and should encourage proper treatment of customers. Because incorporating all these requirements into a program is difficult, sales managers have to strive for proper balance among the requirements.

A firm may use one or more of three basic compensation methods: salary only, commission only, or a combination of salary and commission. In a **salary-only compensation plan,** sales reps are paid a specified amount for a given time period, and this amount remains the same until a pay increase or decrease is put into effect. In a **commission-only compensation plan,** the salesperson's compensation depends solely on the volume of sales in a given time period. A commission may be based on either a single percentage of sales or a sliding scale involving several sales levels and percentage rates.

A unique form of commission payment is used by General Alum & Chemical Corporation, a Holland, Ohio, firm. Its salespeople can earn almost double the standard commission by generating orders for new products from existing customers. Also, the salesperson continues to collect the new-product commission even if transferred to another area. General Alum particularly looks for products that are too small for big companies to produce themselves. It now makes products for Mallory Industries, Oakite Products, and Dow Chemical. These new products account for an additional half-million dollars in sales each year.[6]

Several variations of the combination compensation plan exist. Under the **salary-plus-commission plan,** salespeople receive a fixed salary and a commission based on sales volume. Under the **salary-plus-bonus plan,** sales reps earn a fixed salary but receive a bonus based on either individual or group performance. Some combination programs require the salesperson to exceed a certain sales level before earning a commission; other plans provide for a commission to be paid for any level of sales. Figure 16–3 shows that most companies use salary plus commission and salary plus a bonus.

Figure 16–3   Preferred Methods of Compensation

Top sales representatives earn pay on commission

A new survey of 750 organizations indicates that sales representatives paid on a commission-only basis earned an average $185,600 in 1985, almost four times more than the $47,700 average for salaried representatives. Here's how companies pay sales representatives (percentage):

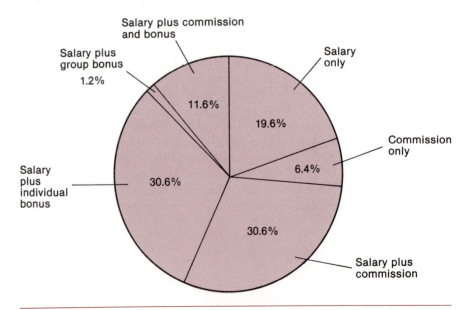

Source: Wyatt Co., as reported in *USA Today,* October 15, 1986, p. 5B. Copyright, 1986, USA TODAY. Adapted with permission.

Setting Up Sales Territories

Setting up sales territories and establishing routing schedules for the sales force should be considered. Small firms can improve their marketing performance by carefully analyzing and controlling their selling activities, especially by assigning specific salespeople clear responsibility for designated territories. Specific objectives include (1) giving each sales representative more definite responsibility, (2) providing management with a valid basis for judging sales representatives' performance, (3) reducing sales expenses, and (4) improving relations with customers.

Supporting and Controlling Sales Personnel

Sales reps should be told good news, such as high earnings or large new orders, as well as bad news, such as product recalls, production problems, and poor sales and earnings, before such news reaches the public. Also, plans for new or changed products, facilities, or services should be provided, along with copies of ads and publicity items for distribution to customers. Salespeople experiencing difficulties in obtaining an account should have support from one of the company's top executives.

A small manufacturer arranged for each member of top management to phone three different salespersons each month to thank them for their sales. Also, important price quotations were mailed to his salespersons to be delivered by them to customers to help in closing sales. Furthermore, salespersons were not asked to be "delivery" persons, bad-debt collectors, repair persons, or clerks. It was recognized that such assignments prevented them from earning commissions. These practices brought managers and salespeople closer together.

Evaluating the Sales Force's Performance

A sales force's performance can be evaluated by analyzing what profit contribution each sales representative makes. **Profit contribution** refers to what's left from the sales dollar after subtracting direct costs and the sales reps' controllable costs.

Optimum Sales Staff Size

A small group of high-quality, highly paid representatives may be preferable to a larger number of less competent salespeople. When only a few customers account for a major proportion of total sales, owner-managers may assign their salespeople accordingly.

In analyzing the firm's accounts, an owner found that 3 percent of the customers accounted for half the total sales and a larger share of the profits. More than 90 percent of the customers accounted for less than 10 percent of the sales. Also, salespeople were spending more time on the small-volume customers than the large ones. Rescheduling the sales staff to emphasize the large-volume customers increased profits.

Retailing

Selling expertise is also needed in retail stores. Advertising may entice customers to come to the store, but advertising alone is not usually sufficient to complete a sale. Customers appreciate good selling and dislike poor service. They believe that salespersons should show an interest in them and assist them in their buying. Often, when competing stores carry the same merchandise, the expertise of the salespeople is the principal reason why one store outsells the other.

The following letter came from a housewife in the Washington, D.C., area:

I went to the Estée Lauder counter at Lord & Taylor, intending to get one or—at the most—two items. Instead, the area sales rep was there and gave me such an overwhelming sales pitch that I ended up buying a horrifying amount of stuff. In addition, they signed me up for the free workshop next week, where they will make me over to show what I should be wearing. After trying *three* Lauder counters in three different stores with no satisfaction, it was nice to have someone *take a personal interest in me* and actually *tell* me what I needed.

In self-service operations, the burden of selling merchandise is placed on the producer's packaging and the retailer's display of the merchandise. Some retailers have found that, of the shoppers who made unplanned purchases, 80 percent bought products because they saw them effectively displayed. Self-service reduces retail costs primarily because it results in small sales salaries and more effective use of store space. However, risks from pilferage and breakage increase.

Some items are packaged differently for self-service. For example, where film is kept behind the counter, the boxes are stacked up in bins; but for self-service, the box has a large extra flap with a hole, permitting it to be hung on an arm, which increases its visibility and also cuts down on shoplifting. Similarly, the same pens that stand en masse in a bin display in a small office supplies store are packaged in hanging blister packs in grocery and variety stores.

A quiet revolution is sweeping department store retailing in an effort to counter such factors as apathy, lack of training, and lack of initiative, which have kept salespeople's productivity (and so their pay) low. Now many retailers are using straight commission, rather than salary or salary plus commission, to pay their salespeople. They hope that the promise of potentially higher pay will motivate existing staff and attract better salespeople (and encourage them to train and develop themselves to be better producers). It seems to be working.

For example, John L. Palmerio, a 25-year veteran of the men's shoe department at Bloomingdale's Manhattan store, has increased his earnings by 25 percent (an extra $175) after switching from a straight hourly scale to a 10 percent commission on sales. Similar experiences are being found at other stores, including the Burdines chain in Florida.[7]

Personal Selling

The largest promotional expenditure for small businesses is almost always for personal selling.[8] Effective sales personnel are especially important to small businesses, which have difficulty competing with large ones in such areas as variety, price, and promotion. Personal selling is one activity where small firms, particularly retailers, can compete with larger competitors—and win!

Effective selling doesn't just happen. Rather, small business managers must work to attain a high level of sales effectiveness in their firms. They should therefore be aware of (1) the different types of salespeople, (2) what the selling process involves, and (3) the attributes of effective salespeople.

Salespeople fall into three main groups: (1) order handlers, (2) order takers, and (3) order getters. **Order handlers** include groups such as grocery store checkers, restaurant cashiers, and ticket sellers at movie theaters, who do only routine selling. Knowledgeable people with pleasing personalities are needed in these jobs. Counter attendants at fast-food restaurants exemplify **order takers,** who may take the order and then suggest that the customer might also wish to buy a particular dessert. As more creativity is needed, pleasing personality, fast service, and suggestion selling all contribute to additional sales. **Order getters,** who do more creative selling, are vital for many businesses. Furniture, jewelry, automobiles, electronic equipment, and large appliances are examples of products that call for people who can handle transactions, take orders, and—most importantly—*get* orders for added sales.

Unfortunately, order handlers and order takers are often assigned to selling positions requiring order getters. Not all selling situations call for order getters, but all salespeople may at times be called upon to sell creatively. Therefore, all salespeople—at the retail and other levels—need a working knowledge of the creative selling process. Unfortunately, it does not appear that most salespeople have this capacity. For example, the consulting firm Learning International Inc. found that 70 percent of sales personnel were rated "ineffective" or only "moderately effective."[9]

Steps in the Creative Selling Process

The creative selling process, as shown in Figure 16–4, may be divided into eight steps. Salespeople should be informed that these steps are needed for effective selling.[10]

Figure 16–4   Steps in the Sales Process

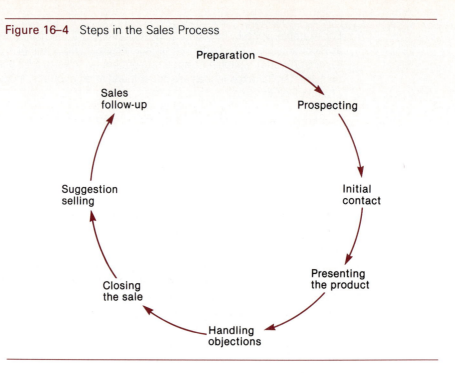

Preparation

Before any customer contact is made, every salesperson should know (*a*) the company's policies, procedures, and rules, (*b*) how to operate equipment, such as the electronic or mechanical cash register, and (*c*) obviously, a great deal about the product, including how and when to use it, its features in comparison with those of other models or brands, and available options (such as color).

Prospecting

Prospecting consists of taking the initiative in dealing with customers by going to them with a product or service idea. There are two types of prospecting: new customer and regular customer.

New customer prospecting takes place when a salesperson tries to attract new customers. For example, a salesperson may contact a prospective bride or new mother and tell her about goods or services that might be appropriate. Regular customer prospecting is effective because a firm's best prospects are its current customers. A salesperson should periodically call regular customers to tell them about products and services, but not so often that they lose the sense of being *special*, or feel they are being badgered.

Initial Contact

In the initial contact with a customer, the salesperson should begin on a positive note. The salesclerk might ask, "May I help you?" The customer replies, "No, thank you. I'm just looking." This common, automatic greeting shows no creativity on the part of the clerk, and the customer's response is equally automatic. Instead, salespeople should treat each customer as an individual, reacting differently to each one. Unfortunately, many sales contacts do not open this way.

Initial contact also includes acknowledging customers when they enter the sales area, even if they cannot be waited on immediately. For example, the salesperson could say, "I'll be with you in a moment." When free, the clerk should be sure to say, "Thank you for waiting." These actions will result in fewer customers leaving without being served and in a higher sales volume. Whenever possible, serving customers should be given top priority. Nothing is more annoying to a customer than waiting while a store clerk straightens stock, counts money, or finishes a conversation with another clerk.

Presenting the Product

In presenting the product to a customer, the salesperson should use product knowledge to best advantage, stressing benefits to the buyer. For example, to a man interested in the fabric and styling of a suit, the clerk could point out how becoming the color is or that the fabric is especially durable or easy to care for. The salesperson should get the customer involved in the presentation. To illustrate, the salesperson can demonstrate several features of a garment and then have the customer try it on for fit, as shown in Figure 16–5.

At this stage, the salesperson should limit the choices the customer has. For example, the rule of three—never show more than three choices at one time—should be applied. If more than three items are placed before the customer, the chance of a sale lessens, and the possibility of shoplifting increases. For this reason, many stores limit the number of clothing items that may be taken to a dressing room. In self-service stores, however, this can be inconvenient for a customer who has to keep getting dressed again to go in search of other sizes or styles.

Canned sales presentations are generally ineffective. So the salesperson should try to establish how much the customer already knows about the product in order to adapt the presentation to the level of the customer's expertise. A sale can be lost both by boring the customer with known facts and by using bewildering technical jargon.

Handling Objections

Objections are a natural part of the selling process. If the customer presents objections, the salesperson should recognize that as a sign of progress, since a customer who does not plan to buy will seldom seek more information in this way. In many cases, an objection opens the way for more selling by the salesperson. For example, if the customer says that a dress looks out of date, the salesperson can meet this objection with one of the following approaches.

Figure 16–5   Presenting the Product

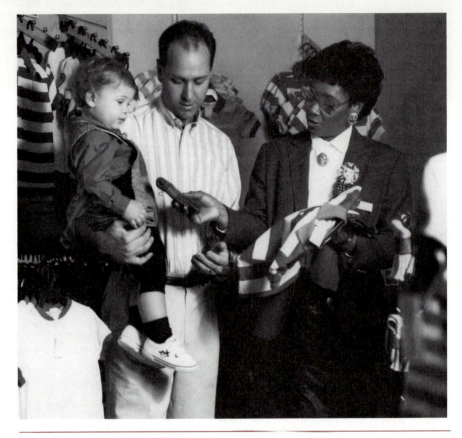

Source: Photo courtesy of William Waldorf.

- Saying "Yes, but": "Yes, it does look old-fashioned, but that style is back in fashion."
- Asking a counterquestion: "Why do you feel it's out of date?"
- Restating the objection: "You feel that the dress looks out of date." The customer may respond, "No, I mean it just looks too young for me."
- Using a direct response: "That dress was first shown at the market this season. It's the latest thing." Although sometimes considered offensive because it contradicts the customer, this approach may be necessary if the customer will not buy unless the untruth can be corrected. Tact is essential in using any of these approaches.

Closing the Sale

Several closing techniques can be used by a salesperson to help the customer make the buying decision. Some of these are:

- Offering a service: "May we deliver it to you this afternoon?"
- Giving a choice: "Do you want the five-piece or the eight-piece cooking set?" "No" should not be one of the choices!
- Offering an incentive: "If you buy now, you get 10 percent off the already low price. If you wait, you may not get the discount."
- Giving reasons for a prompt decision: "If you want this refrigerator, you'd better get it now; it's the last one in stock." The salesperson should be honest, though. If the customer buys and then returns to the store the next day and sees another refrigerator, the sale may have been made, but the customer is lost.

Suggestion Selling

Salespeople should be encouraged to make a definite suggestion for a possible additional sale. Statements such as "Will that be all?" or "Can I get you anything else?" do not constitute a positive suggestion. When a customer buys fabric, the salesperson should offer matching thread and buttons and the appropriate interfacing. The customer who buys a vacuum cleaner should be encouraged to buy a supply of bags. And customers' attention should always be drawn to other items in a line of matching sportswear separates or jewelry. Many customers like to receive valid suggestions, because other shopping trips may be avoided.

Sales Follow-Up

Follow-up should be a part of every sale. The close, "Thank you for shopping with us," is a form of sales follow-up if said with enthusiasm and sincerity. The customer leaves on a positive note, and the potential of repeat business increases. Follow-up may also consist of checking on anything that was promised the customer after the sale. If delivery is scheduled for Friday, the salesperson should check to make sure that the promise will be met and, if not, notify the customer of the problem.

Attributes of a Creative Salesperson

Both large and small companies have tried for a long time to identify and isolate those personal characteristics that can predict a knack for selling. So far, however, evidence indicates that there is no way to successfully determine who will be successful, for salespeople just do not fit a neat pattern.[11] Still, most small firms will try to attract salespeople who have certain attributes that seem to make them more effective in their jobs. These attributes can be categorized as either mental or physical.

Mental Attributes

Judgment—often called common sense, maturity, or intelligence—is essential for good salespeople. For example, effective salespeople do not argue with a customer. Also, they realize that the firm and its personnel should never be "put down" in front of customers. Tact is also needed. For instance, salespeople should avoid confrontations with children who appear to be misbehaving. Finally, a good salesperson has a positive attitude toward customers, products, services, and the firm.

Physical Attributes

To hire only beautiful salespeople is impossible, but personal appearance is important for success. As an example, a slim salesperson would be more appropriate than a larger person for a health spa. Poor personal hygiene, body odor, bad breath, dirty hair, soiled clothes, scuffed shoes, and unkept hands may lead to lost business. An observant manager should watch out for hygiene problems among the staff and, when necessary, counsel offending employees in private about improving their appearance.

Mark H. McCormack, chairman of International Management Group, has found certain prerequisites for good salespeople. His advice is to: (1) believe in your product, (2) believe in yourself, (3) work on your timing, (4) develop a sense of humor, and (5) realize that your customers aren't always telling you what they want.[12]

ADVERTISING

Advertising informs customers of the availability, desirability, and uses of a product. It also tries to convince customers that the products are superior to those of competitors.

The value of advertising to a new small business was illustrated by the example of Steven Freeman, discussed in Chapter 5, who tried to revolutionize Manhattan's residential rest estate market. He attributed part of his failure to relying on word of mouth rather than advertising.[13]

Types of Advertising

Advertising can be categorized as either product or institutional. **Product advertising** is self-explanatory; **institutional advertising** is the selling of an idea regarding the company. The majority of small business advertising is a combination of these two. The advertisements try to keep the public conscious of the company and its good reputation, while also trying to sell specific products.

The institutional type of advertising is done by R. David Thomas, the founder of Wendy's Old Fashioned Hamburgers restaurants. He named the business after his daughter, Melinda Lou, nicknamed "Wendy" by her brothers and sisters.

In May 1989, Thomas began appearing in a series of TV ads built around his daughter and her name. In one ad, he pushes the concept of quality by saying, "The hamburgers have to be good, or I wouldn't have named the place after my daughter." In another ad, a voice chides Thomas about his efforts to align a menu board of Wendy's new products. He finally turns in exasperation and asks, "Wendy, don't you have anything else to do?"

Thomas visits the restaurants and introduces himself with "Hi, I'm Wendy's dad." Market surveys have shown that the consumer identification of Wendy's has jumped about 14 percent.[14]

Source: Photo courtesy of Wendy's International, Inc.

Developing the Program

In order to be most effective, an advertising program should be used over an extended period of time. Intermittent advertising should be limited to (1) preparing customers to accept a new product, (2) suggesting new uses for established products, and (3) calling attention to special sales. Such a program requires four basic decisions: (1) How much money should be budgeted and spent for advertising? (2) What media should be used? (3) What should be said and how should it be said? (4) What are the expected results of the advertising program?

Setting the Budget

Advertising costs are controlled by an *advertising budget,* one means of determining expenses and dividing them appropriately among departments, product lines, or services. The most popular bases for establishing an advertising budget are (1) a percentage of sales or profits, (2) units of sales, (3) objective or task, and (4) executive decision.

Percentage of Sales or Profits

With this method, advertising costs have a consistent relationship to the firm's sales volume and/or profit level. The choice of a percentage figure to use can be made by checking trade magazines and associations and reading reports published by companies such as Dun & Bradstreet and Robert Morris Associates to find out what competitors spend.

One disadvantage of using this method is that advertising may be needed most when sales and profits fall. A cut in advertising may well lead to further reductions in sales and profits, producing a "vicious circle." In the short run, cutting advertising expenditures might result in small additions to profit; in the long run, it could lead to a deterioration in net income.

Units of Sales

Using this method, the firm sets aside a fixed sum for each unit of product to be sold. To illustrate, if it takes, say, 2 cents of advertising to sell a case of canned vegetables and management wants to move 100,000 cases, probably $2,000 should be spent on advertising them. This method is particularly useful for specialty goods and in situations where outside factors limit the amount of product available. On the other hand, this method is difficult to use for advertising divided among many different kinds of products, for sporadic or irregular markets, and for style merchandise.

Objective or Task

This most accurate, most difficult, and least used method for estimating an advertising budget relates the advertising budget to the volume of sales. Specific objectives are set, such as "to sell 25 percent more of Product X by attracting the business of teenagers." Then the medium that best reaches this target market is chosen, and estimates are made concerning costs.

Executive Decision

In this most popular method of all, the *executive decision* method, the advertising or marketing manager decides how much to spend. This method's effectiveness depends on the manager's experience and/or intuition.

Selecting the Media

The most popular advertising media used by small businesses are display ads in newspapers and other periodicals, store signs, direct mail, circulars and handbills, telephone directory Yellow Pages, radio, television, and outdoor signs. Probably the best medium for a small business, though, is word-of-mouth advertising from satisfied customers.

Display ads in the local newspaper are generally appropriate in towns with total newspaper circulation of 50,000 or less; a potential advertiser should talk with other small business advertisers about the effectiveness of display advertising and what days are the most productive. For example, Wednesday afternoons and Thursday mornings are the traditional times for food stores to advertise in newspapers.

High postage rates are making the use of direct mail more expensive. Offset and instant printing have simplified the preparation of small quantities of circulars; however, increased printing and distribution costs and the impact of local ordinances are negative features.

Yellow Pages advertising is most effective for special products, services, and repair shops that potential customers will seek out. Radio advertising is effective for small businesses in some of the less populous parts of the United States.

Television has generally been too costly and wasteful for many small firms to use. Now, however, local cable television systems and low-power TV stations, broadcasting only 15 to 25 miles, have rates low enough to permit small firms to use them.[15] There are now 750 of these low-power stations broadcasting local-interest programs, such as local sports events and community-oriented programs. Thanks to lower operating costs and limited coverage, the advertising rates for both these systems are low enough for smaller firms to afford.

Some examples of media used by small firms are:

- Glamourrammer Beauty Salon (Case I–3) used direct-mail flyers and publicity releases to promote its new "toning" operation.
- Simmons Mountainside Satellite Sales (Case II–3) used ads in the local paper but mostly relied on word of mouth.
- The Mother and Child Shop (Case II–4) used a large sign in front of the store and handbills delivered to homes in the area.

The medium (or media) you choose for your advertising will depend on several factors. We will present only the most important ones here.

Target Market

The media of choice are those that potential customers pay most attention to. Representatives of major media can provide you with a profile of the people who buy their publications or live in their broadcasting area.

Cost

Media cost has two important dimensions: absolute cost and relative cost. Absolute cost is the actual expenditure for running an ad. Relative cost is

"We may not be attractive to boys yet, but we're certainly attractive to advertisers."
Source: Reprinted from *The Wall Street Journal;* permission Cartoon Features Syndicate.

the relationship between the actual cost and the number of consumers the message reaches (typically, the cost per 1,000 consumers reached). Lower relative cost, the most important dimension, will be your objective.

Appropriateness
Your choice of medium may depend on the message you want to convey about a given product. Some will be more appropriate than others. For example, radio carries only sound, while newspapers and other periodicals carry only words and visuals. TV uses sound, (color) pictures, and motion and is therefore the most dramatic. But a print medium may be preferred for conveying complex information, and a catchy radio jingle may suffice for an established product or business.

Availability
The local situation will affect the number and kind of media used. Generally, retailers in small communities have fewer options than those in large cities.

Developing the Message
In newspapers, the ideas or information the advertiser wants to convey should be translated into words and symbols relevant to the target market. The development of the message involves formulating what is to be said, how it is to be said, what form it will take, and what its style and design will be. An ad should have features such as a headline that attracts attention, appeals and benefits enticing to readers, an offer, and a compelling reason to buy now. From an ad, you expect that (1) the business will become better known for the quality of its products, (2) people will be enticed to come to the store or to obtain further information such as a catalog or brochure, and (3) products will be sold immediately to customers who come to the store to buy or who place orders by phone or mail.

Skilled employees of the chosen medium can help develop the ads once you have decided on the central idea. Businesses can also get help from an advertising agency or a graphic arts firm.

When and How to Use an Advertising Agency

Most small business managers plan their own ad programs, particularly when they consider the rather high costs of retaining the services of an advertising agency. This practice is often false economy, however, since materials prepared by professionals differ significantly from those prepared by amateurs. If most of your firm's advertising will be placed in newspapers, however, recognize that most newspaper advertising is developed by skilled persons on the newspaper's staff.

Advertising agencies with experienced specialists can service business firms in many different ways: (1) performing preliminary studies and analyses, (2) developing, implementing, and evaluating an advertising plan, and (3) following up on the advertising. Examples of preliminary studies and analyses include determining the products' advantages and disadvantages relative to competitors' offerings, analyzing present and potential markets, studying distribution channels, and evaluating the advertising media. Development of an advertising plan includes designing, writing, and illustrating the advertisements, forwarding them to the media, placement, and related activities. Follow-up includes checking and verifying advertisements and handling billings and paying for them.

Most small agencies tend to specialize in one area. They can provide their expertise and close relationships with the clients and media involved.

Remember in the Opening Focus of Chapter 15 that Try J. Advertising specialized in the automotive field, especially automobile dealerships.

An advertising agency also coordinates its work with the firm's other marketing activities to ensure the greatest effect from the advertising. And, if the business wishes, the agency can also help (usually for a special fee) in areas such as package design, sales research, sales training, preparation of sales and service literature, design of merchandising displays, preparation of house organs, and public relations and publicity.

Some of the hottest advertising today comes from very small and young entrepreneurial agencies. These agencies tend to attract entrepreneurial clients because they can offer a less structured environment than the bureaucracy of the traditional advertising agency. In addition, these agencies are highly creative and "fast on their feet."[16]

Measuring the Results of Advertising

Measuring the results of advertising—by comparing sales with advertising—is important. Assume that the owners of a small retail firm desire to determine whether their advertising does the job it was intended to do. They would divide the advertising into two kinds: immediate-response and attitude advertising.

Immediate-response advertising attempts to entice potential customers to buy a particular product from the store within a short time—today, tomorrow, this weekend, or next week. This type of advertising should be checked for results shortly after its appearance. Some ways of measuring results of immediate-response ads are coupons (especially for food and drug items) brought to the store, letters or phone requests referring to the ads, the amount of sales of a particular item, and checks on store traffic.

Attitude (image-building) advertising tries to keep a store's name and merchandise before the public. It reminds people about the store's regular products or informs them about new or special policies or services. Effectiveness is more difficult to measure since the sale of a specific product cannot always be attributed to it.

When ads appear concurrently in different media, management should try to evaluate the relative effectiveness of each. Comparing sales during an offer period to normal sales, tallying mail and phone orders, and switching offers between different publications can help determine which medium was more effective.

MERCHANDISING, SALES PROMOTION, AND PUBLICITY

There are some indications that selling activities among the major companies are shifting from advertising to other forms of sales promotion. For example, in 1974, nearly half of an average marketing budget for a major company went for advertising. By 1989, however, the proportion had dropped to about a third.[17] Therefore, merchandising, sales promotion, and publicity are becoming more important in selling a product.

Merchandising

Merchandising is the promotional effort made for a product or service in retailing firms, especially at the point of purchase. It is the way the product is presented to customers, including items such as window displays, store banners, the label and packaging of the product, and product demonstrations.

An effective window display will produce, by estimate, about one-fourth to one-half of the store's sales. A few innovations in window displays have proven effective.

1. *Guessing contests*—such as predictions of scores of baseball, football, or soccer games, used by sporting goods retailers.

2. *Use of motion*—as when a toy and recreational equipment retailer uses an electric train system controlled by buttons near the window on the outside of the store.

3. *Live models*—as when a small-business furrier had models wear fur coats; then a sizable number of coats were sold to women who identified with particular models and the coats they wore.

Window and counter displays should be changed frequently to help bring the merchandise to customers' attention. Some manufacturers and wholesalers advise retailers on how to design better store layouts.

Sales Promotion

Sales promotion, activities that try to make other sales efforts (such as advertising) more effective, consists of consumer promotions, trade promotions, and sales force promotions. **Consumer promotions** comprise coupons, discounts, contests, trading stamps, samples, and so forth. **Trade promotions** include advertising specialties, free goods, buying allowances, merchandise allowances, cooperative advertising, and free items given as premiums.

Like most umbrella manufacturers, Peerless Umbrella Company was hard hit by imports from foreign manufacturers. So it entered the premium market, selling to Japan Air Lines (JAL), which wanted its name printed on umbrellas to be used as premiums.

Based on success with JAL, Gene Moscowitz, just out of business school, prepared a catalog and "hit the streets." Some very big companies were attracted: CBS, New York Times, People Express Airlines, Eastman Kodak, PepsiCo, and Anheuser-Busch. The premium market now accounts for 40 percent of Peerless's business, and revenues have risen sixfold in six years.[18]

Sales force promotions consist of benefits—contests, bonuses, extra commissions, and sales rallies—intended to encourage salespeople to increase their selling effectiveness and efficiency.

Retailers usually promote the opening of their business. A premium (or bonus item) may be given with the purchase of a product. During out-of-season periods, coupons offering a discount may be given to stimulate sales by attracting new customers. Holidays, store remodeling or expansion, store anniversaries, special purchases, fashion shows, or the presence in the store of a celebrity are other events suitable for promotions.

Every promotional activity should be meshed with every other activity. For example, if a store is advertising a certain item, it should reinforce the advertising by devoting window displays, point-of-purchase displays, and direct mail to the item. Customers often need several reminders before they act.

Publicity

Publicity can be considered free advertising. When your firm, your product, or you as the owner become newsworthy, free publicity may result. Many local newspapers are interested in publicizing the opening of a new store or any other business in their area. Take the initiative by sending a publicity release to a news editor for possible inclusion in the newspaper. Also, information about a new product/service or owners or employees who perform various community services may be interesting to the editor.

Public relations entrepreneur Reed Trencher's rapidly growing New York–based firm, Primetime, is using a new approach. He charges clients only if they get favorable coverage. But Trencher turns down clients who do not seem newsworthy.[19]

CONSIDERING ETHNIC DIFFERENCES

There are growing opportunities for small businesses to increase the sales of their product(s) to ethnic groups, for they are growing much faster than the traditional white market. For example, while the U.S. white population was increasing 3 percent from 1980 to 1987, the black population increased 8 percent, and Hispanics increased by 16 percent.[20]

However, these ethnic groups may require special attention in promoting goods or services. Language differences are an obvious example, since more than 10 percent of U.S. families speak a language other than English in their home. Some areas have an even higher percentage. For example, about one out of three households in Miami and San Antonio speaks Spanish.

Small businesses should be careful, however, not to regard all members of an ethnic group as a single target market. Some minority groups seem to be striving for what they perceive as white middle-income standards in material goods. Others disregard these objectives in favor of their traditional values.

The demographics for ethnic groups in this country may vary, too. The median age of U.S. blacks and Hispanics is much lower than that of whites. And many more blacks and Hispanics are in the earlier stages of the family life cycle. They therefore constitute a better market for certain goods, especially durable goods. Separate marketing strategies may be needed for these ethnically or racially defined markets.

For example, in 1988 a Burger King franchise closed on Chicago's South Side after failing to attract customers from the surrounding black neighborhood. Less than a year later, Doc's Great Fish Restaurant, one of three fast-food outlets franchised by Fishy Things Inc., of Chicago, had a thriving restaurant on the site. Its sales of fish sandwiches have beaten projections every month since it opened. Fishy Things now has a chain of 19 company-owned Doc's Restaurants in Chicago and Philadelphia.[21]

The second trend is the growing use of advertising on Hispanic TV stations. The two Spanish-language networks, Telemundo Group Inc. and Univision Inc., attract about 5 percent of the total audience during prime time television viewing. Univision, founded in 1962, reaches about 85 percent of the nation's 6 million Hispanic households. Telemundo, founded in 1986, reaches about 75 percent.[22]

With the U.S. Hispanic population approaching 22 million, or 9 percent of the total population, U.S. companies spent $550 million advertising to it in 1988. Companies such as Domino's Pizza have specialized Hispanic media campaigns for selected areas.[23]

WHAT YOU SHOULD HAVE LEARNED

1. Once the marketing strategy has been chosen, promotion is necessary to actually sell the product. The objectives of promotion are to get attention, to hold interest, to arouse desire, and to obtain action.

2. Promoting the product begins with deciding how to get the product into the users' hands through a distribution channel. A company will need agents or employees to do the selling and promotional activities to make its products and services known and wanted.

   A small business has essentially two choices in choosing a distribution channel: to sell directly to the consumer (or industrial user) or to sell through one or more intermediaries. In making the choice, management will be guided by the nature of the product and traditional practice in the industry. The size of the business and of its market will also affect the channel used.

3. If the small company chooses not to try to sell directly, the usual intermediaries are brokers, independent agencies, wholesalers, and retailers. A broker receives a commission for negotiating purchases or sales of generic merchandise such as produce and crude oil without physically handling the goods. Independent agents, such as selling agents and manufacturers' agents (manufacturers' representatives), also represent clients for a commission, but they may do more actual selling than brokers. Factors to consider in choosing between an in-house sales force and agents are management, cost, control, territory, product, and market knowledge.

   Wholesalers take physical possession of the goods they sell, providing storage, delivery, credit to the buyer, product servicing, and sales promotion. Merchant wholesalers also take legal title to the goods, while agent wholesalers take possession but not title and usually offer fewer services.

   Retailers buy goods from manufacturers or wholesalers and sell them to the ultimate consumer. Retailers serve a local or regional market, determine customer needs, and satisfy them with their choice of location, goods, promotion, prices, and credit policy. The current trends in retailing tend more toward self-service and more automation or computerization.

4. A small business using its own sales force gets involved in a complex operation requiring considerable investment of both capital and management. Good prospective salespeople must be located, hired, trained,

and paid. Their compensation may be paid in the form of a salary or commissions alone or some combination of salary and commissions or bonuses. Sales territories must be established on a geographical, product, or other basis. Salespeople must be motivated and supported and their performance evaluated in terms of profit contribution.

5. Personal selling is required for both retailing operations and those manufacturing concerns that maintain their own sales force. Order handlers and order takers need not be as creative as order getters, but all sales personnel should be aware of the steps in the creative selling process. These steps include preparation, prospecting, initial contact, presenting the product to a customer, handling objections, closing the sale, suggestion selling, and following up on the sale. A creative salesperson should possess judgment, tact, and a good attitude toward customers, products, services, and the firm, as well as an attractive physical appearance.

6. Advertising should be continuous and governed by an advertising budget based on a percentage of sales or profits, a given amount per unit of desired sales, the actual amount required to accomplish the sales objective, or an executive decision.

   Advertising media include newspapers, trade periodicals, store signs, direct mail, circulars and handbills, telephone directory Yellow Pages, radio, television, and outdoor signs. Some factors affecting a company's choice of media are target market, cost, appropriateness, and availability.

   Using an advertising agency to develop and place advertisements may be desirable. Using an agency may not be necessary if most of the business's advertising will be placed in a large newspaper that has a staff trained to prepare advertising copy. The results of advertising should be measured to determine its effectiveness. This is easier in the case of immediate-response advertising than with attitude (image-building) advertising.

7. Merchandising, the promotional effort made in a retail store, especially at the point of purchase, includes window displays, store banners, labeling and packaging of goods, samples, and product demonstrations. Sales promotion consists of activities that try to make other sales efforts more effective. Anything given away to a customer or to a salesperson to encourage sales is a form of sales promotion. Publicity, a form of free advertising, may be achieved when a firm or its owner, products, or employees become newsworthy. Management should make the effort to prepare news releases about such events.

8. Ethnic groups in the United States may require special attention in the promotion of goods and services. Ethnic groups speaking a foreign language may make up a significant portion of the target market, but management should be careful not to lump all members of an ethnic group together, since many blacks and Hispanics, for example, are now adopting the values and tastes of middle America and make up a new and distinct ethnic market.

KEY TERMS

AIDA, *490*

distribution channel, *490*

broker, *493*

independent agents, *493*

wholesalers, *494*

merchant wholesalers, *494*

agent wholesalers, *494*

retailers, *494*

off-price retailers, *495*

telemarketing, *496*

salary-only compensation plan, *497*

commission-only compensation plan, *497*

salary-plus-commission plan, *498*

salary-plus-bonus plan, *498*

profit contribution, *499*

order handlers, *501*

order takers, *501*

order getters, *501*

prospecting, *502*

advertising, *506*

product advertising, *506*

institutional advertising, *506*

immediate-response advertising, *512*

attitude (image-building) advertising, *512*

merchandising, *512*

sales promotion, *513*

consumer promotions, *513*

trade promotions, *513*

sales force promotions, *513*

publicity, *513*

QUESTIONS FOR DISCUSSION

1. What are the four promotional objectives?
2. *(a)* What are the traditional channels of distribution for consumer goods? *(b)* Which one is most frequently used? *(c)* Why?
3. What are three traditional channels of distribution for industrial goods?
4. What factors should be considered in choosing a channel of distribution?
5. *(a)* Name two types of independent agents. *(b)* What are the advantages and disadvantages of using them?
6. *(a)* Why do producers use their own sales force? *(b)* What are some of the problems involved?
7. *(a)* What are the eight steps in the creating selling process? *(b)* Describe each.
8. Describe the attributes of a creative salesperson.
9. Name some current trends in advertising.
10. What basic decisions should be made about an advertising program?
11. What are some important advertising media that can be used by small firms?
12. Distinguish between product and institutional advertising.

13. What are some important functions performed by advertising agencies?
14. What is involved in sales promotion?
15. Describe some opportunities and problems in catering to ethnic differences.

SUGGESTED READINGS

Barnes, Peter W. "Spanish-Language TV Faces Big Changes." *The Wall Street Journal*, April 24, 1986, p. 6.

Bowers, James T. "Your Company's Image Is on the (Phone) Line." *The Wall Street Journal*, December 12, 1988, p. A14.

Browning, J. M., and R. J. Adams. "Trade Shows: An Effective Promotional Tool for the Small Industrial Business." *Journal of Small Business Management* 26 (October 1988): 31–36.

"Do-It-Yourself Promotions for Small Businesses." *Management World*, November–December 1988, pp. 15–18.

Gardner, M. P., and P. Shuman. "Sponsorships and Small Businesses." *Journal of Small Business Management* 26 (October 1988): 44–52.

Gupta, Udayan. " 'Full-Service' Specialty Retailers Draw Venture Capital." *The Wall Street Journal*, May 1, 1989, p. B2.

"How to 'Picture' Your Enterprise." *Kiwanis Magazine*, September 19, 1989, pp. 28–31.

Lipman, Joanne. "New Attempt at Interactive TV Planned to End Passive Viewing." *The Wall Street Journal*, February 23, 1989, p. B11.

Schlichting, Kirsten. "Curb Markets' Appeal Friendly Service, Quality Produce." *Mobile* (Alabama) *Register*, July 17, 1989, p. 7–A.

Stevens, Mark. "Eight Small Ways to Build Sales." *Working Woman*, February 1987, p. 54.

Vaccaro, J. P., and W. W. Cassaye. "Increasing the Advertising Effectiveness of Small Retail Businesses." *Entrepreneurship Theory and Practice* 13 (Fall 1988): 41–47.

ENDNOTES

1. Sometimes they are not sold by the time they reach Chicago, the train's destination, and must be sold at distressed prices or allowed to rot. Then the farmers not only lose the value of their crop but must pay transportation costs as well.

2. Lloyd Gite and Harriet C. Johnson, "Pair Cooks Up Success in Potato Chip Business," *USA Today*, June 20, 1986, p. 4B.

3. Louis E. Boone and David L. Kurtz, *Contemporary Marketing*, 5th ed. (New York: Dryden Press, 1986), pp. 311–12.

4. Martin Sloane, "Shoppers Ring Up Groceries," *Mobile* (Alabama) *Press Register*, May 25, 1986, p. 18–F.

5. David Gabel, "Your Telephone's Best Friend," *Venture*, March 1986, p. 104.

6. "Product Development: New Business from Old Customers," *Inc.*, July 1987, p. 77.

7. Correspondence with Professor Russell Eustice, Husson College, Bangor, Maine.

8. Amy Dunkin and Kathleen Kerwin, "Now Sales People Must Sell for Their Supper," *Business Week*, July 31, 1989, pp. 50, 52.

9. *The Wall Street Journal*, April 4, 1989, p. A1.

10. William H. Bolen, *Creative Selling: The Competitive Edge*, Management Aids No. 4.002 (Washington, D.C.: Small Business Administration, 1985), pp. 1–6.

11. Walter Kiechell, "How to Manage Sales People," *Fortune*, March 14, 1988, pp. 179–80.

12. Mark H. McCormack, "What Makes a Great Salesman," *The Wall Street Journal,* June 20, 1988, p. 18.

13. Keith H. Hammonds, "Pulling the Plug on a Real Estate Data Base," *Business Week,* July 24, 1989, p. 41.

14. Correspondence with Sue Willis of Wendy's International, Inc., and various published sources.

15. William Smith, "Local Cable Comes of Age," *Marketing & Media Decisions,* October 1988, p. 28; and Peter Pae, "Low-Power TV Expands, Fed by New Programming," *The Wall Street Journal,* May 30, 1989, p. B1.

16. Christine Gorman, "Mini-Shops with Maxi Clout," *Time,* September 5, 1988, p. 50.

17. William F. Allman, "Science 1, Advertisers 0," *U.S. News & World Report,* May 1, 1989, p. 60.

18. "High and Dry," *Inc.,* October 1985, p. 128.

19. "The Ultimate in Pay for Performance," *Fortune,* May 25, 1987, p. 14; and Deborah Quilter, "P.R.'s Odd Man Out," *Columbia Journalism Review* 27 (January–February 1989): 12.

20. "Population Trends," *The Wall Street Journal,* May 8, 1987, p. 25.

21. Barbara Marsh, "Fast-Food Firm Finds Niche in Minority Neighborhoods," *The Wall Street Journal,* August 2, 1989, p. B2.

22. Joanne Lipman, "Nielsen to Track Hispanic TV Ratings," *The Wall Street Journal,* July 24, 1989, p. B4.

23. Alfredo Corchado, "Demand for Hispanic Ads Outstrips Specialists in Field," *The Wall Street Journal,* June 29, 1989, p. B1.

17

INTERNATIONAL MARKETING AND MARKETING RESEARCH

Your best customers can sometimes be your best source of information.—John W. Sample, Miller Business Systems

Time and space cannot be discarded, nor can we ignore the fact that we are citizens of the world.—Heywood Broun, author

LEARNING OBJECTIVES

After studying the material in this chapter, you will be able to:

1. Describe the opportunities for small businesses provided by international marketing.
2. Discuss the role of importing and show how it affects small firms.
3. Explain why, and how, small companies can become involved in export marketing.
4. Discuss the need for marketing research in small businesses and describe how it is done.

PORTERFIELD WILSON: FROM SHINING SHOES TO IMPORTING FOREIGN CARS

In 1978, Porterfield Wilson and his wife, Barbara Jean, obtained franchises to import and sell Hondas and Mazdas, which made them the first black dealers in the United States to sell foreign cars. In 1983, they started Ferndale Honda, near Detroit, which Mrs. Wilson runs. What makes this achievement so remarkable is Wilson's classic "rags-to-riches" story.

At age 10, though sometimes barefoot himself, Wilson helped to support himself by shining shoes in front of the Grand Ole Opry in Nashville, Tennessee. At his death, 46 years later, he was one of the most successful automobile dealers in the nation. He had been recognized by *USA Today* as one of the Top 20 Black Businesses in the nation; he was consistently near the top of *Black Enterprise* magazine's Top 100 Black-Owned Businesses; and he was invited to the White House in 1978 to receive a citation for achievement from President Jimmy Carter.

A high school dropout who was raised by an aunt and served as a paratrooper in the Korean War, Wilson moved to Detroit in the 1950s. He worked on a Dodge assembly line during the day and clerked in a drugstore by night. A customer was so impressed with his outstanding sales ability that he encouraged Wilson to become an automobile salesman, which he did.

By 1970, Wilson had saved enough money to buy a Pontiac dealership and become the first black Pontiac dealer in the Midwest. GM's inventory planners expected him to sell about 300 vehicles that first year; he sold 1,000. "I had never seen a financial statement when I started the company," Wilson recalled, "but I was determined to make it work."

Wilson ran his own job-training program, hiring uneducated, unskilled people and giving them free courses in such trades as auto mechanics, while paying them to learn.

Source: Photo courtesy of Porterfield Wilson Pontiac.

His achievements were emphasized when he returned to Nashville after 40 years to receive a key to the city. As he pointed out, "When I was a boy in Nashville, I wasn't allowed to enter the courthouse, and now I have a key to the city. I guess I've come a long way."

Before his death, Wilson conceived and launched Porterfield's Marina Village, a $60 million, 63-acre complex featuring 200 luxury apartments and condominiums, a fine riverside restaurant, a public boat launch, and 450 boat slips. His wife is carrying on the work.

Source: Correspondence with Porterfield Wilson Pontiac; and others, including George White, "Up by the Bootstraps," in "Still the Land of Opportunity," *U.S. News & World Report*, July 4, 1983, pp. 38–39; and *DETROIT 90* (a magazine published by the city of Detroit), pp. 45–47.

Up to this point, we have dealt primarily with domestic operations. Occasionally, we've talked about international influences, such as foreign franchising and the competitiveness resulting from Japanese excellence. But as this Opening Focus shows, we are shifting emphasis in this chapter, which looks at international marketing as an opportunity for small businesses. It also shows the need for, and how to do, marketing research, not only for international operations but also for domestic activities.

OPPORTUNITIES FOR SMALL FIRMS IN INTERNATIONAL MARKETING

As the opening quote by Heywood Broun indicates, "we are citizens of the world," whether as individuals or as small businesspeople. When the Chinese government cracked down on the students in Tiananmen Square in 1989, effectively quashing their bid for independence, it also cracked down on the move toward independence in economic opportunities. When East Germany threw open its borders in 1989, and hordes of East Germans fled west, it also affected us. We can hope that it will also enhance our export opportunities.

In other words, small businesses are affected by what happens in the rest of the world, whether directly involved in international marketing or not. So they must learn to develop marketing relationships with other countries.

Growing Interest in International Marketing

Selling imported foreign goods, as well as exporting our domestic products abroad, has always interested small business owners. There are many reasons for this. They include fascination with foreign products and people, the uniqueness of some of the products involved, the satisfaction that comes from travel, and just being involved in international business transactions.

If you, as a small business owner, do not actually produce a product that's going into international trade, you surely use foreign products in your everyday life. Do you drive an Audi, Honda, Hyundai, Jaguar, Merkur, Saab, Yugo, or Nissan? If so, you're involved in international marketing. Look around you and see how many products originated outside the United States. Your coffee? Tea? Cocoa? What type of music system do you use? Where was your television set or VCR produced? Look at the remote control to your electronic system and see if it was "Assembled in Mexico." What brand of computer do you have? Is it a Leading Edge or Samsung? If so, it is a South Korean product.

Do you get the point? As students, teachers, and small business people, we're surrounded by the evidences of international marketing.

Two Aspects of International Marketing

While all of us are involved in international importing, only a few small firms are directly involved in exporting at this time. That is changing very rapidly. An increasing number of Americans will engage in some aspects of international marketing during their working lives. In fact, we estimate that *over half of you will work in some aspect of international activities during your working life.*

International marketing has two faces. One is **importing,** purchasing the goods of other nations. The other, **exporting,** consists of selling to other nations. We now explore both these faces.

IMPORTING BY SMALL FIRMS

There are essentially two types of small business importers. First, there are those who engage in actual import activities, who import products and sell them to intermediaries or directly to customers. Second—and much more prevalent—there are the millions of small retailers and service businesses that sell international products. Both types are interested in imports for a number of reasons.

Reasons for Importing

First, imported goods may be the product the company sells to customers or raw material for the goods it produces. The small company must decide whether to purchase U.S. products—if available—or import foreign products. If they are imported, does the company purchase the items from a U.S. wholesaler or from firms outside the country?

On the other hand, foreign companies are just as interested in tapping U.S. markets as our producers are in selling to foreign markets. Thus, imported goods may form the main competition for a small business in all stages of buying, producing, and/or selling a product.

Small business managers should recognize that some American buyers

Source: Photo courtesy of William Waldorf.

have a preference for foreign goods or services. Goods such as English china, Japanese sports cars, Italian leather goods, Oriental carpets, Russian caviar, and French crystal are eagerly sought by American consumers.

Also, small U.S. producers should understand that the increasing flow of new and improved products into the country can improve their output or increase their competitive level.

Thus, we see foreign goods flooding U.S. markets at the same time that some of our companies are suffering a lack of customers, or even going bankrupt. For example, foreign-made automobiles, cameras, stereos, television sets, VCRs, clothing, shoes, calculators, and home computers are being found in growing numbers. Although manufactured abroad, these imports provide many opportunities for small firms to sell, distribute, and service those products.

For example, look in the Yellow Pages and see how many franchised dealerships there are for foreign cars such as those mentioned in the Opening Focus. Then look at computers, cameras, and music and entertainment systems to get some idea of the extent of importing by small firms.

Some Problems with Importing

The flip side of the situation is that the benefits of importing must be weighed against its disadvantages. While it is probably true that imports generate more jobs than they eliminate, this is small comfort for those small firms that are adversely affected, as the following example shows.

Kalart Victor Corporation, the last U.S. maker of 16-millimeter movie projectors, called it quits in 1989, a victim of Japanese competition and the popularity of VCRs. Its projectors had been used in school systems and by government bodies—such as U.S. embassies around the world. As these groups began to use VCRs for instructional films, the demand for projectors declined. As the 1970s ended, there were five U.S. makers of projectors, with Kalart alone employing 250 people. By 1989, Kalart, the only producer—with fewer than 50 employees—left the entire market to three Japanese makers.[1]

EXPORTING BY SMALL FIRMS

Along with the fascination we have with foreign business, there are many misconceptions concerning it—including the belief that only large firms can engage in exporting and importing. This is not true, as it has been estimated that nearly three out of four U.S. exporting firms are either medium-sized or small.[2]

Some Common Myths about Exporting

There are many myths that keep small firms from engaging in international exporting. The following are the most significant:

1. *Only large firms can export successfully.*   But small size is no barrier to international marketing. In fact, today's most likely exporters are not the manufacturing giants, but companies with from 1 to 499 employees, according to Cogentics Inc.'s 1990 survey.[3]

2. *Payment for goods sold to foreign buyers is uncertain.*   Not true, as there are fewer credit losses in international sales than there are domestically.

3. *Overseas markets represent only limited sales opportunities.*   On the contrary, around 95 percent of the world's population, and two-thirds of its purchasing power, are outside the United States.

4. *Foreign markets will not buy American products.*   Although some goods may not travel or translate well, most American products have a reputation overseas for high quality, style, durability, and many "state-of-the-art" features, and some products—such as hamburgers, blue jeans, and surfboards—are in demand simply because they are American!

5. *Export start-up costs are high.*   Not necessarily, since you can begin exporting your products through exporting intermediaries at little real cost to you.

Some Opportunities and Risks for Small Firms

There are many opportunities available for small firms in international operations, but there are also many risks involved, as you can see from Figure 17–1.

Figure 17–1   Opportunities and Risks in International Exporting

Opportunities and Challenges for Small Firms
- Expansion of markets and product diversification.
- More effective use of labor force and facilities.
- Lower labor costs in most countries.
- Availability, and lower cost, of certain desired natural resources.
- Potential for higher rates of return on investment.
- Tax advantages.

Problems and Risks
- Possibility of loss of assets and of earnings due to nationalization, war, terrorism, and other disturbances.
- Rapid change in political systems, often by violent overthrow.
- Fluctuating foreign exchange rate.
- High potential for loss, or difficulty or impossibility of retrieving the earnings from investment.
- Unfair competition, particularly from state-subsidized firms.
- Lower skill levels of workers in underdeveloped countries.
- Difficulties in communication and coordination with the home office.
- Attitudinal, cultural, and language barriers.

Source: Adapted from Leon C. Megginson, Donald C. Mosley, and Paul H. Pietri, Jr., *Management: Concepts and Applications,* 3d ed. (New York: Harper & Row, 1989), p. 512.

There Are Many Opportunities

In general, the *opportunities* for small firms are: (1) expansion of markets, and possible market and product diversification, (2) more effective use of resources, including lower labor costs, (3) potentially higher rates of return on investment, and (4) possible tax advantages. As indicated earlier, there is still an effective demand abroad for American goods, especially food, office machines, computers, data processing equipment, and many specialized items of machinery. Also, there's less severe competition in foreign than in domestic markets, and many foreign countries encourage small firms to export to them, as the following example shows.

In the early 1980s, China's powerful State Economic Commission launched a major effort to attract small Western enterprises. It was dissatisfied with large firms—especially Japanese ones—that sell expensive consumer items such as VCRs that do little to advance China's backward economy.

This policy helped Clark Copy International Corporation, a small company making plain-paper copiers in a cramped plant in Melrose Park, Illinois, beat out the industry's world leaders to sign a lucrative contract with China. It agreed to sell 1,000 CMC 2000 copiers and parts for the Chinese to assemble into another 5,000 machines. Clark was also to train 1,600 Chinese technicians to manufacture the copiers and other Clark products for domestic and export sales in a new plant in Kweilin in south China. Clark—which was to be a full partner with the Chinese—was to help lay out and set up the plant.

Otto Clark and representatives of the Chinese government celebrate the signing of the historic contract (April 1982). Left to right: Li Baofeng, Otto Clark, and David Yao.
Source: Photo courtesy of D. C. Heath and Company.

How did Clark do it? According to Clark's founder and president, Otto A. Clark, a Slovak who emigrated to the United States in 1950, "You can't do business in China on a simple buy-and-sell basis, like most multinationals do. Instead, you have to establish a close human relationship and a commitment to stay." That relationship was established with the help of David Yao, Clark's Far East representative, who was born in Shanghai and speaks Chinese. Yao and Clark went to China eight times to negotiate before closing with China's National Bureau of Instrumentation Industries in April 1982.[4]

But There Are Many Risks and Problems

There are also many risks and problems involved in exporting, as shown in Figure 17–1. Several of those risks are (1) the impossibility or difficulty of getting your earnings out of the other country, (2) unfair competition, particularly from state-subsidized firms, and (3) favorable treatment given to local firms and products—this is particularly true in Japan. Now, though, an increasing number of small U.S. manufacturers are tapping Japan's lucrative markets. Also, (4) the political climate can change rapidly, making it more difficult or impossible to engage in international marketing.

A survey of over 1,500 Texas businesses over 10 years old found that 35 percent of those not involved in international trade thought their products were exportable. When asked why they did not export, 56 percent indicated that the main reasons were: (1) government regulations, (2) lack of timely information, (3) difficulty in securing financing, and (4) concern over unforeseen expenses.[5]

A new, and very significant, risk is developing in Europe. With the 1992 implementation of the new European Economic Community (EEC) rules and regulations, small (as well as large) firms must weigh the advantages of building in Europe versus those of just marketing there.[6] The EEC is writing the rules and product specifications to favor firms located within its boundaries and keep out other goods. However, staffing and maintaining plants in Europe are tremendous expenses compared to just maintaining sales offices.

In spite of all the risks and problems involved, the "old entrepreneurial spirit" is definitely at work. Increasing numbers of "little guys" are doing quite well overseas.[7]

For example, See Coast Manufacturing Company, Inc. (Case VII–4), is number one in the world in sales of coin-operated telescopes and binoculars. Its products are operating in 35 foreign countries. It's "holding its own" in Japan, even though a major competitor is Japanese.

Figure 17–2   How to Become Involved in International Exporting

Degree of control over your product	Level of commitment		Risk to you
Great	Fifth:	Produce, as well as market, your product overseas.	Great
	Fourth:	Actually market your product overseas.	
	Third:	Grant licenses to people in other country(ies) to use your product.	
	Second:	Become actively involved in doing exporting.	
Very little	First:	Do some exporting on a casual or accidental basis.	Little

Source: Based on Vern Terpstra, *International Marketing,* 3rd ed. (Hinsdale, Ill.: Dryden Press, 1983). Adapted with permission.

Levels of Involvement

There are at least five levels of involvement in exporting, as shown in Figure 17–2. At the first level, a small business may not even know it's involved in exporting, as the product is sold to an intermediary, who then sells it to foreign buyers. Also, the firm may export only occasionally when there are surplus or obsolete items in its inventory.

At the second level, the small firm actually makes a commitment to seeking export business. This step implies that the firm will make a continuing effort to sell its merchandise abroad.

Level three is reached when the small firm has a formal agreement with a foreign country to produce and/or distribute its merchandise.

At level four, the firm maintains a separate sales office or marketing subsidiary in a foreign country.

Finally, as indicated in the Clark Copy example, a small firm may engage in foreign production and marketing, which is the fifth level. The business can do this by (1) setting up its own production and marketing operations in the foreign country, (2) buying an existing firm to do its business, or (3) forming a joint venture.

As was the case for Clark Copy, in a joint venture the risks, costs, and management of the foreign operations are shared with a partner, who is usually a citizen of the host country.

Does the Firm Have Export Potential?

If a small business chooses to export, it should be willing to commit the resources necessary to make the effort profitable. Thus, it should make sure that it: (1) has a product suitable for export, (2) can reliably fill the needs of foreign countries—as well as satisfy domestic demand, (3) can offer foreign buyers competitive prices and satisfactory credit terms, and (4) is willing to commit the time and skills needed to make export marketing a significant part of the business.

Need for Market Research

The first step in determining potential is to do the sort of market research to be discussed later in this chapter. This research should definitely seek information on such topics as:

1. *What modifications of the product will be needed.*   For example, does the importing country use the metric system? Will the measuring standards be different?

2. *The level of technology involved.*   Some countries will need labor-intensive machines in order to prevent unacceptable levels of unemployment.

3. *The level of distribution of income in the target market.*   Some countries are too poor to buy sophisticated equipment or luxury items, and in other countries, wealth may be concentrated in a way that limits demand.

4. *The level of acceptance of the product.*   For example, birth control pills are just one example of products that would be unwelcome in many countries, as are pork products in others.

Develop an Export Plan

Small companies may be tempted to begin export activities without a careful screening of markets or the options available for market entry. While they may have some measure of success, they may overlook many export opportunities. Instead, it is important for them to formulate an export strategy based on good information and analytical assessment of factors involved. Such a plan makes it more likely that the best options will be chosen, that resources will be used effectively, and that efforts will be carried through to successful completion.[8]

The plan should assemble facts, identify constraints, set goals, and create an action statement of what the firm can—and must—do. It should include specific objectives, set time schedules for implementation, and set goals to achieve in order to measure the degree of success and help motivate those involved. The basic elements of such a plan should include, at a minimum, the questions asked in Figure 17–3.

Choosing the Market to Enter

An important part of developing the export plan is choosing the market to serve. This involves (1) selecting the product(s) to sell and (2) choosing the country or countries to export it to.

Choosing the product.   Table 17–1 shows some of the most popular items the United States exported in 1987, as well as the countries to which

---

Figure 17–3 Types of Questions to Ask in Developing an Export Strategy

- What countries are targeted for sales development?
- What is the best strategy to use in those markets?
- What specific operational steps must be taken?
- When, and in what sequence, should those steps be taken?
- How much money would be required to carry out those operational steps?
- How much management time can be committed to each element of the plan?
- What is the time frame within which the plan will be implemented?
- How will results be evaluated?
- How will evaluations be used to modify future efforts?
- What will be done with the evaluations?

---

they were sold. Although specific products aren't shown in the table, the largest exports were (1) automotive and motor vehicles (which are primarily sold by large companies), (2) office machines and computers, (3) aircraft and parts, (4) electrical machinery, and (5) power-generating machinery. Most of these items can be—and are—exported by small firms. Other important exports by small firms were (1) medical equipment and services, (2)

Table 17–1 What We Exported to Selected Countries in 1987 (in $ billions)

Selected commodities	All countries	Canada	Japan	Mexico	United Kingdom	Germany	South Korea	France	Taiwan
Total, All exports	244	57	27	14	13	11	8	8	7
Machinery	70	13	5	5	6	4	2	3	2
Transport equipment	39	16	2	2	2	1	*	1	*
Chemicals and related products	26	3	3	1	1	1	1	1	1
Crude materials (excluding fuels)	20	2	5	1	1	1	2	*	1
Food and live animals	19	2	5	1	*	1	1	*	1
Manufactured goods	17	5	2	2	1	1	*	*	*
Mineral fuels and related materials	8	1	*	1	*	*	*	*	*
Professional, scientific, and controlling instruments	7	1	1	*	1	1	*	*	*

* Less than $0.5 billion.

Source: Bureau of the Census, Statistical Abstract of the United States, 1989 (Washington, D.C.: Goverment Printing Office, 1989), Table 1371, p. 787.

specialty oil-field parts and machine toolings, (3) electrical components, (4) spare parts of all kinds, (5) specialty chemicals, and (6) technical services.[9]

Choosing the country.   Table 17–1 also shows who the major customers are. Notice that Canada and Japan are far and away the largest buyers of U.S. exports. In 1988, Canada and the United States signed a treaty that essentially opened up free trade between the countries. Small service firms will particularly benefit from the treaty.[10]

Figure 17–4 shows the 10 fastest-growing markets for our exports. Notice

Figure 17–4   The 10 Fastest-Growing Markets for U.S. Exports*

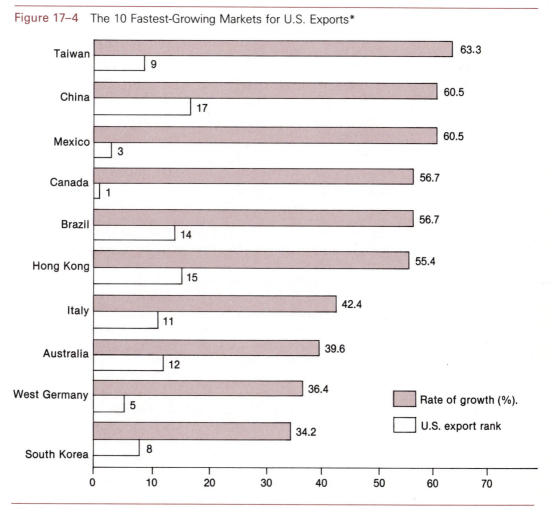

* The shorter the bar, the higher the rank as an importer of U.S. goods.
Source: Department of Commerce data, as reported in Chi B. Anyansi-Archibong, "Challenges and Opportunities as Small Business Goes Global," *Proceedings of the 1989 Small Business Institute Directors' Association National Conference,* ed. Gwen Fontenot (Crystal Gateway Marriott, Arlington, Va., 1989), p. 21.

that all of them are already major U.S. trading partners. The length of the top bar shows the percentage increase in our exports to them; the bottom bar is inverted, so the shorter the bar, the higher the country's rank as an importer of U.S. goods.

The information in these figures—and the text—should help you choose the product and country to target for your export efforts.

Which Approach Should Be Taken?

You saw in Figure 17–2 that there are five levels of involvement in international marketing. These vary from casual, or accidental, exporting to foreign production and marketing. It is important that you choose the approach that fits your needs and abilities—at least initially—as that decision will significantly affect your export plan and marketing strategies.

What Are the Alternatives?

For small businesses, there are only three practical approaches to exporting, which can be used alone or in combination. They are:

1. *Filling orders from domestic buyers, who then export the product.*   From the producer's standpoint, these sales are indistinguishable from domestic sales.

For example, this is the method used by See Coast Manufacturing (Case VII–4) to distribute its telescopes and binoculars.

There are many U.S. and foreign distributors, retailers, and others who purchase for export. With this approach, the buyer bears the risks and handles all the details.

2. *Exporting directly through intermediaries.*   With this approach, you choose intermediary firms (as discussed in Chapter 16) capable of finding and servicing foreign buyers for your product. Export management companies, export trading companies, international trade consultants, and others can provide you with well-established expertise and trade contacts. Yet you still retain considerable control over the process. While your risks increase with this approach, so do your potential profits.

3. *Exporting directly.*   This approach commits you to exporting, and to all the activities required to market products. In addition, you have the international aspects to cope with. It is not appropriate for everyone, or for every product, or for every market. But it does represent the best way to achieve maximum profits and help with long-term growth.

For example, REC Specialties, Inc., of Camarillo, California, a manufacturer of low-voltage solar and battery-operated fluorescent fixtures, uses the direct method of exporting. It was contacted by firms in Argentina, Chile, and Switzerland to distribute its products abroad. According to Patricia Cramer, whose knowledge of five languages has helped her as REC's export manager, the most difficult problem was "finding freight forwarders that knew what they were doing." Now, the export of lamps to 33 countries accounts for 10 percent of the company's annual sales and profits.[11]

Factors to Consider

As indicated, in the *indirect method*, management hires intermediaries to handle the exporting details. There are many of these intermediaries in international marketing because they can handle the entire export function for several manufacturers of similar but noncompeting lines. With their help, small producers can arrange financing through banks that specialize in international trade. It is essential that you determine exactly what services each agent can provide before deciding to use one of them.

The *direct method* does not include those outside aids. Instead, the small exporter must perform all the details. This requires an almost total commitment of time and resources, as there are so many tricky barriers to overcome. Some of these are natural, while others are artificial barriers imposed for protective purposes.

Overcoming Barriers to Exporting

As indicated, there are innumerable natural and artificial barriers that must be overcome if you are to export your product successfully.

Natural Barriers

Some of the natural and inherent barriers are geography, language, sociocultural factors, customs and tradition, religion and religious conflicts, and product and quality standards.

Geography is a natural barrier. For example, the distances from the United States to most major foreign markets make the cost of transportation almost prohibitive for many products.

Language is another natural barrier. While English is now fairly well established as the world's business language, many nationalities, such as the French, prefer to do business with people using their own language. Also, any time you translate from one language to another, problems may result, as shown in Figure 17–5.

Sociocultural factors can be a barrier for businesses entering a foreign market without adequate preparation, particularly in countries with easily identifiable cultural characteristics, as the following examples illustrate.

Mattel found that Barbie dolls did not sell in Japan until they conformed to Japanese standards of beauty. When the eyes and hair were darkened, the bust reduced, and the legs shortened, Barbie became a Japanese craze.

And in a classic "boo-boo," one airline's promotional campaign to give white orchids to passengers as they boarded the plane was not appreciated in many Asian cities where white flowers symbolize death.

Figure 17–5   Some Examples of Communication Breakdowns

The following are some examples of errors and infelicities of translation.

What the advertisers meant	What they didn't know they were saying
Macy's New York	
Headline: "Macy's Introduces the Fabulous Fall Faces by PUPA."	(Polish) *Pupa* = "behind, buttocks."
American Manufacturer	
Product: Hydraulic ram	(Arabic) "water goat"
General Motors	
Product: Chevy Nova	(Spanish) "Chevy does not go."
American Manufacturer	
Product: Touch-toe (pedal-operated) industrial drill, instruction manual.	(Italian) "The dentist takes off his shoe and sock and presses the drill with his toe."
PepsiCo	
Advertisment: "Come alive with Pepsi."	(Chinese) "Pepsi brings your ancestors back from the grave."

Customs and traditions can limit trade. The Japanese reluctance to say "no" to a guest often causes confusion in sales negotiations. And the pride of many Spaniards limits their trading with someone of lower status. Moreover, pride may prevent some of them from doing work they consider beneath their dignity.

For example, an American professor in Madrid needed some typing done. After much effort, he found a Spanish lady who agreed to do it if her family and neighbors never found out. She would pick the work up and return it to him in her grocery shopping bag.

Unfortunately, *religious conflicts*, such as those between Catholics and Protestants in Northern Ireland, Christians and Muslims in Lebanon, and Muslims and Hindus on the Indian subcontinent, are often a limiting factor.

Product standards in other countries often differ from ours, necessitating modifications if products are to be sold there.

For example, our appliances, produced for 110-volt, 60-cycle alternating current (AC) systems and outlets, are incompatible with the 220-volt direct current (DC) systems used in some other countries.

Quality standards may also be a limiting factor. Some products made in the United States often do not fit quality standards of other countries. Therefore, they must be adjusted if they are to compete, which poses a challenge but is not an impossible task.

In 1981, when Japanese demand for lumber far exceeded the supply, Webco Lumber Company, a California company with slack demand, saw an opportunity to export to Japan. Barbara Webb, Webco's president, along with its sales manager, secretary, and treasurer, therefore went to Japan with a trade mission and returned home with several large orders.

However, the Japanese standards and specifications required Webco to change its milling processes. It also changed the type of wood being harvested, cut it to different lengths (13.12 feet, or four meters, instead of the usual 12, 14, or 16 feet), and planed it to finer tolerances than was required in the U.S. market. Satisfying these Japanese standards permitted Webco not only to survive but even to increase its sales.[12]

Artificial Barriers

There are many artificial barriers thrown up by countries to restrict imports. Some of these are **revenue tariffs,** which are imposed on imports to generate tax income, and **protective tariffs,** which are used to discourage imports by setting rates artificially high.

Embargoes prohibit outright the import or export of certain products for military, health and sanitary, moral, or political reasons.

For example, Japan embargoed oranges from California during the "Medfly" scare of the mid-1980s; the United States prohibits the import of certain birds and animals to prevent the spread of disease; and cocaine, heroin, and other harmful substances are barred for moral reasons.

Import quotas place a limit on the amount of a product that can be imported into a country. The quota may be absolute or combined with another barrier to severely restrict or prevent imports.

Exchange controls are often used to control the availability of a country's currency for foreign imports. Developing countries often use this method to discourage or prohibit importing luxury goods, such as cars, whose cost may be more than doubled by the exchange rate.

Attitudinal Barriers

There are at least three attitudinal, or psychological, barriers that inhibit small businesspeople from exporting. These reasons can be summarized as:

1. *Fear of the unknown.* Despite their natural optimism, small business owners fear situations where information is scarce, or where a new location is considered inaccessible.
2. *Fear of long-distance relationships.* Americans—even entrepreneurs—tend to feel uncomfortable with relationships involving long distances.

This is particularly true in an area that may appear unstable, untidy, and fraught with risk.

3. *Fear of complex situations.*   Many owners of small firms fear the complexities of language, legal systems, value systems, and financial matters.

Overcoming These Barriers

Fortunately, the desire of U.S. producers for foreign markets—but especially the demand for American products abroad—can overcome these barriers, as the following example shows.

Kentucky Fried Chicken is a classic example of how much American products are desired overseas. In fact, it is among the leading international restaurant chains. With more then 3,000 restaurants outside the United States, the company has more international outlets than any other chain. The restaurants, located on six continents, produce annual sales of approximately $2 billion.

Kentucky Fried Chicken's international restaurants are operated primarily through franchise and joint venture arrangements, although the corporation owns some units. Franchisees typically pay a percentage of sales to the franchisor for the right to use its name, logo, and operating system. In joint venture arrangements, the corporation holds an equity stake in the operations, from which it earns a percentage of profits.

Japan is one of the company's most successful international markets. Through a joint venture with Mitsubishi, more than 800 KFC restaurants operate in Japan, more than in any other country outside the United States. Even in Japan, half a world away from the Colonel's roots, the company's menu, sign, and packaging are nearly identical to those found in U.S. restaurants, demonstrating the importance of maintaining consistent image and quality from market to market. As you can see from the photo of KFC's Hiroshima restaurant, the name and image of Colonel Sanders are easily recognizable and transcend language barriers.[13]

Colonel Sanders Goes to Japan
Source: Photo courtesy of Kentucky Fried Chicken International.

Help Is *Available*

In spite of the barriers facing you, help *is* available from many sources. This help takes two forms: (1) providing information and guidance and (2) providing financial assistance.

Providing Information and Guidance

Both government and private groups can provide practically unlimited information and guidance, including technical expertise. For example, the SBA offers information on overseas marketing in its pamphlet entitled *Market Overseas with U.S. Government Help.*[14] Other SBA help comes from members of SCORE and ACE, who have many years of practical experience in international trade. Small business institutes and small business development centers provide export counseling and assistance. The SBA also offers financial assistance through its loan guarantees and direct loan programs for small business exporters. Legal advice is provided through an arrangement with the Federal Bar Association.

For example, the district offices of the U.S. Foreign and Commercial Service, U.S. Department of Commerce, with local chambers of commerce, state agencies, and other groups, conduct approximately 5,000 conferences, seminars, and workshops each year. They cover such topics as how to export, documentation and licensing procedures, country-specific market opportunities, and export trading companies.[15]

The U.S. Department of Commerce offers assistance through its International Trade Administration (ITA) and its U.S. and Foreign Commercial Service Agency (USFCSA). It also has district export councils (DECs) that provide exporters with direct contact with seasoned exporters experienced in all phases of export trade. Periodically, it publishes a *Basic Guide to Exporting.*[16]

If you are in Washington, D.C., you can visit the Commerce Department's Export Counseling Center (ECC) for help. Minority exporters can receive help from the department's Minority Business Development Agency (MBDA), which provides a variety of services, including exporters' assistance.[17] The department also has a computer called Dialog that can aid in locating markets for the firm's product(s).

A review of one "best prospects" list from Dialog turned up some unexpected markets for small firms. For example, bicycles were needed in sub-Saharan Africa; the United Kingdom needed candles; Cyprus could not get enough hotel furnishings; fast-food franchises were in short supply in Indonesia; and T-shirts illustrating the Heimlich maneuver were in great demand throughout western Europe.[18]

COMPUTER UPDATE

CENSUS BUREAU PROVIDES NEW ELECTRONIC SERVICE

The U.S. Department of Commerce's Census Bureau has established a National Clearinghouse for Exporter Data Processing Services. On request, the bureau will provide a brochure listing service agencies that have registered with the Census Bureau and have demonstrated that they can provide one or more of the following services:

- Develop or provide computer software.
- Edit raw data.
- Transmit electronic data to the bureau.

- Provide data on computer tape or floppy diskettes.
- Provide current listings of all commodity classifications.

The bureau does not franchise or sponsor the registered organizations and is not responsible for the price or quality of their registered services.

For information, contact the Automated Export Reporting Office at (301) 763–7774, or write to the Census Bureau, (FTD), Washington, DC 20233.

Source: "Good Follow-Up is Vital to Export Success," *Business America*, October 26, 1987, p. 15.

Small companies needing export-related electronic data processing services can get help from the Commerce Department's Census Bureau, as shown in the Computer Update.

Other assistance is available through the U.S. Department of Agriculture's Foreign Agricultural Service (FAS), state development agencies and market development centers, and trade missions and trade shows. Chambers of commerce and trade associations, including American chambers of commerce abroad, are also very helpful, especially in providing contacts with foreign companies. Commercial banks can provide their clients with a wide variety of services, as shown in Figure 17–6.

Figure 17–6   Services Provided by Commercial Banks

Some selected services provided to their exporting clients by commercial banks include the following:
- Advice on export regulations and restrictions.
- Information about exchange rates; exchange of currencies.
- Assistance in financing exports (and imports as well).
- Collection of foreign invoices, drafts, letters of credit, and other foreign receivables.
- Transfer of funds to other countries.
- Letters of introduction and letters of credit for travelers.
- Credit information on potential overseas buyers.
- Credit assistance to the exporter's foreign buyers.

Help with Financing

Financial assistance for small business export programs can be obtained from the Foreign Credit Insurance Association (FCIA) and the Export-Import Bank of the United States (Eximbank).

The FCIA has a program for "new-to-export" businesses. There are no size guidelines, and any exporter, regardless of net worth, that qualifies in all other respects, is eligible for assistance.

At Eximbank, access to small business programs is determined by size, as defined by SBA guidelines. The bank offers small exporters guarantees for short-term working capital loans, backs fixed-rate, medium-term export loans, and offers no-deductible insurance programs.

MARKETING RESEARCH

Marketing research is the systematic gathering, recording, and analyzing of data about problems relating to the marketing of goods and services. It is an orderly, objective way of learning about customers or potential customers and their needs and desires. By observing customers' actions and reactions and drawing conclusions from them, managers of small firms can use marketing research to satisfy their needs.

Angelo's Supermarkets (Case V–3) offers a good example of doing this type of research. The owner's son did a survey of customers' preference for private versus national brands in order to set the company's purchasing policies.

Why Do Marketing Research?

Why should small firms do marketing research? As shown in the above example, small businesses must do it to find out what their customers want. Potentially, small businesses have an edge over larger firms, since their owner-managers are closer to customers and can learn more quickly about consumers' likes and dislikes. Also, owner-managers can react quickly to changes in buying habits, as they are close to, and have a feel for, their customers and markets.

Marketing research is helpful at several points in a small firm's life. Before initiating a business, it can be used to find out whether the location and surrounding population are right for the company's proposed product. After the business is operating, marketing research can help in deciding (1) whether to develop new or different products, expand at the original location, or open additional locations, (2) whether to cut back and, if needed, where, and (3) when and where to change emphasis on activities such as advertising and promotion strategy and channels of distribution.

Entrepreneurs are well advised to use market research to put their gut instincts to the test. "Even if you think that intuitively you have everything in place, it just makes sense to back up your hunches with market research," said Sue Gin, founder and chairman of Flying Food Fare, a Chicago catering firm supplying meals to Midway Airlines.

The primary reason for this new acceptance of marketing research is competition. "It costs a lot more now to make a bum decision than it used to; the price of failure is a lot higher," said Joseph Smith, cofounder and president of Oxtoby-Smith, Inc., a New York marketing research firm.

Marketing research firms are reporting a large increase in the number of entrepreneurial clients. But many clients may be using this technique "because it's the trendy thing to do."[19]

Where Marketing Research Fits into Marketing

Marketing research is part of the overall marketing system. In small firms, it tends to be handled by one or a few persons. By analyzing marketplace data, such as attitudinal, demographic, and lifestyle changes, marketing research can help managers plan their strategic efforts.

Areas where marketing research is effective include:

- Identification of customers for the firm's products.
- Determination of their needs.
- Evaluation of sales potential for the industry and firm.
- Selection of the most appropriate channel of distribution.
- Evaluation of advertising efficiency.

How to Do Marketing Research

Marketing research does not have to be fancy or expensive to meet the small firm's needs. It deals with people and their constantly changing likes and dislikes, which can be affected by many influences. Marketing research tries to find out how things really are (not how managers think they are or should be) and what people really want to buy (not what the firm wants to sell them).

In its simplest form, market research involves defining the problem, then gathering and evaluating information.[20] Many small business managers unknowingly do some form of marketing research nearly every day. For example, they check returned items to see if there is some pattern. They ask old customers on the street why they have not been in recently. They look at competitors' ads to find out what the competition is selling, and at what prices.

At a university small business seminar, a marketing professor emphasized the importance of marketing research in small businesses. Afterward, a panel member, the owner-manager of a wholesaling firm that sold farm equipment and supplies, stated that market research was not relevant in a small business. Later, this panel member told the participants that he visited dealers to learn their needs for shovels and other items before ordering these items for his stock. Without realizing it, he was conducting research.

Defining the Problem

Proper identification of the problem, so obvious but often overlooked, is the most important step in the process, since the right answer to the wrong question is useless. The small business manager should look beyond the symptoms of a problem to get at the real cause. For example, a sales decline is not a cause but rather a symptom of a marketing problem. In defining the problem, the manager should look at influences that may have caused it, such as changes in customers' home areas or in their tastes.

Gathering and Evaluating Information

Marketing research can use existing data or generate new information through research. So managers must make a subjective judgment and weigh the cost of gathering more information against its usefulness. The cost of making a wrong decision should be balanced against the cost of gathering more data to make a better-informed decision.

Using your own sources of information.   Small business managers should "think cheap" and stay as close to home as possible when doing marketing research. Looking at the firm's records and files, such as sales records, complaints, and receipts, can show you where customers live or work or how and what they buy.

The owner of the Cloth Shop (name disguised) used addresses on cash receipts to pinpoint where her customers lived. The addresses were then cross-referenced with products they purchased. This permitted the owner to check the effectiveness of advertising and sales promotion activities.

Credit records can yield valuable information about your market, as customers' jobs, income levels, and marital status can be gleaned from them. Employees are a good source of information about customer likes and dislikes, because they hear customers' gripes about the products and service of the store and its competitors. They are also aware of the items customers request that are not stocked.

Using outside sources of information.   Outside sources of information include publications such as *Survey of Current Business* and *Statistical Abstract of the United States*, trade association reports, chamber of commerce studies, university research publications, trade journals, newspapers, and marketing journals.

An independent manufacturer developed a unique electrical car warmer. The proposed market area was the Edmonton, Canada, trading area as the primary market and the balance of Alberta as the secondary market. The firm wanted to determine the sales potential for its warmer.

A study of census records revealed that vehicle registration totaled 1,253,000 in 1976. The sales potential was calculated after conducting a personal research study of 700 cars to determine how many had warmers installed.[21]

Doing primary research. Primary research can range from simply asking customers or suppliers how they feel about your business to more complex studies such as direct-mail questionnaires, telephone or "on the street" surveys, and test marketing.

Test marketing simulates the conditions under which a product will eventually be sold. However, even a small market test is costly.

Primary research may be reactive or nonreactive. **Reactive research** includes studies such as surveys, interviews, and questionnaires, and usually should be left to experts. Small businesses may use this type of research, but care should be taken to ask the right questions and obtain unbiased answers.

A small company made a product used by meat-packing plants. Its manager wanted to determine the sales potential for an area consisting of 300 counties. From *County Business Patterns,* published by the U.S. Department of Commerce, he determined the total number of meat-packing plants and their employment. Then he sent questionnaires to these plants. Analysis of the responses showed that the average plant bought $200 worth of his product per employee per year. By multiplying the total employment in these plants by $200, he derived the potential annual sales.

Nonreactive research usually involves observing the results of a given action. Sometimes, research methods can be unique, as the following example shows.

During a three-day promotion, a discount merchandiser gave its customers, free of charge, all the roasted peanuts they could eat while shopping in the store. The merchant encouraged customers to "let the hulls fall where they may" and soon had "litter trails" that provided information on the traffic pattern within the store. Trampled peanut hulls littered the most heavily traveled store aisles and were heaped up in front of merchandise displays of special interest to customers. Thus, the merchant learned how customers acted in the store and what they wanted.

Using specialized research techniques. Other techniques include license plate analysis, telephone number analysis, coded coupons, and "tell them Joe sent you" broadcast ads, not to mention just plain people-watching.

In many states, license plates give information about where a car's owner lives—what city or county, for instance. By recording the origin of cars parked at the firm's location, the trade area can be estimated. Similarly, telephone numbers and ZIP codes can tell where people live. This type of data can be found on sales slips, prospect cards, and contest blanks, as well as on personalized checks used for payment.

Coded coupons and "tell them Joe sent you" broadcast ads can be effective, too. The relative effectiveness of a firm's advertising media can be checked by coding coupons and by including in broadcast ads some phrase customers must use to get a discount on a given sale item. If neighborhood newspapers are involved, the business can also get some idea of the area from which customers are drawn. Where they read or heard about the discount offered in the ads may also give information about their tastes. Small businesspeople can learn a great deal about customers just by looking at them. A knowledge-able business owner will notice how customers dress, their age and sex, and whether or not they are married or have children. A tally sheet could be kept for a week to record these types of information.

Using Computerized Data Bases

A wide variety of print information is available at public libraries; many such institutions also offer, for a fee, access to computerized data bases, such as *Standard & Poor's Daily News* and *Cumulative News (Corporation Records)*. (Computerized data bases are covered in Chapter 20.) News about company sales, earnings, dividends, management changes, mergers and acquisitions, and other operations can be found. From these data bases, by gathering data on selected kinds of companies (such as electronics firms producing home videocassettes) or specific geographic areas (such as firms moving into a particular state or city), you can learn about companies expanding operations. Such information may be valuable to small retailers, service businesses, wholesalers, and manufacturers in selecting their target market and marketing strategy.[22]

Many small business owners now solicit information about competitors from their customers. This type of data can be stored in computers to form "profiles" of the competition, which can be used for marketing research.

Example of Market Research

The following is an actual example of market research done by a prospective restaurant owner who wanted to determine the feasibility of opening a restaurant in a given location.

First, he talked to people who worked near the proposed site to see if they would be interested in eating in his restaurant. Then, he surveyed the residents in the area to determine their menu preferences, any dissatisfaction with existing restaurants, and the likelihood of their eating at his prospective restaurant.

After that, he had data gathered about a competing restaurant and its menus.

Then he made a count of customer traffic flow at the competitor's location, used a Department of Transportation traffic survey, and studied census data concerning demographics at the proposed site.

On the basis of the results of these efforts, he modified the marketing and financial information on his business plan. Later, this information was used in advertising and media planning after the restaurant opened.

WHAT YOU SHOULD HAVE LEARNED

1. The opportunities for small firms to become involved in international marketing are growing rapidly. In fact, all of us—students, teachers, consumers, and large and small businesses—are already involved.

2. Millions of small businesses are already involved in importing and selling foreign products, especially automobiles, cameras, stereos, TV sets, VCRs, clothing, shoes, calculators, and home computers. While these imports provide many opportunities for small firms, they also may force some small firms out of business.

3. In general, export opportunities for small firms are: (*a*) expansion of markets, (*b*) more effective use of resources, particularly personnel, (*c*) potentially higher rates of return on investment, and (*d*) tax advantages. Some risks and problems are: (*a*) the impossibility or difficulty of getting earnings out of the other country, (*b*) unfair competition, particularly from state-subsidized firms, (*c*) favorable treatment given to local firms and products, and (*d*) rapidly changing political climates.

   Small firms can become involved in international marketing at one of five levels; namely, (*a*) casual, or accidental, exporting, (*b*) active exporting, (*c*) foreign licensing, (*d*) overseas marketing, and (*e*) foreign production and marketing.

   In deciding to become an exporter, a small firm needs to decide whether it (*a*) has a product suitable for export, (*b*) can reliably supply foreign countries, while still satisfying domestic demand, (*c*) can offer foreign buyers satisfactory prices and credit terms, and (*d*) is willing to commit the time and skills necessary. But extensive market research and an export plan are needed. In choosing the market to enter, you should look at both the product and the country. Our major exports are: (*a*) automotive and motor vehicles, (*b*) office machines and computers, (*c*) aircraft and parts, (*d*) electrical machinery, and (*e*) power-generating machinery. Many of these can be produced by small firms. In choosing the country to enter, keep in mind that the fastest-growing markets are Taiwan, China, Mexico, Canada, and Brazil. Canada is far and away our best customer.

   Barriers to effective export marketing include geography, language, sociocultural factors, customs and traditions, religious conflicts, product and quality standards, tariffs, embargoes, quotas, exchange controls, and attitudinal barriers.

Considerable help is available for exporters and potential exporters. The SBA, U.S. Department of Commerce, U.S. Department of Agriculture, chambers of commerce and trade associations, the Export-Import Bank, and the Foreign Credit Insurance Association provide information and technical assistance, and some help with financing.

4. While relatively few small firms do marketing research, more of them should, as it increases the chance of success and reduces chances of failure. Small firms have an advantage here, as they are closer to customers and can more easily learn customer needs.

Marketing research does not have to be fancy or expensive. In its simplest form, such research involves defining the problem and gathering and evaluating information. Thus, many small business people already do market research by checking returned items to see if there is a pattern, correlating consumer addresses with their purchases and payment records, checking to see what types of ads get the best results, and asking customers for suggestions for improving operations. There are many computerized data bases for small firms that want to do more formal research.

KEY TERMS

importing, *523*

exporting, *523*

revenue tariffs, *535*

protective tariffs, *535*

embargoes, *535*

import quotas, *535*

exchange controls, *535*

marketing research, *539*

test marketing, *542*

reactive research, *542*

nonreactive research, *542*

QUESTIONS FOR DISCUSSION

1. (*a*) Do you believe international marketing is as important as stated? (*b*) Explain.
2. (*a*) Do you really believe the statement that over half of you will work in some aspect of international activities in your working life? (*b*) Explain.
3. (*a*) What are some reasons for importing? (*b*) What are some problems?
4. How involved are you, as an individual or a small business person, in importing?
5. Name and defend *or* reject the five myths about exporting.
6. List the opportunities available in exporting.

7. Describe some of the risks and problems involved in exporting.
8. Explain the five levels of involvement in exporting.
9. If a small business chooses export marketing, what should it do to improve its chances of success?
10. After deciding to export, how does one choose the market to enter?
11. (*a*) Name, or explain, some of the natural barriers to exporting.
    (*b*) Name, or describe, some of the artificial barriers.
12. (*a*) Describe some sources of information and guidance for small firms wishing to export. (*b*) What are some sources of help in financing exports?
13. Why should small firms do marketing research?
14. How does a small firm go about doing marketing research?

SUGGESTED READINGS

"Basic Question: To Export Yourself, or to Hire Someone to Do It for You?" *Business America,* April 27, 1987, pp. 14–17.

Bowman, Russ. "Promotion Research: Taking Measure." *Marketing & Media Decisions,* October 1988, pp. 148–49.

Brockhaus, R. H. "Entrepreneurial Research: Are We Playing the Correct Game?" *American Journal of Small Business* 12 (Winter 1988): 55–61.

Collins, S. H. "Congress: Raising Capital, Backing Exports and More." *Journal of Accountancy* 165 (June 1988): 7–10.

Galante, Steven P. "States Launch Efforts to Make Small Firms Better Exporters." *The Wall Street Journal,* February 2, 1987, p. 27.

"How to Prepare for Business Travel Abroad." *Business America,* June 8, 1987, pp. 11–12.

"How to Prepare Your Product for Export." *Business America,* May 25, 1987, pp. 10–11.

MacPherson, Alan. "New Product Development among Small Toronto Manufacturers: Empirical Evidence on the Role of Technical Service Linkages." *Economic Geography* 54 (January 1988): 62–75.

Revzin, Philip. "Brussels Babble: European Bureaucrats Are Writing the Rules Americans Will Live By." *The Wall Street Journal,* May 17, 1989, pp. A1, A14.

Sherrid, Pamela. "America's Hottest New Export: Entrepreneurship." *U.S. News & World Report,* July 27, 1987, pp. 39–41.

"Small-Firm Exporting Has Growth Potential, Dun & Bradstreet Says." *The Wall Street Journal,* November 3, 1988, p. B2.

ENDNOTES

1. "VCRs Cause Failure of Firm," *Mobile* (Alabama) *Register,* July 31, 1989, p. 2–A.
2. Dan Steinhoff and John F. Burgess, *Small Business Management Fundamentals,* 4th ed. (New York: McGraw-Hill, 1986), p. 295.
3. As reported in "Small Companies Deliver the Goods," *USA Today,* May 7, 1990, p. 1E.
4. Correspondence with Clark Copy International; and various other sources, including "Tiny Copier Maker Taking a Big Step in Deal with China," *The New York Times,* April 26, 1982, p. D–4.

5. John A. Adams, Jr., "Developing a Successful Export Strategy within a Small or Medium-Sized Business," in Fontenot, *Proceedings,* p. 54.

6. William J. Holstein et al., "Should Small U.S. Exporters Take the Big Plunge?" *Business Week,* December 12, 1988, pp. 64–65.

7. William J. Holstein and Brian Bremmer, "The Little Guys Are Making It Big Overseas," *Business Week,* February 27, 1988, pp. 94–96.

8. "Furrowed Brows: Export Policy of Small Businesses," *The Economist,* January 21, 1989, p. 68.

9. Adams, "Developing a Successful Export Strategy," p. 54.

10. See "Opening up Canada," *Nation's Business,* January 1988, p. 12, for the details.

11. Jerry Demuth, "Exporting's Hard Sell," *Venture,* January 1985, pp. 172–73.

12. Erik Larson, "Logging Sales: Small Mill Survives by Setting Its Blades for Export to Japan," *The Wall Street Journal,* May 7, 1982, pp. 1, 14.

13. Correspondence with Richard Detwiler, Director, Public Affairs, Kentucky Fried Chicken International.

14. To order, ask for MA 7.003, *Market Overseas with U.S. Government Help,* U.S. Small Business Administration, Box 30, Denver, CO 80201–0030.

15. "The First Steps in Exporting," *Business America,* February 2, 1987, pp. 5–6.

16. *A Basic Guide to Exporting,* Stock No. 003–009–00487–0, can be obtained from the Superintendent of Documents, U.S. Government Printing Office, Washington, DC 20402 (or phone 202–783–3238).

17. For other assistance for minorities, see Frank McCoy, "Ready for the World," *Black Enterprise,* June 1989, pp. 162–67.

18. "Markets You Might Have Missed," *Inc.,* November 1985, p. 162.

19. Amy Saltzman, "Vision vs. Reality," *Venture,* October 1985, pp. 40–44; and Janice Castro, "She Calls All the Shots," *Time,* July 1988, pp. 54–57.

20. For more details, see "A Step-by-Step Approach to Market Research," *Business America,* March 16, 1987, pp. 10–11.

21. Province of Alberta, Department of Tourism and Small Business, *Marketing for the Small Manufacturer in Alberta,* January 1980, pp. 14–16.

22. J. Ford Laumer, Jr., et al., *Learning about Your Market,* Management Aids No. 4.019 (Washington, D.C.: Small Business Administration, 1985), pp. 1–5.

CASE V–1
CLEANDRUM, INC. (E)

CASE V–2
MEDICAL SERVICES, INC.

CASE V–3
ANGELO'S SUPERMARKETS

CASE V–1
CLEANDRUM, INC. (E)

When Sue Ley formed CleanDrum, Inc. (CDI), three years ago, the original proposal projected annual sales ranging from 31,000 units in 1987 to 50,000 in 1991. In 1989, sales per month ranged from $2,500 to $3,000. While CDI's sales and financial operations had improved, it had lost money from the beginning. Yet CDI's business plan included a Small Business Development Center survey indicating that there was a market that would support another drum-cleaning company, with 200 firms confirming the need for additional quality service.

Since the start of the company, Sue has spent part of her time on the road selling CDI's service. In 1989, she went from two to three days on the road each week making contact with customers. Although she also makes many phone calls to her clients, these "cannot replace face-to-face contacts." When she goes on the road, she designs her travel, within a 200-mile radius, to minimize travel time and mileage. The 200-mile radius is considered the extent of CDI's market. This area is served by five companies, and market size is estimated to be 13,000 drums a month. Currently, CDI's sales volume places it in the middle of the group. Sue estimates that she has over 100 customers.

On Mondays and Fridays, Sue stays in the office and plant doing the company paperwork and managing the plant. In the three middle days of the week, she is on the road selling and buying drums. Sue estimates that CDI now serves about 50 percent of the companies that originally indicated a need, and she is working on the others. About 75 percent of the sales have come from competitors' customers.

Oil and chemical companies are the major customers. Some call in to alert CDI to their need for its service. For example, one of the major customers calls to say, "We have 100 drums ready to be cleaned, and will have

200 by the end of next week." Several companies order twice a month, and some once every six months.

CDI performs two types of service. First, it buys drums with the intention of processing and selling them. This requires finding, pricing, purchasing, transporting, and selling drums. It owns the drums until sold. Second, it has an ongoing drum exchange, whereby it delivers processed drums and picks up drums to be processed. CDI does not own these drums at any time. Sales are about evenly split between the two types of service.

CDI tries to move drums in full trailer loads to keep transportation costs down. A full trailer holds 267 drums. Sometimes, to fill the trailer, the truck has to make several stops. However, CDI tries to avoid situations where the cost of extra transportation eats up the profits. Sue cited the case of a customer who paid $8 above the going price per drum for 20 drums. Delivery took several hours, which eliminated the profit on the job. Now, CDI will not service orders for fewer than 50 drums unless the customer pays the transportation costs.

Sue has been the only person from CDI to contact customers since she started the company. In the first month of operation, she sold only 500 drums. Recently, she has been selling service on 2,500 to 3,000 drums a month and has her eye on sales of 5,000 per month. In forecasting this sales level, she explains that it's possible for several reasons. First, the number of customers has increased steadily since CDI opened. Second, a competing company recently went bankrupt, and Sue picked up most of its customers. Finally, as will soon be discussed, several customers and sales reps from other, noncompeting companies have "boosted" CDI.

At one time, Edie, part owner of CDI, approached Ben, a member of SCORE, about the problem of CDI losing money. Ben studied what information was available and suggested that the problem could lie in the lack of sales volume. Since then, Edie has been advocating reducing labor costs and hiring someone to sell full time or to supervise the shop so Sue can sell full time. Or, as an alternative, hiring a sales representative to allow Sue to supervise the shop full time. Sue has rejected these suggestions because she felt that the company did not have the money to hire any extra people.

Presently, Sue feels that quality and service are the main selling emphasis. Even though CDI has chosen to compete on these points, however, it must also compete with price cutting by some competitors. Pricing practices vary. Sue has heard reports that one competitor quotes a high price for the purchase of good drums and then finds enough wrong with the drums to drive the purchase price down. It can then sell the processed drums for lower prices.

Sue says she has seen delivered drums, processed by others, that have been carelessly processed, while others have not been pressure tested. Early on, CDI "almost lost a good customer because a part-time worker left some refuse in some drums." (Sue has emphasized to the authors how important the workers' performance is to the company.) Sue also cited a customer that was lost because somebody tampered with some of CDI's delivered drums. She hopes to convince potential customers who are currently buying substandard processing that it is in their best interests to obtain quality service.

Some companies, having received poorly processed used drums, now use only new drums. Sue has approached some of these companies asking for a chance to demonstrate the quality of CDI's delivered drums. Although she has not had much success, she says she plans to continue trying.

A large percentage of the drum-cleaning companies label their drums as to quality. Some users of the service have written standards for the quality of drums they will accept. Satisfied customers are referring other companies to CDI. Sue also has other contacts who have referred potential customers to her. She distributed magnetic calling cards to those who may help sales in some way. CDI is the only listing under "Barrels & Drums— Equipment & Supplies" in the Yellow Pages of the local telephone directory, and this seems to be the only logical category under which to list the company. Sue does not know of any publication in which it would be worthwhile to advertise.

Sue is conscious that sales drop considerably during the period from Thanksgiving to Christmas. This tendency has disconcerted her, since the sales record looks good until the last two months come in.

Questions for Discussion

1. *(a)* What are, or appear to have been, CDI's marketing strategies? *(b)* Comment on them.
2. *(a)* From what alternative sources might additional sales be obtained? *(b)* What alternative means might be used to obtain the extra sales?
3. What methods might be used to obtain information on sources in order to evaluate the potential market?
4. Sue, working part time, is the main contributor to obtaining sales. *(a)* Why is Sue succeeding so well? *(b)* What are the problems with this approach? *(c)* What does the future look like?
5. Prepare a program in each of the following areas that are deserving of study: *(a)* use of current personnel to advance marketing effort, *(b)* hiring personnel to advance marketing effort, *(c)* use of sales promotion, and *(d)* doing market research.
6. What steps do you recommend that CDI take?

Source: Prepared by Charles R. Scott, University of Alabama, and William M. Spain, SCORE.

CASE V–2
MEDICAL SERVICES, INC. (MSI)

Dr. Jane Shea was thoughtfully reviewing her notes after completing a strategy review of the medical practice that she shared with two partners, Dr. Fred Hughes and Dr. John Lehmann. The three physicians, upon completion of their internship at a local hospital in 1983, had purchased a family practice, which they had enlarged by opening a minor emergency clinic. Two years later, the combined practice was barely breaking even. One of the more disappointing aspects was the sparse utilization of the emergency clinic.

Dr. Shea had recently attended a short course entitled "Strategic Planning for Services" at a nearby medium-sized (6,000 students) private university. Now she was trying to apply some of the course concepts to her own professional situation.

Product Offered

The product provided by MSI is the medical services of three doctors of osteopathy (D.O.). These services are provided from a converted house located on a main street in a midwestern city of some 400,000 residents. Two different distribution services are used: a private practice office and a minor emergency clinic.

From these units, MSI offers general health care as well as the following medical specialties: pediatrics, internal medicine, surgery, OB/GYN, emergency medicine, orthopedics, and geriatrics. In addition to these purely medical services, the doctors attempt to provide many convenience services, including: personable physicians with experience in health care for the entire family; office hours that extend past normal business hours; a flexible appointment policy to fit patients' needs; minor emergencies treated at a fraction of the cost of a hospital emergency room; workers' compensation injuries treated; doctors available 24 hours a day for emergency calls; payment by Visa, MasterCard, personal check, or cash; and assistance in filing insurance and medicare claims.

Pricing Schedule

Prices that MSI charges for its services are generally about 17 percent lower than competitors' for a standard office visit ($25 versus $30). Many prices are fixed by the cost of the use of an outside facility, such as one of the local hospitals. (See Exhibit 1 for a list of typical fees.) The doctors use a hospital because it can provide many needed services and the use of equipment less expensively than they can provide it themselves. As they become more prosperous, they plan to buy more of their own equipment. Currently, the doctors have the equipment and facilities to handle about 90 percent of their patients' needs. For the remaining 10 percent, they have made arrangements to use outside services at reasonable rates.

Exhibit 1   Medical Services, Inc., Typical Fees

Office visit	$21.00–25.00
Routine physical examination	25.00
Extended physical examination	30.00 and up, depending on services
Electrocardiogram	25.00
X rays	30.00–45.00, depending on part
Small lacerations	35.00–50.00

Market Situation

The market that MSI targets comprises three segments: on-campus students at the nearby university, townspeople within a two-mile radius of the MSI clinic, and the small businesses within that same radius. Details on each of the market segments are given below.

University Students

The doctors realize that the university's faculty and staff have their own health care service, but that the bulk of the on-campus student population does not. The office and clinic are two blocks from the campus, handy for students without cars and for minor emergencies such as minor athletic injuries, cuts, and burns. The clinic's payment policy is flexible and facilitates insurance collections. This should encourage students to utilize MSI's services, but making them aware of the clinic appears to be a major marketing task.

Townspeople

Realistically, many of a doctor's patients come from referrals and personal contact, and this is true of MSI. In addition to students, there are many older people who live in the vicinity. The close proximity of the clinic is an asset that should encourage the local people to use MSI. There are approximately 23,500 residences in the target market, with a median of 2.1 persons per household. Over 10 percent of these people belong to minority groups; the median age of the target market is over 45, with more than 58 percent over that age; over 17 percent of these are married couples with one or more persons under 18 living in the household; the median educational level of the target market is 12.5 years; and the median income is in the low-middle category. This area's method of payment is generally either Medicare or some form of company insurance. The clinic's policy is to assist in filing insurance and Medicare claims, and the doctors encourage patients to use those methods of payment.

Small Businesses

There are approximately 4,000 small businesses in the target area, and the doctors feel that, with adequate promotion through personal and written contact, this market would be wide open to them. While they hesitate to offer "special deals" on medical services, their business policies and close proximity make the clinic attractive for workers' compensation claims and on-the-job minor emergencies. And, as employees come to the office for those reasons, they will also become accustomed to coming in (and bringing their families) for other medical needs. Service contracts are not now being used for small businesses, but this option is currently being considered.

Competitive Situation

Major competitors for MSI's target market segments include three hospitals; Johnson Clinic, Inc.; Nelson Clinic, Inc.; and Dr. Ashley W. Hull (see Exhibit 2). The three hospitals, all located within two miles of MSI, represent the major threat to its minor-emergency operation, as each of them has far greater capability to handle emergencies than does the clinic. There

Exhibit 2 Location of Competing Services

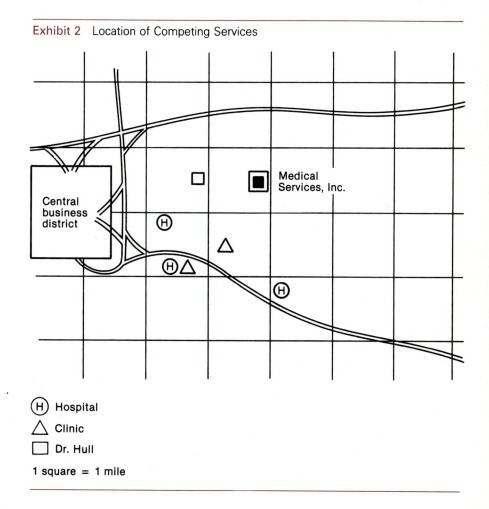

(H) Hospital

△ Clinic

☐ Dr. Hull

1 square = 1 mile

are some negative aspects of the hospitals' emergency care in comparison with MSI, such as cost and customer waiting time: MSI's prices for minor emergencies are substantially lower than those of the hospitals, and, in general, the MSI doctors can treat patients much more promptly than can the typical hospital emergency room.

Johnson Clinic, Inc., specializes in family practice and surgery and is located about a mile and a half southwest of MSI, within two miles of both hospitals. Dr. Kenneth Johnson is a doctor of medicine (as opposed to doctor of osteopathy). The hours of the Johnson Clinic are the normal business hours of 7 A.M. to 4 P.M., Monday through Friday. MSI maintains these hours but also is open late (until 7 P.M.) Monday through Thursday and is open four hours on Saturday. The Nelson Clinic's hours are identical to those of the Johnson Clinic.

Ashley W. Hull, D.O., operates an office within half a mile of MSI. His office hours are 8 A.M. to 5 P.M., Monday through Friday, except that he closes at noon on Thursdays.

While there are several minor emergency clinics and hundreds of doctors (D.O. and M.D.) in the town, these are considered only peripheral competitors because the target markets have been narrowly defined geographically.

Macroenvironmental Factors

Macroenvironmental factors that could impact on MSI include: demographic characteristics and trends, such as population growth, age distribution, urbanization, education, and affluence; and governmental policies intended to reduce health care access inequities.

The city's population growth is slowing. Although it is located in one of the 10 states with the most rapid growth in the 1970s and early 1980s, with annual population increases close to 10 percent, projections are for very slow growth in the next decade. The city's birthrate is also decreasing. The median number of persons per household in the target market is 2.1, down considerably from 10 years ago. This declining population growth will affect the local health care system in many ways. It could, for example, mean that obstetric units will be under pressure to close due to low occupancy, the demand for pediatrics will decline, and there will be less demand for general health services.

The city population, in general, is older than the national average. This has some positive demand effects, as older people tend to need more health care. A growing percentage of the population is over 65 years old; and 58 percent of the target market is over 45 years old. Physician visits are more frequent for older patients (average 7.4 times a year compared to less than 5.0 times a year for patients 17 to 24 years old). Hospital admission rates are also higher for elderly people, and they require longer recuperation and rehabilitation time.

The United States is becoming increasingly urbanized and suburbanized, and city dwellers are more prone to acute respiratory diseases. MSI is located in the central city, but the center of population is 7 or 8 miles to the southeast and moving further out each year.

The United States is also becoming more highly educated, and better-educated people use health care services more than less educated ones. The median educational level in the target market is 12.5 years, which suggests a high level of health care use. Increasing affluence and the reduction (not elimination) of poverty have had a dramatic positive impact on health problems. But affluence creates new health hazards, such as stress-related problems.

With Medicare and Medicaid, health care is increasingly being considered a "right" rather than a "privilege." MSI is located in a low-middle income area, and these insurance methods can be utilized to a great degree.

Exhibit 3 Strategic Situation Analysis

Strengths:
- The doctors' medical education is comprehensive and continually being kept current through postgraduate training in family medicine at the local osteopathic hospital.
- Extended hours at the clinic offer more convenience for patients.
- The doctors inherited many of the files and patients of the previous physicians.
- There are several methods of payment available for patient convenience.
- Patient cost is low in relation to alternative sources of health care.
- The image of osteopathic doctors is better than in the past.

Weaknesses:
- The clinic has a weak history in promoting its services, and there is no advertising budget.
- While there is potential for financial success, currently the clinic is struggling due to lack of patients.
- Management's (the doctors') general business and marketing background is limited.
- The street sign, while informative, is not eyecatching and the grey building is easy to miss while driving by.
- Doctors of osteopathy must continually fight inherited image problems.
- The doctors are young and relatively inexperienced.
- There is little money for advertising and promotion.

Opportunities:
- The on-campus students at the university can be considered a "built-in" market.
- The many small and medium-sized businesses in the area potentially can use a nearby medical facility for low-cost minor emergency care with workers' compensation insurance capabilities.
- There are few competitors in the target area; so market potential should be good.

Threats:
- The target markets are unproven and may be more limited in size than previously estimated.
- Within a mile outside the targeted area, the number of competitors drastically increases. Associated with the hospitals are physicians' buildings, each containing dozens of doctors.

Strategic Situation Analysis

In the planning course Dr. Shea attended, the concept of a strategic situation (SWOT) analysis was introduced and discussed. As she looked over her notes on the product, market, and pricing situation, and on the competitive situation and macroenvironmental factors, Dr. Shea was aware that one of the missing factors was specific information on how patients choose a specific doctor or clinic. In general, she knew that people decide on a specific doctor either on the advice or recommendation of family or friends, from work relationships, by hospital reference, or by reference through another doctor.

It had been a long day. Dr. Shea was the physician on call at the clinic, and this review of the competitive environment was perplexing. She and her two partners needed to devise a strategy for increasing the utilization of the private practice office and the emergency clinic. She decided to review the strategic situation analysis according to the format developed in the short course (see Exhibit 3).

Questions for Discussion

1. What do you believe are the real problems and opportunities facing MSI?
2. (*a*) What is the "product" that MSI is offering? (*b*) Explain.
3. How should MSI prioritize its possible target markets?
4. What would be an appropriate statement of promotional objectives for MSI?
5. Given the target markets and promotional objectives for MSI, what media will best contribute to their success?

Source: Prepared by James W. Cagley and Lester A. Neidell, University of Tulsa. This case was made possible by the cooperation of a medical service that wishes to remain anonymous. Copyright © 1986 by James Cagley and Lester Neidell.

CASE V–3

ANGELO'S SUPERMARKETS

For Sam Angelo, Jr. (Sammy), tomorrow's meeting with his father, Sam, Sr., promised nothing but unpleasantness. During the past year, most meetings of the "management team" of Angelo's Supermarkets had been unpleasant for Sam, Jr., because he and his father had openly disagreed about every store policy that had come up for discussion during the weekly business meetings attended by all store managers, the advertising specialist, the controller, Sammy, and Sam Angelo, Sr. Sammy wondered whether he should simply resign as manager of the east-end store now rather than struggle with evaluating the data spread out before him on his desk. As usual, he had only limited information and very little time within which to make a recommendation, even though the decision to be made tomorrow on adding private brands to normal shelf stock was a very important decision with long-run competitive consequences.

Background

Sam Angelo, Sr., began his career in the food industry in 1927 with two grocery stores that had been liquidated through involuntary bankruptcy procedures. Since that time, Angelo's Supermarkets has enjoyed phenomenal growth and prosperity. According to Sam Angelo, Sr., the success of his supermarkets could be summed up in three words: convenience, service, and national brands. Angelo's Supermarkets has also been an outstanding member of a well-known national franchise for supermarkets since 1932. In addition, Sam, Sr., has been a prominent member of the community, contributing generously to local charitable organizations, serving on the board of a local bank, participating in many local activities and clubs, and donating free food to a local church-sponsored nursery school for disadvantaged children.

Angelo's Supermarkets is a member of one of four major chains. The competitive position of the four supermarket chains as of last year is shown in Exhibit 1.

In the past five years, competitive strategies and market shares for the four chain-store groups have been somewhat stable. For instance, Colonial Food Stores has consistently featured a low-price theme in its weekly newspaper ads. The state chain, Big Bear Grocery Marts, stocks a distinct product mix in that unusual items and brands can often be found within any product category. Big Bear Grocery Marts also offers more convenience foods and prepared foods than the other chain stores. One of the Big Bear stores has a complete in-store bakery. Both Angelo's Supermarkets and Old South Super Savers have the best store locations in the area. Both regularly advertise more food specials than either of the other two chains. However, Old South Super Savers allocates a lot of advertising space to its private brands, whereas Angelo's Supermarkets normally features several well-known national brands as "loss leaders" in a single ad. Moreover, Sam Angelo, Sr., is an avid believer in the "psychological" aspects of loss leader selection,

---

Exhibit 1 Chain Store Market Shares, Dixie Town, USA

Chain	Number of stores	Percentage of sales
Angelo's Supermarkets	5	34.2
Old South Super Savers (regional chain/local franchise)	4	25.6
Colonial Food Stores (national chain)	3	24.1
Big Bear Grocery Marts (state chain)	2	16.1
		100.0

Exhibit 2   Sales Revenue by Supermarket or Chain-Store Groups

	Sales revenue
Angelo's Supermarkets	$15,000,000
Old South Super Savers	11,300,000
Colonial Food Stores	10,600,000
Big Bear Grocery Marts	7,100,000
Warehouse Grocery	6,000,000
Disco Food	8,000,000
Total	$58,000,000

frequently selecting items such as sugar or soft drinks as loss leaders for the week.

Dixie Town is considered by the industry to be very competitive for its size with respect to food stores. The population of Dixie Town is 125,000; yet, in addition to the 14 supermarkets affiliated with one of the four chain-store groups, a warehouse grocery and a discount food store are present. Sales revenue by supermarket or chain-store groups is shown in Exhibit 2.

Recent Events

About six months ago, Sam, Sr. announced to the "management team" of Angelo's Supermarkets that the national franchise association had requested cooperation from its members with regard to distributing a major line of private brands that would be identified with the franchise trademark. Distribution was not mandatory, but each group of stores under one ownership was expected to make a decision about stocking the private brands for a minimum period of five years. Furthermore, the decision had to be made for the entire group.

At the time of the announcement, Sam, Sr., expressed an adverse reaction to the idea of private brands. In his opinion, private brands were not quality products and therefore not suitable for the clientele of Angelo's Supermarkets. In his words, "both Colonial and Old South Super Savers already offer private brands. If our customers wanted private brands, they would shop there!" Sam, Jr., counterargued by pointing out that rising food prices had "changed the picture" and that private brands were gaining in popularity as consumers at all income levels sought to maintain purchasing power. At this point, the controller quietly asked Sam, Sr., about the general price level and gross margin for the proposed line of private brands relative to national brands. Sam, Sr., replied that it was his understanding that the new line of private brands would be priced 10 percent less than national brands of comparable quality. The gross margin on the new line would be anywhere from 20 to 30 percent, compared to 17 to 21 percent for national brands.

The manager of the northeast store expressed concern about the space requirements since his store had a chronic crowding problem. Sam, Sr., agreed that the space problem was "a very serious drawback to stocking the new line because it would require approximately 10 percent of each store's shelf capacity." Sammy angrily protested, stating that "space is not important if the products are well received by our customers. What we need is a consumer survey. No good decision can be made without some insights into customer preferences."

At the request of several members of the management team, Sam, Sr., agreed to delay the decision for six months. During that time, each member of the management team was to prepare a comprehensive recommendation and analysis relative to stocking the proposed line of private brands. For the meeting, Sammy Angelo has collected the two memoranda and the survey responses shown in Exhibits 3, 4, and 5.

Exhibit 3

Memorandum

From: Sammy Angelo
To: Ray Becken, Advertising Specialist
Subject: Consumer survey

The data attached to this memo [Exhibit 4] should be of interest to you. Most of the data come from that consumer survey idea I mentioned in a management team meeting we had several months ago. I feel reasonably comfortable about the survey. It was designed and carried out by a marketing research class at the university here. The sample size (500) seems adequate, and the students who did the work tell me the sample is representative of the area. Since only food shoppers who bought most of their groceries at one of the four chain store groups in town were interviewed, all 500 food shoppers in this survey shop either at one of our stores or at one of our competitors' stores.

The questionnaire used in the survey had questions which provide information about several issues of immediate interest to us in making this difficult decision about the proposed line of private brands.

1. Customer loyalty.
2. Patronage motive. Shoppers were asked for the most important reason they go to the store where they buy most of their groceries.
3. Price knowledge. Food shoppers were scored on their confidence and ability to judge whether each of 32 commonly purchased food items had a reduced or regular price. Half of the 32 items were listed at a reduced price. A separate list of the same products was prepared for each chain so that regular and reduced prices on the list reflect the actual prices charged at that chain. High scores indicate high price knowledge.
4. Opinion about the following strategies for reducing expenditures on food:
   Buying larger sizes of items.
   Buying advertised specials.
   Buying private brands.
   Purchasing cheap cuts of meat.

In addition to the consumer survey, I personally established a 50-item market basket cost for each chain store group. Prices for both a designated national brand and the lowest brand (if available) for each item specification in the market basket were obtained. As you can see from column 4 in Exhibit 3, Angelo's Supermarkets is the most expensive store in town!

Exhibit 4

A. Responses to Survey of Patronage, Price Knowledge, and Cost

#1. Percentage distribution of the supermarket chains patronized.
(Food shoppers named the supermarket at which they bought most of their groceries during the previous month.)

#2. Customers' responses as to whether they bought groceries from more than one chain or supermarket during the preceding month.
(Customers of Angelo's who shop at other stores shop at Old South Super Savers [50%], Colonial [40%], and other miscellaneous stores [20%].)

#3. Price knowledge for chain store customers.

#4. Market basket for national and low-cost brands by chain store group.

Supermarket	(1) Percent	(2) Percent Yes	No	(3) Price knowledge score	(4) National brand	Lowest cost brand
Colonial Food Stores	27.0%	45.9%	54.1%	105.0	$31.90	$29.46
Big Bear Grocery Marts	13.3	73.3	26.7	95.0	32.06	29.46
Angelo's Supermarkets	30.5	52.2	47.8	100.0	32.81	31.41
Old South Super Savers	29.2	50.0	50.0	101.0	31.52	28.31
Number of respondents	500.0	265.0	235.0			

B. Responses on Patronage Motives and Economy Opinions

#1. Primary patronage motives for supermarket most often patronized.

#2. Shopper opinion about the most economical food shopping strategy.

	Percentage distribution for supermarket patronized			
	Colonial	Big Bear	Angelo's	Old South
#1 Primary patronage motives:				
Convenient location	34.4	43.3	39.4	45.5
General price level	42.6	20.0	10.1	21.2
Selection of products/brands	11.5	20.0	13.0	16.7
Advertised specials	0.0	10.0	8.7	1.5
Friendly personnel	4.9	6.7	10.1	4.5
Food stamp redemption	0.0	0.0	1.4	0.0
Trading stamps	0.0	0.0	4.3	3.0
Appearance or atmosphere	3.3	0.0	8.7	1.5
Services offered	0.0	0.0	1.4	0.0
Other	3.3	0.0	2.9	6.1
#2 Strategies:				
Buying larger sizes	44.0	19.0	20.0	14.0
Buying advertised food specials	12.0	29.0	28.0	51.0
Buying private brands	40.0	30.0	32.0	35.0
Purchasing cheap cuts of meat	4.0	22.0	20.0	0.0

Exhibit 5

Memorandum

From: Jack Randall, Controller
To: Sammy Angelo
Subject: Proposed line of private brands

I called Ed Davis at the regional office yesterday to ask a few questions that came up in a recent discussion between you, Ray, and me about the proposed line of private brands. In his opinion, private brands do not attract customers from other stores, except perhaps through advertising. He also said that we could expect sales of the proposed line of private brands to be anywhere from 2 percent to 15 percent of our total sales revenue (7 percent is "average"). Since customers tend to substitute a private brand for a national brand, we could expect our anticipated sales revenue of $20,000,000 for next year to be somewhat less should we decide to stock the new line.

Questions for Discussion

1. Evaluate Sammy's approach to the market survey.
2. (*a*) Would a survey of this sort be feasible for smaller grocery companies? (*b*) Explain.
3. (*a*) Does the addition of the private brands appear to fit Angelo's marketing and management strategies? (*b*) Explain.
4. (*a*) Would the addition of the private brands be profitable? (*b*) Show your analysis.
5. (*a*) What other factors should be considered? (*b*) Explain.
6. (*a*) Should Sammy Angelo recommend stocking the line of private brands? (*b*) How would you present this to the management team?

Source: Prepared by J. B. Wilkinson, Youngstown State University, and J. Barry Mason, University of Alabama.

VI

FINANCIAL PLANNING AND CONTROL

As we have shown throughout this text, a small business is no stronger than its financial strength and vitality. Today, the greatest requirements for success in small business include an appreciation of the importance of financial management; an understanding of how financial relationships affect profit or loss; and the devotion of time, energy, and initiative to these goals. The rewards justify the effort, though, as such planning ensures that the firm not only will survive but also will grow and develop.

Chapter 18 explains the need for and methods of planning for a profit, guiding you through the steps of planning the profit for a hypothetical company. It also covers the basic financial structure of a business.

Chapter 19 explores the basic structure of control. Then it shows the methods of collecting information and comparing actual performance with standard performance. The design and use of budgets and budgetary control are also covered, along with the use of ratio analysis.

Chapter 20 discusses developing the management information system needed for decision making. It covers the importance of storing information, what information is needed, and how to record information. It also deals with the use of computers in small firms.

18

PLANNING FOR PROFIT

Never mind the business outlook; be on the outlook for business.—Anonymous

Earning a profit—staying in business—is still the No. 1 thing. Unless you can make money, you cannot do any of the other things.—Irving Shapiro, on his retirement as chairman of Du Pont

LEARNING OBJECTIVES

After studying the material in this chapter, you will be able to:

1. Explain the need for profit planning for a small business.
2. Discuss what causes changes in the financial position of a company.
3. Understand the financial structure of a business.
4. Explain how a firm's revenues and expenses interact to affect profits.
5. Understand how to plan to make a profit.
6. Plan for a profit for an actual small business.

AVIAN CORPORATION: GETTING OFF THE GROUND

Avian Corporation of St. Petersburg, Florida, seemed to be succeeding in doing what Hertz Rent A Plane and other defunct plane rental businesses had failed to do. It focused almost exclusively on renting and selling planes rather than on providing a wide variety of services to licensed pilots. The company was poised to become the first nationwide aircraft rental business in more than a decade.

Avian was founded in 1982 with $500,000 put up by Bruce J. Micek, Robert H. Rogers, and Timothy C. Bryant and $4 million contributed by others with limited partnership status. The three partners brought to the business a variety of experience. Micek, Avian's president, flew his first plane at the age of seven and opened an aviation sales business in 1979. Rogers, chairman of the company, spent more than 15 years as a marketing executive in the computer industry, then formed his own company as an Apple

manufacturer's representative. Micek taught him to fly so he could cover his territory more quickly, and the two entrepreneurs eventually combined their aviation and computer expertise to form Avian. The third partner, Bryant, is the company's chief financial officer.

Avian's market consisted of the 700,000-plus active licensed pilots in the United States, more than 35 percent of them business users. The recent rental rate was $47 or $58 an hour, depending on the type of plane. The partners planned to phase out their sales activities by 1990, when they expected to have, nationwide, 1,400 planes flying an average of three hours a day at an average rate of $57 an hour. Micek estimated that the predicted volume would result in a 12 percent pretax profit margin.

In 1985, Avian completed its third round of financing, raising $5 million to increase its fleet from 39 to 85 single-engine planes. The planes

(From left to right) Timothy Bryant, Bruce Micek, and Robert Rogers, photographed in front of Avian, at St Petersburg/Clearwater, with a Piper Archer II.
Source: Courtesy of R & B Company.

were then to be sold to a trust or limited partnership and leased back to Avian. The reason for this arrangement, according to Micek, is that "buying planes outright would require a very strong financial sheet and would tie up too much cash." The company planned to make an initial public offering in early 1986 to raise money to buy its own planes and expand into California and the Midwest.

It did not make it. According to the *Tampa Bay Business Journal,* the "company died because it had to grow to stay alive." Apparently, the failure resulted from the repeal of the investment tax credit. Potential investors in the "third round of financing" balked at investing without the tax credit, and that spelled the end of Avian.

In early 1987, the R & B Company attempted to rebuild Avian as a more traditional, fixed-base operation. It stressed the same attention to quality service its predecessors found so appealing to customers. According to William R. Frank, of R & B, "we have not given up on the concept, but we envision a modified approach and ultimate success."

R & B didn't make it! It was out of business by 1989.

Source: Tricia Welsh, "Trying to Make Air Rentals Fly," *Venture,* October 1985, p. 106; correspondence with R & B Company.

As the partners of Avian Corporation and R & B Company discovered, profit cannot be left to chance in small firms. Yet, all too frequently, it is! Even when efforts *are* made to plan for profit, they are often inadequate, for planners tend to assume that historical relationships are fixed and therefore past profits will be repeated in the future. Instead, small business managers must learn to identify all income and costs if a small business is to make a profit. Therefore, each item must be realistically priced, as shown in Chapter 15, and each cost should be accurately computed.

NEED FOR PROFIT PLANNING

To ensure profit, your price must cover all costs and include a markup for planned profit. This chapter will help you determine how much profit you want and show you how to plan to achieve it. The material will also help you learn how to set up an accounting system for your firm and how to read, evaluate, and interpret its accounting and financial figures. Another purpose of this chapter is to serve as a guide in evaluating, or estimating, your firm's financial position. This is not always easy, as the following example shows.

The owner of a compounding company was quite satisfied with the profitability of one of his products. For years, his pricing policy had been to add a 67 percent markup to raw material costs in order to set the selling price. When an outside consultant questioned the validity of this practice, the owner became quite defensive.

A thorough operating-cost analysis was made of that particular product. While raw material costs were $1 per pound and the selling price was $1.68, the total cost of the product, including labor, overhead, and other expenses, was $1.83. While he was really losing 15 cents on each item, he still resisted changing his pricing practice.

This lack of accurate cost information, a recurring problem among small business owners, usually results in profits of unknown quantity—or even a loss. Also, it can foster the illusion of making a greater profit than is really earned—even if one is earned.

The owner of Children's Party Caterer (name disguised) illustrated this point. During the first interview with a small business professor, she said she had "around $400 worth of party materials" in her pantry at home. But, when asked the cost of materials used, or the time involved in preparing for each party, she was vague. The adviser gave her a "homework assignment" to determine the time she spent preparing for and giving each party, and the cost of materials. She was surprised to find she spent around 18 to 20 hours per party, and the cost of materials ranged from $20 to $25. Also, she hadn't included the cost of transportation or the $5 to $6 baby-sitting cost for her two children. Yet she charged only about $20 to $25 for each party.

To the suggestion that she raise her prices to cover these costs, plus a markup for profit, she responded, "People won't pay it." When the adviser replied, "You aren't in the charity business," her exuberant reply was, "Oh, but I enjoy doing it!"

HOW A BUSINESS'S FINANCIAL POSITION CHANGES

The operations of a small business result from decisions made by its owner and managers and the many activities they perform. As decisions are made and operations occur, the firm's financial position constantly changes. Cash received for sales increases the bank balance; sales on credit increase accounts receivable; purchases of material, while increasing inventory, also increase accounts payable or decrease the bank balance. At the same time, machines decrease in value, goods are processed by employees, and utilities are used. Consequently, as the financial position of the business is constantly changing, those changes should be recorded and analyzed, as the following example shows.

The Comprehensive Accounting Corporation (CAC), a nationwide franchised firm specializing in providing accounting services to small firms, warns clients that "tracking month-to-month and year-to-year performance is essential" if they are to survive. Keeping tabs on a firm's health involves maintaining good records, computing results each month, and analyzing these results to see if problems are developing. Such simple analysis can disclose valuable information. For instance, a slight monthly increase in costs may not be so alarming—until it is realized that those costs must be multiplied 12-fold.[1]

How the Financial Position Changes

Throughout its operations, the important question is whether the business is improving its chances of reaching its primary objective, which is to make a profit. However, some small firms make a profit and still fail, since profits are not necessarily cash. Accounts receivable may reflect profits, but many of those accounts may not be collectible. Too much money may be tied up in other assets and not available to pay bills as they come due. In other words, focusing *only* on net income may be foolhardy,[2] unless other variables are also considered. The "bottom line" is *not* an end in itself, but it is the beginning of the more difficult process of tracking cash flow. (See Chapter 19 for more details.)

You may have—or have had—similar problems with your personal finances. Your allowance, earnings, and/or other income may be adequate to pay for food, clothing, and other operating expenses. However, you may need to make some extraordinary purchase, such as to replace a worn-out car, for which you must make a down payment in the form of cash. If your funds are invested in a fixed asset, such as a mortgage on your house, they are not available for paying bills. The same is true of a small business. In fact, as the Computer Update indicates, a small business can use computer programs designed to handle personal finances.

Importance of Accounting

Accounting is quite important in achieving success in any business, especially a small one. Therefore, your accounting records must accurately reflect the changes occurring in the firm's assets, liabilities, income, expenses, and equity. You need to see that the interrelationships among these accounts remain satisfactory. For example, what amount of cash reduces the income-producing possibilities? An increased investment in building and equipment reduces the company's ability to pay operating expenses. Increases in liabilities raise its obligations and monthly payments.

The continued operation of a business also depends—as Irving Shapiro pointed out in the opening quotation—on maintaining the proper balance among its investments, revenues, expenses, and profit. As profit margins are so critical, any decline in them should trigger a search for the cause.

Aubrey D. Boutwell, a certified public accountant (CPA), calls what usually happens in small firms "management by ignorance," for small business owners "don't realize their business is in trouble until it's too late."[3] Many businesses fail without their owners knowing what their problem is—or

COMPUTER UPDATE

USING PERSONAL FINANCE PROGRAMS TO RUN SMALL FIRMS

The computer software market currently offers a plethora of programs designed to handle personal finances. Now many small businesses are finding that they serve equally well for business accounting on a small scale. The personal, user-friendly, but sophisticated software allows small business owners to keep track of the separate accounting for personal and business finances. At least three of these programs—*Financial Navigator,* from MoneyCare Inc.; *Quicken,* from Intuit; and *The Smart Checkbook,* from Softquest Inc.— are quite effective in small firms.

even that they have problems. All they know is that they end up with no money and cannot pay their bills.

Another CPA, Timothy O'Donnell, calls these small business owners "seat-of-the-pants operators" because they fail to monitor all aspects of their businesses. They often consider financial statements "a necessary evil" and think everything is fine as long as sales are increasing and there is money in the bank. "They don't realize [that] what they do in their businesses is reflected in the financial statements. They tend not to pay much attention to the information accountants give them."[4] One young entrepreneur found this out the hard way.

"See no evil, hear no evil, speak no evil . . . I like that in an accountant, Mr. Farouche."
Source: *Management Accounting,* January 1988, p. 13.

For Richard Huttner, the hardest problem in running New York's Parenting Unlimited Inc. was doing the accounting necessary in running its new acquisition, *Baby Talk* magazine. Although *Baby Talk* had revenues of several million dollars a year, it had no financial management, accounting system, general ledger, or bank account when it was acquired. Consequently, while trying to master an ongoing business, Huttner had to spend nearly a third of his time the first three months paying bills and doing accounting. He lamented, "Stanford didn't teach me how long it takes out-of-state checks to clear. We had constant cash flow problems at first because of this."[5]

In discussing financial management in this chapter, we have used a real small business, which we have disguised as The Model Company, to illustrate the concepts. Assume throughout the following discussion that, while the company is owned by Mr. Model, you manage it for him. Therefore, you must make the decisions called for.

FINANCIAL STRUCTURE OF A BUSINESS

The assets, liabilities, and equity of a business are reflected in its financial structure. These accounts, which are interrelated and interact with each other, represent the **financial structure** of a firm, but they change from one period to the next. At regular intervals, a **balance sheet** is prepared to show the value of the business and how its funds are distributed. See Figure 18–1 for the arrangement and amounts of the accounts for our hypothetical business, The Model Company.

Assets

Assets, which are the physical, financial, or other values that a company has, are divided into current and fixed assets.

Current Assets
Current assets are expected to turn over—that is, to change from one form to another—within a year. For example, it is expected that accounts receivable will be paid and converted into cash within a year, while other accounts receivable are being generated.

Cash includes the currency (bills and coins) in the firm's cash registers, the deposits in a checking account, and other non-interest-bearing values that can be converted into cash immediately.

A certain level of cash is necessary to operate a business. However, since cash does not produce income, holding too much of it reduces the income-producing capacity of a business. (This is rather like stuffing your money under a mattress instead of putting it in a savings account.) Therefore,

Figure 18–1

THE MODEL COMPANY
Balance Sheet
December 31, 19—

Assets

Current assets:

Cash	$ 7,054	
Accounts receivable	60,484	
Inventory	80,042	
Prepaid expenses	1,046	
Total current assets		$148,626

Fixed assets:

Equipment	$100,500		
Building.......................................	40,950		
Gross fixed assets		141,450	
Less: accumulated depreciation		16,900	
Net fixed assets			124,550
Total assets			$273,176

Liabilities and Owners' Equity

Current liabilities:

Accounts payable	51,348	
Accrued payables	3,060	
Total current liabilities	$ 54,408	

Long-term liabilities:

Mortgage payable	20,708	
Total liabilities		$ 75,116

Owners' equity:

Capital stock	160,000	
Retained earnings	38,060	
Total equity		198,060
Total liabilities and owners' equity		$273,176

---

while a certain level of cash must be kept, try to keep it at as low a level as is feasible. The question is, what *is* that level?

Alan Goldstein, a partner in Touche Ross & Company's Enterprise Group in Boston, which helps small firms decide how much cash is needed, indicates that small companies are prone to have empty checking accounts creep up on them because they operate on such a thin cushion of cash. He answers the question: "When do everyday nuisances turn into disaster?" by saying: "When you're about to run out of cash."[6]

Accounts receivable result from giving credit to customers, as shown in Chapter 15. While a small company may sell on credit, which helps it maintain a higher level of sales, care must be taken to select customers who will pay within a reasonable length of time. Since credit is a cost to the business, too large an investment in accounts receivable places the firm under considerable strain. Such investments require heavy financial resources and increase the chance of incurring high bad-debt losses.

Inventory provides a buffer between purchase, production, and sales of products (as discussed in Chapter 14). Thus, a business must maintain some level of inventory in order to serve customers. But carrying inventory results in high costs, such as money being tied up, space being used, and products being maintained and/or becoming obsolete or damaged. As a high level of inventory places a financial burden on the small firm because it is *not* an income-producing asset, the amount of inventory to carry depends upon a judicious balancing of income and costs.

Other current asset accounts often carried are called *short-term investment, prepaid items,* and *accrued income.* Usually, these make up only a small percentage of the current assets of a small business and need little attention.

Fixed Assets

Items such as buildings, machinery, store fixtures, trucks, and land, which a business expects to own for a considerable time, are included among its **fixed assets.** Part of their cost is written off each period as depreciation expense.

Different types of fixed assets have different lengths of useful life, as will be seen in Chapter 23. The amount of fixed assets should be related to the needs of the business, and idle fixed assets, a financial drain, should be avoided when possible.

As was shown in Chapter 8, some small firms find it desirable to lease fixed assets instead of owning them. For example, a retailer may rent a store to reduce the need to make a large investment in it, as will be shown in the Opening Focus for Chapter 22. Whether a business decides to rent or own fixed assets will depend on factors such as (1) the availability of rental facilities, (2) the cost of renting as compared to the cost of owning, (3) the availability of capital, and (4) the freedom to operate the business.

Liabilities

A business can obtain funds by owner investment and by borrowing (creating an obligation to pay). The first—which is necessary—is the owners' equity, or the residual ownership of the business. The second results in a liability of the business to pay the funds—plus interest—back to the lender. *The total of liabilities plus owners' equity always equals the total assets of the business.* Prudent small business owners try to maintain a proper balance between the higher risk of borrowing and the limited amount of capital that can be obtained from owners. Borrowing from creditors is divided into current and long-term liabilities.

Current Liabilities

Obligations to be paid within a year are **current liabilities.** They include accounts payable, notes payable, and accrued items (such as payroll), which are for services performed for you but not yet paid for.

Accounts payable are obligations to pay for goods and services purchased, and are usually due within 30 or 60 days, depending on the credit terms. Since any business—especially a small one—should maintain current assets sufficient to pay these accounts, maintaining a high level of accounts payable requires a high level of current assets. Frequent evaluations should be made to determine whether or not early payment is beneficial. Some sellers offer a cash discount for early payment, such as 1 or 2 percent if bills are paid within 10 days, which is a good return on your money if paid within that period.

Notes payable, which are written obligations to pay, usually give the business a longer time than accounts payable before payment is due. An example is a 90-day note.

Long-Term Liabilities

Bonds and mortgages are the usual types of **long-term liabilities,** which have terms of more than a year. A business usually incurs long-term liabilities by purchasing fixed assets. Long-term loans may be used to supply a reasonable amount of **working capital,** which is current assets less current liabilities. This type of borrowing requires regular payment of a fixed amount on the principal, plus interest. The need to make these payments during slack times increases the risk of being unable to meet other obligations. Therefore, small firms use long-term borrowing as a source of funds much less frequently than large ones do.

Owners' Equity

Owners' equity is the owners' share of (or net worth in) the business, after liabilities are subtracted from assets. The owners receive income from profits in the form of dividends or an increase in their share of the company through an increase in retained earnings. The owners also absorb losses, which decrease their equity. (See Chapters 8 and 23 for further details.)

Capital stock is the value the owners invest in a corporation (see Chapter 8 for details). A share of stock, issued in the form of a certificate, has a stated value on the firm's books. Additional shares can be sold or issued in place of cash dividends.

When stock prices are rising, many small firms elect to **go public** by selling common stock, thereby increasing their equity. The funds thus obtained are often used as capital to fund growth in sales and/or production, or to retire outstanding debt—which reduces fixed-interest costs. These actions can result in more favorable financial statements.

Retained earnings are the profits not distributed to the owners as cash dividends. Most firms retain some of the profits to use in times of need, or to provide for growth. Many small firms have failed because the owners paid out too much of the profits as **cash dividends,** thereby reducing current assets. Definite policies should be set up as to what part of your earnings should be retained and what part distributed as dividends.

PROFIT-MAKING ACTIVITIES OF A BUSINESS

The profit-making activities of a business determine its financial structure. These activities are reflected in the revenue and expense accounts, as shown by the formula:

$$\text{Net income (profit)} = \text{Revenue} - \text{Expenses (costs)}$$

During a given period, the business performs services for which it receives revenues. It also incurs expenses for services performed for it by others. These revenues and expenses are shown in the **income statement,** sometimes called the **profit and loss statement** (see Figure 18–2).

Revenue and Expenses

Revenue, also called **sales income,** is the return from services performed or goods sold. The business receives revenue in the form of cash or credit—resulting in accounts receivable. Many companies also have other forms

Figure 18–2

THE MODEL COMPANY
Income Statement
January 1 through December 31, 19—

Net sales	$463,148	
Less: Cost of goods sold	291,262	
Gross income		$171,886
Operating expenses:		
Salaries	$ 83,138	
Utilities	6,950	
Depreciation	10,050	
Rent	2,000	
Building services	4,920	
Insurance	4,000	
Interest	2,646	
Office and supplies	6,550	
Sales promotion	11,000	
Taxes and licenses	6,480	
Maintenance	1,610	
Delivery	5,848	
Miscellaneous	1,750	
Total expenses		146,942
Net income before taxes		24,944
Less: Income taxes		5,484
Net income after taxes		$19,460

of income, such as interest from investments, or rent from unused land or buildings.

Expenses, the costs of paying people to perform services for you (or selling goods to you), include such items as materials, wages, insurance, utilities, transportation, depreciation, taxes, supplies, and advertising and sales promotion. As these obligations are incurred, they become deductions from revenue.

Profit

Profit, also called **income,** is the difference between total revenues received and total expenses paid. Depending on the type of expenses deducted, profit may be called *gross profit, operating profit, net income before taxes,* or *net income after taxes.*

The values of the above items are related to each other and to the financial structure of the business. Changes in sales income require changes in costs—mainly in variable costs, though even fixed costs must be increased at intervals, especially if facilities require updating or expanding.

As your profit margins indicate the relationship between revenues and expenses, a decline in them should trigger a search for the cause. The problem could be a rise in expenses, a per-unit sales revenue decline caused by discounting or pricing errors, or changing the basic operations of the business, as the following example shows.

Pak Malwani, a native of Bombay, India, was an expert in mail-order merchandising when, in 1982, he launched a chain of retail stores specializing in moderately priced imported clothes. His company, Royal Silk Ltd., of Clifton, New Jersey, founded in 1978, had reached a sales level of $42 million by 1988.

But Malwani made a classical mistake: while retailing seemed to be a natural extension of the mail-order business, in fact, the personnel requirements, inventory control, and marketing practices of the two businesses were quite different. Malwani soon found himself focusing almost exclusively on the money-losing retail stores while the mail-order business slipped from a position of profitability in 1987 to a $560,000 loss in 1988. In December 1988, Royal Silk filed for Chapter 11 bankruptcy, listing $14.7 million in liabilities and only $4.8 million in assets.[7]

HOW TO PLAN FOR PROFIT

According to a Dun & Bradstreet report, a well-managed small business has at least the following characteristics:[8]

- It is more liquid than a badly managed company.
- The balance sheet is as important to the owner(s) as the income statement.
- Stability is emphasized instead of rapid growth.
- Long-range planning is important.

Need for Profit Planning

As you study the income statement in Figure 18–2, you may interpret it as saying: "The Model Company received $463,148 in sales, expended $291,262 for costs of goods sold, had $146,942 in other expenses, and had $24,944 left over as profit." Under this interpretation, profit is a "leftover," not a planned amount. Neither you nor Mr. Model can do anything about the past, but you *can* do something about future operations. Since one of your goals is to make a profit, you should plan the operations now in order to achieve your desired profit goal.

Steps in Profit Planning

To achieve your goal during the coming year, you need to take the following steps:

1. Establish a profit goal.
2. Determine the volume of sales needed to make that profit.
3. Estimate the expenses needed to reach that volume of sales.
4. Determine estimated profit, based on plans resulting from Steps 2 and 3.
5. Compare the estimated profit with the profit goal. If you are satisfied with the plans, you can stop at this point.

However, you may want to check further to determine whether improvements can be made—particularly if you are not happy with the results of Step 5. Doing Steps 6 through 10 may help you to understand better how changing some of your operations can affect profit.

6. List some possible alternatives that can be used to improve profit.
7. Determine how costs vary with changes in sales volume.
8. Determine how profits vary with changes in sales volume.
9. Analyze your alternatives, from a profit standpoint.
10. Select an alternative and implement the plans.

Need for Realism in Profit Planning

Be realistic when going through these steps. Otherwise, you may be unable to reach the desired profit goal. You may feel the future is too uncertain to make such plans, but *the greater the uncertainty, the greater the need for planning.*

For example, the president of a small firm said that his forecasts were too inaccurate to be of any help in planning operations, so he had stopped forecasting. His business was so unsuccessful that he had to sell out.

The owner of another small business recently complained that she can't forecast the next year's revenue within 20 percent of actual sales. However, she continues to forecast and plan, for she says she needs plans from which to deviate as conditions change.

"You didn't consider our paper profits real—why do you consider our paper losses real?"
Source: Reprinted from *The Wall Street Journal;* permission Cartoon Features Syndicate.

PROFIT PLANNING APPLIED IN A TYPICAL SMALL BUSINESS

This section uses the above steps to plan profits for The Model Company. As manager, you must start planning for the coming year several months in advance so you can put your plans into effect at the proper time. In order to present a systematic analysis, assume that you are planning for the company for the first time. (Actually, you should be planning for each month at least six months or a year ahead. This can be done by dropping the past month, adjusting the rest of the months in your prior plans, and adding the plans for another month. Such planning gives you time to anticipate needed changes and do something about them.)

Step 1: Establish the Profit Goal

Your desired profit must be a specific target value. To begin, decide what you want to pay yourself. Since you manage the business, pay yourself a reasonable salary. Also, Mr. Model should receive a return on his investment—not only his initial investment, but also any earnings left in the business—for taking the risks of ownership.

To determine the desired profit, compare what you would receive as salary for working for someone else, plus the income Mr. Model would receive if the same amount of money were placed in a relatively safe investment, such as certificates of deposit (CDs), U.S. government bonds, or high-grade stocks. Each of these investments provides a return with a certain degree of risk—and pleasure. If Mr. Model could invest the same amount of money at an 8 percent return with little risk, what do you think the return on his investment in The Model Company should be?

Mr. Model originally invested $160,000 in the company, and has since left about $40,000 of his profits in the business. He made about 10 percent on his investment this past year, which he thinks is too low for the risk he is taking; he feels that about a 20 percent return is reasonable.

As Step 1 in Figure 18–3, you enter his investment, his desired profit, and his estimate of income taxes (from the past and after consultation with his accountant). You determine that he must make $52,000 before taxes, or a 26 percent return on his investment, if he is to reach his desired profit. After you and Mr. Model have set this goal, you should turn to the task of determining what the profit before taxes will be from your forecast of next year's plans.

Step 2: Determine the Planned Sales Volume

A **sales forecast** states the amount a firm expects to sell during a given period. In preparing operating and sales budgets, these forecasts are used to estimate revenues for the next quarter, for the year, or perhaps even for three to five years.

Different parts of the business use these forecasts for planning and controlling their parts of the operations. These forecasts influence decisions such as purchasing raw materials, scheduling production, securing financial resources, purchasing plant or equipment, hiring and paying personnel, scheduling vacations, and planning inventory levels.

In our example, you would probably forecast sales for the coming year on estimates of several factors, such as market conditions, level of sales promotion, estimate of competitors' activities, and inflation. Or you could use forecasts appearing in specialized business and government publications, such as *The Wall Street Journal, Business Week, Kiplinger's Washington Letter, Survey of Current Business, Federal Reserve Bulletin,* and *Monthly Labor Review.* Also, your trade association(s), banker, customers, vendors, and others can provide valuable information.

Using all this information—and assuming 6 percent inflation for the coming year—you estimate that sales will increase about 8 percent to $530,000 ($1,000 per unit × 530 units), which you enter as Step 2 in Figure 18–3.

Step 3: Estimate Expenses for Planned Sales Volume

To estimate expenses for the coming year, look at costs for past years. You decide to use last year's figures and put them in the figure as Step 3. (You also have figures for other years if you need to refer to them.) You should adjust these figures for (1) volume, (2) changes in economic conditions (including inflation), (3) changes in sales promotion needed to attain the planned sales, and (4) improved methods of production.

You compute that about 63 percent of your revenue is to pay for materials

Figure 18–3

THE MODEL COMPANY
Planning the Profit for the Year 19–

Step	Description	Analysis	Comments
1.	*Establish your profit goals.*		
	Equity invested in company	$160,000	
	Retained earnings	40,000	
	Owners' equity	200,000	
	Return desired	40,000	20% × $200,000
	Estimated tax on profit	12,000	
	Profit needed before income taxes	$ 52,000	
2.	*Determine your planned volume of sales.*		
	Estimate of sales income	$530,000	530 units × $1,000/unit

3. *Estimate your expenses for planned volume of sales.*

	Estimated, 19—	Actual, last year
Cost of goods	$333,900	$291,262
Salaries	88,300	83,138
Utilities	7,100	6,950
Depreciation	10,000	10,050
Rent	2,500	2,000
Building services	5,100	4,920
Insurance	5,000	4,000
Interest	3,000	2,646
Office expenses	6,000	5,550
Sales promotion	11,800	11,000
Taxes and licenses	6,900	6,480
Maintenance	1,900	1,610
Delivery	6,500	5,848
Miscellaneous	2,000	1,740
Total	$490,000	$437,204

Step	Description	Analysis	
4.	*Determine your profit, based on Steps 2 and 3.*		
	Estimated sales income	$530,000	
	Estimated expenses	490,000	
	Estimated net profit before taxes	$ 40,000	
5.	*Compare estimated profit with profit goal.*		
	Estimated profit before taxes	$ 40,000	
	Desired profit before taxes	52,000	
	Difference	−$ 12,000	

6. *List possible alternatives to improve profits.*
    A. Change the planned sales income:
        (1) Increase planned volume of units sold.
        (2) Increase or decrease planned price of units.
        (3) Combine (1) and (2).
    B. Decrease planned expenses.
    C. Add other products or services.
    D. Subcontract work.

Figure 18–3 (*concluded*)

7. *Determine how costs vary with changes in sales volume.*

	Total estimated expenses	Fixed expenses	Variable expenses
Goods sold	$333,900		$333,900
Salaries	88,300	$50,000	38,300
Utilities	7,100	6,000	1,100
Depreciation	10,000	10,000	
Rent	2,500	2,500	
Building services	5,100	4,000	1,100
Insurance	5,000	5,000	
Interest	3,000		3,000
Office expenses	6,000	2,800	3,200
Sales promotion	11,800		11,800
Taxes and licenses	6,900	5,000	1,900
Maintenance	1,900	800	1,100
Delivery	6,500		6,500
Miscellaneous	2,000	2,000	
Total	$490,000	$88,100	$401,900

8. *Determine how profits vary with changes in sales volume.*
   Total marginal income = Sales income − Variable expenses
   $$= \$530,000 - \$401,900$$
   $$= \$128,100$$

   Marginal income per dollar of sales income = $128,100 ÷ $530,000
   $$= \$0.242 \text{ per dollar.}$$

   Variable cost per dollar of unit sold = $0.758
   Estimated costs and profits at various sales volumes:

Units sold	=	Sales income*	−	Variable costs†	−	Fixed costs	=	Profits
350		$350,000		$265,300		$88,100		$−3,400
400		400,000		303,200		88,100		8,700
450		450,000		341,100		88,100		20,800
500		500,000		379,000		88,100		32,900
550		550,000		416,900		88,100		45,000
600		600,000		454,800		88,100		57,100
650		650,000		492,700		88,100		69,200
700		700,000		530,600		88,100		81,300

   * Number of units sold × $1,000 per unit.
   † Variable cost per dollar of unit sold × sales income.

9. *Analyze alternatives from a profit standpoint.*
   Increase income by increasing price? Decreasing price?
   Increase income by increasing advertising?
   Decrease variable costs?

10. *Select and implement the plan.*

and labor used directly on the goods you sell. Using this figure, plus 6 percent for inflation, you enter the result, $333,900, as "cost of goods." You then estimate the value of each of the other expenses, recognizing that some expenses vary directly with volume changes, while others do not change at all—or change very little. Enter each expense figure in the appropriate place.

Step 4: Determine Profit from Steps 2 and 3

In this step, you first deduct the figure for total expenses from the sales income and then add the total of any other income, such as interest. You calculate this amount and find that profit before taxes is estimated to be $40,000 ($530,000 − $490,000), which is higher than the $24,944 made last year.

Step 5: Compare Estimated Profit with Profit Goal

Next, you compare the estimated profit ($40,000) with your profit goal ($52,000). As estimated profit is $12,000 less than you would wish, you decide to continue with Steps 6 through 10.

Step 6: List Possible Alternatives to Improve Profits

As shown in Step 6 of Figure 18–3, you have many alternatives for improving profits. Some of these are:

A. Change the planned sales income by:
   1. Increasing the planned volume of units sold through expanding sales promotion, improving the quality of product and/or service, making the product more available, or finding new uses for the product.
   2. Increasing or decreasing the planned price of the units. The best price may not be the planned one. How will price changes affect the profit? What have been the effects of past price changes? How have customer attitudes and economic status changed? If your company sells more than one product, which products' prices should be changed?
   3. Combining (1) and (2). On occasion, some small business owners become too concerned with selling on the basis of price alone. Instead, price for profit and sell quality, better service, reliability, and integrity. Never be entrapped by the cliché "I won't be undersold" or "I will meet any price." The economic path is strewn with many failed businesses whose key to failure was this pricing strategy.
B. Decrease planned expenses by:
   1. Establishing a better control system. Money may be lost by having too many people operating the cash register, by poor scheduling, and/or by having too much money tied up in inventory. Spotting

areas where losses occur and establishing controls may reduce expenses.

2. Increasing productivity of people and machines through improving methods, developing proper motivators, and improving the types and use of machinery.

3. Redesigning the product. Research is constantly developing new materials, machines, and methods for improving products and reducing costs.

C. To reduce costs per unit, add other products or services by:

1. Adding a summer product to a winter line of products.

2. Selling as well as using parts made on machines with idle capacity.

3. Making some customarily purchased parts.

D. Subcontract work

Having listed possible alternatives, you must evaluate each of them. Some may not be good choices at this time; concentrate on the best ones. An understanding of cost and volume relationships is important in evaluating the alternatives.

Step 7: Determine How Costs Vary with Changes in Sales Volume

You should now estimate the probable expenses for the increase in sales volume, as shown in Step 3 of Figure 18–3. You can use a simple **break-even chart** (shown in Figure 18–4) to do this. Notice that as the volume of sales changes, the costs of doing business also change. The use of straight lines adequately approximates costs.

Next, you collect the figures for production volume and costs from the company's records for, say, the past five years. Production figures and costs for items such as direct materials, depreciation, and office supplies appear in Table 18–1. Notice that the cost of direct materials (B) tends to increase in direct proportion to production volume (A). This is to be expected, as amounts of materials used directly in manufacturing the product increase directly as the volume of products increases.

Depreciation (C) is the loss in value of the machinery and equipment as they are used, get older, and wear out. Like the book value of your car, their value decreases with time. Businesses usually deduct the estimated resale value of an item from its cost and divide the balance by the estimated life of the item (in years) to obtain its annual depreciation cost. The formula is:

$$\text{Annual depreciation cost} = \frac{\text{Cost} - \text{Estimated resale value}}{\text{Estimated life (in years)}}$$

Depreciation is considered a fixed cost because its cost per year does not change, regardless of the volume of output, until you buy or sell a fixed asset. Other fixed costs such as rent are paid each period.

The office expenses (D) illustrate semivariable expense. They vary with changes in production and sales but not directly.

Figure 18–4   Break-Even Chart for The Model Company

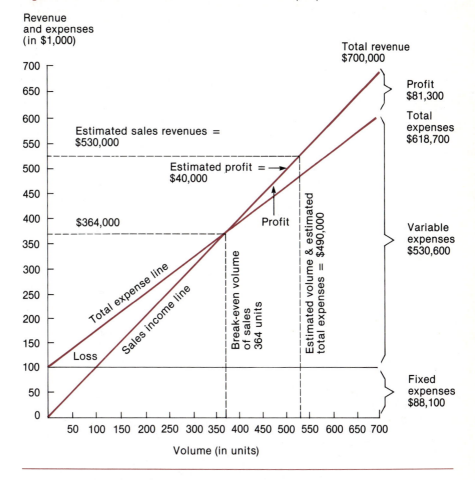

Table 18–1   Data Collected from Model Company's Records

Year	(A) Production volume (units)	(B) Direct materials	(C) Depreciation	(D) Office supplies
1	220	$ 91,800	$ 6,200	$4,300
2	278	108,800	6,200	5,000
3	330	121,400	7,600	3,800
4	410	149,600	8,800	5,600
5	463	170,200	10,050	5,600
6*	530	200,000	10,000	6,000

* Estimated.

While an analysis of past costs is helpful, be aware that:

1. The relationships exist only within limited changes in sales volume. Very high sales volumes may be obtained by such measures as extraordinary sales promotion, added fixed costs of machinery, or overtime. Low sales volumes result in extra costs of idle capacity, lost volume discounts, and so forth.

2. Past relationships may not continue in the future. Inflation or deflation, changing location of customers, new products, and other factors can cause changes in the costs per unit. In our example, you recognize a possible increase in the cost of goods sold for the next year and up the amount budgeted accordingly.

You then compute fixed and variable costs for each item of expense at the planned volume of sales and enter the figures in Step 7 of Figure 18–3.

Step 8: Determine How Profits Vary with Changes in Sales Volume

How much does profit increase for each dollar of sales? You planned for $530,000 of sales and $490,000 of expenses. Therefore, each dollar of sales will incur a cost of $0.92 (or $490,000 ÷ $530,000). However, if you increase your sales by $1, the extra sales should not cost $0.92. For one dollar of sales increase, your cost increase will be:

$$\text{Variable cost} = \$401,900 \div \$530,000 = \$0.758.$$

The increase in profit per dollar of increase in sales volume, often called **marginal income (MI),** is

$$\text{MI} = \$1.00 - \$0.758 = \$0.242.$$

For The Model Company, this means that you can determine the marginal income for each product and show which product is the most profitable—if more than one product is sold.

As shown in Step 8 of Figure 18–3 and plotted graphically in Figure 18–4, you can compute costs and profits at several sales volumes in order to get a picture of the related changes in profit. Notice that the sales income at which the company makes no profit—nor suffers any loss—is between $350,000 and $400,000 (break-even actually occurs at $364,000, or 364 units at $1,000 each). The desired profit can be made only if sales increase to about $580,000.

Step 9: Analyze Alternatives from a Profit Standpoint

Use the marginal analyses to help in decision making, as follows:

1. How much can you reduce your price for a sale to bring in more sales volume? You must not reduce it more than about 22 percent, for if you do, you will be paying out more than the extra sales bring in. A reduction in sales price of less than 22 percent would contribute to reducing the

fixed-cost charges per unit, an increase in profits. (Sales price is greater than variable unit costs.)

2. Is it profitable to increase advertising by $2,000, which you estimate would increase sales by $15,000? For the $2,000 paid out, you should obtain additional profits of $3,630:

$$0.242 \times \$15,000 = \$3,630$$

which would provide an added profit of $3,630 − $2,000 = $1,630.

3. Is it profitable to increase the price 2 percent if a drop of 5 percent in sales can be expected? The price increase would result in an approximate marginal income of $0.262:

$$MI = \$0.242 + \$0.02 = \$0.262$$

The profit would change to about $43,817:

$$(0.262 \times 0.95 \times \$530,000) - \$88,100 = \$43,817$$

This would be preferable to the present expected profit of $40,000.

4. What would a reduction of 5 percent in variable costs do to profit? The MI should increase:

$$MI = \$1.00 - (\$0.758 \times 0.95) = \$0.280$$

and the profit at $530,000 sales volume would be $60,300:

$$(\$530,000 \times 0.280) - \$88,100 = \$60,300$$

This looks very good if the means can be found to reduce the variable cost without hurting other operations.

5. Which product is most profitable?

Other alternatives can be evaluated in much the same manner. Then, having made these economic analyses, you will be ready to make your final plan for action.

Step 10: Select and Implement the Plan

The selection of the plan for action depends on your judgment as to what will most benefit the business. The results of the analyses made in the prior steps provide the economic inputs. These must be evaluated along with other goals. Cost reduction may result in laying off employees or in reducing service to customers. But lowering prices may satisfy your goal for a larger volume of sales. Higher prices are risky because of competition.

Mr. Model has just read this text and has been studying some other management literature. After hearing you present the above analyses to him, he believes that the company can reduce the cost of goods about 2 percent. Figure 18–5 shows a simplified statement of the planned income and outgo for the next year, based on the work you and he have done. How does it look to you?

Figure 18–5

THE MODEL COMPANY
Income Statement
For the Year 19—

Sales income		$530,000
Less:		
Cost of goods sold	$327,200	
Other expenses	156,100	
Total expenses		483,300
Net profit before taxes		$46,700
Pretax return on equity		23.4%
Pretax profit margin		8.8%

WHAT YOU SHOULD HAVE LEARNED

1. Not only do small business owners often fail to plan for a profit, they sometimes do not even know whether they are making a profit or not. Because healthy sales and sizable income do not guarantee a profit, it is important to determine the true cost of a product—raw materials, labor, overhead, sales promotion expenses, and so on—in order to set a fair price and budget and plan accordingly.

2. A business's financial position is not static. For example, every time a product is sold, or money comes in, whenever inventory is bought, or credit given, assets and liabilities fluctuate. Rapid growth and "paper profits" can be the downfall of small business managers who are too busy doing business to sit down and figure out their true financial position. They need to keep accurate records and listen to the conclusions accountants draw from the figures.

3. A company's financial structure consists of its assets, liabilities, and owners' equity. Assets are the physical, financial, or other values that a company has. Current assets, which turn over within a year, include cash, accounts receivable, and inventory, as well as short-term investment, prepaid items, and accrued income. Fixed assets, such as buildings, machinery, store fixtures, trucks, and land, are things the company expects to own for a considerable time. Part of their cost is written off each year as depreciation expense.

   Liabilities are obligations created by borrowing money or buying something on credit. Current liabilities, payable within one year, include accounts payable, notes payable, and accrued items. Long-term liabilities, with terms of a year or longer—such as bonds and mortgages— are used to pay for fixed assets and to acquire working capital.

   Owners' equity is the owners' share of—or net worth in—a business after liabilities are subtracted from assets. Profits are distributed to owners as cash or stock dividends. Profits may be accumulated in the business in the form of retained earnings, which are used to provide for growth or to protect the business from unforeseen losses.

4. Simply stated, a company's profit—or net income—is what is obtained after expenses—the costs of doing business—are subtracted from revenues—the proceeds from sales. These interdependent items are shown on the income—profit and loss—statement. When sales increase, not only does sales income rise, but variable costs change also. To generate more sales—and thus more profit—it may sometimes even be necessary to increase fixed costs.

5. To plan for a profit, a small business must go through at least the first 5 of the following 10 steps:
   (1) Establish the profit goal.
   (2) Determine the planned volume of sales.
   (3) Estimate the expenses for the planned sales volume.
   (4) Determine estimated profit for the planned sales volume.
   (5) Compare the estimated profit with the profit goal.
   (6) If the results of (5) are unsatisfactory, list possible alternatives that can be used to improve the profit position.
   (7) Determine how costs vary with changes in sales volume.
   (8) Determine how profits vary with changes in sales volume.
   (9) Analyze alternatives from a profit standpoint.
   (10) Select an alternative and implement the plans.

   Be realistic when going through these steps; otherwise, the desired profit goals may be unattainable.

6. The chapter concluded by following these steps for a hypothetical company.

KEY TERMS

financial structure, *570*

balance sheet, *570*

assets, *570*

current assets, *570*

cash, *570*

accounts receivable, *571*

inventory, *572*

fixed assets, *572*

current liabilities, *573*

accounts payable, *573*

notes payable, *573*

long-term liabilities, *573*

working capital, *573*

owners' equity, *573*

capital stock, *573*

go public, *573*

retained earnings, *573*

cash dividends, *574*

income (profit and loss) statement, *574*

revenue (sales income), *574*

expenses, *575*

profit (income), 575   depreciation, 582

sales forecast, 578   marginal income (MI), 584

break-even chart, 582

QUESTIONS FOR DISCUSSION

1. Why is planning for profit so important to a small business?
2. In analyzing the changing financial position of a small business, what are some of the things you should look for?
3. (*a*) Is the following statement true? If a small firm is making a profit, there's no danger of its failing. (*b*) Explain your answer.
4. (*a*) What is a firm's financial structure? (*b*) What are the components of this structure?
5. Explain each of the following:

a. Assets	*g.* Owners' equity
b. Current assets	*h.* Capital stock
c. Fixed assets	*i.* Retained earnings
d. Liabilities	*j.* Income (profit and loss) statement
e. Current liabilities	*k.* Balance sheet
f. Long-term liabilities	*l.* Profit

6. What steps are needed in profit planning?
7. How do you establish a profit goal?
8. How do you determine planned volume of sales?
9. How do you determine planned expenses?
10. (*a*) What are some alternatives that could improve planned profits? (*b*) Explain each.
11. How do you determine variations in profit caused by changes in sales volume?

SUGGESTED READINGS

Barnett, F. William. "Four Steps to Forecast Total Market Demand: Without a Total-Demand Forecast, You're Operating in the Dark." *Harvard Business Review* 66 (July–August 1988): 28–33.

Brackey, Harriett J. "Brilliant Deduction: Own a Home." *USA Today*, February 20, 1989, p. 6E.

Croft, Nancy L. "Keeping Your Business Afloat." *Nation's Business*, February 1987, pp. 16–21.

Cullum, Peter F. "Entrepreneurial Finance." *Barron's*, June 6, 1988, Special Advertising Section, pp. 47–54.

Glau, Gregory. *The Small Business Financial Planner*. New York: John Wiley & Sons, 1989.

Gumpert, David E., and Therese Engstrom. "Help! My Business Is Going Under: Five Ways to Protect Your Company—Before Disaster Strikes." *Working Woman*, June 1988, pp. 51–53.

Howard, James S. "Smart Financial Management." *D&B Reports*, January–February 1989, p. 38.

Jaffe, Charles A. "Bad Debts Are Worth Collecting." *Nation's Business*, May 1989, pp. 53–55.

Nichols, Don. "Factors That Let the Cash Flow." *Venture*, June–July 1989, pp. 74–76.

Plewa, Franklin J., and G. Thomas Friedlob. "Are GAAP Statements Worth It?" *Management Accounting*, January 1989, pp. 55–58.

Stevens, Mark. "How Healthy Is Your Business? These Eight Ratios Help You Figure That Out." *Working Woman*, January 1987, pp. 39–42.

Willson, James D. *Budgeting and Profit Planning Manual*. 2d ed. New York: Warren, Gorham & Lamont, 1989.

ENDNOTES

1. Sanford L. Jacobs, "Watch the Numbers to Learn If the Business Is Doing Well," *The Wall Street Journal*, August 26, 1985, p. 19. See also "The American Dream: Your Own Business," *Nation's Business*, November 1988, p. 10, for details of a nationwide survey Comprehensive Accounting Corporation conducted to determine how the American public views small business.

2. Jeffrey M. Laderman, "Earnings, Schmernings—Look at the Cash," *Business Week*, July 24, 1989, pp. 56–57

3. Jacobs, "Watch the Numbers," p. 19.

4. Ibid.

5. Roger Ricklefs and Udayan Gupta, "Traumas of a New Entrepreneur," *The Wall Street Journal*, May 10, 1989, p. B1.

6. David M. Gumpert, "Don't Let Optimism Block Out Trouble Signposts," *USA Today*, May 8, 1989, p. 10E.

7. Echo M. Garrett, "Up Like a Rocket, Down Like a Rock." *Venture*, May 1989, pp. 46–52.

8. James S. Howard, "Smart Financial Management," *D&B Reports*, January–February 1989, p. 38.

19

BUDGETING AND CONTROLLING OPERATIONS

In dealing with accountants, never ask whether something can be done. The correct question is, "How can we do this?"—Robert Dince, Pepperdine University professor

Let us watch well our beginnings, and the results will take care of themselves.—Alexander Clark

LEARNING OBJECTIVES

After studying the material in this chapter, you will be able to:

1. Explain how managers exercise control in a small business.
2. Describe the characteristics of control systems.
3. Discuss how performance standards are set.
4. Explain the different types of budgets, and tell how they are prepared and used.
5. Describe how budgetary control operates.
6. Discuss how information on actual performance can be obtained and used.
7. Explain how ratios can be used to evaluate a firm's financial condition.

VIDEOSTAR CONNECTIONS: THE IMPORTANCE OF STAYING POWER

VideoStar Connections Inc. (VCI) knew it had a problem when Digital Equipment Corporation (DEC) gave a major contract for a permanent satellite network to VideoStar's principal competitor in early 1985. The Atlanta-based company had worked diligently to prepare a winning bid for the Digital contract, which would have secured VCI's position in the rapidly growing corporate market for private television networks. The award of this contract to a relatively new competitor, Private Satellite Network, was a blow.

In the wake of this setback, VCI's top personnel carefully analyzed its strengths and weaknesses. Since its founding in 1980, VideoStar had succeeded in providing temporary satellite networks that could deliver one-time, private television programs to corporate clients. Revenues from such events approached $1 million a day, and VCI had gained a strong reputation for on-time, defect-free performance. VideoStar's earliest business plan also envisioned that its market would evolve to include permanent private corporate networks. VCI's managers believed they could use their expertise, equipment, and financial resources to compete effectively in the new line of business.

They were wrong! The Digital contract went to their competitor for a variety of reasons, including the competitor's strong balance sheet and Wall Street investors. As one analyst said, "Your competitor's financial statements said '$10 million in the bank,' while yours read 'neat and clean premises.'" Major corporations do not like to establish a long-term relationship with financially weak suppliers, particularly when complex, high-technology systems are involved.

The postmortem performed by VCI's top managers revealed several strategic weaknesses. For one thing, although VideoStar claimed it favored permanent networks, its allocation of resources proved otherwise. The bulk of the equipment, personnel, and funding was devoted to the temporary network business. Also while VideoStar's temporary corporate network business was highly successful, a related product line that

Source: Photo courtesy VideoStar Connections Inc.

served commercial television broadcasters was not profitable. It became obvious that VCI needed to reposition both its marketing and its operations resources.

With new strategic plan, VideoStar terminated the unsuccessful product line and restructured the compensation of salespeople to focus on the long-term aspects of permanent satellite networks. The privately held company also publicized its record of revenue growth and solid profitability. Then VCI obtained the help of its equipment suppliers and its major existing permanent network customer in selling the firm's expertise and staying power to prospective customers.

The strategy paid off. A series of permanent networking contracts was signed, topped off by "redemption" at DEC. In late 1986, DEC reopened competition for an expanded network, and VideoStar's bid won out over all competitors.

Source: Correspondence and discussion with VideoStar Connections, Inc., and others in the business television industry.

This Opening Focus illustrates what this text has stressed throughout—especially in the previous chapter—namely, the importance of controlling a small firm's operations. In this chapter, we emphasize the nature, objectives, and mechanics of control. Specifically, we discuss causes of poor performance, characteristics of effective control systems, suggestions for setting up and operating such a system, and the design and use of budgets.

WHAT IS INVOLVED IN CONTROL?

Profit planning alone is not enough! Instead, after developing plans for generating a profit, you must design an operating system to carry out those plans. That system, in turn, must be controlled to see that plans are carried out and objectives reached. This section helps you understand how controls can be used in a small business.

The Role of Control

Each day, we exercise controls over our activities and also are subject to controls. We control the speed of the car we drive; signal lights control the traffic flow. We control our homes' thermostats, which keep the temperature within an acceptable range. Ropes in a bank lobby guide patrons to the next available teller. As you can see, controls are everywhere. They have been established to help accomplish certain objectives.

As shown in Part II, the managerial functions of business include planning, organizing, staffing, leading, and controlling. As discussed in Chapter 5, planning provides the guides and standards used in performing the activities necessary to achieve company goals. A system of controls is essential to ensure that performance conforms to the organization's plans. Any deviation from these plans should point to a need for change—usually in performance but sometimes in the plans themselves.

A machine shop owner with a reputation as a top-rated, skilled machinist developed a special machine to produce wooden display stands for art objects. He arranged to display his machine at a trade show for art dealers in a nearby city. The reception of this new equipment was good, and he received orders for 10 machines.

Returning home, he took a year to raise capital, set up production, and produce the machines. By that time, his orders had evaporated. Since no advance payment had been received, he found himself with 10 unsold machines and an additional materials inventory of $18,000 to $20,000. A system of controls to align delivery with customer needs and to obtain advance payments probably would have eliminated the problem.

Steps in Control

Regardless of where it occurs, the control process consists of these five steps:

1. Setting up standards of performance.
2. Measuring actual performance.
3. Comparing actual performance with the planned performance standards.
4. Determining whether deviations are excessive.
5. Determining the appropriate corrective action required to equalize planned and actual performance.

These steps are performed in all control systems, even though the systems may be quite different. Later in this chapter, these five steps are covered in detail.

CHARACTERISTICS OF EFFECTIVE CONTROL SYSTEMS

Almost all control systems have the same characteristics. They should be timely, cost effective, accurate, quantifiable, and measurable. They should show cause-and-effect relationships, be the responsibility of one individual, and be generally acceptable to those using them or being controlled by their use. Selected controls that have the characteristics described in this section and that enable the manager to meet plans are invaluable in managing a business.

Timely

To keep control systems timely, checks should be made frequently and as quickly as feasible. A small firm cannot wait until the end of the year to find out whether sales meet expectations. Some stores with many small transactions check sales daily. Manufacturers handle fewer transactions on a less regular basis, so weekly or monthly checks may be sufficient. Collecting the totals of an activity, such as sales, takes time. As will be seen in Chapter 20, such data collection has been simplified through the use of computers, cash registers with tapes, and other office technology.

A system for fast checks is valuable. The old adage, "It is too late to lock the stable door after the horse is stolen," applies well to controls. The machine shop owner cited earlier needed a check on customers before starting to produce the special machines. And VideoStar really did need to know what its resources were being used for.

Cost Effective

All controls require the time of a person or of some equipment, both costly. The cost of the control system should be balanced against its value. It is not economical to "spend a nickel to save a penny."

Some systems are simple; others are more complex and costly. The manager should try to reduce the time and paperwork needed to collect information. A systematic, simple inspection of shelf stock may give enough information for control without having a clerk provide a written or tabulated summary. At times, though, extra cost may be justified.

For example, early in his managerial career, Axel L. Grabowsky, CEO of Harte & Company, Inc., a small New York manufacturer and marketer of plastic sheeting, had a compulsion to monitor every detail of his business. The result? "My days got longer, my nights shorter, and my leaden briefcase seemed increasingly likely to unhinge my right shoulder."

His solution? He developed an internal monitoring system to compare a selected set of current figures with the firm's projections. Thus, he concentrates on the most important benchmarks: sales, ratio of gross profit to net sales, direct expenses, other income and expenses, net profit, cash flow, accounts receivable, inventory, and research and development. He compares where they *are* (current figures) with where he *wants to be* (projected figures).[1]

Accurate

If controls are to be useful, they must be reliable; to be reliable, they must be accurate. So, a basic tenet of any control system or procedure is to use accurate data, and then use them accurately.

Quantifiable and Measurable

Although quality must sometimes be judged subjectively, it is much easier to measure and control things that can be expressed in quantitative terms. The choice of measuring units for control is vital. Sales can be measured in dollars, pounds, tons, barrels, gallons, grams, kilograms, meters, or other units. Which will best provide the information needed for control? Which is the least costly? Choose the unit that will give the needed control at the least cost.

Indicative of Causes—When Possible

A report of increasing costs of a product may indicate the actual situation but not tell *why* costs increased. On the other hand, a report stating that the cost per unit of raw materials is higher than planned because a vendor raised prices not only shows the situation but also identifies the source of the higher costs.

Assigned to One Individual

Because small business owners and managers do not have time to control all activities themselves, they need to delegate the authority for some actions to subordinates. They should give those people authority, provide the necessary resources, and then hold them responsible for accomplishments.

Acceptable to Those Involved with Them

People tend to resent controls, especially those they consider unnecessary, unreasonable, unfair, or excessive. They show their resentment by rebelling; that is, by finding a way to "beat the system." Therefore, if controls are to be accepted by those involved, it is important for them to clearly understand the purpose of the controls and feel that they have an important stake in them.

SETTING PERFORMANCE STANDARDS

Performance standards tell employees what level of performance is expected of them. Standards also measure how well employees meet expectations. Standards are usually stated in terms of units consumed or produced or of price paid or charged: (1) standard hours per unit to produce a good or service, (2) miles per gallon of gasoline used, (3) price per part for purchased goods, and so on. These standards are developed from many sources, with the participation of those who are affected. Methods used to determine values of standards include intuition, past performance, plans for desired accomplishment, careful measurement of activities, and comparison with other standards or averages.

Once the standards of performance are set, they should be communicated by means of written policies, rules, procedures, and statements of standards to the people responsible for performance. Standards are valuable in locating sources of inefficient as well as efficient performance.

USING BUDGETS TO SET STANDARDS

As an itemized summary of planned expenditures and income for a given period of time, a **budget** embodies a systematic plan for meeting expenses. The budget system is based on profit plans for the coming period. The most prevalent method of setting standards is through budgets. Budgetary control is then used to ensure that the budget is carried out and objectives reached.

Benefits of Budgets

Budgets should express realistic goals that can be achieved during the planning period. Only with realistic and satisfactory planned goals will the budget serve as an effective method of measuring managerial performance. For planning purposes, then, a budget is a detailed plan or forecast of the results expected from operations, based on the highest reasonable expectations of operating efficiency. It is expressed in monetary terms and covers a quarter, a year, or other specific period.

As each day, week, or month passes, checks must be made to assure progress toward meeting goals. If actual performance conforms to the budget, the company is meeting its goals. If performance differs, decisions can be made about whether changes are needed. Thus, budgets provide guideposts toward achieving goals, indications of where trouble exists, planned actions that need to be taken during the year, and—at planning time—the feasibility of the plans.

Types of Budgets

Larger businesses have many types of budgets. The three most important are (1) a capital budget; (2) an operating budget, which may be broken down into (a) a sales budget, (b) a production budget, and (c) a personnel budget; and (3) a cash flow budget.

A **capital budget** reflects a business's plans for obtaining, replacing, and expanding physical facilities. It requires that management preplan the use of its limited financial resources for needed buildings, tools, equipment, and other facilities.

An **operating budget** forecasts sales and allocates financial resources and supplies. In preparing the operating budget, managers try to anticipate the costs of obtaining and selling their products and the income received from them. By comparing budgeted activities with actual performance, variances can be spotted to help relate deviations from production and selling plans to their causes.

The **cash flow budget** states how much cash will be needed to pay what expenses at what time; it also indicates the sources of cash. The *lack of ready cash resources* is the primary reason that firms get into an **illiquid position** (not enough funds to pay current obligations), causing a forced liquidation. According to a Dun & Bradstreet survey of small business owners, 25 percent felt the most important problem they faced was a cash flow squeeze.[2]

For example, Jerry Rogers and Joe Benson, the owner-managers of Metal Fabricators, Inc. (Case II–5), had such cash flow problems. They often had to refrain from drawing their salaries so that funds would be available to pay employee salaries and buy required materials.

Neil Churchill, professor of entrepreneurship at Babson College, thinks the biggest crisis for small business is lack of cash. Therefore, dealing quickly with cash flow problems can mean the difference between success and failure. His tips on how small firms can cope with this problem are given in Figure 19–1.

For all its importance, the meaning of **cash flow** is not always clear.[3] Our definition is the amount of cash funds a business receives and those it disburses during a given period. The SBA has a form called "Monthly Cash Flow Projection," with instructions for its use, which should help small firms.

Preparing the Operating Budget

The main objective of the operating budget is to plan and control revenue and expenses to obtain desired profits. The sales budget is planned first, giving consideration to production and personnel functions. The production budget is then set to meet the sales budget plans. This budget includes

---

Figure 19–1   How Small Firms Can Cope with Cash Flow Problems

- Make finances your No. 1 priority. Monitor cash flow daily if possible.
- Consider replacing the person who handles your company's finances. Look for a "tough son-of-a-gun" who knows how to keep tighter control over costs.
- Speed up cash flow into the company. One way: Offer discounts to customers who pay their bills within 10 to 15 days versus 30 to 60 days.
- Turn as much inventory as possible into cash, even if it means selling inventory to your competitors.
- Put as many unpaid bills as possible on hold. But be sure to negotiate with your suppliers and your bank to stretch out payments. Don't leave lenders hanging.
- Cut employment. About 80 percent of potential cost savings will come from reducing your work force. As you cut back, though, try to keep your most productive workers.
- Cut your rental costs. Move to cheaper office space or cut back on the amount of space you use.
- Get rid of unproductive assets that cost money, such as outdated machinery that requires costly maintenance.

Source: Reported in David E. Gumpert, "Watch the Purse Strings," *USA Today,* May 8, 1989, p. 10E. Copyright 1989, *USA TODAY.* Excerpted with permission.

---

production, purchasing, and personnel schedules and inventory levels. It includes units such as amount of materials and personnel time, as well as their costs. Next, a personnel budget is developed for the number of people, the training, the pay and employee benefits, and other factors needed. The amount of detail in each of these budgets depends on its value to the company.

The sales budget is the most basic consideration. Its preparation is discussed briefly to illustrate the methodology for budget setting.

Assume you have a sales manager. You and the manager should have worked up the sales plan for the coming year. Now, how much does the sales department need to sell each day? The plan for The Model Company (see Step 2 of Figure 18–3 for computations) calls for sales of $530,000 per year. If the firm plans for 200 sales days per year, it must average $2,650 (or $530,000 ÷ 200) per sales day. But companies have some good days and some poor. You may have noticed seasonal, monthly, or even daily patterns in the past. The daily average can be adjusted upward or downward for each day in the week or for the month.

Using another method to figure goals for daily, weekly, or monthly sales, modify the figures for the past year. If you expect the pattern of sales for the coming year to be the same as that of the past year, merely change last year's daily sales by a given percentage. Remember that Mr. Model planned to increase his sales volume by 8 percent, as shown in Figure 18–3, Step 2.

How often actual sales should be compared to the budget depends on the particular type of business. Weekly, monthly, and year-to-date summaries provide more stable relationships for control than do daily checks. Companies may check at longer intervals and may use other types of checks.

One owner watches the number and size of contracts at the end of each month; other managers watch the units of product sold—by product line, by customer, and/or by territory. For budgeting purposes, a simple tallying of sales in one column of a control pad, the budget in a second column, and the difference in a third column may be adequate.

Preparing the Cash Flow Budget

It surprises some small business managers that their businesses may be making profits and yet go bankrupt because they do not have the cash to pay current expenses. Therefore, provision must be made for adequate cash to pay bills when they are due and payable. This cash planning takes two forms: (1) the daily and weekly cash requirements for the normal operation of the business and (2) the maintenance of the proper balance for longer-term requirements.

Planning Daily and Weekly Cash Needs

The first type of planning tends to be routine. For example, the company may have a fairly constant income and outgo, which can be predicted. Policies can thus be established for the amount of cash to maintain, and procedures should be set up to control that level of cash. These routine demands represent a small part of the needed cash on hand, and they tend to remain fairly constant.

Planning Monthly and Yearly Cash Needs

The second type of planning requires a budget for, say, each month of the year. Payments for rent, payroll, purchases, and services require a regular outflow of cash. Insurance and taxes may require large payments a number of times each year. A special purchase, such as a truck, will place a heavy demand on cash. It takes planning to have the *right* amount of cash available when needed.

Procedure for Cash Planning

Figure 19–2 shows one form of a cash budget for three months ahead. Each month is completed before the next month is shown. Items 1 through 3 give estimates of cash to be received. The Model Company expects to receive 20 percent of its monthly sales in cash (Item 1). A check of its accounts receivable budget (presented in the next section) can provide estimates of the cash to be received in January (Item 2). Other income (Item 3) might come from interest on investments or the sale of surplus equipment.

Expected cash payments, Items 5 through 17, show the items The Model Company might list in its planned budget (see Step 3 in Figure 18–3). Cash is often paid in the month during or after which the service is performed. Examples include payments for electricity and for material purchases. Some cash payments can be made at any one of several times. For example, payments on a new insurance policy can be set up to come

Figure 19–2

THE MODEL COMPANY Cash Budget For Three Months Ending March 31, 19—						
Items that change cash level	January		February		March	
	Budget	Actual	Budget	Actual	Budget	Actual
Expected cash receipts 1. Cash sales						
2. Collections—accounts receivable						
3. Other income						
4. Total cash receipts						
Expected cash payments 5. Goods purchases						
6. Salaries						
7. Utilities						
8. Rent						
9. Building services						
10. Insurance						
11. Interest						
12. Office expenses						
13. Sales promotion						
14. Taxes and licenses						
15. Maintenance						
16. Delivery						
17. Miscellaneous						
18. Total cash payments						
Cash balance 19. Cash balance—beg. of month						
20. Change—item 4 minus item 18						
21. Cash balance—end of month						
22. Desired cash balance						
23. Short-term loans needed						
24. Cash available—end of month						
Cash for capital investments 25. Cash available—line 24						
26. Desired capital cash						
27. Long-term loans needed						

due when other cash demands are low. The cash budget shows when payments are to be made.

The cash balance on the first of January, plus the month's receipts, less the month's cash payments, provides an expected cash balance at the end of January:

$$\frac{\text{Balance at}}{\text{beginning of month}} + \frac{\text{Total cash}}{\text{receipts}} - \frac{\text{Total cash}}{\text{payments}} = \frac{\text{Balance at}}{\text{end of month}}$$

A negative balance will require an increase in cash receipts, a decrease in payments, or the floating of a short-term loan. A company should have a certain amount of cash to take care of contingencies. Item 22 shows the desired amount needed as a minimum balance.

A three-month projection is probably the practical minimum estimation for a cash budget. If sales are seasonal or you expect heavy demands on the cash balance, longer periods may be necessary. Also, at the end of January, actual performance should be checked against the budgeted amounts. Then, the first month (January) should be dropped from the budget and the next month (April) added. Thus, you review the budgets for February and March (Figure 19–2) toward the end of January and budget for April.

Rationale of Cash Flow Budgeting

The cash flow budget controls the flow of cash in a business so that you can make needed payments and not maintain too high a cash balance. Many small businesspeople do not recognize the importance of moving money through their systems as quickly, effectively, and efficiently as possible. Everything else being equal, the faster you can move your money and turn it over in sales and income, the greater profits and the less interest payments should be.

The Computer Update illustrates the use of electronic banking in small business. However, since the name of the game is using money most effectively to make more money, most small and medium-sized companies do not use electronic transfer of funds to pay their bills. They prefer to use, to its maximum, **float time:** the time it takes for a check to go to the vendor, be deposited, and clear the banks.

Robert Anton of Sages Electric Supply Company in Hingham, Massachusetts, says, "We write checks one or two days before they are due. Then we have two days until the check clears the bank. With electronic transfer, we'd lose those two days of float."[4]

USING BUDGETARY CONTROL

By itself, a budget is only a collection of figures or estimates that indicate future plans in financial terms. When the budget is used for control purposes, though, it becomes **budgetary control,** which involves careful planning

COMPUTER UPDATE

THE CHECK IS IN THE COMPUTER

"The whole name of the game is being able to use your money more effectively," said Jayne Palmer, who manages the money in about 20 accounts for Response Communications, an Atlanta telemarketing company.

To use money more effectively, several new businesses have grown up to manage other people's money. For example, Martin Tudor uses a personal computer in his office to: (1) manage the business affairs of several New York actors, (2) check their bank balances, (3) see if a check or deposit has cleared, and (4) move funds between interest-earning and bill-paying accounts. His computer was hooked into his bank's computer system. In effect, he had a branch of the bank in his office.

Neither Palmer nor Tudor used home banking services to pay bills. Palmer used a separate computer for that, and Tudor used checks in order to have proof of payment.

Source: Michael Totty, "Small Businesses Find Electronic Banking Can Be a Useful Tool in Managing Money," *The Wall Street Journal,* July 22, 1986, p. 33. Reprinted by permission of The Wall Street Journal, © Dow Jones & Company, Inc., 1986. ALL RIGHTS RESERVED.

and control of all the company's activities. This also includes frequent and close controls in the areas where poor performance most affects a company. Other areas may be controlled less often. For example, the cost of goods sold by The Model Company is planned for 63 percent of the sales dollar, and utilities are 1.34 percent (see Steps 2 and 3 in Figure 18–3). Cost of goods sold may be divided into material and labor and checked weekly, while utilities might be checked monthly.

Controlling Credit, Collections, and Accounts Receivable

As previously stated, the extension of credit increases the potential for sales. You may have found that the amount of accounts receivable for The Model Company (see Figure 18–1) was large relative to its credit sales. Waiting until the end of the year to find this out is potentially dangerous. Checks should be made often enough to identify customers who are slow in paying and to determine the reason(s) for the slow payments. The average retailer loses more from slow accounts than from bad debts.

The best control of losses on accounts receivable starts with investigating the customer's ability and willingness to pay and by providing clear statements of terms. Then, establish surveillance of past-due accounts each month so that each slow account is followed up promptly. As time passes and an account remains unpaid, the probability of collection decreases. Expect to collect only about one quarter of the accounts over two years old and none of those over five years old.

In budgetary controls, a check should first be made of the total amount of current accounts receivable as compared to previous periods. These figures can be obtained from the balance sheet (such as Figure 18–1) for the desired years. Then, a comparison of your planned figures and the actual amounts (Item 2 in Figure 19–2) indicates how satisfactory the situation is overall.

Next, the accounts can be "aged" by determining the collection period.[5] This means making a tabulation of the accounts receivable by how long they have been unpaid. Thus, The Model Company's accounts receivable might be something like the following:

Accounts receivable by age of accounts					
Less than 30 days	30–60 days	2–6 months	6–12 months	Over one year	Total
$34,300	$16.204	$5,000	$1,980	$3,000	$60,484

What should be done? Give particular attention to accounts over 60 days past due and then to the 30- and 60-day accounts. Remember that most customers are honest and can be expected to be willing and able to pay.

Mr. Model's analysis may lead him to write off some accounts as an expense of bad debts and to provide some incentive for earlier payment by slow-paying customers. Uncollectible accounts receivable create a misstatement of income and therefore an unjustified increase in business income tax liability. Unless there exists a reasonable expectation of collecting the account, a good rule of thumb is to write off all accounts six months old or older at tax time.

Other Types of Budgetary Control

Many other types of budgetary control can be used to control the activities and investments of a company. Any expense can increase gradually without the change being recognized. Have you noticed how fast the cash in your pockets disappears? You know you need to control this, but it is very hard to do. Some call it being "nickeled and dimed to death." A small business has similar problems. Contributing to this creeping increase in the firm's costs may be such diverse situations as a clerk added to process increased paperwork, a solicitor asking for donations, a big customer requesting special delivery, an employee who uses company stamps for personal letters, rising energy costs, and inflation-increased costs. These costs must be controlled if the firm is to survive.

Control over current liabilities relates to expense and cash plans. Fixed assets and long-term liabilities usually change on a fixed basis, except for infrequent changes of equipment and other needs. Capital stock changes are infrequent, and retained earnings change as a result of the operations of the company. Budgets for fixed items can be maintained through a quarterly set of planned financial statements.

Using Audits to Control the Budget

An **audit** of a company consists of a formalized, methodical study, examination, and/or review of its financial records, with the intent of verifying, analyzing, informing, and/or discovering opportunities for improvement. Three main types of auditing occur.

In *financial auditing*, an outside CPA firm usually verifies the records and provides financial and other statements of a company once a year. This audit furnishes management and owners with information on the company's financial status and operations and provides authenticity for anyone using it.

A new wrinkle in auditing is using compact discs for storing information to send to auditors. The discs are the same as those used for music. The primary advantages are reduced storage space and ease of finding citations when doing research. The main disadvantages are that indexing of audit materials is time consuming, and, to keep current, new discs must be sent to auditors as frequently as every three months.[6]

Internal auditing is an independent appraisal of accounting, financial, and/or operations activities with the intention of measuring and evaluating the effectiveness of controls. Such audits function primarily as a service to management for the improvement of its financial controls.

An *operations audit* studies the operations of a company to identify problem areas. It may include studies of functional areas (marketing, finance, production, and purchasing), of organization structure, of personnel, and of planning. Closely related to internal auditing, operations auditing emphasizes operations more than financial activities. The general management self-evaluation in Appendix H at the end of this book can be used as an operations self-audit.

A company should be audited periodically to ensure continued proper operations. Financial statements usually dictate at least an annual financial audit. If any questions arise as to proper controls, inefficient operations, or lost opportunities, some form of internal or operations audit should be performed. A certified public accountant (CPA) or management consultant can perform services of this type.

OBTAINING AND USING INFORMATION ON PERFORMANCE

Information on actual performance comes through some form of **feedback:** observation, oral reports, written memos or reports, and other methods. Observation will probably be most satisfying because you observe at the scene of action and have direct control over the situation. However, this method is time consuming, and you cannot be in all places at one time.

"Never mind the dramatics, Snodgrass—just read the treasurer's report!"
Source: *The Savant* (a SCORE publication), March 1989.

You can justify observation time when your knowledge is needed, your presence may improve the work, or you are present for other purposes.

Oral reports, less simple than personal observation, are also time-consuming. But they provide two-way communication and are the most prevalent type of control used in business. Written memos or reports are prepared when a record is needed and when many facts must be assembled for decision making. This type of feedback is costly unless the reports are the original records. A good record system, as will be discussed in Chapter 20, is a valuable aid, and it should be designed to be a source of reports.

Indirect Control by Means of Reports

New and very small businesses usually lend themselves to the more direct, personal types of control. But indirect controls (by means of reports) may be necessary at later stages of growth. Some guidelines for designing reports include seeing that they (1) cover separate organizational units, (2) can be updated as needed, (3) are factual and not designed just to make someone look good, (4) indicate actions that have been taken or should be taken, and (5) highlight comparisons of performance of various organizational units and/or individuals within the company.

These reports should be given to all managers involved in the activity. Operating on the basis of the need for immediate investigation of the causes of significant variations, whether favorable or unfavorable, a manager should arrange for immediate action to prevent a repetition of bad results or to preserve and continue good results.

Comparing Actual Performance with Standards

Next to providing wanted products, the ability to keep costs low ranks as one of the most important advantages a small company can have. An effective cost accounting system and cost-sensitive controls are vital. For example, small companies are usually labor intensive, and labor costs typically represent a significant cost area that should be watched and controlled.

Information about actual performance, obtained through feedback, can be compared with standards to determine whether any changes are needed. Most often, simple, informal controls can be used. The measures of performance are carried in the manager's head; comparisons are made as feedback is received and decisions made accordingly. This type of control follows the same steps as the more formal types of control needed when delegating authority. Examples of the use of standards were discussed in Chapter 14 and follow the same pattern as control through the use of budgets.

Determining Causes of Poor Performance

Poor performance can result from many factors, both internal and external. A partial list of some of these activities, or nonactivities, would probably include the following:

- Customers not buying the company's product.
- Poor scheduling of production or purchases.
- Theft and/or spoilage of products.
- Too many employees for the work being performed.
- Opportunities lost.
- Too many free services or donations.

A company oriented toward research and development (R&D) was found to be providing customers with special R&D service without reimbursement for the thousands of dollars spent in this manner. This policy was changed, and the company's profits improved.

- Having the wrong objective.

The president of a TV station authorized the purchase of status items such as sports cars for key personnel. Subsequent low profits resulted in his dismissal and in the elimination of the extravagant items.

Once management isolates the true cause(s) of the firm's poor performance, remedies can probably be found. An evaluation of its financial condition should help find the cause.

EVALUATING THE FIRM'S FINANCIAL CONDITION

Having considered the financial structure and operations of a company in Chapter 18, we now consider the methods of evaluating its financial condition. Refer to Figures 18–1 and 18–2, the financial statements of The Model Company. Is the company in a good financial position?

In Chapter 18, we discussed profit planning, which can be used to guide a firm to desired profits. Now, we will discuss how to evaluate the financial status and operations of a small business. The evaluation of a firm's financial condition involves establishing relationships, called **ratios,** between two or more variables. For example, the amount of current assets needed depends on other conditions of a company such as the size of its current liabilities. So the **current ratio**—current assets divided by current liabilities—shows how easily a company can pay its current obligations. Another comparison can be made by subtracting current liabilities from current assets, with the resulting value called **working capital.** Unfortunately, no standard figures have been determined for successes or failures. Yet, a reasonable evaluation is possible and necessary. Two sets of values can be used for evaluation purposes: (1) a comparison of the current value of ratios with those of the past and (2) a comparison of the ratios of your firm with those of similar firms.

Comparing with Firm's Past Performance

A change in the value of selected ratios for a firm indicates a change in its financial position. For example, suppose the current ratio for The Model Company has moved gradually from a value of 1.0 to its present value of 2.73 (which is $148,626 ÷ $54,408 in Figure 18–1). In the past, a ratio of 2:1 has been used as a rule of thumb for the current ratio. However, no one value of a ratio is optimum for all companies. For example, The Model Company has apparently moved to a more liquid position and therefore looks good. However, this improvement may be due to keeping old, uncollectible accounts on the books. In that case, appearances are deceiving. Analysis is needed to determine the causes and to help decide what to do.

Comparing with Similar Companies

Average values and ranges of values for the ratios are published for a variety of small to large companies. Some of these firms will fail, but the averages and ranges provide a guide to what other companies are doing. Suppose the current ratio for companies with assets of $300,000 or less is found to be 1.3:1, while The Model Company has a ratio of 2.73:1. Again, the company's ratio looks good. However, it may be losing income by maintaining too many nonproductive assets in a period of high interest rates.

SOME IMPORTANT RATIOS AND THEIR MEANINGS

As indicated earlier, ratios and percentages help in answering a number of questions that might be asked about a company. Answers to these questions may help correct deficiencies in the operations and structure of the company. When ratios are mentioned, look at Figure 19–3 for the method of computing them. Spaces are provided for computing the ratios for The

Figure 19–3 Financial Ratios

Ratio	Formula	The Model Company	Industry average*
1. Net profit to net worth (ROE)	$\dfrac{\text{Net profit before taxes}}{\text{Net worth}}$ = _____		18.4%
2. Net profit to net sales	$\dfrac{\text{Net profit before taxes}}{\text{Net sales}}$ = _____		3.1
3. Net sales to fixed assets	$\dfrac{\text{Net sales}}{\text{Fixed assets}}$ = _____		5.8
4. Net sales to net worth	$\dfrac{\text{Net sales}}{\text{Owners' equity}}$ = _____		7.5
5. Current ratio	$\dfrac{\text{Current assets}}{\text{Current liabilities}}$ = _____		1.3
6. Acid test (quick ratio)	$\dfrac{\text{Current assets} - \text{Inventory}}{\text{Current liabilities}}$ = _____		1.0
7. Receivables to working capital	$\dfrac{\text{Accounts receivable}}{\text{Working capital}}$ = _____		1.2
8. Inventory to working capital	$\dfrac{\text{Inventory}}{\text{Working capital}}$ = _____		0.4
9. Collection period	$\dfrac{\text{Accounts receivable}}{\text{Average daily credit sales}\dagger}$ = _____		43.0 days
10. Net sales to inventory	$\dfrac{\text{Net sales}}{\text{Inventory}}$ = _____		22.0
11. Net sales to working capital	$\dfrac{\text{Net sales}}{\text{Working capital}}$ = _____		10.0
12. Long-term liabilities to working capital	$\dfrac{\text{Long-term liabilities}}{\text{Working capital}}$ = _____		0.7
13. Debt to net worth	$\dfrac{\text{Total liabilities}}{\text{Net worth}}$ = _____		1.6
14. Current liabilities to net worth	$\dfrac{\text{Current liabilities}}{\text{Owners' equity}}$ = _____		1.1
15. Fixed assets to net worth	$\dfrac{\text{Fixed assets}}{\text{Owners' equity}}$ = _____		1.2

* Times unless otherwise specified.

† If 80 percent of sales are on credit, average daily credit sales are: $\dfrac{\text{Annual sales}}{365} \times 0.80 = \dfrac{}{365} \times 0.80 =$ _____.

Model Company, using the data provided in Figures 18–1 and 18–2. Comparable figures for the industry are provided for comparative purposes.

Are Profits Satisfactory?

Is the owner of The Model Company getting an adequate or reasonable return on his investment? The ratio of *net profit to net worth* (Ratio 1 in Figure 19–3), often called **return on equity (ROE),** or **net worth** is used to evaluate this, but several other ratios should be considered in profit planning and decision making.

How much return does your company make on its sales dollar? The ratio of *net profit to net sales* (Ratio 2) provides this information. Suppose The Model Company does make 4.3 cents profit (after taxes) per dollar of sales. Is the trend up or down? How does it compare with the experience of similar companies? If it is dropping, why? Costs may be increasing without an increase in price; competitors may be keeping their prices lower than yours; you may be trying to obtain a large sales volume at the expense of profit. An increase in sales volume with the same investment and net profit per dollar of sales will increase ROE, but if you reduce the return on a dollar of sales, ROE may decrease.

Are Assets Productive?

Does your company obtain enough sales from its producing assets? The answer is reflected in the ratio of *net sales to fixed assets* (Ratio 3)—fixed assets representing the producing units of the company. So many variables exist (such as leasing instead of owning fixed assets) that the ratio can change with changes in policy. Still, trends and good use of industry data make this a valuable ratio.

Does your company have enough sales for the amount of investment? The ratio of *net sales to net worth* (Ratio 4) provides a guide to this evaluation. This ratio can be combined with the profit-to-sales ratio to obtain the return on equity (ROE) in Ratio 1.

Can the Firm Pay Its Debts?

Can you pay your current obligations? A number of ratios can be valuable in trying to answer this question. The best known is the *current ratio* (5), the ratio of current assets to current liabilities. You may be making a good profit but not be able to pay your debts, for cash does not necessarily increase when you make a profit.

The **acid test (quick ratio)** (6), that is, the ratio of current assets minus inventory to current liabilities, even more rigorously tests the adequacy of liquid financial resources. Another check is obtained by using working capital, or current assets less current liabilities, as a basis. Working capital is the margin of safety a company has in paying its current liabilities. The ratios of *accounts receivable to working capital* (7) and *inventory to working capital* (8) provide an insight into the riskiness of the company's ability to make current payments.

How Good Are the Firm's Assets?

How good are your current assets? Cash in hand is the best current asset. **Accounts receivable** represent what the company will receive in cash from customers sometime in the future. However, the older an account, the greater the expectation of loss. The **collection period ratio** (9), accounts receivable to average daily credit sales, provides a guide to the quality of your accounts receivable. Suppose that The Model Company has set a 30-day payment period for its customers and its collection period ratio is 50 days. As shown earlier, many accounts are less than 30 days old ($34,300). So, many other accounts must be over two months old ($60,484 − $34,300 = $26,184). Apparently, Mr. Model does not adequately check on those to whom he extends credit; he is carrying bad accounts, or he is not exerting enough effort to reduce the slow payment of accounts.

Inventories can be evaluated in about the same way as accounts receivable. Goods in inventory become obsolete if not sold within a reasonable time. Inventory should therefore be turned over during the year. The turnover rate is expressed by the ratio of *net sales to inventory* (10). A turnover of inventory six times each year for a company is good if turnover for the industry is five. If your company turns its inventory over too slowly, you may be keeping obsolete or deteriorating goods. Too high a ratio may result from an inventory so low that it hurts production or from not providing necessary customer services.

Bayview Fabrics (name disguised) had a "going-out-of-business" sale in the summer of 1989. Some of the inventory had been in the store 10 years or longer.

To get an idea of the support that a company receives from its current assets, compute the ratio of *net sales to working capital* (11). Accounts receivable and inventory should increase with an increase in sales, but not out of proportion. Payroll and other expense increases require a higher level of cash outflow. On the other hand, too low a ratio indicates available surplus working capital to service the sales.

How Much Equity Should a Firm Have?

How much equity should your company have? Assets are financed by either equity investments or the creation of liabilities. Retained profits, part of equity, can be used to increase your assets or decrease your liabilities. You can maintain a high level of equity with a relatively low level of risk, or a relatively high level of liabilities with a higher expected return on equity.

Most small companies do not like to maintain a large amount of long-term debt. The risk is too great. The ratios commonly used to check the company's source-of-funds relationships are *long-term liabilities to working capital* (12), *debt to net worth* (13), *current liabilities to net worth* (14), and *fixed assets to net worth* (15). An extremely high value for any of these puts the company in a risky situation. A bad year decreases the income, but the obligation to pay continues. On the other hand, a very good year results in large returns to owners. Positive financial leverage occurs when you earn more on a loan than it costs to borrow. Uncertainty about high interest rates tends to discourage borrowing.

Ratios Are Interrelated

More questions can be asked and more relationships can be developed as a guide to analyzing a company's financial strengths and weaknesses. But each ratio indicates only part of the firm's position. The ratios overlap because a company is a complex system, and a change in the size of one of the accounts, such as cash, affects other values.

The financial ratios for the items on the profit and loss statement can be expressed in percentages of sales. This information is usually hard to obtain from competing firms. High cost of goods sold as a percentage of sales income may indicate a poor choice of vendors, inefficient use of material or labor, or too low a price. A high percentage of salaries may indicate overstaffing of the company.

WHAT YOU SHOULD HAVE LEARNED

1. This chapter repeats a major theme of this book: the importance to small firms of having specific goals and standards for performance, of knowing how performance compares with those goals and standards, and of taking steps to ensure conformity with standards. This is the job of controls.

2. To work effectively, controls should be timely, cost effective, accurate, quantifiable and measurable, indicative of causes rather than just symptoms, administered by one individual, and acceptable to those involved in their use.

3. Before controls can be used, standards of performance must be set and communicated to those responsible for meeting them. One of the most common statements of standards, expressed in monetary terms, is a budget, an itemized summary of planned expenditures and income for a given period of time.

4. Types of budgets needed by small businesses include at least a capital budget, an operating budget (which may be broken down into a sales budget, a production budget, and a personnel budget), and a cash flow budget.

   The most basic consideration in preparing the operating budget is planning for sales. Only when sales are projected can production and personnel budgets be developed. Sales goals should be broken down into daily, weekly, or monthly sales, and actual performance should be checked at these intervals to make sure that sales are within range of the budget.

   Special attention should be paid to the cash flow budget because profit alone will not keep a company solvent. A business must have the cash needed to meet obligations *when* it is needed. The cash flow budget helps a company not only to have enough cash on hand to meet demands but also to avoid maintaining a cash balance that is higher than necessary.

5. When a budget is used for control purposes, it becomes budgetary

control. It is especially important to control accounts receivable, since uncollectible debts reported as assets will be taxed along with the best-paying accounts. Past-due accounts should be swiftly followed up and severely past-due accounts written off as bad-debt losses. Other types of budgetary control can be used to control the activities and investments of the company. Expenses and inventory are among the items that should be closely monitored. Liabilities should be kept in line with earnings.

One way to control the budget is an audit: a formalized, methodical examination of the company's financial records to establish its financial condition. Outside CPA firms usually perform financial audits, but internal audits can also be used to measure and evaluate the effectiveness of controls. Every small company requires periodic audits; a financial audit will be needed at least once a year in preparing the financial statement.

6. Information on actual performance can be obtained by observation or from oral or written reports. A good report covers a specific organizational unit, can be updated as needed, is factual, indicates actions that have been taken or should be taken, and highlights comparisons of the performance of various organizational units or individuals.

    Known performance can be compared to standards in order to determine the causes of poor performance. Only when the causes are known can remedies be found.

7. In evaluating the firm's financial condition, various ratios can be compared to the company's past performance or the performance of similar companies to determine whether profits are satisfactory, whether assets are productive, how well prepared the company is to pay its debts, how good its assets are, and how much equity it has. These ratios are interrelated; a change in one will affect many of the others.

KEY TERMS

performance standards, *595*

budget, *595*

capital budget, *596*

operating budget, *596*

cash flow budget, *596*

illiquid position, *596*

cash flow, *596*

float time, *600*

budgetary control, *600*

audit, *603*

feedback, *603*

ratios, *606*

current ratio, *606*

working capital, *606*

return on equity (ROE) (net worth), *607*

acid test (quick ratio), *608*

accounts receivable, *608*

collection period ratio, *608*

QUESTIONS FOR DISCUSSION

1. What is control?
2. List the steps in an effective control process.
3. What are some characteristics of effective control systems?
4. (*a*) What are performance standards? (*b*) Why are they used?
5. (*a*) What is a budget? (*b*) What are some benefits of using a well-planned budget?
6. Discuss the different types of budgets.
7. (*a*) What is budgetary control? (*b*) How can it be used by a small business?
8. How can auditing be used to control the budget of a small firm?
9. How can information about actual performance be obtained in a small firm?
10. Compute the ratios listed in Figure 19–3 for The Model Company, using the financial data in Figures 18–1 and 18–2.
11. Evaluate the financial condition of The Model Company.
12. What are some recommendations you might make to the owner of The Model Company?
13. Evaluate your personal financial situation and operations, using material developed in this chapter and Chapter 18.
14. Develop a budget for yourself for the coming year.
15. (*a*) Using the formulas shown in Figure 19–3, develop the financial ratios for:

    (1) Wilson's Used Cars (Case I–6).

    (2) Pools Inc. (Case VI–3).

    (*b*) What can you say about the financial position and future of each of these companies?

SUGGESTED READINGS

Bracker, Jeffrey S., Barbara W. Keats, and John N. Pearson. "Planning and Financial Performance among Small Firms in a Growth Industry." *Strategic Management Journal* 9 (November–December 1988): 591–604.

Dwyer, Herbert J., and Richard Lynn. "Small Capitalization Companies: What Does Financial Analysis Tell Us about Them?" *Financial Review* 24 (August 1989): 397–415.

Gallinger, George W., and P. Basil Healey. *Liquidity Analysis and Management.* Reading, Mass.: Addison-Wesley Publishing, 1987.

Glau, Gregory. *The Small Business Financial Planner.* New York: John Wiley & Sons, 1989.

Howard, James S. "Smart Financial Management." *D&B Reports*, January–February 1989, p. 38.

Kyd, Charles W. "Getting the Cash out of Cash Flow." *Inc.*, July 1987, pp. 87–88.

Laderman, Jeffrey M. "Earnings, Schmernings—Look at the Cash." *Business Week*, July 24, 1989, pp. 56–57.

McKeown, Kate. "Go with the Cash Flow." *D&B Reports,* September–October 1988, pp. 30–35.

Peat Marwick Main & Company. *Building the High Technology Business: Guidebook.* New York: Peat Marwick Main & Co., 1988.

Willson, James D. *Budgeting and Profit Planning Manual.* Boston: Warren, Gorham & Lamont, 1989.

ENDNOTES

1. Axel L. Grabowsky, "What to Monitor to Stay in Control," *Inc. Magazine's Guide to Small Business Success,* 1987, pp. 17–18.

2. "Small Business Woes," *The Wall Street Journal,* November 12, 1986, p. 35.

3. James M. Stancell, "When Is There Cash in Cash Flow?" *Harvard Business Review* 65 (March–April 1987): 38–44.

4. "Financial Tactics: The Check Is in the Mail," *Inc.,* June 1985, p. 123.

5. Charles W. Kyd, a consultant for Arthur Young & Company and author of *Financial Modeling Using Lotus 1–2–3* (Berkeley, Calif.: Osborne/McGraw-Hill, 1986), has developed a computerized system for tracking a firm's actual accounts receivable collection history, rather than "days sales outstanding." For details, see his article, "Formula for Disaster?" *Inc.,* November 1986, pp. 123–26.

6. G. Paschal Zachary, "CDs to Store Data Are Music to Auditors' Ears," *The Wall Street Journal,* August 4, 1989, p. B1.

20

USING COMPUTERS AND MANAGEMENT INFORMATION SYSTEMS*

Smart companies get rich using technology; small ones go bankrupt selling it.—Thomas Doerflinger, Paine Webber executive

---

Farms, factories, even tiny one-person businesses are reaping the benefits—and surviving the frustrations—of computerization.—Jared Taylor, business consultant

LEARNING OBJECTIVES

After studying the material in this chapter, you will be able to:

1. Explain the importance of information to a small business.
2. Discuss the need for a management information system (MIS).
3. Describe the growing role of computers in small business.
4. Discuss how accounting is part of a small business's MIS.

---

* The authors thank Charles E. Scott, Loyola College in Maryland, for his major contributions to this chapter.

HERMAN VALENTINE: A STUDY IN MINORITY ENTREPRENEURSHIP

Herman Valentine, the owner of Systems Management American (SMA) Corporation, remembers the time years ago when he shined shoes on the corner of Monticello and Market streets in downtown Norfolk, Virginia. His best customers were executives working in the four-story department store and 16-story Maritime Towers office building across the street. He now owns the store—which serves as headquarters for his company—the office building, and the entire block.

SMA is a computer systems integrator serving the government and private industry. Its capabilities include manufacturing, installation, ruggedization (which is engineering computers to withstand humidity, heat, dust, shock, and other factors that accompany hostile environments), integrated logistics support, software/hardware development, configuration management, command and control, image processing, and data conversion services.

SMA grew from a one-man operation in 1970 into a national corporation with a staff of 430 in 1988. Not realizing how difficult it was going to be, Valentine "put in long hours, borrowed often from banks, and spent a lot of time on proposals for contracts he did not get." But SMA is now one of the largest black-owned businesses in the United States.

An outstanding high school basketball player, Valentine wanted to play in college and professionally, but he wanted a car more! So he took part-time jobs to buy one, finished high school, went into the Army, married, and at age 23 returned to Norfolk. After more part-time jobs and earning a bachelor's degree from Norfolk State University in three years, he became an executive officer for the U.S. Department of Agriculture and later business manager for Norfolk State.

In 1970, he opened Systems Management Associates, a consulting firm for black businesses, with $5,000 he had saved. With an answering service, a post office box, and a part-time secretary, Valentine sold administrative and financial advice to black entrepreneurs and performed data processing and programming for them. Two years later, with 12 employees (mostly part-timers), he

Herman Valentine, chairman and president of Systems Management American Corporation
Source: Courtesy of Systems Management American Corporation.

began bidding on—and winning—small government data processing jobs.

But his business really took off in 1981, when he snagged a U.S. Navy contract (SNAP II) to design, install, and maintain sophisticated recordkeeping computers aboard ships. The Navy thought the job was too big for him, but he persuaded them to send an evaluation team, which found no reason why he couldn't do the job. Revenues skyrocketed for a while, and they have been as high as $60 million. Valentine has pared down his operations somewhat since the SNAP II contract option wasn't exercised, but SMA continues to bid on—and be awarded—government contracts.

He is concentrating on more contract diversification—which includes the government—as well as more emphasis on the private sector, as military budget cuts impact the computer industry. Valentine closed three small offices around the country and cut $4 million out of overhead. Now, he and his staff are "lean and competitive." He trains his employees—many of whom were unskilled workers—to be computer technicians and high-tech specialists.

Valentine worries that 90 percent of SMA's revenue comes from Navy contracts, but is looking for more contract diversification.

Source: Correspondence with Systems Management American Corporation; *Inside Information/Employee Publication of SMA,* December 1988, p. 8; and various others, including Lewis Giles, Jr., "Success: Minority Entrepreneurs Help Their Communities," *Minority Business Today,* May 1989, pp. 19–20.

This Opening Focus illustrates how one person has taken advantage of the specialized need for management information systems on Navy ships. Valentine started a very small company that has now grown into a good-sized operation. This chapter is designed to study the management information systems used in small businesses.

IMPORTANCE OF INFORMATION

Have you ever considered how many records you keep or generate? You probably have in your possession at least a driver's license, credit cards, an ID card, a Social Security card, and a checkbook. Without these items, you would find it difficult to transact much of your daily business. Whenever you use one of these, records (or entries in the records) are generated. For example, suppose you use a credit card. This generates a sales or credit slip, a monthly statement, and a record of payment. You use the statement to write a check and to deduct the amount from your bank balance. All the while, you keep some information in your head to save time in filling out forms.

As you can see, information is a most important resource for a person, as well as for a small business. It should help provide answers to such questions as: Is the product selling properly? Will the cash flow be adequate? Is the inventory management correct for forecasts of the market? Are the employees paid the correct amounts, and are the employment taxes handled properly?

Obviously, these questions cannot be answered without the appropriate data. Your personal records provide data for your decisions. A company collects data for its operations. Data, which are facts, can be inputs, stored, or both. Data that have meaning to the receiver are information for that person. There is a "cycle of information" as data are processed to create information: the recipient receives the information and then makes a decision and takes action; this creates other actions or events, which in turn create a number of scattered data that are captured and serve as inputs; and the cycle starts over.[1]

An efficient information system is needed by small firms—as well as large ones—to convert data to information for management of the company. And, as you will see, many of these information systems are now computerized—even in the small business.

ELEMENTS OF A MANAGEMENT INFORMATION SYSTEM (MIS)

As shown in Chapter 13, all types of systems involve the same basic elements: inputs, processes, and outputs. A **management information system (MIS)** is designed to collect, record, process, report, and/or convert data into a usable form for management. For example, as will be shown later in the chapter, an accounting system records raw and processed data, processes those data, and produces reports. Some systems direct machines and people. A system may be entirely manual or, at the other extreme, almost entirely machine or computer operated. All these systems start with inputs, process the inputs, and furnish outputs. Whether or not computers are used, an organized MIS is necessary for the efficient operation of any business. Figures 20–1 and 20–2 show diagrams of two systems that can be manually or computer operated—or can use some combination of both. Defining the needs of each part of a business for information and its processing and use is the first step in designing an information system.

What Information Is Needed?

Everyone in the small firm should consider the questions: "What would I like to know to do my job better?" and "What information do I have that will help others do their jobs better?" The accumulation of these pieces of information, with analysis of what data are reasonably available, is the initial step in forming an information system. Emphasis should be placed on future demands required by changes—which are constantly occurring. An obvious, but often overlooked, bit of advice: Even the best information system is of no value if it is not used.

One state university graduate and his wife used their savings to open an independent trucking firm. The firm grew, eventually requiring additional funds. The owners approached the SBA, which referred them to a professor for counseling.

The professor asked them to bring their most recent balance sheet and profit and loss statement. The three-month-old statements showed a debt of $185,000 and a substantial loss on operations.

The professor suggested that they raise prices by 10 to 15 percent and acquire a personal computer to maintain current accounting data and prepare financial statements and to cut costs. One of the owners responded, "We can't raise our prices, or our customers will give their contracts to someone else, and we'll be out of business." Several months later, they were out of business anyway!

Figure 20–1   Accounting for Sales

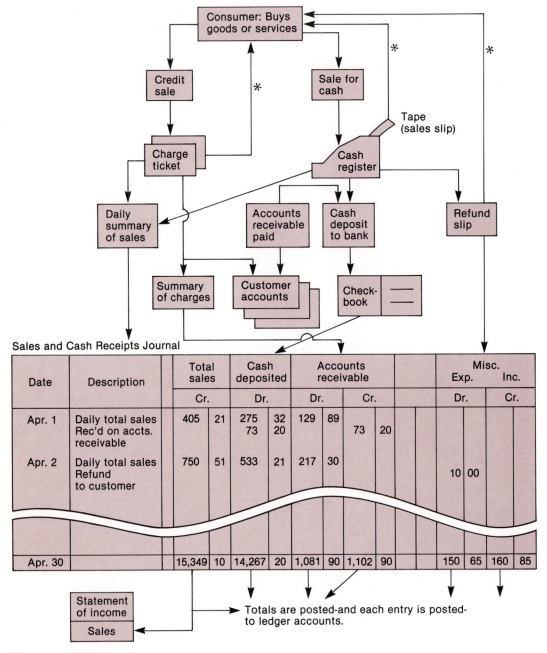

Sales and Cash Receipts Journal

Date	Description	Total sales		Cash deposited		Accounts receivable					Misc. Exp.		Inc.	
		Cr.		Dr.		Dr.		Cr.			Dr.		Cr.	
Apr. 1	Daily total sales	405	21	275	32	129	89							
	Rec'd on accts. receivable			73	20			73	20					
Apr. 2	Daily total sales	750	51	533	21	217	30							
	Refund to customer										10	00		
Apr. 30		15,349	10	14,267	20	1,081	90	1,102	90		150	65	160	85

Statement of income

Sales

Totals are posted-and each entry is posted-to ledger accounts.

*Copy to customer.

Figure 20–2   Accounting for Purchases, Cash Disbursements, and Expenses

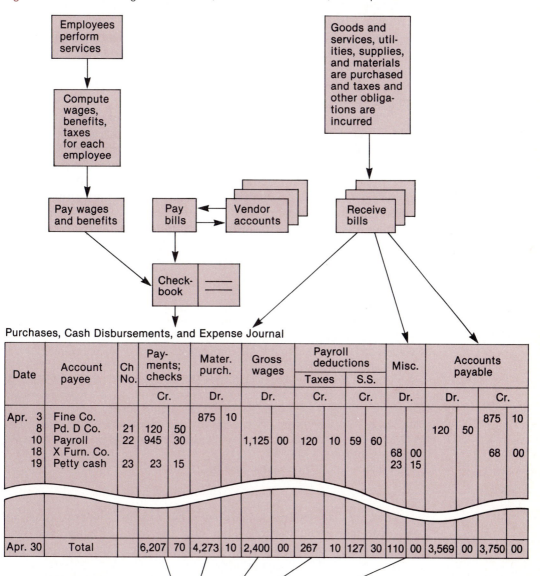

Purchases, Cash Disbursements, and Expense Journal

Date	Account payee	Ch No.	Pay-ments; checks Cr.		Mater. purch. Dr.		Gross wages Dr.		Payroll deductions Taxes Cr.		S.S. Cr.		Misc. Dr.		Accounts payable Dr.		Cr.	
Apr. 3	Fine Co.				875	10											875	10
8	Pd. D Co.	21	120	50											120	50		
10	Payroll	22	945	30			1,125	00	120	10	59	60						
18	X Furn. Co.												68	00			68	00
19	Petty cash	23	23	15									23	15				
Apr. 30	Total		6,207	70	4,273	10	2,400	00	267	10	127	30	110	00	3,569	00	3,750	00

Totals posted, and each entry is posted to ledger accounts.

Purposes for Which Information Is Used

In determining what information is needed, you should ask yourself why you want it. The usual answers are:

1. *To plan a course of action.*   Past information can be used for planning the future. For example, plans can be developed for the amount of goods to purchase (from sales trends), the number of salespeople to hire (from past sales per salesperson), and the amount of accounts receivable to expect (from past payment experience).

2. *To meet obligations.*   Obligations may include, for example, repaying borrowed money, paying for material purchased on credit, making deliveries promised for a certain day at a certain price, and reporting and paying taxes when due.

3. *To control activities.*   Many activities that are routine, but vital to your business, need to be controlled. Suppose, for example, that ordered material has not arrived, inventory has reached the reorder point, losses in supplies are occurring, and/or too much time is being spent on routine work. By having guidelines, instant data retrieval, and "warning flags," the control function discussed in Chapter 19 can be used to prevent trouble.

This was not done by Osborne Computer Company (Case VI–2). At the end of 1982, Adam Osborne, its founder and owner, predicted profits of $20 million on sales of $150 million. When January 1983 sales far exceeded production capacity, an outside CEO was hired to run the company while Osborne concentrated on research and development.

A financial officer was hired to plan for a $50 million public offering of stock. To everyone's shock, it was found that, instead of being a profitable, growing company, Osborne was heading for a serious financial crisis. Due to poor internal controls, costs and inventories were unmanageable. Excess inventories, contract liabilities the firm didn't know it had, and the need for bad-debt and warranty reserves would cause an $8 million loss in 1983.

Later that year, Osborne went bankrupt.

---

4. *To satisfy government regulations.*   For example, federal, state, and local governments collect taxes. They may also require conformance with safety, fair employment, and price control standards and might check on ethical standards of business practice.

5. *To evaluate performance.*   Information is obtained from selected records and reports for review and performance evaluation.

In addition to determining the information needed, you must know how to use it. This involves classifying it into a usable form. For instance, the information for accounting purposes was classified in Chapter 18 as assets, liabilities, owners' equity (or net worth), revenues, expenses, and profit. Many other types of information are needed, such as reports on economic and market conditions, personnel records and capabilities, sources of material, and specifications for products. Systems and procedures must be established to assure the availability of critical information, as the following example shows.

Pools Inc. (Case VI–3) has such a system. A full-time bookkeeper records journal entries daily. At the end of each month, a CPA firm transfers them to the general ledger and prepares an income statement and balance sheet. Thus, Bob Mallard, the owner, can readily tell how Pools Inc. is doing.

Examples of Needed Information

The kinds of information you might need are too numerous to discuss, but the most important are (1) records of service provided to customers and (2) records of services performed for the business.

Records of services provided to customers.   Services to customers provide revenue in the form of cash, checks, or promises to pay. Figure 20–1 shows a diagram of a system for recording sales of goods or services. Both real-time and delayed transactions occur in this system. For example, when videotapes are sold, sales slips are made out to give to customers. Later, the slips are used as daily summaries of sales, sales taxes, and so forth, which are then recorded in journals. Unlike sales, rental of videotapes requires additional transactions.

Records of services performed for the business.   Goods sold to, or services performed for, a small firm become its expenses of doing business. Payments must be made for items such as materials, supplies, electricity, taxes, and advertising. In addition, payments are made to increase assets and reduce obligations. Figure 20–2 diagrams a sample of these transactions.

Records of other activities.   Many nonaccounting matters also result in records. Sources for these records include letters of inquiry or complaint, agreements on sales, implementation of controls over production processes, and employee performance.

Even very small businesses need formal systems for keeping records, as the following example illustrates.

During its early years, Sue Ley kept the records for CleanDrum, Inc. (Case VI–1), in her personal checkbook and in manila folders. When cash was received, she deposited it to her account; she paid bills with her checks. Sales, shipping slips, and invoices were kept in folders and sent to an accountant at the end of the year. A financial package and tax forms were received in return.

The business was losing about $1,000 a month until a member of SCORE was brought in to help.

Timing of Information Flow

Data from activities may be needed (1) at the time of transaction (**real-time processing**) or (2) after transactions accumulate (**batch process-**

ing). For example, as shown in Figure 20–1, a customer is given a sales slip on completion of the sale, which is real time. An MIS can be designed to take care of immediate feedback. For example, portable computers, modems, mobile phones, electronic wands, or radios can be used to collect and provide information quickly, as in the following example.

Ernest Gore, an architect, visited Jean Soor, who was interested in building a house (names disguised). During the discussion, Ernest opened his battery-operated laptop computer and laid out the house plan as Jean described her ideas. Several times, they discussed "what ifs," and he made the changes to show their effects. He left with the plans well developed. Ernest attributes a great deal of his success in making the sale and satisfying the customer to this type of rapid feedback.

Slower turnaround may meet the requirements of the system and be less expensive. So you should balance the speed and convenience of real time with the economy of batch processing.

A chef in a restaurant is a skilled individual who schedules, cooks, and assembles meals. The server is a less skilled person who uses an information system to transmit information from the customer to the producer. Many restaurants use turnstiles for placing orders. First, the orders are written. Then the slips are clipped to a turnstile that the chef can turn to read the order. The slips on the turnstile serve to schedule orders in sequence, and they are also the customers' bills. The turnstile causes a short delay in the MIS but is simple and effective. Also, being impersonal, it does not make the higher-status chef seem to be taking orders from the lower-status servers.

Many restaurants now use computers to store orders. This method is also objective and effective. Some Taco Bell franchises use this system, which contributes to very efficient order processing.

Choosing an MIS

Figure 20–3 presents a checklist to be completed in order to define your company and the types and volume of information it needs. Also, the list includes an explanation of the current MIS, trouble areas, potential future needs, and areas of concern to address. Computer skills present, how much time to spend, and the time frame within which the system is to be installed must be recorded. Completion of this form should help a small firm form a better idea of the system to install.

THE ROLE OF COMPUTERS IN SMALL BUSINESS

Computers are rapidly taking over the roles of recordkeepers, clerks, and analysts as their capabilities mushroom and costs decline. Through the use of personal computers, minicomputers, and time sharing on large sys-

Figure 20–3 Defining What a Company Needs in an MIS

Type of Business
Retail _____ Wholesale _____ Mfg. _____ Professional services _____ Real estate _____
Agriculture _____ Nonprofit _____ Other _____

Business Size
Gross income _____ Net profit as percent of gross income _____

Types of Information Needed
Numerical _____ Textual _____ Graphics _____ Communications _____

Location(s)
Single _____ Dispersed _____ Franchise _____ Subsidiary _____

Transaction Volume
Invoices/month _____ Average accounts receivable _____ Average inventory _____
Inventory turnover _____ Number of inventory items _____ Number of customers _____
Number of employees _____

Current Information System (Describe.)

_____

_____

Trouble Areas (Rank each according to importance and number of people involved. Use more paper if
needed. Be as complete as possible.)

_____

_____

_____

Potential Future Needs (Include all possible needs, as they may be economically feasible in any system
designed.)

_____

_____

Applications
  Business Areas to Be Addressed (Number in order of priority.)
    Accounting _____ Financial reporting _____ Inventory management _____
    Cash flow planning _____ Market and sales analysis _____ Decision support _____ Billing _____
    Scheduling _____ Quality control _____ Payroll _____ Employee benefits _____
    Commissions _____ Customer tracking _____ Portfolio management _____
    Legal defense _____ Long-term planning _____ Tax reporting _____
    Other (be specific) _____

_____

Computer Skills Available in Company

_____

Proposed Budget for MIS
  $ _____ Maximum _____

Time Frame
  Desired start _____ Latest allowed start _____

tems, data can be quickly received, collected, processed, and reported. Even some of the smallest firms have—or have access to—computers. As a business grows, computers become more essential because of the increased volume of relevant information. For certain customers—for example, some government agencies—computerized systems are the only way the mountains of paperwork can be done in the time required. Can you really envision the IRS functioning without computers—or the air traffic control system?

Not only does the IRS use computers to process your return, but some of the returns themselves are now computerized. Over a million returns were filed electronically in 1989. Only those returns with refunds due to the taxpayer can be processed by phone to an IRS computer. The amount of the refund is then wired to the taxpayer's bank account, sent by mail, or applied to the next year's tax.

While this method is faster and cheaper to process than paper forms, the taxpayer must pay for the service. In 1989, H & R Block, which processed 82 percent of such returns in 1988, charged $25 extra, while Electronic Filing Centers, Inc., in Farmingdale, New York, charged $30.[2]

What a Computer System Includes

A **computer** differs from a calculator in that (1) its program, rather than a person, directs the processing of the data, and (2) it can store voluminous quantities of information in its memory. The total computer system is integrated to receive data, recall previously stored data, call up a program, process the data, present results, and store data rapidly, accurately, and without further human help. Computers have the capacity to provide large amounts of information needed for decision making.

The **hardware**—composed of the machines and related equipment—does the processing. A large number of programs—**software**—are available to direct computers to do a wide variety of processing. Much of the value of the computer depends on the software available. Programs designed to perform desired functions may be purchased from computer companies and software publishers, or written by a firm's own qualified people. (See the Glossary of Frequently Used Computer Terms at the end of this book for terms you may need to know when communicating with computer vendors or consultants.)

Strengths and Weaknesses of Computers for Small Firms

The key to whether a computer is an asset or a liability in a small firm is the use made of it. Given the currently available technology, the computer itself is not likely to be a limiting factor. The primary limitation is the availability of software that can economically accomplish the desired tasks. Figure 20–4 gives a representative list of the activities for which software is currently available and a second list of activities for which computers currently offer only limited help. Trying to assign any of the latter group

---

Figure 20–4 What Computers Do Best—and Worst

The computer is most helpful in the following applications, for which software is readily available:
- Repetitive, data-oriented operations, such as accounting, recordkeeping, or mailing lists.
- Organizing data into information, such as financial reporting.
- Codifying and monitoring procedures, such as technical manuals and production control.
- Calculations, such as financial ratios and tax analyses.
- Forecasting, such as trend projection and materials requirements planning.

The computer is less valuable, and may even be a liability, in operations of the following types:
- Solving unstructured problems or those that are not clearly defined, as in invention or innovation.
- Defining and/or establishing true authority in a company, such as leadership roles.
- Identifying new markets or products. The computer can be a major asset here, but only as a tool to assist human workers.
- Interpersonal relations, such as contract negotiations or establishing corporate culture.
- Defining the corporate mission.

---

of tasks to the computer can make the computerized system a liability rather than an asset to the business.

Notice the common theme in the areas in which a computer can be an asset: they are all repetitive, high-volume, quantitative tasks. By contrast, the areas where computers are less useful are the unstructured, open-ended types of activities where human creativity or judgment is required. While the latter are more innovation- or people-oriented activities, the former are the boring, detail-oriented jobs once assigned to lower-paid employees. Now smart small business managers will delegate this category of activities to the computer, with competent staff supervising its activities, freeing themselves to handle the more interesting, long-term problems.[3]

In 1983, four advertising veterans founded Rossin Greenberg Seronick & Hill (RGS&H), an advertising agency in Boston. Neal Hill, as CEO, was responsible for creating an organization to support the others, so they could be creative. He soon found that most of the people's time involved moving information around, leaving little time to create ads.

Hill computerized the noncreative work by getting top management to use word processors. According to one partner, who used one only reluctantly, "My capacity to do the paperwork quadrupled." Then the partners were able to motivate all the employees to use computers.

In a year and a half, billings doubled, while personnel increased only 25 percent![4]

As mentioned above, the problem in using a computer in a small firm is not usually a problem of the economic feasibility of the hardware. Instead, the limitation is likely to be available software. However, as major innovations are constantly being made, a good consultant may be able to identify software that will accomplish the desired activity, even in an area indicated as not an asset in Figure 20–4.

Ideally, the computer and human skills can be combined for more effective performance.

This is done at Plastic Suppliers, Inc. (Case IV–3), which produces parts in its McAllen, Texas, plant for shipment to Mexico for assembly and return for sale in the United States. Its engineering department uses computer-assisted design software to help its highly skilled people design the molds to be used to produce the parts.

Manual versus Computer MIS

The discussion of computers so far has been quite general. It has been phrased in terms of computer versus manual systems instead of discussing the more realistic systems that are partly manual and partly computer operated. All management information systems have some elements of manual operations and some of mechanization. But computers are increasingly involved in the mechanized portion of the MIS. Figure 20–5 compares three levels of mechanization of a company's payroll. The one to choose depends on the comparative output and cost, as well as the company situation.

Avoiding Potential Problems

The introduction of a computer system is risky. Therefore, careful planning is needed to assure accuracy, acceptability, and adaptability. Errors or inadequacies that develop in the system are much easier to detect and correct if the system is carefully designed and if employees are supportive and

---

Figure 20–5   Manual Versus Computer Processing of Employees' Hours

Manual using time cards	Partially computerized using time cards	Fully computerized
Workers clock out.	Workers clock out.	Workers key out.
Clerk collects time cards and records time; calculates regular and overtime; obtains wage rate; calculates pay, taxes, other deductions, and net pay; records in accounting records.	Clerk collects time cards and records time, selects software, and runs software. Computer calculates. Clerk makes entries in accounting records.	Hours are automatically entered in computer system. Computer calculates pay and makes entries in accounting records.
Clerk makes out checks.	Clerk makes out checks.	Computer prints checks.
Resources needed for each process: Time clock, cards, pen, paper, clerk's time, checks, accounts.	Time clock, cards, software, computer, clerk's time, checks, database, accounts, pen.	Time clock attached to computer, computer, software, data base, printer, accounts.

motivated to make it work. But, even when errors and malfunctions are detected, they may not be easy to correct. Have you ever tried to get a computer-generated error on a utility bill or bank statement corrected?

Betty Shaffer does freelance bookkeeping in her Richardson, Texas, home. Doing the work by hand, she says, was "driving me insane"; so she bought an IBM® PC® and an accounting program. She wrestled with the instruction manuals but made only slow progress. Even after she learned to run the program, however, her computer system would not copy data from one magnetic disk to another. Naturally, it all had worked fine in the North Dallas Computerland where she had bought it.

After several painful months nursing the sick computer, she persuaded the store manager to make a house call. He found that the machine worked well when the display monitor was moved from the top of the drive units and put on a table. He suspected that the screen must have been mistakenly given a magnetic coating.

With her computer cured, Mrs. Shaffer's business "took off." Because the computer does the calculations and prints the reports, she can do three times as much work—for three times the income.[5]

The chance of buying the right computer system can be improved by careful identification of the areas, products, resources, and costs affected by the introduction of a computer and then by careful selection, preparation, and implementation of the new system. Even then, you may have difficulties, as the following example illustrates.

A small, family-owned utility company contracted for a computer system. It hired a consultant to design the system, built additional space onto its headquarters, spent considerable time with the consultant defining its needs, and allocated $50,000 for the system. After six months of developmental effort—and $50,000 spent— the firm had a new room and a partially finished (nonfunctional) system. The computer had not even been delivered. At that point, management canceled the whole project.

Three years later, when approached by another consultant about their "obvious need" for a computer system, the company said "not interested." The manager's reaction was: "Once burned, twice shy. No, thank you!"

Another problem caused by the introduction of computerized operations is the need to upgrade your employees' skills. This need can be partially met by other small firms that provide training courses and computer support, as shown in the Computer Update.

Computers Require Added Security

Computers are used for keeping important, often confidential, records, which makes controlling access an important issue. In addition, as more people have access to information, it becomes more important to set up procedures

---

COMPUTER UPDATE

MICRO SUPPORT RESOURCE CORPORATION: TRAINING PEOPLE TO CALL BACK

In March 1985, Deborah Fain and four partners formed Micro Support Resource Corporation (MSR) in Atlanta, Georgia. The company trains and supports employees of client firms using IBM® PCs and/or compatibles.

After one training session of three and a half hours at MSR, the clients' employees can do spreadsheets when they return to their jobs. Afterward, if a problem arises at work, employees are urged to call MSR, whose personnel can answer almost any question about the computer's hardware, software, and peripherals. Once employees are hooked on calling MSR, the company is offered a support contract for future calls.

Fain says her company is ideal for smaller firms that cannot afford in-house computer troubleshooting.

Source: Jack Hayes, "Telephone Support for PC Users," *Venture,* March 1986, pp. 96–98; and Barbara Krasnoff, "MSR: A New Approach to Software Support," *PC Magazine,* January 13, 1987, pp. 259–65.

---

to assure that data are accurately entered and protected from being accidentally (or intentionally) destroyed or altered. This suggests that an important part of an MIS is the procedures set up for entry, updating, and control, which will be discussed more fully in Chapter 21.

The absence of security controls can increase the probability of such undesirable consequences as degraded operations, compromised systems, loss of service, loss of assets, and unauthorized disclosure of sensitive information.[6] Some steps that can be taken to provide security include physical control of facilities, such as guards and emergency power; access control, such as identification of users and specifying authority; and backups, such as appropriate saving of data.

Choosing Software

The primary software applications likely to be needed by a small business include word processing, spreadsheet analysis, account processing, file management, and electronic mail/messaging.[7]

Given the variety of company needs, Figure 20–6 presents a checklist to help you define your software needs and to give you an idea of the options available. It also provides the basis for questions you should ask in making your decision. By consulting a supplier or expert in software, asking probing questions, and then judging for yourself, you may avoid missing out on a good program for your company. It is easy to assume that your business is unique and requires a specially designed system to match your needs. Be wary of this approach, as there are many "off-the-shelf" programs (already designed and available) that may not satisfy all your needs, but might provide a cost-effective solution to most of them.[8]

Figure 20–6   Computer Software Checklist

To identify your area of need, check below:
Word Processor (W/P)
Memos _____ Correspondence _____ Camera-ready originals _____
Spell checking _____ Form letters/mailing lists _____

Spreadsheet (S/S)
Calculations _____ Graphics _____ Presentations _____

Statistical Packages
Summary _____ Regression _____ ANOVA _____ Time series _____

Data Base Management
Small, limited-feature _____ Large, multipurpose _____

Idea Processors
Outliners _____ Expert systems _____ Brainstorming _____

Communications
Internal _____ External _____ Data transfer _____

Graphics
Business: Planning _____ Presentation _____ Camera-ready _____
CAD/CAM: Planning _____ Presentation _____ Camera-ready _____

Integrated
W/P _____ S/S _____ Graphics _____ DTP (Desktop publishing) _____

Accounting
Recordkeeping _____ Financial planning _____ Point of entry _____

Vertical Market Software (specialized by industry)
Shareware _____ Commercial vendor _____ Custom-made _____

Operating System
Single-station _____ Multi-user _____ User interface _____

Utilities
Novice users _____ Intermediate _____ Advanced _____

Programming Languages
Scientific _____ Data processing _____
Prewritten programs _____ User-written programs _____
Other (specify): _____
_____
_____

What you get within price ranges of published software:
Shareware: Developed by individuals; may serve your purposes; minimal cost, minimal support from developer.
Medium-priced: Restricted features, which may include those you need; fully supported by the vendor.
High-priced: Full features, full support; wide variation in features, from specialized to general purpose.

Beware! Although cost is often a deciding factor, it is not always the best indicator of quality. Check head-to-head ratings of the software being considered.

Tailor-made versus published software:
Historically, only custom software was available. Now, there are many excellent off-the-shelf software packages that may fill your needs.

Customized Software
Reasons for using:
1. It is designed for your situation.
2. Efficiency can be built in.

Reasons against using:
1. It may take time to develop.
2. There is more risk.

Figure 20–6   *(concluded)*

3. There will be less testing.
4. The developer may not provide adequate support.
5. It may limit the company to one system or brand of system in the future.
6. The cost and time may considerably exceed original estimates.

Off-the-Shelf Software

Reasons for using:
1. It is available now.
2. It may be cost efficient.
3. It has been tested.
4. User-tested documentation is provided.
5. Other users can provide advice.
6. Vendor support is good.
7. It is less likely to be dependent on specific personnel.

Reasons against using:
1. It may not provide what you need.
2. The user interface is generic.

Choosing Hardware

Having defined the firm's needs and the software desired, you must then choose the hardware. Figure 20–7 is a checklist to help you determine which hardware to choose. (Note that it is completely computer generated.) Since there are many options to consider, the list can form the basis for questioning experts on how to tie into your current system. Most companies need a system somewhere in the middle—not too costly, but one that does the work satisfactorily (see the next Computer Update, page 632).

Figure 20–7 focuses primarily on personal computers because their recently increased speed and capacity has made them capable of handling most of the needs of a small business. An exception would be a company that purchases time on another company's computer system. This **time sharing** is often a cost-effective way of getting computer power without a large initial investment or a long time lag.

Figure 20–8 lists some selected sources of information to help you in your purchase of a computer, software, and peripherals.

THE ACCOUNTING SYSTEM AS AN MIS

There are many parts to the MIS of a small business. For example: forecasting; reporting to tax authorities, management, and workers; inventory control; and personnel records require collecting, storing, and analyzing data. One major MIS is the accounting system, which, historically, has been the first system to be computerized even in very small companies.

The rest of this chapter traces the flow of data for selected transactions in the accounting system. The discussion is based on the flow shown in Figures 20–1 and 20–2. Note the level of detail needed to design systems

Figure 20–7   Hardware Selection Checklist

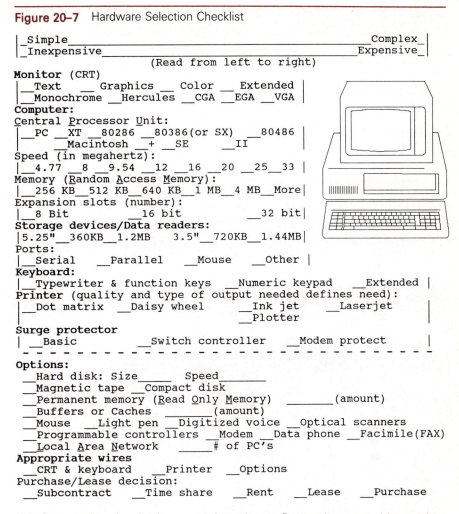

```
|_Simple_____Complex_|
|_Inexpensive_____Expensive_|
                   (Read from left to right)
Monitor (CRT)
|__Text    __ Graphics __ Color __ Extended |
|__Monochrome __Hercules __CGA __EGA __VGA |
Computer:
Central Processor Unit:
|__PC __XT __80286 __80386(or SX)   __80486 |
|   __Macintosh __+ __SE      __II          |
Speed (in megahertz):
|__4.77 __8 __9.54 __12 __16 __20 __25 __33 |
Memory (Random Access Memory):
|__256 KB__512 KB__640 KB__1 MB__4 MB__More|
Expansion slots (number):
|__8 Bit         __16 bit        __32 bit|
Storage devices/Data readers:
|5.25"__360KB__1.2MB   3.5"__720KB__1.44MB|
Ports:
|__Serial   __Parallel   __Mouse   __Other |
Keyboard:
|__Typewriter & function keys __Numeric keypad   __Extended |
Printer (quality and type of output needed defines need):
|__Dot matrix  __Daisy wheel    __Ink jet    __Laserjet   |
                              __Plotter                    |
Surge protector
| __Basic        __Switch controller   __Modem protect   |
- - - - - - - - - - - - - - - - - - - - - - - - - - - - - - - -
Options:
 __Hard disk: Size_____ Speed_____
 __Magnetic tape __Compact disk
 __Permanent memory (Read Only Memory)  _____(amount)
 __Buffers or Caches  _____(amount)
 __Mouse __Light pen __Digitized voice __Optical scanners
 __Programmable controllers __Modem __Data phone __Facimile(FAX)
 __Local Area Network   _____# of PC's
Appropriate wires
 __CRT & keyboard   __Printer __Options
Purchase/Lease decision:
 __Subcontract   __Time share   __Rent   __Lease   __Purchase
```

Note: Be sure to determine what the necessary *interactions* are. For example, memory minimums exist for many software packages; graphics will require the appropriate monitor, video card, software, and printer.

Think ahead to future uses. *Flexibility* of the system should be an important consideration. Rapid technological advances in computers suggest a high depreciation rate. Expect to upgrade or replace in two to five years.

and how the logical flow of data tends to lead to computerization. An expert may be needed to help on the more complex transactions.

Sales

Profits result from the sale of goods or the performance of a service. In every company, large or small, a record must be kept of each sale made. Figure 20–1 showed how a record of sales and cash receipts can be made and accounted for.

COMPUTER UPDATE

THE HAWTHORNE HOTEL: NINETEENTH-CENTURY HOTEL . . .
TWENTIETH-CENTURY TECHNOLOGY

The Hawthorne Hotel, a stylish 89-room inn located in Salem, Massachusetts, and dating back to the seventeenth-century witch hunts, has spent over $2 million restoring its appearance to what it must have been in the nineteenth century. The hotel's manager, Kenneth Boyles, states that the beauty of his hotel is its history, charm, and grace.

To reap the benefits of twentieth-century technology, Boyles bought an Apple® computer. Initially purchased for bookkeeping, its work load has steadily increased. Boyles added financial projections using income statements and balance sheets;

later, he began controlling the food and beverage inventory. Recently, Boyles added an IBM® PC to the inn's system to be used as new reservation system and for night audits. He also integrated the dining room into the system.

Boyles credits his success to two things: a stey-by-step implementation of the computer and help from Tod Riedel, president of First Micro Group Inc. of Boston. Reidel believes that starting small is the best approach for small companies: "It gets technology in the door."

The Hawthorne, Salem's new hotel
Source: Courtesy of Hawthorne Hotel.

The sale of a product generates a sales slip, on which the number and type of items, unit price, and total price are entered. Also, for all items sold, the sales tax must be recorded. Cash sales, when cash registers are used, can be recorded on a tape to be used as the sales slip. Cash registers and computers can record and total sales variables including types of product, salesperson, and department.

Figure 20–8   Sources of Information about Computer Hardware, Software, or Training

The following sources can be used to obtain information to help in choosing hardware, software, and training.

- *Computer stores and consultants.*   These can provide need-specific advice, packaged systems, and ongoing support, but they may be more oriented toward their sale than to your needs. The quality of advice may vary. Future availability of recommended systems is critical.
- *Friends or peers, user groups, bulletin boards, and seminars or workshops.*   These can give more specialized advice, though it may not match your needs. Since hands-on experience is often possible, you may gain a better understanding of your needs if not a specific answer. This is a good source of answers to technical questions, but beware of sales pitches.
- *Magazines, books, and libraries.*   Although these are good sources of background information and comparative evaluations of hardware and software, the volume and technical nature of the information may create information overload problems, and the information is usually not tailored to your needs.
- *Computer company promotion material and mail order.*   This is more oriented to specific software and hardware than to your needs, but it permits comparison of detailed technical specifications. Some mail-order firms offer ongoing support, but be sure to check, as this is important.
- *Industry associations.*   These may have systems already fully designed to handle your specific problems, may have data that could be useful to you, but may include a membership cost or licensing fee.
- *Government publications and SCORE/SBA.*   These are inexpensive sources of information, data services, consultant referrals, and possibly even funding, but the quality may vary and may not include the most recent technology.

Information on the sales forms is used to accumulate the sales income, to reduce inventory, to make analyses for future plans, and—in the case of a credit sale—to enter in the accounts receivable a record for the customer. A computer is particularly needed to help with this problem, as the following example shows.

According to Dun & Bradstreet, companies with fewer than 10 employees have 27 percent of their receivables past due, compared to only 20 percent for those with 50 or more employees. The smaller firms take on riskier accounts and then don't have the information and resources needed to make collections.[9]

Daily summaries of sales, sales on account, cash received (including charges to bank credit cards such as Visa, MasterCard, and Discover), sales by department, and other vital data can be recorded on multicolumnar or computer paper. Then, periodically, the total is entered in the ledger account. An analysis of this sheet can provide valuable information on sales trends, where the major volume is, or who is selling the most.

Cash Income and Outgo

Recorded sales totals must equal the total of recorded cash, credits, and other values if your accounts are to balance. Since cash is acceptable anywhere, the recording system for it should be designed and established with care so as to minimize mishandling and consequent losses. For cash sales, goods sold and cash received should be recorded independently of each other, if possible.

A waitress makes out the bill for a customer at a restaurant, and a cashier receives the money. At a gas station, gas pumps record the total gallons pumped, the price, and the total amount of the sale, and the attendant collects the cash. The cash register, placed in view of the customer paying a bill, allows the customer to check the cash recording.

Also, to maintain control, only certain people should be allowed to handle the cash and then only on an individual basis: each person starts with a standard amount for change, and the cash balance is reconciled each day or more often. The reconciliation makes sure that the cash on hand equals the beginning cash on hand, plus cash sales, less cash returns.

While some companies accept only cash, many others accept checks, but require identification such as a driver's license. Past experience with payment plans often determines the policy to follow. As far as credit is concerned, the proper balance should be maintained between safeguarding against losses and making the customer feel that a personal privilege is being extended in the granting of credit.

At the end of each day, businesses deposit in the bank the cash income received that day, less the change needed for the next day's operations. The deposited amount is added to the checkbook stub.

The business then makes payments by check or with petty cash. The checkbook is a journal that can be balanced by adding bank deposits to the last balance and deducting each check on a checkbook stub. Each check is entered in the cash journal to identify the account to which it is charged.

Small bills (say $5) are paid out of a **petty cash fund** of perhaps $50. Each payment is recorded and periodically transferred to appropriate accounts.

Accounts Receivable

When customers buy goods using open accounts or a store's credit card, each sale is entered on a customer account record, as shown in Figure 20–1. At the end of each period—usually a month—each customer's account is totaled and a bill sent requesting payment. As payments are received, the amount is posted to each customer's account and totaled for entry in the sales and cash receipts journal. (See Chapter 15 for a discussion of credit practices.)

Sales to customers using outside credit cards are treated as cash sales and processed as cash through the bank. Gross sales are then entered as sales income, as are accounts receivable and cash sales, and the accounts receivable or cash account (depending on the procedure) posted.

Some transactions—such as installment sales, handling damaged or lost goods, and settling insurance claims on damaged equipment—require more complex accounting procedures than we present here. For these, we recommend consulting an accountant or studying a basic accounting text.

Accounts Payable

As shown in Figure 20–2, a business incurs many obligations for materials purchased, utilities, wages, and taxes. The bills and invoices for these are entered in the purchases or expense journal or computer and may be filed by date to be paid. The journals can be multicolumnar to show how the money is spent. Columns are for categories with many similar items, such as material purchases, and the miscellaneous column is for categories, such as insurance, that require few entries.

The individual files keep track of whom to pay, when to pay, and how much to pay. After payment, they are filed for future reference. The paid bill amount is entered on the check stub and in the purchases and cash disbursements journal.

Inventory

Among the most troublesome records to keep are those dealing with inventory. While the physical planning and control of inventory were discussed in Chapter 14, we will discuss here the accounting aspects of inventory.

Inventory Accounting

After items such as materials and goods are purchased, their costs are entered into inventory, and then the used portion is charged as a material expense, as diagrammed in Figure 20–9. The diagram shows purchases of $100, an expense of $80, and an inventory of $20 at the end of the month. In another method, often used by high-volume purchasers, purchases are charged to expense as they are received, and then, at the end of the month, the unused portion is moved to inventory.

Periodically, the number of units in stock is counted. Once a year, most firms physically count inventory to verify or correct their records. This extra effort is valuable for tax purposes. A business selling a high volume of many items—a grocery store, for example—depends on periodic visual inspection of the items on the shelves. Holograph scanners, connected to a computer, are often used to read the product number, comparing the amount in inventory with expected needs and entering the amount that needs to be ordered. The introduction of computers has made the use of **perpetual inventory records,** for timely control, more feasible.

Figure 20–9   Examples of Recording and Adjustment of Transactions

1. (a) Receive shipment of material X, $100, entered in books when received.
   (b) Used $80 of material X, entered at end of period.

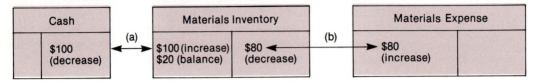

2. (a) Paid insurance policy premium of $600, entered when paid.
   (b) Monthly expense of insurance, $50 (1/12 of annual $600), entered at end of period.

3. (a) Wages paid to workers this month, $4,000 (160 hours × $5.00 per hour × 5 workers) (from payroll book).
   (b) $800 (32 hours × $5.00 per hour × 5 workers) was for work done and charged to last month's expenses.
   (c) Work done, and charged, this month but not yet paid.

4. Have machine which cost $1,300. From machine records, machine expense, $20 = (Machine cost [$1,300] − Estimated scrap value [$100]) ÷ Estimated life (5 years [6 months]).

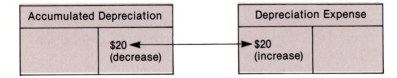

Costing Inventory

Items may be purchased at different prices, and in different quantities, over a period of time. What cost should be charged to sales as some of these items are used up? The most commonly used methods of valuing inventory and computing costs are:

1. *First-in, first-out (FIFO).*   This method is like "first come, first served." It charges sales with the cost of goods received first; inventory is charged at the cost of goods received last. When prices rise, this method tends to inflate computed profits.

2. *Last-in, first-out (LIFO).*   This method is like "last come, first served." It charges sales with the last or current cost; inventory is valued at the first or old cost. When prices rise, this method understates the value of inventory.

3. *Average costs.*   This method averages the prices of all items on hand and then charges the average cost to sales. This method requires considerable calculation, but use of a computer makes it feasible.

For tax purposes, the Internal Revenue Service (IRS) requires new businesses to select a method of valuing or costing inventory. A business must use the same method for the entire inventory and from year to year. Any changes in method must be approved by the IRS.

Most small firms use the FIFO method. When inflation begins to rise, however, many of them switch to the more complicated LIFO method to save on taxes.

For example, Chicago Heights Steel Company boosted the level of cash by 5 to 10 percent (by lowering income taxes) when it switched to LIFO in 1989.[10]

Expenses

A business purchases services from other businesses, and these become expenses. Material is transformed and sold, electricity is used, machines decrease in value, and insurance protection lapses. The bases of payments for these costs of doing business vary from a daily basis to several years. To determine true profit, say for March, income and expenses must be determined for March.

Taxes

Taxes deserve special treatment because of their importance and complexity. A small firm must account for and pay most of the following taxes: sales, property, license, corporate income, Social Security, unemployment insurance, and individual income. Chapter 23 discusses their characteristics. Taxes must be computed according to the latest regulations. The firm pays some taxes; others are collected from employees or customers for forwarding to the appropriate authority, such as the Social Security Administration. Timing of collection and payment is important. Small business owners and managers are advised to study state and federal tax regulations carefully or to consult a qualified tax accountant before designing an accounting system or paying the taxes.

Handling Expenses on a Cash or Accrual Basis

Many small businesses compute their profit on a cash basis rather than on an accrual basis because it is simpler. The **cash basis** assumes that payments and use occur in the same time period. But payment is not always received (or made) in the same period in which services are performed—as in the case of credit sales, for example. The **accrual basis** makes adjustments to reflect the actual expense of a service and the income received for it in a given time period, not past expenses or anticipated income. The accrual method is illustrated in Figure 20–9, discussed earlier. In deciding which method to use, balance the value of accuracy against the cost of the two methods.

Procedure for using the accrual method.   To calculate expenses by the accrual method, (1) obtain the values of all assets, payments, and obligations, (2) determine how much of each has been used during the period, and (3) transfer the used portion to expense, reduce the asset, or increase the obligation.

Examples of the accrual method.   A number of examples of this procedure are described here (see Figure 20–9 for sample recordings of each).

1. *Material for sale in a retail store* (discussed earlier).

$$\text{Expense of material} = \frac{\text{Beginning}}{\text{inventory}} + \text{Purchases} - \frac{\text{Ending}}{\text{inventory}}$$

2. *Insurance.*   Insurance may be paid monthly, quarterly, or annually for the period ahead. Usually, annual payments reduce the cost and are prorated as shown in Figure 20–9, example 2. In the illustration, $600 is charged to prepaid insurance (an asset) when it is paid by the small firm, with $\frac{1}{12}$, or $50, charged to expenses each month. This adjustment may not be necessary if premiums on various policies are due at different times of year.

3. *Wages and salaries.*   These expenses are paid regularly after employees have performed a service for the business. Salaries paid at the end of the month count as expenses of the month and need no adjustment. When wages are paid weekly or biweekly, adjustments must be made. Figure 20–9, example 3, shows the end-of-month adjustment for wages. The cash payment of $4,000 during the month includes $800 for work done last month. Similarly, this month's wage expense includes $1,000, a liability, which will not actually be paid until next month. Subsidiary records are kept to compute the wages, salaries, employee benefits, company payments for Social Security, and so forth.

4. *Machinery, equipment, and buildings.*   These facilities are used over a number of years, and so their value is consumed gradually. In order to assign a part of their expense to each period, an accounting method must reflect their **depreciation,** or gradual loss of value. The most

common method, **straight-line depreciation,** depreciates a machine at a constant rate over its useful life. The amount to be charged for each month may be determined by the following formula.

$$\frac{\text{Cost of machine} - \text{Sale (or scrap) value at end of expected life}}{\text{Expected life (in months)}}$$

The amount that has already been attributed to expenses is called **accumulated depreciation.** Figure 20–9, example 4, shows the adjustment of the two depreciation accounts by the amount thus arrived at. Consult an accounting text for the formulas for other methods of depreciation, such as sum-of-the-years'-digits and depreciation by use.

Many other items of expense and income need the same types of adjustment just discussed. The main issues to decide are: How much of the cost is used up during the accounting period? How much remains as an asset? How much expense is incurred but remains unpaid, as a liability? Find the easiest way to assign the proper values to expenses, income, assets, and liabilities. These records can then be used for analysis and for making reports.

Financial Statements

During each period—daily or weekly—a few critical accounts (such as sales) should be checked for trends and other changes taking place. This permits anticipating managerial adjustments that may be needed.

As shown in Chapter 18, financial statements, prepared from accounting records, aid management in its analyses. They are usually the balance sheet and income statement. Income statements should be prepared monthly, while the balance sheets can be prepared less often.

Tax reports are completed for the various government divisions many times during the year. These include reports for income, sales, Social Security, and excise tax.

WHAT YOU SHOULD HAVE LEARNED

1. Information is an important resource for small businesses as well as for people. Companies collect and process data, make decisions, act on those decisions, and start the cycle anew.

2. A management information system (MIS) collects, processes, records, reports, and/or directs data into usable form for management. These data, with meaning, become information. Managers usually want the MIS to meet the needs of planning, meeting obligations, controlling activities, satisfying government demands, and evaluating performance. Data can be processed in "real time," with instantaneous feedback, or batch processed later at a lower cost. Records of transactions between the company and both customers and suppliers can be recorded on

multicolumnar pages for management use. Records are also needed for many other activities.

3. Computers are becoming very important in small firms, as they can process data quickly. Personal computers, minicomputers, and time sharing are computer system options. A computer—hardware—is physical equipment used for storage, processing, and presentation of large quantities of data. Programs—software—direct the computers to process the data. Much of the value of the computer systems comes from the software.

   In a small business, computers are used to process data related to accounting, employees, forecasting, operations, and machine direction. Most systems involve both manual and computer operations, and the choice of the appropriate system depends on output, cost, and the situation in the business. A good system design anticipates employee resentment, dealing with technical complexities, the need for management control, and the need for the system to grow with the business.

   In choosing a computer system, checklists are used to analyze the present situation and available software and hardware. Many sources of information are available to help in choosing the systems.

4. Accounting systems are part of a firm's MIS. The sale of goods starts a series of accounting entries using sales slips, cash register receipts, credit card receipts, multicolumnar paper (or computer files), and ledgers to record changes in cash, sales, and accounts receivable. Computers can facilitate this process and enhance its value.

   Secure systems must be designed to handle cash because stolen cash is not traceable and can be spent anywhere. When a check is used to pay for a sale, the customer should be asked to show personal identification. Bank credit cards are treated as cash, but require payments and additional processing.

   When a sale uses company credit, the amount of the sale on a sales slip is entered into accounts receivable, and the customer is billed monthly.

   Bills for purchases and other items used are recorded in suppliers' accounts for proper payment. Monthly, the amount used during the month is moved to an expense account.

   Keeping track of inventory can be one of the greatest challenges for any business. Depending on the nature of the stock and the transactions, either keep a perpetual inventory record, logging each item in and out, or "take inventory" at intervals. The usual methods of valuing inventory are first-in, first-out (FIFO); last-in, first-out (LIFO); and averaging. Most small firms use FIFO.

   Expenses can be recorded on either a cash or an accrual basis. The simpler cash basis charges items as they are actually paid. The accrual basis assigns the amount of revenue and expenses to the period in which they occur.

KEY TERMS

management information system (MIS), *617*

real-time processing, *621*

batch processing, *621*

computer, *624*

hardware, *624*

software, *624*

time sharing, *630*

petty cash fund, *634*

perpetual inventory records, *635*

cash basis, *638*

accrual basis, *638*

depreciation, *638*

straight-line depreciation, *639*

accumulated depreciation, *639*

QUESTIONS FOR DISCUSSION

1. What are some of the management decisions small business owners or managers must make?
2. What types of information do they need to make those decisions?
3. What are some of the ways in which the needed information can be classified?
4. What are some of the sources of the needed information?
5. How would you answer the argument of "Once burned, twice shy" offered by the small utility company in the example on page 627?
6. In the example on page 617, what information did the trucking firm not have that was badly needed?
7. Discuss manual versus computer processing in a company you are acquainted with.
8. Complete one or more of the forms in Figures 20–3, 20–6, and 20–7 for a company you know or in one of the cases in this book.
9. Develop arguments for and against purchasing a computer for your home.
10. (*a*) Design a computer system or flow diagram for the accounting for sales (see Figure 20–1). (*b*) For accounting for purchases (Figure 20–2).
11. How might a computer be used in (*a*) a library, (*b*) a drugstore, or (*c*) a fast-food restaurant?
12. Discuss the use of each of the methods of valuing inventory under changing economic conditions.

SUGGESTED READINGS

Berney, Kevin. "Computerizing with Confidence." *Nation's Business,* April 1987, pp. 22–24.

DeLong, David. "Toss out Useless Paperwork." *Inc. Magazine's Guide to Small Business Success,* 1987, pp. 16–17.

Farmaian, Roxane. "Does Computing Really Help?" *Working Woman,* March 1988, pp. 42–43.

Hoffer, William. "The Electronic Blackboard." *Nation's Business,* April 1988, pp. 85–86.

Kainen, Bertha. "7 Mistakes That Can Kill Your Business and How to Avoid Them." *Changing Times,* August 19, 1988, pp. 45–48.

Long, Larry. *MIS Case Study: ZIMCO.* Englewood Cliffs, N.J.: Prentice-Hall, 1988.

McDougall, Ian, and Charles K. Hoyt. "Computers: The Electronic Pencil: One Small Firm's Approach." *Architectural Record,* June 1987, pp. 45–46.

Totty, Michael. "Small Businesses Find Electronic Banking Can Be a Useful Tool in Managing Money." *The Wall Street Journal,* July 22, 1986, p. 33.

"Ventures in Software: Prestarted Start-Ups." *The Wall Street Journal,* August 25, 1989, p. B1.

White, Ron. "You Can't Judge a Clone by Its Cover." *PC Computing,* April 1989, pp. 74–81.

ENDNOTES

1. John G. Burch and Gary Grudnitski, *Information Systems,* 5th ed. (New York: John Wiley & Sons, 1989), p. 4.
2. "The Return Is in the Computer," *The Wall Street Journal,* April 12, 1989, p. A1.
3. See Mark Stevens, "Six Small-Business Problems Computers Can Solve," *Working Woman,* September 1987, pp. 33–36, for more uses of computers in small firms.
4. Tom Richman, "Break It to Me Gently," *Inc.,* July 1989, pp. 108–110.
5. Jared Taylor, "Keeping up with the Computer," *The Wall Street Journal,* Special Report, May 20, 1985, p. 84c.
6. Burch and Grudnitski, *Information Systems,* p. 484.
7. "Office Technology: Software Use," *Inc.,* May 1989, p. 123.
8. See Neil L. Shapiro, "Money Matters," *MacUser,* November 1987, pp. 69–70, for information about software costs for small business start-ups.
9. "Odds and Ends," *The Wall Street Journal,* December 7, 1988, p. B1.
10. "Inflation Jitters Prompt Small Companies to Shift Accounting Methods," *The Wall Street Journal,* April 27, 1989, p. A1.

CASE VI–1
CleanDrum, Inc. (F)

CASE VI–2
Osborne Computer Company (A) and (B)

CASE VI–3
Pools Inc.

CASE VI–4
Horne Box, Inc.

CASE VI–5
What Is Profit?

CASE VI–1

CLEANDRUM, INC. (F)

CleanDrum, Inc. (CDI), formed three years ago by Sue Ley to clean drums for oil, chemicals, and other products, has made some progress toward profitability, but Sue feels she needs to make more changes. She decides to review the history of CDI's finances.

Originally, Sue obtained a loan of $60,000 from the bank and put $25,000 of her own money into the business. At the end of the first year, she was $30,000 in the hole, so she went to the bank for another loan. The bank lent her $12,000, and she mortgaged her house to keep CDI going.

The financial position of the company had not improved when Edie came into the picture. With no business experience—but with a degree in environmental engineering, a husband who owned a successful business, and an interest in investing—Edie bought a 50 percent share of CDI for the $32,000 CDI owed.

Soon after that, Edie came to Ben, a member of SCORE, to obtain counseling about the company's finances. She reported that CDI was losing about $1,000 a month. Company information indicated to Ben that overhead (as a percentage of sales) was high, labor and material costs were low, and, apparently, greater sales volume was necessary. He suggested that CDI do some advertising and/or hire a sales representative to help increase sales. Edie said that the company could not afford either of those plans. Ben pointed out that "there is no way you can solve your problem by 'economizing.' Your overhead—not your direct costs—is your problem, and it is practically irreducible." He suggested that a 5 percent reduction in price would produce a 15 to 20 percent increase in sales, allowing CDI to make a profit.

Edie approached Sue about reducing costs—in particular the labor costs. In answer to this, Sue pointed out that the workers were being paid the minimum wage and yet were putting forth "a good level of effort." Then Edie recommended hiring someone either to manage the plant or to go out selling. Sue said that CDI did not have the money to pay another employee.

The six workers in the plant started work at the minimum wage of $3.35 per hour. One of them, who has worked for CDI since it was formed, is the group leader now and is paid more than $6 an hour. Three have been with CDI less than two years and are paid about $4 an hour. The average wage is about $4.50 an hour. The workers mostly do manual, inspection, and machine-tending activities. Sue has talked about giving a bonus to recognize good work, but the problem is "How do you pay them?"

Sue and the landlord have been discussing expanding the plant by 50 percent. This will give more "breathing room" for the workers and make it easier to expand production from under 3,000 drums per month to about 5,000. The rent of the building will increase by 50 percent.

CDI's price structure varies but is about as follows. Used drums are purchased (about 50 percent of sales) from various sources for about $4 apiece, depending on their condition. Those needing straightening and/or rust removal can be purchased at lower prices. After processing, a cleaned and painted drum is sold for about $12 to $13. Customers' drums are processed and returned to them for about $7 a drum—again depending on the condition before processing. Drums sold for waste and part storage are sold for about $5 each. Pricing varies, but Sue feels that, in general, CDI's pricing is in line with its competitors'. (One competitor sells drums at a lower price, but he does not pressure test and appears to be able to obtain dirty drums at lower prices than CDI.)

The company truck brings in a trailer load of dirty drums, leaves the loaded trailer, and picks up clean drums to be delivered to customers. CDI has a policy of limiting orders so that near trailer loads are moved. It does not accept orders for less than about 25 drums unless the customer arranges to pay for transportation. This past year, CDI has been having trouble with truck breakdowns and repairs.

During the early years of the company, Sue used her checkbook for the accounting. When cash was received, she entered it into the checkbook. When she paid a bill, she paid it by check. She used sales and shipping slips to keep track of sales and invoices received. At the end of the year, she took all the slips, invoices, and checks to the firm's accountants and received in return a financial package, plus completed tax forms. See Exhibits 1 and 2 for CDI's financial statements for the three years in business.

During 1989, losses continued to mount—even with sales of about 30,000 clean drums. More money had to be borrowed, and Sue had to sell her house to keep herself and the business going. Acting under necessity, she

Exhibit 1

CLEANDRUM, INC.
Balance Sheet
December 31, 1989
($000s)*

	1989	1988	1987
Assets			
Current assets:			
Cash in bank	$ —	$ —	$ 6.7
Accounts receivable	26.7	22.7	12.8
Inventory	10.5	14.7	7.7
Total current assets	37.2	37.4	27.2
Property and equipment:			
Equipment	87.2	78.5	78.5
Leasehold improvements	—	5.5	5.5
Less: accumulated depreciation	−52.8	−36.1	−19.8
Net property and equipment	34.4	47.9	64.2
Total assets	$ 71.6	85.3	91.4
Liabilities and Stockholders' Equity			
Current liabilities:			
Accounts payable	$ 28.2	$ 36.1	$ 38.9
Current long-term debt	25.0	25.0	16.4
Notes payable	85.0	85.1	59.0
Accruals	5.4	9.4	11.8
Total current liabilities	143.6	155.6	126.1
Long-term debt	91.0	80.0	96.5
Total liabilities	234.6	235.6	222.6
Stockholders' equity:			
Common stock	1.0	1.0	1.0
Added paid-in capital	16.7	9.0	9.0
Accumulated deficit	(180.7)	(160.3)	(141.2)
Total stockholders' equity	(163.0)	(150.3)	(131.2)
Total liabilities and stockholders' equity	$ 71.6	$ 85.3	$ 91.4

* Values have been converted to thousands for ease of study.

stabilized her work force and called on Ben for further counseling. This time Ben and Archie, another SCORE member, joined forces in analyzing costs and seeking solutions to CDI's problems. As one practical way of helping, Archie helped design and install a simple accounting system.

Now, Sue fills in a multicolumnar sheet as income is received and expenses are paid. At the end of the month, she makes up a profit and loss sheet from this. Of the new system, Sue says, "Until Ben and Archie came in, I didn't know how many units CDI needed to sell each month to break even. We have figured that that level is 2,000 to 3,000 drums. Any units sold beyond this level will be making a profit." Sue decided at the end of this past year to have the accounting firm do the tax preparation as usual, but not the annual reports—so as to save $1,000.

Exhibit 2

CLEANDRUM, INC.
Profit and Loss Statements
($000s)*

Item	1989	1988	1987
Sales	$320.4	$303.3	$161.2
Cost of sales:			
Materials	99.1	104.2	98.9
Labor	64.6	86.2	48.1
Freight	42.0	19.3	—
Total cost of sales	205.7	209.7	147.0
Gross profit	$114.7	$ 93.6	$ 14.2
Operating, administrative, and selling costs:			
Depreciation	16.7	16.4	15.9
Payroll taxes	10.0	10.4	6.4
Repair and maintenance	14.5	3.9	11.3
Rent	7.2	7.2	13.3
Utilities	18.0	19.6	13.2
Salaries	20.9	15.7	13.0
Insurance	14.5	11.2	11.0
Office expense	3.6	1.5	1.5
General tax, legal, accounting	0.5	2.9	4.3
Selling, travel, automobile	10.4	3.4	3.2
Telephone	7.6	4.6	3.8
Sales taxes	—	—	—
Miscellaneous	0.5	1.8	2.9
Total operating, administrative, and selling costs	124.4	98.6	99.8
Operating profit	(9.7)	(5.0)	(85.6)
Income-legal	10.1	—	—
Interest expense	19.9	14.0	17.6
Net income	$(19.6)	$(19.0)	$(97.4)

* Values have been converted to thousands for ease of study.

Recently, Sue obtained a state loan to replace numerous loans that, because CDI's rating was low, were at rates of interest above the prime. (The state loan program has been made available to start or operate small businesses that need help.) CDI has a loan for two years at 8.5 percent interest. During the year, when CDI did not have $3,000 to pay a bill, Sue paid it from her own bank account but did not record it on CDI's books.

Questions for Discussion

1. (*a*) Analyze the financial statements. (*b*) What does the analysis tell you? (*c*) What would you tell Sue?

2. *(a)* Evaluate CDI's reports and the accounting system as management tools. *(b)* What advice would you give Sue on these?
3. *(a)* At what volume of sales does CDI appear to be breaking even? *(b)* What might be done to reduce the break-even volume?
4. How much profit should CDI make to be a satisfactory operation?
5. Archie changed CDI's bookkeeping system. *(a)* Was this a step forward? *(b)* Can you recommend further improvement? *(c)* Use of a computer?
6. What recommendations would you give Sue? Give your reasoning.

Source: Prepared by Charles R. Scott, University of Alabama, and William M. Spain, SCORE.

CASE VI–2
OSBORNE COMPUTER COMPANY (A): FROM BRAGS TO RICHES TO RAGS

To a publicist, the story of the Osborne Computer Company through January 1983 might have seemed an epic tale of the "Great American Dream." Here was a British expatriate who had parlayed a simple business idea into a rapidly growing, $100 million company in less than two years. Lionized by the press, Adam Osborne seemed on the verge of phenomenal wealth since his privately held company was planning a public stock offering during the coming spring.

By the end of 1983, Osborne's dream had become a nightmare. The stock offering had long since been canceled, over 800 people had been laid off, and in September the company had filed for protection from creditors under Chapter 11 of the federal bankruptcy code.

Adam Osborne's Background

In many ways Adam Osborne was the typical entrepreneur. The son of a British professor, he was born in Bangkok, Thailand, in 1939. He emigrated to the United States in 1961, earned a Ph.D. in chemical engineering, and then joined Shell Oil Company. Osborne soon became frustrated by the bureaucratic structure, so he left Shell in 1970 to found a company to do computer consulting and publishing.

Although he had had no training in electronics, computer science, or even business, Osborne quickly established himself as one of the computer industry's most respected commentators. In addition to writing almost a dozen books on computers (one of which, *Introduction to Microcomputers*, sold over 300,000 copies from 1975 to 1982), Osborne also branched out into technical publishing, and his company published about 40 books. But it was as a magazine columnist that he built his formidable reputation.

Osborne's most damning critiques were leveled at the pricing policies of microcomputer producers. Instead of cutting prices to enlarge the computer market and bring computing power within the reach of ordinary people, he claimed, manufacturers were reaping short-term profits. Not content with mere criticism, Osborne decided to start his own manufacturing company.

Most of the initial capital for the Osborne Computer Company came from the sale of Adam Osborne's publishing firm to McGraw-Hill in 1979. When he founded the new company in 1981, Osborne announced that his computer would be fully portable, would have ample memory, would come complete with at least five popular software packages, and would sell for under $2,000. The industry consensus was that such a computer couldn't be built and that Osborne would quickly be bankrupt.

It took Osborne only four months to build his first machine from cheap, easily obtainable parts. It took only a little over an hour and only 40 screws to assemble the Osborne 1. The small unit had 64K of memory, weighed only 24 pounds, had a 5-inch display screen, and was packaged in a plastic container that fit under an airplane seat. With a portable power pack, it could be used in courtrooms, in the wilds of Africa, in war-torn Afghanistan, or on Osborne's boat. He shipped the first units in July 1981.

The Osborne 1 computer was an immediate, phenomenal success. Unlike his critics, Adam Osborne had done his homework well and in only four months had developed a rugged, functional computer which he began selling for $1,795. The price included five of the most popular software packages, which would have retailed separately for over $1,500. As one distributor said, "It was like selling the software, and throwing in a computer for free." The introduction of the Osborne 1 was accompanied by an effective advertising campaign that stressed both the portability and the price of the new computer.

It was soon clear that the fledgling company's founder was not only an effective publicist—few corporate executives have handled the press as effectively as Adam Osborne—he was also a brilliant entrepreneur. The Osborne 1 was manufactured using standard, off-the-shelf parts, and the company was able to realize a 30 percent pretax operating margin even at the low sales price. In another innovative move, Osborne negotiated deals with the major software publishers whereby they would cut the cost of the software they provided in exchange for stock in the new company. All in all, Adam Osborne had created an impressive package.

Peak Years and Competitive Pressures

The years 1981 and 1982 were glorious for the Osborne Computer Company. By the end of 1981, the firm had 140 employees, and by June 1982 over 30,000 Osborne 1s had been sold. Such success made Adam Osborne expansive. In February 1982, he predicted that the company would reach $1 billion in annual revenues by 1984, and in November he predicted that the company would earn $20 million on sales of $150 million during 1982—

and double that during 1983. By the end of 1982, over 125,000 Osborne 1s had been sold.

It was during 1982, however, that serious competitive pressure began to build. During 1981, no other firm in the industry had been able to meet Osborne's combination of price and performance, but soon other comparable portable computers appeared. In particular, Kaypro Corporation's portable computer was similar to the Osborne 1 in price and performance, but had a larger screen. The entire microcomputer industry was being transformed by the IBM® Personal Computer (PC)—which during 1982 was establishing its market dominance.

The fortunes of Adam Osborne seemed to peak during January 1983. After a Christmas during which demand for the Osborne 1 had exceeded his company's production capacity, he announced that Robert Jaunich II, then president of Consolidated Tools, would become Osborne's president and CEO. The company was then shipping 10,000 computers per month, and Osborne announced there would be a $50 million public stock offering in the spring.

Jaunich had been hired to bring professional management to what was no longer a small entrepreneurial company. He immediately hired four new vice-presidents, including Don Waite as chief financial officer. Jaunich instituted formal managerial controls and initiated an internal audit.

The results of Waite's internal audit were a shock to everyone concerned. Instead of showing a profitable, growing company, it revealed a company heading for serious financial troubles. Due to poor internal controls, costs and inventories had become unmanageably large. Excess inventories and software contract liabilities the firm didn't know it had and the need for greater bad-debt and warranty reserves would lead to an annual loss of $8 million.

Since virtually all power had resided with Adam Osborne, internal communication and long-term planning were inadequate. Competitors were rapidly catching up with Osborne Computer Company. By early 1983, Kaypro was shipping 7,500 machines per month, and by spring Compaq Computer Company would begin selling an IBM-compatible portable computer.

Once Osborne's problems became clear to Jaunich, he canceled the forthcoming stock offering. In spite of pressure from Osborne investors to proceed, and in spite of the fact that going public would have made him a multimillionaire, Jaunich said his personal integrity wouldn't allow him to be party to an equity offering when the continued existence of Osborne was in doubt. Instead, he announced that the company would seek to obtain needed financing privately.

While Osborne Computer Company's new management team was trying to come to grips with a myriad of difficulties, the company's founder was making a rare public relations blunder. The company planned to launch a new computer, the Executive, in the spring, but was having production problems. Adam Osborne launched an advertising and publicity blitz timed for when the machine should have come to market. Publicity about the new computer caused dealers to cut their orders for the Osborne 1 in anticipation of ordering the new Executive.

The results of this publicity were catastrophic. Osborne had envisioned the Executive as a new product—not as a replacement for the Osborne 1. When orders for the old machine evaporated, the Executive was still not ready for distribution because of production problems. The inevitable result was a vicious cash flow squeeze. As Adam Osborne said, "We had an April without income."

To try to fill the cash flow gap, Osborne raised about $9.1 million from private investors during April. It wasn't enough. By the time volume shipments of the Executive began in May, the company had been seriously injured. Drastic steps were being taken to halt the financial losses, which for the 12 months ending May 28 totaled $26.5 million. Layoffs began, and all of Osborne's engineering resources were committed to the development of an IBM-compatible Executive II. During July, the price of the Osborne 1 was slashed 35 percent to $1,295, in a futile attempt to generate sales revenue. The second and third quarters of 1983 were periods of mounting competitive pressures and financial losses throughout the personal computer industry. In fact, an industry shakeout had begun.

In early September, suppliers refused to extend credit, and dealers were complaining about a lack of service support for Osborne products. Osborne laid off 300 employees (retaining only 80), and then filed for bankruptcy. The company was $45 million in debt, and had a negative net worth. While Osborne managers stressed that the company would remain in business (selling out of inventory and developing an IBM-compatible machine), few observers gave them much of a chance. However, Osborne promised that he would be back!

Questions for Discussion

1. (a) In your opinion, why did Osborne Computer Company fail?
   (b) Explain.
2. What does this case show about the "problems of success"?
3. What does this case illustrate about the need for innovative and creative entrepreneurship?
4. What does this case illustrate about the need to either (a) hire professional managers or (b) learn to become a manager?
5. What does this case show about the relationships among the primary business functions of production, marketing—especially advertising—and financing?
6. (a) Should Osborne Computer have gone public in the spring of 1983?
   (b) Give reasons for and against going public at that time.
7. What does the case show about the need for accurate and timely recordkeeping?

8. What does the case show about (*a*) the importance of cash flow? (*b*) the relationship among revenue (income), expenses (costs), and profits (or losses)?

Source: Prepared by William L. Megginson, University of Georgia.

OSBORNE COMPUTER COMPANY (B): OSBORNE REBORN

In the months immediately after the Osborne Computer Corporation (OCC) filed for bankruptcy, skeptics of the company saw that chances for recovery were poor. Within one month of the Chapter 11 bankruptcy filing on September 13, 1983, almost 90 percent of the U.S. retailers who had been selling Osborne computers had dropped the line, and the personal relationship between Adam Osborne and his hand-picked president, Robert Jaunich II, had deteriorated badly. The company ceased all manufacturing activities, and sales of the Osborne 1 from inventory were running at 1,000 units monthly as opposed to a monthly sales rate of 6,000 to 7,000 units immediately before the bankruptcy filing.

Even during this bleak period, however, some signs were positive. First, sales of the company's products in international markets (particularly in Europe) remained strong. In 1982, Osborne held 5 percent of the rapidly growing European personal computer market, and this enduring base of support would later provide one of the principal legs of the company's recovery plan. The fact that Xerox Corporation moved swiftly to offer service support for Osborne Computers after the company filed for Chapter 11 was a second positive signal that Osborne might be able to make a comeback. This move reflected the large number of Osborne computer owners who would be demanding technical support as well as follow-on products. Finally, by March 1984, Jaunich had resigned as president and had been replaced by Ronald J. Brown. When Adam Osborne resigned as chairman in the summer of 1984 (although both he and Jaunich remained on the board of directors), the debilitating management infighting had ended.

In the spring of 1984, OCC filed a reorganization plan with the federal bankruptcy court. At the time, President Brown claimed that the firm had a positive cash flow (not a great accomplishment for a company selling goods from inventory), and the centerpiece of his recovery plan called for the company to capitalize on its strong position in international markets. Further, the company pledged to pay off its $10.5 million bank debts in full; in fact much of this debt had already been repaid. Unsecured creditors fared much less well. When OCC entered bankruptcy, 850 creditors had had claims of over $30 million, and the company promised to repay only

$5 million in cash. In return, creditors would receive 20 percent of the company's equity. The company's reorganization was accepted by the court in July 1984.

The reorganized Osborne Computer Corporation emerged from Chapter 11 in January 1985 and immediately raised $3 million in a public stock offering limited to investors in the state of California. The company was still selling most of its products overseas, and its plans for the United States called for the company to position itself as a "vertical market supplier," effectively abandoning the general microcomputer market to larger companies such as IBM®, Apple®, and COMPAQ®. Its hopes were pinned on two new products. The first of these, the Osborne 3, was a follow-on to the popular Osborne 1. The second product was the $1,295 Vixon, which came complete with such popular software as WordStar®, and was MS-DOS® compatible. All of these computers were manufactured by other companies. The once-proved maker of the revolutionary Osborne 1 had been reduced essentially to an export-oriented marketing company trying to capitalize on its famous (infamous?) name.

Meanwhile, Adam Osborne himself had been a busy entrepreneur. After his company's fall, Osborne was besieged with lecture offers from groups eager to hear firsthand accounts of the rise and fall of one of Silicon Valley's most dramatic innovators. Partly to satisfy this interest and partly to present his own version of what caused OCC's bankruptcy, Adam Osborne coauthored a book entitled *Hypergrowth: The Rise and Fall of Osborne Computer Corporation.* In it, he documented some of the monumental problems the company had encountered as orders for the firm's products far exceeded the employees' capacity to cope. On a more controversial note, Osborne and his coauthor stopped just short of accusing Robert Jaunich of deliberately driving OCC into bankruptcy.

Osborne also pursued a new venture as a software publisher. In the spring of 1984 he persuaded an electronics distributor to invest $200,000 in his venture, Paperback Publishing International, and he then invested an additional $250,000 of his own funds. In January 1985, Osborne took his new company public, selling 6 million shares on the "penny stock market" and raising $540,000. The company raised an additional $600,000 by calling the warrants on the initially issued shares. By the spring of 1985, the company was still losing money, although Osborne claimed that sales were increasing.

In late 1989, Osborne was chief executive officer of Paperback Software Company in Berkeley, California. Its most popular product was a Lotus 1-2-3®–compatible spreadsheet called *V-P Planner.* Lotus has sued the company for copyright infringement.*

---

* For more information on Osborne, see Patricia A. Bellow, "Osborne Tries for Comeback in Computer," *The Wall Street Journal,* October 12, 1984, p. 33; Wendy L. McKibbin, "The Humpty Dumpty Game," *Infosystems,* November 1984, p. 40; Patricia A. Bellow, "Modern Phoenixes: Fallen Entrepreneurs in Silicon Valley Find Failure Is No Disgrace," *The Wall*

Questions for Discussion

1. How would you evaluate the company's efforts to remain afloat?
2. What would you have advised them to do if you had been called in as a consultant?
3. How would you evaluate Adam Osborne's activities after leaving the management of OCC?

Source: Prepared by William L. Megginson, University of Georgia.

CASE VI–3

POOLS INC.

In the initial interview with the Small Business Institute student team, Bob Mallard, owner-manager of Pools Inc., commented:

My immediate goal is to get the business to the point where my wife and I can leave the firm for a few months, if we desire, and let the employees run it. Our strategy to reach this goal consists of quality products and superior workmanship, determination, competitive prices, well-trained employees, tight control over collections, and adequate financing.

Bob believed that this goal had been attained earlier in the year, and he and his wife left for an extended vacation. An employee, Jay, who had been with the firm for almost a year, was placed in charge and given guidelines to follow in managing the operations. Four months later, the Mallards' CPA called to tell them that he had not received any financial information from the firm. The Mallards returned and found that Jay had fired several employees and replaced them with friends, had lowered the prices of the pools, and had increased sales commissions substantially. No inventory records had been kept, and he had bought materials from different vendors at higher prices. "My firm will lose about $160,000 this year due to this situation, and I'm charging him with embezzlement," Bob declared.

Products and Services

Pools Inc. was a swimming pool construction and supplies firm owned by Bob Mallard and his wife in a southwest city of about 350,000. Two types of in-ground swimming pools were constructed. The Gunite® pools were considered to be of excellent quality, and the average price for construction

---

Street Journal, April 30, 1985, pp. 1, 14; "PC Makers Try Again: Franklin, Osborne End Chap. 11 Options," *Electronic News,* January 14, 1985, pp. 21–22; Paul Freiberger and Dan McNeill, "That Was Then, This Is Now," *Compute,* September 1988, pp. 26–28; and "Readers' Report," *Business Week,* September 18, 1989, p. 12.

was $22,000. The average price of the good-quality, vinyl-lined pools was $9,000. A top line of spas, pool and patio furniture, pool equipment, tableware, and chemicals was carried. Mallard remarked: "The furniture is hard to sell to my customers. They pay a high price for their pools but buy cheap furniture to set around it." Future plans were to downgrade the type of furniture carried in order to increase sales. As a service to their customers, water samples could be brought to the storeroom and analyzed, without charge, by a computer owned by the firm.

The firm began operations six years ago when Mallard found that swimming pool companies' charges for repairing a neighborhood pool were excessive. He believed that he could do the work for a much lower cost, and that his experience as a drilling engineer and degree in business administration gave him a competitive edge in operating a pool building and repair firm. His company grew from a one-man operation in his garage to an S Corporation with annual sales of $1.2 million and 10 employees.

Mallard believed that superior quality and his determination to succeed were the firm's most important attributes. To him, there was only one other local competitor that built concrete pools of comparable quality. He believed there was great market potential for pool construction in the southwest city and its environs. The pools were constructed by subcontractors, and Mallard hired only the most competent.

People started thinking about buying pools in March and April. Construction started in April and ended in mid-August. Spas sold best during October through the spring months. To help boost income during the winter months, Pools Inc. started selling Christmas gifts and supplies. "We'll continue to incur a loss in this line for a short while; but in a few years, it will be profitable," Bob predicted.

Marketing

Marketing was considered important by Mallard. The majority of Pools Inc.'s promotion was done during March and April. The firm advertised in various local magazines. Six billboards had been placed around the metropolitan area. Newspaper advertising was used occasionally to advertise the vinyl-lined pools. Customers were the base for advertising Christmas gifts. Mallard advertised last Christmas season but stated that it was a waste of money and that word-of-mouth advertising was better for the unique items carried.

Telephone solicitation was used to remind present pool customers of various sales and times to purchase chemicals during the year. The firm had had the second largest booth at the home and garden show the previous year, and put together for prospective customers a brochure consisting of pool scenes, a history of the company, and Mallard's background.

The firm had two salesmen who were located at the office and answered people's calls for information. Mallard did not have them make sales phone calls. He was always promoting Pools Inc. and occasionally got involved in selling. He said: "The buyers of our vinyl-lined pools are mainly blue-collar workers or young professionals who cannot afford the more expensive Gunite® pools and whose principal concern is price."

Operations

The present location served as a showroom, warehouse, and office area. Mallard's private office was easily accessible for prospective customers to talk with him. There were two other offices—one for the secretary and bookkeeper and the other for layout work and drafting. These offices were simply, but functionally, furnished.

The warehouse section of the building contained offices for water sample testing by the computer and for the job supervisor to receive shipments and organize jobs. "Our warehouse is disorganized due to lack of space for inventories of furniture, diving boards, and various mechanical devices used for construction," Bob admitted.

The following procedure was used in pool construction: A salesperson sold the pool or spa unit. A drawing was developed for the construction plans. Once these were finalized, Mallard started contacting the subcontractors. He and the job supervisor directed operations to be certain that they were performed correctly.

Mallard stated that his firm's major problems were (1) lack of qualified and reputable subcontractors, (2) inability to recruit skilled workers, and (3) difficulty in finding a responsible supervisor.

Management

Bob Mallard did the planning for the firm. He hired the subcontractors, acted as consultant on difficult jobs, did public relations work, and kept track of job costs. Mrs. Mallard supervised bookkeeping and recordkeeping and shared the controlling function with her husband.

An organization chart is presented in Exhibit 1. According to Mrs. Mallard, the job supervisor assisted her husband in the hiring of subcontractors and supervising field construction. One employee was in charge of shop retail sales; another the warehouse and purchasing; and another the bookkeeping. A controller kept track of actual job costs versus estimated costs. An inventory clerk kept track of inventory. Two salespeople worked out of the shop, and two full-time construction employees installed the vinyl-lined pools. Mallard engaged a CPA for consultation. According to Mrs. Mallard, there were few formal reports. Employees reported to her on their activities whenever she thought it was needed. However, in the inventory control system, an employee filled out a requisition form for materials needed, which was given to the inventory clerk to mark it off the inventory list. The warehouse supervisor then obtained the materials for the employee.

Mallard and his wife were supported by her income obtained from buying gold and diamonds for resale. They both worked full time in Pools Inc., but neither drew a salary. Mallard preferred to retain their salaries in the firm so that it could survive.

Mallard defined these goals: a large building with a courtyard containing

Exhibit 1   Organization Chart

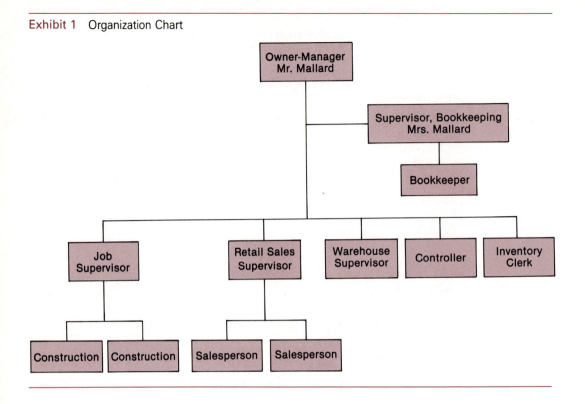

three or four pools, a full-time landscape artist, a fleet of service trucks, and a large volume of new pool construction (at least 600 pools) in three years.

Accounting and Finance

A full-time bookkeeper recorded journal entries daily; and, at the end of each month, an employee from the CPA firm transferred these entries into the general ledger. Financial statements—a balance sheet and an income statement (Exhibits 2 and 3)—were usually prepared monthly.

"When I started the firm, my financial goal was to be worth $1 million after five years," Bob Mallard declared. However, this goal was not achieved. "Now my goal is to achieve $4 million in sales next year. Sales should reach $1.6 million this year."

Mallard commented: "My major financial problem is obtaining adequate financing for the firm." So far he had used only personal loans since he had not been able to obtain a bank loan. "Banks require too much collateral for a business loan, and they only lend you money if you prove you do not need it." He planned to continue to finance future expansion through

Exhibit 2

POOLS INC.
Balance Sheet
December 31, 19—

Assets

Cash		$ 28,809
Accounts receivable		24,049
Inventories		56,931
Total current assets		109,789
Property and equipment, at cost	$122,181	
Less: accumulated depreciation	42,259	79,922
Total assets		$189,711

Liabilities and Stockholders' Equity

Current liabilities:		
Accounts payable	$211,567	
Accrued payables	1,302	
Current maturities of long-term debt	41,005	
Total current liabilities		$253,874
Long-term debt, less current maturities		22,009
Total liabilities		275,883
Stockholders' equity:		
Capital stock	500	
Retained earnings (deficit)	(86,672)	
Total stockholders' equity		(86,172)
Total liabilities and stockholders' equity		$189,711

personal loans. He stated that other problems were: (1) getting customers to pay for the last 5 percent of the pool and (2) cost overruns. The latter was more serious because it usually involved more money. His goal was to attain a 25 to 30 percent profit margin before taxes; but, due to cost overruns, only 14 percent had been obtained. A new job costing system had been developed recently, and it had been effective on the last few jobs.

Pools Inc. had a payment schedule on pools which helped to reduce accounts receivable. This schedule required at least $250 down when the contract was signed, and this portion was not returned if the customer withdrew from the contract. Further payments required 30 percent when the pool was dug; 30 percent when the walls were constructed; 30 percent when the concrete was poured; 5 percent when the decking was installed; and the last 5 percent, minus the deposit, was paid after the job was complete. (Mallard had taken unpaid claims to the small claims court). All other products were paid for when they were bought. An exception was made for a few regular customers who bought supplies and chemicals from the firm, for whom charge accounts were established.

Exhibit 3

POOLS, INC.
Statement of Income and Expense
Year Ended December 31, 19—

Revenue:

Construction	$336,002
Sales, service and retail	186,660
Total revenue	522,662
Cost of sales	282,667
Gross margin	239,995

Expenses:

Salaries	114,467
Advertising	35,756
Auto, truck, tools, and equipment	23,805
Commissions	13,513
Depreciation and amortization	21,115
Dues, subscriptions, and professional fees	7,329
Entertainment	1,940
Freight	7,498
Insurance, casualty losses, and warranties	15,599
Interest	9,420
Office expense	7,608
Rent	12,300
Repairs and maintenance	4,601
Taxes	14,866
Travel	3,413
Uniforms	2,160
Utilities	5,593
Warehouse	1,550
Miscellaneous	1,138
Total expenses	303,671
Net profit (loss)	$ (63,676)

Questions for Discussion

1. (*a*) When the Mallards took their vacation, had Jay been developed effectively to become the firm's manager? (*b*) Why or why not?
2. Evaluate the policy of having Christmas gifts and supplies in Pools Inc.'s product line.
3. Evaluate the firm's advertising and sales promotion program.
4. Evaluate the firm's organization structure.
5. What should be done to improve Pools Inc.'s operations?
6. Evaluate the firm's financial position. What are its (*a*) current ratio and (*b*) quick ratio?
7. What do you see as the firm's future?

Source: Prepared by Lyle R. Trueblood, University of Tulsa.

CASE VI–4
HORNE BOX, INC.

John Horne, owner-president of Horne Box, Inc. (HBI), is very optimistic about its future. He states that he now has sufficient capacity for sales of about $9 million and looks forward to having no worries about adding to capacity for a number of years. Recently, he acquired a new machine at favorable terms to expand the capacity of the plant, and he has been working with a Japanese firm in locating and expanding its production of a product related to packaging products. Through this collaboration, production can be shifted from one plant to another as needed.

Formation of HBI

For 39 years, John has been associated with the printing and sale of paperboard boxes such as those used for fast food, snack food, and bakery items. Nine years ago, he started his own business to take advantage of the low costs of in-line offset printing equipment. He had been president of the last company he worked for. When that company needed to expand and was looking for a new plant location, it had considered an existing plant in a small town in Clay County, the present location of HBI. John had been involved in the search for a new plant location.

John had a noncompete contract with his former company. It stated that, if he left the company, he would not go into the same box business, using the same type of printing presses, for four years. In the Clay County plant, an offset printing press (Press A) that complied with his noncompete contract was in place. The equipment was designed to produce a wide variety of products but was unproven in America for the quality of boxes needed. John felt that the machine could produce quality work at competitive prices, but others in the industry said it could not.

Ten years ago, John formed his own company and leased the plant in Clay County. Financing was arranged mainly for the large printing machine, and the company hired about 76 employees. It took about two months for the company to get the large machine operational and to train the workers. The company started producing in September 1980.

Equipment

In 1982, HBI purchased a second large press, which gave the company flexibility in its operations and increased HBI's capacity to about $6.5 million of output. However, cash flow dropped to the point where the company had to sell the machine in 1984 to obtain more liquidity.

In 1986, HBI installed a conventional press (Press B), which broadened demand for HBI's output through increased versatility. A year later, the company added a third press (Press C). About a year after that, the Japanese plant became operational. HBI now operates three presses, which represent the bulk of its $1.8 million investment in machinery and equipment and perform the most critical operations. Press B's operating costs are the highest per unit, but it performs the jobs demanding the highest quality. Press A can process up to six colors at one pass, has the highest rate of output of the three machines, and has the lowest cost per unit. Press C, a small version of A, is limited to four colors per pass and currently is used to produce for only one customer.

This past year, technical changes have been developed to improve the surface quality of boxes. One method required a heavy equipment investment and three times the cost for ink but resulted in a very high-quality output. The second method cost less and did not result in as high quality, but met customer quality demands. John opted for the latter. The plant next door, which is associated with Horne but makes boxes for higher quality needs, installed the more costly method.

Some operations are subcontracted. Sometimes the subcontracting presents problems. At one time, HBI subcontracted the making of offset printing plates to a company about 150 miles away. The subcontractor supplied new and replacement plates when needed. At times, a new plate was not satisfactory, resulting in downtime and/or additional resetting of the press. Recently, HBI spent over $8,000 on equipment to make plates, eliminating the need for subcontracting that work.

Operations

Customers of HBI order boxes annually and send releases when shipments are desired. HBI can anticipate the approximate time and size of a requested release. Usually, customers want the releases shipped the same day so that they can keep their inventories of boxes at a low level. All boxes produced are presold, some for future and some for current delivery.

HBI processes each order as follows: When a release is received, inventory is checked to determine whether the items are in stock. If so, the items are placed in cartons and shipped. If not, the boxes must be made. Usually HBI has the item in stock; one of its selling points is that it will ship the day it receives requests. Some items, however, do not require immediate delivery.

To make up an order, raw materials must be obtained. Until recent years, HBI was supplied by large paper mills located several hundred miles away. Two years ago, a nearby paper mill upgraded and revised its paper products. Now, HBI is that company's main customer for one product, and the company has added two other mills; each mill supplies a different type and quality of paperboard. In discussing the paperboard supply situation, John said that the board was in short supply and the price had increased somewhat. More important were the relations with suppliers. In the past, large users had clout and tended to obtain discounted prices; small users had little clout and had to pay the going price. John feels that the mills are taking care of the small buyers now so that HBI does not have trouble obtaining the supply it needs. Also, HBI has been able to take advantage of discounts for cash payments.

Machines A and C require a crew of three each, and, for an order of one to six colors, each averages about 4,500 sheets per hour. Machine B is slower. The setup process for Press A takes two or three operators working 8 to 12 hours; the other machines take somewhat less time. The processing of an order on a machine may take the rest of a week to complete. The three machines are capable of producing boxes to support $9 million of sales annually. At present, they are operating at 50 percent of capacity. The three machines can be scheduled to be set up and run concurrently.

The company employs 50 workers in the plant, two in sales, and two in the office, plus John and his wife. John says that his wife could take over the operation of the company if anything happened to him.

John keeps close control over operations—primarily output and downtime. Standards have been set by product and machine so that actual and standard can be compared. For example, one week the plant, on average, ran about 5 percent better than standard. However, one machine was 30 percent above standard, while another was 30 percent below.

One customer requires special treatment of its boxes. Because an electronic product is to be inserted in the box, the boxes must receive special handling to ensure that no static or particles of dirt are present. This requires specially trained people, and processing takes longer than for regular boxes, but these orders are more profitable than the other sales.

Sales

When John formed the company in 1980, he anticipated sales of about $6 million within a year or so. He planned the organization and operations for this level. As can be seen in Exhibit 1, sales have ranged between $3.1 and $5.1 million. Planning for too high a capacity caused added expenses. When the third-year sales dropped to first-year levels, John cut

---

Exhibit 1

HORNE BOX, INC.
Statement of Income
For Selected Years Ending June 30
(in $000s)

	1981	1982	1983	1986	1987	1988	1989*
Net sales	$3,101	$4,564	$3,319	$3,548	$4,092	$5,094	$3,321
Cost of goods sold	2,813	4,102	3,033	3,134	3,856	4,587	2,871
Gross profit	288	462	286	414	236	507	450
Selling expenses	56	96	111	63	45	44	76
Administrative expenses	132	242	153	141	162	175	144
Net operating income	100	124	22	210	29	288	230
Other income (charges)	(96)	(301)	(246)	(70)	(163)	(134)	(128)
Net income before taxes	4	(177)	(266)	140	(134)	154	102
Income taxes	—	—	—	5	—	47	
Net income (loss)	$ 4	$ (177)	$ (266)	$ 135	$ (134)	$ 107	$ 102

* Eight months only.

back on some of his expenses. He reduced the space he was renting and dropped some of the employees. Now he feels he has the costs under better control.

John spends about half his time in selling and half in production. A significant part of HBI's sales is obtained by a salesperson on commission. John feels that HBI has stiff competition, the number of companies is not growing, the sophistication is rising, and integration of processes is increasing. John says HBI's prices for boxes are in line with the competition or only slightly higher.

Financing

John started HBI by investing $1,000 as equity and obtaining an SBA loan of $250,000, secured by his personal assets. Manufacturing equipment was obtained through capital leasing agreements, office equipment was financed through a note payable, material was purchased on the basis of trade accounts payable, and wages were paid at the end of working periods.

During the first year, the firm was able to make a small profit but piled up a large obligation for trade accounts. Management found that it had to pay for materials and many other items before customers paid their bills. This was and is because material is ordered, stored, processed, and stored again before shipping to customers. Using the same terms for supplier and customer payments leaves a gap that HBI must finance. By the end of the year, suppliers were requiring HBI to pay at the time of delivery of goods. This widened the gap and increased the burden on the cash flow. This caused considerable concern, and steps were taken to reduce the loss. Rented space was reduced, production workers and office personnel were laid off, and some overhead items were reduced or deleted. Still, cash was in short supply.

At times, the company's debt was such that it had to pay interest rates ranging from 15 to 19 percent, with some rates stated as 2 percent above the prime rate.

Customers have worked with HBI management in making payments somewhat ahead of their normal schedules. Also, accounts receivable have been factored, and interest rates have dropped. The issuance of preferred stock has provided funds. All these actions have helped the company meet its obligations. However, the cash flow situation is still serious.

During the past year, HBI was forced to purchase the land and building that it was leasing. This increased HBI's debt, financed mainly by banks and finance companies. Interest rates range from 8.5 to 15.8 percent. The notes are scheduled to be paid off at the rate of $250,000 a year. HBI is in litigation for about $100,000 from the sale of a machine in 1984. The accountants believe HBI has a strong enough case to pursue legal proceedings, but nothing appears to be coming of it at this time. Exhibits 1 and 2 show most of the statements of income and the balance sheets from the origin of the company through March 31, 1989.

John bases much of his control on HBI's marginal income (MI), that is, sales income (SI), less materials. The MI by products and as a percentage

Exhibit 2

HORNE BOX, INC.
Balance Sheet
June 30
(in $000s)

	1981	1982	1985	1986	1987	1988
Assets						
Current assets:						
Cash	$ 11	$ 36	$ 22	$ 39	$ 70	$ 26
Accounts receivable	213	182	185	117	227	244
Inventories, FIFO or market	329	453	206	346	241	406
Total current assets	553	671	413	502	538	676
Land, plant, equipment, leasehold:						
Land and building	—	—	—	—	—	466
Machinery and equipment	930	1,868	980	1,479	1,494	1,816
Other fixtures and improvements	47	52	50	52	53	21
Total	977	1,920	1,030	1,531	1,547	2,303
Less accumulated depreciation	55	174	287	363	480	598
Net fixed assets	922	1,746	743	1,168	1,067	1,705
Other assets	10	20	—	13	10	18
Total assets	$1,485	$2,437	$1,156	$1,683	$1,615	$2,399
Liabilities and Stockholders' Equity						
Current liabilities:						
Trade accounts payable	$ 513	$ 879	$ 236	$ 314	$ 406	$ 305
Accrued expenses	56	25	47	43	72	56
Current part of long-term debt	94	233	113	152	193	253
Notes payable	—	—	45	37	42	30
Total current liabilities	663	1,137	441	546	713	644
Total long-term liabilities	817	1,222	642	915	814	1,514
Stockholders' equity:						
Common stock	1	1	1	1	1	1
Additional paid-in capital	—	250	268	281	281	281
Preferred stock	—	—	134	135	135	135
Retained earnings (deficit)	5	(173)	(330)	(195)	(329)	(176)
Total equity	5	78	73	222	88	241
Total liabilities and						
stockholders' equity	$1,485	$2,437	$1,156	$1,683	$1,615	$2,399

of sales ranges from about 30 to 40 percent. John estimates that he spends about 70 percent of his time in planning and monthly studies of his reports showing the year to date and developing sales projections. He receives information for each of his 15 products.

The Future

John is very optimistic about the future but unsure about what decisions to make. He feels that the company is in a favorable position to expand its sales. It has the capacity to produce the product for sales over $9 million. He expects that in a number of years he will need more machinery. The sales predictions indicate growth in sales. HBI has a good supplier, and

John feels he has good relations with HBI's customers. John is working closely with the Japanese management next door. But he is concerned about the heavy debt and ups and downs of profit. He believes that steps can be taken to improve the situation.

Questions for Discussion

1. (*a*) Calculate the financial ratios for HBI. (*b*) What do the results seem to say?
2. How does John Horne appear to compare with other entrepreneurs in his approach to the operation and financing of his company?
3. Considering HBI's financial situation, what should be done about the capacity problem?
4. (*a*) What are the major current problems for HBI? (*b*) What alternatives might be available for solving them?
5. (*a*) What do you recommend that Horne do? (*b*) Not do?

Source: Prepared by Charles R. Scott, University of Alabama.

CASE VI–5
WHAT IS PROFIT?

The Powell Company was organized in a small metal building two years ago to sell and service small boats. In order to start operating, the company had to hire some experienced personnel from an established competitor. Phil Powell, the owner, approached several of these potential employees and offered them (in some cases) the same wages they were earning from their current employers. In other cases, the wages offered were slightly less than those that were being paid by the competitor. Since there was little to be gained financially by the job change, the prospective employees were told of the advantages of getting in on the ground floor of the newer, though smaller, organization. The interested individuals were told that as the firm grew and sales and profit increased, it would be management's policy to pay a higher basic wage and also larger employee benefits.

The recruiting policy was relatively successful, and several employees were indeed enticed away from the competition.

During the company's first year in business, sales did not come up to Powell's expectations. After analyzing the situation, he decided that, in order to increase sales, he should move to a more desirable location, where modern equipment and facilities could improve production. The search for a new location was begun, and the employees—both the experienced ones who had been hired from the competition and the inexperienced ones who were being trained—were excited at the prospect of being located in a newer building with expanded facilities and the latest tools and equipment.

While the new facilities were being readied, there were few personal problems and morale was high. Employee performance was superior, and Powell was proud that none of his employees were clock-watchers.

When the facilities were completed and occupied, morale improved even further. During the first few months, more orders were obtained by the sales force than the firm was able to fill, but production quotas were met and surpassed. To all concerned it appeared that the company was well on its way to becoming a leader in its field.

With the new and expanded facilities, though, came new and unexpected problems. For example, overhead greatly expanded, there was a larger tax burden, and costs incurred for insurance, utilities, and personnel increased. All these factors contributed to a significant increase in operating expenses. So, while revenues were obviously increasing, expenses were increasing faster, and the business wasn't breaking even, much less making a profit.

Powell felt he could not fulfill his promise to increase wages and add more employee benefits. He told the employees that they would just have to wait until the financial position improved before receiving what he had promised them. He said that the increases would not be given until the company's sales became sufficiently higher than expenses to provide a profit.

Bob Benjamin, the production manager, agreed with Powell that wages could not be raised at that particular time, but he felt that seeds of trouble had been sown among the employees. He reported that as far as the employees were concerned, they could see only that sales were high and that production was exceeding expectations. Benjamin believed that unless they were shown a detailed report of expenses, they would continue to believe that the firm was making a substantial profit and had gone back on its word.

Powell, although he realized that this situation existed, said he also felt the employees had no justification for looking into the company's financial situation. In view of this, he said, he knew of but one alternative—the one he had previously outlined.

Questions for Discussion

1. What does this case show about the role of expectations in wage and salary administration?
2. What does it show about the relationships among income, expenses, and profits (losses)?
3. What did the move to new facilities do to the firm's break-even point?
4. (*a*) Should the owner show the books to the employees? (*b*) Why or why not?
5. What would you do now if you were the owner?

Source: Prepared by Gayle M. Ross, University of Mississippi Medical Center, Jackson, Mississippi.

VII

PROVIDING PRESENT AND FUTURE SECURITY FOR THE BUSINESS

Most of the general aspects of managing a small business have been covered in the preceding parts. However, we need to look into some special considerations before we are through.

First, Chapter 21 discusses a business's need to minimize the risks incurred in owning and operating a small business. By establishing insurance and reserves, most losses can be minimized. In properly planned operations, crime prevention, including security measures, can further reduce the chances—or magnitude—of other losses.

Chapter 22 covers some of the most important laws affecting small firms. It also discusses the need for social responsibility and the practice of business ethics.

Chapter 23 focuses on the taxes that small firms must pay. It also deals with the problems of collecting, handling, and reporting those taxes.

Chapter 24 deals with the need to provide for management succession. It also discusses family and manager problems with the firm. Many business owners do not like to talk about the question of succession. However, to be realistic in assuring the continuance of the firm or in providing a going concern for family members to operate, this question must be looked at analytically.

The cases found at the end of this part integrate the material covered in the text.

Finally, Appendix I at the end of this book shows a form for the self-evaluation of the general management of an organization. This form will provide a guide for deciding whether or not to become a small business owner-manager.

21

RISK MANAGEMENT, INSURANCE, AND CRIME PREVENTION

Everything is sweetened by risk.—Alexander Smith

Carrying liability insurance these days is almost a liability in itself. . . . Premiums are rising at a fantastic rate . . . [and] in some cases insurance coverage has become impossible to obtain—at any cost.—Charles W. Patchen, CPA and writer

LEARNING OBJECTIVES

After studying the material in this chapter, you will be able to:

1. Define risk and explain how to manage it.
2. Explain what insurance is and show how it can be used to minimize risk.
3. Discuss crime prevention as a way to reduce risk and protect assets.
4. Describe how to safeguard employees with preventive measures.

BUSINESS RISKS INTERNATIONAL INC.: CORPORATE PROTECTION

Recent years have witnessed a dramatic increase in white-collar crime, substance abuse by employees, terrorist threats against corporate executives, and other criminal risks facing business. A new breed of entrepreneur has come to the fore to help companies navigate through this minefield of shady risks—the private security specialist. Many of these people, and their newly formed companies, have successfully carved a niche in the U.S. security industry, which is now a $26 billion-a-year business and growing at an 8 to 12 percent compound annual rate.

Don Walker, a lawyer and former FBI agent, founded Nashville-based Business Risk International Inc. (BRI) in 1985. Previously he had been director of security for several firms and assistant general counsel at Genesco.

BRI now has 24 offices in the United States, 1 in London, and 5 in Asia—Bangkok, Hong Kong, the Phillipines, Singapore, and Taiwan. The company has benefited from trends that cause other companies major headaches, such as the growth of crime and terrorism. BRI helps firms reduce their exposure to risks. Companies, increasingly aware of the costs associated with these risks, often use outside resources to identify and eliminate or reduce the problem—just as they use other resources, such as attorneys, accountants, and management consultants. Small firms use BRI's services instead of starting their own security department; larger companies use them to augment, or add to, their current staff. In either case, BRI reduces the business's hiring costs and overhead expenses.

Among the services that BRI provides is investigating prospective employees and potential business associates. The pervasiveness of alcohol and drug abuse among employees has caused a dramatic increase in the demand for effective screening and investigation of workers, especially since a federal law passed in 1988 severely restricts (and usually prohibits) polygraph tests in preemployment screening. Now, the Drug-Free Omnibus Act of 1988 requires firms with a

Source: Photo courtesy of Business Risks International Inc.

contract of $25,000 or more with the U.S. government to have a "drug-free workplace" program. This affects *many* companies.

Walker tells of a case where BRI agents, working undercover, purchased cocaine from 35 employees manufacturing equipment for the U.S. military. In another case, BRI investigated a prospective foreign business partner for one of the firm's clients. A South American businessman was on the verge of being awarded a franchise for a major fast-food chain when BRI discovered that the man was a key figure in one of the cocaine cartels operating out of Colombia. According to Walker, this finding saved the chain "a lot of embarrassment and potential problems."

The future definitely looks bright for security firms such as BRI. As the nation girds itself for a major new war on drugs, demand for their services should continue to skyrocket.

Source: Jack Cavanaugh, "Running Scared," *Venture,* January 1989, pp., 31–33; and correspondence with Business Risks International Inc.

This Opening Focus deals with only a few of the many risks a small business faces. In this chapter, we will discuss some of the most prevalent risks facing small companies and show how to cope with them. The first part deals with risk and its management, the second part with using insurance to minimize loss due to risk; the third part deals with crime prevention; and the last part explains how security systems can protect your assets.

RISK AND ITS MANAGEMENT

Small business losses of money and property occur as a result of such things as fire, weather, theft, lawsuits, bankruptcy, and politics, as well as the death, disability, or defection of key personnel. For example, a physical peril like a hurricane, fire, or tornado may destroy the property outright. Or remodeling, street repairs, or flooding may temporarily close a shop, thereby reducing income. Goods may be stolen, damaged, destroyed, or spoiled in transit, for which the common carrier isn't liable. Improper storage facilities may cause unexpected spoilage. Forgery of warehouse receipts may result in product losses. Banks may either call in or refuse to renew loans. Customers may become insolvent and be unable to pay accounts receivable. The government may cut back on military spending. A competitor may hire one of your key employees. Given this rogues' gallery of lurking perils, what's a small business to do?

The answer is to use **risk management,** which is the process of conserving a firm's earning power and assets by minimizing the financial shocks of such accidental losses. It lets a firm regain its financial balance and operating effectiveness after suffering an unexpected loss. Some ways of accomplishing this are paying a short-term fixed loss (the premium paid for insurance) in order to minimize long-term loss from risks, or using crime prevention tactics.

Types of Risk

There are different types of risk, of course. A **pure risk** is uncertainty as to whether some unpredictable event that can result in loss will occur. Pure risk always exists when the possibility of a loss is present but the possible extent of the loss is unknown. For example, the consequences of a fire, the death of a key employee, or a liability judgment against you cannot be predicted with any degree of certainty. Many of these risks, however, can be analyzed statistically and are therefore insurable.

On the other hand, a **speculative risk** is uncertainty as to whether a voluntarily undertaken activity will result in a gain or a loss. Production risks, such as building a plant that turns out to have the wrong capacity, or keeping an inventory level that turns out to be too high or too low, are speculative risks.

Speculative risk is the name of the game in business. For example, Texas Instruments risked lowering the price of its TI 99/4A computer to increase sales, but financial losses were so great that it dropped its line of low-priced computers entirely. Levi Strauss risked selling its jeans through mass merchandisers such as Sears and Penney's, only to have department stores turn to Lee jeans.

As you can see from these examples, some business risks are insurable and others uninsurable. And, as you know, the greatest risk facing any small business—the ever-present possibility that it will be unprofitable—is uninsurable. Other uninsurable risks are associated with the development of new products, changes in customers' preferences, price fluctuations, and changes in laws. In this chapter we deal only with **insurable risk.**

Ways of Coping with Risk

The main ways for a small business to cope with risk are (1) risk avoidance, (2) risk prevention, or loss control, (3) risk transfer, and (4) risk assumption.

Risk avoidance is refusing to undertake—or abandoning—a venture in which the risk seems too costly. For instance, a New York bank experimented with having depositors of less than $5,000 either pay a fee to see a teller or use an automatic teller machine. When customers rebelled, the project was dropped as too risky.[1]

Risk prevention, or **loss control,** consists of using any of various methods to reduce the probability that a given event will occur. The primary control technique is prevention, including safety and protective procedures. For example, groups like the American Cancer Society are trying to reduce lost earnings due to cancer through improved testing and protective measures. If your business is large enough, it might try to control losses by providing first aid offices, driver training, and work safety rules, not to mention security guards to prevent pilferage, shoplifting, and other forms of theft.

Risk transfer means shifting the risk to persons or organizations outside your business. The best-known form of risk transfer is **insurance,** which is the process by which an insurance company agrees, for a fee (a premium) to pay an individual or organization an agreed-upon sum of money for a given loss.

Risk assumption usually takes the form of **self-insurance,** whereby a firm sets aside a certain amount of its own funds to meet losses that are uncertain in size and frequency. This method is usually impractical for very small firms, as they do not have the large cash reserves needed to make it feasible.

Generally, more than one method of handling risks is used at the same time. For example, a firm may use self-insurance for automobile damage, which costs relatively little, while using commercial insurance against liability claims, which may be prohibitively great.

USING INSURANCE TO MINIMIZE LOSS DUE TO RISK

The principal value of insurance lies in its reduction of risk. In buying insurance, you trade a potentially large but uncertain loss for a small but certain one (the cost of the premium). In other words, you trade uncertainty for certainty. But, if the insurance premium is a substantial proportion of the value of the property, do not buy the insurance.

The annual premium for a $50-deductible automobile collision insurance policy is $35 more than the premium for $100 deductible. By opting for a $50-deductible policy, the insured would in effect be paying $35 each year for $50 of additional coverage.

A well-designed insurance program not only compensates for losses but also provides other values, including reduction of worry, freeing funds for investment, suggestions for loss prevention techniques, and easing of credit.

Determining Need for Insurance

In deciding what to do about business risks, you—as a small business owner or manager—should ask yourself some important questions. Without adequate insurance, what will happen to my company if:

1. I die or suddenly become incapacitated?
2. A fire destroys my firm's building(s) and/or inventories?
3. There is theft by an outsider, a customer, or an employee, or an employee embezzles company funds?
4. A customer is awarded a sizable settlement after bringing a product or accident liability suit against the business?
5. Someone, inside or outside the firm, obtains unauthorized information from my computer?

Often, when such disasters occur in small companies with inadequate insurance protection or none at all, the owners are forced out of business or operations are severely restricted.

Do you remember the example of Don Albright and his Speedy Bicycle Shop from Chapter 5? His wife owned a day-care center, and both businesses operated on such a tight budget that they did not carry hospitalization insurance.

Later, when Don needed heart and abdominal surgery, they were wiped out financially. They had to sell the shop and give the day-care center to their church.

Types of Insurance Coverage

Some of the major types of insurance to consider include:

- Fire.
- Casualty.
- Liability.
- Workers' compensation.
- Employee health and life.
- Business continuation life.
- Fidelity and surety bonds.[2]

The basic **fire insurance policy** insures only for losses from fire and lightning and those due to temporary removal of goods from the premises because of fire. In most instances, this policy should be supplemented by an **extended-coverage endorsement** that insures against loss from windstorm, hail, explosion, riot, aircraft, vehicle, and smoke damage. **Business interruption coverage** should also be provided through endorsement, because such indirect losses are frequently more severe in their eventual cost than are direct losses. To illustrate, while rebuilding after a fire, the business must continue to pay fixed expenses such as salaries of key employees and such expenses as utilities, interest, and taxes. You also need this type of insurance for other types of business interruption.

To ensure reimbursement for the full amount of covered losses, most property insurance contracts have a **coinsurance** provision. It requires policyholders to buy insurance in an amount equal to a specified percentage of the property value—say 80 percent.

Casualty insurance consists of automobile insurance, both collision and public liability, plus burglary, theft, robbery, plate glass, and health and accident insurance. Automobile liability and physical-damage insurance are necessary because firms may be legally liable for the trucks and passenger cars used in their behalf, even those the company does not own. For example, when employees use their own cars on company business, the employer is liable in case of an accident.

Liability insurance, especially product liability, is particularly important because, in conducting business, companies are subject to common and statutory laws governing negligence to customers, employees, and anyone else with whom they do business. One liability judgment, without adequate insurance, can easily result in the liquidation of a business.

Today's legal and social environment makes the liability of the producer or seller of a product or service increasingly significant. Premiums for **product/service liability** coverage are becoming almost prohibitive. In fact, the crisis has reached such proportions that the first of 60 recommendations made to Congress by the 1986 White House Conference on Small Business was to "enact sweeping reforms affecting liability."[3] At least 10 states have adopted legislation limiting punitive damage awards.[4]

Small business owners are not always aware that they need product liability coverage. Through ignorance, they may not realize the potentially disastrous consequences of a lawsuit resulting from someone's purchase or use of their product. Or they may just not ever have considered the problem.

For example, Jeanne Parnell had given little thought to insurance—particularly product liability coverage—for The Beary Best Cookies (Case III–3) until a friend mentioned it to her.

Workers' compensation and **employer liability insurance** are related to common-law requirements that employers provide employees with a safe place to work, hire competent fellow employees, provide safe tools, and warn employees of any existing danger. State laws govern the kinds of benefits payable under workers' compensation policies. These policies typically provide for medical care, lump sums for death and dismemberment, benefits for disablement by occupational disease, and income payments for disabled workers or their dependents. As shown in Chapter 11, this type of coverage is required by federal law.

Another growing problem for small firms is what to do about liability when sponsoring athletic teams or some potentially dangerous activities. Employers are facing the problem in two ways. Some are trying to get reasonably priced insurance coverage. When this isn't feasible, many small firms are abandoning the practice.

Employee health and life insurance can be used in several ways in small firms. A firm can buy, or help buy, group life and group health insurance policies for its employees. **Life insurance** provides protection for an employee's estate when he or she dies while still in the income-producing years, or lives beyond that time but has little or no income. **Health insurance** provides protection against the risk of medical expenses, including doctor and hospital bills and prescription expenses.

Health insurance costs are becoming almost critical for small firms. Insurance companies treat large and small businesses differently. If a big company—one with over 100 employees—has a bad year and a high total health bill, the insurer regards it as almost a natural occurrence and figures that health costs will decline the following year. But it's common for rates at a small business—one with 10 to 20 people covered—to skyrocket if just one employee racks up huge health claims during the year.

For example, Mike Lower had trouble finding an insurer for his two Corydon, Indiana, businesses. The spouse of one of his three employees has a serious illness—which seems to be under control. Still, the insurers willing to cover him would charge an expensive $300 a month or more per employee.[5]

Business owner's insurance, an important coverage, consists of (1) protection of owner or dependents against loss from premature death, disability, or medical expenses and (2) provision for the continuation of a business following the premature death of an owner.

Business continuation life insurance, as previously discussed, is used in closely held corporations to provide cash on the death of an owner, while a trust agreement provides for its use. The cash can be used to retire the interest of a partner or, in case of death, to repurchase the stock of a closely held corporation.

Insurers issue fidelity and surety bonds to guarantee that employees and others with whom the company transacts business are honest and will fulfill their contractual obligations. **Fidelity bonds** are purchased for employees occupying positions that involve the handling of company funds. **Surety bonds** provide protection against the failure of others to fulfill contractual obligations.

Guides to Selecting an Insurer

In choosing an insurer, consider the financial characteristics of the insurer, the insurer's flexibility in meeting your requirements, and the services rendered by the agent. While insurance companies have agents representing them, independent agents represent more than one company. These independent agents use the following logo:

Financial Characteristics and Flexibility of Insurer

The major types of insurers are stock companies, mutual companies, reciprocals, and Lloyd's groups. While mutuals and reciprocals are cooperatively organized and sell insurance "at cost," in practice their premiums may be no lower than those of profit-making companies. In comparing different types of insurers, you should use the following criteria:

- *Financial stability.* In addition to your insurance agent, a good source of financial ratings and analyses of insurers is *Best's Insurance Reports.*

- *Specialization.* Some insurers specialize in certain types of coverage and offer the advantage of greater experience in these lines. For example, Lloyd's groups often underwrite unusual risks that other insurers do not assume.

Figure 21–1 Steps to Ease the Pain When Insurance Coverage Comes Up for Renewal

1. Consult your agent for methods of minimizing your premium.
2. Be selective in hiring employees and reassign existing high-risk employees to less sensitive jobs.
3. Eliminate risk wherever possible. Spell out tasks and rules in writing.
4. Consider boosting your policy deductibles to keep premium costs within manageable limits.
5. Before renewal time arrives, shop around among several agents for coverage.
6. Find out if your professional organization offers lower-cost coverage for its members.
7. Check out the special risk pools.
8. Consider alternatives to insurance coverage, such as self-insurance or coinsurance.

Source: Charles W. Patchen, "Accountant's Admonitions," *Tulsa World,* October 5, 1986, p. G-3. By permission, *The Tulsa World.*

- *Flexibility in coverage.*   Some insurers offer greater flexibility by tailoring their policies to meet your needs. Tailoring can be accomplished by inserting special provisions in the contracts and/or providing certain services to meet particular requirements.
- *Cost of protection.*   Only when you are satisfied with the first three criteria should you consider cost. Valid comparisons of insurance costs are difficult to make, but your insurance brokers, independent insurance advisers, or agents can assist you. In addition, a few things you can do to ease the pain when your insurance comes up for renewal are shown in Figure 21–1.

Services Rendered by the Agent

Decide which qualifications of agents are most important, then inquire about agents among business friends and others who have had experience with them. In comparing agents, look for contacts among insurers, professionalism, degree of individual attention, quality of service, and help in time of loss. Choose an agent who is willing and able to: (1) devote enough time to your individual problems to justify the commission, (2) survey exposure to loss, (3) recommend adequate insurance and loss prevention programs, and (4) offer alternative methods of insurance.

Noninsurance Methods for Dealing with Risk

Methods other than insurance for handling risk include noninsurance, loss prevention, risk transfer, and self-insurance. One or more of these methods, combined with insurance, may reduce costs related to risks.

Noninsurance is used to some extent by all firms, for they must inevitably assume some risks. To cover all potential losses is simply impossible. Noninsurance makes sense when the severity of the potential loss is low and when the risks are predictable, preventable, or reducible.

Loss prevention programs, by design, reduce the probability of loss. Examples include programs for preventing fire and burglary. Such programs usually result in reductions in insurance premiums, but they add to other expenses.

As mentioned earlier, *risk transfer* involves transferring the risk of loss to others, as in leasing an automobile under a contract whereby the lessor buys the accident insurance; whereas *self-insurance*—acting as an insurance company for oneself—requires adequate finances and broadly diversified risks.

CRIME PREVENTION

Small business owners need to practice crime prevention as a way of reducing risks and protecting their assets. Not only do they need to prevent major crimes, such as armed robbery, theft, and white-collar crimes, they also need protection from trespassing, vandalism, and harassment.

For example, Glammourrammer Beauty Salon (Case I–3) had a considerable problem with trespassers who defaced its property. The losses were so great that it installed a $3,000 surveillance unit and a high fence to keep undesirables from trespassing.

An awareness of the potential dangers helps to minimize the risks involved and reduces losses from crime. It seems impossible to have a security program that will prevent all criminal acts against a business. One can only hope to minimize their occurrence and severity. Figure 21–2 lists the five most common security problem areas for small businesses. The source article also describes steps that can be taken to address these problem areas.

Law enforcement agencies and the business community are learning to identify areas particularly susceptible to crime. Crimes appear to fall into patterns. Armed robbery occurs frequently in one type of neighborhood, theft in another, and both in a third. A prospective business owner needs to evaluate a potential site with this problem in mind. Examples of sites that appear to be particularly vulnerable to criminal acts are public housing projects, low-rent neighborhoods, areas of high unemployment, and areas with a high incidence of illiteracy.

Figure 21–2   The Five Most Common Security Problem Areas for Small Firms

1. Easily defeated door locks.
2. Lack of (computerized) information backup system.
3. Little or no control over distribution of keys or access codes.
4. False sense of security provided by insurance.
5. Improperly secured equipment.

Source: Paul Gassaway, ''Identifying Security Risks,'' *Business Age,* April 1989, p. 29.

Interface, a New York public policy group, found that, because of crime, the city creates new jobs at only a third of the national rate. In a survey of 350 New York small businesses, it found that 26 percent of them have trouble hiring workers, 18 percent say sales have suffered, 17 percent remain open fewer hours, 14 percent say employees have quit, and 12 percent have shelved plans to expand—all because of crime. After spending an average of $8,385 each year on security, each store had had an average of $10,746 in merchandise stolen and $4,202 in property damage over the past three years.[6]

Criminal acts have forced not only small but even large businesses into insolvency. Armed robbery, theft, and white-collar crimes are the major crimes affecting small firms.

Armed Robbery

In recent years, the number of armed robberies has increased significantly. An armed person enters the premises with the intent of obtaining cash or valuable merchandise and leaves as quickly as possible in order to minimize the risk of identification or apprehension. Since time is critical in such circumstances, locations that afford easy access and relatively secure escape routes seem most vulnerable. This type of robber usually wants to be in and out of the location in three minutes or less, and the pressure of the situation tends to make the robber more dangerous.

Several measures can be taken to reduce the chances of being robbed. They include modifying the store's layout, securing entrances, using security dogs, controlling the handling of cash, and redesigning the surrounding area.

Modifying Store Layout

Location of the cash register and high visibility inside and from outside the store are important in preventing armed robbery. If robbers cannot dash in, scoop up the cash, and dash out again within a short time, they are not as likely to attempt the robbery.

One convenience food chain removed from the windows all material that would obstruct the view into the store. In addition, it encouraged crowds at all hours with various gimmicks and attracted policemen by giving them free coffee. The average annual robbery rate dropped markedly.

Securing Entrances

The security of entrances and exits is extremely important in preventing robbery. Windows and rear doors should be kept locked and barred. In high-crime neighborhoods, many businesses use tough, shock-resistant transparent materials in their windows instead of glass.

Using Security Dogs

Security dogs are trained to be vicious on command. Businesspeople have found these animals to be effective deterrents against armed robbers. The animals may be purchased outright or rented. If you purchase a dog, you may wish to have it periodically run through a refresher course to keep it effective. Health and sanitation regulations in some jurisdictions may prevent the use of dogs.

When 589 convicted criminals were asked how best to foil burglars, the largest number—15.8 percent—said to have a dog. Next, at 15.1 percent, was to have an alarm system.[7]

Controlling the Handling of Cash

Daily deposit of cash, varying the deposit time from day to day, is highly recommended. Banks and other businesses rigidly enforce *minimum cash on hand* rules for cash drawers in order to reduce losses in the event of an armed robbery. Many businesses hide safes in unobtrusive hiding places and limit knowledge of their combinations to only one or two people. It is not uncommon for a sign to be posted on the safe, or near it, advising that the person on duty does not have access to the combination, or "Notice: Cash in drawer does not exceed $50." Other stores, such as gas stations, use locked cash boxes and accept only correct change, credit cards, and/or payment through secured windows during certain hours.

Redesigning the Surroundings

Well-lighted parking lots help deter robbers. If possible, try to keep vehicles from parking too near the entrance to the business. Armed robbery can be reduced by making access less convenient. For example, many convenience food store parking lots have precast concrete bumper blocks so distributed as to deter fast entry into and exit from the lot.

Some businesses find it advisable to use silent alarms, video cameras to photograph crime in action, or video cameras tied to TV monitors in a security office.

In a return to the Old West style, 33 Boston-area financial institutions have formed the Metropolitan Holdup Alert Team (HALT) to offer rewards for information leading to the capture of bank robbers. In monthly ads, photos of suspects snapped by surveillance cameras are published, and posters offering a $1,000 reward for their capture are also put in bank lobbies.

Since its start in February 1986, four rewards have been paid. In addition, armed robbery decreased by 25 percent among member banks.[8]

Theft

Theft has become a serious problem for businesses for numerous reasons: drug use, inflation, unemployment, and challenge, for example. People resort to stealing to maintain a standard of living or to subsist when unemployed. Sometimes, stealing is a game, a challenge. (Can I get away with it?) Unfortunately, in some circumstances, it is a bid for peer approval. Many national merchandising businesses add a factor of 2 to 3 percent to their prices to cover the cost of theft, but even this may not be enough to compensate for the total loss.

For instance, U.S. retailers lost approximately $1.8 billion, or 2.2 percent of sales, in 1987 to theft and paperwork errors. The favorite targets were women's apparel, records and tapes, and consumer electronics.[9] Supermarkets alone lost $1.1 billion.[10]

Types of Theft

Essentially, two types of theft occur: that done by outsiders, usually known as *shoplifting*, and that done by employees, *employee theft*. Retailers sometimes refer to losses from both kinds of theft as *shrinkage*.

Shoplifting.   **Shoplifting** may be done by the amateur, the kleptomaniac, or the professional. The amateur may be a thrill seeker who takes an item or two to see whether or not he or she can get away with it. (This is often the case with children and teenagers.) Or the person may not be able to purchase the item, but the desire for it overcomes self-control. The **kleptomaniac** has an uncontrollable urge to take things, whether they are needed or not. The professional shoplifter may wear specially prepared or large garments, carry a large handbag, or ask for an empty box to conceal stolen merchandise.

Sometimes, shoplifters walk in with an air of confidence (as if they were delivery persons or clerks), pick up merchandise, and calmly walk out of the store. Business owners and managers often find the various techniques that people use to remove merchandise from their premises shocking.

A well-known matron was at the checkout counter. Upon inspection, her large purse was found to contain several prepackaged steaks and packages of luncheon meat. The store owner observed: "I thought she was one of our best customers. She has been coming here for years. I wonder how much she has taken."

A man entered a store during the rush hour, picked up a large box, moved to the cigarette display, filled the box with cartons of cigarettes, hoisted it onto his shoulder, and proceeded to pass through the checkout as if he had an empty box. Suddenly the box separated, and 30 cartons of cigarettes fell to the floor. The culprit departed in haste. Not easily discouraged, the culprit returned the following day with a well-taped box. Recognized immediately, he was escorted from the premises.

Retailers are now striking back at shoplifters by means of a new tactic called **civil recovery,** or **civil restitution.** Since 1973, 35 states have passed laws permitting stores to send letters to shoplifters or their parents demanding payment for the items taken. Some states permit not only recovery of the amount stolen but also damage awards for additional costs of crime prevention, damage to displays, or injuries resulting from the act.

Civil Demand Associates, of Sherman Oaks, California, is a four-year-old firm specializing in this type of recovery. One of several law firms dedicated to this new weapon against shoplifting, it has clients nationwide.[11]

Employee theft.   Employee theft is a major source of loss. It may range from the act of an individual who takes only one or two items (such as pens or paper clips) to raids by groups that remove truckloads of merchandise.

A fast-food place lost $20,000 worth of raw chicken in a six-month period: not by the piece or even as whole chickens, but by the case—out the back door.

Construction materials may be stolen by either employees or outsiders. Two or more employees may conspire to cheat their employer by stealing. Lack of controls, looseness of accountability, and the minimal or nonexistent security at many storage yards and job sites lead to this type of pilferage.

Workers loaded materials to take to a job site, but no tally sheet identifying the quantity or kind of material was filled out. The trucks were detoured to the site of a side job being done after hours by the employees, and a portion of the material was unloaded.

Placing too much confidence in employees may result in problems. Employees sometimes conspire with outsiders to steal from their employer. They may do this in various ways—for example, by charging the outsiders a lower price or by placing additional merchandise in their packages.

A service station attendant serviced a friend's car, changing the oil, lubricating it, and putting in $4 worth of gasoline. He charged the friend only $1. And a tire dealer's service attendant sold four first-line tires to a customer for $50, then pocketed the cash.

Figure 21–3   Stealing at Work

A study of 453 employees caught stealing from their company showed that:
- 90 precent are under 30 years old.
- 78 percent steal without an accomplice.
- 63 percent are male.
- 60 percent are full-time workers.
- 60 percent steal merchandise.

Source: Security Management magazine, as reported in *The Wall Street Journal,* November 11, 1986, p. 39. Reprinted by permission of *The Wall Street Journal,* © Dow Jones & Company, Inc., 1986. ALL RIGHTS RESERVED.

How serious is employee theft? It has been estimated that it costs all businesses between $70 and $100 billion annually. In one year, the FBI reported $2.19 billion in embezzlements alone.[12] Small firms are particularly vulnerable to embezzlement because they often cannot afford to have different employees (*a*) handle and (*b*) record and report on their finances.

Who Steals?

Investigators say that employees who think their income is too low, or stagnating, steal more often and in greater amounts than other employees. A University of Minnesota study of 5,000 workers at stores, hospitals, and electronics manufacturing plants in the Minneapolis area concluded that the most likely employee thieves are young, ambitious clerks, and professionals who feel frustrated in their jobs.[13]

As you can see from Figure 21–3, another study showed that those who steal tend to be young, full-time employees operating alone, and they steal merchandise more often than cash. The computer can be used to help identify employees who steal (see Computer Update).

Techniques for Preventing Theft

Several loss prevention techniques can be used by retail establishments and construction firms.

Retail establishments.   These firms have found the use of some of the following measures effective in reducing theft:

1.   Wide-angle and one-way mirrors to observe employee or customer behavior.
2.   TV cameras, tied to monitors, to observe a large area of the store.
3.   Electronic noise activators—some visible, some not—to warn of unprocessed merchandise leaving the store.
4.   Security guards, when economically feasible.
5.   Security audits, such as the following:
     a.   Unannounced spot checks of critical activity areas, such as cash registers, employees' packages, car trunks, lunch pails, and waste disposal holding areas.

COMPUTER UPDATE

KROY SIGN SYSTEMS: WATCH THAT SIGN—IT MAY BE WATCHING YOU!

Kroy Sign Systems of Scottsdale, Arizona, has proposed the security system of the future. According to John Glitsos, Kroy's vice president and general manager, the computer and burglar alarm system that "sees" all would implant motion-detecting sensors in hallway signs and link them to a central computer. A tiny microchip transmitter would be installed in employees' and visitors' name badges. Anyone walking in the area without a valid name tag would activate the sensors, which would set off an alarm. Although the system does not yet exist, it could easily be created, says Glitsos.

Source: "Computer 'Watches' Where You Go," *USA Today*, November 24, 1986, p. 4B. Copyright 1986, USA TODAY. Reprinted with permission.

---

    b. Visible security surveillance of work activities.

    c. Weekly, monthly, or quarterly physical inventory checks.

6. Using paper-and-pencil tests of a potential employee's honesty, such as the Compu-Scan Pre-Employment Risk Analysis (see Computer Update in Chapter 10).

Construction contractors. These firms should take special care to prevent or minimize theft. Planning and control of the timing and amount of materials purchasing and scheduling of operations can be used to arrange for just-in-time delivery. One contractor found that by scheduling low-inventory

"The salesman said it was the most effective home security system on the market."

Source: Reprinted from *The Wall Street Journal;* permission Cartoon Features Syndicate.

levels on weekends, he could substantially reduce his losses. Such improvements also help maintain more effective control over costs.

In addition to dogs and security guards (discussed earlier), other security measures are possible:

1. Fencing and lighting storage yards and clearing the area adjacent to the fence.
2. Using locking systems that are difficult to jimmy. A locksmith or hardware dealer may provide the latest lock systems.
3. Assigning a knowledgeable employee the responsibility for checking materials into the job site. Unfortunately, too many people fail to recognize the importance of this activity and permit it to be dealt with haphazardly. They say, "Put it over there and check back with me when you've finished unloading." Unannounced rotation of the person responsible for receiving materials may serve as a deterrent to collusion with the delivery person.

A contractor purchased a mobile concrete mixer and sent it to the site of one of his jobs. Those responsible for the mixer left it outside the fenced-in area that night, and it was stolen. Later, the contractor found that a subordinate had failed to record it for insurance coverage.

White-Collar Crime

Another category of serious abuse against business is white-collar crime, especially employee theft and computer crimes, which have been rising rapidly. Possibly, the losses total more than in other categories.

Types of White-Collar Crimes

White-collar crimes include the removal of cash; falsification of accounts; fraudulent computer manipulation; external accessing of the computer; bribery of purchasing agents and other employees; collusion that results in unrecorded transactions; sale of proprietary information; and sabotage of new technology, new or old products, or customer relations. According to the FBI special agent-in-charge in Cleveland, Ohio, white-collar crime adds 15 percent to the price of everything we buy. It costs us at least $200 billion each year, which is far more than robbers take.[14]

Computer security is becoming a real problem for small firms. There are two problems as far as computer use is concerned. They are: (1) fraudulent use and (2) unintentional destruction of data. "Only about half the companies [with computers] have any computer rules at all."[15] Guidelines, rules, and passwords should be changed frequently. Thieves working with computers can be real "big-time operators." Not only has the number of such crimes increased; so has their magnitude.

Steve Albrecht, of Brigham Young University, has estimated that thieves working with computers average $500,000 each time they strike, as opposed to an average of $23,500 for each white-collar crime, while armed robbers average only $250 per grab.[16]

A new kind of white-collar criminal is called *the credit doctor*. These computer con artists gain access to credit bureau computer files to steal the personnel data of people who have good credit histories, which they sell to people with bad credit records.[17] Lenders then grant credit to these poor risks and end up footing the bill when a credit applicant stops making payments, or vanishes.

Ways to Minimize White-Collar Crime

Special measures must be taken to minimize crimes by white-collar personnel. One way might be to publicize the dangers of such crime.

A new federal study of forgers, counterfeiters, defrauders, and embezzlers by the Bureau of Justice Statistics shows that white-collar crime does not pay. In its first study to find out how white-collar offenders fared, the bureau found that white-collar defendants were prosecuted and convicted at rates similar to those accused of violent, property, and public order crimes.[18] But they are more likely to be sent to minimum-security or "country club" prisons.

Other deterrents to white-collar crime include audits, officer-handled adjustments, work habits vigils, identification, and insurance. As mentioned above, since computer crimes are increasing in frequency, small firms that use computers may need the services of a firm with computer security expertise.

Audits.   **Audits** of data such as past sales transactions, inventory levels, purchase prices, and accounts receivable may uncover undesirable activities. Cashiers and disbursing agents have been known to prepare bogus or forged invoices, purchase orders, receiving reports, and so forth. Purchasing agents have also taken bribes. The kind of detective work required to uncover these crimes entails a more thorough audit than sometimes takes place. But spot audit of documents and of receiving areas should help in reducing losses, at a low cost.

Officer-handled adjustments.   Sales adjustments on large items should be handled by an officer of the company, not the salesperson. This policy reduces the chances of collusion and cash compromises to the customer's and salesperson's advantage. Appropriate reports showing adjustments made on each customer's account should aid in revealing any misdeeds.

Work habits vigils.   Be aware of white-collar employees' work habits. They may all be open and aboveboard, but they should be checked. You should ask such questions as: Do they work nights regularly? Do they never take a day off? Do they forgo their usual vacation? Standards of living, dress, car, housing, entertainment, and travel that seem to cost more than an employee should be able to afford often signal economic misconduct.

Identification.   Proper identification, along with a device that takes pictures of a check and the person cashing it, tends to discourage bad-check artists. Although this practice may be too expensive for a small firm, its bank may assist in developing effective identification procedures.

Small businesses have used their clout to get 20 states to pass "bad-check laws." These laws permit the business that receives a bad check to collect not only its face value but also double to triple damages in small claims court. At least a dozen other states have similar bills pending.

Since credit cards frequently are stolen, additional identification should be required. Be sure that the signature corresponds to the one on the card.

Recently, a professional thief stole a credit card from a home. The card had never been used by the owner, but the thief used it to purchase an airline ticket, some personal items, and a new set of burglar tools. He signed the purchase tickets by crudely printing the name that was on the card. Carelessness in accepting the card cost the airlines and merchants $750.

As in the case of credit cards, be sure to ascertain the validity of trade documents, such as invoices and securities. Each year, millions of dollars are lost by businesspeople through carelessness that allows others to palm off bogus documents. A careful check with the appropriate bank or company can prevent many of these losses.

Fidelity bonding.   **Fidelity bonding** helps insure against employee fraud or theft. The employer pays a premium to an insurance company, which then assumes the risk and reimburses the company for any loss.

Document Security

Our personal experience in working with small businesses, as well as press releases in recent years, have made us aware of the importance of document security. As shown in Chapter 20, *information is a vital factor in managing and controlling business activities,* and its management and maintenance help to assure the continuation of the business. The life of an organization depends on the appropriate recording of information, its transmission to the appropriate person, and its security. Recorded information can be classified as either confidential or nonconfidential. Records with confidential information should be stored in bank lockboxes, safes, or restricted areas, and only authorized persons should have access to them. And all records should be protected by backups, as shown in the next Computer Update.

COMPUTER UPDATE

COMPUTERIZING ACCOUNTS RECEIVABLE: A TWO-EDGED SWORD

Personal computers have become ubiquitous in businesses large and small in recent years. One of the most common, and most productive, uses of this new technology has been computerizing a firm's accounts receivable using one of the many standard receivables software packages on the market. While this has been a major boon in most cases, it can also prove disastrous to those firms that do not routinely have backup storage in another location. Loss of, or damage to, data on a disk means loss of the balance showing how much each customer owes the business. Proper "information maintenance" programs and supplementary insurance policies can reduce the risk of loss.

Source: "The *Inc.* Insurance Advisory Panel" (Special Advertising Section), *Inc.*, April 1989.

The proprietary nature of confidential business records and various documents makes it essential to protect them from unauthorized eyes and hands. The trade secrets and competitive advantage of the firm may be lost if this information passes into the wrong hands. Therefore, a list of authorized personnel should be prepared and frequently updated. This list should be provided to those responsible for document security.

An unbending rule should be that under no circumstance is it permissible to remove confidential material from the restricted area or from the business premises. Some business owners think they can save on personnel costs by permitting material to be carried to an employee's residence where the employee works on the firm's records after hours. The chance of loss, the opportunity for access by unauthorized persons, and the risk of a claim for adequate compensation make this practice inadvisable.

SAFEGUARDING EMPLOYEES WITH PREVENTIVE MEASURES

Within a business, various types of accidents and health problems occur, causing potential losses. The use of insurance to eliminate or minimize disastrous financial losses in a company was discussed earlier in this chapter. In addition, safeguards can be instituted to reduce human suffering as well as costs to a company and employees.

In Chapter 12, we discussed the importance of providing for health, safety, and security within a company. The Occupational Safety and Health Administration (OSHA) received special attention. This agency provides much valuable information to help a company attain good working conditions. OSHA has established procedures for enforcing compliance with set safety standards, all of which have resulted in improved health, safety, and security.

Employees—just as much as money—are assets that a small business can protect through proper safety procedures. These procedures should be preventive in nature. Not only should the business provide a safe place for workers but, in addition, employees must work safely; most accidents occur because of human error, such as driving an automobile carelessly or handling equipment improperly.

Guards over moving tools, devices to keep hands away or stop machines, employee protective gear, warnings of unsafe conditions, and medical treatment are some items or steps used to protect employees from accidents and health problems and to prevent lawsuits.

Usually, when there is corporate wrongdoing, the company takes the rap because it is so difficult to prove knowledge of illegal acts in a huge, decentralized organization. But in a landmark case, three executives of Film Recovery Systems Inc. (FRS) were found guilty in June 1985 of murdering an employee because they "knowingly created a strong probability of death." FRS operated in close quarters, had a "hands-on hierarchy," and worked closely with plant employees but ignored their complaints. The executives were therefore presumed to know the dangers Stefan Golab was exposed to in working over "140 vats of bubbling cyanide."

In another case, executives of a Detroit concern were charged with involuntary manslaughter of a worker who died from carbon monoxide poisoning. They allegedly knew the company van was defective. They were convicted of murder in 1986.[19]

WHAT YOU SHOULD HAVE LEARNED

1. One of the greatest challenges for small businesses is dealing with risk. Risk management minimizes financial shocks. Pure risk is uncertain but is often measurable and insurable. Speculative risk occurs with voluntary decisions. Risk may be avoided, prevented, assumed, or transferred.

2. Insurance minimizes losses due to risks. Small businesses must determine their insurance needs and then provide insurance coverage for them.

   Businesses usually need several types of insurance coverage, including (*a*) fire, (*b*) casualty, (*c*) liability, (*d*) workers' compensation, (*e*) employee health and life, (*f*) business continuation life insurance, and (*g*) fidelity and surety bonds. Product/service liability insurance, which is similar to a doctor's or lawyer's malpractice insurance, has become almost prohibitive in cost, but is essential.

   In choosing an insurer, consider its financial characteristics, flexibility in meeting your requirements, and the services rendered by the agent. An insurance company can be judged on financial stability, specialization in types of coverage, flexibility in the offering of coverage, and cost of protection. Some things to look for in an agent are contacts among insurers, professionalism, degree of individual attention, quality of service, and help in time of loss.

Alternatives to insurance include noninsurance (recommended where losses would be trivial or the cost of coverage is close to its value), loss prevention, risk transfer, and self-insurance.

3. Although businesses should be insured against losses, they should also take steps to prevent crime. Three important areas for preventive efforts are armed robbery, theft, and white-collar crime, especially computer crimes. Measures that can reduce the chances of being robbed include modifying the store's layout, securing entrances, using security dogs, controlling the handling of cash, and redesigning the surrounding area.

Theft includes shoplifting by outsiders and employee theft. Shoplifters may be amateurs, kleptomaniacs, or professionals. Employee theft may be committed by individuals or groups on a very small or incredibly large scale, especially where construction materials are concerned. Security measures to reduce theft include mirrors, TV cameras, electronic noise activators on merchandise, security guards, security audits (spot checks on critical activities), and screening of prospective employees.

White-collar crime includes removal of cash, falsification of accounts, fraudulent computer manipulation, external accessing of the computer, bribery of purchasing agents or other employees, collusion resulting in unrecorded transactions, sale of proprietary information, and sabotage of new technology, new or old products, or customer relations. Ways to deal with white-collar crime include publicizing the risks, audits of records, requiring officers to make sales adjustments, observing employees' work habits, requiring proper identification with checks and credit cards, and fidelity bonding.

Confidential documents should be stored in bank lockboxes, safes, or restricted areas. A limited number of employees should be authorized to have access to them, and no one should be allowed to take the documents home.

4. A small firm has a special responsibility to protect employees, to provide a safe workplace, and to encourage employees to maintain safe work habits.

KEY TERMS

risk management, *670*

pure risk, *670*

speculative risk, *670*

insurable risk, *671*

risk avoidance, *671*

risk prevention (loss
   control), *671*

risk transfer, *671*

insurance, *671*

risk assumption, *671*

self-insurance, *671*

fire insurance policy, *673*

extended-coverage
   endorsement, *673*

business interruption
coverage, *673*

coinsurance, *673*

casualty insurance, *673*

liability insurance, *673*

product/service liability, *673*

workers' compensation, *674*

employer liability insurance, *674*

life insurance, *674*

health insurance, *674*

business owner's insurance, *675*

business continuation life
insurance, *675*

fidelity bonds, *675*

surety bonds, *675*

noninsurance, *676*

loss prevention programs, *676*

shoplifting, *680*

kleptomaniac, *680*

civil recovery (civil
restitution), *681*

white-collar crimes, *684*

computer security, *684*

audits, *685*

fidelity bonding, *686*

QUESTIONS FOR DISCUSSION

1. What is meant by risk management?
2. Distinguish between pure risk and speculative risk as they apply to small businesses.
3. Discuss four ways small firms can cope with risk.
4. What are some considerations in determining a small business's need for insurance?
5. (*a*) What types of insurance are commonly carried by small businesses? (*b*) Describe each type of coverage.
6. What criteria should you use in choosing (*a*) an insurer? (*b*) an insurance agent?
7. Discuss the methods a small business can use to reduce the chances of being robbed.
8. What measures have been found effective in reducing theft?
9. (*a*) What is meant by white-collar crime? (*b*) What are some ways to minimize it?
10. Discuss the importance of document security, especially with regard to computerized records.
11. What are some methods used to safeguard employees?

SUGGESTED READINGS

Asinof, Lynn. "Specialty Insurance Products Start to Make a Comeback." *The Wall Street Journal,* April 27, 1989, p. B1.

"Getting Past the Liability Crisis." *Nation's Business,* August 1986, pp. 69–71.

"Heading Off Crime Losses." *Nation's Business,* February 1985, p. 12.

Lewyn, Mark. "Virus Cleanup: About $96 Million." *USA Today,* November 11, 1988, p. 4B.

"Liability: Trying Times." *Nation's Business,* February 1986, pp. 22–27.

Miles, Gregory L. "Information Thieves Are Now Corporate Enemy No. 1." *Business Week,* May 5, 1986, pp. 120–22.

Myers, Kenneth N. "How to Keep Your Business Running." *Management Accounting,* April 1989, pp. 39–41.

Pillsbury, Dennis H. "Insurance Alternatives for Growing Corporations." *Inc.,* June 1986, pp. 89–91.

"Small Firms Have Many Cost-Cutting Options." *Business Insurance,* April 21, 1986, p. 20.

Striarchuk, Gregory. "Businesses Crack Down on Workers Who Cheat to Help the Company." *The Wall Street Journal,* June 13, 1986, p. 25.

Wells, Chris, and Christopher Farrell. "Insurers under Siege." *Business Week,* August 21, 1989, pp. 72–79.

ENDNOTES

1. "Citibank's Test of Paying to See Tellers Doesn't Pay," *The Wall Street Journal,* May 26, 1983, p. 6.

2. For a complete discussion of the major insurance issues facing small business owners, or risk managers, see the "1989 *Inc.* Insurance Advisory Panel" (Special Advertising Section), *Inc.,* April 1989.

3. As summarized by Roger Thompson, "Small Business: What's Next?" *Nation's Business,* October 1986, p. 48, the complete recommendation was:

    Enact sweeping reforms affecting liability insurance in four areas. Under civil justice reform, return to a fault-based standard of liability, severely restrict joint and several liability (which permits any one defendant to pay the full damage award regardless of degree of fault), limit noneconomic (pain and suffering) damages to a maximum of $250,000, restrict punitive damage awards to cases involving willful and malicious conduct and impose a statute of limitations on all civil liability actions. Also, enact uniform federal standards for product, professional and commercial liability; consider regulating the insurance industry at the federal level; and educate the public about the negative social impact of the liability crisis.

4. See "1989 *Inc.* Insurance Advisory Panel."

5. Ben Z. Hershberg, "The Ills of Small Firms," *USA Today,* September 25, 1989, p. 3B.

6. "Crime Robs New York of Business Growth," *The Wall Street Journal,* May 23, 1989, p. B1.

7. "To Stop a Thief," *U.S. News & World Report,* May 1, 1989, p. 76.

8. "Rewards Seen Cutting Bank Robberies," *Mobile* (Alabama) *Press Register,* December 7, 1986, p. 2–A.

9. Andrea Stone, "Season's Greetings: Tighter Security," *USA Today,* November 18, 1988, p. 1B.

10. "Smugglers at the Supermarket," *U.S. News & World Report,* March 13, 1989, p. 73.

11. Arlene Levinson, "Retailers Strike Back at Shoplifters via Letter Campaign," *Mobile* (Alabama) *Press Register,* May 13, 1989, p. 5–A.

12. Peter Pae, "Small Firms Are Easy Prey for Embezzlers," *The Wall Street Journal,* August 3, 1989, pp. B1, B2.

13. *The Wall Street Journal,* January 6, 1981, p. 1.

14. "White-Collar Crime Deserves Jail Time," *USA Today,* October 27, 1989, p. 14A.

15. *CPA Client Bulletin,* February 1984, p. 3.

16. "High-Tech Success," *The Wall Street Journal,* November 22, 1988, p. 1A.

17. Bob Kirby, "New Kind of Doctor . . . ," *Mobile* (Alabama) *Register,* May 18, 1989, p. 1–B.

18. "Study: White-Collar Crime Not Overlooked," *USA Today,* November 17, 1986, p. 3A.

19. Joshua Hyatt, "Behind Bars: Murder Verdict May Be Fatal for Small Firms," *Inc.,* November 1985, p. 17; and R. McCrory, "Murder on the Shop Floor," *Across the Board,* June 1986, pp. 24–27.

22

BUSINESS LAWS AND BUSINESS ETHICS

No man shall be judged except by the legal judgment of his peers or the law of the land.— The Magna Charta (1215)

Business has a soul, and management has social responsibilities as a major partner in the community, alongside capital and labour.—Oliver Sheldon, *The Philosophy of Management* (1923)

I want as few government mandates on small business as possible.—Susan Engeleiter, SBA administrator

LEARNING OBJECTIVES

After studying the material in this chapter, you will be able to:

1. Understand the legal system in which small businesses operate.
2. Explain some basic business laws affecting small firms.
3. Discuss the role played by government assistance.
4. Describe some of the burdensome aspects of government regulation and paperwork.
5. Explain how to choose a lawyer.
6. Describe what is ethical and socially responsible behavior.

GEORGIO CHERUBINI: ENGINEER-TURNED-RESTAURATEUR COOKS UP THREE-STAR SUCCESS

Georgio Cherubini, an Italian immigrant living in Minneapolis, Minnesota, had long dreamed of owning his own restaurant. But since he needed the security of a steady income, the restaurant had to wait while he earned a living. However, his security was shattered when he was laid off after cutbacks by his company, for economic reasons. Fortunately, with the help of Marcel Sutton, a counselor at the Service Corps of Retired Executives Chapter 2 in Minneapolis, he was able to turn misfortune into opportunity and use his vision and motivation to enter the restaurant business.

Cherubini's success was not based on luck— although that did come into play, as you will see. Instead, he was well prepared for the venture. He received his training as a cook and in restaurant operation in his native Florence. After immigrating to the United States, he worked as an engineer until 1985, when he lost his job. He took a job as a waiter at the Rosewood Room, one of Minneapolis's finer dining spots.

On December 5, 1985, Cheribini contacted the SCORE office for counseling. His case was turned over to Marcel Sutton, who counseled Cherubini at the SCORE office a week later. After that, Sutton worked with Cherubini several times, including telephone discussions.

Cherubini's proposed 60-table restaurant, specializing in regional Tuscan cooking, would require about $300,000 for leasehold improvements, equipment, decor, and other start-up needs. But he had only $10,000 available for investment. Sutton tried to get him an SBA-guaranteed bank loan, but it could not be negotiated because of the lack of required capital investment and collateral needed for a $300,000 loan.

However, there was one possibility that he could open such a restaurant with his limited capital. First, he had to find a suitable location where a previous restaurant had gone into bankruptcy, and then lease the location with all the equipment now owned by the landlord as part

Georgio Cherubini credits SCORE with putting him on the path to success with his Hosteria Fiorentina in downtown Minneapolis. Sampling some of Cherubini's Tuscan cooking is his counselor, Marcel Sutton.
Source: *Photo courtesy of Marcel Sutton.*

of the lease. Thus, his $10,000 capital would be sufficient for the operating expenses of the restaurant.

Cherubini had been looking at options for a year and a half when, in May 1987, he found such a restaurant in a good downtown location.

Additional information was provided to the owner in a 12-page outline on *Starting a Small Restaurant,* by Daniel Miller. Sutton used that to emphasize five important ingredients for a successful restaurant setup:

1. Excellent food.
2. Excellent service.
3. Appropriate advertising.
4. Overhead expense control.
5. Developing satisfied customers to help by word-of-mouth advertising.

When Hosteria Fiorentina opened in May 1987, its different and excellent Tuscan cooking and service succeeded immediately. In its second week of operation, it was showing a profit, and by September it had received the *Minneapolis Star-Tribune*'s coveted three-star rating. Business increased to the point where the restaurant had to turn customers away on weekends.

Now, Cherubini and his staff of 28 employees continue to practice the five rules stressed by Marcel Sutton as they serve lunch and dinner daily and a brunch on Sunday.

Source: Correspondence and discussions with Marcel Sutton; and others, including "Success in SCORE: Engineer-Turned-Restaurateur Cooks Up 3-Star Recipe," *The Savant,* March 1989, p. 8.

A small business is inevitably involved in a legal and governmental environment that sets rules and regulations for activities from starting the business to going out of business, as the Opening Focus demonstrated. Throughout the book, we've talked about the operation of a small business within the framework of government assistance and regulation. We have shown how the government assists small firms not only in getting started but also in such activities as training employees, obtaining capital, and exporting their products. Also, we've mentioned some of the laws and regulations affecting hiring personnel, paying them, maintaining their health and safety, and dealing with legal representatives. In addition, some influences of the government on financial and profit planning were shown.

Now we would like to concentrate on this legal environment. We will look at some of the most important government laws and regulations affecting small firms, as well as show how governments provide assistance and control. Then we will discuss how to choose a lawyer and how to maintain ethical and socially responsible behavior.

UNDERSTANDING THE LEGAL ENVIRONMENT

As it is so important to know and obey government laws and regulations, we will give you an overview of the subject. For further coverage, you should obtain competent legal assitance from someone familiar with local business conditions.

Some Basic Legal Principles

Before looking at specific laws that apply to small firms, let's see how the legal system as a whole works. Many U.S. legal concepts grew out of British **common law,** which is the body of law arising from judicial decisions based on unwritten customs and usages generally accepted by the people. Much of common law has now been converted to **statute law,** which consists of the laws passed by federal, state, and local governments.

The U.S. legal system has many built-in safeguards. Probably the most basic principle of our system is that *everyone is equal under the law.* Because we have a government of laws—not individuals—everyone, regardless of status or position, is expected to obey those laws.

A second principle is that *all laws must be based on the federal or a state constitution.* The **interstate commerce clause** of the U.S. Constitution gives Congress the right to "regulate Commerce with foreign nations, and among the several States." The right of states to regulate business is based on the use of **police power,** which is the right to use the forces of the state to promote the general welfare of its citizens.

The third principle is that *everyone is entitled to a day in court.* This **due process** provision means that legal procedures must be applied evenly under conditions of decency and fairness.

A fourth basic protection is that *a person is presumed to be innocent until proven guilty.*

A fifth concept, and one that people in other countries find difficult to understand, is that *we have multiple levels of government.* This means that there are federal, state, county, and municipal laws that are administered by their respective units. And sometimes these laws are contradictory.

A final principle is that *the making, administering, and interpreting of laws are separated into three distinct branches of government.* Thus, the **legislative branch**—such as the U.S. Congress, a state legislature, or a town or county council—passes laws; the **executive branch**—such as the president, a governor, the president of a county commission, or a mayor—enforces the law through regulatory agencies and decrees; and the **judicial branch**—the courts—interprets those laws and sees that they are enforced.

Different Types of Laws

There are essentially two types of laws affecting business.[1] First, **public law** deals with the rights and powers of the government. This type of law is usually **criminal law,** which is concerned with punishing individuals who commit illegal acts against society.

Suppose you own an apartment house. You go to collect the rent and one of the tenants slams the door in your face, knocking you down, causing lost teeth and multiple fractures. The tenant has probably broken a criminal law and can be charged with assault and battery and prosecuted by the state.

Private law is administered between two or more private citizens. It usually takes the form of **civil law,** which deals with violations against another person who has been harmed in some way.

Suppose that the tenant does not pay you. You can file suit in a civil court to obtain the rent and any interest.

From Figure 22–1, which shows the different bases and sources of laws affecting business, you can gather how complex the legal environment really is. Thus, while prospective small business owners and managers don't need a law degree, they should at least understand how to deal with the legal aspects of their problems—and know when to hire a good lawyer.

Figure 22–1   Bases and sources of laws affecting business

		Sources and forms of laws			
Government level	Basis of laws	Statutory acts	Executive decrees	Regulations (administrative laws)	Court decrees
Federal	United States Constitution, as amended	Legislation passed by Congress	Executive orders of the president, as authorized by Congressional statute or the Constitution	Issued by federal regulatory agencies, as authorized by Congress	Based on court decisions and interpretations of laws, orders, and regulations
State	Constitution, as amended	Legislation passed by legislatures	Orders issued by the governor, as authorized by the legislature or constitution	Issued by state regulatory agencies, as authorized by the legislature	Same as above
County	Charter	Legislation passed by the county's legislative body	Orders of the chief executive officer, as authorized by legislative act or the county's legislative body	Issued by county regulatory agencies, as authorized by the state legislature and county governing body	Same as above
City	Charter	Acts of state legislature or ordinances passed by city council or board of aldermen	Orders of the chief executive officer, as authorized by legislative act or city ordinance	Issued by city regulatory agencies, as authorized by state legislature and city governing body	Same as above

Source: Leon C. Megginson, Lyle R. Trueblood, and Gayle M. Ross, *Business* (Lexington, Mass.: D. C. Heath, 1985), p. 620.

SOME BASIC BUSINESS LAWS

The most important laws, as far as small firms are concerned, are those dealing with

1. Contracts.
2. Sales.
3. Property.
4. Patents, copyrights, and trademarks.

5. Agency.
6. Negotiable instruments.
7. Torts.
8. Bankruptcy.

Influencing all of these—and influenced by them—is the Uniform Commercial Code.

The Uniform Commercial Code

Since laws affecting business vary greatly from state to state, an effort was made to draft a set of uniform model statutes to govern business and commercial transactions in all 50 states. The result was the **Uniform Commercial Code (UCC),** consisting of the following 10 parts:[2]

1. General provisions.
2. Sales.
3. Commercial paper.
4. Bank deposits and collections.
5. Letters of credit.

6. Bulk transfers.
7. Documents of title.
8. Investment securities.
9. Secured transactions.
10. Effective date and repealer.

The code has been adopted by all states, the U.S. Virgin Islands, and the District of Columbia, with minor exceptions. For example, Louisiana, which still has many laws based on the Code Napoléon, the French Civil Code that has been in effect there since the Louisiana Purchase, has adopted only Articles 1, 3, 4, and 5.

Instead of trying to describe the entire UCC, we will look at the most important of the business laws.

Contracts

The law of contracts deals with legal business relationships resulting from agreements between two or more individuals or businesses. A **contract** is an agreement between two parties, be they individuals or groups, that is enforced by law. A contract may be valid and enforceable whether it is oral or written. Without contracts there would be no business as we know it, for contract law affects almost all business operations. Figure 22–2 illustrates a simple, but most binding, contract.

For a contract to be legal in the United States, the following conditions must be met:

1. Both parties must be legally competent to act. This means not only being of sound mind but also being the authorized representative of a group or corporation.

Figure 22–2   Simple Contract

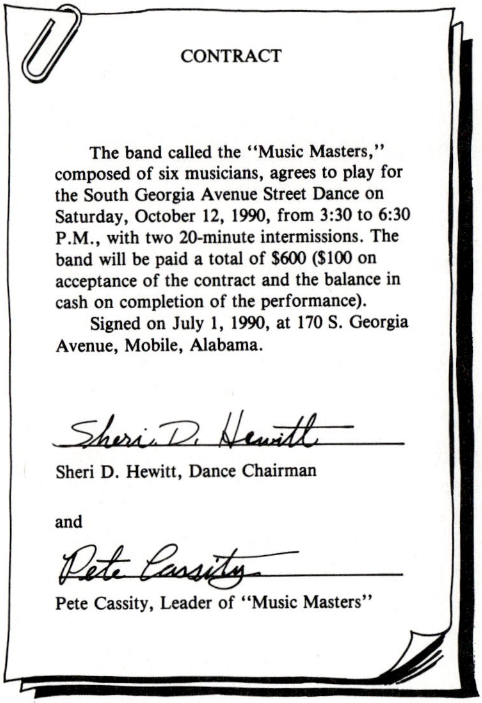

> **CONTRACT**
>
> The band called the "Music Masters," composed of six musicians, agrees to play for the South Georgia Avenue Street Dance on Saturday, October 12, 1990, from 3:30 to 6:30 P.M., with two 20-minute intermissions. The band will be paid a total of $600 ($100 on acceptance of the contract and the balance in cash on completion of the performance).
>
> Signed on July 1, 1990, at 170 S. Georgia Avenue, Mobile, Alabama.
>
> *Sheri D. Hewitt*
> _____
> Sheri D. Hewitt, Dance Chairman
>
> and
>
> *Pete Cassity*
> _____
> Pete Cassity, Leader of "Music Masters"

In our sample contract, both Pete Cassity, the leader of the Music Masters band, and Sheri Hewitt, elected by the residents of Georgia Avenue, were authorized representatives.

2. The agreement must not involve illegal actions or promises.

For example, the street dance was legal, as it had written permission from the City of Mobile and met other legal requirements.

3. A valid offer to enter into an agreement must be made by one party, in a serious manner, not in jest. The offer may be explicit—an automobile salesperson may offer to sell you the Super Deluxe Whizbang for "only $15,000 plus your old car." Or it may be implicit—a retailer marks a VCR on display "$299.99."

Notice that the Music Masters made a valid offer to provide music for the street dance.

4. The second party must voluntarily accept this offer, equally seriously, without duress (physical force or other compulsion) or "undue influence."

The South Georgia Avenue residents, through their agent, Sheri Hewitt, accepted the Music Masters' offer.

5. Each party must promise the other some form of **consideration,** which is something of value, such as money, services, goods, or the surrender of some legal right.

The Georgia Avenue residents offered $600 as consideration, $100 of which was guaranteed and paid in advance. In return, the Music Masters agreed to play for three hours with two intermissions.

6. The contract must be in a legal form, even if oral, but may really be quite simple (as Figure 22–2 illustrates). It must contain at least four elements to be a valid contract—the identity of the two parties, an offer, consideration, and acceptance—but little else is needed.

Sales

Laws affecting the sale of products are really part of contract law, except that when we pay the stated price for a product without negotiation, we don't usually realize that we are actually entering into an **implied contract,** which can be inferred from the actions of the parties.

For example, if you go to a physician, state your symptoms, and receive treatment, a valid contract can be inferred.

If two parties negotiate and reach an agreement, an **express contract** is formed, even if nothing is written down.[3]

For example, if a prospective buyer makes an offer on a house and it is accepted by the seller, a contract exists even before it has been put in writing.

Warranties

A **warranty,** which is a representation made by the seller to the buyer regarding the quality and performance of a product, may be express or implied. **Express warranties,** which are specific representations made by the seller regarding the product, often come in the form of warranty cards to be completed and returned by the buyer. **Implied warranties** are those legally imposed on the seller. For example, the FDA defines what is meant by "ice cream," as opposed to "ice milk," "cheese," as opposed to "pasteurized process cheese food," and a seller who labels a product with one of those names implies that the buyer has as right to expect that it will be as defined. Unless implied warranties are disclaimed before the sale, in writing, by the seller, they are automatically applied. The law of warranties for sales transactions is set forth in the UCC.

Product Liability

A serious problem these days is product liability. An ever-present question facing a small business is "How safe *should* the product be?" Much attention is now being focused on the design of products and quality control to ensure product safety. But if all possible safety precautions were built into all products and their production, they'd be prohibitively expensive—and sometimes impossible to use. Thus, the degree of safety required depends on the product itself. While a defective compact disc may present only a minor inconvenience, the proper functioning of a heart pacemaker is a matter of life and death, so each pacemaker must be perfect.

In 1989, Cordis Corporation, a medical equipment manufacturer, pleaded guilty to charges of selling thousands of defective pacemakers and batteries prone to corrode. Cordis agreed to pay $764,000 in penalties in the *criminal case.* Earlier, it had agreed to pay $5 million to settle a *civil fraud claim* filed by the U.S. government.[4]

Property

Property law involves the rights and duties resulting from the ownership or use of personal or real property. Contract, sales, and other types of law also apply to the transfer of such property. **Real property** is land, or anything attached more or less permanently to it, such as a house, factory, research laboratory, or oil well. **Personal property** is anything of value, aside from land, that can be owned or used by an individual.

Real property is usually transferred to a new owner by means of a **deed,** a written document. A person may obtain the use of property for a limited time by means of a **lease,** a written agreement issued by the owner.

Personal property may be **tangible property**—that is, some material good or product such as a car, stereo, or clothing—or **intangible property**—such as a share of stock or a deposit slip. The transfer of personal property from one party to another is usually achieved by conveying the **title,** or the legal right to possess and use it. When this isn't done, use of the property constitutes fraud.

Patents, Copyrights, and Trademarks

The legal protection of personal property also includes protecting patents, copyrights, and trademarks.

A **patent** is a grant from the U.S. Patent and Trademark Office giving the inventor of a product the exclusive right to make, use, or sell the invention in the United States for 17 years from the issuing date. After that time, the patent expires and cannot be renewed. In order to be patented, a device must be new, useful, and not obvious to a person in the related field of ordinary skill or knowledge. Redesign patents—extending for 3½, 7, or 14 years—may be given to inventors who make new, original, and ornamental changes in a product.

Inventors can enhance their chances of getting a patent by following the basic steps suggested by the Patent and Trademark Office.[5] Also, they can get help from **patent practitioners,** who are patent attorneys or patent agents with the Patent Office. Only those registered attorneys and agents may represent inventors seeking patents.

A **copyright** is the exclusive right that protects creators of "original works of authorship" such as artistic, literary, dramatic, and musical works. It protects only the form in which the idea is expressed, not the idea itself. While you can copyright something merely by claiming the right to do so, Form TX must be filed with the Copyright Office of the Library of Congress to register the copyright. A valid copyright lasts for the life of the creator, plus 50 years. When a copyright expires, the work becomes public property and can be used by anyone, free of charge. The international recognized symbol © is used to designate a copyrighted work.

A **trademark** is any distinctive name, term, word, design, symbol, or device used to identify the origin of a product, or to distinguish it from other products on the market. Registration of a trademark prevents others from employing a similar mark to identify their products. In the United States, a trademark cannot be reserved in advance of its use. Instead, the owner must establish the right to a trademark by actually using it.

A registered trademark cannot keep anyone else from producing the same item, or from selling it under a different trademark. It merely prevents others from using the same or a confusingly similar trademark for the same or a similar product.

Johnny Carson, host of NBC's "Tonight Show," is welcomed with the phrase, "Here's Johnny!" The phrase has become so closely identified with him that he's licensed its use by a restaurant and for a line of clothing.

To register a trademark, the applicant must prove that it is distinctive. As long as a producer continues to use a trademark, no one can legally infringe upon it. But an owner may lose the exclusive right to a trademark if it loses its unique character and becomes a generic name. *Aspirin, cellophane, thermos, yo-yo,* and even *shredded wheat* were once enforceable trademarks but, because of common usage, can no longer be licensed as a company's trademark. On the other hand, Ping-Pong®, Fiberglas®, Velcro®, Spackle®, Realtor®, Kelly Girl®, Xerox®, and Kleenex® are still valid trademarks fiercely protected by their owners.

Agency

The term **agency** describes the legal relationship between a principal and an agent. The **principal** is the person who wants to do something but is unable or unwilling to do it personally. The **agent** is the person or company engaged to act on behalf of the principal. All types of business transactions, and many personal ones, involve agency. Directors, officers, and sales personnel act as agents for a business or other group. Partners act as agents for each other, and most professional athletes, actors, artists, writers, and musicians have agents.

In our sample contract (Figure 22–2), notice that Sheri Hewett was acting as agent for the South Georgia Avenue residents, not for herself alone.

Negotiable Instruments

Special laws are needed to deal with buying, owning, and selling negotiable instruments. A **negotiable instrument** is some form of financial document, such as a check, bank draft, or certificate of deposit, that's transferable from one party to another. The law requires that negotiable instruments be written, not oral; signed by the maker; good for the promise of a specified sum of money; and payable when endorsed by the payee.

Torts

Laws concerning torts cover the responsibilities and obligations of people involved in business dealings, other than those already discussed. A **tort** is a wrongful act by one party, not covered by criminal law, that results in injury to a second party's person, property, or reputation, for which the first party is liable. Laws dealing with torts provide for the performance of duties and compensation for the physical, mental, or economic injuries resulting from faulty products or actions of employees. This usually involves some form of economic restitution (monetary payment) for damages or losses incurred.

For example, a man who tried to commit suicide by throwing himself in front of an incoming New York Metropolitan Transit Authority subway train won a $650,000 settlement because the train's operator "demonstrated negligence."[6]

Bankruptcy

Under **bankruptcy law,** people or businesses can petition the courts to be relieved of the obligation to pay debts they can't repay. There are two types of bankruptcy, voluntary and involuntary. **Voluntary bankruptcy** occurs when a debtor files an application with a court claiming that debts exceed assets and asks to be declared bankrupt. When one or more creditors file the bankruptcy petition, it's called **involuntary bankruptcy.** The Bankruptcy Reform Act of 1978 provides for quick and efficient handling of both types.

Chapter 11 of this act contains a provision for reorganizing the bankrupt business, whether the bankruptcy petition is filed voluntarily or involuntarily. Thus, the firm can continue to operate while its debts are being repaid. If the business is so far gone that it can't keep operating, it must be liquidated.

Occasionally, through no fault of its own, a small business encounters problems in protecting its assets. The small business owner should be aware both of risks and of defensive measures to use (1) when a customer or debtor company goes bankrupt or (2) when the business itself seems financially insolvent.

Protection from Debtors' Insolvency

In the first case, the firm will probably lose money. However, it should have taken steps with all its loans, such as accounts and notes receivable, to protect them from such occurrences. Two ways to do this are (1) to obtain security (such as a lien on property) for the loan when possible and (2) to follow up quickly on delays in loan repayment. A delay indicates trouble. If a customer files in court for bankruptcy, the amount of money received by a firm depends on the type of bankruptcy selected, the amount of security on loans, and the amount of money available.

Protection When the Business Itself Becomes Insolvent

If the small business itself becomes insolvent, it can:

1. Arrange for a **composition of creditors,** a contractual agreement between a business firm and its creditors to enable the firm to continue operations and to provide, over a reasonable time period, for satisfying the claims of creditors. This agreement, supervised by a trustee, results in lower legal and accounting expenses than those incurred in filing for bankruptcy.
2. File for rehabilitation (Chapter 11). This procedure gives the business a fresh start and assures that debtors deal fairly with creditors in dispersal of assets.
3. File for liquidation (Chapter 7). The firm will not be rehabilitated, and all assets will be distributed according to some prescribed method.

A firm should consult a lawyer as soon as possible whenever it is affected by a bankruptcy situation.

GOVERNMENT HELP FOR SMALL BUSINESSES

Many examples of assistance to small businesses have been given throughout this text, especially in Chapters 3, 8, and 17. As most such help is provided by the SBA and the U.S. Department of Commerce, their assistance will be summarized.

Small Business Administration (SBA)

As was shown in Chapter 8, the SBA provides many types of direct and guaranteed loans for small firms. Its publications, such as its series of Management Aids; local workshops; small business development centers; and small business institutes provide help for small firms. Also, information on overseas marketing is provided in the pamphlet *Market Overseas with U.S. Government Help.*

Help for women takes many forms. The SBA has an Office of Women's Business Ownership, which enforces the Women's Business Ownership Act of 1988. It also has a National Women's Business Council, which submits plans to Congress for helping women entrepreneurs.

Assistance for minorities also comes in many forms, such as the Office of Minority Small Business, Capital Ownership, and the Minority Business Development Agency. The SBA's Minority Small Business and Capital Ownership Development units oversee the 8(a) program, which grants government contracts to economically disadvantaged firms.

In addition, the SBA sponsors the **Service Corps of Retired Executives (SCORE).** SCORE's 750 chapters and satellites nationwide comprise 13,000 volunteer members who specialize in helping people develop their business ideas. They are retired but active men and women from all areas of business and industry, and their services are free!

SCORE can match one or more of these counselors to a specific business. It can also call on its extensive roster of public relations experts, bankers, lawyers, and the like to answer the important and detailed questions you might have about setting up a business. They'll even work with you as long as you need after you start your business. Some clients consult with SCORE counselors for several years.

SCORE chapters also offer, for a nominal fee, one- to two-day workshops covering a variety of business topics, such as taxes, personnel procedures, and inventory control.

In the past 25 years, over 2.5 million people have taken advantage of the experience SCORE counselors can draw on. They attest to the success SCORE has brought them.[7]

Another way the SBA helps is to encourage small business owners to try to perform more effectively. It does this by making state and national awards for the "Small Business Persons of the Year." Figure 22–3 shows President Bush announcing the 1989 awards at the White House.

Figure 22–3 Small Business Honorees

President Bush honors the 1989 small business persons of the year at a White House ceremony. From the left are Chad Olson of Bountiful, Utah, tie for third; Carolyn Stradley of Marietta, Georgia, tie for third; Richard Barlow of Salina, Kansas, second; and small businessman of the year Ted Bretting of Ashland, Wisconsin.
Source: Photo courtesy of Michael Sargent, White House photographer.

U.S. Department of Commerce

As indicated in earlier chapters, especially Chapter 17, the U.S. Department of Commerce offers assistance through its International Trade Administration (ITA), its U.S. and Foreign Commercial Service Agency (USFCSA), and its District Export Counsels (DECs). It also publishes a *Basic Guide to Exporting.* Additionally, it provides assistance through the Export Counseling Center (ECC) and its Minority Business Development Agency (MBDA). Finally, the department's Census Bureau furnishes much demographic information. For those small firms in a hurry, data may be obtained electronically, as shown in the next Computer Update.

Other Government Agencies

Among the other agencies helping small business are the Foreign Credit Insurance Association (FCIA) and the Export-Import Bank, which provide financial assistance.

COMPUTER UPDATE

THE COMMERCE DEPARTMENT REPORTS BY COMPUTER

Many small business owners need information and economic reports from the government much more quickly than they can receive it by mail. Now, the U.S. Department of Commerce makes electronic data available to small businesses that have computers and modems. Data can be obtained on subjects such as consumer prices, trade figures, retail sales, housing starts, gross national product and other timely topics of interest.

The department charges small firms a $25 registration fee, which includes two hours of free access time. The charge for additional time is 10 cents per minute in the daytime and 5 cents per minute at night. For more details about this service, call the Commerce Department at (202) 377–1986.

Source: "Reports by Computers," *Management Accounting,* September 1989, p. 17.

The U.S. Department of Agriculture provides assistance through the Cooperative Extension Service, the Federal Land Bank Association, the Production Credit Association, and the Farmers Home Administration.

The Internal Revenue Service helps small firms obtain an IRS tax number. Called an **employer identification number,** it is needed for all your business tax returns and many other documents.[8] The IRS also provides assistance in filing your income tax return. In addition, a wide range of state and local agencies provide help when contacted.

HANDLING GOVERNMENT REGULATIONS AND PAPERWORK

If you want to see a small businessperson become incensed, mention government regulations and paperwork, which are a growing problem. At one time, smaller firms were exempt from many federal regulations and even some state and local ones. Today, though, these firms tend to be regulated the same as their larger competitors. Equal employment opportunity, occupational safety and health, environmental protection, and other laws now tend to apply to small businesses, often adding greatly to their operating costs. These regulations are numerous, complex, costly, and often contradictory.

About 41,000 regulations, stemming from 200 laws and 111 precedent-setting court cases, affect the production and sale of hamburgers and add 8 to 11 cents to the cost of each burger sold. Similarly, 310 federal regulations, covering 40 pages of documents, govern what goes into a pizza.[9]

It is difficult to understand and comply with governmental requirements. While most businesspeople are willing to obey the law, compliance is complex, arduous, time-consuming, and expensive.

CleanDrum, Inc. (Case III–1), with only six full-time employees, had to complete 104 W–2 forms in one year because of high turnover. One hiree had lasted half an hour, others for "a day or so," and only two had stayed the whole year.

Dealing with Regulatory Agencies

In theory, a **regulatory agency** is more flexible and sensitive to the needs of society than Congress can be, since less time is needed for an agency to develop and issue new regulations than for Congress to enact new legislation. Experience, however, doesn't seem to support this theory. Many small business managers believe, for example, that on occasion an agency's findings may be arbitrary or may protect its own security or that of the industry it's supposed to regulate. Figure 22–4 shows some of the more important regulatory bodies and their duties. There were 54 such agencies in 1989, employing around 400,000 people.

Some Benefits of Regulation

Do the benefits of government regulation outweigh its costs? Since there's no profit mechanism to measure this, as there is in private business, and since both costs and benefits are hard to determine, estimates must be made. Even with these measurement limitations, though, it's been shown that some regulations are truly cost effective.

For example, air pollution requirements have provided economic benefits that far outweigh the costs of complying with them, according to the White House Council on Environmental Quality.[10]

An important benefit to small business is that the marketplace is kept relatively free from restrictive monopolistic practices. The Federal Trade Commission (FTC) enforces the laws designed to maintain relatively unrestricted competition, especially the Sherman Antitrust Act, the Clayton Act, and the Celler-Kefauver Act. These laws prohibit companies from buying out a competing firm, or entering into a joint venture, in order to decrease competition.

Price fixing is also prohibited. The Robinson-Patman Act outlaws price discrimination that cannot be justified on the basis of quality or quantity differences, or that injures competition. Thus, a store can't offer you a discount for trading with it unless the same discount is offered to everyone in the same demographic group—such as senior citizens. A store may, however, offer a discount for cash or to anyone who buys in large quantities.

Figure 22–4   Some U.S. Regulatory Agencies with Which Small Firms Must Deal

Antitrust Division, Justice Department, enforces antitrust and antimonopoly laws to maintain competition.

Consumer Product Safety Commission issues and enforces performance and safety standards for more than 10,000 products, including toys, lawn mowers, tools, and clothing.

Drug Enforcement Administration controls illegal distribution and sale of narcotics and dangerous drugs and hunts down traffickers in illicit drugs.

Environmental Protection Agency protects the nation's water and air by monitoring discharges and emissions from factories, sewer systems, and other polluters.

Equal Employment Opportunity Commission investigates complaints of discrimination in hiring, training, and promotion of workers on the basis of race, religion, sex, physical handicap, or age.

Federal Communications Commission grants operating licenses for radio and TV stations and citizen's-band radio owners, oversees interstate telephone operations, including rates on long-distance calls, and sets standards for cable TV and communications satellites.

Federal Deposit Insurance Corporation insures the deposits held by banks belonging to the Federal Reserve System and establishes standards for the proper operation of financial institutions.

Federal Reserve System sets monetary policy and regulates banks belonging to the system.

Federal Trade Commission ensures that firms compete fairly—without price fixing, deceptive advertising, and other questionable practices.

Food and Drug Administration inspects and tests drugs, cosmetics, and food products before they are offered to the public.

Food Safety and Quality Service certifies the wholesomeness, grade, and quality of meats, poultry, and fresh fruits and vegetables.

Immigration and Naturalization Service controls the flow of newcomers into the United States and enforces rules for citizenship and employment of aliens.

Internal Revenue Service enforces federal tax laws and rules in tax-related disputes.

Interstate Commerce Commission establishes railroad and truck rates, investigates complaints against carriers, and oversees transportation mergers.

National Highway Traffic Safety Administration sets rules for fuel efficiency and safety standards for cars and trucks.

National Labor Relations Board oversees elections on union representation of workers and investigates employer-worker disputes.

Occupational Safety and Health Administration makes and enforces rules for protecting employees' health and safety.

Patent and Trademark Office protects the rights of inventors and producers of new goods and services and prevents infringement upon established products.

Securities and Exchange Commission regulates trading in stocks and bonds and gathers financial information on firms.

U.S. Forest Service regulates the cutting of timber on federal lands and provides national leadership in forestry.

For example, a local hardware store gives a 20 percent discount to anyone who buys air filters by the case of a dozen, and a dry cleaning business gives 25 percent off for having five men's suits cleaned at once.

Some Problems with Regulation

There are at least three areas of concern that small firms have with government regulations. The first problem is the *difficulty of understanding some of the regulations*, as well as the confusing, and often restrictive nature of some laws and regulations, as the following example illustrates.

For 18 years, Wilfred Allick, Jr., like his father before him, ran a charter boat service to the Buck Island Reef National Monument near St. Croix, in the U.S. Virgin Islands. But in the mid-1970s, believing there were too many charter boat operators carrying tourists to Buck Island, the National Park Service (NPS) began licensing operators and regulating charter rates to stop "predatory price cutting." According to Leonard Hall, in charge of concessions for NPS in the southeastern United States, including the Virgin Islands, Allick is one of the best operators around and has done nothing to harm the National Monument.

In 1982, however, when Allick took longer than the Park Service allowed to replace the mast on his sailboat, the agency terminated his permit. Allick worked for other charter boat operators for a while, then reapplied for a Buck Island permit in 1988, but it was denied.

Explaining that "I just want to make an honest living," Allick feels very frustrated. In 1989, he was trying to start his own charter service to other sites in the area. Also, he considered filing suit against the NPS.

The Park Service's policy of stopping price cutting has apparently worked, for where there were once 23 operators, there were only 7 in 1989. In fact, according to Hall, the Park Service is currently more worried about "price gouging" than price cutting.[11]

Buck Island Reef National Monument, Virgin Islands
Source: Photo courtesy of the National Park Service

A second problem is the *enormous amount of paperwork involved in preparing and handling the reports* needed to comply with government regulations and in maintaining the records needed to satisfy the regulators.

A third problem is the *difficulty and cost of complying with the regulations.* The costs are greater than just the administrative expenses; bringing actual operations into compliance with the regulations is also expensive.

For example, the Service Station Dealers of America estimated in 1989 that it would cost each station up to $125,000 to comply with the president's new clean-air standards.[12] Moreover, independent station owners had already spent an average of $37,000 on tank and underground leak monitors to comply with the EPA's rules to prevent underground gas tanks from leaking into our water supplies.[13]

How Small Firms Can Cope with Regulations

What can small business managers do about burdensome government regulations and paperwork? There are several approaches to consider.

1. Learn as much as you can about the law, particularly if it is possible that a law can help you.

For example, when population growth and drought led local and national lawmakers to mandate water conservation, Massachusetts and some other states passed laws requiring that toilets use only 1.6 gallons of water for each flush. Conventional toilets used five gallons, but a Michigan company, Water Control International Inc., made one using an air pressure boost that used only 1.6 gallons. The company worked 100 hours per week in 1989 to keep up with demand.[14]

---

2. Challenge detrimental or harmful laws, perhaps by appearing before a Congressional small business committee or by joining organizations such as the National Federation of Independent Business, the National Small Business Association, and National Small Business United.

In order to give small firms more clout with federal agencies, small business lobby groups had the Equal Access to Justice Act passed in 1981. In an effort to prevent agencies from making unwarranted tax and regulatory rulings, the law permits small firms to petition to recover legal fees incurred in successfully defending themselves against actions brought by U.S. agencies, except the IRS. Previously, many firms found it cheaper to accept penalties rather than incur heavy legal fees.[15]

---

3. Become involved in the legal-political system to elect officials of your choosing who will help change the laws.

4. Find a better legal environment, if possible, even if it means moving to a different city, county, or state.
5. Learn to live with the laws and regulations.

CHOOSING AND USING A LAWYER

You can see from the previous discussion that it isn't easy to start and operate a small business. From a legal point of view, many technicalities must be met. Therefore, one of the first things you should do when forming a business is to hire a competent lawyer. Actually, your attorney should be retained at the time you are developing your business plan, as well as when you are obtaining financing—not when you get in trouble.

Choosing the Lawyer

You should choose a lawyer as you would a consultant, an accountant, or anyone else who provides services. Comparison shop. Check the credentials of different attorneys. Discuss fees with them candidly. And, whatever you do, don't forget to talk with them about the wisdom of retaining legal counsel. For example, does it make sense to spend $500 in legal fees and court costs to recover a $100 bad debt?

How do you look for a lawyer? The first and most obvious step is to define the nature of your legal problem. You will be wasting your time as well as an attorney's if you bring a simple real estate transaction to a criminal defense specialist.

Where to Look

Once you have defined the problem, there are a number of ways to find a lawyer to help you with it. The American Bar Association recommends four sources:[16]

Personal referral.   Begin by asking advice from an acquaintance or someone whose opinion you value, such as your banker, your minister, a relative, or another lawyer. Other common referral sources are law school teachers and administrators, consumer groups, public interest organizations, and women's associations.

Martindale-Hubbell Law Directory.   You can also find some answers in this directory in the public library. For more than 100 years, it has published as complete a roster as possible of the members of the bar in the United States and Canada. The directory gives brief biographical sketches of many lawyers and describes the legal areas in which law firms practice.

Lawyer referral services.   Most bar associations in larger cities have a Lawyer Referral and Information Service (LRS) that can refer you to competent and reliable lawyers. Although the name may vary, you can usually find a bar-sponsored lawyer referral service in the Yellow Pages of your telephone directory under "Attorneys." Under an LRS plan, a lawyer will consult with you on a legal problem for half an hour either without charge or for a prescribed, nominal fee and then render whatever other services are requested for a fee you both agree on.

Advertising.   From 1908 to 1977 lawyers were forbidden to advertise their services. This prohibition came about through fear of "puffery" and the belief that even the best executed advertising could be unintentionally false, misleading, or deceptive because of the complex nature of legal services. A 1977 ruling of the United States Supreme Court (*Bates* v. *State Bar of Arizona*) changed the rules to a degree. Lawyers are now permitted to advertise certain information in newspapers and Yellow Pages and on radio and television.

What to Look For

Look for certain characteristics in the lawyer you choose to represent you. First, he or she should have appropriate experience with your type of small business. While you may not necessarily rely on the lawyer for business advice, the one chosen should at least have sufficient background and information about the particulars of your business and its problems to represent you effectively.

The employees of a rural New York state grocery chain learned this lesson the hard way. After paying a local attorney to arrange a buyout of the company, they found problems with their employee stock ownership plan. Later, an educational consultant providing training for ESOP owners suggested that the new owners hire James Steiker, a Philadelphia ESOP specialist, to straighten out the mess. The owners were so pleased with his professional competence that they hired him as their new general counsel.[17]

Second, since there should be compatibility between lawyer and client, observe the lawyer's demeanor, the style and atmosphere of his or her office, and any clients—if possible—before making your choice.

Third, does the lawyer have time for you and your business? If you have difficulty getting an appointment, or are repeatedly kept waiting on the phone, you should probably look elsewhere.

Finally, since cost is an important consideration, do not hesitate to discuss fees with the prospective attorney, for performance must be balanced against the cost of the service provided. Lawyers' time is expensive. For example, New York lawyers typically charge from $90 to $300 an hour.[18] While fees may be lower in other areas, they're still costly.

Maintaining Relationships with Attorneys

Lawyers usually have three basic ways of charging for their services. First, a flat fee may be charged for a specific assignment. For example, a fee of $1,000 might be charged for handling an incorporation procedure. Thus,

Figure 22–5 A Sample Contract for a Lawyer's Services

I, Joe Blo, hereby agree to employ the law firm of Suzy Q. Glutz to represent me and act on my behalf and in my best interest in presenting a claim for any and all damages, including personal injury, resulting from an accident which occurred on or about June 29, 1990, near Bethesda, Maryland.

I agree to pay to said firm an amount equal to 30 percent of any and all sums collected by way of settlement or from legal action. In the event of trial (as determined as of the time a jury is impaneled), I agree to pay said firm an amount equal to 50 percent of any amounts received.

Be it further understood that no settlement will be made without consent of client.

It is understood that if nothing is obtained on client's behalf, then client owes nothing to said law firm, except for the expenses associated with handling this case.

Said law firm agrees to act on client's behalf with all due diligence and in client's best interest at all times in prosecuting said claims.

DATED this _____ day of _____, 19_____

_____

Suzy Q. Glutz

By: _____

---

the cost of the service is known, and funds can be allocated for it. Second, the lawyer may charge an hourly fee based on the type of activities to be performed and the amount of staff assistance required. Third, a contingency fee may be set. If the stakes are really high, and if time and risks are involved, the attorney may charge a percentage (say 30 percent) of the negotiated settlement, or even more if the amount is obtained through a trial (as high as 50 percent), as shown in the sample contract in Figure 22–5.

Also, the lawyer will expect to be reimbursed for out-of-pocket expenses, such as mileage, parking, long-distance calls, postage, transcripts of testimony, and other costs. In long, involved cases, the lawyer should provide periodic reports, including a statement of expenses.

Being Your Own Counsel

While we do not recommend it, it is possible to be your own counsel. With legal fees increasing, many small businesspeople are looking for ways to minimize legal expenses. And their options are growing. One way is to do your own legal work. And there are now do-it-yourself legal books and software packages available that explain such tasks as how to form a corporation, make out a sales contract, or file for bankruptcy protection. For prices ranging from about $10 to around $130, you can obtain help, as shown in Figure 22–6.

Figure 22–6 Self-Help Available for Small Firms

Title	Publisher	Price	Topics covered
The Partnership Book	Nolo Press	$ 18.95	How to write agreements that cover disputes, buy-outs, and a partner's death.
The Complete Legal Kit	Running Press	17.95	More than 150 ready-to-use legal forms, including deeds, leases, and escrow agreements.
The Basic Book of Business Agreements	Enterprise Publishing	69.95	Letters, contracts, sales agreements, and other forms (available on computer diskette).
California Incorporator	Nolo Press	129.00	Software package for setting up a corporation in California.
Start Your Subchapter S Corporation	John Wiley & Sons	14.95	Advice and forms for setting up a small corporation.
Complete Book of Corporate Forms	Enterprise Publishing	69.95	108 lawyer-prepared forms for documenting employer-employee relations (available on computer diskette).
How to Avoid Lawyers	Fawcett Crest	4.95	A general guide to such matters as divorce, wills, and bankruptcy.
How to Register a Copyright and Protect Your Creative Work	Charles Scribner's Sons	10.95	What you can copyright, and how.

Source: Adapted from Wayne E. Green, "Taking Your Own Counsel," *The Wall Street Journal,* May 8, 1989, p. B1. Reprinted by permission of *The Wall Street Journal,* © Dow Jones & Company, Inc., 1989. ALL RIGHTS RESERVED.

SOCIALLY AND ETHICALLY RESPONSIBLE BEHAVIOR

While most small businesspeople have long accepted—and practiced—social responsibility and ethical behavior, considerable external emphasis is now being placed on these topics.

Social Responsibility

The term **social responsibility** refers to a business's obligation to set policies, make decisions, and follow courses of action that are desirable in terms of the values and objectives of society. Whether that term is used or not, it means that the business acts with the best interests of society in mind, as well as those of the business.

Anita Roddick, founder of The Body Shop in 1976, says the money from her company funds her environmental campaigns. "I'm in the cosmetics industry, which I loath, but I make money in it." When the name of a franchisee came up, Roddick said, "She's doing wonderful work with blind people." "Business is not just the profit and loss sheet," she says. "You can play the game and not lose your soul. . . . You can educate your staff and your customers to have a more holistic approach to business."

Sales of The Body Shop were over $100 million in 1989.[19]

There have been three periods in the 19th and 20th centuries when government has passed laws to force businesses to act even more responsibly. In the late 1800s and early 1900s, Congress passed three rigorous laws aimed at restricting abusive business practices. They are still in effect. The Interstate Commerce Act prohibits railroads from giving rebates and special rates to favored customers; the Sherman Antitrust Act attempts to reduce monopoly and encourage competition, at least among large corporations; and the Pure Food and Drug Law, designed to eliminate the filthy and dangerous conditions in the meat-packing industry, has now been extended to many other areas.

During the 1930s, Congress passed more laws to protect employees and consumers from big businesses and their managers. For example, the National Labor Relations Act gives employees the right to join unions and bargain collectively with management; the Social Security Act provides for unemployment insurance, old-age pensions, and disability and health insurance; the Fair Labor Standards Act sets minimum wages and maximum hours for employees; the Wheeler-Lea Act empowers the Federal Trade Commission to prevent unfair competition and false advertising; and the Securities Act and Securities Exchange Act give a measure of protection to investors.

In the 1960s and early 1970s, another surge of legislation encouraged social responsibility on the part of business. Equal employment opportunity is provided by the Civil Rights Act and other laws that were discussed in Chapter 10. Environmental protection, in the form of conservation and pollution control, is provided for through laws such as the Clean Air Act and the National Environmental Policy Act, which set up the Environmental Protection Agency (EPA). Finally, employee safety and health have improved because of the Occupational Safety and Health Act and other laws.

Consumerism is the organized efforts of independent, government, and business groups to protect consumers from undesirable effects of poorly designed and poorly produced products. The consumerism movement became popular during the 1960s and 1970s. The Traffic and Motor Vehicle Safety Act requires manufacturers to notify new car purchasers of safety defects discovered after the car is delivered to the customer. The Child

Protection and Toy Safety Act set up the Consumer Product Safety Commission (CPSC) to set safety standards, require warning labels on potentially unsafe products, and require recall of products found to be harmful.

Business Ethics

Business ethics are the standards used to judge the rightness or wrongness of a business's relations to others. Small businesspeople are expected to deal ethically with employees, customers, competitors, and others. For example, ethical behavior is expected in decisions concerning bribery, industrial theft and espionage, collusion, tax evasion, false and/or misleading advertising, and conflicts of interest, as well as in personal conduct, such as loyalty, confidentiality, respecting others' privacy, and truthfulness.[20]

As a minimum, the public expects small business owners and managers to obey both the letter *and* the spirit of laws affecting their operations. Finally, they should go beyond laws and social responsibility to behavior based on ethical considerations. Sometimes, though, it is difficult for the small business to act ethically and still satisfy the customer.

For example, do you remember how Kevin Wilson, president of Wilson's Used Cars (Case I–6), wanted to give customers the lowest acceptable price on cars? But the customers wouldn't accept that as the lowest price and still wanted to negotiate. Only when he "played the game" did Wilson sell any cars.

Perhaps the best test of ethical behavior is Rotary International's Four-Way Test. In making a decision, ask yourself:

1. Is it the truth?
2. Is it fair to all concerned?
3. Will it build goodwill and better relationships?
4. Will it be beneficial to all?

WHAT YOU SHOULD HAVE LEARNED

1. The U.S. legal system is based on British common law, as modified by laws passed by our federal, state, and local governments. The system is based on several principles; namely, that (*a*) everyone is equal under the law, (*b*) all laws must be based on the federal or a state constitution, (*c*) everyone is entitled to a day in court, (*d*) a person is presumed to be innocent until proven guilty, (*e*) there are multiple levels of government, such as federal, state, county, and municipal, and (*f*) the making, administering, and interpreting of laws are separated into three distinct branches of government: the legislative, executive, and judicial branches.

2. There are different types of business laws. The most important areas for small firms are (*a*) contracts, (*b*) sales, (*c*) property, (*d*) patents, copyrights, and trademarks, (*e*) agency, (*f*) negotiable instruments, (*g*) torts, and (*h*) bankruptcy. Many of these laws, which differ in the various states, have been codified into the Uniform Commercial Code, which has been adopted—with minor exceptions—by all 50 states.

3. Both the federal and local governments provide considerable assistance for small businesses, as shown in this chapter and in Chapters 3, 8, and 17. The Small Business Administration, the U.S. Department of Commerce, the U.S. Department of Agriculture, the Internal Revenue Service, and other agencies provide considerable assistance to small business people.

4. Although there is much assistance for small firms from government agencies, there is also considerable regulation and paperwork. There are around 54 federal agencies regulating and controlling small business activities. This regulation causes three problems for small firms. They are: (*a*) difficulty of understanding some of the regulations, which may be confusing and even contradictory, (*b*) the enormous amounts of paperwork needed to comply with government regulations, and (*c*) the difficulty and cost of complying with the regulations.

    But regulations provide many benefits. Often, the regulations will lead to net savings and expenditures. Also, regulation provides relatively free competition and restricts monopolistic practices. Price fixing is also prohibited.

    Small firms can cope with regulation by: (*a*) learning about the laws and using them for their benefit, (*b*) challenging detrimental or harmful laws and trying to get them modified or repealed, (*c*) becoming involved in the legal-political system to elect sympathetic officials, (*d*) finding a better legal environment—if possible—and (*e*) learning to live with the laws.

5. Choosing a lawyer is not easy. Still, you should obtain a lawyer familiar with small business activities, as well as the problem you are facing, before you even start your business. You can use the local lawyer referral service, talk to friends, or use word of mouth in searching for a competent lawyer.

    Some criteria for choosing a lawyer are: (*a*) the lawyer is knowledgeable about your type of business, (*b*) you and the lawyer are compatible, (*c*) the lawyer has time to deal with you and your business, and (*d*) the costs are not prohibitive.

    While we do not recommend it, it is possible—with the books, software, and videocassettes now available—to be your own counsel. There are do-it-yourself legal books and software packages available that explain such tasks as how to incorporate, make out a sales contract, or file for bankruptcy.

6. Small businesses are expected to act in an ethical and socially responsible manner in dealing with employees, customers, and the public. Acting socially responsibly means considering not only the owners, but others in making decisions that affect them.

    Most small businesses have always acted responsibly. Yet, around the turn of the century, during the 1930s, and again in the 1960s and 1970s, Congress passed many laws to force businesses—particularly large ones—to be more responsible.

    Ethical behavior is expected from small businesses, especially as it pertains to false and/or misleading advertising and tax evasion. As a minimum, small business managers are expected to obey both the letter *and* the spirit of laws affecting them.

KEY TERMS

common law, *695*

statute law, *695*

interstate commerce clause, *695*

police power, *695*

due process, *695*

legislative branch, *695*

executive branch, *695*

judicial branch, *695*

public law, *695*

criminal law, *695*

private law, *696*

civil law, *696*

Uniform Commercial Code (UCC), *697*

contract, *697*

consideration, *699*

implied contract, *699*

express contract, *699*

warranty, *700*

express warranties, *700*

implied warranties, *700*

real property, *700*

personal property, *700*

deed, *700*

lease, *700*

tangible property, *700*

intangible property, *700*

title, *700*

patent, *701*

patent practitioners, *701*

copyright, *701*

trademark, *701*

agency, *702*

principal, *702*

agent, *702*

negotiable instrument, *702*

tort, *702*

bankruptcy law, *703*

voluntary bankruptcy, *703*

involuntary bankruptcy, *703*

Chapter 11, *703*

composition of creditors, *703*

Service Corps of Retired Executives (SCORE), *704*

employer identification number, *706*

regulatory agency, *707*

social responsibility, *714*

consumerism, *715*

business ethics, *716*

QUESTIONS FOR DISCUSSION

1. Explain the six basic principles on which the U.S. legal system is based.
2. Distinguish between public/criminal and private/civil law.
3. What is the Uniform Commercial Code?
4. *(a)* What is a contract? *(b)* What are the six elements necessary to make a contract legal?
5. *(a)* What is a warranty? *(b)* Distinguish between express and implied warranties.
6. *(a)* What is product liability, and *(b)* why is it a problem for small businesses?
7. What is *(a)* a patent, *(b)* a copyright, and *(c)* a trademark? *(d)* How are these protected under U.S. law?
8. *(a)* What is agency law? *(b)* What is a principal? *(c)* What is an agent?
9. *(a)* What are negotiable instruments? *(b)* What does the law say about them?
10. Distinguish between *(a)* voluntary and involuntary bankruptcy, and *(b)* Chapter 11 and Chapter 7 bankruptcy.
11. Describe some of the assistance available from government agencies to help small firms.
12. *(a)* Why are regulatory agencies important to small firms? *(b)* Name and explain at least 10 U.S. government agencies.
13. *(a)* Describe at least three problems small businesses have with government regulation. *(b)* What are some benefits of such regulation?
14. Explain the five ways in which small firms can cope with regulations.
15. *(a)* Describe the characteristics you should look for in a lawyer. *(b)* How would you find such a lawyer? *(c)* How are lawyers compensated for their services?
16. *(a)* What is social responsibility? *(b)* Why is it important to small firms?
17. What are business ethics, and why are they so important?

SUGGESTED READINGS

Bacon, Donald C. "Small Business Briefs Mr. Bush." *Nation's Business,* January 1989, p. 20.

Bailey, Jeff. "Tightening the Rules." *The Wall Street Journal,* February 24, 1989, pp. R27, R28.

Carlson, Eugene. "Private Mail Firms Put Pressure on U.S. Postal Service." *The Wall Street Journal,* August 9, 1989, p. B2.

Gupta, Udayan. "Red Tape Tangling Those Least Suited to Handling It." *The Wall Street Journal,* October 25, 1989, p. B1.

Hagedorn, Ann. "Turning Safety into a Competitive Issue." *The Wall Street Journal,* July 25, 1989, p. B1.

Hoffman, Francis. "The Mice That Roared; Against All Odds." *Entrepreneur,* February 1989, pp. 92–94.

"Minority Contract Programs Reformed." *Journal of Accountancy,* January 1989, pp. 92–95.

Paul, Bill. "Small Businesses Parcel Out Donations in Varied Ways." *The Wall Street Journal,* December 27, 1988, p. B1.

Saddler, Jeanne. "Federal Regulators Draw Fire on TV Ad." *The Wall Street Journal,* May 3, 1989, p. B2.

Tannenbaum, Jeffrey A. "Tiny Firm Faces Legal Might of Wrathful Multinational." *The Wall Street Journal,* October 16, 1989, p. B2.

ENDNOTES

1. Douglas Whitman et al., *Law and Business* (New York: Random House, 1987), Chapter 1.

2. For some selected sections from the UCC, see Whitman, *Law and Business,* pp. 781–855.

3. Ibid., p. 83.

4. "Selling Faulty Pacemakers Costs Firm Plenty," *Mobile* (Alabama) *Register,* March 29, 1989, p. 2–A.

5. For more details on how to get a patent, call the U.S. Patent Office at 703–557–3158. To register a trademark, write the U.S. Trademark Association at 6 East 45th Street, New York, NY 10017. See also Harriet C. Johnson, "When It's Time to Get a Patent," *USA Today,* May 8, 1989, p. 5E.

6. *Fortune,* January 23, 1984, p. 31.

7. To learn more about SCORE, contact the National SCORE Office, 1825 Connecticut Avenue, Suite 503, Washington, DC 20009 (202–653–6279). Or contact your local SCORE chapter. Check in the blue pages of your phone book under the U.S. Small Business Administration.

8. To get this identification number, call 1–800–424–1040 and ask for Form SS–4, or go to your local IRS office and fill one out.

9. See Leon C. Megginson, Lyle R. Trueblood, and Gayle M. Ross, *Business* (Lexington, Mass.: D. C. Heath, 1985), pp. 625–28, for more details.

10. U.S. Department of Commerce, *Survey of Current Business* (Washington, D.C.: U.S. Government Printing Office, August 1983), p. 24.

11. John R. Emshwiller, "Agencies Block Competition by Small Firms," *The Wall Street Journal,* July 26, 1989, pp. B1, B2. Reprinted by permission of The Wall Street Journal, © Dow Jones & Company, Inc., 1989. ALL RIGHTS RESERVED.

12. Jeanne Saddler, "Small Talk," *The Wall Street Journal,* July 27, 1989, p. B2.

13. David Landis, "Tighter Rules Put Squeeze on Firms," *USA Today,* May 26, 1989, p. 2B.

14. "Toilet Maker Profits with Special Flush to Meet Water Limits," *Mobile* (Alabama) *Register,* April 24, 1989, p. 8–B.

15. "Heeding Equal Access," *Nation's Business,* December 1987, p. 12.

16. *How to Choose and Use a Lawyer* (Chicago, Ill.: American Bar Association). For information contact the ABA at 750 N. Lake Shore Drive, Chicago, IL 60611.

17. Jeffrey A. Tannenbaum, "Small-Business Owners Must Pick a Lawyer Judiciously," *The Wall Street Journal,* February 15, 1989, p. B2.

18. Amy Dockser, "Tips for Finding Legal Assistance at Modest Rate," *The Wall Street Journal,* April 26, 1989, p. B8.

19. Roland Flamiñi, "Anita Roddick," *European Travel & Life,* March 1990, pp. 59–61.

20. The Annenberg/CPB Project has a new audio and video series dealing with "Ethics in Business." A preview can be arranged by writing The Annenberg/CPB Project, c/o Intellimation, P.O. Box 4069, Santa Barbara, CA 93140, or calling 1–800–LEARNER.

23

TAXES AND THEIR TREATMENT

Our Constitution is in actual operation; everything appears to promise that it will last; but in this world nothing can be said to be certain but death and taxes.—Benjamin Franklin

Noah must have taken two taxes into the ark—and they have been multiplying ever since!
—Will Rogers

LEARNING OBJECTIVES

After studying the material in this chapter, you will be able to:

1. Explain how the U.S. tax system operates.
2. Name and describe the taxes imposed on the small business itself.
3. Name and describe employment-related taxes.
4. Explain how the ownership of the business results in direct taxation of the owner.
5. Show how taxes may be reduced by careful estate planning.
6. Understand the importance of recordkeeping and tax reporting.

JACK BARES: ESTATE PLANNING TO MINIMIZE TAXES

Jack Bares is an unusual entrepreneur. Not only did he establish his own company—Milbar Corporation, a Chagrin Falls, Ohio, hand-tool manufacturing company—but he also started planning his estate at the birth of his first child in 1960, shortly after starting Milbar. He worked out a practical three-stage approach to correspond with the life cycle of his growing family and business.

In 1960, in the first stage, he wrote a will leaving the new business and his other assets to his wife—and "bought plenty of life insurance." Then he set up a family partnership, combining a standard family partnership agreement with a sale-leaseback strategy. After placing Milbar's few assets in the partnership, the corporation leased the assets back from the partnership. The result was that the corporation basically owned only its working capital, while the family partnership owned everything else.

Jack and his wife were equal partners with the children in the partnership. The parents made annual tax-free contributions to the partnership in each child's name. They started with $3,000 per parent per child, the IRS limit at that time, and have worked up to the current maximum of $10,000. The parents were the general partners, operating and controlling the partnership's business. Because of the family partnership leasing strategy, the income earned by the partnership, which was primarily leasing fees, was taxed at a personal rate—which was lower than the corporate rate.

The first stage of the estate plan was flexible enough to adjust to the changing needs of a growing business, without a lot of unnecesssary paperwork and administrative cost.

When the Bareses' first child went to college, Bares entered the second stage of his estate plan by concentrating on the best tax-saving device available at that time; namely, the estate freeze. (Note: Although estate freezing was wiped out

Milbar Corporation CEO Jack Bares
Source: Photo © Bruce Zake, 1989.

by the Tax Reform Act of 1986, its elimination was not made retroactive.) Under a stock recapitalization plan, he transferred nonvoting common stock to the children, while he retained the voting stock. Thus, he continued to run, build, and profit from the business while passing along the ownership of the company to the children, at large tax savings.

He recently entered the third stage. He and his wife reduced their share of the business to only 0.5 percent each, and the remaining shares were split equally among their four children. He promoted a vice president to the president's spot and named three outside businesspeople as board members. The role of these four people is either to ensure a smooth transition to new family management or, if none of the family want to stay involved, to sell the company.

Source: Jill Andresky Fraser, "Planning Ahead: Estate Planning Isn't Just for Your Heirs. It Can Save Your Company," *Inc.*, August 1989, pp. 125–27. Reprinted with permission of *Inc.* magazine. Copyright © 1989 by Goldhirsh Group, Inc., 38 Commercial Wharf, Boston MA 02110.

No one denies the truth of Benjamin Franklin's statement that "nothing is certain but death and taxes," especially small business owners. The Opening Focus dramatizes these owners' need to lower their taxes. **Taxes,** which are the charges levied by a government on persons and organizations subject to its jurisdiction, are inevitable. Therefore, we'll try to explain how the U.S. tax system affects small businesses.

HOW THE U.S. TAX SYSTEM OPERATES

The theory underlying taxation is simple enough. The government uses its power to tax in order to have funds to spend on essential goods and services. In the past, it's been considered desirable to have taxes levied according to the *ability of the payer to pay,* not according to the value of the benefits used. Thus, state and federal income taxes are imposed directly on companies and individuals to raise the funds needed to meet the government's regular budgetary needs. In general, the amount paid varies according to the ability to pay.

A consideration that's now becoming more important, though, is the *consequences of the tax*—that is, the effects a tax bill will have on the economy. An example is the capital gains tax. In 1978, we were suffering from **stagflation**—a stagnant economy with a high inflation rate. Congress passed the **Tax Reform Act of 1978,** lowering the marginal rate for long-term capital gains from 35 percent to 28 percent in order to stimulate the economy. The results were dramatic. The commitment of new funds just from venture capitalists rose from $68 million in 1977 to $4.9 billion in 1987.[1] In 1989, after the rate had increased to 33 percent in 1986, President Bush requested a reduction in the rate to 19 percent in order to stimulate the economy.

The U.S. tax system includes all the federal, state, and local tax systems. However, each of these systems has at least two parts. The first part is the system for determining what the taxes will be and who will pay them. The processes involved are legislation, imposing the tax, and determining the liability of each individual or institution. The second part is the system for collecting the taxes.

Who Pays the Taxes?

Taxes can be either indirect or direct. **Indirect taxes** are paid not by the person or firm against which they're levied but by someone else. Since indirect taxes are part of the cost of doing business, they must either be added to the price of the firm's goods or services or shifted backward to the persons or firms who produced the goods or services.

Direct taxes are paid directly to the taxing authority by the person or business against which they're levied.

For example, the owner of a building containing a retail shop pays the property tax (direct) to the tax collector, but the amount of the tax is included in the rent paid by the retailer to the owner (indirect). In turn, the retailer includes this tax in the price that a customer pays for the goods or services that are being sold (indirect).

Also, as will be shown later, you pay tax on your income (direct) even though your employer may withhold it and send it to the tax collector for you.

Figure 23–1 gives an overview of some selected taxes on small businesses. It shows the kind of tax, the taxpayer, the point of collection, and the governmental unit collecting the tax.

Figure 23–1   Some Selected Direct Taxes Paid by Small Firms

Kind of tax	Taxpayer	Point of collection	Collecting agency
Corporate income tax	Corporations	Tax collectors	Internal Revenue Service State revenue departments City tax collectors
Corporate franchise tax (on capital stock)	Corporations	Tax collectors	States
Undistributed profits tax	Corporations	District IRS office	Internal Revenue Service
Customs duties	Corporations	Customs agents	U.S. Customs Service
Excise taxes	Businesses Customers	Utility companies Wholesale distributors Tax collectors	Internal Revenue Service State revenue departments
Motor fuel taxes	Businesses	Wholesale distributors	Internal Revenue Service State revenue departments
Highway use tax	Motor transport businesses	Interstate Commerce Commission	Interstate Commerce Commission
Unemployment compensation	Employers	Internal Revenue Service	Internal Revenue Service
Licenses, permits	Businesses	Tax collectors	City tax collectors State revenue departments CAB, ICC, FCC, etc.
Old Age, Survivors, Disability, and Hospital Insurance (OASDHI)	Employers Employees	Businesses	Internal Revenue Service
Sales and use taxes	Customers	Businesses	City and state revenue departments
Property tax	Businesses	Local tax collectors	City and county tax collectors
Inventory or floor tax	Businesses	Local and state tax collectors	County and state tax collectors
Public utility taxes	Utility companies	City, county, and state tax collectors	City, county, and state tax collectors

Note: This table applies to direct taxes only; the shifting of taxes from the point of collection backward or forward isn't considered.
Source: Adapted from Leon C. Megginson, Lyle R. Trueblood, and Gayle M. Ross, *Business* (Lexington, Mass.: D. C. Heath, 1985), p. 636.

How Taxes Affect Small Businesses

Taxes affect almost every aspect of operating a small business. First, there is the direct taxation of business income, whether in the form of sales taxes levied as a tax on business receipts or as an income tax on corporate profits.

Second, employers must withhold a variety of employment-related taxes levied on their employees, and often must match them. The most important of these taxes are federal and state income taxes on personal wage and salary incomes, and federal taxes levied to fund the Social Security system.

Third, small business owners must pay personal taxes on their salaries, bonuses, stock options, dividends, and other ownership-related income they withdraw from the business. And, if part of their wealth is invested outside the business, entrepreneurs face taxes on the investment income they receive. When they decide to sell their business, the tax treatment of the sale can critically affect the net value received for a lifetime's work.

Fourth, taxes are levied on the intergenerational transfer of ownership of the business, so the small business owner must approach estate planning with a keen eye to minimizing the tax bite on an inheritance, as shown in the Opening Focus and as will be discussed later.

As extensive as the above list seems, it is far from complete. Taxes also affect business decisions on other levels, as well. For example, the choice of the best form of business organization—proprietorship, partnership, corporation, or S Corporation—largely depends on the profitability of the business and the tax status of the owner(s).

Finally, the administrative cost of being a tax collector for the government is becoming burdensome. As shown in Figure 23–1, it's the small business's responsibility to collect several taxes for the government by withholding sums from the employees' paychecks or by adding the tax (such as sales or use taxes) to the price of the products sold to customers. These administrative costs become very expensive in terms of personnel, time, and money.

Get Professional Help!

The purpose of this chapter is to make you aware of the current tax environment in which small firms operate, and to raise some basic tax issues important to every small business owner. It is *very important* for someone in every small firm to understand the tax system in order to take advantage of the opportunities available for deductions, credits, and tax savings. Therefore, it is wise to hire a competent bookkeeper or CPA to advise you on tax matters. However, the final responsibility for determining and paying your taxes rests with you.

While the U.S. Internal Revenue Service, as well as state and local agencies, will willingly help you determine whether you owe additional taxes, *they accept no responsibility for the accuracy of their over-the-counter or telephone advice.* The responsibility is yours, so get professional help! Also, you should familiarize yourself with the *Tax Guide for Small Business,*[2] which covers income, excise, and employment taxes for individuals, partnerships, and corporations.

Types of Taxes

Since it is impossible to discuss all the taxes small firms have to pay, we've grouped them into four categories: (1) taxes imposed on the business itself, (2) employment-related taxes, (3) personal taxes that owners pay, and (4) estate taxes.

TAXES IMPOSED ON THE BUSINESS ITSELF

Numerous taxes are imposed on the small firm as a condition of its doing business. We've grouped those together as: (1) taxes paid for the "right" to operate the business, (2) excise and intangible property taxes, (3) state and local taxes on business receipts, and (4) federal, state, and local income taxes.

Taxes Paid to Operate the Business

Some license fees, incorporation taxes, and the cost of permits must be paid before the business actually begins operating. Figure 23–2 illustrates the most important of these.

Figure 23–2   Selected Licenses, Permits, and Registrations Required of Small Firms

- *Business license (city, county, state).*   Generally, you must apply for one or more business licenses. Often a tax identification number will be printed on your business license, and you'll use the number when filing various tax returns. Your state Department of Revenue can assist you in defining your reporting requirements.
- *Employer's federal ID number (SS-4) (federal).*   A federal ID number is needed to identify an employer on all federal tax fillings. Some local jurisdictions also require the federal ID number on various filings. The SS-4 form is available from the IRS.
- *Incorporation or partnership registration (state).*   You should plan on using an attorney to assist with registering your company as a corporation or partnership. If you are a corporation, you'll also need articles of incorporation, bylaws, stock certificates, a corporate seal, and other items.
- *Trade name registration (state).*   You'll need to register any trade names used in your business (e.g., if your legal incorporated name is Superior Semiconductors of California, Ltd., but you generally go by the name "Superior," you'll need to register your alternative name.)
- *Zoning permits (city or county).*   If your business constitutes an "alternative use" or other special case, you'll need appropriate zoning permits.
- *Building permits (city or county).*   If you are doing any remodeling, construction, or related work, be sure you have appropriate permits.
- *Mailing permits (federal).*   Check with your post office about any bulk, first class, business reply card, or other mailing permits.
- *Professional registrations (state).*   Generally these are employee specific, such as registered engineer, notary public, etc. You may, however, wish to reimburse employees for any job-related expenses.

Source: Building the High Technology Business: Positioning for Growth, Profitability, and Success (New York: Peat Marwick Main & Co., 1988), p. 59.

Most cities, counties, and states require business operators to obtain numerous licenses and permits in order to comply with various laws and regulations. These fees and permits are often intertwined with taxes, insurance, capital requirements, and the nature and scope of the business itself.

Business Licenses

Many cities and counties require different types of licenses. In addition to the initial license fee, some agencies receive a percentage of gross sales. Unfortunately, many of these permits and licenses must be obtained from numerous locations, often widely dispersed. But many cities, counties, and states are now permitting "one-step permitting," whereby these permits can be obtained in one office—or at least in one building.

Your state, county, and city revenue agencies should be able to assist you in determining what is required of you.

Note that Mick and Cathy obtained their city and state licenses for the Mother and Child Shop (Case II–4) several weeks before it opened.

The federal government also requires certain operators and businesses to have federal licenses. For example, television and radio stations, meat processors, common carriers, and certain investment advisory services must be licensed. The Federal Trade Commission can tell you if you require such a license.

Employer Identification Number

If you employ one or more persons in your small firm, you must have a federal **employer identification number** for tax purposes. Also, if your state has an income tax, you must obtain an identification number from it as well. This number must be used when reporting and paying income taxes and Social Security taxes.

State Incorporation or Partnership Registration

As shown in Chapter 9, businesses are incorporated by the state, with each state setting its own rules and regulations. Thus, if you choose incorporation, it must be done through your secretary of state. As Figure 23–2 shows, you will need bylaws, stock certificates, and a corporate seal as well as the charter and articles of incorporation.

If you draw up articles of co-partnership with your partner(s), they will need to be recorded also.

Trade Name Registration

As discussed in Chapter 22, you need to register with the secretary of state any trade names you use in your home state and in other states in which you operate.

Zoning Variances

If you plan to construct a new building or use an existing building for a different use from its previous one, or if extensive remodeling is required, you should check for local zoning and building codes. If the zoning regulations do not permit your type of operation, you can file for a **zoning variance,** a zoning change, or a conditional use permit. This may take 90 days or longer, and the filing fee may be as high as $1,500.

Building Permits

In most zoned areas, a building permit is required for construction of a new building, remodeling of an existing one, or other modifications. You, or your contractor, will need to get plumbing, electrical, and other construction permits.

Mailing Permit

If you intend to do bulk mailing, use business reply cards, or make any other special use of mailing privileges, you will need to check with the U.S. Postal Service for permits—and pay the appropriate fees.

Occupational and Professional Registration

Many states require occupational permits or certification licenses for people engaged in specific professions and occupations. Often, these individuals must pass state examinations, after intensive training programs, before being licensed. Some of these occupations are registered engineer, notary public, licensed psychologist, insurance agent, real estate broker or agent, and anyone providing services to the human body, such as doctors, nurses, and barbers.

Other Permits Required

Many cities and counties require special permits in order to regulate or control such concerns as air and water quality, fire safety, health maintenance, alcohol consumption, and size, location, lighting, and type of signs.

Excise and Intangible Property Taxes

The federal government places an **excise tax** on many items such as tires for automobiles and other moving vehicles, cigars and cigarettes, and alcoholic beverages. Many states also apply such taxes.

Taxes on intangibles such as copyrights, patents, and trademarks are another source of income for many states. Some states even have a tax on inventories in stock.

State and Local Sales and Use Taxes

Many states and localities have sales and use taxes, which generate large sums. **Use taxes** are usually imposed on the use, consumption, or storage of goods within the taxing jurisdiction. This type of tax is often applied to automobiles and other moving vehicles that are purchased outside the jurisdiction and brought in for future use.

Sales taxes are usually based on the gross amount of the sale for goods sold within the taxing jurisdiction. A new trend is to tax sales in other locations as well, so you will need to check for your liability for sales taxes in those locations. Exemptions from sales taxes are often provided for goods to be resold and for machinery or equipment used exclusively in processing or assembling other goods. Service businesses are often totally exempt, as are drugs, unprepared foods, and agricultural products in certain states.

For example, in Maryland, not only are drugs and food items in grocery stores exempt but also prepared foods under $1 (such as concession sales and restaurant orders such as a cup of coffee). Some states don't charge sales tax on alcoholic beverages, which already bear a state tax stamp, or cigarettes for the same reason.

You need to contact your state or local revenue offices for information on the tax rate and the law in your area so that you can adapt your bookkeeping to the appropriate requirements. Sales and use taxes are often reported on a monthly basis. *One word of caution:* Even if you do not collect these taxes from your customers or clients, you will probably be held liable for the full amount of the uncollected taxes.

Federal, State, and Local Income Taxes

Income taxes have been very much in the news during the past decade. The **Tax Reform Act of 1986** made sweeping changes in the structure of tax rates and other features of the tax code for businesses and individuals.[3] These changes affect almost all Americans who must pay taxes.

States and localities have also instituted or modified their tax laws during the decade. Because of the variation and complexities of the state and local laws, and because space in this text is limited, we will discuss only the federal law.

From the very beginning of your business, you should have a qualified accountant to provide you with information and help you make important decisions, compiling facts for accurate tax returns, and protecting you from costly errors.

There are three major decisions involving taxes that you must make at the start, namely: (1) the method of handling your income and expenses, (2) the time period for paying taxes, and (3) the form of business to use, as that form will largely determine your tax rates and other tax considerations.

Accounting Method and Tax Period

Choosing the appropriate accounting method and the period of your business "year" can save your company unnecessary future tax liabilities, so it is important to have your accountant's assistance early in the life of your firm.

Cash versus accrual method.   As discussed in Part VI, under the **accrual method** of accounting, income and expenses are charged to the period in which they occur, regardless of whether the money has been received or paid out.

For example, if you sell goods on credit, and they have not been paid for, you still record them as income for the period of sale.

Also, if you have unpaid expenses incurred during the period, you can still take the deduction for that expense.

For example, if employees work the last two weeks of a month, and you pay them in the next month, you can deduct their earnings as expenses, since they have earned the money.

The accrual method is required for businesses using inventories, for purchases and sales, and for most corporations and partnerships. However, some corporations and partnerships with annual gross receipts of less than $5 million can choose either the cash or the accrual method.

Calendar versus fiscal year period.   Tax returns for your business may be prepared on a calendar- or fiscal-year basis. If the tax liability is calculated on a calendar-year basis, the tax return must be filed with the IRS no later than April each year. To pick a favorable filing month, many small firms use a fiscal-year basis. Again, the decision should be made with the help of your accountant.

How the Form of a Business Affects Its Taxes

As discussed in Chapter 9, the amount and methods of handling income taxes affect the choice of business form.[4] As shown in Figures 9–3 and 9–4, a small business owner may choose a partnership or proprietorship rather than pay higher taxes on corporate income and then pay individual taxes on dividends.

Current U.S. tax laws are prompting some professional corporations to seek S Corporation status.[5] S Corporation shareholders are taxed at individual rates, which are lower than corporate rates; yet they still enjoy the legal protection that comes with corporate status.[6] But S Corporations do have disadvantages, such as restrictions on benefit plans, a limitation on the number of shareholders, and possible recognition of built-in gains.

Finally, as shown in Chapter 8, the use of employee stock ownership plans (ESOPs) can lead to tax advantages as well as cash flow advantages.

Figure 23–3   How Business Form Affects Flow of Income and Amount of Taxes

Company operations	Tax treatment

A. Sole proprietorship: Company A

Schedule C, Form 1040

Sales . . . . $XXX,XXX Deductible expenses . . . . . . XX,XXX Net income . . . . $ X,XXX (No income tax paid on business income.)	Owner pays personal taxes on business income, after deducting itemized expenses. $X,XXX

B. Partnership: A & B Company

Schedule C, Form 1040

Sales . . . . $XXX,XXX Deductible expenses . . . . . . XX,XXX Net income . . . . $ X,XXX (No income tax paid on partnership income, but IRS Form 1065 must be filed showing total net income.*)	*Partner A:* Takes share of net income out of business and pays personal taxes at his or her individual rate. $X,XXX
	Partner B: Takes share of net income out of business and pays personal taxes at his or her individual rate. $X,XXX

C.   Corporation: ABC Corporation

Form 1040

Sales . . . . $XXX,XXX
Deductible expenses . . . . . .   XX,XXX
Net income . . . . $ X,XXX
 	
Corporate income
  tax paid (IRS
  Form 1120)† . . . . $ XXX
Available for
  dividends $ XXX
	Stockholder A:
	Income from dividend taxed at individual rate. $ XXX

	Stockholder B: Income from dividend taxed at individual rate. $ XXX
	Stockholder C: Income from dividend taxed at individual rate. $ XXX

* See U.S. Department of the Treasury, Internal Revenue Service, *Tax Information on Partnerships* (Washington, D.C.: U.S. Government Printing Office, December 1987), for details.

† See U.S. Department of the Treasury, Internal Revenue Service, *Tax Information on Corporations* (Washington, D.C.: U.S. Government Printing Office, December 1987), for details.

Figure 23–3 shows how the business form affects the flow of income from sales into net income into taxes.

As state and federal laws are so varied and complex, we will discuss only federal corporate income taxes.

Treatment of Federal Corporate Income Taxes

There are three questions small corporations need to answer when handling their federal income taxes. They are:

1. What tax rate applies to the business?
2. What is taxable income?
3. What are deductible expenses?

What Tax Rates Apply?

The corporate federal income tax on small firms is simple in one respect—there are only three basic rates, as shown in Table 23–1. Thus, after taxable income and deductible expenses are computed, it is simple to compute the taxes.

For example, if a corporation has net income of $100,000, it would pay federal income taxes as follows:

$$
\begin{array}{rl}
0.15 \times \$50,000 = & \$\ 7,500. \\
0.25 \times\ \ \ 25,000 = & 6,250. \\
0.34 \times\ \ \ 25,000 = & \underline{8,500} \\
\text{Total income tax} = & \$22,250
\end{array}
$$

What Is Taxable Income?

For income tax purposes, **taxable income** is defined as total revenues minus deductible expenses. While this definition sounds simple, problems arise in measuring both income and expenses. Accounting associations have developed a set of procedures known as **generally accepted accounting principles (GAAP)** that are used by both businesses and income tax people for handling these problems.

While the government has set the rules for calculating income for tax purposes, the firm may have discretion in reporting income to its stockholders.[7]

Table 23–1   Federal Tax Rates for Corporations

Taxable income	Tax rate
0–$50,000	15%
$50,000–$75,000	25
Over $75,000	34

Source: U.S. Department of the Treasury, Internal Revenue Service, *Tax Information on Corporations,* Publication 542 (Washington, D.C.: U.S. Government Printing Office, December 1987), p. 1.

What Expenses Are Deductible?

Normally, deductions from income are classified as cost of goods sold, selling expenses, and administrative expenses. Rather than try to cover all the expenses that can be deducted from revenue to determine net income, we discuss only the following selected ones:

1. Administrative expenses.
2. Depreciation.
3. Inventory valuation.
4. Interest payments.
5. Business lunches, entertainment, and travel.
6. Automobile, home, and computer expenses.

Administrative expenses.   These expenses are those that are needed to run a business office, such as rent, accounting and legal expenses, telephone and other utilities, dues and subscriptions to business publications, and professional services.

Depreciation.   The determination of the amount of depreciation to be deducted from income tax each year is an example of the effect that different accounting procedures can have on income. For example, you can use cash-value depreciation or tax-related depreciation.

Cash value depreciation is based on the difference between the cost of a piece of equipment and its fair market value at the end of a given period of time.

For example, if a piece of equipment costing $15,000 is bought in January 1990 and has a market value of $11,000 in December 1990, the cash value depreciation for that year would be $4,000.

Tax-related depreciation, on the other hand, is an accounting device to maximize the allowable deduction permitted by tax laws in figuring your net taxable income.

Aside from land, which is normally not considered a depreciable asset, depreciation on assets can be computed on either a straight-line method or an accelerated cost recovery system basis. Under the **straight-line method,** the value of the asset, divided by its useful life in years, gives the amount that can be deducted each year. Under the **accelerated cost recovery system (ACRS),** there are some formulas to be used to deduct the greatest amount of depreciation of assets during their earlier years.[8] Table 23–2 shows some selected types of assets and their useful life, as permitted by the IRS.

Inventory valuation.   Another accounting decision to make is how to value inventory that is used during the year. The problem is particularly acute when prices are changing and/or when a firm holds inventory for long

Table 23–2 Useful Life of Selected Assets for Federal Taxes

Type of asset	Normal recovery period (years)
Certain short-lived property and special-purpose tools	3
Automobiles, buses, and light trucks; technological equipment, computers, and information systems; and construction, electronic, and semiconductor manufacturing equipment	5
Most manufacturing equipment; heavy trucks; and office furniture and equipment	7
Water transport vehicles, such as barges and tugs; and some heavy manufacturing equipment	10
Land improvements, such as sidewalks; sewage treatment plants; and electric generation equipment	15
Nonresidential real property	20

periods of time. As shown in Chapter 20, the three methods of computing inventory used in production are: (1) the **first-in, first-out (FIFO) method,** (2) the **last-in, first-out (LIFO) method,** and (3) the **average-cost method.** The decision on which method to use should be made in the first year of operations. After one method is chosen, it is difficult to change it, according to IRS regulations. In general, when prices are rising, small firms tend to switch to the LIFO method to save taxes.

For example, as shown in Chapter 20, the Chicago Heights Steel Company boosted its cash holdings by 5 to 10 percent, and thus lowered its income taxes, by switching to LIFO in 1989.[9]

Interest payments. The U.S. Revenue Code has a built-in bias toward the use of debt by small firms, as interest on debt is deductible, while dividends paid to stockholders are not (see Figure 23–3). The total amount of interest paid is deducted from revenue to find taxable income.

Business lunches, entertainment, and travel. Only 80 percent of the cost of business meals and entertainment expenses is deductible. To deduct any meals and entertainment expenses, you must keep records of (1) whom you entertained, (2) the purpose of the meeting, (3) the amount spent, and (4) when and where it took place.

Travel, food, and lodging expenses for out-of-town business travel are deductible if you stay overnight. Such costs as air, bus, or auto transportation, hotel cost, meals, taxes, and tips are deductible. The cost of seminars, conferences, and conventions is also deductible.

Automobile, home, and computer expenses. Many small businesses operate out of the home(s) of the owner(s). Deductions for these expenses can be quite valuable to small businesspeople. Certain expenses, such as operating a car, utilities, repairs and maintenance, computer operations and maintenance, and home insurance and taxes can be deducted from income taxes if they are business related. But there are restrictions, which are enforced. For an automobile, you can either deduct the actual cost of running your car or truck, or take a standard mileage rate. You must use actual costs if you use more than one vehicle in your business. In 1989, the standard mileage rate was 24 cents per mile up to 15,000 miles, and 11 cents for each mile after that, in addition to parking fees and tolls.

When you work out of your home, you can claim actual business-related expenses, such as telephone charges, business equipment and supplies, postage, photocopying, and clerical and professional costs.[10] A deduction is also allowable for any portion of your home used "exclusively" and "regularly" as your principal place of business. For example, you can deduct expenses for taxes, insurance, and depreciation on that portion of your home that is used exclusively as your office. The ratio of the square footage used to the total area of the residence is a good basis for apportionment. Another method is to use the ratio of the number of rooms in the home and those used for business purposes.

The **Deficit Reduction Act of 1984** limits the conditions under which computers used in the home can be deducted as business expenses. The simple test is: If you use a home computer for business purposes over 50 percent of the time, it qualifies for the appropriate credits or deductions.

EMPLOYMENT-RELATED TAXES

Employment-related taxes are the largest costs for most small firms since they are due even if there is no profit. So careful consideration should be given to computing and paying them.

As shown in Chapter 11, employers are legally required to provide their employees with **Social Security, unemployment compensation insurance,** and **industrial insurance** (commonly called **workers' compensation**). In addition, the employer must withhold taxes from employees for city, county, state, and federal income taxes. Also, since 1986, the **Employee Retirement Income Security Act (ERISA)** has required employers with 20 or more employees to continue health insurance programs for limited periods for employees who are terminated and for widows, divorced spouses, and dependents of employees.

Income Tax Withholding

The IRS and certain states, counties, and localities require you to withhold the appropriate amount of income tax from each employee's earnings during each pay period. The amount of this pay-as-you-go tax depends on each employee's total wages, number of exemptions claimed on his or her withholding exemption certificate, marital status, and length of pay period. Each employee must complete and sign a W-4 form for your files.[11] See

---

Figure 23–4 Selected Employee-Related Tax Forms Needed by Small Firms

A. Federal Tax Forms
    For companies with paid employees:
    ■ Form SS–4, Application for Employer Identification Number
    ■ Form W–2, Wage and Tax Statement
    ■ Form W–2P, Statement for Recipients of Periodic Annuities, Pensions, Retired Pay, or IRA Payments
    ■ Form W–3, Transmittal of Income and Tax Statements
    ■ Form W–4, Employee's Withholding Allowance Certificate, for each employee
    ■ Form 940, Employer's Annual Federal Unemployment (FUTA) Tax Return
    ■ Form 941, Employer's Quarterly Federal Tax Return
    ■ Form 1099–MISC, Statement for Recipients of Nonemployee Compensation

    Income tax forms and schedules, which vary depending on your organizational status, type of income/losses, selection of various elections, etc.

    ERISA Form 5500 series, depending on your status under the Employee Retirement Income Security Act

B. State and Local Forms
    Income and/or business and occupation taxes.
    Industrial insurance ("workers' compensation").
    Unemployment compensation insurance.

Source: *Building the High Technology Business: Positioning for Growth, Profitability, and Success* (New York: Peat Marwick Main & Co., 1988), p. 63.

Figure 23–4 for the more important employee-related forms needed by small firms.

The amount withheld from all employees must be submitted to the IRS, along with Form 941, on a quarterly basis. However, if $3,000 or more has been withheld from employees during the month, that deposit must be made within three banking days following the end of the month.

Form W–2, Wage and Tax Statement (Figure 23–5), must be completed and mailed to each employee by January 31 immediately following the taxable year.

As shown in the next Computer Update, employers submitting 250 or more W–2 or W–2P forms must transmit those forms to the IRS by magnetic media.

Social Security Taxes

As shown in Chapter 11, the Social Security program, as set up by the **Social Security Act of 1935,** requires employers to act as both tax collectors and taxpayers. Not only do you have to withhold a certain percentage of each employee's income, but you must also match it with a payment of your own. These taxes are technically for the **Federal Insurance Contributions Act (FICA)** but are usually referred to as the Social Security tax. In 1989, the employer had to collect 7.51 percent of an employee's

Figure 23–5   Form W–2, Wage and Tax Statement

1 Control number			
		OMB No. 1545-0008	

2 Employer's name, address, and ZIP code		3 Employer's identification number	4 Employer's State number
		5 Statutory employee ☐ De-ceased ☐ Pension plan ☐ Legal rep. ☐ 942 emp. ☐ Sub-total ☐ Deferred compensation ☐ Void ☐	
		6 Allocated tips	7 Advance EIC payment

8 Employee's social security number	9 Federal income tax withheld	10 Wages, tips, other compensation	11 Social security tax withheld
12 Employee's name, address, and ZIP code		13 Social security wages	14 Social security tips
		16	16a Fringe benefits incl. in Box 10
		17 State income tax	18 State wages, tips, etc. 19 Name of State
		20 Local Income tax	21 Local wages, tips, etc. 22 Name of locality

Form **W-2 Wage and Tax Statement 1989**   Copy 1 For State, City, or Local Tax Department ☐
Employee's and employer's copy compared.

total earnings—up to $48,000—and then match that amount out of business revenues. These taxes are sent to the IRS each quarter, along with Federal Form 941, Employer's Quarterly Federal Tax Return. Self-employed people must pay the combined employee's and employer's amount of taxes, which amounted to 15.02 percent in 1989.

Unemployment Compensation Insurance

Unemployment compensation insurance has two parts. First, a small basic amount is paid to the U.S. government as a **federal unemployment tax** to administer the program. A second part, which is determined by the states, builds up a fund from which employees are paid in case they are laid off. Figure 23–6 shows that these payments are not insignificant.

For example, while all employers paid an average of $224 per worker for federal and state unemployment taxes, Alaska employers paid an average of $984.

Federal Form 940, Employer's Annual Federal Unemployment (FUTA) Tax Return, must be filed annually. However, you may be liable for periodic tax deposits during the year.

COMPUTER UPDATE

MAGNETIC MEDIA REPORTING

Beginning in 1988, for the tax year 1987, employers reporting 250 or more Forms W–2 or W–2P must transmit those forms by magnetic media. You can file your W–2 data on magnetic film or diskette, but Form W–2P data must be filed on magnetic tape. The IRS has certain waiver requirements if an employer can show undue hardship.

Many service bureaus have agreed to prepare these magnetic reports and submit them directly to the Social Security Administration, saving their customers the time and trouble of filing their own reports on copy A of the W–2.

Write to Magnetic Media Reporting, Social Security Administration, P.O. Box 2312, Baltimore, MD 21203, for more information.

Source: A Message from Social Security to All Employers, SSA Pub. No. 05–10155, January 1988, pp. 10–11.

Figure 23–6   Top States for Jobless Taxes

Employers paid an average $224 per worker in federal and state unemployment taxes in 1988 (including $58 per worker in federal unemployment tax). States with the highest unemployment taxes per worker:

Source: Laurdan Associates, Inc., as reported in *USA Today,* May 18, 1989, p. 1B. Copyright 1989, USA TODAY. Adapted with permission.

Workers' Compensation

The Social Security Act of 1935 requires employers to provide industrial insurance for employees who are harmed or killed on the job. These payments are usually funded through an insurance program, with higher rates for higher-risk employees.

PERSONAL TAXES PAID BY OWNERS THEMSELVES

There are several methods of withdrawing cash from the business for your own use. Some of these are taxable to you, and some are taxable for the firm.

Taxes on Amounts Withdrawn from the Business

First, salaries and bonuses received from the business are an expense to the business. But individual income taxes are also paid on those sums, at the rate shown in Table 23–3. You can also withdraw cash from a proprietorship or partnership, and these sums are also taxable to you as an individual.

For example, Jeanne Parnell (Case III–3) filed a joint return with her husband. She included the "profits" from The Beary Best Cookies with her husband's earnings. As their recordkeeping was haphazard, they weren't really sure of the profit. In fact, Jeanne counted all sales as profits because her costs were so low, and that figure was used for tax purposes.

From a corporation, owners receive dividends, which are taxed twice. The corporation gets no tax deduction, and owners must pay taxes at their individual rates.

Table 23–3   Federal Tax Rates for Individuals

Income of		Amount of taxes
At least	But not more than	
Single taxpayers:		
$ 0	$ 17,850	$ 0 + 15% of income over $ 0
17,850	43,150	2,678 + 28 of income over $ 17,850
43,150	89,560	9,762 + 33 of income over $ 43,150
89,560	. . .	25,077 + 28 of income over $ 89,560
Married taxpayers filing jointly:		
$ 0	$ 29,750	$ 0 + 15% of income over $ 0
29,750	71,900	4,463 + 28 of income over $ 29,750
71,900	149,250	16,265 + 33 of income over $ 71,900
149,250	. . .	41,790 + 28 of income over $149,250

Source: U.S. Department of the Treasury, Internal Revenue Service, *1988 Forms and Instructions, 1040* (Washington, D.C.: U.S. Government Printing Office, 1988), p. 47.

Although not in the form of cash, employees can also receive tax-free benefits from the business, which are deductible by the firm. These include such things as medical and legal reimbursements, tuition assistance, and other fringe benefits, as well as travel and entertainment expense reimbursements.

Finally, there are many pension and profit-sharing plans, the payment of which is deductible by the business. Payments from the plans are not taxable to the recipients until they are received.

Taxes on Amounts Received from Sale of the Business

There is an almost infinite variety of terms that can be negotiated when a business is sold. Usually, when entrepreneurs sell their companies, the contracts contain the following important provisions: (1) the purchase price—whether it is paid in cash, with a promissory note, in stock in the acquiring company, or with some combination; (2) the contingent earnout, which is a bonus based on the post-sale performance of the company being sold; (3) a noncompeting clause from the seller; and (4) warranties and representations by the seller about the debt and liabilities of the company being sold.

Before the Tax Reform Act of 1986, it was almost a toss-up whether the owner of a business being sold was willing to receive cash, a promissory note, or stock in the acquiring company. Under the new law, however, most asset sales are subject to double taxation, both corporate and personal, as shown earlier, and so many transactions now involve the exchange of stock. Therefore, the form in which the proceeds are to be received can be as critical as the price and should be included in negotiations between buyer and seller.

The interests of the buyer and seller tend to be diametrically opposed. In general, sellers want cash, often to fund their next venture. Or they may want stock for tax reasons, as mentioned. On the other hand, the purchaser often prefers to give stock or a promissory note. The final terms may therefore be a compromise, with part of the payment in cash and part in stock of the new company.

Jan and Al Williams started a business in their garage in southern California in the early 1960s. The company product, a polyurethane form pad used to prevent bedsores in individuals, was quite popular. So by 1985, Sunrise Medical, Inc., a Torrance, California, company, was willing to pay $7.2 million for the Williamses' Bio Clinic Company.

The Williamses, who were in the process of divorcing at the time of the sale, wanted different things when they negotiated the terms of sale. Jan wanted stock, as she expected the stock of Sunrise to appreciate. Al, on the other hand, wanted as much cash as possible. The parties worked out a compromise—$2 million in stock, and $5.2 million in cash.[12]

In summary, the tax consequences from the sale of a business are: (1) you pay an immediate capital gains tax on cash payments from the sale (at rates that, in 1990, were the same as the individual tax rate), or (2) if you receive part of the payment in stock, you may be able to defer some taxes to a later period.

ESTATE PLANNING TO MINIMIZE TAXES

No one wants to pay more taxes than necessary. This is especially true when you're trying to pass the benefits of the estate you've built up over the years to your family: you want to reduce taxes to the minimum so that they will get the maximum.

Notice that Jack Bares (in the Opening Focus) did that for his children. He planned his estate for 29 years so they would gain control of the business but pay only a minimum in taxes.

To give you an idea of the problem, until 1993, the tax on gifts and bequests between $2.5 million and $3 million is $1.026 million, plus 53 percent of the amount over $2.5 million. For gifts and estates from $3 million to $10 million, the rate is even higher: $1.291 million, plus 55 percent of amounts over $3 million. So you can see that it becomes almost impossible to convey the estate to your children and leave them a viable business.

Estate Planning Issues

For entrepreneurs, there are several issues involved in estate planning. The most important of these are (1) trying to minimize taxes, (2) retaining control of the business, and (3) maintaining flexibility of operations.

Estate Planning Techniques

While it is impossible—and probably undesirable—to avoid all inheritance taxes, there are some ways of at least reducing the amount of tax paid. They include: (1) family gifts, (2) family partnerships, (3) stock sales to family members, and (4) living trusts.

Make Gifts to Family

One way to reduce taxes on your estate is to start giving parts of it to your family as soon as feasible. The rules are:

1. The gifts must be of "present interest," such as a direct cash gift, rather than a "future interest," such as gifts of cash that go into a trust fund for later distribution.
2. The first $10,000 in gifts made by each spouse to each person during a year is tax free. Thus, the effective annual exclusion can be as high

as $20,000 per year for each person receiving gifts if both spouses are involved.

3. Gifts of up to $300,000 by a single person, or $600,000 from a couple, are essentially tax free. If the entire credit of $10,000 per person per year is used, a married couple will have exhausted its lifetime gifts in 30 years.

These gifts, which are based on the fair market value of the property at the time of the gift, can be cash, bonds, real estate, the family business, interest in a partnership, and so forth. The gifts do not have to be treated as income by the recipient.[13]

Establish Family Partnerships

You can form a family partnership to take money out of your company at lower tax rates. It must be a passive partnership that owns some type of property but does not operate the business. Because this type of tax shelter is very complex, *don't try to do it by yourself;* get professional help.[14]

Sell Stock to Children

A third way to minimize taxes is to sell all or a part of your business to your children. There is a high price tag on this method, however. First, your children will need a source of income to make nondeductible payments to you for the stock. And second, you must pay capital gains tax on the stock you sell.

This method may be combined with gifts to the family. If the value of your business is greater than the amount that you can give as gifts during your lifetime, you may want to give up to the maximum and sell stock for the rest of the business.

Establish a Living Trust

A **living trust** is a legal document that resembles a will, but, in addition to providing for distribution of personal assets upon the maker's death, it also contains instructions for managing those assets should the person become disabled. A living trust does not go through probate, thus relieving the family of the emotional and financial cost of the court procedure, and assets can be distributed according to the owner's instructions in a short period of time.

Benefits of a living trust. Living trusts are more difficult to contest than wills. Also, the firm's assets are not frozen, but are immediately and privately distributed to the beneficiaries. Finally, a living trust can save on estate taxes. As you can see from Table 23–4, if you have a will for an estate valued at more than $600,000, federal estate taxes must be paid at your death, at a rate beginning at 37 percent. A living trust, on the other hand, lets you and your spouse pass on up to $1.2 million to your beneficiaries tax free. When one of you dies, the trust is divided into two separate trusts, each with a $600,000 estate tax exemption.

Table 23–4 A Living Trust Can Save a Family Thousands of Dollars in Estate Taxes and Probate Fees

Estate size	With a simple will			With an A-B living trust		
	Estate taxes	Probate fees*	Total	Estate taxes	Probate fees	Total
$ 100,000	$ 0	$ 6,300	$ 6,300	$0	$0	$0
300,000	0	14,300	14,300	0	0	0
600,000	0	26,300	26,300	0	0	0
750,000	55,500	32,300	87,800	0	0	0
1,200,000	235,000	46,300	281,300	0	0	0

* Minimum combined for attorney and executor in California.

Source: Schumacher and Company, Los Angeles, California, as reported in Louis Austin, Vickie Schumaker, and Jim Schumacher, "Living Trusts Replace Wills as Estate Planning Tools," *Small Business Reports,* March 1989, p. 93.

Disadvantages of a living trust.   As with other aspects of estate planning, there is also a "down" side. First, when you establish such a trust, you must also change the title on all real estate, securities, and other assets to the name of your trust. From a legal point of view, you no longer own these properties, so there is nothing to probate when it becomes time to distribute your assets. Most people with wills serve as their own trustees, eliminating management fees. Or you and your spouse may find it advantageous to become joint trustees in order to bypass the probate process.

Another problem is that people often either forget to put all their property into the trust or procrastinate. And anything left out must be probated. Finally, another weakness of this technique is that if you decide to refinance your home or another asset, some lenders may refuse to refinance it if it is in a trust.

RECORDKEEPING AND TAX REPORTING

The importance of recordkeeping has been emphasized throughout this text, especially in Chapter 20. There are essentially two reasons for keeping business records. First, tax and other records are required by law, and second, they help you manage your business better. While the IRS allows some flexibility in records systems, it does require that records be kept, be complete, and be separate for each individual business.

Maintaining Tax Records

As shown in Chapter 5, when you start your business, you should establish the type and arrangement of records most suitable for your particular operations. And as you go along, you should keep in mind that the records should be readily available to compute, record, and pay taxes as they become due and payable.

Figure 23–7   List of Selected Tax-Reporting Periods

Tax	Reporting period
Estimated income tax deposits	Quarterly
Income tax withholding deposits	Quarterly
FICA tax deposits	Quarterly
FUTA tax deposits	Quarterly
Income tax	Annually
Income tax withholding	Annually
Self-employment tax	Annually
FICA (Social Security) tax	Annually
FUTA (unemployment) tax	Annually

Note: Even though tax deposits are made quarterly, a return (which reports income and the bases for calculating the tax due) is filed only annually.

The IRS requires you to maintain your tax records for up to three years after you file your tax return. If there is any reason to suspect fraud on your part, the IRS may look at tax returns at any time. Fraud may be suspected when deductions seem excessive or appear to have been claimed with the intent to defraud the government out of tax revenues, or when income seems unnaturally low. The IRS has up to three years from the date of filing to look at your records. By the same token, you have up to three years from the date of filing to straighten out tax matters as the circumstances demand. If changes are needed, you may file a one-page amended return, on Form 1040X.[15]

Reporting Your Taxes

Every federal, state, and local government entity having jurisdiction over your business requires that you submit a report in writing, on a monthly, quarterly, or annual basis. Since the requirements vary so much for state and local agencies, we will list only the federal reporting requirements, which are shown in Figure 23–7.

WHAT YOU SHOULD HAVE LEARNED

1. The U.S. tax system is very complex. Federal, state, and local governments impose taxes directly on companies and individuals, and also require businesses to collect taxes from others. Taxes may be direct, and paid to the taxing authority by the person or business owing them, or indirect, being collected by the business from someone else and paid to the taxing authorities. Since taxes affect small firms in so many ways, their owners should get professional help with tax problems.

     This chapter looked at four types of taxes: (*a*) those imposed on the firm itself, (*b*) employment-related taxes, (*c*) personal taxes paid by the owners, and (d) estate taxes. Taxes imposed on the business itself include (a) taxes paid for the "right" to operate the business, (b) excise and property taxes, (c) state and local taxes on business receipts, and (d) federal and state income taxes.

2. Taxes paid to operate the business include fees paid for (or the paperwork and expense necessary to obtain) a business license, state incorporation or partnership registration, zoning variances, building permits, mailing permits, occupational or professional registration, and other such licenses.

   Excise and intangible property taxes are paid on such items as tires; cigars, cigarettes, and alcoholic beverages; and intangibles such as copyrights, patents, and trademarks.

   State and local sales and use taxes are imposed on the purchase, use, consumption, or storage of goods. Exceptions are often made for service businesses, drugs, and industrial goods.

   Income taxes are imposed at the federal and local levels. The Tax Reform Act of 1986, as well as state and local tax revisions during the last decade, drastically changed the rules. To comply with income tax laws, a small business must choose the method of handling income and expenses—cash or accrual method; the time for paying taxes—on a calendar or fiscal year; and what form the business should take to minimize taxes.

   We treat only the federal corporate income tax, from three points of view: (a) what tax rates apply to your business, (b) what is income, and (c) what are deductible expenses.

   The three federal tax rates are 15 percent of the first $50,000, 25 percent on the next $25,000, and 34 percent on all income above that. Taxable income is total revenues minus deductible expenses, normally including cost of goods sold, selling expenses, and administrative expenses. We discussed them as (a) administrative expenses, (b) depreciation, (c) inventory, (d) interest, (e) business lunches, entertainment, and travel, and (f) automobile, home, and computer use.

3. Small employers are required to provide Social Security, unemployment compensation insurance, and industrial insurance (commonly called workers' compensation) for all employees, and to withhold taxes from them. The amount of taxes withheld depends on the employee's wages, number of exemptions, marital status, and length of the pay period. Each employee must complete a W–4 form. The withheld amounts must be submitted to the IRS, along with Form 941, on a quarterly basis. A Form W–2 must be mailed to each employee by January 31 of the following year.

   A percentage of each employee's earnings must be withheld and matched as Social Security taxes. These taxes are sent, along with Form 941, to the IRS each quarter.

   Unemployment compensation insurance payments build up a fund from which a state can pay employees if they are laid off.

4. The owners themselves must also pay taxes on funds withdrawn from the business. Funds can be withdrawn through *(a)* receiving salaries or bonuses, which are deductible by the business but taxable for the individual, *(b)* withdrawing sums from a proprietorship or partnership, on which taxes must be paid, *(c)* receiving dividends from a corporation, which are not deductible by the business and are taxable for the individuals, *(d)* receiving tax-free benefits from the business, which are also deductible by the firm, and *(e)* receiving pension and profit-sharing benefits, which are deductible for the business but taxable to recipients when received.

    When you sell the business, a contract should be written. You must pay taxes on the capital gain received. In general, sellers prefer cash, while buyers prefer to offer stock. A combination can be worked out.

5. Estate planning can be used to minimize taxes. In doing so, you must consider *(a)* the amount of taxes, *(b)* retaining control of the business, and *(c)* maintaining flexibility of operations. The currently available techniques for lowering taxes through estate planning are *(a)* giving gifts from the business to the family, *(b)* forming family partnerships, *(c)* selling stock to family members, and *(d)* setting up a living trust. All these have advantages and disadvantages, so have professional help in using them.

6. From the time you begin your business, you should maintain complete and accurate tax records. For tax purposes, records must be retained up to three years after the date of filing the return. If for any reason the IRS suspects fraud, there is no time limitation.

KEY TERMS

taxes, *724*

stagflation, *724*

Tax Reform Act of 1978, *724*

indirect taxes, *724*

direct taxes, *724*

employer identification number, *728*

zoning variance, *729*

excise tax, *729*

use taxes, *729*

sales taxes, *730*

Tax Reform Act of 1986, *730*

accrual method, *731*

taxable income, *733*

generally accepted accounting principles (GAAP), *733*

cash value depreciation, *734*

tax-related depreciation, *734*

straight-line method, *734*

accelerated cost recovery system, *734*

first-in, first-out (FIFO) method, *735*

last-in, first-out (LIFO) method, *735*

average-cost method, *735*

Deficit Reduction Act of 1984, *736*

Social Security, *736*

unemployment compensation insurance, 736

industrial insurance (workers' compensation), 736

Employee Retirement Income Security Act (ERISA), 736

Form W–2, Wage and Tax Statement, 737

Social Security Act of 1935, 737

Federal Insurance Contributions Act (FICA), 737

unemployment compensation insurance, 738

federal unemployment tax, 738

living trust, 743

QUESTIONS FOR DISCUSSION

1. What is included in the U.S. tax system?
2. How do taxes affect a small business?
3. Name the three types of taxes a small firm must pay.
4. Name and explain at least five taxes a firm must pay for the "right" to do business.
5. (a) What are sales and use taxes? (b) Is the sales tax a direct or an indirect tax? (c) Explain.
6. What are the three major decisions a business must make about income tax?
7. How does the form of a business affect its taxes?
8. For federal income tax purposes, (a) what is income, and (b) what are the usual deductible expenses?
9. Name and explain the three types of employment-related taxes.
10. (a) How can funds be withdrawn from a small business, and (b) how are they treated for tax purposes?
11. (a) What are the three main issues in estate planning? (b) What are the ways a small business owner can reduce estate taxes?
12. Why are records so important for tax purposes?

SUGGESTED READINGS

"A Look to the Future: Home Is Where the Office Is." *Working Age* (an AARP newsletter), November/December 1989, p. 3.

Boroughs, Don L. "Giving Workers the Boss's Benefits." *U.S. News & World Report,* April 10, 1989, p. BC–1.

Brackey, Harriet. "You Can File Electronically for Speedy Return." *USA Today,* January 12, 1990, p. 1B.

"Don't Expect Any Capital-Gains Tax Cut to Nourish Startups." *Business Week,* April 24, 1989, p. 20.

Foster, Mike. "A Battle of Words with the IRS: Advice on Tax Deductions for Entrepreneurs." *Nation's Business,* March 1989, pp. 42–43.

Saddler, Jeanne. "Small Business Celebrates Flow to Tax Code Section 89." *The Wall Street Journal,* September 18, 1989, p. B2.

Strassels, Paul N. "It's Your Money." *Nation's Business,* October 1989, p. 88.

"Which Courts Handle What Tax Cases." *Small Business Records,* May 1989, pp. 61–62.

Wiener, Leonard. "Separating Your Business from Your Personal Life." *U.S. News & World Report,* October 2, 1989, p. 67.

Yang, Cathy. "Want a Tax Shelter—and a Good Conscience?" *Business Week,* October 5, 1989, p. 130.

ENDNOTES

1. James M. Poterba, "Venture Capital and Capital Gains Taxation," Working Paper No. 2832 (Cambridge, Mass.: National Bureau of Economic Research, January 1989).

2. U.S. Department of the Treasury, Internal Revenue Service, *Tax Guide for Small Business,* Publication 334 (Washington, D.C.: U.S. Government Printing Office, November 1988).

3. An excellent discussion of these changes can be found in *Explanation of the Tax Reform Act of 1986 for Business,* IRS Publication 921 (August 1987).

4. Kurt R. Majette and Thomas P. Rohman, "Choice of Business Entity after the Tax Reform of 1986: The Brave New World," *Review of Taxation for Individuals,* Winter 1988, pp. 38–65.

5. "Tax Briefs," *Small Business Reports,* December 1988, p. 61.

6. See U.S. Department of the Treasury, Internal Revenue Service, *Tax Information on S Corporations,* Publication 589 (Washington, D.C.: U.S. Government Printing Office, November 1987), for more details.

7. Gordon Alexander and William F. Sharpe, *Fundamentals of Investments* (Englewood Cliffs, N.J.: Prentice-Hall, 1987), pp. 72–73.

8. Since these methods are too technical to be explained in this text, for more information, see Alexander and Sharpe, *Fundamentals of Investments,* pp. 73–74.

9. "Inflation Jitters Prompt Companies to Shift Accounting Methods," *The Wall Street Journal,* April 27, 1989, p. A1.

10. See U.S. Department of the Treasury, Internal Revenue Service, *1989 Forms and Instructions, 1040* (Washington, D.C.: U.S. Government Printing Office, 1989), Instructions for Schedule C, Profit or Loss, for instructions and limitations.

11. For more information see U.S. Department of the Treasury, Internal Revenue Service, *1989 Federal Employment Tax Forms,* Publication 393 (Washington, D.C.: U.S. Government Printing Office, 1989).

12. Sandra Salmans, "Cutting the Deal," *Venture,* January 19, 1988, pp. 32, 34.

13. See Irving L. Blackman, "Family Gifts," *Inc.,* January 1989, p. 125, for details.

14. See Irving L. Blackman, "Family Partnerships as Tax Shelter," *Inc.,* April 1988, p. 131, for further details and illustrations.

15. The IRS has a free listing of publications and other information for tax-related services. To obtain your copy of this listing, call 1–800–424–3676 and ask for publication 910, *Guide to Free Tax Service.*

24

PLANNING FOR THE FUTURE

Time present and time past
Are perhaps both contained in time future,
And time future contained in time past.
—T. S. Eliot

And 'tis a shameful sight,
When children of one family
Fall out, and chide, and fight.
—Isaac Watts

LEARNING OBJECTIVES

After studying the material in this chapter, you will be able to:

1. Discuss some of the problems involved in the organization and operation of small family-owned businesses.
2. Explain how family relationships can affect the company operations.
3. Discuss the importance and method of preparing for management succession.
4. Describe the activities needed to prepare the next generation to enter the firm.
5. Discuss the need for estate planning in small companies.

TO CONTINUE OR NOT TO CONTINUE?

George Landry, Jr., and Bill Gillespie are very similar in many ways. They are both respected community leaders and owners of successful small second-generation family enterprises. But they differ in one significant way. Landry, the owner-manager of a Brewer, Maine, appliance store, will probably see his business kept in the family by his son and daughter. Gillespie and his brothers, on the other hand, plan to sell their St. Joseph, Michigan, pharmacy.

George Landry, Sr., died two years after founding Landry's in 1945. Ruth, his widow, managed the business until 1979, when she sold it to her son, George, Jr. Today, the staff consists of George Landry, his wife, two children, a sister, a nephew, and four nonfamily employees. Landry, 60 years old, does not plan to retire soon. But when he does, the dealership will go to his daughter Stephanie and son David.

Conversely, nobody in the Gillespie family wants the 81-year-old pharmacy. Believed to be one of the two oldest pharmacies in Michigan, Gillespie's was founded by Frank Gillespie in 1905. Of Gillespie's six children, four became pharmacists. Shortly before he died in 1955, Gillespie divided his estate into six equal shares. A separate agreement was drawn up to cover the transition of the business from the founder to his children.

Bill, Bob, and Collins Gillespie became owners of the pharmacy. For a while, Ruth Grootendorst, a sister, worked there as a clerk. Another brother,

George Landry, Jr.
Source: Photo courtesy of George Landry.

Dick, opened his own drugstore, and Tom, the other brother, was St. Joseph's police chief for many years.

Now, Collins is 76, Bob is 68, and Bill is 61, and all plan to retire soon. Among them, they have seven sons, but none are pharmacists, nor do the sons want to manage the business. So the brothers plan to sell Gillespie's to someone outside the family.

Source: Kiwanis Magazine, April 1986, p. 21.

The Gillespies' predicament is far from unique. Many small business owners put off selecting a successor until it is too late. Many family-business executives, facing possible retirement, feel that finding a successor can be done quickly. But the odds are against them. Only 30 percent of U.S. family businesses pass successfully from the first to the second generation, and only 15 percent make it to the third generation, according to Nancy Drozdow, project manager for the Family Business Program at Wharton School of Business.[1]

Over 80 percent of all U.S. businesses—large, medium, and small—are family owned. Yet, as indicated, only about one out of seven of them makes it to the third generation, often because of unwillingness or inability to deal with the challenges that are unique to family-run enterprises.[2] But most small business owners do not like to talk about the question of succession. Perhaps this reflects a denial of their own mortality, the same instinct that makes people reluctant to make a will. However, to be realistic in assuring the continuation of the business, or in providing a going concern for family members to operate, this question must be looked at analytically. We do that in this chapter.

ROLE OF FAMILY-OWNED BUSINESSES

Family-owned businesses provide a living and personal satisfaction for many people. But they must be managed just like any other small firm if they are to succeed. Previous chapters have presented the basics of running small businesses, whether family owned or not. While family businesses are the backbone of America, they can also be a source of unresolved family tensions and conflicts, which can create obstacles to achieving even the most basic business goals.[3] When close relatives work together, emotions often interfere with business decisions. Also, unique problems, such as the departure of the founder-owner, develop in family-owned firms.

As shown in Chapter 9, a small business can be organized as a sole proprietorship, a partnership, or a corporation. In the corporation, ownership tends to be separated from management, while in the other two, ownership and management are often the same. When more than one family member is involved, particularly in a partnership, emotions and differing value systems can cause conflicts between members.

This happened in the Manhattan Distributing Company when its owner, Joseph Rothberg, brought his son-in-law, Nolan Crane, into the family business as his successor. With little discussion, the two men agreed to work together—and spent the next six years feuding.

Rothberg was a self-made man who had spent 32 years pushing, prodding, and nurturing his business to make it grow and prosper. Crane, on the other hand, had spent 10 years working for large corporations. He entered the family business seeking security, economic stability, and a chance to get ahead faster. While willing to work to get ahead, he was not willing to devote his entire life to the business.

Source: Cartoon copyright 1989 by Doug Blackwell. Reprinted with permission.

Only after Crane resigned did his wife resolve the problems between her husband and father. Crane later returned to run the company.[4]

The Family and the Business

We usually think of family businesses as being started, owned, and operated by the parents, with children helping out and later taking over. This has been the normal pattern, as many examples in the text have shown.

For example, Albert Shaffer and his father and mother started Shaffer's Drive Inns (Case I–5). The parents put up the money, while Albert contributed many of the ideas and "a lot of energy." After a few years, he bought out his parents' interest.

There are two contrary trends now occurring. First, many young people are going into business for themselves—and tapping their parents for funds to finance their ventures. In return, the children often give one or both parents an executive position in the company, including a seat on the company's board. Also, many retirees want to work part time for the children's businesses, without assuming a lot of responsibility.

For example, the two brothers who run the Levy Organization in Chicago employ their mother as a hostess at one of their restaurants. They even named a deli after her and use her recipes. According to Mark Levy, the company's vice chairman, "My mom is a very integral part of our business."[5]

Another trend is the large number of spouses doing business together. We used to think of married couples running a small neighborhood store, toiling long hours for a modest living. Now, though, a new breed of husband-and-wife entrepreneurs has emerged, typically running a service enterprise out of their home and using computers, modems, and phone lines as the tools of their trade. As shown in Figure 2–4, while there was a 42 percent increase in all proprietorships from 1980 to 1986, the SBA found that joint proprietorships of husbands and wives jumped 63 percent.

Although ownership of a small firm is usually controlled by one or a few family members, many others in the larger family are often interested participants. The spouse and children are vitally interested because the business is the source of their livelihood. Some relatives may be employed by the firm; some may have investments in it; and some may perform various services for the company. Older relatives may have a parental concern for the owner. Investors are concerned about profits and dividends. Those employed want income, promotions, and a voice in company decisions. Each interested family member has a particular viewpoint toward the firm which, when brought to family council, can be very beneficial, or traumatic.

The founder-owner may set any one or more of a variety of goals, such as: large profits now and sale later; adequate income and perpetuation of the business; high sales; service to the community; support of family; and production of an unusual product, just to name a few. This variety of goals exists in all companies, but, in family firms, strong family ties can improve the chances of consensus and support, while dissensions can lead to disagreement and/or disruption of activities.

Family Hierarchy

Usually the founder—or a close descendant—is the head of a small business. Relatives may be placed in high positions in the company, while other positions are filled by nonfamily members. In some cases, it is expected that the next head of the firm will be a family member and other members will move up through the ranks according to their position in the **family hierarchy.** Family ties can cause friction when ownership and management are not dealt with separately. When family members are treated preferentially, nonfamily employees may become disgruntled or quit.[6]

On the other hand, when everybody finds family advancement desirable, the company receives the benefits of greater satisfaction, less complaining, and enhanced family interest and pride. Motivation can be high, turnover low, and antagonisms minimal. Members feel that they are taking care of other members of the family. All these factors tend to motivate family workers to perform at a high level, and nonfamily employees tend to understand their position.

Family Interactions

Family members often assume a positive attitude of "It's our business." This can be a strong, positive motivator in building the business and leading to greater cooperation.

For example, Dot and Jiggs Martin and their married daughters, Michele Statkewicz and Renee Sossaman, started a small business, Bloomin' Lollipops Inc., making chocolate flowers, hard candy lollipops, and candy animals to go in gift baskets, mugs, vases, boxes, carousels, and so forth. They began their research six months before opening their store. They worked closely together on all aspects of organizing, promoting, opening, and operating the business. The family members searched for and tried many recipes for candy, then developed their own by combining the ones they liked best. Although each person has a job specialty—making candy, arranging the lollipops creatively in containers, or delivering the candy bouquets— each one has learned every phase of the enterprise. Not only are they doing an outstanding job of running the business, but they are also enjoying social interaction with each other and with other family relations.[7]

(The photographs on the next page show the Martin family at work.)

Of course, the opposite can be true. As shown by the Manhattan Distributing Company example, where the attitude was negative, it can be a detriment. Conflicts can occur because each relative looks at the business from a different perspective. Relatives who are silent partners, stockholders, or directors may see only dollar signs when judging capital expenditures, growth, and other important matters. Relatives involved in daily operations judge those matters from the viewpoint of marketing, production or operations, and personnel necessary to make the firm successful.

How to Deal with Incompetent Family Members

A related problem can be the inability of family members to make objective decisions about one another's skills and abilities. Unfortunately, their quarrels and ill feelings may spread to include nonfamily employees. One possible solution is to convince family members, as well as nonfamily employees, that their interests are best served by a profitable firm with strong leadership.

The Chapman House grew into a profitable chain of restaurants, motels, and textile industries. In time, the second generation took over more and more from the matriarch, and the third generation began its entry into the business. However, too many chiefs resulted in a proliferation of activities, an increase in internal conflicts, and a decrease in profitability.

The death of the matriarch was followed by 90 days of internal strife. Then, a third-generation family member with an M.B.A. from State University and outside employment experience in a major industrial corporation formulated some centralized objectives and an organizational structure appropriate to reaching the objectives.

The Martin family of Bloomin' Lollipops Inc.

Source: Mobile Press Register photographs, February 8, 1990, p. 4–B. © 1990. All rights reserved.

Most family members recognized that they should keep the business intact and expand only in those areas offering the best return on investment.

Some members want to become chief executive officer of the business but do not have the talents or training needed. Some others may have the talents, but because of youth, inexperience, or some similar reason, their talents may not be recognized. Small businesses usually do not have the professional staff to evaluate family members for the top position.

Family members with little ability to contribute to the firm can be placed in jobs where they do not disturb other employees. Sometimes, though, relatives can demoralize the business by their dealings with other employees or customers or by loafing on the job, avoiding unpleasant tasks, or taking special privileges. They may be responsible for the high turnover rate of top-notch nonfamily managers and employees. Such relatives should be assigned to jobs allowing minimal contact with other employees. In some cases, attitudes may be changed by formal or informal education.

How to Compensate Family Members

Compensating family members and dividing profits among them can also be difficult because some family members may feel they contribute more to the success of the firm than others. Wages paid should be based on job performance, not family position. Fringe benefits can be useful as financial rewards, but they must conform to those given to nonfamily employees. Stock can be established as part of the compensation plan. Deferred profit-sharing plans, pension plans, insurance programs, and stock purchase programs can all be effective in placating disgruntled family members.

Family Limitations

Founders of companies are usually not general managers but rather specialists in one of the functional areas, such as marketing, production, or finance. While the broader skills can be developed over a period of time through education, training, and/or experience, the skill of evaluating, and sometimes saying no to, family members wanting to enter the business may still be missing.

Another problem is that family managers of the firm may feel it is necessary to clear routine matters with top family members. Also, bottlenecks that work against efficient operations can be caused by personality clashes and emotional reactions. Lines of authority in the company must be clear and separated from those of the family. Age more often sets the lines of authority in a family than in a business, where ability tends to be the primary guide.

The number of family members from whom to choose the managers of the company is limited. Some members do not want to join—or are not capable of joining—the company in any position; some are only capable of filling lower-level jobs; and some are not willing to take the time or expend the effort to prepare themselves for a management position. Of those remaining, some cannot cope with family scheming and conniving, and family blocs may be formed to put someone else in the position. But it is amazing that so many family businesses have such good leadership—family and nonfamily. As the leadership grows older, it must keep up with the times and guard against letting past successes lead to idolizing and conforming to the things of the past by trying to maintain the status quo.

For example, the five stockholders of Donald & Asby, engineers, established a policy of encouraging growth. One of the younger stockholders suggested using media advertising to obtain new business. Mr. Donald, who had helped found the firm 30 years earlier, indicated that this would produce an undesirable type of growth. He suggested that they continue to depend on the company's reputation to expand requests for job proposals. How do you think the stockholders decided? Why?

Some families form their businesses into corporations and hire professional managers to run them when no members are in positions to manage or no agreement can be reached on who should run the company. This solution has the advantages of using professional management, freeing family time for other purposes, reducing friction, and having employees treated more fairly. However, the disadvantages are loss of a personal touch, reduced family employment, lower income, concentration of power in small cliques, and difficulties in finding and keeping a good management team.

Family Resources

The amount of capital available within the family may limit expansion. While family resources and contacts may be adequate for a small business, as the company grows, the borrowing power is limited by the amount of family assets. Then, family members may disagree about the amount to borrow and the risks to take, or other issues such as: Should money be obtained by borrowing, issuing stock, selling assets, or other financial techniques? Should planning be for the short or long run? Because of the diversity of opinion, even the choice of a consultant can be controversial.

Preparing the Next Generation

It might be assumed that children (or grandchildren) automatically want to enter the family business. But, as you saw in the Opening Focus, this isn't always true.

What does lead children to follow in Mom or Dad's footsteps? A survey by Nancy Bowman-Upton, of Baylor University, found that the two primary reasons were money and liking the business. Figure 24–1 shows how important these and other reasons for joining the firm were.

Start at Part-Time or Full-Time Job(s)?

The children of business owner(s) can be given opportunities to work on simple jobs, or on a part-time or summer basis. This provides insights

Figure 24–1   Reasons Why Children Join Family Businesses*

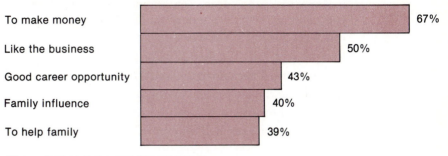

To make money — 67%
Like the business — 50%
Good career opportunity — 43%
Family influence — 40%
To help family — 39%

* Respondents could give more than one answer.

that may influence them into or away from the business. The experience often leads them into finishing their education. They may also try to get work experience in another company in order to broaden their training and background. Such experience helps justify moving a family member into the family business.

A study by the Los Angeles accounting firm of Laventhal & Horwath, for example, found that the vast majority of owners of family firms thought children should have outside experience, either as their own boss or working for someone else, before joining the family business. See Figure 24–2 for details.

Figure 24–2   When Should Children Join Family Businesses?

When asked when their children should join the company, surveyed owners of family businesses said:

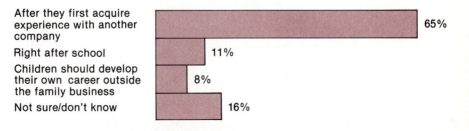

After they first acquire experience with another company — 65%
Right after school — 11%
Children should develop their own career outside the family business — 8%
Not sure/don't know — 16%

Start at Entry-Level or Higher-Level Position?

Should a family member start in an entry-level job in the family business in order to learn it from the ground up? There is disagreement on this point, but none about the need for knowing the business. Some techniques that have worked for others include:

- Never allowing a child to work in senior management until he or she has worked for someone else for at least two years.
- Rotating the person in varying positions.
- Giving promotions only as they are earned.
- Devoting at least half an hour each day to face-to-face teaching and training.
- Not bringing business matters home.[8]

If the newcomer is really to learn the business, true responsibility must be given. Otherwise, the person cannot learn to manage the business.

For example, a son who successfully took over his father's business said, "My father had difficulty trusting me. It's not what you might think. He just did not want to see me fail. When he saw that something I was doing might not pan out, he injected himself into the situation. I never had a chance to fail."

The son was never given full responsibility for anything more than a typical sale. Thus, when he took over the agency, he knew the table of organization, but making it work was something else.[9]

PREPARING FOR MANAGEMENT SUCCESSION

All businesses must be prepared for changes in the top management of the company. It is not enough to select a person to step into the top job when it becomes vacant. Instead, that key job requires much training and experience, as the decisions the person makes can vitally affect the company and its future. Owners do not want to bring in outsiders as nonfamily companies do. Instead they prefer to prepare and bring in children or other family members to run the business.

For example, John Horne and his wife share the management of operations of Horne Box, Inc. (Case VI–4). She's sufficiently trained and experienced to step in and run the business if anything happens to him.

Why Succession Is a Problem

When preparing someone for management succession, many small business owners have some grave concerns about passing the business on to their children. In the survey by Nancy Bowman-Upton previously mentioned,

Figure 24–3   Who Will Take Charge?

Family-business owners with two or more children working for the company were surveyed. Here's a breakdown of how they said they intend to resolve the issue of who will take over when the owners step aside:

35% plan to groom one child from an early age to take over.

25% plan to let the children compete and to choose one or more successors with help from the board of directors.

15% plan to let the children compete and choose one or more successors without input from a third party.

15% plan to form an "executive committee" of two or more children.

10% plan to let the children choose their own leader, or leaders.

Source: John Ward, professor at Loyola University of Chicago's Graduate School of Business, as reported in Buck Brown, "Succession Strategies for Family Firms," *The Wall Street Journal,* August 4, 1988, p. 23. Reprinted by permission of *The Wall Street Journal,* © Dow Jones & Company, Inc., 1988. ALL RIGHTS RESERVED.

it was found that the main concern was treating all children fairly. Of the entrepreneurs surveyed, 31 percent gave this as their main concern. Another 22 percent were concerned about the reaction of nonfamily employees. And 20 percent gave family communication conflict and estate taxes as concerns.[10]

Another trend today is having two or more children succeed the parent in running the business. For example, a study by John Ward, a professor at Loyola University's Graduate School of Business, found that 55 percent of family-owned firms say they want to include two or more children in future ownership or management of the family business.[11] Figure 24–3 shows how the owners expect to have their children prepare to take over the company.

When Somer Obernauer retires in another year, his daughter, Lorie, and her brother, Somer, Jr., will split ownership and management of the firm. She'll be executive vice president, in charge of sales, while he will be president, in charge of accounting. They are already essentially running the Keystone Ribbon & Floral Supply Company, according to Lorie: "I'm in charge out front, and he's in charge in back. We each have our own territory."[12]

If family members are going to be used to run the business, rather than bring in outsiders, training should begin early and be ongoing. Early on, one or more replacements should be started on the path toward taking over the reins of the firm. This process sometimes works, but sometimes it does not.

For example, Ralph Simmons' son-in-law, who had just graduated from college with a technical degree, helped set up Simmons Mountainside Satellite Sales (Case

II–3) and install its operating system. So Mr. Simmons is willing to turn the business over to him.

In contrast, Art Carroll is very concerned that his son-in-law, Fred Clayton, a former naval officer with a degree in geology, is not developing to take over Carroll Sales Company (Case VII–5). After 16 years of training and experience in the company, Clayton is "unhappy . . . and completely unmotivated to succeed."

When the choice of replacements is limited, the owner may consider reorganizing the present assignments and using present managers more effectively. The job specifications for a new manager may be written more broadly to widen the range of choices. All present managers—family and nonfamily—should participate in this planning so that they feel they have contributed to the decision. They may then accept the newcomer more readily. In fact, some family firms have set up regular discussion meetings for this purpose.

An Overlooked Problem

In most firms, the development of managerial personnel and the provision for management succession are greatly neglected, often until it is too late to do anything about it. According to one expert, "The lack of planning for the company's future is the most common, and most fatal, flaw in family businesses."[13] Therefore, once your firm is operating successfully, you should answer several questions such as these: Is there someone to operate the firm so that I can take vacations or go to training programs or conventions? Who will fill my shoes so that I can retire when I choose? If my business is a proprietorship, do I want my spouse or child(ren) to manage it when I leave? If my company is a partnership and I leave it, do I want my spouse or child(ren) to be a partner? How will my death or incapacity affect my small firm?

In 1947, 27-year-old Carl Rosen succeeded his father as head of Puritan Skirt and Dress Company. Then, in mid-1982, Carl learned that he had cancer. He immediately initiated careful steps to speed up the grooming of his son, Andrew, then 25 years old, to become the third-generation Rosen to run the firm.[14]

PLAN AHEAD!

To avoid family succession problems, entrepreneurs should start planning for their replacements as much as 10 to 15 years ahead of the actual passing of power, according to John Schoen, the family business executive in residence at Baylor University's Institute for Family Business in Waco, Texas.[15] Such a comprehensive succession plan involves more than just laying out the role of the younger generation in the business. In addition, provision must be made for the parent's retirement income and the ownership of the business. When operating authority passes from one generation to the next, so should stock ownership.

Management succession occurs when the family leader (1) dies, (2) becomes incapacitated, (3) elects to leave the company, or (4) decides to retire.

Sudden Departure

A successful business must continue to operate even when the owner-manager leaves. Plans can easily be made for vacations because they are of short duration, they require a limited number of decisions, and the vacationer is available if needed. In fact, when the owner takes a vacation, a form of on-the-job training is provided for those left in charge. Those persons can take over temporarily under other circumstances.

But the sudden death or incapacity of the owner can be very disruptive if not adequately provided for. If the owner has left no will or instructions on what to do, family members will probably have conflicting opinions about what should be done. For this reason, an owner should make a will, and keep it current, including instructions about what should be done in—or with—the business.

As shown in Chapter 21, the firm can take out life insurance on the owner(s), the proceeds from which will go to the company at death. This money can be used to help the business operate until it recovers from the loss of its owner-manager.

Planned Departure

When owners plan to leave or retire, they have a number of options, as shown in Figure 24–4. If the company is a corporation, the replacement top officer should be known by the time the owner departs, and the transition will probably go smoothly. The board of directors can select a family or nonfamily employee, or an outsider, for the top job. The handling of the stock can be delayed, but stock retention may give the new key executive the feeling that the departed one is still looking over his or her shoulder. The corporation tends to be the most impersonal of the three types of organization and consequently the one with the least controversy in choosing a new head.

In proprietorships and partnerships, the entire family tends to become involved in the replacement decision. Therefore, in planning for departure, the owner should look for someone in the family able and willing to take over. This person(s) may already be recognized as the "heir apparent."

Notice in the Keystone Ribbon & Floral Supply Company, for example, that both the daughter (Lorie) and the son (Somer, Jr.) were designated "heirs apparent."

Figure 24–4   Options for Replacing Family Management

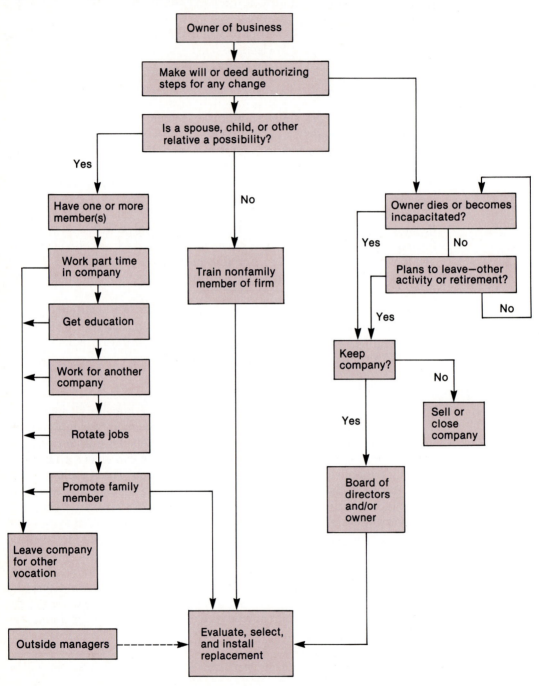

Selling to Family Member(s)

If the transition is to be complete, the business should be sold to the offspring so that full responsibility is handed over to them. The advantages of this type of change for the original owner are:

- The business stays in the family.
- It provides a source of employment for family members.
- The family's stature is maintained.
- The former owner is free to relax or travel.
- There is pleasure when the successor is successful.

Such a transition can strengthen family bonds rather than produce additional family friction.

Selling to Outsiders

If no relative will assume responsibility for the running of the business, the owner can sell out to a partner or an outsider, or can even close the business. Selling to outsiders can also have a salutary effect on family relationships.

For example, this occurred when one family business was sold. The reaction of one child was: "A number of financially enmeshed families were liberated to pursue individual courses. A company had shed its burdensome past and could look forward to a renaissance under new leadership. Ray, Joyce, and I are no longer wrangling siblings polarized in an ugly triad. We are free to be friends."[16]

Selling to someone outside the family may mean loss of family identification and resulting sadness, as it marks the end of years of effort and the loss of something the founder built. Yet the advantages of this choice are:

- Assured income.
- Lack of worry about what subsequently happens.
- Possible opportunity to consult.
- Release of family tension.
- Relief from further responsibility.

For example, one of the authors ran into O'Beal and Ray Belk at a football game. When asked about the recent sale of their grocery store, O'Beal answered, "Now both of us can go together to the high school football games. For 30 years, one of us had to tend the store until 11 P.M."

Helpful Hints on Selling Your Business

When you've decided to sell the business, you've done the easy part. The difficult part is going through with it. It can take a year or longer to negotiate a trouble-free transfer of ownership—so start planning early!

According to Ric Zigmond, head of the small business practice at Laventhal & Horwath, a Los Angeles tax accounting partnership, there are some basic things to consider, such as:

1. Decide on your goal. If you plan to retire immediately, this may reduce the firm's attractiveness, as some buyers want to keep the founder-owner around during the transition.
2. Set a price, with professional help in evaluating assets.
3. Shift some assets to your heirs, to lower or spread out taxes.
4. Build up profits, to make the company more attractive to buyers.
5. Update financial records to truly reflect your firm's worth.
6. Consider what you'll lose by selling—such as pension, health insurance, company car, and club dues—and set the selling price accordingly.
7. Check tax considerations such as the state sales tax on assets, or transfer taxes, as well as state and federal income taxes.[17]

Making the Transition Easier

What preparations should be made by an owner planning to retire, or otherwise to turn the business over to someone else? Too often, a small firm suffers under these circumstances, and sales may decrease or production lag.

For the Owner

To make transitions easier for themselves, owners need to broaden their focus. The narrower the owners' experience and skills, the more difficult it will be to make a smooth transition to other activities after leaving their businesses. Owners should also begin to devote more time to hobbies and outside group activities, which should help develop a sense of worth apart from the business.

Finally, the transition can be made in phases, by gradually turning part of the business over to the successors.

Do you remember Joe and Margaret Teague from the Opening Focus for Chapter 13? They ran a moving company and a carpet cleaning business for over 30 years. In 1989, they turned the operations of the moving company over to their daughter and son-in-law, Dottie and Don Wesley. The Wesleys are buying the business from

Joe and Margaret Teague
Source: Mobile (Alabama) *Press Register,* August 6, 1989, p. 13–E. Photo by J. P. Schaffner. Mobile Press Register photograph, © 1989. All rights reserved.

the Teagues. Dottie, as president, and Don, as vice president, are completely reorganizing the operations, with the Teagues' blessing.

For the New Manager

To minimize the problems for the new owner or manager, be prepared to have him or her pick up where you leave off. The key is to make available to the successor the specialized knowledge you have accumulated over the years. To accomplish this, an inventory of the various kinds of information can be developed, including your goals and objectives, facts about the general management of the company, data concerning the firm's finances, and information about operational and technical aspects. This type of inventory should also help in estimating the value of the firm at any time and in making projections of cash flow and profit or loss.

The Moment of Truth

Ultimately, the moment arrives when the owner must turn over to someone else the business created by his or her own ambition, initiative, and character. Built well, it will survive as a testament to that creativity. But a successful changeover requires advance preparation and transition.

TAXES, ESTATE PLANNING, AND THE FUTURE OF THE BUSINESS

In projecting the future of the business, planning is needed to minimize estate taxes. A business and its assets may appreciate in value much more than the owners are aware. Therefore, estate plans should be reviewed frequently, along with possible estate tax liability and the provisions for paying such taxes.

Tax Planning

In planning the firm's future activities, consider the influence taxes will have on profits and the business's capital structure. Since tax laws and regulations change frequently, stay current in the knowledge of these matters. (Business owners should have an annual planning conference with a CPA well versed in business tax matters.)

Estate Planning

Estate planning prepares for the transfer of the equity of an owner when death occurs. The major concern here is the perpetuation of a small or family business. Tax rates on estates are now such that the assets bequeathed to beneficiaries may be needed to pay taxes, resulting in removal of equity from a business. By planning for the transition, this problem can be minimized.

From the small firm's standpoint, estate planning can (1) reduce the need for beneficiaries to withdraw funds, (2) help maintain beneficiaries' interest in keeping funds in the firm, and (3) provide for a smooth transition. Estate planning for the above objectives can be in the form of:

1. *Gifts to children.*   Currently, gifts up to $20,000 per year per child are nontaxable if given by a couple. As shown in Chapter 23, however, the 1986 Tax Reform Act institutes some tax ramifications for the child. These should be investigated before making the gift.
2. *A trust.*   The owner establishes a trust to receive business income and gifts, and the trust then distributes a specified income to beneficiaries.
3. *Recapitalization of the firm.*   Beneficiaries are given common stock.
4. *Insurance.*   A company can take out life insurance on owners, the proceeds from which, on their death, will go to the company. The insurance premiums can be an expense of doing business.

In addition to the above planning, the designated beneficiaries of pension plans should be individuals or trusts, not estates. Also, appropriate steps should be taken to assure compliance with IRS regulations. Three methods for determining the true value of a business are: (1) determining the value of a comparable business that is publicly traded, (2) ascertaining the business's value by capitalizing its earnings, and (3) estimating the business's value by determining its book value.

Buy/Sell Agreement

Certain actions are possible to assure that the IRS is bound by a predetermined agreement. One way of accomplishing this is to use a predetermined shareholder buy/sell agreement, whereby the corporation agrees to buy back the stock or sell it for the shareholder. Such an agreement becomes binding on the IRS. In addition, a properly prepared buy/sell agreement assures a market for the stock. It also provides protection for the minority stockholder. If such a stockholder is terminated without such an agreement, he or she may be placed at a serious disadvantage.

A young woman held 28 percent of the stock in her employer's corporation; a majority of her personal assets were tied up in the stock. Without warning, she lost her job, and her unsympathetic ex-employer was unwilling to redeem the stock.

A number of references may be used to aid in estate and tax planning, but we recommend using the services of a lawyer, accountant, and/or professional tax planner, as well.

DOING A MANAGEMENT SELF-EVALUATION

When a small business owner asks, "How well am I actually doing?" his or her individual situation can be determined by doing a management self-evaluation. A questionnaire for this purpose is presented in Appendix H at the end of this book. This material has been field-tested and has proved useful in helping current and prospective business owners and managers take an objective look at their managerial status and the status of their business.

This is a self-appraisal. Therefore, as with the other questionnaire, you should answer the questions as completely, objectively, and honestly as you can. When you have finished, you may want to go over it again, objectively evaluating how you are doing. As an alternative, submit the evaluation to someone you trust—a consultant, banker, or friend—and have him or her evaluate how you are doing.

WHAT YOU SHOULD HAVE LEARNED

1. This chapter concentrates on the operations of the 80 percent of small businesses that are family owned. It shows that family members have different viewpoints depending on their relationships in the family and

to the business. Founders expect that some family member(s), especially their child(ren), will follow them into the firm.

2. To the extent feasible, ownership and management should be separated from family affairs in order to be fair to nonfamily employees and to reduce antagonisms and turnover. Accepted upward movement of family and other employees in the business can generate positive motivation, but evaluation of family members' skills is difficult. Disruptive members should be isolated, delegation should be practiced, and compensation should be fair—and based on job performance if possible. Family and nonfamily relations are important, yet difficult to maintain.

3. Family businesses are usually limited in the number and caliber of people from whom to choose managers, and in the money available for expansion. Age may hamper the progress of younger family members, and it may lead to disagreements on money matters. Forming a corporation tends to remove family stress within the company. An ongoing training procedure—including early employment in the business, rotating job positions, and personal contact with the owner—is recommended for developing younger members.

4. Start planning for succession early in the game; early training can help smooth any sudden transition. If the new officer is known early, planning has been good; if not, selection must be made under adverse conditions. If the new officer is a family member, the owner should sell his or her interest to that person to transfer full responsibility.

    Transfer of the firm to other family members has many advantages, including continuity and family support. Selling the company to outsiders can be sad; closing out the company can be even more traumatic.

5. Planning for the future should also include estate planning to minimize the tax burden of the business owner's heirs. Strategies exist to reduce beneficiaries' need to withdraw funds, maintain their interest in leaving funds in the firm, and provide for a smooth transition. These strategies include gifts to children, a trust, recapitalization of the firm, and insurance. In doing such planning, owners should assure that IRS regulations are met. To determine the true value of the estate, you can capitalize its earnings, determine its book value, or determine the value of a comparable business. A predetermined shareholder buy/sell agreement can also be useful. In all such planning, owners are advised to consult professionals such as lawyers, accountants, or professional tax planners.

KEY TERMS

family hierarchy, 754   estate planning, 768

QUESTIONS

1. *(a)* Why is management succession so important an issue for any small firm? *(b)* For a family firm?

2. *(a)* Why is it often difficult to make reasonable decisions in a family business? *(b)* What problems are caused by a family organization structure?

3. What problems face a company when a key officer leaves suddenly?

4. You start a business when you are in your 20s. Should you do anything about your replacement? Explain.

5. Suppose you have a successful business now but decide you want to leave it. *(a)* What might be some reasons for leaving it? *(b)* What alternatives do you have for the business? *(c)* Which might you try? *(d)* Why?

6. *(a)* How important is estate planning? *(b)* How can you do it?

7. Why would you want to do a management audit?

SUGGESTED READINGS

Aisenberg, Linda. "The Daughter Also Rises." *Canadian Business,* February 1988, pp. 52–57.

DeQuine, Jeane. "Going Public Can Be Emotional." *USA Today,* May 8, 1989, p. 10E.

Gumpert, David E., and Therese Engstrom. "Help! My Business Is Going Under: Five Ways to Protect Your Company—Before Disaster Strikes." *Working Woman,* June 1988, pp. 51–53.

Jaffe, Charles A. "How to Sell Your Business." *Nation's Business,* November 1988, pp. 38–41.

Johnson, Harriet C. "Ready to Sell? Helpful Tips from Experts." *USA Today,* May 9, 1988, p. 11E.

"Nobody's Business but Your Own." *Forbes,* April 4, 1988, p. 117ff.

Peavy, T. R., and W. G. Dyer. "Power Orientations of Entrepreneurs and Succession Planning." *Journal of Small Business Management* 27 (January 1989): 47–52.

Thompson, Terri. "When It's Time to Sell Out." *U.S. News & World Report,* June 26, 1989, pp. 62–64.

Woolley, Suzanne. "Rule No. 1 for Selling Your Company: Don't Rush." *Business Week,* April 3, 1989, pp. 114–15.

ENDNOTES

1. Hank Gilman, "The Last Generation," *The Wall Street Journal,* May 20, 1985, p. 29C.

2. "When Business Is All in the Family," *Mobile* (Alabama) *Press Register,* February 23, 1986, p. 1–C.

3. Jean K. Mason, "Selling Father's Painful Legacy," *Nation's Business,* September 1988, p. 30.

4. Margaret Crane, "How to Keep Families from Feuding," *Inc. Magazine's Guide to Small Business Success,* 1987, pp. 32–34.

5. "The New Business: Smith & Parents," *The Wall Street Journal,* December 8, 1988, p. B1.

6. Daniel M. Morris, "Why Family Businesses Fail," *Business Credit,* February 1989, p. 47.

7. Betty Jo Lagman, "Lollipop Bouquets Sweeten the Days for Entrepreneurs," *Mobile* (Alabama) *Register,* February 8, 1990, p. 4–B.

8. David L. Epstein, "Prepare Your Heir," *Restaurant Business,* January 20, 1988, p. 70.

9. "So You're Going to Take over the Family Business," *Agency Sales Magazine,* July 1988, p. 34.

10. John R. Emshwiller, "Handing Down the Business," *The Wall Street Journal,* May 19, 1989, p. B1.

11. Sharon Donovan, "Boss's Daughter, Son Get Down to Business," *USA Today,* May 8, 1989, p. 10E.

12. Ibid.

13. Priscilla Donegan, "A Fight for Survival," *Progressive Grocer,* September 1988, p. 22.

14. Dennis Kneale, "How Third Generation Came to Take Control at Puritan Fashions," *The Wall Street Journal,* September 6, 1983, pp. 1, 22.

15. "Planning Ahead Can Ease Succession," *The Wall Street Journal,* May 19, 1989, p. B1.

16. Mason, "Selling Father's Painful Legacy," p. 35.

17. Harriet C. Johnson, "Ready to Sell? Helpful Tips from Experts," *USA Today,* May 9, 1988, p. 11E.

CASE VII–1
CLEANDRUM, INC. (G)

CASE VII–2
OUR HERO RESTAURANT (D)

CASE VII–3
THE ROXY DINNER THEATRE

CASE VII–4
SEE COAST MANUFACTURING COMPANY, INC.

CASE VII–5
THE SON-IN-LAW

CASE VII–1

CLEANDRUM, INC. (G)

CDI was formed three years ago by Sue Ley to clean empty drums for customers to reuse for storage and transportation of liquids. Because CDI had lost money each year of its existence, Sue was discouraged. But the recent first-quarter results indicate a turnaround. Sue started the business with only a vague understanding of what it entailed, but now, she says, she has overcome many obstacles and has the experience needed to run CDI. She has gradually increased sales to give the best financial quarter that CDI has had, the first quarter of 1990 (see Exhibit 1). "We have been selling well over 3,000 drums each month—3,400 last month and 2,000 in the first half of this month. If we can maintain these sales levels, we should soon be in good shape." While sales volume is not yet up to the 44,000 drums set for 1989 in the initial proposal for the firm, the past quarter does indicate a trend toward the 50,000 drums set for 1990.

In early 1990, Sue started preparing monthly financial statements according to the new bookkeeping system designed and implemented by Archie, a member of SCORE. Sue had not had monthly statements before. She said she found it very easy to total the columns at the end of the month and draw off the profit and loss statements.

Currently, CDI is still having trouble with its cash flow, as indicated by the delay in paying for some drums. However, it had raised its cash balance from zero to $6,700 at the beginning of 1990. In January, it was able to make large payments due on a loan and on past sales tax; in February, it planned to pay off an overdue account.

Exhibit 1

CleanDrum, Inc.
Profit and Loss Sheets
1990
(in thousands)*

	Months		
Item	January	February	March
Sales	$30.0	$34.7	$31.0
Cost of sales:			
Beginning inventory	$10.4	$ 8.9	$ 8.7
Drums purchased	4.0	10.4†	4.6
Paint	.0	1.5	.0
Micellaneous supplies	.1	2.1	.6
Direct labor	3.8	4.7	5.7‡
Freight	2.0	3.0	2.8
Less ending inventory	−8.9	−8.7	−6.8
Total cost of sales	$11.4	$21.9	$15.6
Gross profit	$18.6	$12.8	$15.4
Operating, administrative, and selling costs:			
Payroll taxes	$ 2.0	$ 1.8	$ 2.1
Repair and maintenance	.0	1.6	.8
Rent	.6	.6	.6
Utilities	1.1	1.7	1.4
Salaries	1.3	1.3	2.0
Insurance	.6	.6	1.9
Office expenses	.3	.6	.1
General tax, legal, and accounting expenses	.0	.2	.1
Selling (travel and auto) expenses	.5	.8	.5
Telephone	.4	1.1	.4
Interest	.0	1.0	1.0
Sales taxes§	5.9	.4	.4
Miscellaneous (loan principal)	6.3	1.3	1.3
Total operating, administrative, and selling expenses	$19.0	$13.0	$12.6
Net income	$ (0.4)	$ (0.2)	$ 2.8

* Values have been converted into 1,000s for ease in study.
† Paid Coger Bros. $5,600 for drums purchased in 1989.
‡ Three payrolls in this month.
§ In January, accumulated unpaid sales taxes were paid.

The increased volume of sales is requiring increased production, which, in turn, is increasing the number of drums in process. At times, drums between operations block movement in the plant. Sue has an agreement with the landlord to expand the plant by 50 percent, but construction has not yet begun. This change will increase the rent 50 percent, and moving and installing machines is also expected to be expensive. Sue plans to use the plant workers for most of the machine movement and installation.

Recently, repairs on the tractor pulling the trailers have been substantial. Still, Sue has expressed concern about its reliability on the highway.

Sue has had differences with Edie, co-owner of CDI, about the managing and running of the company. Edie owns 50 percent of the company stock and has loaned the company about $80,000, on which she receives interest. "Edie calls up or comes in about every three months. She asks me what we are doing and how many drums we have sold. Then she tells us to sell more, cut costs, and so forth." Sue works full time at CDI, managing its affairs and buying and selling drums. Ben, a member of SCORE, asked if Sue had a buy-back agreement. Sue said, "Yes, but where am I supposed to get the money when I don't have any?"

Last year, Sue bought a three-acre residential lot on a local lake for $45,000. Later, a real estate agent urged her to set a sale price for a client who wanted to buy the lot. After some discussion, she set the price at $125,000. The agent countered with a price of $100,000. Ben asked why she did not sell the lot and put the money into the business. She responded, "That property is one-of-a-kind."

Sue is elated by the increase in sales, yet her financial situation still appears to be unsettled.

Questions for Discussion

1. (a) Evaluate the financial information presented in the profit and loss sheets. (b) Should changes be made in the information?
2. Discuss the method of collecting and presenting the monthly financial information.
3. (a) Show the change in cash during the first three months of 1990. (b) Estimate the cash flow for the next month. (Assume needed values.)
4. Show how the profits and cash flow would change if the plant expansion were started and completed soon.
5. (a) Would it be wise for Sue to buy out Edie? (b) If so, what kind of settlement might be fair to both parties? (c) Explain.
6. Can the purchase-sale situation of the residential lot have any bearing on Sue's decisions in CDI? Explain.

Source: Prepared by Charles R. Scott, University of Alabama, and William M. Spain, SCORE.

CASE VII–2

OUR HERO RESTAURANT (D)

The Chappells' thinking about the possibility of a new location several states distant had its real origins in two circumstances. One was Steve Chappell's determination to make the business grow and to diversify it.

"After two years of operations, we had the upper hand on the business and had become financially secure; we were ready to expand into a new venture."

The other circumstance—and the one that gave form to the new possibility—was learning of an investment group of Our Hero franchise owners that had been brought together to open several stores in Georgia. Unfortunately the group was already complete, but its proposed method intrigued Steve Chappell.

The Georgia investment group was to form a Subchapter S corporation, with each of the 10 investors holding an equal share. Since each of the five proposed stores required an investment of $20,000 plus working capital, the eventual total commitment would exceed $100,000. It was planned, however, to develop the stores in stages so that only $2,500 per investor would be required initially to start the first store. When it became profitable, another increment would be committed with which to develop Store 2, and the same pattern would be followed with Stores 3 through 5, with the expectation of returning profits once Store 5 had gotten under way.

The Georgia group proposed to hire a resident general manager who would at first be involved directly in operations from behind the counter but later, as the additional stores were constructed, would limit activities to overall supervision and management. It was further proposed to retain an auditing firm to prepare statements and verify records and books from the individual stores.

Although the Georgia group had formulated scenarios that dealt with various contingencies of limited success and even failure, the true belief was that the probabilities of the situation justified optimism. According to Steve Chappell:

The chances of success are high. Typically 75 percent of Our Hero sandwich shops exceed break-even volume levels within the first 30 days of operation. The return on investment, using this approach, can be substantial. Many stores that are currently in operation have a return on investment well exceeding 100 percent per annum. It would not be unreasonable to expect a 40 percent to 60 percent return on investment from an operating group such as this.

Although the Georgia group was closed to Barbara and him, Steve Chappell had thought late the second year, "Why not develop a similar group myself?" He could see hiring Pete Sherman, who was about to graduate from NEU, making him general manager, forming an investment group as the Georgia people had done, and generally following the path of development they had indicated.

But he knew that before these tactical steps could be taken, some major strategic questions should be asked and answered. Not the least of these was whether the Waretown Our Hero's success could really be transplanted to a distant point in a new territory strange to Our Hero. Indeed, how he should go about identifying a territory with potential for several stores was worth pondering. As he reflected on these matters, he realized that still other strategic aspects deserved attention too.

Questions for Discussion

1. (*a*) Should the Chappells expand into a new venture? (*b*) Why or why not?

2. (*a*) Evaluate the Georgia investment group's proposal. (*b*) Would you recommend that the Chappells participate with this group if they could? (*c*) Why or why not?

3. Evaluate the Chappells' plan to initiate a similar group.

4. (*a*) Which plan would you recommend? (*b*) Why?

Source: Adapted from a case prepared by John Clair Thompson, University of Connecticut.

CASE VII–3

THE ROXY DINNER THEATRE

Tom Thayer sat alone in the dark of the empty stage. "I really love this business," he thought, "but some changes have to be made if we are to survive." Tom, president of South Stage Theatre Corporation, which owns the Roxy Dinner Theatre, had just left the cast party where the cast was still celebrating the Roxy's first full month of operation. Without doubt, it had been an artistic success, but now Tom must consider the business side of the Roxy's first month.

The Roxy is located in downtown Clarksville, Tennessee. Constructed in the 1930s, it enjoyed many years of profitable operation as a motion picture theater showing first-run cinema classics such as *Casablanca, Gone with the Wind,* and Roy Rogers westerns. When shopping center cinemas took most of the old theater's patrons, the Roxy was forced to close its doors.

The Roxy lay dormant and fell into a state of disrepair until a minor renovation was attempted by a community theatre group. This attempt failed, and the Roxy once again was dark.

It seemed there was little hope for the Roxy, and it was slated for demolition to make room for parking in the downtown area. It was then that a group of young entrepreneurs decided to establish a theatre in Clarksville, saving the old building in its historic downtown location.

South Stage Theatre Corporation

A group of five young people from varied theatrical backgrounds formed the South Stage Theatre Corporation and leased the Roxy building. Each of the five owners held an equal $2,000 share in the corporation and occupied a seat on the board of directors. Each had unique qualifications and played a personal role in the operation of the theatre. None of them could invest any more money.

Four of the five owners graduated from the local high school, and the fifth became interested when he met Tom Thayer. Their ages range from the mid-20s to the upper 30s. Tom Thayer has been in the theatre since age 12 and has taught dramatic arts. He functions as primary director, choreographer, designer, writer, coach, carpenter, and general business manager.

Carmello Roman has studied acting and is a graphic artist. Roman designs makeup and costumes for the Roxy and assists in direction, acting techniques, and choreography. She also does all the graphics, brochures, and posters for the theatre.

Ginger Mulvey, vice president for marketing and general house manager, has had extensive acting experience in the Clarksville area and has worked as an actress in New York. Her duties include the hiring of staff, inventory, serving as hostess, taking reservations, some accounting and marketing, and publicity photos.

Exhibit 1   Statement of Purpose

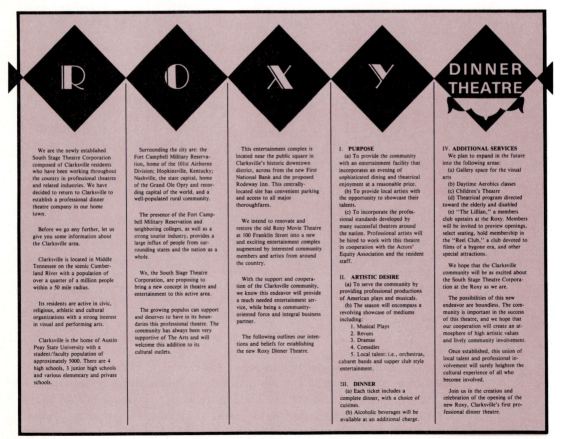

We are the newly established South Stage Theatre Corporation composed of Clarksville residents who have been working throughout the country in professional theatres and related industries. We have decided to return to Clarksville to establish a professional dinner theatre company in our home town.

Before we go any further, let us give you some information about the Clarksville area.

Clarksville is located in Middle Tennessee on the scenic Cumberland River with a population of over a quarter of a million people within a 50 mile radius.

Its residents are active in civic, religious, athletic and cultural organizations with a strong interest in visual and performing arts.

Clarksville is the home of Austin Peay State University with a student/faculty population of approximately 5000. There are 4 high schools, 3 junior high schools and various elementary and private schools.

Surrounding the city are: the Fort Campbell Military Reservation, home of the 101st Airborne Division; Hopkinsville, Kentucky; Nashville, the state capital, home of the Grand Ole Opry and recording capital of the world, and a well-populated rural community.

The presence of the Fort Campbell Military Reservation and neighboring colleges, as well as a strong tourist industry, provides a large influx of people from surrounding states and the nation as a whole.

We, the South Stage Theatre Corporation, are proposing to bring a new concept in theatre and entertainment to this active area.

The growing populus can support and deserves to have in its boundaries this professional theatre. The community has always been very supportive of The Arts and will welcome this addition to its cultural outlets.

This entertainment complex is located near the public square in Clarksville's historic downtown district, across from the new First National Bank and the proposed Rodeway Inn. This centrally-located site has convenient parking and access to all major thoroughfares.

We intend to renovate and restore the old Roxy Movie Theatre at 100 Franklin Street into a new and exciting entertainment complex augmented by interested community members and artists from around the country.

With the support and cooperation of the Clarksville community, we know this endeavor will provide a much needed entertainment service, while being a community-oriented force and integral business partner.

The following outlines our intentions and beliefs for establishing the new Roxy Dinner Theatre.

I. PURPOSE
(a) To provide the community with an entertainment facility that incorporates an evening of sophisticated dining and theatrical enjoyment at a reasonable price.
(b) To provide local artists with the opportunity to showcase their talents.
(c) To incorporate the professional standards developed by many successful theatres around the nation. Professional artists will be hired to work with this theatre in cooperation with the Actors' Equity Association and the resident staff.

II. ARTISTIC DESIRE
(a) To serve the community by providing professional productions of American plays and musicals.
(b) The season will encompass a revolving showcase of mediums including:
  1. Musical Plays
  2. Revues
  3. Dramas
  4. Comedies
  5. Local talent: i.e., orchestras, cabaret bands and supper club style entertainment.

III. DINNER
(a) Each ticket includes a complete dinner, with a choice of cuisines.
(b) Alcoholic beverages will be available at an additional charge.

IV. ADDITIONAL SERVICES
We plan to expand in the future into the following areas:
(a) Gallery space for the visual arts
(b) Daytime Aerobics classes
(c) Children's Theatre
(d) Theatrical program directed toward the elderly and disabled
(e) "The Lillian," a members club upstairs at the Roxy. Members will be invited to preview openings, select seating, hold membership in the "Reel Club," a club devoted to films of a bygone era, and other special attractions.

We hope that the Clarksville community will be as excited about the South Stage Theatre Corporation at the Roxy as we are.

The possibilities of this new endeavor are boundless. The community is important in the success of this theatre, and we hope that our cooperation will create an atmosphere of high artistic values and lively community involvement.

Once established, this union of local talent and professional involvement will surely heighten the cultural experience of all who become involved.

Join us in the creation and celebration of the opening of the new Roxy, Clarksville's first professional dinner theatre.

Tom Griffin, the technician, is the son of a theatre professional. He's in charge of all technical aspects, including the design of lighting for plots and sets, construction of sets, lighting of performances, inventory and procurement of set materials, directing, and performing.

John McDonald has had acting experience in soap operas and off-Broadway shows, has taught acting, and has been director of the children's threatre and workshops.

The group is tightly knit, with a great drive to make the Roxy succeed. The group's primary objective, as evidenced by the Statement of Purpose shown in Exhibit 1, is to bring the performing arts to Clarksville and the surrounding community. While profit is necessary, it is not the group's primary motivation.

Performing Arts in the Middle Tennessee Area

Clarksville, a town of about 60,000 people, is located in Montgomery County, which has a population of about 90,000 people. The primary employer in the area is Fort Campbell, where 20,000 military personnel, plus additional civilian support personnel, work. Austin Peay State University has approximately 5,000 students, faculty, and staff. Forty different plants employ approximately another 5,000 people. Agriculture is a major contributor to the economy.

The Roxy faces competition from primary as well as secondary competitors, as follows:

1. The Barn Dinner Theatre is located in Nashville, 40 miles away. For $17.25, its patrons receive a catered meal similar to those offered by the Roxy. The schedule is similar to the Roxy's, but nationally known talent is sometimes featured. Seating capacity is 110.

2. The Fort Campbell Cabaret Dinner Theatre charges $11 for a ticket that includes a meal. It is open all year on Friday and Saturday nights and showcases local Fort Campbell talent in modern plays similar to the Roxy's fare. Seating capacity is 150.

3. The Soldier Show Theatre at Fort Campbell is a motion picture cinema that charges $2 per ticket on Friday and Saturday nights. Seating capacity is 220.

4. The Tennessee Performing Arts Center frequently features Broadway shows with the original casts. Five shows per season, usually on Friday and Saturday evenings, are offered at prices ranging from $10 to $25. Cocktails and other beverages are offered during intermissions. Seating capacity is 2,800.

5. The Austin Peay State University Theatre and Music Department offers free performances with no meals or refreshments. Shows, offered year-round, usually feature student talent, but occasionally a professional Shakespearean group or other talent is offered on a Thursday, Friday, or Saturday. Seating capacity is 180.

6. The Kiwanis Club Community Theatre offers four performances each of three different plays per year at a cost of $8 to $10 per ticket. The plays are presented on Fridays and Saturdays, and no meals or beverages are available. Seating capacity is 250.

7. The high school drama club offers three free performances of two modern plays each year on weekends. Seating capacity is 450.

8. The Capri Twin and Martin 4 motion picture theaters charge $3.75 per ticket, and their combined seating capacity is 700.

The Roxy Opens

Extensive physical renovation of the building was necessary before the Roxy could open. In fact, the doors themselves could not be opened until they were replaced by fire doors. The interior stage and seats were re-arranged, replaced, renovated, or repainted. The theatre has a seating capacity of 200. The renovation was financed by a National Bank loan of $50,000.

Operating the Theatre

The Roxy staff has established a production schedule of 144 performances per year, based on 12 performances each month, a different show each month. Six of the 12 shows are to be musicals. Each show is to run three weeks, with four performances each week. This leaves one week per month between shows to prepare for the next show's three-week run.

Shows are available without dinner for $8 a person, and for $13, $15, or $17 with a meal, depending upon place of seating. On Sundays, a brunch performance is featured for $11. Dinners are catered by a local restaurant, and waiters serve all meals. The Roxy does not have a liquor license and sells only beer and soft drinks. Separate records of beverage sales and costs are not maintained, and brown bagging by patrons is permitted. Seating is highly flexible, consisting of small tables and chairs that can be clustered to create many different seating arrangements.

Open auditions are held, and performers, selected from the community, donate their time and talents. The available supply of talent limits the types of performances the Roxy can present.

The primary motivational tool is advertising in the entertainment section of the local newspaper. This advertising is "donated" in exchange for tickets. There is no other charge if the finished copy is provided. The first season's lineup of plays is shown in Exhibit 2.

The members of the staff perform a variety of tasks, as noted in the position descriptions, that are often rotated and shared. Specialization is not possible because of the mercurial nature of theatre operations. One day might require intensive work on costumes or choreography, while another might demand greater attention to sets or rehearsal. The flexibility of the members is a plus, and the feelings of cohesiveness and camaraderie within the group appear strong. Members work in the cold building during winter months to save on utility bills and often rely on the "happy hour" at a nearby hotel for food.

Exhibit 2   The Roxy's First Season (November–February)

MACK AND MABEL
Nov. 3,4,5,6,10,11,12,13,17,18,19,20
The musical romance of Mack Sennett's funny and fabulous Hollywood featuring the Keystone Cops, bathing beauties, and the scandal surrounding screen star Mabel Normand.
By Michael *(42nd Street)* Steward and Jerry *(Hello Dolly)* Herman

ONCE IN A LIFETIME
Dec. 1,2,3,4,8,9,10,11,15,16,17,18
Love, laughter and romance follow this happy trio's journey from the final days of vaudeville to the early days of the "talkies."
By George S. *(The Royal Family)* Kaufman and Moss *(You Can't Take It With You)* Hart

BARNUM
Dec. 29,30,31, Jan. 1,5,6,7,8,12,13,14,15
A three-ring circus spectacular detailing the fantastic life of big tent impresario P. T. Barnum, with Tom Thumb, Jenny Lind, and Jumbo the Elephant along for the ride.
By Cy *(Sweet Charity)* Coleman and Michael Stewart

TOYS IN THE ATTIC
Jan. 26,27,28,29, Feb. 2,3,4,5,9,10,11,12
A true American classic, brilliantly conceived by America's foremost authoress, Lillian *(The Little Foxes)* Hellman.

Also coming this year . . .

I Love My Wife / *Vanities* / *She Loves Me* / *Mornings at Seven* / *Tintypes* / *GEORGE M!* / *Two by Two* / *Tartuffe (alias 'The Preacher')*

However, the flexible style of the group often causes confusion concerning reservations, advertising, and cash disbursements. Accounting records for purchases, bills to be paid, receipts, and disbursements are not kept on a regular basis. Check stubs often are not identified. Funds are frequently not available to pay bills when they are due. The staff has discovered that it costs less to bounce a check at the bank than to pay a reconnection fee for utilities. Therefore, it has become their unwritten policy to write checks with insufficient funds to pay bills.

Funds are provided from several sources: the sale of tickets, meals, and beverages; cash donations by patrons, who are noted in the program as "angels" or "saints" according to the size of the gift; and donations of old clothes, furniture, rugs, and the like by concerned friends.

Expenses for a performance consist of costumes, sets, script rentals, royalty payments, advertising, printing, food, labor costs, musicians (for musicals), and overhead items, such as utilities. As cash is limited, expenditures are limited to the most necessary items. Often, old sets are cannibalized to create new ones. Additional props or parts are sometimes borrowed from local businesses in exchange for tickets, donated by concerned patrons, or purchased at the least possible cost.

For musicals, the Roxy staff has an agreement with a pianist to provide music for $600 per show. Royalties for musicals are expected to average $975 per run, while royalties for a play average $250 per run. The first production was a play.

Labor expenses include the cost of a bartender at $75 per week and four waiters who work approximately 16 hours a week at $2.05 per hour, plus tips, during the run of the show (three weeks). The cost of a catered meal is $6.50 per plate.

The fixed costs associated with operating the Roxy include a $910 monthly lease payment, $540 per month (half of which is interest) to repay the renovation loan, and $150 per month for insurance. The principals pay themselves a total of $1,175 per month, which includes the $235 rent for the apartment used by two of the owners. In addition, they retain an attorney to keep track of royalties, entertainment taxes, and other required record-keeping and reporting. Entertainment taxes are 6.75 percent of ticket sales. The telephone bill is expected to average $220 per month. Gas expense will probably average $1,000 per month during the four months of winter and $50 per month during the warmer months; electricity averages $400 per month.

The First Month

The first month of operation was an exciting time for the members of the group. Ticket sales amounted to $10,734, and the average attendance was only 118. Friday and Saturday audiences were about twice the size of Thursday and Sunday audiences. However, Tom says he is concerned because he does not know how many free tickets were issued and has no record of meals sold, given away, or spoiled. He also does not know how many tickets of each price have been sold. Tom's impression of the Roxy's first-month audiences is that they were between 25 and 55 years of age, college educated, middle- and upper-income, white-collar workers from the Clarksville area.

Tom has a cigar box filled with notes, receipts, bills and canceled checks. Upon examination of its contents, Tom finds the following information:

1. A bill for $303.33 for graphic design of advertising and programs.
2. A bill for $460.00 for the printing of programs.
3. A receipt from the U.S. Postal Service for $88.00.
4. A bank statement indicating monthly service and NSF charges of $57.75.
5. A note from Tom that the corporation owes him $33.37 for the use of his personal auto for business trips.
6. Receipts totaling $331.74 for props.
7. A laundry receipt for $300.28 for cleaning costumes.
8. Several bills from plumbers and electricians for repairs to the old building, totaling $893.45. Tom isn't sure whether such expense might be incurred every month.

9. Canceled checks indicating several purchases of supplies (napkins, cleaning supplies, and so on), totaling $391.82.
10. Other miscellaneous items totaling $312.50.
11. Canceled checks to the caterer totaling $4,722.92.
12. A bill for $115 for attorney fees.

Tom believes that he can construct an income and expense statement and that he can find out how many tickets the Roxy must sell to break even. But he is more concerned about how to control disbursements, free tickets, meals, and other operational problems. More important, Tom is concerned about filling the house with a paying audience and keeping the group together. Is the market for the Roxy's productions viable? Will people from the larger city travel to the smaller town for entertainment? Since the Roxy has not advertised outside Clarksville, it is difficult for Tom to know.

In his discussions with friends, Tom finds that many believe that the majority of the area residents are apathetic toward the arts. The statement that, "If it's in Clarksville, it can't be very good," has been expressed by more than one acquaintance. One person responded that there was a limited audience for anything more intellectually stimulating than a tractor pull and an inherent distrust of any form of entertainment out of the norm. Others seem hesitant to spend more than the price of a movie ticket for any form of entertainment. Some thought the transient population, with wide cultural backgrounds, afforded by Fort Campbell was unaware of cultural events in the local community.

Tom wonders whether serving alcoholic beverages might increase the audience size. The State Alcoholic Beverage Commission indicated that, following an inspection of a business's premises, a liquor license can be granted under the following constraints:

For businesses seating 75–125 persons, the minimum fee per year is $600; business tax licenses from the city and county are $600 each, and a $10,000 bond must be put up. The bond may be procured through a bonding company for 10 percent of the bond value. The fee for a business seating 126–175 persons is $750.

Once the liquor license was secured, an outlay of up to $5,000 would be necessary to stock liquor and mixers. An experienced bartender would be required, at a wage of $5 an hour.

A study of some local restaurants that serve both dinner and liquor shows that 25 to 30 percent of their total profits comes from bar business. Bars usually earn a 70 percent profit per dollar on liquor sales. This is an after-tax profit estimate.

Questions for Discussion

1. Describe the nature of the dinner theatre business.
2. What do you think of the mission statement of South Stage Theatre Corporation?

3.   What are the objectives of the Roxy group?

4.   What are the strengths and weaknesses of the organization's members?

5.   What is your opinion of planning at the Roxy?

6.   (*a*) Name the opportunities and threats in the Roxy's environment?
     (*b*) How would you deal with each?

7.   (*a*) Identify the internal strengths and weaknesses of the Roxy.
     (*b*) What changes would you suggest?

8.   How profitable was the Roxy's first month?

9.   What annual profit do you project for the Roxy at its present level of operations?

10. What is the maximum annual profit potential of the Roxy?

11. (*a*) Should the Roxy acquire a liquor license? (*b*) Why or why not?

12. Summarize your recommendations.

Source: Prepared by John E. Oliver, Valdosta State College, and Steven J. Anderson, Christoph Nussbaumer, Albert J. Taylor, and Jeanne Whitehead, Austin Peay State University.

CASE VII–4
SEE COAST MANUFACTURING COMPANY, INC.

If the phrase "For Distant Viewing" has ever enticed you to drop a quarter into a coin-operated telescope or binoculars, chances are the instrument was made by See Coast Manufacturing Company in Fairhope, Alabama. Although it has only eight employees and until recently was operating out of a building in its owners' backyards, the company, one of only two in the United States and four in the world making coin-operated telescopes and binoculars, has tangible assets of over $1 million, an income "in the mid six figures," and over 85 percent of the domestic market in sales of coin-operated telescopes and binoculars. It is number one in sales in the world and number two in concessions. See Coast telescopes are located in over half the 50 states and in 35 foreign countries.

Background

Although the company is still small, it was once almost nonexistent. In the late 1950s, Kenneth Cain, a former merchant marine and pipefitter, among other things, was working seven days a week in Fairhope's only restaurant. He didn't get to see much of his family—his wife, Dorothy, and two sons—and so a friend who operated pinball and vending machines suggested that he place several coin-operated telescopes at the Pensacola Municipal Auditorium, then under construction on the waterfront in Pensacola, Florida. It wasn't a very lucrative venture, as the three telescopes sometimes brought in as little as 30 cents a day (at a dime for three minutes), but the coin boxes held only $150 and so required periodic trips to Pensacola (about 50 miles away) to empty them. These trips became the family vacations, as the Cains would camp and fish and eat out at Morrison's Cafeteria in Pensacola.

Although the family placed several more telescopes on fishing piers along the Gulf Coast, the operation remained a sideline until the late 1950s, when Cain, a lifelong workaholic, was hospitalized for suspected tuberculosis. In his enforced idleness in the sanatorium, he contemplated the fact that, although he couldn't work, his telescopes (10 or 15 of them by that time) were still earning money for him. If he had hundreds of them, he reasoned, they could earn a living for him, and as soon as he was released he went into high gear.

Cain had been buying the telescopes from Echols Electronics in Evansville, Indiana, for $300 apiece, but he believed he could make them for $150 each. Though deeply in debt from his years in the sanatorium, he was able to sell some rental properties for enough to launch the new venture. He had done some research and learned that the mechanical patent on the telescopes he was buying had expired in 1907 and was not renewable, and so he and some machinist friends examined their construction and copied them to make the company's first five telescopes.

The Cains traveled farther and farther south in Florida, placing the telescopes on fishing piers and arranging to pay the pier owners a percentage of their receipts. Within a year they had reached Tampa. Living frugally, they camped out in state parks and never stayed at motels. Instead, they plowed all their profits back into the business and built new telescopes whenever they could afford the parts.

Meanwhile, the two Cain sons went off to college. The older one single-mindedly pursued his ambition to become an engineer, graduating from the Georgia Institute of Technology. But the younger son, Geoffrey, was in his junior year at the University of Southern Mississippi, majoring in psychology and minoring in philosophy, without any clear career goals, when his father realized he needed help. Geoff was almost relieved to leave school and go home to join the family business. Like his father, mother, and brother, he had graduated from the Marietta Johnson School of Organic Education, whose philosophy stresses educating the body along with the mind; and Geoffrey, like his father, had always enjoyed working with his hands. Beginning with aluminum welding, he gradually learned the skills involved in making the telescopes. A job as a draftsman for a civil engineering firm in Fairhope had given him the ability to think in design terms, and this was also helpful.

By the late 1960s, the Cains had 50 telescopes in Florida and were spending six months of the year on the road. Since Geoff had just married and Kenneth was looking toward retirement, they decided there had to be a better way to do business. So when they expanded their operations into the state parks of Georgia, they experimented with a different concession basis, giving the operators a larger share of the receipts but making them responsible for collecting the coins and remitting the Cains' share. This proved to be a much more satisfactory plan, and they used it to expand into the state parks of Alabama, Mississippi, Tennessee, and Louisiana.

They also began to produce a new model, the Mark II, which is a non-coin-operated binocular, intended for use in national parks. Stewart Udall (Secretary of the Interior from 1961 to 1969) endorsed these binoculars for national parks in eight regions of the country, and See Coast was able to expand its operations still further.

Sometime in the early 1970s, See Coast began selling telescopes as well as putting them out on concessions. The first significant sale, in 1975, was to the John Hancock Center in Chicago. This marked a giant step for See Coast because it was able to outbid American Science Center, the Chicago-based company that had acquired the telescope business from which Kenneth Cain had bought his first telescopes. After being beaten in its own backyard again when See Coast got the contract for telescopes on the Sears Tower, American Science Center lost interest in its telescope division and agreed to sell it to See Coast in 1979.

Change to Professional Management

Kenneth Cain had retired in 1973, and Geoffrey was now in charge of the company. The acquisition of American Science Center's customer list and inventory had doubled the size of the company, and Geoff saw the need to put operations on a more professional footing. Till then, plans for the telescopes had existed only in the Cains' heads, and development was by trial and error. Now, with 13 employees, Geoff realized that this was not satisfactory, and so, using the drafting skills he had gained working for the engineering firm, he reduced the plans to blueprints. The company was also incorporated at that time.

It was at about that same time that Geoff saw the need for coin-operated binoculars. It took 18 months to develop the design for the Mark III (see Exhibit 1), which is totally different from the Mark II, but luckily this development was fully paid for by an advance sale to Stone Mountain Park in Georgia.

The subsequent history of See Coast has been one of continued growth. See Coast telescopes or binoculars, which now sell for around $2,400 and give 80 seconds of viewing for a quarter, are located at Rock City in Chattanooga, at the World Trade Center in New York City, at the International Trade Mart in New Orleans, on the Space Needle in Seattle, and on the CN Tower in Toronto, Ontario, among other places. They have been at the world's fairs in Knoxville and New Orleans and can be found at every Six Flags amusement park except one. Since the telescopes, located along the seacoast, at theme parks, and on tall buildings and mountains, are used primarily by vacationers, Cain considers his business a leisure industry, although he has three different standard industrial classifications.

Exhibit 1 Design and Specifications of Mark I and Mark III

Mark I & Mark III are constructed of Rigid Aluminum alloys for maximum strength and durability. Optical interiors are anodized and sealed for maximum protection against corrosion. Exteriors are painted with an extremely durable finish to withstand harsh weather conditions.

Precision ground lenses and prisms are hard coated and the front and rear lenses are protected by optically flat glass plates.

Cash Boxes are specifically designed to provide protection against vandalism or public abuse and will hold approximately $200.00 in coins. They are secured by special barrel locks.

Each viewer has a counter to record coins deposited and may be equipped with 25¢ coin chute. (Foreign coinage, tokens or other denominations available by special order.)

Viewer head may be removed from the column by simply unlocking pedestal cap barrel lock for storing ease during your "off season" or for safekeeping.

The Mark I telescope and Mark III binocular are covered by a 6 month warranty against defective workmanship or materials.·

Mark I telescope $2,395.00*

Mark III binocular $2,395.00*

(Prices include base)
*Prices subject to change without notice.

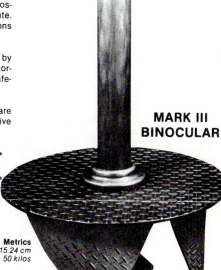

MARK III BINOCULAR

Mark III specifications: **Metrics**
Height: 59 Inches   15.24 cm
Weight: 105 Lbs.   50 kilos
Castings: 356 Alum. Alloy
Column: 4'1/2" Dia. Alum. Pipe   114.5 mm
Standard Base: 30" Dia.   7.62 cm
Binocular Length: 22 Inches   5.59 cm
Binocular Width: 12 Inches   3.05 cm
Housing Movement 360º Rotation,
50º Up and Down
Power 10x
Field of View: 183' at 1,000 yards   55.78 m at 9.14 meters
Coin Chute; 25¢ Standard (U.S. coins)
Timing Mechanism: 1 min. 20 sec.
Standard Color: Dove Gray

Competition

See Coast has rapidly overtaken its competition. Its acquisition of American Science Center's telescope division left only one American competitor, Tower Optical Company, South Norwalk, Connecticut, which is owned by Towers W. Hamilton and a brother. Both men are in their 70s, with no children interested in perpetuating the business; so they are understandably less entrepreneurial than Geoffrey Cain. Hamilton still has an exclusive concession at the Empire State Building, but Tower Optical and See Coast share Niagara Falls. International competitors are Pentax in Japan and Graphoscope in West Germany. Graphoscope has saturated France and Spain, but Cain has heard reports that the company's quality and maintenance are slipping, and he foresees an opening for competition in these countries eventually. Underbidding Pentax for the Seattle Space Needle was also very satisfying.

Marketing

Although Cain still travels extensively in the Southeast, all international business and some in the United States is handled by distributors, who work on a commission basis. Some are stocking distributors, while others merely take orders. They are located in Miami, Los Angeles, San Francisco, Detroit; Galveston, Texas; Hartford, Connecticut; and Wilmington, North Carolina, in the United States, as well as in San Juan, Puerto Rico; Toronto, Ontario; Vancouver, British Columbia; Reykjavik, Iceland; Jönköping, Sweden; Penang, Malaysia; Sydney, Australia; and Singapore. Cain laughs about a newspaper article that claimed he had "10 offices dotting the globe." "Yes," he jokes, "and every one of them is a phone booth." Although friends of Cain's have reported seeing his telescopes in Thailand and Saudi Arabia, and a picture of one in Japan appeared in a newspaper, Cain cannot specify where they are located, as they are sold not only through his many distributors but also to exporters in Miami and New York.

Why has See Coast been so successful? Cain is an aggressive marketer, engaging in personal selling and advertising in publications aimed at the leisure industry. See Coast is also the only manufacturer of coin-operated telescopes listed in the *Thomas Register,* an index of manufacturing companies that is available in libraries and also in all U.S. embassies, a boost to foreign sales. But Cain says the telescopes really sell themselves. People see them when they travel and inquire about them, especially the ones at the World Trade Center in New York.

Production

Anyone who inquires about See Coast telescopes will probably get a good report, too, as the company's real secret of success is quality. The telescopes are ruggedly built, and they do not become obsolete: the first telescope Kenneth Cain made, now 26 years old, is still in operation. Although See Coast constantly strives to improve the design of the telescopes, each innovation must be compatible with older models. Cain's greatest challenge came when the manufacturer from whom he was buying coin chutes stopped making the model he used. A new coin chute was available, but Cain had to figure out how to incorporate it into new telescopes in such a way that it could be retrofitted into the existing ones.

The concession telescopes are overhauled about every two years. In the meantime, they are simple to maintain, with little for the operator to do except empty the coin box. Sometimes a $20 part must be replaced if the operator has neglected to oil it. The company's biggest problem is vandalism, but fewer than 1 percent of the telescopes are lost to vandals each year. The telescopes come with a one-year warranty, but See Coast has never had a warranty claim. For his concession operators, Cain provides training in maintenance of the telescopes. Buyers get written instructions or a videotape demonstrating the required maintenance procedures.

Cain smiles about Ford's slogan, "Quality is Job 1." At See Coast, he says, that is literally true, as his telescopes are meant to last forever. He cannot understand manufacturers who are willing to produce as low a grade of quality as the market will bear. He encountered this attitude in the maker of his timers. Since he was buying only 500 to 1,000 a year, a very small fraction of the company's output, his complaints about the difficulties he was having with the timers were not taken very seriously. Although Cain knew that other customers were having the same problems, the company pointed out that no one else had complained. When Cain was able to demonstrate a simple way to make the timers more reliable, however, the company was ultimately convinced, with the result that Cain and all the other customers benefited from the improved device.

See Coast now makes its own timers. The company produces all but about 20 percent of its parts and subassemblies and is working toward complete autonomy. Cain buys optics from Japan but plans soon to produce his own; in fact, the rate of exchange is currently so favorable to buyers in Japan that See Coast is negotiating with a Japanese firm to supply lenses to them.

Production capacity now exceeds 300 telescopes per year, with a production run of 50 to 60. Until recently, all production operations were carried out in a 2,600-square-foot machine shop in the back of Kenneth and Geoffrey Cain's adjoining house lots. The business was handled in a 700-square-foot office in Geoff's basement. But in September 1985 the company moved into a 5,100-square-foot facility in an industrial section of town, and further expansion is projected for the near future. "To show you how crowded we were," says Cain, "when we moved in here, we didn't buy a single thing—not one machine nor a bit of office furnishing—and yet we immediately filled the place up."

Organization

Of the telescopes made each year, about 25 percent are put out on concessions, and the firm's income comes about equally from sales and concessions. The manufacture and sale of the telescopes are in a separate division from the concessions. Leased telescopes are sold by the manufacturing division to the concession division, and each telescope concession is maintained as a separate profit center. Although the performance record of each concession is maintained by computer, this method naturally generates a lot of paperwork. Of See Coast's eight employees, only four are engaged in production. The other four, under the direction of Cain's wife, Gerri, the company's secretary-treasurer, are needed to keep up with the paperwork.

Not much of this paperwork is government generated, though Cain did mention the red tape involved in selling to the U.S. government. He has also sold equipment to Parks of Canada and much prefers dealing with that country.

The Future?

Although Cain enjoys the challenge of sales, he still likes to work with his hands and is especially happy when he is creating a new design. He expects to be producing a revolutionary new telescope within six months. It will have a new timer, new optics, and a more attractive appearance, in addition to being virtually indestructible. See Coast's market standing seems secure, but Cain is not concerned about profits. "If you enjoy what you're doing and are willing to work hard," he says, "remuneration is automatic. Forget quantity and stress longevity, and the sales will be there."

Questions for Discussion

1. (*a*) Evaluate the way See Coast was founded. (*b*) What does it show about the characteristics of successful entrepreneurs?
2. Discuss the way the business developed under the original owner, Kenneth Cain.
3. How did the nature of the business change under the son, Geoffrey?
4. What are the strengths and weaknesses of the present company?
5. (*a*) Evaluate the firm's marketing activities. (*b*) Should they be changed? (*c*) Explain.
6. (*a*) Evaluate the firm's production activities. (*b*) Should they be changed? (*c*) Explain.
7. How do you explain the success of See Coast, while the competition seems to be deteriorating?
8. (*a*) Was it a wise move to incorporate? (*b*) Explain.

Source: Prepared by Suzanne S. Barnhill, Fairhope, Alabama.

CASE VII–5

THE SON-IN-LAW

Fred Clayton, a college graduate with a degree in geology, was inducted as a commissioned officer in the Navy. While in the service, he married the daughter (and only child) of Art Carroll, a prosperous manufacturers' agent in the electronics industry.

When Fred's military service was terminated, he accepted a sales position in his father-in-law's organization, the Carroll Sales Company. Carroll had high hopes that Fred would take an interest in the business and eventually relieve him of some of the managerial responsibilities. Fred was trained for a short while in the home office and was assigned a territory in which to make sales calls and to promote the products offered by his company. A new car and a liberal expense account were provided. He presented a pleasing personal appearance to the customers. However, it was soon evident to Carroll that Fred did not possess the necessary characteristics to become a good salesman.

For a number of years, Fred continued to receive a share of the available business in his area with little sales effort. This condition was primarily due to the tremendous demand for electronic equipment, which far exceeded the supply at that time.

Carroll was concerned with the fact that Fred was not spending sufficient time in his territory. He would frequently leave town on Tuesday and return on Thursday of the same week after attempting to cover an area which, to be properly serviced, would normally take from Monday through Friday. Fred's expenses were extremely high for the time he spent in the field. On occasion, Carroll would discuss Fred's progress with him. Carroll requested that his son-in-law, as a future officer in the company, set an example for the other sales personnel by putting in more time in his territory and by cutting down on his weekly expenses. After these talks, Fred would improve, but within a short time he would return to his original routine.

The company continued to prosper and to expand due to good sales effort from most of the sales force and because of the continued demand for their products. Five years ago the company covered a sales area consisting of nine states. At that time, the son-in-law was appointed district sales manager of a two-state territory and was responsible for the supervision of a warehouse and five salespeople. Fred did not work closely with any of his sales personnel, but he took time to scrutinize all expense accounts and often returned them with items marked "not approved." The salespeople felt he was very petty about this and were frequently infuriated by his actions. He also controlled all of their correspondence and information flowing to and from the territory. The other sales districts within the company had more liberal expense accounts and salespeople could make decisions on their own. The district under the supervision of Fred Clayton never led the company in sales, although it had the greatest potential of all the districts.

Carroll was quite disappointed in the lack of sales progress in Fred's division. He was also very concerned over the results of a survey which indicated that Fred's district had an unusually high turnover of sales personnel.

About a year ago, Carroll took his son-in-law out of sales. He still hoped that there might be some position in the firm where the younger man would be a real asset. With this thought in mind, he placed Fred in charge of operations to supervise and regulate the operation of the warehouses. Fred was to control inventories. He continued to have problems with personnel, causing so much unrest among employees that a number of key employees talked of leaving.

A year later, Carroll realized the situation was critical. He asked himself, "Why, after 16 years with the company, is Fred unhappy? Is he completely unmotivated to succeed because he thinks he doesn't have to? Doesn't he feel at least a moral obligation to try to get along with his associates? How have I failed to give his best abilities an opportunity? How far must I go in trying to fit him into the situation?"

Questions for Discussion

1. Comment on Fred's capabilities for managing a small business.
2. What could Carroll do to help Fred become a better manager?
3. (*a*) What qualities should a good manager possess in a company such as this? (*b*) Does Fred possess them?
4. (*a*) Who was responsible for developing Fred into a capable executive? (*b*) Has Fred or Carroll succeeded or failed? (*c*) Explain the success or failure of each.
5. How do you explain the unusually high turnover of sales personnel in Fred's district?
6. How would you answer each of Carroll's questions?
7. What does the case show about the problem of management succession in a small family-owned business?

Source: Prepared by Gayle M. Ross of the University of Mississippi Medical Center, Jackson, Mississippi.

APPENDIXES

In this section, we have included some information that should be helpful to you in learning about small business. While this information is not an integral part of the text, it should help you learn more about the subject, in addition to providing practical information for those engaged in a small business.

The following appendixes are included:

A   Help for Women
B   Help for Minorities
C   Some Useful Publications for Potential Entrepreneurs
D   Deciding Whether to Buy an Existing Business, Start a New One, or Buy a Franchise
E   A Sample Business Plan
F   Things You Can Do When a Union Tries to Organize Your Company
G   Things You Cannot Do When a Union Tries to Organize Your Company
H   General Management Self-Evaluation

HELP FOR WOMEN

Women own 4.6 million businesses and are starting twice as many as men. Here's where to get help:

National Association for Female Executives
127 West 24th Street
New York, NY 10011
212-645-0770

National Association of Black Women Entrepreneurs
P.O. Box 1375
Detroit, MI 48231
313-341-7400

National Association of Women Business Owners
600 South Federal
Chicago, IL 60605
312-922-0465

American Women's Economic Development Corporation
60 East 42nd Street, Suite 405
New York, NY 10165
800-222-2933 (out of state)
800-442-2933 (in state)
212-692-9100 (Manhattan)

Office of Women's Business Ownership
U.S. Small Business Administration
1441 L Street NW, Room 414
Washington, DC 20416
202-653-8000

HELP FOR MINORITIES

The following organizations offer help to minority-owned firms:

U.S. Hispanic Chamber of Commerce
4900 Main, Suite 700
Kansas City, MO 64112
816-531-6363

National Minority Supplier Development Council
1412 Broadway
New York, NY 10018
212-944-2430

Office of Minority Small Business, Capital Ownership
U.S. Small Business Administration
1441 L Street NW, Room 602
Washington, DC 20416
202-653-6407

Minority Business Development Agency, Communications
U.S. Department of Commerce
14th and Constitution NW, Room 5073
Washington, DC 20230
202-377-2414

Source: USA Today, May 11, 1989, p. 4B. Copyright 1989, USA TODAY. Used with permission.

SOME USEFUL PUBLICATIONS FOR POTENTIAL ENTREPRENEURS*

A. From the Bureau of the Census
   1. *Bureau of the Census Catalog*
   2. *Census of Manufacturers* (published every five years)
   3. *Census of Population* (published every 10 years)
   4. *Census of Retail Trade* (published every five years)
   5. *County Business Patterns* (published annually)
   6. *Enterprise Statistics* (published every five years)
   7. *Location of Manufacturing Plants by County, Industry, and Employment Size* (published every five years)

B. From the U.S. Government Printing Office
   1. *Business Statistics* (published every two years by the Bureau of Economic Analysis, U.S. Department of Commerce)
   2. *Statistical Abstract of the United States* (published annually by the Bureau of the Census)
   3. *U.S. Industrial Outlook* (published annually by the U.S. Department of Commerce)

C. From the U.S. Small Business Administration
   1. *Directory of Business Development Publications* (Form 115A)
   2. *ABC's of Borrowing* (FM 1)
   3. *Advertising Media Decisions* (MT 6)
   4. *Basic Budgets for Profit Planning* (FM 3)
   5. *The Business Plan for Homebased Business* (MP 15)
   6. *Creative Selling: The Competitive Edge* (MT 10)
   7. *Developing a Strategic Business Plan* (MP 210)
   8. *Going into Business* (MP 12)
   9. *Marketing for Small Business: An Overview* (MT 2)
   10. *Planning and Goal Setting for Small Business* (MP 5)
   11. *Recordkeeping in a Small Business* (FM 10)
   12. *Research Your Market* (MT 8)

D. Various trade associations, their personnel, and publications. These provide a timely and—usually—well-informed source of information about a specific industry.

E. Trade journals

* Write to the appropriate agency at the following addresses: Bureau of the Census, U.S. Department of Commerce, Washington, DC 20233; U.S. Government Printing Office, Washington, DC 20402; U.S. Small Business Administration, Box 15434, Fort Worth, TX 76119.

DECIDING WHETHER TO BUY AN EXISTING BUSINESS, START A NEW ONE, OR BUY A FRANCHISE

"Should I start a new business, buy an existing one, or buy a franchise?" At this point in your career, this is a very important question. The material in this appendix can aid you in making this choice. We recommend that you answer the questions as conscientiously as you can for any business you have in mind.

If, after covering the material in Checklist A, you decide to enter an established business rather than start one of your own, then proceed to the material in Checklist B. Checklist C, to be completed after Checklist A or A and B, is used to determine whether to operate a franchise or nonfranchise business. Complete this form for each specific business you are considering entering.

Checklist A: Starting a New Business or Buying an Existing One

Before deciding whether you will establish a new business or purchase an established business, you need to give consideration to the positive and negative features of each. More important, you should rate each point a plus or minus as you perceive the significance of the point and its value to you.

1. Define the nature of the business:

   _____

   _____

   _____

2. Favorable points for establishing a new business (plus [+] or minus [−]):
   a. Opportunity to create the type of physical facilities I prefer. _____
   b. Ability to take advantage of the latest technology in selecting equipment, materials, and tools. _____
   c. Opportunity to utilize the most recent processes and procedures. _____
   d. Opportunity to obtain a fresh inventory. _____
   e. Opportunity to have a free hand in selecting, training, developing, and motivating personnel. _____
   f. Opportunity to design my own management information system. _____
   g. Opportunity to select my competitive environment, within limits. _____

3. Favorable points for selecting an established business (plus [+] or minus [−]):

    a. Avoiding the difficulty of a business with an unproved
performance record in sales, reliability, service,
and profits.   _____

    b. Avoiding the problems associated with assembling
the composite resources—including location, building,
equipment, material, and people.   _____

    c. Avoiding the necessity of selecting and training a
new work force.   _____

    d. Avoiding the lack of an established product line.   _____

    e. Avoiding production problems associated with the
start-up of a new business.   _____

    f. Avoiding the lack of an established market channel for
distribution.   _____

    g. Avoiding the problems in establishing a basic
accounting and control system.   _____

    h. Avoiding the difficulty in working out the "bugs"
that develop in the initial operation.   _____

4. Checking back over the points covered in 2 and 3 above,
I conclude that:
    a. I want to establish a new business.   _____
    b. I prefer to enter an established business.   _____

5. If you checked *4b*, then proceed with Checklist B below.

Checklist B: Analyzing the Desirability of an Existing Business*

Considerations for selecting an established business, your responses, those
of the present owner, and the facts concerning the status of the business
should guide you to a comfortable decision as to whether this business is
for you.

1. Why is the business available for purchase?

   _____

   _____

2. What are the intentions of the present owner?

   _____

   _____

    a. Does the present owner plan another business to compete with
you? Yes _____ No _____

    b. Is the present owner in good health? Yes _____ No _____

    c. Does the present owner wish to retire? Yes _____ No _____

    d. Does the present owner wish to continue to be associated with
the business? Yes _____ No _____

3. Are demographic factors changing?
    a. Population: Up _____ Stable _____ Down _____
    b. Neighborhood: Better _____ Stable _____ Worse _____

---

* Note: See Chapters 4, 6, and 7 for short explanations of the items in this checklist. These
and subsequent chapters discuss these items in greater detail.

    c.   Demand: Up _____ Stable _____ Down _____

    d.   Other factors: Better _____ Stable _____ Worse _____

4.   Are physical facilities suitable? Yes _____ No _____

    a.   Worn-out or outdated? Yes _____ No _____

    b.   Proper size for demand? Yes _____ No _____

    c.   Laid out properly? Yes _____ No _____

5.   Is the business operating efficiently? Yes _____ No _____

    a.   How effective are the personnel?

        (1)   What is the rate of labor turnover? _____%

        (2)   What is the rate of absenteeism? _____%

        (3)   Is the business unionized? Yes _____ No _____

        (4)   Is productivity high? Yes _____ No _____

    b.   What is the amount of waste?

        (1)   Material: _____% $_____ per day

        (2)   Machine time: _____% $_____ per day

        (3)   Personnel time: _____% $_____ per day

    c.   Is the quality of product/service good? Yes _____ No _____

        (1)   What portion of product is wasted? _____

        (2)   How many complaints about service are received? _____ per year

        (3)   Are deliveries on time? Yes _____ No _____

    d.   Are content and level of inventory satisfactory? Yes _____ No _____

        (1)   Does the inventory contain mostly "dead stock"? Yes _____ No _____

        (2)   Is its level appropriate for the firm? Yes _____ No _____

6.   What is the financial condition of the firm?

    Good _____ Fair _____ Poor _____

    a.   Have you had a reputable CPA appraise the firm's assets and liabilities? Yes _____ No _____

    b.   Validity of financial statements:

    Accurate _____ Overstated _____ Understated _____

    Warning, check to see: Relationship of book value of fixed assets to replacement costs; percentage of total accounts receivable over 90 days (_____%); records kept of age of accounts receivable? (Yes _____ No _____); dollar amount of bad debts charged off last 6 months ($_____), 12 months ($_____), 36 months ($_____).

    c.   Cash position: Cash on hand: $_____ Cash in bank: $_____

    d.   Is cash flow adequate to meet obligations? Yes _____ No _____

    e.   Current ratio: (current assets/current liabilities) _____

    f.   Quick ratio: ([current assets − inventories]/[current liabilities]) _____

    g.   Debt to equity ratio: (debt [current liabilities, notes, bonds] ÷ owner's funds [common stock, preferred stock, capital surplus, and retained earnings]) _____

    h.   Ratio of net income to sales: (net income/net sales) _____ *i.*   Ratio of net income to equity or investment: (net income/equity or investment) _____

    j.   Amount of debt: Notes: $_____ Bonds: $_____

    k.   Terms of debt: _____

    l.   Adequacy of cost data: Can you accurately determine the cost of the product or service? Yes _____ No _____

    m.   Are there available data to enable you accurately to break down the price of a product or service into costs and profit? Yes _____ No _____

    n.   Is the business solvent? Yes _____ No _____

7. How much investment is needed? $_____

8. What is the estimated return on your investment? _____%

9. What is your decision? _____
_____
_____
_____

Checklist C: Desirability of Buying a Franchise

Is a franchise the type of business you need? Your responses to, and the ranking of, the issues raised below should aid you in this determination. The ranking should vary from "1," for the highest order of need, to "10," for the lowest ranking of need. (Franchise opportunities were discussed in Chapter 4.)

Ranking (1 to 10)	Do I Need:	Yes	No
_____	1. The benefit of a special training program?	____	____
_____	2. The assistance provided by a standardized accounting and cost control system?	____	____
_____	3. Financial assistance?	____	____
_____	4. Assistance in site selection?	____	____
_____	5. Counsel for erecting and equipping a facility?	____	____
_____	6. The benefit of an efficient production system?	____	____
_____	7. The benefit of a system that minimizes labor cost?	____	____
_____	8. The benefit of a local, regional, or national image?	____	____
_____	9. A well-planned and -implemented regional or national advertising program?	____	____
_____	10. To be supervised in setting and maintaining customer service standards?	____	____
_____	11. A continuing program of management assistance, training, and guidance?	____	____
_____	12. Assistance in sensitivity and responsiveness to changing marketing opportunities?	____	____
_____	13. Assistance in obtaining a purchasing advantage?	____	____
_____	14. Access to a proven successful operating system?		
	Checking over the answers and ranking above, I conclude:	____	____
	a. I want to obtain a franchise.	____	____
	b. I want to operate an independent business.	____	____

A SAMPLE BUSINESS PLAN

RECYCLE AMERICA, LTD.
12 Main Street
Athens, GA 30605
(404) 555–0950
General Partner: Jerry Zykling
Formulation Date: January 1, 1990

EXECUTIVE SUMMARY

Recycle America, Ltd. (hereafter referred to as the Company), is a start-up company developed by the president and chief operating officer, Jerry Zykling. Operations will begin in March of 1990. The Company is in the recyclable product curbside pickup business.

Background

Jerry Zykling has a Master of Business Administration degree in corporate finance and entrepreneurship/new venture formation. He has financial management experience and some entrepreneurial familiarity.

The business concept itself is relatively new. At least one similar operation is being run in Marin County, California.

Objectives and Goals

The Company's goals are a high volume of business and operating efficiencies so as to minimize expenses. Growth and development are planned for several years.

The Business

Recycle America, Ltd., as mentioned before, is a recyclable product curbside pickup service whose profit results from the sale of recyclable materials picked up from households or businesses.

The population of Athens, Georgia, will be solicited through advertisements to participate, and, if they choose to, they will be given plastic containers in which to separate their waste into various recyclables. Initially, the focus will be on retrieving aluminum, glass, and newspaper products.

Trucks will pick up the separated waste at curbside once a week and drop it at a local recycling plant for weighing and payment.

The Market

The test market is the 10,000 residences of Athens, Georgia. Since it is a college town, Athens' consumption patterns and attitude should make it a good test market.

The Company will be relying on environmental issues to promote its idea. Recycling is an attractive alternative to landfill and incineration and also preserves dwindling natural resources.

Market penetration is expected to reach 40 percent residential and 35 percent of selected restaurants and bars in the area. Growth is expected to reach 60 percent of the residences and 40 percent of the restaurants and bars by the end of the fourth year.

There is currently no competition in Athens or the Southeast.

Management and Staff

The organizational structure consists of a general partner acting as the chief operating officer, an office assistant, and four field officers. Three limited partners will not actively participate in managing the business.

The chief operating officer is to be compensated at the rate of $22,000 per year, plus a bonus of 2 percent of gross revenue. The office assistant and field operators will be paid an hourly rate. In addition, the field operators will receive a monthly incentive payment based on pounds of recyclable goods collected.

Financial Projections

Cash flow is expected to become positive in fiscal year 1993. Beginning at that time, dividends of 15 percent will be payable annually to each limited partner. Capital appreciation in excess of 200 percent is expected after the third year of operation.

Financing Required

Three limited partners will contribute $6,000 each and may each be required to contribute up to $2,500 more in the event of a cash shortage. A short-term loan of $10,000 will be required, as well as a $5,000 to $10,000 line of credit for a one-year period. Cash flow should be sufficient in fiscal year 1992 to retire any existing bank debt.

BUSINESS PLAN

Table of Contents

I. Background
   A. The General Partner
   B. History of the Concept

II. The Business
   A. Recycle America, Ltd.
   B. Objectives and Goals

III. Operations
   A. Start-up
   B. Day-to-Day Operations
   C. Expected Growth and Expansion
   D. The Future

IV.   Marketing
    A.   Environmental Issues and Legislation
    B.   Target Market
    C.   Market Penetration
    D.   Prices
    E.   Competition
V.   Management and Staff
    A.   Organizational Structure
    B.   Employee Policies and Compensation
VI.   Financial Projections
    A.   Revenue Forecasts
    B.   Projected Expenses
    C.   Projected Profit (Loss)
VII.   Financing Required
    A.   Equity Capital
    B.   Bank Financing
VIII.   Conclusion
IX.   References

BACKGROUND

The General Partner

Jerry Zykling, 25, received his undergraduate degree in English from the University of Florida. He continued his education in the Master of Business Administration program at the University of Georgia, concentrating in corporate finance and entrepreneurship/new venture formation. For the past two years, he has worked for the Coca-Cola Company as a financial analyst. Zykling paid for the last four years of his education by running a small computer distributorship. He is the general partner for the project.

History of the Concept

Companies similar to Recycle America have proven to be very successful in other parts of the country. In Marin County, California, Marin Recycling has seen its volume increase from 2 million pounds in 1982 to 40 million pounds in 1986 and 46 million pounds in 1987. The 250,000 residents presently recycle 22 percent of their waste, and curbside participation in Marin Recycling's efforts is 55 percent. Participation in that company's growth is expected to approach 75 percent by 1992.

THE BUSINESS

Recycle America, Ltd.

Recycle America, Ltd. (the Company), is a recyclable waste curbside pickup and disposal company. The profit margin is the difference between the gross revenue obtained from selling the recyclable products to a recycling plant and the expenses incurred in picking up the recyclables and getting them to the plant.

Objectives and Goals

The Company's initial focus will be on market penetration and community acceptance. After initial acceptance is achieved, the focus will change to attracting high volume, since this is the key to profitability. Also, initial expenses must be kept to a minimum in order to maintain what will be a relatively small profit margin.

Other goals are expansion and growth into other markets and adding services related to recyclable product curbside pickup. This objective is discussed in a later section.

Finally, employees and the community can look to the following mission statement for the motivation behind the Company's activities: Recycle America is proud to take a part in keeping America clean and preserving our raw materials for future generations.

OPERATIONS

Start-up

The items needed for initial start-up will be discussed later in the plan, but they will be mentioned here so that daily operations can be more easily explained. They are as follows:

Two 2-ton payload pickup trucks with truck beds modified for pickup and delivery of the recyclable waste.

Approximately 4,000 plastic five-gallon containers supporting drop-off for an initial 2,000 residences; 4,000 more will be required in the second month.

A small office, with room for a secretary and the general partner/chief operating officer, and a small amount of office equipment.

A fenced-in area of land beside the office for parking trucks when not in use.

Rental of a mini-warehouse for storage of unused containers.

To gain initial acceptance and market penetration, the Company plans to use public service radio and television advertisements, newspaper notices, and hand-distributed fliers. These ads will focus on the environmental benefits of recycling and should generate immediate response. The initial target is 2,000 residences (20 percent of the total), to be achieved within one month of first public notice. Bars and restaurants in the area will also be targeted. The initial penetration there is also expected to be 20 percent.

Persons agreeing to separate their garbage and place it out for weekly curbside pickup will be provided with two plastic five-gallon containers. Businesses—depending on their contributed volume—will have pickups more than once a week. As soon as the containers have been distributed, waste collection will begin.

Day-to-Day Operations

Four employees, two per truck, will do the curbside collection. Using commonly available routing techniques, these collectors will travel on scheduled routes around the city, collect the recyclables, and deliver them to a local recycling plant. At first, the two trucks will not be heavily utilized, but when the number of households subscribing reaches the first-year estimate of 4,000, both trucks will need to be serving 400 houses a day, or 50 per hour, with eight-hour days. The two-person teams picking up regular garbage average 60 stops per hour; so even at a 40 percent saturation level, the trucks and teams will not reach full capacity by the end of the first year, as it should take significantly less time to pick up relatively small amounts of waste. With the excess capacity, the teams will make two or more trips to the recycling plant daily and make pickups at the subscribing bars and restaurants.

Residents will be asked to separate their refuse into three recyclable products: aluminum, glass, and newspaper. The two five-gallon containers will hold the aluminum and glass. The people will be asked to tie up the newspaper or put it into some sort of paper container such as a grocery bag. Then, on the appointed day of the week, they will put the containers and bundles near the street or road. One of the pickup teams will then come by the person's house on that day and empty the containers into their respective compartments on the truck.

When the pickup truck's payload is full, the collectors will drive to the recycling plant and make a delivery. The products will then be weighed, and the driver will receive a receipt for what was delivered. This receipt will be checked against weekly payment from the recycling plant via the mail. Security and incentive measures will be implemented to prevent collusion between pickup teams and plant personnel and to maintain efficient operations.

Expected Growth and Expansion

Within the first year of operation, market penetration is expected to reach 40 percent for residential prospects and 35 percent for selected bars and restaurants. Residential figures are expected to climb 10 percent a year in years two and three, reaching a level currently being achieved by a similar operation in Marin County, California. Bar and restaurant participation is expected to grow to 40 percent by the end of the third year.

This growth could possibly be accompanied by the addition of needed staffing and a third truck. Also, if warranted by the size of the operation in the future, a larger truck, with certain features more conducive to the waste removal business, might be necessary. The new trucks would feature low-entry, right-side (sit-down or stand-up) steering wheel-operated cabs so that the driver could stop and pick up garbage as well as drive, thereby reducing the number of people per truck to one. Added features could include hydraulic lifts under each of the truck's three containers for easier disposal and scales built into the trucks for more accurate measuring of the recyclables' weight.

Sometime in the fourth year, operations will be expanded into the Atlanta metropolitan area, then into other large cities in the southeastern United States after further testing. Further geographic expansion is anticipated if the concept is successful in the Southeast. The Company will rely on reputation, innovation, and efficiency to fend off anticipated competition. Being one of the first companies exploring this niche will give Recycle America an advantage over later entries.

The Future

Curbside pickup of aluminum, glass, and newspaper is not the only area of recycling the Company plans to be involved in. To start, there are other products that can be recycled, such as steel and rubber. The Company will eventually become involved in lobbying against the use of plastic products. These products are made of a valuable resource, oil, and cannot be recycled. In addition, plastics produce toxic fumes when burned, further limiting their disposal prospects.

Tree limbs, shrub cuttings, compost, and other such fibrous material are also valuable products and can be used. Today, at least one recycling plant in the country is run completely from electricity generated by burning such material.

Another logical step for the Company is to go into recycling itself. If the curbside pickup service produces enough volume to support a plant, then Recycle America would certainly be interested in bypassing other processors and reaping the benefits of selling the actual recycled products themselves.

MARKETING

Environmental Issues and Legislation

Recycle America, Ltd., focuses on the expanding opportunities available in the recycling industry. Boosted by the mounting garbage crisis, recycling offers a viable alternative to landfills and incinerators. Not only are these two disposal methods encountering increased opposition from environmental activists, waste disposal costs are soaring as available sites dwindle. For example, at this time the landfill rates in Athens are $6.50 per ton, but rates of $20 per ton or more are common in other parts of the country. Furthermore, experts predict that half of America's cities will run out of landfill space by the early 1990s. Establishing new dumps and incinerators ignites fierce local opposition, as communities nearly always take a "not in my back yard" stance toward any such proposals.

Adding to the recycling industry's attractiveness are the facts that several states have already passed mandatory recycling laws and that new technology allows more kinds of waste to be recycled and reused. One Athens official expects the city to pass a recycling law by 1990. In fact, the Environmental Protection Agency expects that, by 1992, at least 25 percent of the nation's yearly waste will be recycled. By comparison, Japan already recycles 50 percent of its household and commercial waste. The most successful programs have Japanese residents separate their waste into seven categories. Since events such as the infamous "garbage barge" of 1987 have heightened awareness of the waste disposal problem, Americans have shown a willingness to make recycling a priority.

Target Market

The Company chose March 1, 1990, to begin test marketing the concept in Athens, Georgia. A university town with approximately 10,000 residences, Athens was selected as the test market for several reasons. First, the general partner received his education here and is familiar with the area. Also, in doing research on the subject, he has developed contacts in the Athens Waste Management Department who have helped him in working out the logistics of a curbside pickup service. It should be noted that these officials feel that local landfill sources will be filled by 1994.

The city is also a good choice because of the large student population. A university community is generally more liberal and better educated than average and would therefore be more receptive to the idea of separating its waste for recycling. Also, student consumption patterns make the collection of glass and aluminum profitable.

Market Penetration

The participation rate for the first year is projected at 40 percent of the market, or 4,000 residences. Participation in the second year is estimated to be 50 percent of residences, growing to 60 percent in the third year. In addition, Recycle America intends to provide service to 35 percent of selected bars and restaurants by the end of the first year. These student-oriented businesses will generate about 400 pounds of glass and 10 pounds of aluminum weekly.

Prices

Although prices for paper, aluminum, and glass have historically been very volatile, markets have stabilized somewhat over the last few years. Athens has three recyclers, contributing to the stability of the market. Paper prices remain the most volatile, ranging from one to two cents per pound. Currently, the price is one cent per pound. Glass prices have remained steady over the short term, with a current value of two cents per pound. Aluminum has a market price of 45 cents per pound. Although these prices are subject to change, we are certain that they represent conservative, accurate figures as a basis for our financial projections.

Competition

There is little competition, although the threat of government involvement is always present. Should the city of Athens undertake a recycling effort, it would be a formidable opponent. However, we believe that, by having our operation in place and running successfully, we can overcome the challenges brought about by competition, and we hope that having an operation under way will also deter government entry.

MANAGEMENT AND STAFF

Organizational Structure

The organizational structure of Recycle America is shown in the chart below.

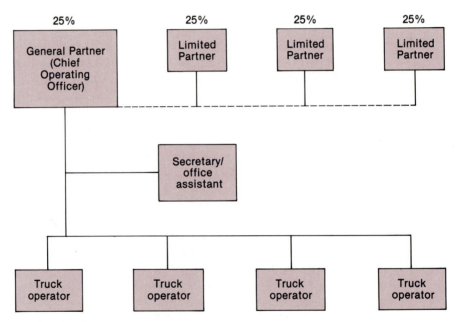

This structure emphasizes cost efficiency and direct control by one individual. The general partner, who is also the chief operating officer (COO), will operate the entire business with the assistance of one part-time or full-time office aide/secretary. He will direct all activities of the truck operators, including their working hours and pickup schedules, and also handle the cash receipts and disbursements, with a secretary to help in critical areas of internal control.

The first advantage of this simple, efficient structure is cost minimization in the start-up phase. The truck operators and office assistant will be used on the basis of pickup schedule demands. The only "fixed" wage expense is the COO's monthly salary of $1,833.

Another important advantage of this simplified structure is that direct responsibility for all operations is in the hands of one person—the chief operating officer. The structure also encourages entrepreneurial independence and motivation, which are essential ingredients in the success of a new business venture.

Employee Policies and Compensation

There are three groups of employees in the organization:

1. *Management.*   Chief operating officer.
2. *Staff.*   Secretary/office assistant.
3. *Field operations.*   Truck operators and pickup personnel.

A brief discussion of job descriptions and compensation by employee type follows.

Management

The only manager is the chief operating officer (COO). He is responsible for daily operations, including scheduling weekly routes for pickup of recyclable goods, distribution of plastic containers to residences and businesses, cash receipt and disbursement, preparing the payroll, and promotion and advertising. Monthly duties include preparation and distribution of monthly cash flow information to the limited partners and applicable creditors, as well as preparation of monthly statistics and financial information. Annual duties include assistance with yearly review/audit and coordination and presentation of the annual meeting with the limited partners. The COO has blanket responsibility for all ongoing activities within Recycle America, Ltd.

The COO will receive an annual salary of $22,000, paid biweekly, plus a bonus of 2 percent of gross revenue, paid semiannually. The second payment of the bonus each year shall be based on annual gross revenue as determined by the annual review/audit by an independent CPA, less the first semiannual bonus payment.

This COO compensation package will be in effect for two years, subject to renewal and/or revision at the beginning of fiscal year 1993.

Staff

The staff position consists of only one clerical staff worker, part-time or full-time, known as the *office assistant.* The office assistant will be responsible for daily word processing, bookkeeping, invoice and check preparation, payroll records (except for the COO's and his/her own), and container inventory.

Staff members shall receive an hourly rate of $5.70 per hour, payable biweekly. Adjustments to the hourly rate will be considered every six months and will be based on a performance review.

Field Operations

Field operations will be performed by the truck operators and pickup personnel. Their duties include following weekly routes and work schedules prepared by the COO; picking up the recyclable aluminum, paper, and glass from residential and business locations; and transporting the recyclable goods to a designated recycling center. In addition, field operators are responsible for the care of the vehicles, distribution of containers, and distribution of promotional and instructional materials.

Field operators will receive a rate of $5.30 per hour, plus a monthly incentive payment based on the number of pounds collected, by category of recyclable goods, and allocated to each person on the basis of the number of hours worked. The incentive payment will be $0.015 per pound of aluminum and $0.002 per pound of paper and glass.

FINANCIAL PROJECTIONS

Revenue Forecasts

The projected revenues for the first year of operations are shown in Exhibit 1. They are expected to vary from $6,900 for the first two months to $13,675 for the last two. Total revenues are projected to be $126,775 for the first year of operations.

Exhibit 2 projects revenues increasing to $202,500 for the second year and $242,400 for the third year.

Projected Expenses

The expense projections are as follows:

Salaries and wages:

Chief operating officer: $1,833 per month

Office assistant: 20 hours per week for March–April 1990
30 hours per week for May–October 1990
40 hours per week after October 1990

Truck operators: Three workers for March–April 1990
Four workers after April 1990

Bonuses:

Chief operating officer: 2 percent of gross revenue, payable semiannually

Truck operators: Based on pounds of aluminum and paper/glass, payable monthly

Container expense (based on two containers per household served):
March 1990:   4,000 buckets at $1.90 = $7,600
April 1990:   4,000 buckets at $1.90 = $7,600

Rent:

> Office space lease at $500 per month, plus $500 security deposit in March 1990
>
> Mini-warehouse space for container inventory at $100 per month

Insurance:

> Trucks: Liability and collision with $1,000 deductible
> General business liability coverage
> Fire and casualty
>
> Total coverage costs approximate $200 per month.

Advertising and promotion:

> Athens newspaper: 4 column inches at $40 per column inch = $160 per ad
>> March 1990:   One week (five days) = $800
>> June 1990:   Two days = $320
>> September 1990:   One week = $800
>
> Direct distribution:
>> March 1990: 3,000 copies at $0.07 = $210
>> September 1990:   3,000 copies at $0.07 = $210

Truck maintenance:

> $300 per truck per year = $600 per year = $50 per month

Gasoline:

> Trucks travel approximately 35 miles each per day
> Two trucks × 35 miles × 22 days = 1,540 miles per month
> 1,540 miles per 10 mpg = 154 gallons per month
> 154 gallons per month × $1.05 per gallon = $161.70 per month

Utilities:

> Telephone: $75 per month
> Electricity: $50 per month

Licensing:

> Business license at $129 in March 1990

Truck finance payments:

> Two trucks (2-ton pickup trucks)
> $2,000 down payment in March 1990
> $660 payments beginning April 1990, based on $25,000 loan at 12% for 48 months
>
> Interest attributable to loan is $2,721 for the year 1991, $2,064 for 1992, and $1,324 for 1993.

Computer and furnishings:

> The office will require the following capital expenditures in March 1990 to furnish it and make it operable:

Exhibit 1

RECYCLE AMERICA, LTD
Revenue Projections
Fiscal Year 1991

		March	April	May	June	July
Price per pound:						
Paper	$0.01					
Glass	0.02					
Aluminum	0.45					
Residential pickup:						
Residences (number)	10,000					
Residential participation (%)		20%	20%	25%	25%	30%
Weight:*						
Paper	35	70,000	70,000	87,500	87,500	105,000
Glass	30	60,000	60,000	75,000	75,000	90,000
Aluminum	5	10,000	10,000	12,500	12,500	15,000
Residential sales:						
Paper		$ 700	$ 700	$ 875	$ 875	$ 1,050
Glass		1,200	1,200	1,500	1,500	1,800
Aluminum		4,500	4,500	5,625	5,625	6,750
Restaurant/bar pickup:						
Establishments (number)	50					
Commercial participation (%)		20%	20%	20%	25%	25%
Weight:†						
Glass	1,600	16,000	16,000	16,000	20,000	20,000
Aluminum	40	400	400	400	500	500
Commercial sales:						
Glass		$ 320	$ 320	$ 320	$ 400	$ 400
Aluminum		180	180	180	225	225
Revenue totals:		$6,900	$6,900	$8,500	$8,625	$10,225

* Pounds per residence per month.

† Estimated pounds per establishment per month.

Two filing cabinets	$ 150
Two desks	600
Two chairs	350
Leasehold improvements	800
Computer with monitor	2,000
Printer	500
Total	$4,400

Depreciation expense:

   The trucks, computer and printer, furnishings, and leasehold improvements are considered five-year property under the current tax law. They will be depreciated as follows:

August	September	October	November	December	January	February	For year 1991
30%	30%	35%	35%	40%	40%	40%	31%
105,000	105,000	122,500	122,500	140,000	140,000	140,000	1,295,000
90,000	90,000	105,000	105,000	120,000	120,000	120,000	1,110,000
15,000	15,000	17,500	17,500	20,000	20,000	20,000	185,000
$ 1,050	$ 1,050	$ 1,225	$ 1,225	$ 1,400	$ 1,400	$ 1,400	$ 12,950
1,800	1,800	2,100	2,100	2,400	2,400	2,400	22,200
6,750	6,750	7,875	7,875	9,000	9,000	9,000	83,250
30%	30%	30%	30%	35%	35%	35%	28%
24,000	24,000	24,000	24,000	28,000	28,000	28,000	268,000
600	600	600	600	700	700	700	6,700
$ 480	$ 480	$ 480	$ 480	$ 560	$ 560	$ 560	$ 5,360
270	270	270	270	315	315	315	3,015
$10,350	$10,350	$11,950	$11,950	$13,675	$13,675	$13,675	$126,775

	Cost	Depreciation expense		
		1991	1992	1993
Trucks	$27,000	$5,400	$ 8,640	$5,184
Computer and printer	2,500	500	800	480
Furniture	1,100	220	352	211
Leasehold improvements	800	160	256	154
Total	$31,400	$6,280	$10,048	$6,029

Based on these projections, total expenses will be $134,194 for the first fiscal year, $143,330 for the second, and $154,967 for the third.

Exhibit 2

RECYCLE AMERICA, LTD
Revenue Projections
Fiscal Years 1991–1993

		1991	1992	1993
Residential pickup:				
Residences (number)	10,000			
Residential participation (%)		31%	50%	60%
Weight:*				
Paper	35	1,295,000	2,100,000	2,520,000
Glass	30	1,110,000	1,800,000	2,160,000
Aluminum	5	185,000	300,000	360,000
Residential sales:				
Paper		$ 12,950	$ 21,000	$ 25,200
Glass		22,200	36,000	43,200
Aluminum		83,250	135,000	162,000
Restaurant/bar pickup:				
Establishments (number)	50			
Commercial participation (%)		28%	35%	40%
Weight:†				
Glass	1,600	268,000	336,000	384,000
Glass	40	6,700	8,400	9,600
Commercial sales:				
Glass		$ 5,360	$ 6,720	$ 7,680
Aluminum		3,015	3,780	4,320
Revenue totals:		$126,775	$202,500	$242,400

* Pounds per residence per month.

† Estimated pounds per establishment per month.

Projected Profit (Loss)

As shown in Exhibit 3, income statements for 1991–1993, a loss of $7,419 is projected for the first year of operations. But a profit of $59,170 is projected for the second year, and $87,433 for the third. Exhibit 4 shows the balance sheets for the Company for 1990–1992.

FINANCING REQUIRED

Financing of this venture will come from both equity and debt financing.

Equity Capital

As previously indicated, operations will begin with three limited partners, each with a 25 percent interest in the business. The required initial capital contribution is $6,000 each. (The COO is given the remaining 25 percent interest, with no required monetary contribution.) The limited partners require monthly cash flow statements, due by the 15th of the following month, and periodic meetings with the COO—at their discretion. They

Exhibit 3

RECYCLE AMERICA, LTD.
Income Statements
February 28, 1991–1993

	1991	1992	1993
Revenue:			
Aluminum	$ 86,265	$138,780	$166,320
Paper	12,950	21,000	25,200
Glass	27,560	42,720	50,880
Total revenue	126,775	202,500	242,400
Operating expenses:			
Salaries and wages	82,363	90,540	99,594
Bonuses	10,763	17,148	20,520
Container expense	15,200	5,000	6,000
Rent	7,200	7,560	7,950
Insurance	2,400	2,520	2,650
Advertising and promotion	2,340	3,000	4,000
Truck maintenance	550	600	1,000
Gasoline	1,848	2,000	2,400
Utilities	1,500	1,650	1,800
Depreciation	6,280	10,048	6,029
Interest	2,721	2,064	1,324
Taxes and licenses	129	0	200
Miscellaneous	900	1,200	1,500
Total operating expenses	134,194	143,330	154,967
Net profit (loss)	$ (7,419)	$ 59,170	$ 87,433

shall have the right to an annual accounting of operations (review or audit by an independent CPA), to be presented by April 30 of each year. In the first year of operations, a six-month review of operations shall be presented to the limited partners by the COO to ensure that revenue goals stated in the financial section are met. In event of a cash shortfall at that time, the limited partners will be required to make an additional cash contribution not to exceed $2,500 each ($7,500 collectively).

After two years of operations, the limited partners and the general partner will receive a 15 percent annual dividend based on their balance of contributed capital. The general partner will receive a dividend as if he had contributed 25 percent of all contributed capital.

Bank Financing

Based on our cash flow projections for the first year (see Exhibit 5), a short-term (one-year) loan for $10,000 will be required to cover the shortfall from April 1990 to December 1990. In addition, a line of credit for an additional $5,000 to $10,000 should be available in the event of unanticipated cash shortages brought on by promotional activities and purchase of additional containers due to increased demand. Cash flow in the second year, FY 1992, should be sufficient to retire any existing debt.

Exhibit 4

RECYCLE AMERICA, LTD.
Balance Sheets

	3/1/90	2/28/91	2/28/92
Current Assets:			
Cash	$ 3,300	$ 6,917	$43,577
Accounts receivable	500	500	500
Container inventory.......................	7,600	0	6,000
Prepaid expenses	200	220	250
Total current assets	11,600	7,637	50,327
Fixed assets:			
Trucks..................................	27,000	27,000	51,000
Furniture and equipment	3,600	3,600	5,600
Leashold improvements..................	800	800	800
Total fixed assets	31,400	31,400	57,400
Less: Accumulated			
depreciation	0	(6,280)	(16,328)
Net fixed assets	31,400	25,120	41,072
Total Assets..............................	$43,000	$32,757	$91,399
Current liabilities:			
Accounts payable	$ 0	$ 400	$ 600
Payroll liabilities.........................	0	1,500	2,500
Total current liabilities.................	0	1,900	3,100
Long-term liabilities:			
Lease obligation—Trucks	25,000	20,276	14,948
Dividend payable.......................	0	0	3,600
Total long-term liabilities	25,000	20,276	18,548
Net worth (owners' equity)	18,000	10,581	69,751
Total liabilities and net worth	$43,000	$32,757	$91,399

Exhibit 5

RECYCLE AMERICA, LTD.
Cash Flow Projections—1991
(by month)

	For year 1991	March	April	May	June	July	August	Sept.	Oct.	Nov.	Dec.	Jan.	Feb.
Cash receipts	$144,775	$24,900	$ 6,900	$8,500	$ 8,625	$10,225	$10,350	$10,350	$11,950	$11,950	$13,675	$13,675	$13,675
Operating expenses:													
Salaries and wages	82,364	5,703	5,703	6,991	6,991	6,991	6,991	6,991	6,991	7,253	7,253	7,253	7,253
Bonuses	10,763	448	448	551	560	663	1,703	672	775	775	887	887	2,394
Container expense	15,200	7,600	7,600										
Rent	7,700	1,100	600	600	600	600	600	600	600	600	600	600	600
Insurance	2,400	200	200	200	200	200	200	200	200	200	200	200	200
Advertising and promotion	2,340	1,010			320			1,010					
Truck maintenance	550		50	50	50	50	50	50	50	50	50	50	50
Gasoline	1,848	154	154	154	154	154	154	154	154	154	154	154	154
Utilities	1,500	125	125	125	125	125	125	125	125	125	125	125	125
Taxes and licenses	129	129											
Miscellaneous	900	75	75	75	75	75	75	75	75	75	75	75	75
Finance payments—Trucks	9,260	2,000	660	660	660	660	660	660	660	660	660	660	660
Computer and furnishing	4,400	4,400											
Total cash disbursements	139,354	22,944	15,615	9,406	9,735	9,518	10,558	10,537	9,630	9,892	10,004	10,004	11,511
Cash balance—Beginning	0	0	1,500	(7,215)	(8,121)	(9,231)	(8,524)	(8,732)	(8,919)	(6,599)	(4,541)	(870)	1,500
Net cash flow	5,422	1,956	(8,715)	(906)	(1,110)	707	(208)	(187)	2,320	2,058	3,671	3,671	2,164
Cash available	5,422	1,956	(7,215)	(8,121)	(9,231)	(8,524)	(8,732)	(8,919)	(6,599)	(4,541)	(870)	2,801	3,664
Desired cash balance	1,500	1,500	1,500	1,500	1,500	1,500	1,500	1,500	1,500	1,500	1,500	1,500	1,500
Short-term financing needed	0	0	8,715	9,621	10,731	10,024	10,232	10,419	8,099	6,041	2,370	0	0
Cash balance—Ending	$ 1,500	$ 1,500	($ 7,215)	($8,121)	($ 9,231)	($ 8,524)	($ 8,732)	($ 8,919)	($ 6,599)	($ 4,541)	($ 870)	$ 1,500	$ 1,500

CONCLUSION

From all indications, this is a viable project, satisfying a demonstrated—and rapidly growing—need. The management and staff of Recycle America, Ltd., have the experience and expertise needed to satisfy that need. And with the given equity financing and the expected debt financing, the company should be an operating and financial success by the second year.

REFERENCES

Prices of recyclable materials:

Prospect Recycling Company
333½ North Avenue
Athens, Georgia

Dothel Edwards, Director
Department of Solid Waste
City of Athens
1005 College Avenue
Athens, Georgia

Truck leasing:

Jim Biggers, Salesman
Brack-Rowe Chevrolet
2625 Atlanta Hwy.
Athens, Georgia

Number of residences in Athens:

Dothel Edwards, Director
Department of Solid Waste
City of Athens

Number of residences that can be served in one day:

Dothel Edwards, Director
Department of Solid Waste
City of Athens

Mr. Trash/Northeast Waste
    Disposal
Choice Waste Services, Inc.
4057 Lexington Road
Athens, Georgia

Recyclable weights per household (paper):

Dothel Edwards, Director
Department of Solid Waste
City of Athens

Athens Daily News
Circulation = 60,000

Percentage of expected participation:

Dothel Edwards, Director
Department of Solid Waste
City of Athens

One More Time [film]
Subject: Curbside/dumpsite
    recycling in Marin County,
    California
California Video Production

Source: Prepared by William Berg, Brad Crawford, David Herman, and Jamie Fristoe, of the University of Georgia School of Business, under the supervision of Dr. William L. Megginson.

THINGS YOU CAN DO WHEN A UNION TRIES TO ORGANIZE YOUR COMPANY

1. Keep outside organizers off premises.
2. Inform employees from time to time of the benefits they presently enjoy. (Avoid veiled promises or threats.)
3. Inform employees that signing a union authorization card does not mean they must vote for the union if there is an election.
4. Inform employees of the disadvantages of belonging to the union, such as the possibility of strikes, serving in a picket line, dues, fines, assessments, and rule by cliques or one individual.
5. Inform employees that you prefer to deal with them rather than have the union or any other outsider settle grievances.
6. Tell employees what you think about unions and about union policies.
7. Inform employees about any prior experience you have had with unions and whatever you know about the union officials trying to organize them.
8. Inform employees that the law permits you to hire a new employee to replace any employee who goes on strike for economic reasons.
9. Inform employees how their wages and benefits compare with those in unionized or nonunionized concerns where wages are lower and benefits less desirable.
10. Inform employees that the local union probably will be dominated by the international union, and that they, the members, will have little to say in its operations.
11. Inform employees of any untrue or misleading statements made by the organizer. You may give employees corrections of these statements.
12. Give opinions on union and union leaders, even in derogatory terms.
13. Distribute information about unions, such as disclosures of Congressional committees.
14. Reply to union attacks on company policies or practices.
15. Give legal position on labor-management matters.
16. Advise employees of their legal rights, provided you do not engage in or finance an employee suit or proceeding.
17. Declare a fixed policy in opposition to compulsory union membership contracts.
18. Campaign against a union seeking to represent the employees.
19. Insist that no solicitation of membership or discussion of union affairs be conducted during working time.

20. Administer discipline, layoff, and grievance procedures without regard to union membership or nonmembership of the employees involved.
21. Treat both union and nonunion employees alike in making assignments of preferred work or desired overtime.
22. Enforce plant rules impartially, regardless of the employee's membership activity in a union.
23. Tell employees, if they ask, that they are free to join or not to join any organization, so far as their status with the company is concerned.
24. Tell employees that their *personal* and *job* security will be determined by the economic prosperity of the company.

THINGS YOU CANNOT DO WHEN A UNION TRIES TO ORGANIZE YOUR COMPANY

1. Engage in surveillance of employees to determine who is and who is not participating in the union program; attend union meetings or engage in any undercover activities for this purpose.

2. Threaten, intimidate, or punish employees who engage in union activity.

3. Request information from employees about union matters, meetings, etc. Employees may, of their own volition, give such information without prompting. You may listen but not ask questions.

4. Prevent employee union representatives from soliciting memberships during nonworking time.

5. Grant wage increases, special concessions, or promises of any kind to keep the union out.

6. Question prospective employees about their affiliation with a labor organization.

7. Threaten to close up or move the plant, curtail operations, or reduce employee benefits.

8. Engage in any discriminatory practices, such as work assignments, overtime, layoffs, promotions, wage increases, or any other actions that could be regarded as preferential treatment for certain employees.

9. Discriminate against union people when disciplining employees for a specific action and permit nonunion employees to go unpunished for the same action.

10. Transfer workers on the basis of teaming up nonunion employees to separate them from union employees.

11. Deviate in any way from company policies for the primary purpose of eliminating a union employee.

12. Intimate, advise, or indicate, in any way, that unionization will force the company to lay off employees, take away company benefits or privileges enjoyed, or make any other changes that could be regarded as a curtailment of privileges.

13. Make statements to the effect that you will not deal with a union.

14. Give any financial support or other assistance to employees who support or oppose the union.

15. Visit the homes of employees to urge them to oppose or reject the union in its campaign.

16. Be a party to any petition or circular against the union or encourage employees to circulate such a petition.

17. Make any promises of promotions, benefits, wage increases, or any other items that would induce employees to oppose the union.

18. Engage in discussions or arguments that may lead to physical encounters with employees over the union question.

19. Use a third party to threaten or coerce a union member, or attempt to influence any employee's vote through this medium.

20. Question employees on whether or not they have or have not affiliated or signed with the union.

21. Use the word *never* in any predictions or attitudes about unions or their promises or demands.

22. Talk about tomorrow. When you give examples or reasons, you can talk about yesterday or today instead of tomorrow, to avoid making a prediction or conviction that may be interpreted as a threat or promise by the union or the NLRB.

GENERAL MANAGEMENT SELF-EVALUATION

You should now have successfully completed reading and studying the material in this text. We hope it has been of help to you in deciding whether to become an independent business owner-manager or, if you are already in that position, to continue as one. Those of you who currently own a small or independent business may wish to complete the following form as an evaluation of the general management of your organization.

As with the other appendixes, you should answer the questions as completely, objectively, and honestly as possible. When you have completed this, you may want to go over it again, objectively evaluating how you are doing. As an alternative, submit this to someone you trust—a consultant, banker, or friend—and have him or her evaluate how you are doing.

Good luck to you!

1. Organization
   a. Do you have a board of directors? Yes _____ No _____
   b. Who constitutes your board? _____
   _____
   _____
   c. How often do you meet?
      Monthly _____ Quarterly _____ Semiannually _____
      Yearly _____
   d. Are these meetings of any actual benefit? Yes _____ No _____
   e. Does any action result from suggestions made in board meetings?
      Yes _____ No _____

2. President—function and status
   a. How old are you? _____
   b. What is the state of your health?
      Excellent _____ Good _____ Fair _____ Poor _____
   c. Do you have any specific health problems? _____
   _____
   d. What do you do in running your company? _____
   _____
   _____
   e. Who looks after things when you are away? _____
   _____
   f. Are you satisfied with what goes on in your absence?
      Yes _____ No _____
   g. If, for some reason beyond your control, you were not able to be there to run the business, what would happen? _____
   _____
   _____

h. Could your business continue if you were killed in an automobile accident? Yes _____ No _____

i. Are you training someone to assume your managerial responsibilities? Yes _____ No _____

j. How long have you been training this person? _____

k. Why did you select him or her? _____

_____

l. How much consideration have you given to detailing the activities that take place in your company? _____

_____

_____

m. Have you assigned specific people to be responsible for specific activities? Yes _____ No _____

n. Are you happy with everybody's performance in his or her assigned role? Yes _____ No _____
With whose performance are you not happy?

_____

_____

Why? _____

_____

_____

o. Do you ever go through your organization and evaluate the performance effectiveness of those people assigned to some type of managerial responsibility? Yes _____ No _____

p. Do you expect these people to evaluate the people they supervise? Yes _____ No _____

q. Construct an organization chart of your business. First do it by functional activity without the people, then add the people.

3. Management information: Provide information that reveals what actually has occurred in a specific time frame. This information should be utilized to determine accurate costs, to plan more effectively for profits, and to determine asset-and-liability status.

4. Paper-flow analysis (Sales orders → Who → What happens → Where?)

a. What happens when an order is received? _____

_____

_____

Is a credit check obtained? Yes _____ No _____

b. How is it recorded? _____

_____

_____

c. If it is recorded on a sales order, what is the sequence of events that follows? Who handles it (step-by-step through production and shipment)? At the end, who takes final action and files orders?

_____

_____

_____

    d.   How do you maintain a file of orders? _____

_____

    e.   Who is responsible for seeing that orders are filled and shipped?

_____

    f.   Are the sales orders dated and numbered?
Yes _____ No _____

    g.   Are purchase orders issued on prenumbered forms?
Yes _____ No _____

    h.   How are purchase orders initiated? _____

_____

    i.   Trace the paper flow of purchase orders. _____

_____

    j.   What system of recordkeeping exists for purchases? Do you check invoices against purchase orders?
Yes _____ No _____

    k.   Do you have receiving reports? Yes _____ No _____ Who gets them? _____

_____

    l.   Are they matched against purchase orders and incoming invoices? Yes _____ No _____

    m.   Do you invoice your orders on prenumbered invoice forms?
Yes _____ No _____

    n.   How many copies of invoices are made? _____
Who receives them? _____

_____

    o.   When are invoices issued? _____

    p.   In sending invoice to customer, do you send copies of all appropriate documents, bill of lading, other related information?
Yes ___ No ___

    q.   What procedures control sales invoices? Are they transferred to accounts receivable, accounts receivable aged, etc? _____

_____

    r.   Is it possible that a salesperson or other person might make up an invoice, collect for it, and not turn in such receipts?
Yes _____ No _____

    s.   Do you keep a record of adjustments?
Yes _____ No _____

    t.   Who is authorized to make adjustments? _____

_____

There is danger of collusion between salesperson and customer in making adjustments. Do you permit salespeople to make adjustments?
Yes _____ No _____

u. Do you get sales reports on calls activity, information obtained, indication of expected activity or lack of it?
Yes _____ No _____

v. Do you develop a monthly sales expense, by salesperson?
Yes _____ No _____

w. Do you develop a production order? Yes _____ No _____
For what time period?

Daily	_____	Semiannually	_____
Weekly	_____	Quarterly	_____
Monthly	_____	Yearly	_____
Every six weeks	_____		

x. List paper-flow distribution by time through operating period.

_____
_____
_____
_____

5. Profit analysis
   a. Cost breakdown
      (1) Overhead _____
      (2) Operating
         (a) People _____
         (b) Material/goods _____
   b. How do you price your product? _____

   _____
   _____
   _____

   c. Collection cycle? _____
   d. How do you plan for profit? Bottom line? Pricing formula? Explain.

   _____
   _____

6. Marketing: What plans and what activities are taking place in your organization to assure a future market?
   a. Are you replacing retiring dealers with younger people?
   Yes _____ No _____
   b. Are you promoting the development of new customers to assure a continuing market? Yes _____ No _____
   c. How are you approaching the market to accommodate the changing age distribution in the population? Are you developing products with special appeal to the younger generation?
   Yes _____ No _____
   d. Other: _____

   _____
   _____
   _____

FREQUENTLY USED BUSINESS TERMS

accounts payable A delay in the required payment for a product that a vendor provides to the buyer.

accounts receivable Forms a current asset that results from giving credit to customers when they buy goods or services.

accruals Continually recurring short-term liabilities, such as accrued wages, accrued taxes, and accrued interest.

advertising A method of informing potential customers about, and for promoting sale of, company products or services.

affirmative action programs (AAPs) Guidelines developed to help firms eliminate discrimination against such groups as women and minorities during their recruitment, training, promotion, and other employment activities.

agent A person or business that acts as intermediary between purchaser and seller without actually taking title to the goods involved. See also *principal*.

amortize To liquidate on an installment basis. An amortized loan is one in which the principal amount of the loan is repaid in installments during the life of the loan.

angel capitalists Wealthy local businesspeople and other such investors usually willing to accept lower rates of return and make smaller investments than professional venture capitalists.

annuity A series of payments of a fixed amount for a specified number of years.

apprenticeship training Used to train workers performing skilled, craft-type jobs. It blends the learning of theory with practice in the techniques of the job.

articles of copartnership Drawn up during the preoperating period to show rights, duties, and responsibilities of each partner.

articles of incorporation The instrument by which a private corporation is formed and organized under the general corporation laws of a given state.

assets The physical, financial, and other values that a company has.

audit A formalized, methodical study, examination, and/or review of financial records in a company.

balance sheet A statement of the assets, liabilities, and owner's equity of a business at a given point of time.

bankrupt The state of a person or firm being unable to pay creditors, and therefore judged legally insolvent upon voluntary or creditor petition.

Better Business Bureau   A community organization, sponsored by local businesses, which acts to police unfair business practices.

board of directors   A group of people elected by the stockholders to represent their interests in running a corporation.

bona fide occupational qualification (BFOQ)   The provable requirement (or need) of a person of a specific sex for a given job.

bond   A long-term debt instrument used to finance the capital needs of a business or government unit. See also *fidelity bond*.

bonding   An obligation made binding by a money forfeiture.

book value   The accounting value of an asset, as recorded in a firm's accounting records.

break-even point   The volume of production or sales at which the firm's total costs equal its total income, so there's no profit or loss.

broker   An agent who negotiates contracts of purchase or sale but does not take control of the goods.

budget   An itemized summary of probable expenditures and revenues for a given period of time, with a systematic plan for achieving those figures.

budgetary control   Involves careful planning and control of all the company's activities, so that budgeted figures are reached.

business cycle   In business activity, a definable pattern of changes that is periodically repeated.

business ethics   Individual, personal guidelines that indicate how one should act rightly and justly in a business situation.

business incubators   Usually old buildings renovated, subdivided, and rented to new companies by private and governmental units to shelter young enterprises, offer moral support, and provide support services until they are ready to go on their own.

business plan   A statement, written by the individual(s) responsible for starting and operating a company, setting forth its objectives, the steps necessary to achieve them, the industry conditions, and the firm's financial needs that must be met.

buyer   The person who makes the purchase decision.

cafeteria-style benefit plan   Employees are told the dollar value of benefits they are entitled to receive, and then permitted to say how they want to receive the voluntary benefits.

capital   See *owner's equity*.

capital asset   An asset that has a life of more than one year and that is not bought and sold in the ordinary course of business. See also *assets*.

capital budgeting   The process of planning expenditures on assets whose returns are expected to extend beyond one year.

capital, debt   See *debt funding*.

capital, equity   See *equity capital*.

capital gains (losses)   Profits (or losses) on the sale of capital assets owned for six months or more.

capital stock   The value of the owners' investment in a corporation.

carrying costs   Costs associated with holding inventory, such as interest charges on funds invested in inventory, storage costs, and costs of inventory devaluation due to physical change, obsolescence, or market changes.

cash   Any easily transferred negotiable assets, such as coin, paper money, checks, money orders, and money on deposit in banks.

cash flow budget   A statement of how much cash will be needed to pay what expenses at what time, including cash income and cash expenditures.

casualty insurance   Automobile insurance (both collision and public liability) plus burglary, theft, robbery, plate glass, and health and accident insurance.

channels of distribution   See *marketing channel*.

chattel mortgage   A mortgage on any tangible, movable article of personal property (not real estate), such as equipment.

chemical dependency   Alcohol and drug addiction. See also *substance abuse*.

Civil Rights Act of 1964   A federal law that was passed to eliminate job discrimination based on race, color, religion, sex, or national origin and to ensure due process and equal protection under the law.

Clayton Act A statute that prohibits certain practices in commerce if they might substantially lessen competition.

coinsurance A provision requiring policyholders to buy insurance in an amount equal to a specified percentage of the property value, usually 80 percent.

commercial bank An ordinary bank of deposit and discount, with checking accounts, as distinguished from a savings bank.

commission Incentive compensation directly related to the sales or profits achieved by a salesperson.

common stock The ownership element of a corporation represented by shares of stock.

competitive edge A particular characteristic that makes a firm more attractive to customers than its competitors.

computer A calculator that is programmed to direct processing and can store large amounts of data.

consignment Goods placed by the supplier in the inventory of the consignee, with no payment being made until after the goods are sold.

consumer goods (products) Includes both goods and services; purchased for ultimate satisfaction of personal and/or household needs. See also *industrial goods*.

consumerism A consumer movement prodding business to improve the quality of its products and services and to expand consumer knowledge of them.

contingency fund Cash set aside for unexpected expenditures.

convenience goods Goods sold to the customer whose shopping time is limited and who buys frequently and routinely in many different stores. See also *impulse goods, shopping goods,* and *specialty goods*.

cooperative An organization composed of independent producers, wholesalers, retailers, consumers, or a combination thereof that acts collectively in buying or selling or both.

copyright The exclusive right that protects creators of "original works of authorship," such as artistic, literary, dramatic, and musical works.

corporation A business formed and owned by a group of people, called stockholders, and given certain rights, privileges, and liabilities by law.

cost-benefit analysis An analytic technique of weighing the costs of a project or investment against the benefits derived therefrom.

cost-plus pricing Pricing based upon the cost of producing the good or service.

credit limit Represents the maximum amount of credit to be extended to customers based on their financial condition.

credit line A guide for approving customers' requests to charge purchases.

credit trade See *trade credit*.

credit union An organization, usually composed of employees, whose purpose is to provide financial services for employees.

current assets Assets that turn over within one year.

current liabilities Obligations to be paid within one year.

current ratio Current assets divided by current liabilities.

debenture A bond backed by the faith and credit of the issuing firm.

debt funding Funding consisting of money that a firm has borrowed and has contracted to pay interest on and to repay by a certain date.

depreciation The accounting procedure for apportioning the cost of fixed assets as a part of the expense of each period. Thus, the cost is amortized over a defined period of time.

distribution channels See *marketing channel*.

double-entry system A system of accounting that requires a transaction to be entered in two places.

Dun & Bradstreet A mercantile agency that offers credit ratings, financial analyses, and other financial services, usually on a contractual basis.

EBIT Abbreviation for earnings before interest and taxes.

economic order quantity (EOQ) The optimum (lowest-cost) quantity of merchandise that should be purchased per order.

EEOC   See *Equal Employment Opportunity Commission.*

employee benefits   The rewards and services provided to workers in addition to their regular earnings.

employee referral   A present employee recommends a friend or acquaintance for a job in the same business.

employee stock ownership plan (ESOP)   A modification of profit sharing where the ESOP borrows money, purchases a block of the company's stock, and allocates it to the employees on the basis of salaries and/or longevity.

employer liability insurance   Provides for medical care, lump sums for death and dismemberment, benefits for disablement by occupational disease, and income payments for disabled workers or their dependents.

entrepreneur   A person who organizes, manages, and assumes the risks of a business venture.

Environmental Protection Agency (EPA)   An administrative agency set up to protect and improve the quality of the environment.

EOQ   See *economic order quantity.*

EPA   See *Environmental Protection Agency.*

Equal Employment Opportunity Commission (EEOC)   The federal administrative agency responsible for enforcing the provisions of the Civil Rights Act of 1964 and promoting voluntary action programs for equal employment opportunities.

equity   The net worth of a business, consisting of capital stocks, capital (or paid-in) surplus, earned surplus (or retained earnings), and, occasionally, certain net worth reserves.

equity capital   The assets of the firm that the owner(s) have invested.

estate planning   The preparation for the transfer of equity of an owner when death occurs.

ethics, business   See *business ethics.*

excise tax   A tax on the manufacture, sale, or consumption of specified commodities.

executive summary   A brief summary of the most important information in a business plan.

export marketing   The practice of selling a firm's products or services to international markets.

factoring   A method of financing accounts receivable under which a firm sells its accounts receivable (generally without recourse) to a financial institution (the factor).

Fair Labor Standards Act (FLSA)   An act covering minimum wages, maximum working hours per week, payment of overtime, and restrictions on child labor.

FDA   See *Food and Drug Administration.*

Federal Trade Commission (FTC)   An independent administrative agency that assists in the enforcement of the Clayton Act and other laws for maintaining free competitive enterprise as the keystone of the American economic system.

fidelity bond   An insurance bond usually written to cover those people who have control over a business's funds, to protect the business against loss.

FIFO (first-in, first-out)   Accounting method used to value inventory for pricing purposes, which charges sales with the cost of goods received first.

financial structure   Consists of the assets, liabilities, and equity accounts of a company at a given time.

fixed assets   Business assets that are of a relatively permanent nature and are necessary for the functioning of the firm.

fixed costs (expenses)   Costs that do not vary with changes in output.

flexitime   An arrangement under which employees may schedule their own hours for starting and stopping work, as long as they are present during certain required hours.

Food and Drug Administration (FDA)   An agency that acts to protect the nation against impure and unsafe foods, drugs, cosmetics, and other potential hazards.

401(k) plans   Permit workers to place up to a certain amount of their wages each year in tax-deferred retirement savings plans.

franchise   An agreement through which a retailer is given exclusive rights to sell specified goods or to use a particular product name.

fringe benefits See *employee benefits.*
FTC See *Federal Trade Commission.*

general partnership Each partner participates as an equal in managing the business and is held liable for the acts of other partners.

implied warranty See *warranty, implied.*
impulse goods Goods bought on sight by consumers in order to satisfy a desire that is strongly felt at the moment. See also *convenience goods, shopping goods,* and *specialty goods.*
incentive wage The extra compensation paid for all production over a specified amount.
incubator, business See *business incubators.*
individual retirement account (IRA) Accounts open to employees to replace pension programs.
industrial goods (products) Include both goods and services, bought for use in a firm's operations or to make other products. See also *consumer goods.*
industrial insurance See *workers' compensation.*
inflation The phenomenon of generally rising prices, attributed to the injection into the economy of more currency than volume of goods and services.
internship training Combines education at a school or college with on-the-job training at a cooperating business.
inventory The total of items of tangible property that a firm will use up or sell during a short time, including goods, material, and supplies.
investment capital See *owners' equity.*

job specifications Written statement of details of work assignment and of qualifications needed to fulfill the job acceptably.
Job Training Partnership Act (JTPA) Underwrites the most important public training programs currently being used to help small business.
joint venture A form of temporary partnership whereby two or more persons or firms join together in a single endeavor to make a profit.

just-in-time delivery (JIT) Process by which the materials are delivered to the user at the time needed for production.
Keogh retirement plans Permit self-employed persons and partnerships to set aside a certain amount of the person's eligible total earnings and deduct it from income taxes.
layout The arrangement of the fixtures, equipment, machinery, furnishings, and other physical aspects of the business.
lead time The time between one event and another; e.g., the time from ordering an item until it is received in stock.
leased manpower Employees obtained from some outside firm that specializes in performing a given service. They may work full time for a leasing firm and only part time for a small employer.
leverage The use of external funds (as opposed to equity) to generate profits.
leveraged buyout (LBO) A practice of purchasing the assets or stock of a company by the use of a significant amount of borrowed funds.
liabilities Financial obligations of a business.
LIFO (last-in, first-out) Inventory costing method that charges sales with last, or current, cost of inventory.
limited partnership An agreement between two or more people to conduct a business with one or more special partners who contribute capital but who do not participate in management, and are not held liable for the debts of the partnership.
line of credit An arrangement whereby a financial institution commits itself to lend to a firm or individual a specified maximum amount of funds during a specified period.
liquidity A firm's cash position and its ability to meet maturing obligations.
living trust A legal document that resembles a will, but, in addition to providing for distribution of personal assets upon death, contains instructions for managing those assets should the person become disabled.
long-term liabilities Obligations to pay someone, with terms of one year or longer. Examples are bonds and mortgages.

loss leader   A product priced at a loss or no profit for the purpose of attracting patronage to a store.

management by objectives (MBO)   A management technique of defining goals for subordinates through agreement of supervisor and subordinates. It offers continual feedback to subordinates.

management information system (MIS)   A system designed to process, record, report, and/or direct information into a usable form.

manufacturer   A maker, producer, or processor of raw material into a finished product.

marginal income   Increase in profit per dollar of increase in sales volume.

marketing   Activities concerned with the sale and distribution of a firm's products or services according to needs of customers.

marketing channel   The pipeline through which a product flows on its way to the ultimate consumer.

marketing concept   The way in which a firm chooses to give special consideration to the needs, desires, and wishes of prospective and present customers.

marketing mix   A blend, in the proper proportions, of the basic elements of product, price, promotion, and place into an integrated marketing program.

marketing strategy   Consists of setting objectives, choosing target market(s), and developing an effective marketing mix.

market research   The systematic gathering, recording, and analyzing of data about problems relating to the marketing of goods and services.

market segmentation   A marketing strategy consciously developed to produce a product or service that embodies characteristics preferred by a small, select part of a total market.

market share   The percentage of the total market that the firm has or can obtain.

markup   The percentage change from the purchase price or the cost of goods sold to the selling price.

MBO   See *management by objectives.*

merchandising   The promotional effort made for a product or service in a retailing firm.

merger   The process by which one firm acquires the assets and liabilities of another firm.

mission   The long-term vision of what the firm is trying to become.

modes of transportation   See *transportation modes.*

mortgage loan   A long-term debt secured by real property to be used to repay the loan in case of default.

motivation   The inner state that activates or moves a person, including drives, desires, and/or motives.

National Labor Relations Act (NLRA)   The basic labor law of the land, which requires management to bargain with the union if a majority of its employees desire to unionize.

negotiable instrument   An instrument in writing and signed, containing an unconditional order or promise to pay a specific amount of money to order or to bearer at a definite time or on demand.

notes payable   Written obligations to pay, which give the company a longer period before payment is required and usually require payment of interest. An example is a 90-day note.

objectives   Purposes, goals, and desired results for the company and its parts.

Occupational Safety and Health Act   Establishes specific safety standards and requires the installation of safety appliances by employers and the use of safety equipment by employees.

odd pricing   Setting the price of goods to end in an odd number, such as $9.95.

on-the-job training (OJT)   Involves actual performance of work duties by the employee under the supervision and guidance of the owner, manager, or a trained worker or instructor.

operating budget   Its purpose is forecasting sales and allocating financial resources and supplies.

overhead   All the costs of a business other than direct labor and materials.

owner's equity   Those assets left over after all creditors have been paid. The two sources of equity are owner investment and retained earnings from profitable operations.

partnership A business owned by two or more persons and in which one or more owners have unlimited liability for the firm's debts. See also *general partnership* and *limited partnership*.

penetration pricing Pricing strategy involving the use of a relatively low entry price as compared with competitive offerings, based on the theory that this initial low price will help secure market acceptance. Compare with *skimming pricing*.

PERT (program evaluation and review technique) Used to schedule complicated sequences of operations, each of which may be dependent on completing other activity(ies).

policies Overall guides for action and decision making to provide some consistency in company operations.

preferred stock A type of company financing that has characteristics fitting between bonds and common stock.

price-earnings ratio The ratio of price per share to earnings per share.

principal A person who agrees to let an agent act on his or her behalf. See also *agent*.

producer See *manufacturer*.

production (operations) The creation of value or wealth by converting inputs to outputs that customers buy.

product life cycle Comprises four stages: introduction, growth, maturity, and decline.

product line A group of products that are closely related because they satisfy a class of needs, are used together, are sold to the same customer groups, are marketed through the same type of outlet, or fall within a given price range.

product/service liability The concept that producers and marketers are responsible for injuries or damages caused by their product(s).

profit (income) The difference between total revenue received and total expenses paid out.

profit and loss statement A statement prepared periodically showing revenues, expenses, and profit (or loss) from doing business.

profit motive The desire to enter a business or take an action in business in order to make a profit.

profit sharing An arrangement whereby employees receive a prescribed share of the company's profits.

proprietorship See *sole proprietorship*.

quality Characteristics of products being assessed; the probability that products will meet established standards.

quality circles (QC) Small, organized work groups meeting periodically to find ways to improve quality and productivity.

quality control The process by which a producer ensures that finished goods and services meet customer expectations.

ratios The established relationships between two or more variables that evaluate a firm's financial condition.

reorder point The inventory level at which the business places an order to replenish inventory up to a predetermined level.

retailer A merchant or agent whose main business is to buy goods for resale to the ultimate consumer.

retained earnings The accumulation of the profits that are not distributed to the owners in the form of cash dividends.

return on equity (ROE) The ratio of net profit to net worth used to evaluate the percentage return owners receive on the net worth of their company. Also called *return on net worth* and *return on investment (ROI)*.

revenue (sales income) The return from services performed or goods sold, received by the company in the form of cash or credit.

right-to-work laws Effective in 21 states, these laws prohibit the union shop agreement, whereby workers must join a union as a condition of employment.

salary A fixed compensation paid regularly to employees for services performed.

sales promotion Consists of activities that try to make other sales efforts more effective.

SBA See *Small Business Administration*.

SBICs See *small business investment companies*.

S Corporation A special type of corporation used to eliminate multiple taxation and its attendant paperwork.

self-insurance   Acting as an insurance company for oneself. Requires adequate finances and broadly diversified risks.

service business   A firm filling nonproduct needs of customers. Examples include banking and repairing firms.

Service Corps of Retired Executives (SCORE)   A volunteer group of retired and active men and women from all walks of business and industry formed into chapters around the nation that specialize in helping people develop their business ideas.

service objectives   The aim of producing and selling to meet the needs of customers at a fair price.

shopping goods   Items for which buyers are willing to put forth considerable effort in planning and making the purchase. See also *convenience goods, impulse goods,* and *specialty goods.*

short-term loans   Loans scheduled to be repaid within one year. Also called *short-term securities.*

simplified employee pension (SEP) plan   Called a SEP/IRA, it helps workers provide for their own retirement by opening an IRA and having the employer pay up to a certain percent of their salary into it each year.

skimming pricing   A pricing strategy involving the use of a relatively high initial price compared to the prices of competitive offerings, in order to "skim off the cream" of profits rapidly. Compare with *penetration pricing.*

small business   A firm that is independently owned and operated and is not dominant in its field of operation.

Small Business Administration (SBA)   A governmental unit formed to aid small businesses and their establishment.

small business investment companies (SBICs)   Private, licensed, and regulated firms that make "venture" investments in small enterprises.

social responsibility   The aim of being a responsible citizen in treatment of people internal and external to the company.

Social Security   A federal government program that provides support for the retired, widowed, disabled, and their dependents.

software   Programs designed to direct computers in performing desired work.

sole proprietorship   A business owned by one person who has unlimited liability for the firm's debts.

specialty goods   Items that are bought infrequently at particular outlets after a special effort. See also *convenience goods, impulse goods,* and *shopping goods.*

standard   A measure to which performance should conform, such as for quality, productivity, cost, or conduct.

stock   Evidence of equity in a corporation, in the form of either common or preferred stock.

stock dividend   A dividend paid in additional shares rather than in cash.

stock-out   A situation in which the demand for an item cannot be filled from inventory.

strategic plan   A major, comprehensive, long-term plan providing direction for a firm to accomplish its mission.

strategy   A plan of action to attain objectives.

substance abuse   Alcohol and drug addiction are increasingly posing a problem for small businesses as well as large ones. See also *chemical dependency.*

surety bond   An insurance provision providing protection against the failure of others to fulfill contractual obligations.

target market   The segment of the total market selected for a concentration of promotional effort.

telemarketing   Using computers to dial phone numbers, deliver a short prerecorded message, and take a message requesting more information.

temporaries   Short-time or limited-time workers.

test marketing   Process of selecting specific areas considered reasonably typical of the total market and introducing the product with a marketing campaign in that area.

trade credit   Inter-firm debt arising through credit sales and recorded as an account receivable by the seller and as an account payable by the buyer.

trademark   A brand name or logo that is given legal protection because it refers exclusively to a product. It may be used only by the trademark owner.

transportation modes   Methods used to take products (and people) from place to place.

trust   An entity designed to hold and distribute assets for the benefit of others. See also *living trust*.

unemployment insurance   Insurance that is provided for by the Social Security Act.

Uniform Commercial Code (UCC)   A set of uniform model statutes to govern business and commercial transactions in all 50 states.

unit pricing   Provides for the listing of the product's price in terms of some measurement such as an ounce, a pint, or a yard.

variable costs (expenses)   Expenses that change in relation to output: when production is low the expenses are low, and when production rises the expenses rise also.

venture capital clubs   Groups set up by private and public organizations to bring together people with new business concepts and those interested in financing such ideas. For a fee, a member can apply for funding from a venture capitalist.

venture capitalists   Firms composed of wealthy individuals who make equity investments in small firms with fast-growth opportunities.

wages   A payment for labor or services, usually of money, according to contract, at an hourly, daily, or piecework rate.

warranty   A guarantee to the buyer that the producer will replace a product or refund its purchase price if the product proves to be defective during a specified period of time.

warranty, express   A specific representation made by the seller regarding the product, often in the form of a warranty card to be completed and returned by the buyer.

warranty, implied   Consists of the sanctions legally imposed on sellers by the nature of their operations, as buyers have a right to expect a certain quality from a product. Unless disclaimed before the sale in writing, they automatically apply.

wholesaler   A business unit that buys and resells merchandise to retailers and other merchants and/or to industrial, institutional, and commercial users.

workers' compensation   Payments made to employees for losses from accidents and occupational diseases.

working capital   Current assets less current liabilities.

FREQUENTLY USED COMPUTER TERMS

baud   Transmission speed of a modem or printer driver.

bit   Binary digit, smallest unit of computer information.

bulletin board   Computer network with data and programs available to others.

byte   Unit of information for PCs (equals 8 bits).

CAD/CAM   Computer Aided Design/Computer Aided Manufacture—hardware and software.

chip   Processing unit for computer.

communications package   See *modem.*

compatibility   Ability of components of a system to work together.

compile   See *programming language.*

CPU   Central processing unit—"brains" of the computer.

CRT   Cathode ray tube—video display of a PC.

data   Facts.

data base management software   Program that organizes and presents large amount of data.

desktop publishing package   Software that combines graphics and text into camera-ready printout.

disk controller   Computer board needed for disk drive communication.

disk drive   Large-capacity storage device; can be floppy disk or hard disk/card.

DOS   Disk operating system—software to start and run other programs.

expert system   Program mimicking "expert" decision making.

fax   Facsimile; machine to send and receive photocopy.

floppy disk   See *disk drive.*

general-purpose software   Programs for a variety of applications.

graphics package   Program for creating pictures, graphs, or charts.

hard disk/card   See *disk drive.*

hardware   Physical computer equipment.

hertz   Cycles per second; electronic measure of speed.

idea or **thought processors**   Software designed to facilitate organizing ideas.

information   Data organized in such a way that it has meaning.

information service   Sources from which information can be bought.

integrated software   Multipurpose software package.

interpreter   See *programming language.*

LAN   *Local Area Network*—interconnected microcomputers.

laptop   Small portable computer.

light pen   Pointer for selecting options from video screen.

Macintosh®   Apple microcomputer known for its easy user interface or "user-friendliness" and its graphics capabilities.

magnetic tape   High-volume sequential storage device.

mainframe   Large multiuser computer.

MB   *Megabyte*—binary million bytes—common unit of storage.

megahertz   Unit of computer processing speed.

microcomputer or **personal computer (PC)**   Small, desktop computer.

minicomputer   Small multiuser computer.

MIPS   *Millions of instructions per second.*

modem   *Modulator/demodulator*; device to connect a computer with another over a telephone line; needs *communications package* to use.

mouse   External mechanical device to move cursor on a computer screen to select options.

MS-DOS   *Microsoft's DOS*—an industry standard.

netware   Software necessary to run a local area network.

OS   *Operating system*—control program for computer.

OS/2   New Microsoft DOS designed for new technology.

package   Term applied to software with a specific purpose.

PC   Personal computer.

PC-DOS   Version of DOS created for IBM® PC.

programming language   Language to direct the computer (BASIC, Pascal, FORTRAN, COBOL, C, and Assembler); must be translated into computer language by an *interpreter*—which runs as it translates—or a *compiler*—which translates and then runs.

RAM   *Random Access Memory*—usable internal computer memory.

ROM   *Read Only Memory*—unchangeable computer memory used for specialized applications.

software   Programs to run a computer.

spreadsheet   Program for tabular manipulation of numeric data.

terminal   Input/output device; includes keyboard and video display.

time sharing   Piecemeal use of large computer by unrelated users.

user interface   Means of user-computer communication.

video board   Printed circuit board that controls video display (current standards include Hercules, CGA, EGA, and VGA).

word processors   "Intelligent typewriter" software.

workstation   Single-user, special-purpose microcomputer.

A

Ability Based on Long Experience (ABLE), 457
Accelerated cost recovery system, 734
Accounting
  accounts receivable recording, 634–35
  for expenses, 637–39
  inventory records, 635–37
  MIS and, 630–33
  payables recording, 635
  recording cash, 634
  small business and, 568–70
  systems, 166
  taxes and, 730–31, 744–45
Accounts payable, 573
  recording of, 635
Accounts receivable, 571–72
  budgetary control and, 601–2
  collectability of, 608–9
  computerization of, 687
  recording, 634–35
Accrual basis, 638
  tax accounting and, 731
Accumulated depreciation, 639
Acid test, 608
Activities, 385
Activities-oriented manager, 48
Advertising, 279, 506
  developing the message, 510–11
  measuring results of, 511–12
  media selection, 508–10
  program development, 507
  setting the budget, 508
  types of, 506–7
  using agencies, 511
Age Discrimination in Employment Act of 1967, 294
Age-groups, 455
Agency, 702
Agent, 702
Agent wholesalers, 494
Agricultural loans, 216
Agriculture, U.S. Department of, 706
AIDA, 490
AIDS, 288

Alcoholism, 339
American Association of Community and Junior Colleges, 8
American Business Information, 59
American Express, 21
American Motors, 11
Anchor stores, 382
Anders Book Stores, 401–2
Angel capitalists, 206
Angelo's Supermarkets, 556–61
Apple Computer, 10, 63, 73
Apprenticeship training, 290
Armed robbery, 678
Articles of copartnership, 230
Articles of incorporation, 232
Asian small businesses, 71–72
Aspirations, 49
Assets, 570
  productivity of, 608
Associated Credit Bureaus, Inc., 475
Association of Collegiate Entrepreneurs (ACE), 9
Atomic Energy Act, 333
Attitude (image-building) advertising, 512
Attitudes, 49–51
  communication and, 306–7
Audit, 603
  white-collar crime and, 685–86
Autocratic leadership, 304
Automatic teller machines (ATM), 496
Automotive franchises, 99
Average-cost method, 637, 735
Avian Corporation, 565–66

B

Baby-boomers, 455–57
Background information, applicant, 281–84
Bacon, Francis, 56
Balance sheet, 570
Bankruptcy, 703
Banks, 209
Bares, Jack, 723
Basic Guide to Exporting, 705
Batch processing, 621–22
Beary Best Cookies, 32, 740
  case study, 356–63

Ben & Jerry's Homemade, Inc., 302
Ben Franklin Stores, 4
Best Western Motels, 87
Biographical information, 282–83
Black Enterprise, 67
Blacks
  demographics, 514
  small business and, 67–69
Block layout, 389
Blue Cross/Blue Shield, 38
Board of directors, 233
Bodenstab, Charles J., 176
Bona fide occupational qualification (BFOQ), 294
Bonds, 199
Bonuses, 317
Boutwell, Aubrey D., 568
Bowman-Upton, Nancy, 758, 760
Break-even chart, 582
  illustrated, 583
Broker, 493
Broun, Heywood, 520
Budgetary control, 600
  auditing and, 603
  credit/accounts receivable, 601–2
Budgets, 162
  for advertising, 508
  benefits of, 595
  types of, 596
Building contractor
  pricing and, 469
  theft prevention and, 683–84
Building permits, 729
Burch, John G., 186
Bureau of Labor Statistics, 8
  growth industries and, 58–59
  statistics on safety, 332
Burger King, 273
Burke, Edmund, 222
Burstiner, Irving, 38
Busby, Jim, 177
Business continuation life insurance, 675
Business cycles, 6
Business environment
  buying decision and, 143–44
  industry future and, 60–62
Business format franchising, 86–90

Business incubators, 206–7
Business interruption coverage, 673
Business objectives, achieving, 33–34
Business plan, 178
　Asian entrepreneurs and, 72
　components of, 181–85
　implementation of, 187–88
　preparation of, 180–81
　presentation of, 186–87
　purpose of, 178–79
　sample, 803–20
Business Plan for Small Manufacturers, 186
Business Risks International, Inc., 669
Business Week Newsletter for Family-Owned Businesses, 11
Buying roles, 450

C

Cadwell, Carlton, 222
Cafeteria-style pension plans, 322
Campus recruitment, 280
Capital, 44
　acquiring, 42
Capital budget, 596
Capital leases, 198
Capital stock, 573
Cappo, Joe, 456
Careers USA, Inc., 101
Carnegie, Andrew, 272
Carnegie, Dale, 488
Carson, Johnny, 701
Cash, 570
　crime prevention and, 679
Cash basis, 638
Cash budgets, 195–96
Cash dividends, 574
Cash flow, 44, 596
Cash flow budget, 596
　preparation of, 598–600
　rationale for, 600
Cash requirements, 168–71
Cash value depreciation, 734
Casualty insurance, 673
Census, U.S. Bureau of, 15, 19, 705
　electronic service, 538
　market research data and, 136
Certified Development Company Program, 215
Chappell, Barbara, 48
Chapter 11, 703
Charter, corporate, 232
Chattel mortgage loan, 199–200

Cherubini, Georgio, 693–94
Chrysler, 11, 68
Churchill, Neil, 44
Cironi's Sewing Center, 113–17
Civil law, 696
Civil recovery, 681
Civil restitution, 681
Civil Rights Act, 293, 715
Clark, Alexander, 590
Clayton, Fred, 791–92
CleanDrum, Inc., 42, 94, 166, 200, 492, 621, 707
　case study (A), 107–9
　case study (B), 247–51
　case study (C), 352–54
　case study (D), 432–36
　case study (E), 548–50
　case study (F), 643–47
　case study (G), 773–75
Coaching, 292
Codex Corporation, 280
Coinsurance, 673
Collection period ratio, 608–9
Collection procedures, 476
Combination layout, 388–89
Commerce, U.S. Department of, 705
　on franchise sales, 82
　franchising and, 87–88, 94, 98
　market research and, 136
　small business help and, 704
Commercial banks, 209–10
Commercial finance companies, 211
Commission-only compensation plan, 497
Commissions, 317
Committee for Economic Development, 11
Commitment, 50
Common law, 695
Common stock, 198
Common stockholders, 196
Communication, 304
　barriers to, 306
　improvement of, 306–7
　process of, 305–6
COMPAQ Computer, 208–9
Compensation
　accounting for, 638
　family business and, 757
　legal influences, 314–15
　managerial/professional personnel and, 318
　preferred methods of, 498
　sales people, 497–98
　setting rates of pay, 315

Competition, 136
　computer profiles, 161
　estimating size of, 137–38
　marketing strategy and, 481
　small firms and, 19
Competitive edge, 159
　seeking, 452–53
Composition of creditors, 703
Comprehensive Accounting Corporation, 7, 567–68
Compu-Scan, 286
Computerized business start-ups, 130
Computers, 624
　computerized credit companies, 217
　inventory and, 414
　security and, 627–28
　small business innovation and, 18
　small business role, 622–24
　strength/weaknesses of, 624–26
Computer security, 684
Connie's Confections, 436–38
Consideration, 699
Consignment selling, 209
Consumer behavior, 449
Consumer decision process, 449
Consumerism, 452
Consumer products, 459
　distribution channels for, 490–91
Consumer Product Safety Commission (CPSC), 716
Consumer promotions, 513
Contracts, 697–99
Control, 73
Controlling operations, 592–93
　performance feedback, 603–5
　systems for, 593–94
Convenience goods, 380
Convenience stores, 99, 380
Conversion process, 370–71
Cooperative Extension Service, 216, 706
Cooperatives, 234–35
Copyright, 701
Corporate officers, 233
Corporation, 225
　defined, 230–32
　federal income taxes, 733–36
　formation of, 232
　governing process of, 233
Cost-plus pricing, 469
Counseling, 336
　areas needing, 337–41
　employees, 336–37
Cover sheet, 181

Credit cards, 474
  marketing research and, 541–42
  sales summaries and, 633, 635
Credit doctor, 685
Credit management, 473
  budgetary control and, 601–2
  methods of payment, 473–74
  policies and, 474–76
Credit risks, 475
Credit sales, 195–96
  budgetary control and, 601
Crime prevention, 677–78
Criminal law, 695
Critical path method (CPM), 424
Critical path scheduling, 424–25
Cultural networks, 71
Current assets, 570–72
  collectability of, 608–9
Current liabilities, 573
  budgetary control and, 602
Current ratio, 606
  debt management and, 608
Customer needs, 450–51
Cycle of information, 616

D

Davidow, William H., 446
Debentures, 199
Debt capital, 196
Debt financing
  commercial and industrial institu-
    tions, 209–11
  SBA and, 211–15
Debt management, 217
  ratios for measuring, 608
Debtor's insolvency, 703
Debt securities placement, 199
Deed, 700
Deficit Reduction Act of 1984,
  736
Delaware corporation, 232
Delegation, 237
  small-firm problem, 238–39
  and time management, 47
Delivery system, 373
  location and, 377
Democratic (participative) leader-
  ship, 304
Depreciation, 582, 638
  accounting for, 638–39
  taxes and, 734
Digital Equipment Corporation, 63
Dince, Robert, 590
Direct loans, 214–15
Direct taxes, 724

Discipline, employee, 338
  documenting cases, 342
  encouraging self-discipline, 341
  graduated penalties, 343
  methods for, 342–44
Disclosure documents, 91
Discontinuances, 74
Discounts and allowances, 469–70
Distribution channel, 490; *see also*
  Intermediary selling
  consumer goods and, 490–91
  factors in choosing, 492–93
  industrial goods and, 491–92
District Export Councils (DECs),
  537, 705
Dividends, 574
Division of labor, 238
Doerflinger, Thomas, 614
Domino's Pizza, 373, 515
Downtown locations, 381
Drozdow, Nancy, 752
Drucker, Peter, 368, 400
Drug addiction, 339
Drug-Free Workplace Act, 340
Drug-Free Workplace Rules, 340
Due process, 695
Dun & Bradstreet, 575

E

Ebony, 39
Exchange controls, 535
Eckert, J. Presper, 19, 33, 188
Economic Development Adminis-
  tration (EDA), 215–16
Economic order quantity (EOQ),
  413–14
EEO; *see* Equal employment oppor-
  tunity (EEO)
Electronic Data Systems (EDS), 38
Electronic scanners, 137
Electronics franchises, 99
Eliot, T. S., 750
Embargoes, 535
Employee
  identification, 686
  theft and, 681–82
Employee benefits, 319–20
  legal requirements and, 320
  voluntary benefits, 320–22
Employee complaints, 341
Employee evaluation, 313
Employee referrals, 280
Employee Retirement Income Secu-
  rity Act (ERISA), 321, 736
Employees
  external hiring sources, 276–79

Employees—*Cont.*
  internal hiring sources of, 273–76
  learning experience and, 9
  recruiting, 279
  selection process, 281
  termination of, 295
Employee Stock Ownership Plans
  (ESOPs), 208–9
  monetary motivations and, 318
  taxes and, 731
Employer identification number,
  706, 728
Employer liability insurance, 674
Employment
  franchising and, 83
  small business and, 15–16
Employment agencies, 280
Employment at will, 295
Employment tests, 284
Engeleiter, Susan, 692
Entrepreneur(s), 15, 92
  characteristics for, 10
  self-test, 51
  useful publications for, 797
Entrepreneurial checklists
  analyzing the desirability of an ex-
    isting business, 800–802
  desirability of buying a franchise,
    802
  start a new business or buy an
    existing one, 799–800
Entrepreneurial venture, 13
  and small business compared, 12–
    15
Entrepreneurial Woman, 11
Environment, external, 156–57
Environmental Protection Agency
  (EPA), 336, 715
Equal employment opportunity
  (EEO), 280
  application of laws, 294–95
  enforcing laws, 295
  interviewing and, 287
  laws pertaining to, 293–94
Equal Employment Opportunity
  Commission (EEOC), 295
Equal Pay Act of 1963, 315
Equity, 196
  optimum level of, 609
Equity capital, 196
Equity financing, 200
  angel capitalists and, 206
  role of, 196–97
  SBICs and, 201–2
  venture capitalists and, 202–6
Equity securities, 198
Estate planning, 742–44, 768
Ethics, business, 716

Ethnic differences, 514–15
European Economic Community (EEC), 527
Evans, Murry, 301
Excise tax, 729
Exclusive bargaining agent, 344
Executive branch, 695
Executive development programs, 292
Executive summary, 181–83
  venture capitalists and, 205
Expenses, 575
  profit planning and, 578
  tax deductible, 734
Expertise, 45
Export Counseling Center (ECC), 705
Export-Import Bank, 539, 705
Exporting, 523
  artificial barriers to, 535
  attitudinal barriers to, 535–36
  choosing entry-market, 529–32
  choosing method of, 532–33
  developing plan, 529
  financial help, 539
  firm's potential for, 528–29
  information and guidance for, 537–38
  natural barriers to, 533–35
  small firms and, 524–25
Express contract, 699
Express warranties, 700
Extended-coverage endorsement, 673

F

Facilities layout, 386
  crime prevention and, 678–80
  types of, 387–91
Facilities planning, 385–86
  implementation of, 392
Failures, business, 74
  financing and, 22
  rates of, 61
  threat of, 74–75
Fair Labor Standards Act of 1938, 294, 314, 715
Fair trade laws, 16
Falvey, Jack, 488
Family Business Magazine, 11
Family hierarchy, 754
Family-owned businesses, 752–53
  capital availability, 758
  compensation in, 757
  family hierarchy and, 754
  family role in, 753–54

Family-owned businesses—*Cont.*
  incompetent family members and, 755–57
  managerial limitations, 757–58
  ownership succession and, 758–60, 762–64
  selling of, 765–67, 769
Family partnerships, 743
Farmers Home Administration, 216, 706
Farr, Mel, 68, 489
Fast foods, 98
Federal Bar Association, 537
Federal Credit Insurance Association (FCIA), 539
Federal Insurance Contributions Act (FICA), 737
Federal Land Bank Administration, 706
Federal Land Bank Association, 216
Federal Mine Safety Act, 333
Federal Trade Commission (FTC), 91, 715
Federal Unemployment Tax, 738
Feedback, 603–4
Fidelity bonds, 675
  white-collar crimes and, 686
Financial analysis, 185
Financial audit, 603
Financial condition
  evaluation of, 605–6
  profit evaluation and, 607–8
  using ratios and, 606–7
Financial incentives, 315–18
Financial leverage, 197
Financial needs, estimating, 194–96
Financial planning, role of, 166
Financial position, changes in, 567–68
Financial resources, 159
Financial statements, 639
Financial structure
  fixed assets, 570–71
  liabilities, 572–73
  owner's equity, 573–74
  profit-making activities and, 574
Fire insurance policy, 673
First-in, first-out (FIFO), 637, 735
501/502 loans, 215
Five-year plan, 385
Fixed assets, 572
Fixed expenses, 168
Flexitime, 312
Float time, 600
Ford, 11, 45, 68
Foreign Agricultural Service, 538

Foreign Commercial Service Agency (USFCSA), 705
Foreign Credit Insurance Association (FCIA), 705
Formal failures, 74
Form W-2, 737
Fortune, 67
Foster, Dennis L., 94
401K plans, 322
Franchise, 85; *see also* Franchising
  buying process, 92–93
  checklist for, 93
  dream to reality, 101–2
  investigation of, 94–96
  reasons for/against buying, 146–48
Franchise Annual, 86
Franchisee, 85
Franchise offering circular, 96
Franchise Opportunities, 92
Franchise Opportunities Handbook, 94
Franchising
  areas of growth, 98–99
  benefits from, 147
  defined, 85–86
  extent of, 82–83
  franchise listings, 83–85
  growing importance of, 90–91
  international markets and, 99–100
  minority ownership and, 100–101
  types of systems, 86–90
Franchising in the Economy, 83
Franchising World, 86
Franchisor, 85
  services provided by, 146
Francis, Clarence, 313
Franklin, Benjamin, 722
Free enterprise system, 6
Free-standing locations, 81
Fringe benefits, 319

G

Gates, William, 10
General construction firms, 12
General Electric, 10
General layout, 389–91
Generally accepted accounting principles (GAAP), 733
General Motors, 11, 68, 302
General partnerships, 228
Gillespie, Bill, 751–52
Glammourramer Beauty Salon, 109–12

Goal-centered performance appraisals, 312
Gomez, Salvador, 69
Go public, 573
Goudreau Corporation, 198
Government help, 704
  SBA, 704–5
Government regulations, 694, 706–7
  coping with, 44–45, 710–11
  dealing with, 707–10
  information systems and, 620
  location and, 377–78
  OSHA, 335
  paperwork and, 22
Grapevine communication, 241
Graphology analysis, 284–85
Group-centered individuals, 48
Growth industries, 58–60
  franchising and, 90–91
Growth objectives, 35
Growth pattern, 73–74
Guaranteed loans, 212–14

H

Haagen-Daz, 97–98
Haake, Alfred, Dr., 302
Handicapped workers, 277
Hannaford Brothers, 137
Hannah, David, 153
Hardware, computer, 624
  choosing, 630
  selection checklist, 631
Hawken, Paul, 330
Hazard Community Standard, 335
Health insurance, 674
Hershey Chocolate Company, 468
Hill, Sherri, 57–58, 423
Hispanic Chamber of Commerce, U.S., 69
Hispanics
  demographics, 514–15
  small business and, 69–70
Hofer, Charles W., 26
Hoffman-La Roche, Inc., 340
Honeywell, Inc., 281
Horne Box, Inc., 659–64
Human relations, 302–3
Human resources, 159
  management of, 42
Hunter, George, 286

I

IBM, 10, 18–19, 38, 63, 188
Illiquid position, 596

Illness, employee, 339
Image consciousness, 452
Immediate-response advertising, 512
Immigration Reform and Control Act of 1986, 294
Implied contract, 699
Implied warranties, 700
Importing, 523
  small firms and, 523–24
Import quotas, 535
Inbreeding, 22
Incentive wage, 316
Income, 575
  taxable, 733
Income and expenses, 167–68
Income statement, 574
Incorporation, 728
Independence, 37–38
  poorly planned growth and, 72–73
  small business start-up and, 28–30
Indirect taxes, 724
Individualist, 48
Individual retirement accounts (IRAs), 321
Industrial development corporations (IDCs), 215
Industrial engineering, 392
Industrial insurance, 736
Industrial products, 459
  distribution channels for, 491
Inflation rate, 578
Informal leader, 241
Informal organization, 240
Information; *see also* Management information system (MIS)
  document security and, 686–87
  necessity of, 616–17
  performance feedback and, 603–5
  small business management and, 42
Innovation, 17–19
  marketing strategy and, 482
  suggestions for small firms, 64
Inputs, 370
Institute for Family Business, 762
Institutional advertising, 506
Insurable risk, 671
Insurance, 232
  accounting for expense of, 638
  determining needs for, 672
  family businesses and, 763
  selecting insurer, 675–76
  transfer of risk and, 671–72
  types of coverage, 673–75

Insurance companies, 211
Intangible property, 700
Interest payment, 200
  taxes and, 735
Intermediary selling
  brokers and, 493
  exporting and, 532
  independent agents and, 493–94
  retailers, 494
  wholesalers, 494
Intermediate-term securities, 199
Internal audit, 603
Internal resources, 159
Internal Revenue Service, 15, 706
  computers and, 624
  tax help and, 726
International Franchise Association, 97
International marketing, 522–23
  levels of involvement, 528
  market research and, 529–32
  opportunities for small firms, 525–27
  risks for small firms, 527–28
International Trade Association (ITA), 90, 537, 705
Internship training, 290–91
Interstate Commerce Act, 715
Interstate commerce clause, 695
Interviewing applicants, 285–87
Inventory, 572
  carrying costs of, 417
  carrying inventory, 414–15
  computers and, 414
  costing, 636–37
  order quantities, 418–19
  recording of, 635
  reorder points, 417–18
  taxes and, 734–35
  types of, 415–17
Investment
  buying decision and, 144
  initial investment estimate, 168–71

J

Jacobs, Sanford, 300
Japanese companies, 202
Jargon, 306
Job
  classifications, 238
  enrichment, 311
  rotation, 292
  satisfaction, 310
  sharing, 312
  specifications, 273

Job description, 237, 273
  illustrated, 274
Jobs, Steven, 38, 63, 73
Job shops, 422
Job-splitting, 312
Job Training Partnership Act
  (JTPA), 291
Johnson, John H., 39
Joint ventures, 236
*Journal of Small Business Manage-
  ment,* 11
Judicial branch, 695
Just-in-time delivery, 404

K

Keeping Records in Small Business,
  166
Kentucky Fried Chicken, 80, 536
Keogh retirement plan, 321
Kiam, Victor K., II, 27, 34, 36, 38
Kleiner, Bruce, 368
Kleptomaniac, 680
Kloss, Henry E., 223–24
Kostecka, Andrew, 90
Kroc, Ray, 81
Kurtz, Sandra, 10

L

Laissez-faire (free-rein) leadership,
  304
Landry, George, Jr., 751
Last-in, first-out (LIFO), 637, 735
Laws, basic business, 697
Leadership, 303
  family business and, 755–57
  styles, 304
Lead time, 418
Lease contract, 197, 700
Leased manpower, 278
Legal advise; *see* Professional advice
Legal environment, 694
  basic principles in, 695
  types of laws, 695–96
Legislative branch, 695
Lenders' credit requirements, 216–
  17
Leon, Raymond O., 180
Lester, John, 446
Leveraged buyout (LBO), 197
Lever Brothers, 27
Levitt, Theodore, 126
Levy, Michael, 331
Liability, product/service, 673
Liability insurance, 673

Liabilities, 572–73
Licenses, business, 728
Life insurance, 674
Limited partnerships, 228–29
Line-and-staff organization, 240
Line of credit, 210
Line organization, 240
Listening, 307
Live to Win, 27
Living trust, 743–44
Location
  factors affecting, 376–79
  researching potential sites, 375–
    76
  retail stores and, 381–83
  selection of, 374–75
Long-term liabilities, 573
  optimum-equity level and, 609
Long-term securities, 199
Loss control, 671
Loss leaders, 469
Loss prevention programs, 676–
  77

M

McDonald's, 68
  genesis of, 81–82
McGregor, Douglas, 303
McKay, Foster, 8
McRae Bluebook, 405
Magnetic Media Reporting, 739
Mailing permit, 729
Maine Line Company, 43
Management
  accounting system and, 630–33
  business failure and, 22
  business plan and, 185
  family businesses and, 760–62
  self-evaluation, 825–28
  small business success and, 41
  types of, 48
Management by objectives (MBO),
  160–61
  motivation and, 312
  performance appraisal and, 313
Management information system
  (MIS), 617
  defining system, 623
  information needs and, 617–19,
    621
  information uses and, 620–21
  versus manual system, 626–27
  timing/flow of information and,
    621–22
Managerial development, 291–92
  methods for, 292

Manufacturing firms, 12
  locating operations of, 383–84
Marginal income (MI), 584
Market
  analysis, 480
  definition, 41–42, 184
  estimating size of, 137
  penetration of, 482
Marketing concept, 448–49
  implementation of, 451–52
  marketing research and, 540
  service business and, 478
Marketing mix, 458
Marketing research, 136, 539–40
  computerized data bases and, 543
  illustrative example, 543–44
  methods used for, 136–38
  process of, 540–43
Marketing strategy, 453
  growth stage, 481–82
  implementation of, 480
  introductory stage, 480–81
  operational planning and, 165
Marketing system, 373
*Market Overseas with U.S. Govern-
  ment Help,* 537
Market share, 136
  estimating size of, 138
Markon, 466
Markup, 465–66
Martin Marietta, 45
Massachusetts Bay Transportation
  Authority (MBTA), 206
Master franchising, 91
Maturity, 199
Mauchly, John, 19, 33
*Measuring Markets: A Guide to the
  Use of Federal and State Statisti-
  cal Data,* 136
Medical Services, Inc., 551–56
Mental abilities, 49
Merchandising, 512–13
Merchant wholesalers, 494
Merit increases, 316
Merit rating, 313
Metal Fabricators, Inc., 262–67
Methods, 162
Microsoft, 10
Miller Business Systems, Inc., 161
Minimum wage, 314
Minorities
  exporting assistance and, 537
  franchising and, 100–101
  help organizations, 795
  SBA direct loans and, 214
  small business and, 66–67

Minority Business Development Agency (MBDA), 66, 101, 537, 704–5
Minority Vendor Profile System, 101
Minota Corporation, 21
MIS; *see* Management information system (MIS)
Mission, 157
Mom-and-Pop operation, 12, 202
  Asians and, 71
  Hispanics and, 69–70
  minorities and, 68
Morgan, Roy, 193
Mortgage loan, 199
Motels, 99
Mother and Child Shop, 130, 132
  case study, 258–62
Motivating employees, 307–8
  integrated approach, 322–24
  methods for, 310–12
  monetary incentives and, 312–13, 315–18
  reasons for, 309–10
Motivation, 308–9
  technique and, 313

N

National Apprenticeship Act of 1937, 291
National Association of Investment Companies, 66
National Association of Women Business Owners, 65
National Council on Alcoholism, 339
National Federation of Independent Business (NFIB), 5, 9
National Federation of Small Business, 21
National Institute of Occupational Safety and Health, 334
National Institute of Alcohol Abuse and Alcoholism, 339
National Labor Relations Act of 1935 (NLRA), 344, 715
National Labor Relations Board (NLRB), 344
National Safety Council, 334
National Women's Business Council, 66, 704
Net worth, 607
  ratios and, 609
New business failures, 21
New Business Opportunities, 11
New firms, 59
Next, Inc., 63
Nichols, June, 2, 7

Nonfinancial institutions, 211
Noninsurance, 676
Nonreactive research, 542
Notes payable, 573

O

Objectives, 33, 156
  business plan and, 185
  meshing of, 35–36
Occupational-professional registration, 729
Occupational Safety and Health Act (OSHA), 333, 715
  employee/employer under, 334
  management rights under, 334
Occupational Safety and Health Administration (OSHA), 333
  improving enforcement and, 335–36
  preventive safety and, 687
O'Donnell, Timothy, 569
Off-price retailers, 495
On-the-job training (OJT), 289–90
Operating budget, 596
  preparation of, 596–98
Operating leases, 198
Operating system, 371–73
  defined, 370
  start-up and, 373–74
Operational improvements
  collecting and analyzing information, 393–94
  new methods, 394
  problem recognition, 392–93
Operational planning, 156
  control and, 420, 425
  demand variations, 420–21
  physical facilities and, 385–86
  process of, 162–66
  role of, 161
  scheduling operations, 421–25
Operations, 371, 385
  improvement of, 392
Operations audit, 603
Opportunities, 58
Order getters, 501
Order handlers, 501
Order processing, 473
  exporting and, 532
Order takers, 501
Organization chart, 242–43
Organization structure
  basic concepts in, 236–38
  grouping activities and, 241–42
  operational planning and, 164–65

Organization structure—*Cont.*
  selecting legal form, 224–26
  types of authority and, 240–41
Organizing, 236
Orientation, employee, 288
Osborne Computer Company, 620
  case study (A), 647–51
  case study (B), 651–53
OSHA; *see* Occupational Safety and Health Administration (OSHA)
Our Hero Restaurant, 48, 381, 410
  case study (A), 107–9
  case study (B), 251–54
  case study (C), 354–56
  case study (D), 775–77
Out-of-pocket expenses, 195
Outplacement, 281
Outputs, 371
Owner's equity, 573–74

P

Packaging, 462–63
Parnell, Jeanne, 32, 740
Partnerships, 225
  defined, 227–28
  registration, 728
  tests of, 230
  types of, 228–30
Partridge, Mary H., 331
Part-time workers, 278
Past-due accounts, 601
Patchen, Charles W., 668
Patent practitioners, 701
Patents, 701
Penetration price, 464
Penny, J. C., 4
Pension programs, 321–22
Pepper Bush, 364–65
Performance, job, 309
  appraisals of, 312
  counseling and, 337
Performance standards, 394–95, 595
  budgets and, 595–600
  comparisons to actual, 604–5
  information systems and, 620–21
Perot, H. Ross, 38
Perpetual inventory records, 635
Personal analysis, 47
Personal budget, 168
Personal finance programs, 569
Personal (informal) failures, 74
Personal problems, 339–41
Personal property, 700
Personnel appraisal, 313

Personnel development, 288
  training nonmanagerial employ-
    ees, 289–91
Personnel Journal, 339
Personnel planning
  employees need, 272–73
  personnel sources, 273–79
Peters, Tom, 56, 300
Peterson, C. D., 39
Petty cash fund, 634
Physical distribution, 472–73
Physical examinations, 288
Physical resources, 159
  buying decision and, 144
  facilities planning, 385
  marketing strategy and, 481
  operational planning and, 163
Piece rate, 316–17
Planned progression, 292
Planning, 154
  cash needs, 598–600
  small business and, 154–56
  types of, 156
Plastic Suppliers, Inc., 439–43
Polaroid Corporation, 409
Police power, 695
Policies, 162
Polygraph tests, 284
Pools, Inc., 653–58
Positive discipline, 342
Powell Company, 664–65
Power centers, 382
Preferred stock, 198
Preferred stockholders, 196
Preliminary screening, 282
Pricing, 470–72
  cost-oriented, 465–66
  establishing policy, 463–65
  retailers and, 468
  service firms and, 466–68, 478
Primary research, 542
Principal, 702
Private employment agencies, 280
Private industry councils (PICs),
  291
Private law, 696
Procedures, 162
Process layout, 388
Procter & Gamble, 404
Producers, 378
  pricing and, 469
  sales force, 496–500
Producers Credit Association, 706
Product
  business plan and, 184
  facilities planning and, 385

Product—*Cont.*
  identification, 130–31
  liability, 700
  life cycle of, 458–61
  market study and, 135–36, 480–
    81
  mix, 462
  and organization structure, 241
  promoting sales of, 489–90
  selection of, 131–33
  types of, 459
Product advertising, 506
Product and trademark franchising,
  86
Product identification, 130–31
Production, 371
Production Credit Association, 216
Production system, 373
Product life cycle, 458, 459–60
  growth stage, 460–61
  introduction stage, 460
  maturity-decline stage, 461
Professional advice
  choosing a lawyer, 711–12
  franchises and, 96–97
  relationship with attorneys, 712–
    13
  taxes and, 726–27
Profit, 575
  case study, 664–65
  evaluation of, 607–8
  goal, 577–78
  retained, 609
Profit and loss statement, 574
Profit contribution, 499
Profit objectives, 34–35
Profit planning, 566–67
  determining profit levels, 581–82
  establishing goal, 577–78
  estimating expenses and, 578–81
  marginal analysis and, 584–85
  process of, 575–77
  sales forecast and, 578
  volume relationships and, 582–85
Profit sharing, 317
Program evaluation and review
  technique (PERT), 424
Promoting personnel, 276
  EEO laws and, 295
Property law, 700–701
Property taxes, intangible, 729
Proprietorships, 225
  defined, 227
Prospecting, 502
Protection and Toy Act, 716
Protective tariffs, 535
Publicity, 513–14

Public law, 695
Public warehouses, 472
Pugsley, Judy, 447–48
Purchase orders, 413
Purchasing, 403
  importance of, 403–4
  responsibility for, 404–5
Purchasing procedures, 410–12
  processing purchase orders, 412–
    13
  receiving inventory, 413–14
Pure Food Drug Law, 715
Pure risk, 670
Push money (PM), 317

Q

Quality, 426
  control and improvement of, 427–
    28
  small business and, 426–27
Quality assurance, 427–28
Quality circles (QCs), 311
Quality control, 427
  service business and, 478
Quartermaine, William, 400
Quick ratio, 608

R

Radio Shack, 318
Rating Guide to Franchises, 94
Ratios, 606
  interrelationship of, 609–10
  summary of, 607
Reactive research, 542
Real estate investment trust (REIT),
  234
Real property, 700
Real-time processing, 621
Recapitalization, 768
Receivables aging, 602
Recording system, 165–66
Recruitment, 279
  EEO laws and, 294–95
References, employment, 287
Regulatory agencies, 707–10
  listing of, 708
Reich, Robert B., 6
Remington Products, Inc., 27
Reorder point, 417
Reports, performance, 604
Requests for bids, 407
Responsibilities, 49
Results-oriented manager, 48
Retailers, 12, 378, 494
  intermediary selling and, 494–96
  locating stores, 379

Retailers—*Cont.*
  preventing theft, 682–83
  pricing and, 468–69
  types of locations, 381–83
  types of stores, 380–81
Retail sales, franchising and, 82–83
Retained earnings, 573
Retained profits, 609
Retirement counseling, 338
Return on equity (ROE), 607
Return on investment (ROI), 144–45
Revenue, 574
Revenue tariffs, 535
Right-to-work laws, 344
Risk
  coping with, 671
  noninsurance methods for handling, 676–77
  types of, 670–71
Risk assumption, 671
Risk avoidance, 671
Risk management, 670
Risk prevention, 671
Risk taker, 50
Risk transfer, 671
Robot Center, 61
Rock, Arthur, 270
Rogers, Will, 722
Romans, Phil, 152
Roper Organization, 7
  undergraduate student poll, 8
Rousseau, Jean-Jacques, 192
Roxy Dinner Theatre, 777–84
Rucker, John B., Jr., 286

S

Safety
  counseling and, 338
  factors influencing, 332–33
  preventive measures and, 687–88
Salary-only compensation plan, 497
Salary-plus-bonus plan, 498
Salary-plus-commission plan, 498
Sales contract, 699
Sales force
  creative sales person, 505–6
  optimum size of, 499–501
  performance of, 499
  personal selling and, 501
  personnel selection, 496–97
  personnel training, 502–5
  producers and, 496–500
  retailing, 500–501
Sales force promotions, 513

Sales forecast, 578
Sales income, 574
Sales promotions, 513
Sales territories, 499
Sales volume, 136
  expanding markets and, 481–82
Sample, John W., 520
Samuel, Jerry, 127
Sanders, Harlan, Colonel, 80, 91
Sanyo E&E Corporation, 13
Saving and loan associations (S&Ls), 210
Sawyer, Sam, 363–64
SBA; *see* Small Business Administration, U.S. (SBA)
SBICs; *see* Small business investment companies (SBICs)
Schedule irregularity of, 50
Scheduling, 421
Schoen, John, 762
S Corporations, 233–34
  tax laws and, 731
Scouting, 280–81
Securities
  debt, 199–200
  equity, 198–99
Security
  documentation of, 686–87
  dogs and, 679
  entrances and, 678
See Coast Manufacturing Company, Inc., 784–90
Selection, employee, 281
Self-confidence, 50–51
Self-counsel, 713–14
  self-help listing, 714
Self-discipline, 50
Self-employment, 8–9
Self-help groups, 134–35
Self-insurance, 671
Self-service operations, 500
Selling business
  buy/sell agreement, 769
  family-owned, 765–67
  tax implications, 741
Selling process, 501–5
Service business, 12, 378
  growth and, 58–59
  marketing strategies for, 478–80
  nature of, 476–77
  pricing, 466–68
  promotion of, 478–80
Service Core of Retired Executives (SCORE), 92, 186, 537, 704
  accounting systems and, 166
  choosing a business and, 133

Service objectives, 34
Sex discrimination, 294
Shaffer's Drive Inns, 118–20
Shapiro, Irving, 564, 568
Sheldon, Oliver, 692
Sherman Antitrust Act, 715
Shoplifting, 680
Shopping centers, 381–83
Shopping goods, 380
Short-term securities, 199
Simmons, Ralph, 41
Simmons Mountainside Satellite Sales, 13, 41
  case study, 254–57
Simplified employee pension (SEP) plan, 322
Site-rating sheet, 375
Skimming price, 464
Slack time, 424
Sloan, John, Jr., 26
Small business, 12; *see also* Family-owned businesses
  ageless attraction, 9–11
  definition of, 11–12
  diversity of, 12
  future leaders in, 63
  Great American Dream and, 4
  new-employment generator, 5–6, 59
  organizational problems in, 238–40
  practical ideas for, 62–64
  profit planning and, 577
  publications for, 11
  reasons for start-up, 28
  selling of, 765–67
  successful management of, 41–47
  unique contributions of, 16–17
Small Business Administration, U.S. (SBA), 6, 11, 59
  business classifications and, 12
  business planning and, 186
  direct loans and, 214–15, 537
  financing and, 211–12
  franchising and, 91–92
  guaranteed loans and, 212–14
  health/safety loans, 335
  market research and, 136
  minority programs, 66
  participating loans, 216
Small Business Handbook, The, 38
Small business investment companies (SBICs), 201–2
  SBA loans and, 215
Small Business Journal, 11
Small business owner, 14
  areas for concern, 72–75

Small business owner—*Cont.*
  business entry and, 41
  characteristics for success, 36–37
  choosing a business, 133–35
  dedication and, 40
  ownership challenges, 62
  personal taxes and, 740–41
  personal/family considerations, 39
  quick-concrete results and, 39–40
  sense of enterprise, 38–39
Small business start-up
  buy existing business, 140–41, 143
  buying decision, 141–44
  capital investment and, 194
  cultural networks and, 71
  income motivation and, 30–32
  personal objectives and, 28–32
  providing new products and, 32–33
  reasons for/against, 138–40
  steps in starting, 128–30
Smith, Alexander, 668
Social objectives, 35
Social responsibility, 714–15
Social Security, 320, 637, 736
Social Security Act of 1935, 737
Software, computer, 624
  choosing, 628–30
Sorkin, Sylvia, Dr., 306
Sources of funds, 171–72
  banks and institutions, 209–11
  customers as, 208–9
  quasi-governmental sources, 215–16
  SBA and, 211–15
  SBICs and, 215
  trade credit, 209
Sources of supply, 163–64
  location and, 376, 383
Space Service, Inc., 153
Span of control, 238
Specialization, 238
Specialty goods, 380–81
  purchase-order quantities and, 405
  scheduling of, 422
Speculative buying, 405
Speculative risk, 670
Sperry Corporation, 27
Stable personality, 50
Stagflation, 724
Standards, 162
Standing orders, 413
Starr, Edward, 16

Starting inventory, 168
State employment agencies, 280
Statistical Abstract of the United States, 541
Statute law, 695
Staubach, Roger, 32
Stockholders, 233
Stockouts, 404
Straight-line depreciation, 639
  taxes and, 734
Strategic planning, 156
  mission and objectives, 157–60
  role of, 157
  strategies, 160–61
Strategies, 160
Subfranchising, 91
Substance abuse, 339
Success rates, industry, 60
Sun Microsystems, 63
Supreme Plumbing and Heating Company, 271
Surety bonds, 675
Survey of Current Business, 541
System definition, 449
Systems approach, 451
Systems coordination, 373

T

Tangible property, 700
Target market, 453
  advertising-media selection and, 509
  market segmentation and, 454
  shifting composition of, 454–58
Taxable income, 733
Taxes, 724
  accounting for, 637–39, 730–31
  business start-up and, 31
  business withdrawals, 740–41
  estate planning and, 742–44, 768–69
  form of business and, 731–32
  hiring handicapped and, 277
  income, 730–33
  operating taxes, 727–28
  owner's personal taxes, 740–41
  planning for, 768
  professional help, 726–27
  property, 729
  sale of business and, 741–42
  sales and use, 729–30
  small businesses and, 725–26
  types of, 727
  U.S. tax system, 724

Taxes, employment-related, 736
  income tax withholding, 736–37
  Social Security, 737–38
  unemployment compensation insurance, 738–39
  worker's compensation, 740
Tax Guide for Small Business, 726
Tax Reform Act of 1978, 202, 724
Tax Reform Act of 1986, 197, 206, 321, 730
  gifts and, 768
  selling business and, 741
Tax-related depreciation, 734
Taylor, Jared, 614
Teague Brothers Rug and Carpet Cleaners, 369–70
Temporary workers, 278
Termination, employee, 338
Test marketing, 542
Theft
  prevention of, 682–84
  types of, 680–82
Theory X/Y, 303
Thinking Machines Corporation, 63
Thomas, J. Neal, 152
Thomas Register of American Manufacturers, 405
Time management, 45–47
Time schedule, 166
Title, 700–701
Torts, 702
Total rent concept, 382
Trade credit, 209
Trademark, 701–2
Trade name registration, 728
Trade promotions, 513
Traffic and Motor Vehicle Safety Act, 715
Training, 285–90
Transferring personnel, 276
Transportation, 473
  location and, 383–84
Transportation mode, 383
Treasury Department, U.S., 5
Trusts, 234, 768
TRW Credit Data, Inc., 217

U

Undercapitalization, 22
Unemployment compensation insurance, 320, 736, 738–39
Unfair labor practice, 346
Uniform Commercial Code (UCC), 697
Uniform Partnership Act, 227
Unions
  illegal means of opposition to, 823–24

Unions—*Cont.*
  legal means of opposition to, 821–22
  living with agreement, 348
  negotiating agreement, 347
  union-management relations, 344–47
Union shop clause, 344
Unit pricing, 468
Unity of command, 236–37
Univac Corporation, 19, 33
Upgrading personnel, 276
Use taxes, 729–30
Utilities, 376

V

Valentine, Herman, 67, 615–16
Values analysis, 47–48
Vancouver Computerized Trading System (VCT), 204–5
Vancouver Stock Exchange (VSE), 204
Variable expenses, 168
Vendors
  evaluating performance, 409
  investigating suppliers, 407–9
  maintaining good relations with, 409–10
  number of, 406–7

Vendors—*Cont.*
  selecting, 405–6
  types of, 406
Venture, 36, 88, 179
Venture capital clubs, 207–8
Venture capitalists, 202–6
  foreign stock exchanges and, 204
  Japanese companies and, 202
Venture capital networks, 206
VideoStar Connections, Inc. (VCI), 591
Vocational rehabilitation programs, 291
Von Companies, 70

W

Wage and Tax Statement, 737
Wage discrimination, 295
Walker, Don, 669
Wall Street Journal, 62
Wal-Mart Stores, 3, 15, 404
Walton, Sam, 3–4, 11, 15, 28
Ward, John L., 270
Warranty, 700
Watson, Thomas J., Jr., 188
Watts, Isaac, 750
Wells Fargo, 7
Wheeler-Lea Act, 715

White-collar crime, 684
  minimizing, 685–86
  types of, 684–85
White Sewing Machine Company, 113–17
Wholesalers, 12, 494
  pricing and, 469
Wilson, Porterfield, 521
Wilson, Woodrow, 330
Wilson's Used Cars, 120–24, 716
Women
  equal pay and, 315
  help organizations, 66, 795
  SBA direct loans and, 214
  small business and, 64–66
Women's Business Ownership Act of 1988, 66, 704
Worker's compensation, 320
  common-law requirements, 674
  taxes and, 740
Workforce, 376
Working capital, 195, 573
  financial evaluation and, 606
Work simplification, 392
Wozniak, Steve, 73
Wysocki, Bernard, Jr., 2

Z

Zero defects, 311
Zigmond, Ric, 766
Zoning variances, 729